文物进出境外国法律文件选编与述评

彭　蕾　编著

文物出版社

图书在版编目（CIP）数据

文物进出境外国法律文件选编与述评 / 彭蕾编著
. -- 北京：文物出版社，2019.12
ISBN 978-7-5010-6480-9

Ⅰ. ①文… Ⅱ. ①彭… Ⅲ. ①文物—出入境管理—法律—研究—世界 Ⅳ. ①D912.160.4

中国版本图书馆 CIP 数据核字（2019）第 273002 号

文物进出境外国法律文件选编与述评

编　　著：彭蕾

责任编辑：许海意
封面设计：谭德毅
责任印制：张道奇
出版发行：文物出版社
社　　址：北京市东直门内北小街 2 号楼
邮政编码：100007
网　　址：http：//www.wenwu.com
邮　　箱：web@wenwu.com
经　　销：新华书店
印　　刷：北京京都六环印刷厂
开　　本：710mm × 1000mm　1/16
印　　张：46.75
版　　次：2019 年 12 月第 1 版
印　　次：2019 年 12 月第 1 次印刷
书　　号：ISBN 978-7-5010-6480-9
定　　价：180.00 元

编者的话

文物进出境管理是我国文化遗产保护事业的重要组成部分，也是《文物保护法》赋予文物部门的一项重要职责，依法开展文物进出境审核，是把好国门，防止珍贵文物流失境外的最后一道关口。党和政府历来高度重视文物进出境管理工作。我国的文物进出境管理制度和法规体系基本建成，以《文物保护法》为统领，《文物保护法实施条例》《文物进出境审核管理办法》《文物出境审核标准》等一系列法规文件为配套；管理机构得到进一步加强和优化；责任鉴定员队伍不断扩大，资质管理、人才培养和联合执法等各项工作稳步推进。总体来说，全国文物进出境管理机构以及其他相关机构的同志们本着对国家负责、对历史负责、对文物保护事业负责的态度，克己奉公，严格执法，为文化遗产保护事业做出了重大贡献。

当前，由于收藏热的持续增温，私人携运文物进出境数量激增，文物犯罪案件高发，盗掘、盗窃及非法贩运文物犯罪活动依然猖獗，这要求我国应抓紧完善文物进出境法律法规，加强文物进出境管理，加强与国际社会紧密合作，维护国家文物安全，保证文物合法流通，这也是中国加入相关国际公约后对国际社会和其他缔约国应当履行的责任。

完善中国文物进出境法律制度，对构建新时代中国特色社会主义文物保护法治体系具有重大意义。为了广泛了解和借鉴外国在文物进出境管理中的先进立法经验、立法技术、立法角度和立法成果，本书特别选取并翻译了十个国家（或地区）包含但不限于文物进出境管理的法律文件，并在每个国家（或地区）的法律之前做简要述评作为导言，最终形成《文物进出境外国法律文件选编与述评》一书。这些国家（或地区），分布在美洲、欧洲、大洋洲、非洲、亚洲，既包括通常意义上的文物市场国，也包括文物出口国。在多年的文物进出境管理实践中，上述国家（或地区）逐渐形成了自己的管理特色，也同时存在一些共通之处。本书试图引发读者思考，哪些规定可以转化为符合中国国情的、符合中国文物管理特点的、符合中国语言习惯的规定，希冀对我国的文物进出境法规制定，进而对我国立法活动带来一些有意义的启示。同时也希望为广大文物工作者和相关研究人员提供一份读取便利的参考资料。

另外应当说明的是，意大利显然对文物进出境管理和流失文物返还工作非常重视，也取得了出色的成绩。《意大利文化与景观遗产法典》[①]是意大利有关文化和环境遗产的立法汇编，从中可见相关法律也是比较严密的。这部法典由184条和附件A组成。正文分为总则、文化财产、享用和强化、景观资产、处罚以及法律的暂行规定、废除和生效等五个部分。根据法典规定，文化遗产由文化财产和景观资产组成。法典第10条列举了受法律保护的文化财产的范围。关于文化财产进出境问题，法典第二部分第一编的第五章做出了较为详细的规定。这一章涉及文化财产的出口、进口、从欧盟成员国领土出口和非法出境的文化财产的归还等几方面的问题。内容很丰富，欲进一步了解详细规定，可参见《意大利文化与景观遗产法典》一书。故本书未收录意大利相关法律。

法律文件翻译很不容易，本书的问世，历经数次反复琢磨、推敲、讨论，凝聚了许多人的努力和心血。本书收录文件的初步翻译由中国文化遗产研究院余建立副研究馆员、重庆大学法学院周超副教授、延边大学崔景日老师、中国嘉德国际拍卖有限公司李睿琦，以及中央编译翻译服务有限公司的老师们共同翻译完成，英文部分的初校主要由中国政法大学霍政欣教授、余萌博士后以及研究生王成岳、王鈊平、徐书林、荣煜、陈月迷、陈锐达负责，德国、日本、韩国法律的初校由最初翻译人负责。在此特别对所有人的付出表示由衷谢忱！全书由彭蕾终校、统稿并撰写述评。

特别声明，本书的主要内容孵化于国家文物局2017年度项目“文物进出境法规建设及管理制度”，部分内容收录于项目报告的附件，在此特别鸣谢国家文物局邓超副司长、吴旻处长和其他领导的大力支持，以及承担单位中国文化遗产研究院领导和专家们的悉心指教。最后还要特别致谢中国文物信息

① 国家文物局编译：《意大利文化与景观遗产法典》，北京，文物出版社，2009年。

咨询中心刘铭威主任为本书统稿和章节设计提供了很多宝贵经验，使本书最终成为现在的样子，并得以顺利出版。本书主要统稿校对工作系编者调至中国文物信息咨询中心后完成。

本书翻译如有不当，请各位同仁不吝赐教，欢迎指正。

目 录

Foreign Laws Concerning the Import and Export of Cultural Relics: Compilation and Commentary

Peng Lei

Cultural Relics Press

THE UNITED STATES OF AMERICA

UNITED KINGDOM OF GREAT BRITAIN AND NORTHERN IRELAND

GERMANY

SWITZERLAND

CANADA

AUSTRALIA

THE ARAB REPUBLIC OF EGYPT

JAPAN

REPUBLIC OF KOREA

EUROPEAN UNION

THE UNITED STATES OF AMERICA

(See also *19 U.S.C. 2601 etseq.*)

CONVENTION ON CULTURAL PROPERTY IMPLEMENTATION ACT

Partial text of Public Law 97-446 [H.R. 4566], 96 Stat. 2329, approved January 12, 1983; as amended by Public Law 100-204 [H.R. 1777], 101 Stat. 1331, approved December 22, 1987

AN ACT To reduce certain duties, to suspend temporarily certain duties, to extend certain existing suspensions of duties, and for other purposes.

Be it enacted by the Senate and House of Representatives of the United States of America in Congress assembled,

TITLE III - IMPLEMENTATION OF CONVENTION ON CULTURAL PROPERTY

SECTION 301. SHORT TITLE.

This title may be cited as the "Convention on Cultural Property Implementation Act". [1]

SECTION 302. DEFINITIONS.

For purposes of this title-

(1) The term "agreement" includes any amendment to, or extension of, any agreement under this title that enters into force with respect to the United States.

(2) The term "archaeological or ethnological material of the State Party" means-

(A) any object of archaeological interest;

(B) any object of ethnological interest; or

(C) any fragment or part of any object referred to in subparagraph (A) or (B); which was first discovered within, and is subject to export control by, the State Party. For purposes of this paragraph-

(i) no object may be considered to be an object of archaeological interest unless such object-

(I) is of cultural significance;

(II) is at least two hundred and fifty years old; and

(III) was normally discovered as a result of scientific excavation, clandestine or accidental digging, or exploration on land or under water; and

(ii) no object may be considered to be an object of ethnological interest unless such object is-

(I) the product of a tribal or nonindustrial society, and

(II) Important to the cultural heritage of a people because of its distinctive characteristics, comparative rarity, or its contribution to the knowledge of the origins, development, or history of that people.

(3) The term "Committee" means the Cultural Property Advisory Committee established under section 206. [2]

(4) The term "consignee" means a consignee as defined in section 483 of the Tariff Act of 1930 (19U.S.C.1483).

(5) The term "Convention" means the Convention on the means of prohibiting and preventing the illicit import, export, and transfer of ownership of cultural property adopted by the General Conference of the United Nations Educational, Scientific, and Cultural Organization at its sixteenth session.

(6) The term "cultural property" includes articles described in article 1 (a) through (k) of the Convention whether or not any such article is specifically designated as such by any State Party for the purposes of such article.

(7) The term "designated archaeological or ethnological material" means any archaeological or ethnological material of the State Party which-

(A) is-

(i) Covered by an agreement under this title that enters into force with respect to the United States, or

(ii) subject to emergency action under section 304, and

(B) is listed by regulation under section305.

(8) The term "Secretary" means the Secretary of the Treasury or his delegate.

(9) The term "State Party" means any nation which has ratified, accepted, or acceded to the Convention.

(10) The term "United States" includes the several States, the District of Columbia, and any territory or area the foreign relations for which the United States is responsible.

(11) The term "United States citizen" means-

(A) any individual who is a citizen or national of the United States;

(B) any corporation, partnership, association, or other legal entity organized or

existing under the laws of the United States or any State; or

(C) any department, agency, or entity of the Federal Government or of any government of any State.

SECTION 303. [3] AGREEMENTS TO IMPLEMENT ARTICLE 9 OF THE CONVENTION.

(a) AGREEMENT AUTHORITY. -

(1) [4] IN GENERAL. -If the President determines, after request is made to the United States under article 9 of the Convention by any State Party-

(A) that the cultural patrimony of the State Party is in jeopardy from the pillage of archaeological or ethnological materials of the State Party;

(B) that the State Party has taken measures consistent with the Convention to protect its cultural patrimony;

(C) that-

(i) the application of the import restrictions set forth in section 307 with respect to archaeological or ethnological material of the State Party, if applied in concert with similar restrictions implemented, or to be implemented within a reasonable period of time, by those nations (whether or not State Parties) individually having a significant import trade in such material, would be of substantial benefit in deterring a serious situation of pillage, and

(ii) remedies less drastic than the application of the restrictions set forth in such section are not available; and

(D) that the application of the import restrictions set forth in section 307 in the particular circumstances is consistent with the general interest of the international community in the interchange of cultural property among nations for scientific, cultural, and educational purposes; the President may, subject to the provisions of this chapter, take the actions described in paragraph(2).

(2) [5] AUTHORITY OF PRESIDENT. -For purposes of paragraph (1), the President may enter into-

(A) a bilateral agreement with the State Party to apply the import restrictions set forth in section 307 to the archaeological or ethnological material of the State Party the pillage of which is creating the jeopardy to the cultural patrimony of the State Party found to exist under paragraph (1) (A); or

(B) a multilateral agreement with the State Party and with one or more other nations (whether or not a State Party) under which the United States will apply such restrictions, and the other nations will apply similar restrictions, with respect to such material.

(3) REQUESTS.- A request made to the United States under article 9 of the Convention by a State Party must be accompanied by a written statement of the facts known to the State Party that relate to those matters with respect to which determinations must be made under subparagraphs (A) through (D) of paragraph (1).

(4) 5 IMPLEMENTATION.-In implementing this subsection, the President should endeavor to obtain the commitment of the State Party concerned to permit the exchange of its archaeological and ethnological materials under circumstances in which such exchange does not jeopardize its cultural patrimony.

(b) EFFECTIVE PERIOD.-The President may not enter into any agreement under subsection (a) which has an effective period beyond the close of the five-year period beginning on the date on which such agreement enters into force with respect to the United States.

(c) RESTRICTIONS ON ENTERING INTO AGREEMENTS.-

(1) IN GENERAL.-The President may not enter into a bilateral or multilateral agreement authorized by subsection (a) unless the application of the import restrictions set forth in section 307 with respect to archaeological or ethnological material of the State Party making a request to the United States under article 9 of the Convention will be applied in concert with similar restrictions implemented, or to be implemented, by those nations (whether or not State Parties) individually having a significant import trade in such material.

(2) EXCEPTION TO RESTRICTIONS.-Notwithstanding paragraph (1), the President may enter into an agreement if he determines that a nation individually having a significant import trade in such material is not implementing, or is not likely to implement, similar restrictions, but-

(A) such restrictions are not essential to deter a serious situation of pillage, and

(B) the application of the import restrictions set forth in section 307 in concert with similar restrictions implemented, or to be implemented, by other nations (whether or not State Parties) individually having a significant import trade in such material would be of substantial benefit in deterring a serious situation of pillage.

(d) [6] SUSPENSION OF IMPORT RESTRICTIONS UNDER AGREEMENTS.

If, after an agreement enters into force with respect to the United States, the President determines that a number of parties to the agreement (other than parties described in subsection (c)(2) having significant import trade in the archaeological and ethnological material covered by the agreement-

(1) have not implemented within a reasonable period of time import restrictions that are similar to those set forth in section 307, or

(2) are not implementing such restrictions satisfactorily with the result that no substantial benefit in deterring a serious situation of pillage in the State Party concerned is being obtained, the President shall suspend the implementation of the import restrictions under section 307 until such time as the nations take appropriate corrective action.

(e) [7] EXTENSION OF AGREEMENTS.

The President may extend any agreement that enters into force with respect to the United States for additional periods of not more than five years each if the President determines that-

(1) the factors referred to in subsection (a)(1) of this section which justified the entering into of the agreement still pertain, and

(2) no cause for suspension under subsection (d) exists.

(f) [8] PROCEDURES.-If any request described in subsection (a) is made by a State Party, or if the President proposes to extend any agreement under subsection (e) of this section, the President shall-

(1) publish notification of the request or proposal in the Federal Register;

(2) submit to the Committee such information regarding the request or proposal (including, if applicable, information from the State Party with respect to the implementation of emergency action under section 304) as is appropriate to enable the Committee to carry out its duties under section 306(f); and

(3) consider, in taking action on the request or proposal, the views and recommendations contained in any Committee report-

(A) required under section 306(f)(1) or (2) of this title, and

(B) submitted to the President before the close of the one-hundred-and-fifty-day period beginning on the day on which the President submitted information on the request or proposal to the Committee under paragraph (2).

(g) [9] INFORMATION ON PRESIDENTIAL ACTION.-

(1) IN GENERAL.-In any case in which the President-

(A) enters into or extends an agreement pursuant to subsection (a) or (e), or

(B) [10] applies import restrictions under section 304, the President shall, promptly after taking such action, submit a report to the Congress.

(2) REPORT.-The report under paragraph (1) shall contain-

(A) a description of such action (including the text of any agreement entered into),

(B) the differences (if any) between such action and the views and recommendations contained in any Committee report which the President was required to consider, and

(C) the reasons for any such difference.

(3) INFORMATION RELATING TO COMMITTEE RECOMMENDATIONS.-If any Committee report required to be considered by the President recommends that an agreement be entered into, but no such agreement is entered into, the President shall submit to the Congress a report which contains the reasons why such agreement was not entered into.

SECTION 304. [11] EMERGENCY IMPLEMENTATION OF IMPORT REST RICTIONS.

(a) EMERGENCY CONDITION DEFINED.-For purposes of this section, the term "emergency condition" means, with respect to any archaeological or ethnological material of any State Party, that such material is-

(1) a newly discovered type of material which is of importance for the understanding of the history of mankind and is in jeopardy from pillage, dismantling, dispersal, or fragmentation;

(2) identifiable as coming from any site recognized to be of high cultural significance if such site is in jeopardy from pillage, dismantling, dispersal, or fragmentation which is, or threatens to be, of crisis proportions; or

(3) a part of the remains of a particular culture or civilization, the record of which is in jeopardy from pillage, dismantling, dispersal, or fragmentation which is, or threatens to be, of crisis proportions; and application of the import restrictions set forth in section 307 on a temporary basis would, in whole or in part, reduce the incentive for such pillage, dismantling, dispersal or fragmentation.

(b) [12] PRESIDENTIAL ACTION.-Subject to subsection (c), if the President determines that an emergency condition applies with respect to any archaeological or ethnological material of any State Party, the President may apply the import restrictions set forth in section 307 with respect to such material.

(c) LIMITATIONS.-

(1) The President may not implement this section with respect to the archaeological or ethnological materials of any State Party unless the State Party has made a request described in section 303(a) to the United States and has supplied information which supports a determination that an emergency condition exists.

(2) In taking action under subsection (b) of this section with respect to any State Party, the President shall consider the views and recommendations contained in the Committee report required under section 306(f)(3) if the report is submitted to the President before the close of the ninety-day period beginning on the day on which the President submitted information to the Committee under section 303(f)(2) on the request of the State Party under section 303(a).

(3) [13] No import restrictions set forth in section 307 of this title may be applied under this section to the archaeological or ethnological materials of any State Party for more than five years after the date on which the request of a State Party under section 303(a) is made to the United States. This period may be extended by the President for three more years if the President determines that the emergency condition continues to apply with respect to the archaeological or ethnological material. However, before taking such action, the President shall request and consider, if received within ninety days, a report of the Committee setting forth its recommendations, together with the reasons therefor, as to

whether such import restrictions shall be extended.

(4) [14] The import restrictions under this section may continue to apply in whole or in part, if before their expiration under paragraph (3), there has entered into force with respect to the archaeological or ethnological materials an agreement under section 203 [15] or an agreement with a State Party to which the Senate has given its advice and consent to ratification. Such import restrictions may continue to apply for the duration of the agreement.

SECTION 305. [16] DESIGNATION OF MATERIALS COVERED BY AGREEMENTS OR EMERGENCY ACTIONS.

After any agreement enters into force under section 303, or emergency action is taken under section 304, the Secretary, after consultation with the Director of the United States Information Agency, shall by regulation promulgate (and when appropriate shall revise) a list of the archaeological or ethnological material of the State Party covered by the agreement or by such action. The Secretary may list such material by type or other appropriate classification, but each listing made under this section shall be sufficiently specific and precise to insure that

(1) the import restrictions under section 307 are applied only to the archeological and ethnological material covered by the agreement or emergency action; and

(2) fair notice is given to importers and other persons as to what material is subject to such restrictions.

SECTION 306. [17] CULTURAL PROPERTY ADVISORY COMMITTEE.

(a) ESTABLISHMENT.-There is established the Cultural Property Advisory Committee.

(b) MEMBERSHIP.-

(1) The Committee shall be composed of eleven members appointed by the President as follows:

(A) Two members representing the interests of museums.

(B) Three members who shall be experts in the fields of archaeology, anthropology, ethnology, or related areas.

(C) Three members who shall be experts in the international sale of archaeological, ethnological, and other cultural property.

(D) Three members who shall represent the interest of the general public.

(2) Appointments made under paragraph (1) shall be made in such a manner so as to insure-

(A) fair representation of the various interests of the public sectors and the private sectors in the international exchange of archaeological and ethnological materials, and

(B) that within such sectors, fair representation is accorded to the interests of regional and local institutions and museums.

(3)

(A) [18] Members of the Committee shall be appointed for terms of three years and may be reappointed for one or more terms. With respect to the initial appointments, the President shall select, on a representative basis to the maximum extent practicable, four members to serve three-year terms, four members to serve two-year terms, and the remaining members to serve a one-year term. Thereafter each appointment shall be for a three-year term.

(B)

(i) [19] A vacancy in the Committee shall be filled in the same manner as the original appointment was made and for the unexpired portion of the term, if the vacancy occurred during a term of office. Any member of the Committee may continue to serve as a member of the Committee after the expiration of his term of office until reappointed or until his successor has been appointed.

(ii) The President shall designate a Chairman of the Committee from the members of the Committee.

(c) EXPENSES.-The members of the Committee shall be reimbursed for actual expenses incurred in the performance of duties for the Committee.

(d) TRANSACTION OF BUSINESS.-Six of the members of the Committee shall constitute a quorum. All decisions of the Committee shall be by majority vote of the members present and voting.

(e) STAFF AND ADMINISTRATION.-

(1) The Director of the United States Information Agency shall make available to the Committee such administrative and technical support services and assistance as it may reasonably require to carry out its activities. Upon the request of the Committee, the head of any other Federal agency may detail to the Committee, on a reimbursable basis, any of the personnel of such agency to assist the Committee in carrying out its functions, and provide such information and assistance as the Committee may reasonably require to carry out its activities.

(2) The Committee shall meet at the call of the Director of the United States Information Agency, or when a majority of its members request a meeting in writing.

(f) REPORTS BY COMMITTEE.-

(1) The Committee shall, with respect to each request of a State Party referred to in section 303(a), undertake an investigation and review with respect to matters referred to in section 303(a)(1) as they relate to the State Party or the request and shall prepare a

report setting forth-

(A) the results of such investigation and review;

(B) its findings as to the nations individually having a significant import trade in the relevant material; and

(C) its recommendation, together with the reasons therefor, as to whether an agreement should be entered into under section 303(a) with respect to the State Party.

(2) The Committee shall, with respect to each agreement proposed to be extended by the President under section 303(e), prepare a report setting forth its recommendations together with the reasons therefor, as to whether or not the agreement should be extended.

(3) The Committee shall in each case in which the Committee finds that an emergency condition under section 304 exists prepare a report setting forth its recommendations, together with the reasons therefor, as to whether emergency action under section 304 should be implemented. If any State Party indicates in its request under section 303(a) that an emergency condition exists and the Committee finds that such a condition does not exist, the Committee shall prepare a report setting forth the reasons for such finding.

(4) Any report prepared by the Committee which recommends the entering into or the extension of any agreement under section 303 or the implementation of emergency action under section 304 shall set forth-

(A) such terms and conditions which it considers necessary and appropriate to include within such agreement, or apply with respect to such implementation, for purposes of carrying out the intent of the Convention; and

(B) such archaeological or ethnological material of the State Party, specified by type or such other classification as the Committee deems appropriate, which should be covered by such agreement or action.

(5) If any member of the Committee disagrees with respect to any matter in any report prepared under this subsection, such member may prepare a statement setting forth the reasons for such disagreement and such statement shall be appended to, and considered a part of, the report.

(6) [20] The Committee shall submit to the Congress and the President a copy of each report prepared by it under this subsection.

(g) [21] COMMITTEE REVIEW.-

(1) IN GENERAL.-The Committee shall undertake a continuing review of the effectiveness of agreements under section 303 that have entered into force with respect to the United States, and of emergency action implemented under section 304.

(2) ACTION BY COMMITTEE.-If the Committee finds, as a result of such review, that-

(A) cause exists for suspending, under section 303(d), the import restrictions imposed under an agreement;

(B) any agreement or emergency action is not achieving the purposes for which entered into or implemented; or

(C) changes are required to this title in order to implement fully the obligations of the United States under the Convention; the Committee may submit a report to the Congress and the President setting forth its recommendations for suspending such import restrictions or for improving the effectiveness of any such agreement or emergency action or this title.

(h) [22] FEDERAL ADVISORY COMMITTEE ACT.-The provisions of the Federal Advisory Committee Act (Public Law 92-463;5 U.S.C. Appendix I) shall apply to the Committee except that the requirements of subsections (a) and (b) of section 10 and section 11 of such Act (relating to open meetings, public notice, public participation, and public availability of documents) shall not apply to the Committee, whenever and to the extent it is determined by the President or his designee that the disclosure of matters involved in the Committee's proceedings would compromise the Government's negotiating objectives or bargaining positions on the negotiations of any agreement authorized by this title.

(i) CONFIDENTIAL INFORMATION.-

(1) IN GENERAL-Any information (including trade secrets and commercial or financial information which is privileged or confidential) submitted in confidence by the private sector to officers or employees of the United States or to the Committee in connection with the responsibilities of the Committee shall not be disclosed to any person other than to-

(A) officers and employees of the United States designated by the Director of the United States Information Agency;

(B) members of the Committee on Ways and Means of the House of Representatives and the Committee on Finance of the Senate who are designated by the chairman of either such Committee and members of the staff of either such Committee designated by the chairman for use in connection with negotiation of agreements or other activities authorized by this title; and

(C) the Committee established under this title.

(2) GOVERNMENTAL INFORMATION.-Information submitted in confidence by officers or employees of the United States to the Committee shall not be disclosed other than in accordance with rules issued by the Director of the United States Information Agency, after consultation with the Committee. Such rules shall define the categories of information which require restricted or confidential handling by such Committee considering the extent to which public disclosure of such information can reasonably be expected to prejudice the interests of the United States. Such rules shall, to the maximum extent feasible, permit meaningful consultations by Committee members with persons affected by proposed agreements authorized by this title.

(j) NO AUTHORITY TO NEGOTIATE.-Nothing contained in this section shall be construed to authorize or to permit any individual (not otherwise authorized or permitted) to participate directly in any negotiation of any agreement authorized by this title.

SECTION 307. [23] IMPORTRE STRICTIONS.

(a) DOCUMENTATION OF LAWFUL EXPORTATION.-No designated archaeological or ethnological material that is exported (whether or not such exportation is to the United States) from the State Party after the designation of such material under section 305 may be imported into the United States unless the State Party issues a certification or other documentation which certifies that such exportation was not in violation of the laws of the State Party.

(b) CUSTOMS ACTION IN ABSENCE OF DOCUMENTATION.-If the consignee of any designated archaeological or ethnological material is unable to present to the customs officer concerned at the time of making entry of such material-

(1) the certificate or other documentation of the State Party required under subsection (a); or

(2) satisfactory evidence that such material was exported from the State Party-

(A) not less than ten years before the date of such entry and that neither the person for whose account the material is imported (or any related person) contracted for or acquired an interest, directly or indirectly, in such material more than one year before that date of entry, or

(B) on or before the date on which such material was designated under section 305. the customs officer concerned shall refuse to release the material from customs custody and send it to a bonded warehouse or store to be held at the risk and expense of the consignee, notwithstanding any other provision of law, until such documentation or evidence is filed with such officer. If such documentation or evidence is not presented within ninety days after the date on which such material is refused release from customs custody, or such longer period as may be allowed by the Secretary for good cause shown, the material shall be subject to seizure and forfeiture. The presentation of such documentation or evidence shall not bar subsequent action under section 310.

(c) DEFINITION OF SATISFACTORY EVIDENCE.-The term "satisfactory evidence" means-

(1) for purposes of subsection(b)(2)(A)-

(A) one or more declarations under oath by the importer, or the person for whose account the material is imported, stating that, to the best of his knowledge-

(i) the material was exported from the State Party not less than ten years before the date of entry into the United States, and

(ii) neither such importer or person (or any related person) contracted for or acquired an interest, directly or indirectly, in such material more than one year before the date of entry of the material; and

(B) a statement provided by the consignor, or person who sold the material to the importer, which states the date, or, if not known, his belief, that the material was exported from the State Party not less than ten years before the date of entry into the United States, and the reasons on which the statement is based; and

(2) for purposes of subsection(b)(2)(B)-

(A) one or more declarations under oath by the importer or the person for whose account the material is to be imported, stating that, to the best of his knowledge, the material was exported from the State Party on or before the date such material was designated under section 305, and

(B) a statement by the consignor or person who sold the material to the importer which states the date, or if not known, his belief, that the material was exported from the State Party on or before the date such material was designated under section 305, and the reasons on which the statement is based.

(d) RELATED PERSONS.-For purposes of subsections (b) and (c) of this section, a person shall be treated as a related person to an importer, or to a person for whose account material is imported, if such person-

(1) is a member of the same family as the importer or person of account, including, but not limited to, membership as a brother or sister (whether by whole or half blood), spouse, ancestor, or lineal descendant;

(2) is a partner or associate with the importer or person of account in any partnership, association, or other venture; or

(3) is a corporation or other legal entity in which the importer or person of account directly or indirectly owns, controls, or holds power to vote 20 percent or more of the outstanding voting stock or shares in the entity.

SECTION 308. [24] STOLEN CULTURALPROPERTY.

No article of cultural property documented as appertaining to the inventory of a museum or religious or secular public monument or similar institution in any State Party which is stolen from such institution after the effective date of this title, or after the date of entry into force of the Convention for the State Party, whichever date is later, may be imported into the United States.

SECTION 309. [25] TEMPORARY DISPOSITION OF MATERIALS AND ARTICLES SUBJECT TO TITLE.

Pending a final determination as to whether any archaeological or ethnological material, or any article of cultural property, has been imported into the United States in violation of section 307 section 308, the Secretary shall, upon application by any museum or other cultural or scientific institution in the United States which is open to the public, permit such material or article to be retained at such institution if he finds that-

(1) sufficient safeguards will be taken by the institution for the protection of such material or article; and

(2) sufficient bond is posted by the institution to ensure its return to the Secretary.

SECTION 310. [26] SEIZURE AND FORFEITURE.

(a) IN GENERAL.-Any designated archaeological or ethnological material or article of cultural property, as the case may be, which is imported into the United States in violation of section 307 or section 308 shall be subject to seizure and forfeiture. All provisions of law relating to seizure, forfeiture, and condemnation for violation of the customs laws shall apply to seizures and forfeitures incurred, or alleged to have been incurred, under this title, insofar as such provisions of law are applicable to, and not inconsistent with, the provisions of this title.

(b) ARCHAEOLOGICAL AND ETHNOLOGICAL MATERIAL.-Any designated archaeological and ethnological material which is imported into the United States in violation of section 307 and which is forfeited to the United States under this title shall-

(1) first be offered for return to the State Party;

(2) if not returned to the State Party, be returned to a claimant with respect to whom the material was forfeited if that claimant establishes-

(A) valid title to the material,

(B) that the claimant is a bona fide purchaser for value of the material; or

(3) if not returned to the State Party under paragraph (1) or to a claimant under paragraph (2), be disposed of in the manner prescribed by law for articles forfeited for violation of the customs laws. No return of material may be made under paragraph (1) or (2) unless the State Party or claimant, as the case may be, bears the expenses incurred incident to the return and delivery, and complies with such other requirements relating to the return as the Secretary shall prescribe.

(c) ARTICLES OF CULTURAL PROPERTY-

(1) In any action for forfeiture under this section regarding an article of cultural property imported into the United States in violation of section 308, if the claimant establishes valid title to the article, under applicable law, as against the institution from which the article was stolen, forfeiture shall not be decreed unless the State Party to which the article is to be returned pays the claimant just compensation for the article. In any action for forfeiture under this section where the claimant does not establish such title but establishes that it purchased the article for value without knowledge or reason to believe it was stolen, forfeiture shall not be decreed unless-

(A) the State Party to which the article is to be returned pays the claimant an amount equal to the amount which the claimant paid for the article, or

(B) the United States establishes that such State Party, as a matter of law or reciprocity, would in similar circumstances recover and return an article stolen from an institution in the United States without requiring the payment of compensation.

(2) Any article of cultural property which is imported into the United States in violation of section 308 and which is forfeited to the United States under this chapter shall-

(A) first be offered for return to the State Party in whose territory is situated the institution referred to in section 308 and shall be returned if that State Party bears the expenses incident to such return and delivery and complies with such other requirements relating to the return as the Secretary prescribes; or

(B) if not returned to such State Party, be disposed of in the manner prescribed by law for articles forfeited for violation of the customs laws.

SECTION 311. [27] EVIDENTIARYREQUIREMENTS.

Notwithstanding the provisions of section 615 of the Tariff Act of 1930 (19 U.S.C. 1615), in any forfeiture proceeding brought under this title in which the material or article, as the case may be, is claimed by any person, the United States shall establish

(1) in the case of any material subject to the provisions of section 307, that the material has been listed by the Secretary in accordance with section 305; and

(2) in the case of any article subject to section 308 of this title, that the article-

(A) is documented as appertaining to the inventory of a museum or religious or secular public monument or similar institution in a State Party, and

(B) was stolen from such institution after the effective date of this title, or after the date of entry into force of the Convention for the State Party concerned, whichever date is later.

SECTION 312. [28] CERTAIN MATERIAL AND ARTICLES EXEMPT FROM TITLE.

The provisions of this chapter shall not apply to-

(1) any archaeological or ethnological material or any article of cultural property which is imported into the United States for temporary exhibition or display if such material or article is immune from seizure under judicial process pursuant to the Act entitled "An Act to render immune from seizure under judicial process certain objects of cultural significance imported into the United States for temporary display or exhibition, and for other purposes," approved October 19, 1965 (22 U.S.C. 2459); or

(2) any designated archaeological or ethnological material or any article of cultural property imported into the United States if such material or article-

(A) has been held in the United States for a period of not less than three consecutive years by a recognized museum or religious or secular monument or similar institution, and was purchased by that institution for value, in good faith, and without notice that such material or article was imported in violation of this chapter, but only if-

(i) the acquisition of such material or article has been reported in a publication of such institution, any regularly published newspaper or periodical with a circulation of at least fifty thousand, or a periodical or exhibition catalog which is concerned with the type of article or materials sought to be exempted from this title,

(ii) such material or article has been exhibited to the public for a period or periods aggregating at least one year during such three-year period, or

(iii) such article or material has been cataloged and the catalog material made available upon request to the public for at least two years during such three-year period;

(B) if subparagraph (A) does not apply, has been within the United States for a period of not less than ten consecutive years and has been exhibited for not less than five years during such period in a recognized museum or religious or secular monument or similar institution in the United States open to the public; or

(C) if subparagraphs (A) and (B) do not apply, has been within the United States for a period of not less than ten consecutive years and the State Party concerned has received or should have received during such period fair notice (through such adequate and accessible publication, or other means, as the Secretary shall by regulation prescribe) of its location within the United States; and

(D) if none of the preceding subparagraphs apply, has been within the United States for a period of not less than twenty consecutive years and the claimant establishes that it purchased the material or article for value without knowledge or reason to believe that it was imported in violation of law.

SECTION 313. [29] REGULATIONS.

The Secretary shall prescribe such rules and regulations as are necessary and appropriate to carry out the provisions of this title.

SECTION 314. [30] ENFORCEMENT.

In the customs territory of the United States, and in the Virgin Islands, the provisions of this title shall be enforced by appropriate customs officers. In any other territory or area within the United States, but not within such customs territory or the Virgin Islands, such provisions shall be enforced by such persons as may be designated by the President.

SECTION 315. EFFECTIVE DATE.

(a) IN GENERAL.-This title shall take effect on the ninetieth day after the date of the enactment of this Act or on any date which the President shall prescribe and publish in the Federal Register, if such date is-

(1) before such ninetieth day and after such date of enactment; and

(2) after the initial membership of the Committee is appointed.

(b) EXCEPTION.-Notwithstanding subsection (a), the members of the Committee may be appointed in the manner provided for in section 306 at any time after the date of the enactment of this Act.

NOTES

[1] 19 U.S.C. 2601.

[2] This reference to Section 206 should probably be a reference to Section 306.

[3] 19 U.S.C. 2602

[4] The functions conferred upon the President by Section 303(a)(1) concerning determinations to be made prior to initiation of negotiations of bilateral or multilateral agreements were delegated to the Director of the United States Information Agency, acting in consultation with the Secretary of State and the Secretary of the Treasury, by Executive Order 12555 of March 10, 1986, 51 F.R. 8475.

[5] The functions conferred upon the President by secs. 303(a)(2) and 303(a)(4) were delegated to the Secretary of State, acting in consultation with and with the participation of the Director of the United States Information Agency and in consultation with the Secretary of the Treasury, by Executive Order 12555 of March 10, 1986, 51 F.R. 8475.

[6] The functions conferred upon the President by Section 303(d) with respect to the determinations concerning the failure of other parties to an agreement to take any or satisfactory implementation action on their agreement were delegated to the Director of the United States Information Agency, acting in consultation with the Secretary of State and the Secretary of the Treasury, by Executive Order 12555 of March 10, 1986, 51 F.R. 8475. The Order required, however, that the Secretary of State remain responsible for interpretation of the agreement. To the extent they involve suspension of import restrictions, functions were delegated to the Secretary of the Treasury.

[7] The functions conferred upon the President by Section 303(e) relating to the determinations to be made prior to the initiation of negotiations for the extension of any agreement were delegated to the Director of the United States Information Agency, acting in consultation with the Secretary of State and the Secretary of the Treasury, by Executive Order 12555 of March 10, 1986, 51 F.R. 8475.
Functions relating only to negotiation and conclusion of extensions of agreements under this Act were delegated to the Secretary of State, acting in consultation with and with the participation of the Director of the United States Information Agency and in consultation with the Secretary of the Treasury.

[8] The functions conferred upon the President by this Section 303(f) relating to the actions to be taken upon receipt of a request made by a State Party were delegated to the Director of the United States Information Agency, acting in consultation with the Secretary of State and the Secretary of the Treasury, by Executive Order 12555 of March 10, 1986, 51 F.R. 8475.

[9] Except with respect to subsection 303(g)(1)(B), the functions conferred upon the

President by Section 303(g) were delegated to the Secretary of State, acting in consultation with and the participation of the Director of the United States Information Agency and the Secretary of the Treasury, by Executive Order 12555 of March 10, 1986, 51 F.R. 8475.

[10] The functions conferred upon the President by Section 303(1)(b) relating to the notification of Presidential action and furnishing of reports to Congress were delegated to the Director of the United States Information Agency, acting in consultation with the Secretary of State and the Secretary of the Treasury, by Executive Order 12555 of March 10, 1986, 51 F.R. 8475.

[11] 19 U.S.C. 2603. The functions conferred upon the President by this section to the extent that they involve the application of import restrictions set forth in Section 307 and the extension of such import restrictions pursuant to Section 304(c)(3) were delegated to the Secretary of the Treasury, acting in consultation with the Director of the United States Information Agency and the Secretary of State, by Executive Order 12555 of March 10, 1986, 51 F. R. 8475.

[12] The functions conferred upon the President by Section 304(b) to the extent that they involve determinations by the President that an emergency condition applies with respect to any archaeological or ethnological material of any State Party to the convention, subject to the limitations of secs. 304(c)(1), 304(c)(2), and 304(c)(3), were delegated to the Director of the United States Information Agency, acting in consultation with the Secretary of State and the Secretary of the Treasury, by Executive Order 12555 of March 10, 1986, 51 F.R. 8475.

[13] The functions conferred upon the President by Section 304(c)(3) to the extent that they involve determinations to be made and the receipt and consideration of an advisory report from the Cultural Property Advisory Committee by the President prior to extensions of emergency import restrictions were delegated to the Director of the United States Information Agency, acting in consultation with the Secretary of State and the Secretary of the Treasury, by Executive Order 12555 of March 10, 1986, 51 F.R. 8475.

[14] The functions conferred upon the President by Section 303(c)(4) to the extent that they involve the negotiation and conclusion of agreements subject to the advice and consent to ratification by the Senate were delegated to the Secretary of State, acting in consultation with and with the participation of the Director of the United States Information Agency and in consultation with the Secretary of the Treasury by Executive Order 12555 of March 10, 1986, 51 F.R. 8475

[15] This reference to Section 203 probably should have been a reference to Section 303.

[16] 19 U.S.C. 2604

[17] 19 U.S.C. 2605

[18] Subsection (3)(A) was amended and restated by Section 307(a) of the Foreign Relations

Authorization Act. Fiscal Years 1988 and 1989 (Public Law 100-204; 101 Stat. 1380). Section 307(c) of the same act makes subsection (3)(A) apply to those members of the Cultural Property Advisory Committee first appointed after enactment of Public Law100-204.

[19] Subsection (3)(B) was amended and restated by Section 307(b) of the Foreign Relations Authorization Act, Fiscal Years 1988 (Public Law 100-204; 101 Stat.1380).

[20] The functions conferred upon the President by Section 306(f)(6) were delegated to the Director of the United States Information Agency, acting in consultation with the Secretary of State and the Secretary of the Treasury, by Executive Order 12555 of March 10, 1986, 51 F.R. 8475.

[21] The functions conferred upon the President by this subsec. relating to the receipt of reports were delegated to the Director of the United States Information Agency, acting in consultation with the Secretary of State and the Secretary of the Treasury, by Executive Order 12555 of March 10, 1986,51F.R. 8475.

[22] The functions conferred upon the President by this section relating to the determinations to be made about the disclosure of matters involved in the Committee's proceedings were delegated to the Director of the United States Information Agency, acting in consultation with the Secretary of State and the Secretary of the Treasury, by Executive Order 12555 of March 10, 1986, 51 F.R. 8475.

[23] 19 U.S.C. 2606

[24] 19 U.S.C. 2607

[25] 19 U.S.C. 2608

[26] 19 U.S.C. 2609

[27] 19 U.S.C. 2610

[28] 19 U.S.C. 2611

[29] 19 U.S.C. 2612

[30] 19 U.S.C. 2613

UNITED KINGDOM OF GREAT BRITAIN AND NORTHERN IRELAND

STATUTORY INSTRUMENTS

2003 No. 2759

CUSTOMS AND EXCISE

The Export of Objects of Cultural Interest (Control) Order 2003

Made - - - -	*17th November 2003*
Laid before Parliament	*18th November 2003*
Coming into force - -	*1st May 2004*

The Secretary of State, in exercise of the powers conferred upon her by sections 1, 5 and 7 of the Export Control Act 2002 (**1**) hereby makes the following Order:

Citation, commencement and interpretation

1. —(1) This Order may be cited as the Export of Objects of Cultural Interest (Control) Order 2003 and shall come into force on 1st May 2004.

(2) In this Order, unless the context otherwise requires-

"the Act" means the Export Control Act 2002;

"the Commissioners" means the Commissioners of Customs and Excise;

"Community Licence" means an authorisation granted by the Secretary of State (whether before or after commencement of this Order) under the Regulation;

"cultural goods" shall have the same meaning as that given in the Regulation;

"exportation" includes shipment as stores and, unless the context otherwise requires, means exportation from the United Kingdom to any destination except for the Isle of Man;

"objects" mean objects of cultural interest of a description specified in and not excluded from the Schedule to this Order;

"prescribed sum" has the same meaning as in the Customs and Excise Management Act 1979 (**2**); and

"the Regulation" means Council Regulation (EEC) No 3911/92 of 9 December 1992 on the export of cultural goods (**3**).

(**1**) 2002 c. 28

(**2**) 1979 c. 2.

(**3**) OJ No. L 395, 31.12.92, p.1, as amended by Council Regulation (EC) No 2469/96 (OJ No. L 335, 16.12.96, p.9), Council Regulation (EC) No 1103/97 (OJ L 162, 17.06.97, p.1) and Council Regulation (EC) No 974/2001 (OJ No L 137, 19.05.01, p.10).

Controls on the export of objects of cultural interest

2. Subject to the provisions of this Order, all objects are prohibited to be exported to any destination except under the authority of a licence in writing granted by the Secretary of State, and in accordance with all the conditions attached to the licence.

Licences

3.—(1) A Community Licence or licence granted by the Secretary of State under article 2 may be:

(a) general or specific;

(b) unlimited or limited so as to expire on a specified date unless renewed; and

(c) subject to or without conditions, and any such condition may require any act or omission before or after the exportation of objects under the licence.

(2) Any such licence may be varied, suspended or revoked by the Secretary of State at any time and in such circumstances and on such terms as the Secretary of State thinks fit, by serving a notice to that effect on the holder of the licence.

Misleading applications for licences etc.

4.—(1) Where for the purpose of obtaining a licence under article 2 or a Community Licence, any person either—

(a) makes any statement or furnishes any document or information which to his knowledge is false in a material particular; or

(b) recklessly makes any statement or furnishes any document or information which is false in a material particular,

he shall be guilty of an offence.

(2) A person guilty of an offence under paragraph (1) above shall be liable—

(a) on summary conviction to a fine of the prescribed sum, and

(b) on conviction on indictment to a fine of any amount, or imprisonment for a term not exceeding 2 years, or to both,

and any licence which may have been granted in connection with the application for which the false statement was made or the false document or information furnished, shall be void as from the time it was granted.

Failure to comply with licence conditions

5.—(1) Subject to the provisions of paragraph (2) below, any person who—

(a) has done any act under the authority of a licence granted under article 2 or a Community Licence; and

(b) fails to comply with any condition attaching to that licence, shall be guilty of an offence.

(2) A person guilty of an offence under paragraph (1) shall be liable—

(a) on summary conviction to a fine of the prescribed sum, and

(b) on conviction on indictment to a fine of any amount, or imprisonment for a term not exceeding 2 years, or to both.

(3) No person shall be guilty of an offence under paragraph (1) where—

(a) the licence condition in question had been previously modified by the Secretary of State;

and

(b) the alleged failure to comply would not have been a failure had the licence not been so modified; and

(c) the condition with which he failed to comply was modified, otherwise than with his consent, by the Secretary of State after the doing of the act authorised by the licence.

Customs powers to demand evidence of destination

6.—(1) Any person who exports or ships objects or cultural goods, shall, if so required by the Commissioners, furnish within such time as the Commissioners may determine, evidence of the destination to which the objects or cultural goods were delivered and, if he fails to do so, he shall be guilty of an offence.

(2) Any person guilty of an offence under paragraph (1) shall be liable on summary conviction to a fine not exceeding level 4 on the standard scale.

Application of the Customs and Excise Management Act 1979

7.—(1) It shall be the duty of the Commissioners to take such action as they consider appropriate to secure the enforcement of this Order.

(2) It shall be the duty of the Commissioners to take such action as they consider appropriate to secure the enforcement of the Regulation in respect of the export of cultural goods.

Use and disclosure of information

8.—(1) This article applies to information which is held by—

(a) the Secretary of State, or

(b) the Commissioners,

in connection with the operation of controls imposed by this Order or by any directly applicable Community provision on the exportation of cultural goods.

(2) Information to which this article applies may be used for the purposes of, or for any purposes connected with—

(a) the exercise of functions in relation to any control imposed by this Order or by any order made under the Act;

(b) giving effect to any European Community or other international obligation of the United Kingdom;

(c) facilitating the exercise by an authority or international organisation outside the United Kingdom of functions which correspond to functions conferred by or in connection with any activity subject to any control by this Order or by any order made under the Act,

and may be disclosed to any person for use for these purposes.

(3) No disclosure of information shall be made by virtue of this article unless the Secretary of State is, or the Commissioners are, satisfied that the making of the disclosure is proportionate to what is sought to be achieved by it.

(4) For the purposes of this article "information" is any information that relates to a particular business or other activity carried on by a person.

(5) Nothing in this article shall be taken to prejudice any power to disclose information which exists apart from this article.

(6) The information that may be disclosed by virtue of this article includes information obtained before the commencement of this Order.

Tessa Jowell
Secretary of State for Culture, Media and Sport,
Department of Culture, Media and Sport

17th November 2003

SCHEDULE 1

Article 1

OBJECTS OF CULTURAL INTEREST

1. Any objects of cultural interest manufactured or produced more than 50 years before the date of exportation except:

(a) postage stamps and other articles of philatelic interest;

(b) birth, marriage or death certificates or other documents relating to the personal affairs of the exporter or the spouse of the exporter;

(c) letters or other writings written by or to the exporter or the spouse of the exporter; and

(d) goods exported by, and being the personal property of, the manufacturer or producer thereof, or the spouse, widow or widower of that person.

EXPLANATORY NOTE

(This note is not part of the Order)

This Order replaces the remaining provisions of S.I.1992/3092 that have been revoked by the Export Control Act 1992 (c.28).

A Regulatory Impact Assessment has not been prepared for this Order.

STATUTORY INSTRUMENTS

2009 No. 2164

CUSTOMS AND EXCISE

The Export of Objects of Cultural Interest (Control) (Amendment) Order 2009

Made - - - -	*5th August2009*
Laid before Parliament	*6th August2009*
Coming into force - -	*28th August2009*

The Secretary of State makes the following Order in exercise of the powers conferred by sections 1, 5 and 7 of the Export Control Act 2002 (**1**):

Citation and commencement

1. This Order may be cited as the Export of Objects of Cultural Interest (Control) (Amendment) Order 2009 and comes into force on 28th August 2009.

Amendment of the Export of Objects of Cultural Interest (Control) Order 2003

2. For the definition of "the Regulation" in article 1(2) of the Export of Objects of Cultural Interest (Control) Order 2003 (**2**) substitute "'the Regulation' means Council Regulation (EC)No116/2009 of 18 December 2008 on the export of cultural goods (**3**).".

Gerry Sutcliffe
Minister of State
5th August 2009 Department for Culture Media and Sport

(**1**) 2002 c. 28.
(**2**) S.I. 2003/2759
(**3**) OJ L 39, 10.02.2009, p.1-7.

EXPLANATORY NOTE

(This note is not part of the Order)

This Order amends the definition of "the Regulation" in article 1(2) of the Export of Objects of Cultural Interest (Control) Order 2003 (S.I. 2003/2759) by deleting the reference to Council Regulation (EEC) No. 3911/92 ("the 1992 Regulation") and substituting a reference to Council Regulation (EC) No 116/2009 ("the codified Regulation"). The codified Regulation does not make any substantive change; it consolidates the provisions of the 1992 Regulation and the amendments made to the 1992 Regulation by Council Regulation (EC) No. 2469/96; Council Regulation (EC) No 947/2001 and Council Regulation (EC) No 806/2003.

Dealing in Cultural Objects (Offences) Act 2003

2003 CHAPTER 27

An Act to provide for an offence of acquiring, disposing of, importing or exporting tainted cultural objects, or agreeing or arranging to do so; and for connected purposes.

[30th October 2003]

BE IT ENACTED by the Queen's most Excellent Majesty, by and with the advice and consent of the Lords Spiritual and Temporal, and Commons, in this present Parliament assembled, and by the authority of the same, as follows: —

1. Offence of dealing in tainted cultural objects

(1) A person is guilty of an offence if he dishonestly deals in a cultural object that is tainted, knowing or believing that the object is tainted.

(2) It is immaterial whether he knows or believes that the object is a cultural object.

(3) A person guilty of the offence is liable—

(a) on conviction on indictment, to imprisonment for a term not exceeding seven years or a fine (or both),

(b) on summary conviction, to imprisonment for a term not exceeding six months or a fine not exceeding the statutory maximum (or both).

2. Meaning of "tainted cultural object"

(1) "Cultural object" means an object of historical, architectural or archaeological interest.

(2) A cultural object is tainted if, after the commencement of this Act—

(a) a person removes the object in a case falling within subsection (4) or he excavates the object, and

(b) the removal or excavation constitutes an offence.

(3) It is immaterial whether—

(a) the removal or excavation was done in the United Kingdom or elsewhere,

(b) the offence is committed under the law of a part of the United Kingdom or under the law of any other country or territory.

(4) An object is removed in a case falling within this subsection if—

(a) it is removed from a building or structure of historical, architectural or archaeological interest where the object has at any time formed part of the building or structure, or

(b) it is removed from a monument of such interest.

(5) "Monument" means—

(a) any work, cave or excavation,

(b) any site comprising the remains of any building or structure or of any work, cave or excavation,

(c) any site comprising, or comprising the remains of, any vehicle, vessel, aircraft or other movable structure, or part of any such thing.

(6) "Remains" includes any trace or sign of the previous existence of the thing in question.

(7) It is immaterial whether—

(a) a building, structure or work is above or below the surface of the land,

(b) a site is above or below water.

(8) This section has effect for the purposes of section 1.

3. Meaning of "deals in"

(1) A person deals in an object if (and only if) he—

(a) acquires, disposes of, imports or exports it,

(b) agrees with another to do an act mentioned in paragraph (a), or

(c) makes arrangements under which another person does such an act or under which another person agrees with a third person to do such an act.

(2) "Acquires" means buys, hires, borrows or accepts.

(3) "Disposes of" means sells, lets on hire, lends or gives.

(4) In relation to agreeing or arranging to do an act, it is immaterial whether the act is agreed or arranged to take place in the United Kingdom or elsewhere.

(5) This section has effect for the purposes of section 1.

4. Customs and Excise prosecutions

(1) Proceedings for an offence relating to the dealing in a tainted cultural object may be instituted by order of the Commissioners of Customs and Excise if it appears to them that the offence has involved the importation or exportation of such an object.

(2) An offence relates to the dealing in a tainted cultural object if it is—

(a) an offence under section 1, or

(b) an offence of inciting the commission of, or attempting or conspiring to commit, such an offence.

(3) Proceedings for an offence which are instituted under subsection (1) are to be commenced in the name of an officer, but may be continued by another officer.

(4) Where the Commissioners of Customs and Excise investigate, or propose to investigate, any matter with a view to determining—

(a) whether there are grounds for believing that a person has committed an offence which relates to the dealing in a tainted cultural object and which involves the importation or exportation of such an object, or

(b) whether a person should be prosecuted for such an offence,

the matter is to be treated as an assigned matter within the meaning of the Customs and Excise Management Act 1979 (c. 2).

(5) Nothing in this section affects any powers of any person (including any officer) apart from this section.

(6) "Officer" means a person commissioned by the Commissioners of Customs and Excise under section 6(3) of the Customs and Excise Management Act 1979.

5. Offences by bodies corporate

(1) If an offence under section 1 committed by a body corporate is proved—

(a) to have been committed with the consent or connivance of an officer, or

(b) to be attributable to any neglect on his part,

he (as well as the body corporate) is guilty of the offence and liable to be proceeded against and punished accordingly.

(2) "Officer", in relation to a body corporate, means—

(a) a director, manager, secretary or other similar officer of the body,

(b) a person purporting to act in any such capacity.

(3) If the affairs of a body corporate are managed by its members, subsection (1) applies in relation to the acts and defaults of a member in connection with his functions of management as if he were a director of the body.

6. Short title, commencement and extent

(1) This Act may be cited as the Dealing in Cultural Objects (Offences) Act 2003.

(2) This Act comes into force at the end of the period of two months beginning with the day on which it is passed.

(3) This Act does not extend to Scotland.

GERMANY

Bundesrat **Drucksache** **346/16**

24.06.16

K

Gesetzesbeschluss

des DeutschenBundestages

Gesetz zur Neuregelung des Kulturgutschutzrechts

Der Deutsche Bundestag hat in seiner 179. Sitzung am 23. Juni 2016 aufgrund der Beschlussempfehlung und des Berichts des Ausschusses für Kultur und Medien – Drucksache 18/8908 – den von der Bundesregierung eingebrachten

Entwurf eines Gesetzes zur Neuregelung des Kulturgutschutzrechts
– Drucksache 18/7456 –

in beigefügter Fassung angenommen.

(1) (2)

---

(1) Fristablauf: 15.07.16

(2) Erster Durchgang: Drs. 538/15

Vertrieb: Bundesanzeiger Verlag GmbH, Postfach 10 05 34, 50445 Köln

Telefon (02 21) 97 66 83 40, Fax (02 21) 97 66 83 44, www.betrifft-gesetze.de

ISSN 0720-2946

Gesetz zur Neuregelung des Kulturgutschutzrechts*

Vom 31.Juli 2016

Der Bundestag hat mit Zustimmung des Bundesrates das folgende Gesetz beschlossen:

Kapitel 1
Allgemeine Bestimmungen

§ 1 Anwendungsbereich

Das Gesetz regelt

1. den Schutz nationalen Kulturgutes gegen Abwanderung,
2. die Ein- und Ausfuhr von Kulturgut,
3. das Inverkehrbringen von Kulturgut,
4. die Rückgabe unrechtmäßig eingeführten Kulturgutes,
5. die Rückgabe unrechtmäßig ausgeführten Kulturgutes und
6. die Rückgabezusage im internationalen Leihverkehr.

§ 2 Begriffsbestimmungen

(1) Im Sinne dieses Gesetzes ist oder sind

1. „archäologisches Kulturgut“ bewegliche Sachen oder Sachgesamtheiten, die von Menschen geschaffen oder bearbeitet wurden oder Aufschluss über menschliches Leben in vergangener Zeit geben, sich im Boden oder in einem Gewässer befinden oder befunden haben oder bei denen aufgrund der Gesamtumstände dies zu vermuten ist,
2. „Ausfuhr“ die Verbringung von Kulturgut aus dem Bundesgebiet,
3. „Drittstaat“ jeder Staat, der kein Mitgliedstaat der Europäischen Union ist,
4. „Eigenbesitzer“ die Person, die die tatsächliche Sachherrschaft über das Kulturgut für sich selbst ausübt,
5. „Einfuhr“ die Verbringung von Kulturgut in das Bundesgebiet,
6. „Fremdbesitzer“ die Person, die die tatsächliche Sachherrschaft über das Kulturgut für andere ausübt,

---

* Artikel 1 dieses Gesetzes dient der Umsetzung der Richtlinie 2014/60/EU des Europ.ischen Parlaments und des Rates vom 15. Mai 2014 über die Rückgabe von unrechtmäßig aus dem Hoheitsgebiet eines Mitgliedstaats verbrachten Kulturgütern und zur Änderung der Verordnung (EU) Nr. 1024/2012 (Neufassung) (ABl. L 159 vom 28.5.2014, S. 1).

7. „Haager Konvention“ die Haager Konvention vom 14. Mai 1954 zum Schutz von Kulturgut bei bewaffneten Konflikten (BGBl. 1967 II S. 1233, 1235),
8. „Herkunftsstaat“ ein Mitgliedstaat oder Vertragsstaat, in dem das Kulturgut entstanden ist oder der eine so enge Beziehung zu dem Kulturgut hat, dass er es zum Zeitpunkt der Verbringung aus seinem Hoheitsgebiet als nationales Kulturgut unter Schutz gestellt hat,
9. „Inverkehrbringen“ von Kulturgut das Anbieten, das Verkaufen, die Vermittlung, der Vertrieb, das Absetzen, die unentgeltliche Weiter- oder Abgabe zum Zweck der wirtschaftlichen Verwertung oder die wirtschaftliche Verwertung in sonstiger Weise im eigenen oder fremden Namen,
10. „Kulturgut“ jede bewegliche Sache oder Sachgesamtheit von künstlerischem, geschichtlichem oder archäo logischem Wert oder aus anderen Bereichen des kulturellen Erbes, insbesondere von paläontologischem, ethnographischem, numismatischem oder wissenschaftlichem Wert,
11. „Kulturgut bewahrende Einrichtung“ jede Einrichtung im Bundesgebiet, deren Hauptzweck die Bewahrung und Erhaltung von Kulturgut und die Sicherung des Zugangs der Öffentlichkeit zu diesem Kulturgut ist, insbesondere Museen, Bibliotheken und Archive,
12. „Mitgliedstaat“ jeder Mitgliedstaat der Europäischen Union außer der Bundesrepublik Deutschland,
13. „Protokoll zur Haager Konvention“ das Protokoll zur Konvention vom 14. Mai 1954 zum Schutz von Kul turgut bei bewaffneten Konflikten (BGBl. 1967 II S. 1233, 1300),
14. „rechtswidrig ausgegraben“ ein Kulturgut, wenn es unter Verstoß gegen eine inländische oder ausländische Rechtsvorschrift zum Schutz von archäologischem oder paläontologischem Kulturgut, insbesondere ohne eine nach einer solchen Rechtsvorschrift erforderliche Genehmigung, ausgegraben worden ist,
15. „Rückgabe“ die Verbringung des Kulturgutes in das Hoheitsgebiet des ersuchenden Staates zur Erfüllung eines Rückgabeanspruchs,
16. „Sachgesamtheit“ mehrere zusammengehörige Kulturgüter, insbesondere Archivbestände, Bibliotheksbe stände, Nachlässe, Sammlungen oder Teile davon,
17. „UNESCO-Übereinkommen“ das Übereinkommen über Maßnahmen zum Verbot und zur Verhütung der rechtswidrigen Einfuhr, Ausfuhr und Übereignung von Kulturgut (BGBl. 2007 II S. 626, 627),
18. die Verbringung von Kulturgut
    a) „vorübergehend“, wenn sie für einen von Anfang an befristeten Zeitraum von höchstens fünf Jahren erfolgt,
    b) „dauerhaft“, wenn sie für einen Zeitraum von mehr als fünf Jahren erfolgt,
19. „Vertragsstaat“ jeder andere Staat außer der Bundesrepublik Deutschland, für den das UNESCO-überein kommen bindend ist,
20. „Verzeichnis national wertvollen Kulturgutes“ ein Verzeichnis eines Landes, in das es Kulturgut als national wertvoll einträgt.

(2) Keine Ein-und Ausfuhr im Sinne dieses Gesetzes ist

1. die Herausgabe von Kulturgut durch Rechtshilfe im Sinne des § 66 des

Gesetzes über die internationale Rechtshilfe in Strafsachen in der Fassung der Bekanntmachung vom 27. Juni 1994 (BGBl. I S. 1537), das zuletzt durch Artikel 163 der Verordnung vom 31. August 2015 (BGBl. I S. 1474) geändert worden ist,
2. die Rückgabe von unrechtmäßig verbrachtem Kulturgut nach Kapitel 5 und
3. die Rückgabe von Kulturgut an einen anderen Staat oder aus einem ausländischen Staat aufgrund bilateraler völkerrechtlicher Vereinbarungen.

§ 3 Zuständige Behörden

(1) Zuständige Behörden im Sinne dieses Gesetzes sind die zuständigen Behörden der Länder, soweit in diesem Gesetz nichts anderes bestimmt ist. Die Länder benennen die zuständigen Behörden durch Gesetz oder Rechtsverordnung.

(2) Die zentrale Stelle der Bundesrepublik Deutschland im Sinne des Artikels 4 der Richtlinie 2014/60/EU des Europäischen Parlaments und des Rates vom 15. Mai 2014 über die Rückgabe von unrechtmäßig aus dem Hoheitsgebiet eines Mitgliedstaats verbrachten Kulturgütern und zur Änderung der Verordnung (EU) Nr. 1024/2012 (Neufassung) (ABl. L 159 vom 28.5.2014, S. 1), die durch die Berichtigung der Richtlinie 2014/60/EU des Europäischen Parlaments und des Rates vom 15. Mai 2014 über die Rückgabe von unrechtmäßig aus dem Hoheitsgebiet eines Mitgliedstaats verbrachten Kulturgütern und zur Änderung der Verordnung (EU) Nr. 1024/2012 (ABl. L 147 vom 12.6.2015, S. 24) berichtigt worden ist, für die Kontaktaufnahme und Zusam menarbeit zwischen den Mitgliedstaaten ist die für Kultur und Medien zuständige oberste Bundesbehörde.

§ 4 Internetportal zum Kulturgutschutz

(1) Die für Kultur und Medien zuständige oberste Bundesbehörde ist verpflichtet, ein zentrales Internet portal zum Kulturgutschutz zu errichten und zu unterhalten. Das Internetportal dient insbesondere der Unterrich tung der Öffentlichkeit und der Herstellung von Transparenz im Kulturgutschutz, namentlich durch die
1. Darstellung der Aufgaben und Ziele des Kulturgutschutzes,
2. Darstellung der nationalen und internationalen Rechtsgrundlagen des Kulturgutschutzes,
3. Unterstützung der Verwaltungsverfahren etwa durch Bereitstellung von Formularen und Leitfäden,
4. Datenbank zur Dokumentation geschützten Kulturgutes und
5. Information über zuständige Behörden und Ansprechpartner.

(2) Die Datenbereitstellung im Internet erfolgt durch die für Kultur und Medien zuständige oberste Bun desbehörde und die zuständigen obersten Landesbehörden in deren jeweiliger Verantwortlichkeit.

(3) Bund und Länder richten einen Verwaltungsausschuss zur koordinierten Erfüllung der maßgeblichen Aufgaben nach diesem Gesetz und zur Gewährleistung der

einheitlichen Verwaltungspraxis der Länder ein, ins besondere zur
1. Beschlussfassung über Grundsätze der Veröffentlichung der Verzeichnisse national wertvollen Kulturgutes nach § 16,
2. Beschlussfassung über Grundsätze des gemeinsamen Verfahrens nach § 79 und
3. Zusammenarbeit zwischen Bund und Ländern.

Der Verwaltungsausschuss berät darüber hinaus die oberste für Kultur und Medien zuständige Bundesbehörde bei dem Betrieb des Internetportals. Ihm gehören zwei Vertreter oder Vertreterinnen der für Kultur und Medien zuständigen obersten Bundesbehörde und ein Vertreter oder eine Vertreterin jedes Landes an.

(4) Der Verwaltungsausschuss trifft seine Beschlüsse mit der Mehrheit der abgegebenen Stimmen. Bei Entscheidungen über Fragen, die nicht die Aufgaben der Länder nach diesem Gesetz betreffen, kann ein Beschluss nicht gegen die Stimmen der Vertreter der für Kultur und Medien zuständigen obersten Bundesbehörde getroffen werden. Die Beschlüsse sind verbindlich für alle Länder, wenn sie mit einer Mehrheit von drei Vierteln der abge gebenen Stimmen getroffen werden. Ein Mehrheitsbeschluss im schriftlichen Verfahren ist möglich, wenn nicht drei Viertel der Mitglieder des Verwaltungsausschusses dem widersprechen.

(5) Zur Klärung weiterer Verfahrensfragen und zur Regelung der Aufgaben im Einzelnen gibt sich der Verwaltungsausschuss eine Geschäftsordnung.

Kapitel 2
Schutz von Kulturgut vor Abwanderung

Abschnitt 1
Unterschutzstellen des nationalen Kulturgutes

§ 5 Grundsatz

Nationales Kulturgut unterliegt als Teil des kulturellen Erbes Deutschlands dem Schutz gegen Abwanderung aus dem Bundesgebiet nach diesem Gesetz.

§ 6 Nationales Kulturgut

(1) Nationales Kulturgut ist Kulturgut, das
1. in ein Verzeichnis national wertvollen Kulturgutes eingetragen ist,
2. sich in öffentlichem Eigentum und im Bestand einer öffentlich-rechtlichen Kulturgut bewahrenden Einrich tung befindet,
3. sich im Eigentum und im Bestand einer Kulturgut bewahrenden Einrichtung befindet, die überwiegend durch Zuwendungen der öffentlichen Hand finanziert wird, oder
4. Teil einer Kunstsammlung des Bundes oder der Länder ist.

(2) Nur mit Zustimmung des Verleihers oder Deponenten gegenüber der zuständigen Behörde gilt Kultur gut in einer öffentlich-rechtlichen Kulturgut bewahrenden Einrichtung oder einer solchen, die überwiegend durch Zuwendungen der öffentlichen Hand finanziert wird, für die Dauer des Leih- oder Depositalvertrages vorüberge- hend ebenfalls als nationales Kulturgut. Der Verleiher oder der Deponent kann seine Zustimmung jederzeit wi derrufen. Die Einrichtung hat den Verleiher oder Deponenten über die Rechtsfolgen des Verzichts auf den Schutz als nationales Kulturgut nach den §§ 69 und 70 zu unterrichten. Dieser Schutz endet mit der Kündigung oder mit dem Ablauf des Leih- oder Depositalvertrages.

§ 7 Eintragung in ein Verzeichnis national wertvollen Kulturgutes

(1) Kulturgut ist von der obersten Landesbehörde in ein Verzeichnis national wertvollen Kulturgutes ein zutragen, wenn

1. es besonders bedeutsam für das kulturelle Erbe Deutschlands, der Länder oder einer seiner historischen Re gionen und damit identitätsstiftend für die Kultur Deutschlands ist und
2. seine Abwanderung einen wesentlichen Verlust für den deutschen Kulturbesitz bedeuten würde und deshalb sein Verbleib im Bundesgebiet im herausragenden kulturellen öffentlichen Interesse liegt.

Werke lebender Urheber oder Hersteller dürfen nur mit deren Zustimmung eingetragen werden.

(2) Eine Sachgesamtheit ist auch dann nach Absatz 1 in ein Verzeichnis national wertvollen Kulturgutes einzutragen, wenn die Sachgesamtheit als solche, nicht aber zwingend ihre einzelnen Bestandteile die Kriterien nach Absatz 1 erfüllen. Einer Eintragung steht nicht entgegen, wenn eine Sachgesamtheit

1. teilweise zerstört ist,
2. an unterschiedlichen Orten im Inland aufbewahrt ist oder
3. teilweise im Ausland aufbewahrt ist.

(3) Zuständig für die Eintragung in ein Verzeichnis national wertvollen Kulturgutes ist die oberste Landes- behörde des Landes, in dem sich das Kulturgut zum Zeitpunkt der Einleitung des Eintragungsverfahrens befindet. Die Zuständigkeit bleibt bestehen, bis die Entscheidung über die Eintragung unanfechtbar geworden ist.

(4) Die Eintragung von Kulturgut im Eigentum der Kirchen und der als Körperschaften des öffentlichen Rechts anerkannten Religionsgemeinschaften richtet sich nach § 9.

§ 8 Nachträgliche Eintragung

(1) Ist Kulturgut unter Verstoß gegen § 24 ausgeführt worden, so kann es von der zuständigen obersten Landesbehörde auch nach der Ausfuhr in ein Verzeichnis national wertvollen Kulturgutes eingetragen werden, wenn die Voraussetzungen nach §

7 Absatz 1 und 2 erfüllt sind.

(2) Die örtliche Zuständigkeit für die Eintragung richtet sich nach dem Ort der letzten dauerhaften Bele genheit im Bundesgebiet. Ist dieser Ort nicht feststellbar, bestimmt die für Kultur und Medien zuständige oberste Bundesbehörde die zuständige oberste Landesbehörde. Dabei hat sie die besondere Verbindung des Kulturgutes mit einem Land aus historischen oder anderen Gründen zu berücksichtigen.

(3) Die Befugnis zur nachträglichen Eintragung in ein Verzeichnis national wertvollen Kulturgutes endet, wenn die zuständige oberste Landesbehörde das Eintragungsverfahren nicht innerhalb eines Jahres eingeleitet hat, nachdem sie von der unrechtmäßigen Ausfuhr und dem Ort der neuen Belegenheit Kenntnis erlangt hat.

(4) Mit der Einleitung des Eintragungsverfahrens gilt das Kulturgut nach Absatz 1 als nationales Kulturgut, bis die Entscheidung über die Eintragung unanfechtbar geworden ist.

§ 9 Kulturgut im Eigentum der Kirchen und Religionsgemeinschaften

(1) Die Kirchen und die als Körperschaften des öffentlichen Rechts anerkannten Religionsgemeinschaften können bei der zuständigen obersten Landesbehörde beantragen, dass Kulturgut, das sich in ihrem Eigentum be findet, in ein Verzeichnis national wertvollen Kulturgutes eingetragen wird. § 7 Absatz 1 und 2 ist entsprechend anzuwenden.

(2) Bei einer nachträglichen Eintragung nach § 8 kann der Antrag nur innerhalb der Frist nach § 8 Absatz 3 gestellt werden. Die zuständige oberste Landesbehörde unterrichtet unverzüglich die Kirche oder die als Körper- schaft des öffentlichen Rechts anerkannte Religionsgemeinschaft, wenn sie von Umständen Kenntnis erhält, die einen Antrag nach Absatz 1 ermöglichen.

(3) Die Kirchen und die als Körperschaften des öffentlichen Rechts anerkannten Religionsgemeinschaften können bei den obersten Landesbehörden beantragen, dass für einzelne Sachgesamtheiten ihrer Kulturgut bewah renden Einrichtungen und für das Inventar ihrer liturgischen Räume § 6 Absatz 1 Nummer 3 entsprechend anzu wenden ist mit der Maßgabe, dass an die Stelle der Finanzierung durch die öffentliche Hand die Finanzierung durch die Kirchen oder Religionsgemeinschaften tritt.

§ 10 Ausnahmen zur Eintragung von Kulturgut bei Leihgaben aus dem Ausland und nach Rückkehr in das Bundesgebiet

(1) Für ehemals im Bundesgebiet belegenes Kulturgut, das sich mehr als fünf Jahre vor dem 6. August 2016 wieder in das außerhalb des Bundesgebietes befunden hat und nach dem 6. August 2016 wieder in das Bundesgebiet eingeführt werden soll, kann die zu- ständige oberste Landesbehörde, wenn eine Eintragung nach § 7 in Betracht kommt, auf Antrag einer Kulturgut bewahrenden Einrichtung vor der Einfuhr dem Eigentümer des Kulturgutes zusichern, dass das Kulturgut nicht nach § 7 in ein

Verzeichnis national wertvollen Kulturgutes eingetragen wird, sofern der Eigentümer die Gewähr dafür bietet, dass das Kulturgut für mindestens fünf Jahre

1. sich ohne Unterbrechung im Bundesgebiet befinden wird und
2. bei der antragstellenden Einrichtung als Leihgabe öffentlich ausgestellt oder für die Forschung zugänglich gemacht wird.

(2) Die oberste Landesbehörde kann die Zusicherung davon abhängig machen, dass die Kulturgut bewah rende Einrichtung nach Absatz 1 mit dem Eigentümer des Kulturgutes einen Vertrag über einen möglichen An kauf des Kulturgutes schließt.

(3) Die Zusicherung nach Absatz 1 ist von der zuständigen obersten Landesbehörde mit Nebenbestimmun gen zu versehen, die sicherstellen, dass die Voraussetzungen nach Absatz 1 Nummer 1 und 2 eingehalten werden. Weitere Nebenbestimmungen sind zulässig.

(4) Die zuständige oberste Landesbehörde kann über die Zusicherung nach Absatz 1 auch einen öffentlich- rechtlichen Vertrag mit dem Eigentümer schließen.

(5) Wird Kulturgut nach Ablauf des vereinbarten Zeitraums nach Absatz 1 ausgeführt, so unterliegt es nicht der Genehmigungspflicht nach § 24 Absatz 1 Nummer 2.

(6) Wird Kulturgut unter Verstoß gegen die Nebenbestimmungen zur Zusicherung nach Absatz 1 oder ge gen den nach Absatz 4 geschlossenen öffentlich rechtlichen Vertrag ausgeführt, gilt das Kulturgut als unrechtmäßig ausgeführt. Dies gilt auch dann, wenn der Eigentümer bei der Ausfuhr gegen eine Vereinbarung verstößt, die er mit der zuständigen Behörde oder mit einer Kulturgut bewahrenden Einrichtung nach Absatz 1 getroffen hat.

(7) Wird ein Leihvertrag zwischen einem Verleiher mit nicht nur vorübergehendem Wohnsitz oder Sitz im Ausland und einer Kulturgut bewahrenden Einrichtung im Inland abgeschlossen, so kann die zuständige oberste Landesbehörde außer in den Fällen einer Rückkehr des Kulturgutes nach Absatz 1 auf Antrag des Entleihers dem Verleiher vor der Einfuhr des Kulturgutes schriftlich zusichern, dass für die Dauer von bis zu sechs Monaten nach Ende des Leihvertrages kein Verfahren zur Eintragung in ein Verzeichnis national wertvollen Kulturgutes einge leitet wird. Auf Kulturgut, das sich vor dem 6. August 2016 auf der Grund lage eines Leihvertrages im Sinne des Satzes 1 im Inland befindet, findet § 7 Absatz 1 und 2 ebenfalls für die Dauer von bis zu sechs Monate nach Ablauf des Leihvertrages keine Anwendung. Die Ausfuhr bis zu sechs Monaten nach Beendigung eines Leihvertrages nach den Sätzen 1 und 2 unterliegt nicht der Genehmigungspflicht nach § 24 Absatz 1 Nummer 2.

§ 11 Ortswechsel von eingetragenem Kulturgut

(1) Wird Kulturgut, das in ein Verzeichnis national wertvollen Kulturgutes eingetragen ist, für weniger als ein Jahr von einem Land in ein anderes Land verbracht, so behält die Eintragung in das Verzeichnis national wertvollen Kulturgutes ihre Wirkung.

(2) Wird Kulturgut, das in ein Verzeichnis national wertvollen Kulturgutes eingetragen ist, für mehr als ein Jahr in ein anderes Land verbracht, so wird es in das Verzeichnis

national wertvollen Kulturgutes des Landes übertragen, in das es verbracht worden ist. Der unmittelbare Besitzer hat den Ortswechsel und den Zeitpunkt des Ortswechsels der nunmehr zuständigen obersten Landesbehörde schriftlich oder elektronisch mitzuteilen.

§ 12 Steuerliche Begünstigung von national wertvollem Kulturgut, Ausgleich bei Verkauf infolge wirtschaftli cher Notlage

(1) Kulturgut, das in ein Verzeichnis national wertvollen Kulturgutes eingetragen ist, wird bei der Heran ziehung zu Steuern begünstigt nach

1. § 13 Absatz 1 Nummer 2 Buchstabe b Doppelbuchstabe bb des Erbschaftsteuer- und Schenkungsteuergeset zes in der Fassung des Artikels 8 des Gesetzes vom 31. Juli 2016(BGBl. I S. 1914) sowie
2. § 10g des Einkommensteuergesetzes in der Fassung des Artikels 7 des Gesetzes vom 31. Juli 2016(BGBl. I S. 1914).

(2) Wird die Genehmigung zur dauerhaften Ausfuhr nach § 23 rechtskräftig versagt und ist der Eigentümer national wertvollen Kulturgutes infolge wirtschaftlicher Notlage zum Verkauf gezwungen, so hat die oberste Lan desbehörde des Landes, in dem sich das Kulturgut befindet, im Einvernehmen mit der für Kultur und Medien zuständigen obersten Bundesbehörde auf einen billigen Ausgleich unter Berücksichtigung der Steuervorteile nach Absatz 1 hinzuwirken.

§ 13 Löschung der Eintragung

(1) Haben sich die das Kulturgut betreffenden Umstände, die zur Eintragung des Kulturgutes in ein Ver zeichnis national wertvollen Kulturgutes geführt haben, wesentlich verändert, so kann die Eintragung von Amts wegen oder auf Antrag des Eigentümers von der obersten Landesbehörde gelöscht werden.

(2) Eine Änderung wesentlicher Umstände nach Absatz 1 ist stets gegeben, wenn rechtskräftig oder durch eine abschließende Regelung der Beteiligten im Hinblick auf einen Entzug festgestellt ist, dass das Kulturgut zwischen dem 30. Januar 1933 und dem 8. Mai 1945 aufgrund der Verfolgung durch den Nationalsozialismus einem früheren Eigentümer entzogen worden ist und es aus dem Bundesgebiet ausge führt werden soll, um es an außerhalb des Bundesgebietes lebende ursprüngliche Eigentümer oder deren dort lebende Rechtsnachfolger zurückzugeben.

(3) Ist Kulturgut nach § 11 Absatz 2 in das Verzeichnis eines anderen Landes übertragen worden, so gibt die oberste Landesbehörde vor ihrer Entscheidung über die Löschung der ursprünglich für die Eintragung zustän digen obersten Landesbehörde die Gelegenheit zur Stellungnahme.

(4) Für das Verfahren zur Löschung der Eintragung ist § 14 Absatz 1 bis 5 entsprechend anzuwenden.

Abschnitt 2
Verfahren und Mitwirkungspflichten; Veröffentlichung

§ 14 Eintragungsverfahren

(1) Die Einleitung des Verfahrens auf Eintragung in ein Verzeichnis national wertvollen Kulturgutes erfolgt von Amts wegen oder auf Antrag des Eigentümers. Der Antrag ist an die oberste Landesbehörde zu richten und muss folgende Angaben enthalten

1. die Bezeichnung des Kulturgutes,
2. den Namen und die Anschrift des Eigentümers und des Besitzers,
3. die Belegenheit zum Zeitpunkt der Antragstellung und
4. die Begründung der Eintragungsvoraussetzungen nach § 7 Absatz 1 Satz 1 Nummer 1 und 2.

(2) Die obersten Landesbehörden berufen Sachverständigenausschüsse, die keiner Weisung unterliegen. Diese bestehen aus fünf Sachverständigen und werden für die Dauer von fünf Jahren berufen, wobei Wiederbe rufungen möglich sind. Bei der Berufung sind sachkundige Personen aus dem Kreis der Kulturgut bewahrenden Einrichtungen, der Wissenschaft, des Kunsthandels und Antiquariats sowie der privaten Sammlerinnen und Sammler zu berücksichtigen. Verbände und Organisationen aus diesen Bereichen können Vorschläge für die Be rufung einreichen. Eine der sachkundigen Personen ist auf Vorschlag der für Kultur und Medien zuständigen obersten Bundesbehörde zu berufen. Die Zusammensetzung der Sachverständigenausschüsse der Länder ist im Internetportal nach § 4 zu veröffentlichen. Die Ausschüsse können vor ihrer Entscheidung auch externe sachkun dige Personen anhören.

(3) Kulturgut darf nur im Benehmen mit dem Sachverständigenausschuss eingetragen werden. Die zustän dige oberste Landesbehörde hat nach Herstellung des Benehmens mit dem Sachverständigenausschuss und vor ihrer Sachentscheidung den Eigentümer des Kulturgutes zu hören.

(4) Die zuständige oberste Landesbehörde gibt vor ihrer Entscheidung über die Eintragung in ihr Verzeich nis national wertvollen Kulturgutes anderen Ländern die Gelegenheit zur Stellungnahme, sofern das Kulturgut zu diesen Ländern insbesondere aus historischen Gründen eine besondere Verbindung hat.

(5) Zur Wahrung eines gesamtstaatlichen Interesses kann auch die für Kultur und Medien zuständige oberste Bundesbehörde die Eintragung in ein Verzeichnis national wertvollen Kulturgutes beantragen.

(6) Das Eintragungsverfahren endet mit der Entscheidung der zuständigen obersten Landesbehörde über die Eintragung. Erfolgt diese Entscheidung nicht binnen sechs Monaten nach Einleitung des Verfahrens, so gilt das Verfahren als ohne Eintragung beendet. Verhandlungen des Eigentümers mit der zuständigen obersten Lan desbehörde, Rechtsmittel des Eigentümers im Verfahren sowie in begründeten

Ausnahmefällen bei der Einholung externen Sachverstands nach Absatz 2 Satz 7 hemmen die Frist. Die Frist ist ferner gehemmt, wenn der Eigentü mer seinen Mitwirkungspflichten nach § 15 nicht nachkommt oder das Verfahren sonst verzögert. Ist das Verfah ren ohne Eintragung beendet und die Beendigung nach § 17 bekannt gemacht worden, so kann ein erneutes Ver fahren zur Eintragung, auch in einem anderen Land, nur eingeleitet werden, wenn sich die Umstände, die zur Beendigung des Verfahrens geführt haben, wesentlich verändert haben.

(7) Der Eigentümer kann, sofern er nachweist, dass das Kulturgut die Alters- und Wertgrenzen der in § 24 Absatz 1 Nummer 1 in Bezug genommenen Verordnung übersteigt, entsprechend Absatz 1 auch unter Darlegung seines berechtigten Interesses und der Versicherung der Vollständigkeit und Wahrheit seiner Angaben beantragen, dass die zuständige Behörde verbindlich feststellt, dass die Voraussetzungen der Eintragung in das Verzeichnis national wertvollen Kulturgutes nicht vorliegen. Die zuständige Behörde kann den nach Absatz 2 berufenen Sach verständigenausschuss beteiligen. Die Absätze 4 und 6 Satz 5 gelten entsprechend. Die Ausfuhr von Kulturgut, für das eine solche verbindliche Feststellung vorliegt, unterliegt nicht der Genehmigungspflicht nach § 24 Ab satz 1 Nummer 2.

§ 15 Mitwirkungspflichten während des Eintragungsverfahrens

(1) Im Verfahren zur Eintragung in ein Verzeichnis national wertvollen Kulturgutes ist der Eigentümer, hilfsweise der unmittelbare Besitzer, verpflichtet, der obersten Landesbehörde

1. die zur eindeutigen Identifizierung des Kulturgutes erforderlichen Angaben, die Eigentumsverhältnisse und den Aufbewahrungsort mitzuteilen,
2. geeignete Abbildungen des Kulturgutes zur Verfügung zu stellen oder deren Herstellung durch die zustän dige oberste Landesbehörde oder eines oder einer durch sie Beauftragten zu gestatten und
3. nicht ausschließliche, zeitlich unbefristete, weltweite Rechte zur Vervielfältigung und öffentlichen Zugäng lichmachung der identifizierenden Angaben sowie der Abbildungen zur Nutzung für das Verzeichnis natio nal wertvollen Kulturgutes einzuräumen oder zu übertragen.

Urheberrechtliche Vorschriften bleiben unberührt.

(2) Der Eigentümer, hilfsweise der unmittelbare Besitzer, ist während des Eintragungsverfahrens verpflich tet, jede Änderung der mitgeteilten Angaben nach Absatz 1 Satz 1 Nummer 1 unverzüglich der obersten Landes behörde mitzuteilen.

§ 16 Führung und Veröffentlichung der Verzeichnisse national wertvollen Kulturgutes

(1) Die Länder führen ihre Verzeichnisse national wertvollen Kulturgutes in dem gemeinsamen Verfahren nach § 79 Absatz 1 Satz 1 und veröffentlichen sie zentral und

länderübergreifend im Internetportal nach § 4.

(2) Personenbezogene Daten des Eigentümers oder des Besitzers und der Ort der Belegenheit des eingetra genen Kulturgutes dürfen nicht veröffentlicht werden. Dies gilt nicht, soweit diese Angaben für die eindeutige Bezeichnung des Kulturgutes erforderlich sind.

(3) Die für Kultur und Medien zuständige oberste Bundesbehörde hat bei der Veröffentlichung durch or ganisatorische und dem jeweiligen Stand der Technik entsprechende technische Maßnahmen sicherzustellen, dass die Eintragungen während ihrer Veröffentlichung unversehrt, vollständig sowie aktuell bleiben und jederzeit ih rem Ursprung nach zugeordnet werden können.

(4) Für den Zugang zu einer Veröffentlichung ist § 15 Absatz 2 Satz 1 bis 3 des E-Government-Gesetzes entsprechend anzuwenden.

(5) Einzelheiten der Führung und Veröffentlichung der Verzeichnisse werden durch für alle Länder ver bindliche Beschlüsse des Verwaltungsausschusses nach § 4 Absatz 4 geregelt.

§ 17 Öffentliche Bekanntmachung

(1) Die zuständige oberste Landesbehörde hat jede Einleitung und jede Beendigung eines Verfahrens zur Eintragung, jede Eintragung, jede Löschung oder jede sonstige Änderung einer Eintragung in ein Verzeichnis national wertvollen Kulturgutes öffentlich im Bundesanzeiger bekannt zu machen und den Beteiligten mitzutei len.

(2) § 16 Absatz 2 ist entsprechend anzuwenden.

Abschnitt 3
Beschä digungsverbot und Mitteilungspflicht

§ 18 Beschädigungsverbot

(1) Es ist verboten, Kulturgut, das in ein Verzeichnis national wertvollen Kulturgutes eingetragen ist, zu zerstören, zu beschädigen oder dessen Erscheinungsbild nicht nur unerheblich und nicht nur vorübergehend zu verändern, sofern dieses nicht zur fachgerechten Konservierung und Restaurierung oder zur Forschung nach an erkannten wissenschaftlichen Standards erfolgt. § 304 Absatz 1 und 2 des Strafgesetzbuches bleibt unberührt.

(2) Absatz 1 gilt auch, wenn für ein Kulturgut das Verfahren zur Eintragung in ein Verzeichnis national wertvollen Kulturgutes eingeleitet ist.

§ 19 Mitteilungspflichten

(1) Der unmittelbare Besitzer eines Kulturgutes, das in ein Verzeichnis national

wertvollen Kulturgutes eingetragen ist, ist verpflichtet, der zuständigen obersten Landesbehörde unverzüglich das Abhandenkommen, die Zerstörung, die Beschädigung oder die nicht nur unerhebliche und nicht nur vorübergehende Veränderung des Erscheinungsbildes des Kulturgutes mitzuteilen. Bei Besitzwechsel ist der neue, hilfsweise der frühere unmittel bare Besitzer, zur Mitteilung verpflichtet.

(2) Sind der Eigentümer und der unmittelbare Besitzer des Kulturgutes nicht dieselbe Person, so gilt die Mitteilungspflicht nach Absatz 1 hilfsweise auch für den Eigentümer.

(3) Bei einem Eigentumswechsel ist der neue Eigentümer des Kulturgutes, hilfsweise der frühere Eigentü mer, verpflichtet, der zuständigen obersten Landesbehörde diesen Eigentumswechsel unverzüglich mitzuteilen.

(4) Die Absätze 1 bis 3 sind entsprechend anzuwenden, wenn für ein Kulturgut das Verfahren zur Eintra gung in ein Verzeichnis national wertvollen Kulturgutes eingeleitet ist.

Kapitel 3
Kulturgutverkehr

Abschnitt 1
Grundsatz

§ 20 Kulturgutverkehrsfreiheit

Kulturgut kann ein- oder ausgeführt sowie in Verkehr gebracht werden, soweit nicht dieses Gesetz oder andere Rechtsvorschriften, insbesondere unmittelbar geltende Rechtsakte der Europäischen Union, Verbote oder Beschränkungen vorsehen.

Abschnitt 2
Ausfuhr

§ 21 Ausfuhrverbot

Die Ausfuhr von Kulturgut ist verboten, wenn

1. für das Kulturgut das Verfahren zur Eintragung in ein Verzeichnis national wertvollen Kulturgutes eingelei tet worden ist und die Entscheidung über die Eintragung noch nicht unanfechtbar geworden ist,
2. für das Kulturgut keine nach den §§ 22, 23, 24, 27 Absatz 1 bis 3 erforderliche Genehmigung vorliegt oder nach den §§ 25, 26 oder § 27 Absatz 4 erteilt worden ist,
3. das Kulturgut nach § 32 Absatz 1 unrechtmäßig eingeführt worden ist,
4. das Kulturgut nach § 33 Absatz 1 sichergestellt ist oder

5. das Kulturgut nach § 81 Absatz 4 angehalten wird.

§ 22 Genehmigung der vorübergehenden Ausfuhr von nationalem Kulturgut

(1) Genehmigungspflichtig ist die vorübergehende Ausfuhr von nationalem Kulturgut nach § 6 in einen Mitgliedstaat oder Drittstaat.

(2) Die Genehmigung ist zu erteilen, wenn der Antragsteller die Gewähr dafür bietet, dass das zur Ausfuhr bestimmte Kulturgut in unbeschadetem Zustand und fristgerecht in das Bundesgebiet wieder eingeführt wird.

(3) Zuständig für die Erteilung der Genehmigung ist die oberste Landesbehörde des Landes, in dessen Ver zeichnis national wertvollen Kulturgutes das Kulturgut nach § 6 Absatz 1 Nummer 1 eingetragen ist oder in dem sich das Kulturgut nach § 6 Absatz 1 Nummer 2 und 3 zum Zeitpunkt der Antragstellung befindet. Ist der Antrag steller eine juristische Person mit mehreren Sitzen, so ist sein Hauptsitz im Bundesgebiet für die örtliche Zustän digkeit maßgeblich. Die oberste Landesbehörde kann die Zuständigkeit nach Maßgabe des Landesrechts auf eine andere Landesbehörde übertragen.

(4) Die Ausfuhrgenehmigung kann der Eigentümer oder ein bevollmächtigter Dritter beantragen.

(5) Eine durch Drohung, Bestechung oder Kollusion erwirkte oder durch unrichtige oder unvollständige Angaben erschlichene Genehmigung ist nichtig.

§ 23 Genehmigung der dauerhaften Ausfuhr von nationalem Kulturgut

(1) Genehmigungspflichtig ist die dauerhafte Ausfuhr von nationalem Kulturgut nach § 6 in einen Mit gliedstaat oder einen Drittstaat.

(2) Die Genehmigung ist zu versagen, wenn bei Abwägung der Umstände des Einzelfalls wesentliche Be lange des deutschen Kulturgutbesitzes überwiegen.

(3) Die Genehmigung ist zu erteilen, wenn rechtskräftig oder durch eine abschließende Regelung der Be teiligten im Hinblick auf einen Entzug festgestellt ist, dass das Kulturgut zwischen dem 30. Januar 1933 und dem 8. Mai 1945 einem früheren Eigentümer aufgrund der Verfolgung durch den Nationalsozialismus entzogen wor den ist und es aus dem Bundesgebiet ausgeführt werden soll, um es an außerhalb des Bundesgebietes lebende ursprüngliche Eigentümer oder deren dort lebende Rechtsnachfolger zurückzugeben.

(4) Zuständig für die Erteilung der Genehmigung ist die für Kultur und Medien zuständige oberste Bun desbehörde. Vor der Entscheidung hört sie die zuständige oberste Landesbehörde und einen Sachverständigen- ausschuss an. Hinsichtlich der Zusammensetzung des Sachverständigenausschusses ist § 14 Absatz 2 entsprechend anzuwenden. Im Falle eines Ortswechsels nach § 11 Absatz 2 ist auch die ursprünglich für die Eintragung zuständige oberste Landesbehörde anzuhören.

(5) Mit der Genehmigung der dauerhaften Ausfuhr endet die Unterschutzstellung nach § 6 Absatz 1. Ein getragenes Kulturgut ist nach der Ausfuhr von der zuständigen

obersten Landesbehörde aus dem Verzeichnis national wertvollen Kulturgutes zu löschen.

(6) Wird die Genehmigung zur dauerhaften Ausfuhr von eingetragenem Kulturgut abgelehnt, so unterrich tet die oberste für Kultur und Medien zuständige Bundesbehörde die nach Absatz 4 angehörten obersten Landes behörden. Auf Antrag des Eigentümers klären die oberste für Kultur und Medien zuständige Bundesbehörde und die nach Satz 1 unterrichteten Landesbehörden unter organisatorischer Leitung der Kulturstiftung der Länder bin nen zwölf Monaten die nach Abwägung der beteiligten Interessen angemessenen Bedingungen für einen mögli chen Ankauf des Kulturgutes durch oder für eine Kulturgut bewahrende Einrichtung im Bundesgebiet, die das Kulturgut der Öffentlichkeit zugänglich macht. Zur Klärung dieser Bedingungen gehören insbesondere

1. die Klärung, zum Bestand welcher Kulturgut bewahrenden Einrichtung das Kulturgut passen würde,
2. die Festlegung eines angemessenen Preises unter Berücksichtigung der Steuervorteile des Eigentümers nach § 11 Absatz 1 oder sonstiger Vorteile des Eigentümers,
3. die Klärung ob und gegebenenfalls wann und in welcher Höhe eine Kulturgut bewahrende Einrichtung nach Nummer 1 Fördermittel für einen Ankauf aus öffentlichen und privaten Mitteln erhalten könnte,
4. die sonstigen Modalitäten eines möglichen Ankaufes.

Für die Festlegung eines angemessenen Preises nach Nummer 2 zieht die Kulturstiftung der Länder externen Sachverstand heran.

(7) Sind die Bedingungen eines Ankaufes nach Absatz 6 geklärt, kann eine Kulturgut bewahrende Einrich tung nach Absatz 6 Nummer 1 dem Eigentümer auf dieser Basis und sofern die Finanzierung gesichert ist, ein Ankaufsangebot machen. Weist der Eigentümer nach, dass er den Ausfuhrantrag aufgrund einer wirtschaftlichen Notlage gestellt hat, wirken die beteiligten Bundes- und Landesbehörden darauf hin, dass die Finanzierung eines Ankaufes gesichert ist, und die Kulturgut bewahrende Einrichtung ein Ankaufsangebot unterbreitet. § 12 Absatz 2 bleibt unberührt.

(8) Der Eigentümer kann das Angebot nach Absatz 7 binnen sechs Monaten annehmen. Kommt ein Ankauf nicht zustande, kann ein neuer Ausfuhrantrag erst nach einer Frist von fünf Jahren nach Ablehnung des vorherge henden Antrages gestellt werden.

(9) In besonderen Einzelfällen kann auf Antrag des Landes die für Kultur und Medien zuständige oberste Bundesbehörde die Genehmigung nach Absatz 1 auch für eine erst zukünftige Ausfuhr anlässlich eines öffentlich- rechtlichen Vertrages zwischen dem Eigentümer und der obersten Landesbehörde erteilen, wenn die Vorausset zungen nach § 10 Absatz 1 Nummer 1 und 2 für mindestens 15 Jahre vorliegen. Die für Kultur und Medien zu ständige oberste Bundesbehörde soll diese Zustimmung davon abhängig machen, dass die Einrichtung im Bun desgebiet mit dem Eigentümer des Kulturgutes einen Vertrag über einen möglichen Ankauf des Kulturgutes trifft. Weitere Nebenbestimmungen sind zulässig.

(10) § 22 Absatz 4 und 5 ist entsprechend anzuwenden.

§ 24 Genehmigungspflichtige Ausfuhr von Kulturgut; Verordnungsermächtigung

(1) Genehmigungspflichtig ist die Ausfuhr von Kulturgut

1. in einen Drittstaat nach der unmittelbar geltenden Verordnung (EG) Nr. 116/2009 des Rates vom 18. De zember 2008 über die Ausfuhr von Kulturgütern (Kodifizierte Fassung) (ABl. L 39 vom 10.2.2009, S. 1),
2. in einen Mitgliedstaat, sofern das Kulturgut den Kriterien nach Absatz 2 bei Ausfuhr in den Binnenmarkt unterfällt und nicht Eigentum des Urhebers oder Herstellers ist.

(2) Für die Ausfuhr in den Binnenmarkt sind die Altersuntergrenzen und das Doppelte der Wertuntergren zen nach Anhang I der Verordnung (EG) Nr. 116/2009 mit der Maßgabe anzuwenden, dass bei den nachstehenden Kategorien folgende weiter heraufgesetzte Mindestuntergrenzen bei Kulturgut nach Anhang I Kategorie A gelten:

1. Nummer 3: 75 Jahre und 300 000 Euro;
2. die Nummern 4 und 7: 75 Jahre und 100 000 Euro;
3. die Nummern 5, 6, 8 und 9: 75 Jahre und 50 000 Euro;
4. Nummer 12: 50 Jahre und 50 000 Euro;
5. Nummer 14: 150 Jahre und 100 000 Euro;
6. Nummer 15: 100 Jahre und 100 000 Euro.

Münzen gelten nicht als archäologische Gegenstände nach Kategorie 1 des Anhangs I der Verordnung (EG) Nr. 116/2009, wenn es sie in großer Stückzahl gibt, sie für die Archäologie keinen relevanten Erkenntniswert haben und nicht von einem Mitgliedstaat als individualisierbare Einzelobjekte unter Schutz gestellt sind. Im Übrigen sind die Kategorien nach Absatz 2 Satz 1 im Lichte der Auslegung der Kategorien des Anhangs I der Verordnung (EG) Nr. 116/2009 anzuwenden.

(3) Das für Kultur und Medien zuständige Mitglied der Bundesregierung wird ermächtigt, die Wertgrenzen zur Anpassung an die Preisentwicklungen in den für die in Absatz 2 Satz 1 genannten Kategorien relevanten Märkten in einer Rechtsverordnung, die der Zustimmung des Bundesrates bedarf, anzuheben.

(4) Der für die Genehmigungspflicht nach Absatz 1 maßgebliche finanzielle Wert des Kulturgutes ist der innerhalb der letzten drei Jahre gezahlte Preis bei einem An- oder Verkauf, in sonstigen Fällen ein begründeter inländischer Schätzwert zum Zeitpunkt der Antragstellung.

(5) Die Genehmigung ist zu erteilen, wenn zum Zeitpunkt der Entscheidung über den Antrag kein Ausfuhr- verbot nach § 21 Nummer 1, 3, 4 und 5 besteht.

(6) Zuständig für die Erteilung der Genehmigung nach Absatz 1 ist die oberste Landesbehörde des Landes, in dem sich das Kulturgut zum Zeitpunkt der Antragstellung befindet, sofern sich in Fällen des Absatzes 1 Num mer 1 keine andere Zuständigkeit aus Artikel 2 der Verordnung (EG) Nr. 116/2009 ergibt. Als Ort der Belegenheit wird der Wohnort oder Sitz des Antragstellers widerleglich vermutet. § 22 Absatz 3 Satz 2 ist entsprechend an zuwenden.

(7) Über den Antrag auf Erteilung der Genehmigung hat die oberste Landesbehörde innerhalb von zehn Arbeitstagen nach Einreichung der vollständigen Antragsunterlagen zu entscheiden. Diese Landesbehörde kann die Zuständigkeit nach Maßgabe des

Landesrechts auf eine andere Landesbehörde übertragen.

(8) Die Genehmigungspflicht nach Absatz 1 Nummer 2 entfällt, wenn das Kulturgut sich nachweisbar nur vorübergehend bis zu zwei Jahre im Bundesgebiet befindet. Dies gilt nicht für Kulturgut, das

1. unrechtmäßig eingeführt wurde (§ 28) oder
2. zuvor ohne Genehmigung nach Absatz 1 ausgeführt wurde.

(9) § 22 Absatz 4 und 5 ist entsprechend anzuwenden.

§ 25 Allgemeine offene Genehmigung

(1) Für die vorübergehende Ausfuhr von Kulturgut kann die zuständige oberste Landesbehörde einer Kul turgut bewahrenden Einrichtung auf Antrag eine zeitlich befristete generelle Genehmigung (allgemeine offene Genehmigung) erteilen, wenn diese Einrichtung regelmäßig Teile ihrer Bestände vorübergehend für öffentliche Ausstellungen, Restaurierungen oder Forschungszwecke ausführt. Die allgemeine offene Genehmigung kann mit Nebenbestimmungen versehen werden.

(2) Die allgemeine offene Genehmigung kann erteilt werden für die Ausfuhr in Mitgliedstaaten oder Dritt staaten. Beide Genehmigungen können in einem Bescheid erteilt werden.

(3) Der Antragsteller muss die Gewähr dafür bieten, dass das zur Ausfuhr bestimmte Kulturgut in unbe- schadetem Zustand und fristgerecht wiedereingeführt wird.

(4) Die Geltungsdauer einer allgemeinen offenen Genehmigung darf fünf Jahre nicht überschreiten. Die zuständige oberste Landesbehörde veröffentlicht im Internetportal zum Kulturgutschutz nach § 4 diejenigen Kul turgut bewahrenden Einrichtungen, denen eine allgemeine offene Genehmigung erteilt worden ist.

(5) Teile des Bestandes einer Kulturgut bewahrenden Einrichtung können von der allgemeinen offenen Genehmigung durch die zuständige oberste Landesbehörde ausgenommen werden.

§ 26 Spezifische offene Genehmigung

(1) Für die regelmäßige vorübergehende Ausfuhr von Kulturgut kann die zuständige oberste Landesbe hörde dem Eigentümer oder rechtmäßigen unmittelbaren Besitzer auf Antrag eine zeitlich befristete, auf ein be stimmtes Kulturgut bezogene Genehmigung (spezifische offene Genehmigung) erteilen, wenn das Kulturgut im Ausland wiederholt verwendet oder ausgestellt werden soll.

(2) Die spezifische offene Genehmigung kann erteilt werden für die Ausfuhr in Mitgliedstaaten oder Dritt staaten. Beide Genehmigungen können in einem Bescheid erteilt werden.

(3) Die Genehmigung darf nur erteilt werden, wenn der Antragsteller die Gewähr dafür bietet, dass das zur vorübergehenden Ausfuhr bestimmte Kulturgut in

unbeschadetem Zustand und fristgerecht wiedereingeführt wird.

(4) Die Geltungsdauer einer spezifischen offenen Genehmigung darf fünf Jahre nicht überschreiten.

§ 27 Genehmigung der Ausfuhr von kirchlichem Kulturgut

(1) Für die vorübergehende Ausfuhr von nationalem Kulturgut, das sich im Eigentum einer Kirche oder einer als Körperschaft des öffentlichen Rechts anerkannten Religionsgemeinschaft befindet, erteilt die Kirche oder Religionsgemeinschaft die Genehmigung nach § 22 im Benehmen mit der zuständigen Landesbehörde.

(2) Bei einem Verfahren zur Genehmigung nach § 23 für die dauerhafte Ausfuhr von nationalem Kulturgut nach § 6 Absatz 1 Nummer 1 in Verbindung mit § 9 Absatz 1 wird bei Kulturgut, das sich im Eigentum einer Kir che oder einer als Körperschaft des öffentlichen Rechts anerkannten Religionsgemeinschaft befindet, abweichend von § 23 Absatz 4 Satz 2 ausschließlich die betroffene Kirche oder die als Körperschaft des öffentlichen Rechts anerkannte Religionsgemeinschaft angehört. Sofern es sich um nationales Kulturgut nach § 9 Absatz 3 handelt, erteilt die Kirche oder Religionsgemeinschaft die Genehmigung im Benehmen mit der zuständigen obersten Lan desbehörde.

(3) Die Kirchen und die als Körperschaften des öffentlichen Rechts anerkannten Religionsgemeinschaften können beantragen, dass für Kulturgut, das sich in ihrem Eigentum befindet, die Genehmigung für die Ausfuhr in einen Mitgliedstaat nach § 24 Absatz 1 Nummer 2 nicht erforderlich ist. In diesem Falle ist eine nachträgliche Eintragung in ein Verzeichnis national wertvollen Kulturgutes nach § 8 ausgeschlossen.

(4) Die §§ 25 und 26 sind für Kirchen und die als Körperschaft des öffentlichen Recht anerkannten Religi onsgemeinschaften sowie für die von ihnen beaufsichtigten Einrichtungen und Organisationen mit der Maßgabe entsprechend anzuwenden, dass die Genehmigung nur im Einvernehmen mit der zuständigen Kirche oder Religionsgemeinschaft erteilt werden kann.

Abschnitt 3
Einfuhr

§ 28 Einfuhrverbot

Die Einfuhr von Kulturgut ist verboten, wenn es

1. von einem Mitgliedstaat oder Vertragsstaat als nationales Kulturgut eingestuft oder definiert worden ist und unter Verstoß gegen dessen Rechtsvorschriften zum Schutz nationalen Kulturgutes aus dessen Hoheitsgebiet verbracht worden ist,
2. unter Verstoß gegen im Amtsblatt der Europäischen Union veröffentlichte unmittelbar geltenden Rechtsakte der Europäischen Union, die die grenzüberschreitende

Verbringung von Kulturgut einschränken oder ver bieten, verbracht worden ist oder
3. unter Verstoß gegen Abschnitt I Nummer 1 des Protokolls zur Haager Konvention aufgrund eines bewaff neten Konflikts verbracht worden ist.

§ 29 Ausnahmen vom Einfuhrverbot

Das Einfuhrverbot ist nicht anzuwenden auf Kulturgut, das
1. sich zum 6. August 2016 rechtmäßig im Bundesgebiet befunden hat, soweit nicht unmittelbar geltende Rechtsakte der Europäischen Union Abweichendes anordnen, oder
2. zum Schutz vor den Gefahren eines bewaffneten Konflikts im Sinne des Abschnitts II Nummer 5 des Proto kolls zur Haager Konvention im Bundesgebiet deponiert werden soll, um es zeitweilig zu verwahren.

§ 30 Nachweis der Rechtmäßigkeit der Einfuhr

Wer Kulturgut einführt, hat, sofern es von einem Mitgliedstaat oder Vertragsstaat als nationales Kulturgut eingestuft oder definiert worden ist, zum Nachweis der Rechtmäßigkeit der Ausfuhr aus dem Herkunftsstaat im Sinne von § 28 Nummer 1 entsprechende Unterlagen mitzuführen. Ein solcher Nachweis sind Ausfuhrgenehmi gungen des Herkunftsstaates sowie sonstige Bestätigungen des Herkunftsstaates, dass das Kulturgut rechtmäßig ausgeführt werden konnte.

Abschnitt 4
Unrech tmßiger Kultu rgutverk ehr

§ 31 Unrechtmäßige Ausfuhr von Kulturgut

(1) Die Ausfuhr von Kulturgut ist unrechtmäßig, wenn sie unter Verstoß gegen die §§ 21 bis 27 erfolgt oder unter Verstoß gegen Verordnungen der Europäischen Union, die die grenzüberschreitende Verbringung von Kulturgut ausdrücklich einschränken oder verbieten.

(2) Einer unrechtmäßigen Ausfuhr stehen auch jede nicht erfolgte Rückkehr nach Ablauf der Frist für eine vorübergehende rechtmäßige Ausfuhr und jeder Verstoß gegen eine Nebenbestimmung zur Genehmigung der vorübergehenden Ausfuhr gleich.

§ 32 Unrechtmäßige Einfuhr von Kulturgut

(1) Die Einfuhr von Kulturgut ist unrechtmäßig,
1. wenn das Kulturgut bei der Ausfuhr aus einem anderen Staat entgegen den in

diesem Staat geltenden Rechts vorschriften zum Schutz nationalen Kulturgutes verbracht worden ist

a) nach dem 31. Dezember 1992 aus dem Hoheitsgebiet eines anderen Mitgliedstaates oder

b) nach dem 26. April 2007 aus dem Hoheitsgebiet eines Vertragsstaates,

2. wenn die Einfuhr gegen § 28 verstößt oder
3. wenn die Einfuhr gegen sonstige in der Bundesrepublik Deutschland geltende Rechtsvorschriften verstößt.

(2) Kann die Herkunft von Kulturgut in mehreren heutigen Staaten liegen und lässt sich keine eindeutige Zuordnung vornehmen, so ist das Kulturgut unrechtmäßig eingeführt, wenn das Kulturgut nach dem Recht jedes in Frage kommenden Staates das Kulturgut nicht ohne Ausfuhrgenehmigung hätte ausgeführt werden dürfen und eine solche Ausfuhrgenehmigung nicht vorliegt.

§ 33 Sicherstellung von Kulturgut

(1) Die zuständige Behörde hat Kulturgut sicherzustellen,

1. wenn der hinreichende Verdacht besteht, dass es
   a) entgegen einem Verbot nach § 21 ausgeführt werden soll oder
   b) entgegen einem Verbot nach § 28 eingeführt worden ist, oder
2. wenn bei der Einfuhr die nach § 30 erforderlichen Unterlagen nicht vorgelegt werden.

(2) Nach Sicherstellung des Kulturgutes ist dem bisherigen Gewahrsamsinhaber eine Bescheinigung aus zuhändigen, die das sichergestellte Kulturgut und den Grund der Sicherstellung nennt. Kann eine Bescheinigung nicht ausgehändigt werden, so ist über die Sicherstellung eine Niederschrift aufzunehmen, die auch erkennen lässt, warum eine Bescheinigung nicht ausgestellt worden ist.

(3) Widerspruch und Anfechtungsklage gegen die Sicherstellung des Kulturgutes haben keine aufschie bende Wirkung. Die Sicherstellung hat die Wirkung eines Veräußerungsverbots im Sinne des § 136 des Bürger lichen Gesetzbuches; das Verbot umfasst auch andere Verfügungen als Veräußerungen.

(4) Die Sicherstellung des Kulturgutes ist durch die zuständige Behörde unverzüglich der für Kultur und Medien zuständigen obersten Bundesbehörde zur Erfüllung der Aufgaben nach § 62 mitzuteilen.

(5) Es ist verboten, sichergestelltes Kulturgut zu zerstören, zu beschädigen oder dessen Erscheinungsbild nicht nur unerheblich und nicht nur vorübergehend zu verändern.

§ 34 Verwahrung sichergestellten Kulturgutes

(1) Sichergestelltes Kulturgut ist von der zuständigen Behörde in Verwahrung zu nehmen. Sie kann das Kulturgut, sofern der Zweck der Sicherstellung dadurch nicht

gefährdet ist, durch die Person, der der Gewahrsam entzogen worden ist, oder durch einen Dritten verwahren lassen. In diesem Fall darf das Kulturgut nur mit schrift licher oder elektronisch übermittelter Zustimmung der zuständigen Behörde an andere Personen oder Einrichtun gen weitergegeben werden.

(2) Zu Beginn und nach Ende der Verwahrung soll der Erhaltungszustand des sichergestellten Kulturgutes von der zuständigen Behörde oder einem von ihr beauftragten Dritten festgehalten werden.

(3) Die zur Erhaltung des Kulturgutes erforderlichen Maßnahmen werden von der zuständigen Behörde getroffen oder veranlasst.

§ 35 Aufhebung der Sicherstellung

(1) Die Sicherstellung des Kulturgutes ist von der zuständigen Behörde aufzuheben, wenn

1. der hinreichende Verdacht nach § 33 Absatz 1 Nummer 1 entfallen ist,
2. die Voraussetzungen des § 33 Absatz 1 Nummer 1 Buchstabe a entfallen sind,
3. im Fall des § 33 Absatz 1 Nummer 1 Buchstabe b
   a) die Voraussetzungen des Rückgabeanspruchs nach Kapitel 5 dieses Gesetzes offensichtlich nicht vor liegen oder
   b) die Verjährung des Rückgabeanspruchs nach Kapitel 5 dieses Gesetzes eingetreten ist,
4. im Falle des § 33 Absatz 1 Nummer 1 Buchstabe b die Sicherstellung im Hinblick auf einen Anspruch aus § 50 oder § 52 erfolgt ist und
   a) nicht innerhalb von sechs Kalendermonaten nach Unterrichtung nach § 62 Absatz 1 Nummer 1 oder Absatz 2 Nummer 1 um eine Rückgabe nach § 50 oder § 52 ersucht worden ist,
   b) eine gütliche Einigung zwischen dem ersuchenden Mitgliedstaat oder Vertragsstaat und dem Rückgabe schuldner erzielt worden ist oder
   c) die Entscheidung über die Klage auf Rückgabe rechtskräftig geworden ist,
5. im Falle des § 33 Absatz 1 Nummer 1 Buchstabe b die Sicherstellung im Hinblick auf einen Anspruch aus § 51 erfolgt ist und eine Rückgabe erfolgen soll,
6. im Falle des § 33 Absatz 1 Nummer 1 Buchstabe b die Sicherstellung im Hinblick auf einen Anspruch aus § 53 Absatz 1 erfolgt ist und eine Rückgabe erfolgen soll oder,
7. sobald sich im Falle des § 33 Absatz 1 Nummer 2 kein hinreichender Verdacht ergibt, dass das Kulturgut unrechtmäßig eingeführt worden ist.

(2) Hat ein Mitgliedstaat oder Vertragsstaat ein Rückgabeersuchen nach § 59 bereits gestellt oder ist ge klärt, welcher Mitgliedstaat oder Vertragsstaat ein solches Ersuchen stellen könnte, so kann die Sicherstellung nur mit Zustimmung dieses Mitgliedstaates oder Vertragsstaates aufgehoben werden, es sei denn, der Anlass der Sicherstellung ist zwischenzeitlich entfallen.

§ 36 Herausgabe sichergestellten Kulturgutes

(1) Ist die Sicherstellung aufgehoben worden, so ist das Kulturgut herauszugeben
1. in den Fällen des § 35 Absatz 1 Nummer 1 bis 3, 4 Buchstabe a und Nummer 7 an den Eigenbesitzer,
2. in den Fällen des § 35 Absatz 1 Nummer 4 Buchstabe b und c an den Berechtigten,
3. in den Fällen des § 35 Absatz 1 Nummer 5 an den betreffenden Mitgliedstaat oder Vertragsstaat oder
4. in den Fällen des § 35 Absatz 1 Nummer 6 an die jeweils zuständige Behörde des Herkunftsgebiets.

(2) In den Fällen der Herausgabe an den Eigenbesitzer ist diesem eine Mitteilung über eine Frist zur Abho lung zuzustellen. Die Frist ist ausreichend zu bemessen. Die Mitteilung hat den Hinweis zu enthalten, dass das Kulturgut eingezogen wird, wenn es nicht innerhalb der Frist abgeholt wird.

§ 37 Einziehung sichergestellten Kulturgutes

(1) Sichergestelltes Kulturgut soll von der zuständigen Behörde eingezogen werden, wenn es in den Fällen des § 36 Absatz 1 Nummer 1 nicht an den Eigenbesitzer herausgegeben werden kann, weil
1. der Eigenbesitzer nicht bekannt ist und nicht mit einem vertretbaren Aufwand zu ermitteln ist oder
2. der Eigenbesitzer das Kulturgut nicht innerhalb der Frist nach § 36 Absatz 2 Satz 2 abholt.

Die Anordnung der Einziehung ist nach Landesrecht öffentlich bekannt zu machen und im Internetportal nach § 4 zu veröffentlichen. Sie ist unverzüglich der für Kultur und Medien zuständigen obersten Bundesbehörde zur Er füllung der Aufgaben nach § 62 mitzuteilen.

(2) Die zuständige Behörde kann das eingezogene Kulturgut einer Kulturgut bewahrenden Einrichtung in Verwahrung geben.

§ 38 Folgen der Einziehung; Entschädigung

(1) Wird sichergestelltes Kulturgut eingezogen, so gehen der Besitz an dem Kulturgut mit der Anordnung der Einziehung und das Eigentum an dem Kulturgut mit der Bestandskraft der Anordnung auf das Land über. Rechte Dritter erlöschen mit der Bestandskraft der Anordnung.

(2) Der Eigentümer, dessen Recht an dem Kulturgut durch die Entscheidung erloschen ist, wird von dem Land, in dessen Eigentum das Kulturgut übergegangen ist, unter Berücksichtigung des Verkehrswertes angemes sen in Geld entschädigt, es sei denn, es wird rückübereignet, Zug um Zug gegen den Ersatz einer möglichen Entschädigung an den Dritten nach Absatz 3.

(3) War das Kulturgut mit dem Recht eines Dritten belastet, das durch die

Einziehung erloschen ist, so wird auch der Dritte von dem Land, in dessen Eigentum das Kulturgut übergegangen ist, unter Berücksichtigung des Verkehrswertes angemessen in Geld entschädigt.

(4) In den Fällen des Absatzes 2 wird eine Entschädigung nicht gewährt, wenn

1. der Eigentümer mindestens leichtfertig dazu beigetragen hat, dass die Voraussetzungen der Sicherstellung und die Voraussetzungen der Einziehung des Kulturgutes vorlagen,
2. der Eigentümer das Kulturgut in Kenntnis der Umstände, die die Sicherstellung zugelassen haben, erworben hat oder
3. es nach den Umständen, welche die Sicherstellung und Einziehung begründet haben, aufgrund anderer ge setzlicher Vorschriften zulässig wäre, das Kulturgut dem Eigentümer ohne Entschädigung dauernd zu ent ziehen.

Satz 1 ist nicht anzuwenden, soweit die Nichtgewährung der Entschädigung eine unbillige Härte wäre.

(5) In den Fällen des Absatzes 3 wird eine Entschädigung nicht gewährt, wenn

1. der Dritte wenigstens leichtfertig dazu beigetragen hat, dass die Voraussetzungen der Sicherstellung des Kulturgutes vorlagen,
2. der Dritte das Recht an dem Kulturgut in Kenntnis der Umstände, die die Einziehung zugelassen haben, erworben hat oder
3. es nach den Umständen, die die Sicherstellung und Einziehung begründet haben, aufgrund anderer gesetzli cher Vorschriften zulässig wäre, das Recht an dem Kulturgut dem Dritten ohne Entschädigung dauernd zu entziehen.

Satz 1 ist nicht anzuwenden, soweit die Nichtgewährung der Entschädigung eine unbillige Härte wäre.

(6) Der Anspruch auf Entschädigung nach den Absätzen 2 oder 3 erlischt 30 Jahre nach der Bekanntma chung der Anordnung der Einziehung.

§ 39 Kosten für Sicherstellung, Verwahrung, Erhaltung und Herausgabe

Die notwendigen Kosten und Auslagen für die Sicherstellung, Verwahrung, Erhaltung und Herausgabe des Kulturgutes trägt die Person, der der Gewahrsam entzogen worden ist. Die §§ 66 bis 68 bleiben unberührt. Die zuständige Behörde setzt den zu erstattenden Betrag durch Bescheid fest.

Kapitel 4
Pflichten beim Inverkehrbringen von Kulturgut

§ 40 Verbot des Inverkehrbringens

(1) Verboten ist das Inverkehrbringen von Kulturgut, das abhandengekommen ist, rechtswidrig ausgegra ben oder unrechtmäßig eingeführt worden ist.

(2) Verpflichtungs- und Verfügungsgeschäfte, die nach Absatz 1 verboten sind, sind nichtig.

(3) Verpflichtungs- und Verfügungsgeschäfte über Kulturgut, das entgegen § 21 ausgeführt worden ist, sind verboten.

(4) Derjenige, der das Kulturgut unter Verstoß gegen das Verbot in Absatz 1 in Verkehr gebracht hat, ist dem Erwerber zum Ersatz des Schadens unter Einschluss des Ersatzes der Aufwendungen anlässlich des Erwerbs und der Aufwendungen zur Erhaltung des Kulturgutes verpflichtet. Dies gilt nicht, wenn derjenige, der das Kul turgut in Verkehr gebracht hat, nachweist, dass er den Verstoß nicht zu vertreten hat.

§ 41 Allgemeine Sorgfaltspflichten

(1) Wer Kulturgut in Verkehr bringt, ist verpflichtet, zuvor mit der erforderlichen Sorgfalt zu prüfen, ob das Kulturgut

1. abhandengekommen ist,
2. unrechtmäßig eingeführt worden ist oder
3. rechtswidrig ausgegraben worden ist.

(2) Die allgemeine Sorgfaltspflicht nach Absatz 1 ist von der Person, die Kulturgut in Verkehr bringt, an zuwenden, wenn sich einer vernünftigen Person die Vermutung aufdrängen müsste, dass einer der in Absatz 1 genannten Tatbestände in Betracht kommt. Diese Vermutung ist insbesondere anzunehmen, wenn bei einem früheren Erwerb des Kulturgutes, das in Verkehr gebracht werden soll,

1. ein außergewöhnlich niedriger Preis ohne nähere Begründung gefordert worden ist oder
2. der Verkäufer bei einem Kaufpreis von mehr als 5 000 Euro Barzahlung verlangt hat.

(3) Die erforderliche Sorgfalt umfasst die Prüfung einschlägiger Informationen, die mit zumutbarem Auf wand zu beschaffen sind, oder jede andere Prüfung, die eine vernünftige Person unter denselben Umständen des Inverkehrbringens von Kulturgut unternehmen würde.

§ 42 Sorgfaltspflichten beim gewerblichen Inverkehrbringen

(1) Wer in Ausübung seiner gewerblichen Tätigkeit Kulturgut in Verkehr bringt, ist verpflichtet, zuvor zusätzlich zu den Pflichten nach § 41

1. Name und Anschrift des Veräußerers, des Einlieferers, des Erwerbers oder des Auftraggebers festzustellen,
2. eine Beschreibung und eine Abbildung anzufertigen, die geeignet sind, die Identität des Kulturgutes festzu stellen,
3. die Provenienz des Kulturgutes zu prüfen,
4. Dokumente, die eine rechtmäßige Ein- und Ausfuhr belegen, zu prüfen,
5. Verbote und Beschränkungen zur Ein- und Ausfuhr sowie zum Handel zu prüfen,
6. zu prüfen, ob das Kulturgut in öffentlich zugänglichen Verzeichnissen und

Datenbanken eingetragen ist, und
7. eine schriftliche oder elektronisch übermittelte Erklärung des Einlieferers oder Veräußerers einzuholen, dass dieser berechtigt ist, über das Kulturgut zu verfügen.

Die Pflichten nach Satz 1 Nummer 2 lassen urheberrechtliche Vorschriften unberührt. Die Pflichten nach Satz 1 Nummer 3 bis 6 sind nach Maßgabe des zumutbaren Aufwandes, insbesondere der wirtschaftlichen Zumutbarkeit, zu erfüllen.

(2) Die zusätzlichen Sorgfaltspflichten nach Absatz 1 sind nicht anzuwenden
1. für den gewerblichen Buchhandel mit Ausnahme des Antiquariatshandels und
2. für den gewerblichen Handel mit Bild- und Tonträgern.

(3) Die zusätzlichen Sorgfaltspflichten nach Absatz 1 sind ferner nicht anzuwenden für Kulturgut,
1. das kein archäologisches Kulturgut ist und
2. dessen Wert 2 500 Euro nicht übersteigt.

Münzen gelten nicht als archäologisches Kulturgut im Sinne des Satzes 1 Nummer 1, wenn es sie in großer Stück zahl gibt und sie für die Archäologie keinen relevanten Erkenntniswert haben. Maßgeblicher Wert ist bei einem Kauf der gezahlte Preis, in sonstigen Fällen ein begründeter inländischer Schätz wert.

§ 43 Erleichterte Sorgfaltspflichten beim gewerblichen Inverkehrbringen

Erleichterte Sorgfaltspflichten gelten, wenn
1. der Urheber oder Hersteller des Kulturgutes dieses in Verkehr bringt oder
2. jemand das Kulturgut unmittelbar von dessen Urheber oder Hersteller erworben hat und es in Verkehr bringt oder
3. jemand für den Urheber oder Hersteller das von diesem geschaffene Kulturgut in Verkehr bringt.

Die erleichterten Sorgfaltspflichten umfassen zusätzlich zu den Pflichten nach § 41 nur diejenigen nach § 42 Absatz 1 Nummer 1 und 2. § 42 Absatz 2 und 3 ist entsprechend anzuwenden.

§ 44 Erhöhte Sorgfaltspflichten beim gewerblichen Inverkehrbringen

Beim gewerblichen Inverkehrbringen ist der Maßstab des zumutbaren Aufwandes nach § 42 Absatz 1 Satz 3 nicht für Kulturgut anzuwenden,
1. bei dem nachgewiesen oder zu vermuten ist, dass es zwischen dem 30. Januar 1933 und dem 8. Mai 1945 aufgrund der Verfolgung durch den Nationalsozialismus entzogen worden ist, es sei denn, das Kulturgut ist an seinen ursprünglichen Eigentümer oder dessen Erben zurückgegeben worden oder diese haben eine andere abschließende Regelung im Hinblick auf den Entzug getroffen,
2. das aus einem Mitgliedstaat oder Vertragsstaat stammt, für den der Internationale Museumsrat eine Rote Liste gefährdeter Kulturgüter veröffentlicht hat, oder
3. für das ein Verbot zur Ein- oder Ausfuhr sowie zum Inverkehrbringen nach einer

Verordnung der Europäi schen Union maßgebend ist.
Auf Kulturgut nach Satz 1 ist § 42 Absatz 3 nicht anzuwenden.

§ 45 Aufzeichnungs- und Aufbewahrungspflichten

(1) Wer in Ausübung einer gewerblichen Tätigkeit Kulturgut in Verkehr bringt, ist verpflichtet, über die Prüfungen und Feststellungen nach § 42 Aufzeichnungen zu führen. Die Aufzeichnungen und die Sicherung ent sprechender Unterlagen können in elektronischer Form erfolgen.

(2) Die Aufzeichnungen nach Absatz 1 sind mit den dazugehörigen Unterlagen und Nachweisen vom Auf zeichnungspflichtigen 30 Jahre lang aufzubewahren. Absatz 1 Satz 2 ist entsprechend anzuwenden.

(3) Aufzeichnungen nach anderen Rechtsvorschriften stehen den Aufzeichnungen nach Absatz 1 gleich, sofern sie den Prüfungen und Feststellungen nach § 42 entsprechen und die in diesem Gesetz geforderte Feststel lung der Identität des Kulturgutes nach § 42 Absatz 1 Nummer 2 ermöglichen. Für die Aufbewahrungsfrist ist Absatz 2 Satz 1 anzuwenden.

§ 46 Auskunftspflicht

(1) Wer in Ausübung einer gewerblichen Tätigkeit Kulturgut in Verkehr bringt, ist verpflichtet, der zustän digen Behörde auf Verlangen

1. die Aufzeichnungen nach § 45 vorzulegen oder
2. Auskunft über die nach § 41 Absatz 1 über ein Kulturgut gewonnenen Informationen zu erteilen.

Die nach Satz 1 vorzulegenden Aufzeichnungen und zu erteilenden Auskünfte beschränken sich auf die Informa tionen, die für die zuständigen Behörden zur Durchführung ihrer Aufgaben nach diesem Gesetz erforderlich sind.

(2) § 29 der Gewerbeordnung bleibt unberührt.

§ 47 Rechtsfolge bei Verstößen

Hat die zuständige Behörde belegbare Erkenntnisse darüber, dass wiederholt gegen Aufzeichnungs-, Aufbe wahrungs- und Auskunftspflichten nach den §§ 45 und 46 Absatz 1 verstoßen worden ist, so teilt sie diese Er kenntnisse der Gewerbeaufsicht zur Prüfung der Zuverlässigkeit im Sinne des § 35 der Gewerbeordnung mit.

§ 48 Einsichtsrechte des Käufers

(1) Wird ein Erwerber eines Kulturgutes gerichtlich nach diesem Gesetz oder

aufgrund zivilrechtlicher Vorschriften auf Herausgabe des Kulturgutes in Anspruch genommen, so hat er gegenüber demjenigen, der das Kulturgut nach den §§ 42 bis 44 in Verkehr gebracht hat, einen Anspruch auf Einsicht in die Aufzeichnungen nach § 45, wenn er das Kulturgut nach dem6. August 2016 erworben hat.

(2) Absatz 1 ist auch anzuwenden im Falle der außergerichtlichen Inanspruchnahme bei Geltendmachung

1. eines Rückgabeanspruchs eines Mitgliedstaates oder Vertragsstaates oder
2. eines Entzuges dieses Kulturgutes aufgrund der Verfolgung durch den Nationalsozialismus.

Kapitel 5
Rückgabe unrechtmäßig eingeführten Kulturgutes

Abschnitt 1
Rückgabeanspruch

§ 49 Öffentlich-rechtliche Rückgabeansprüche

(1) Ansprüche auf Rückgabe von Kulturgut nach diesem Abschnitt sind öffentlich-rechtliche Ansprüche. Zivilrechtliche Ansprüche bleiben davon unberührt.

(2) Rückgabeschuldner ist der unmittelbare Eigenbesitzer, hilfsweise der unmittelbare Fremdbesitzer.

§ 50 Rückgabeanspruch eines Mitgliedstaates

Auf Ersuchen eines Mitgliedstaates ist Kulturgut zurückzugeben, wenn es

1. nach dem 31. Dezember 1992 aus dem Hoheitsgebiet eines Mitgliedstaates unter Verstoß gegen dortige Rechtsvorschriften verbracht worden ist und
2. vor oder nach der Verbringung von dem ersuchenden Mitgliedstaat durch nationale Rechtsvorschriften oder durch Verwaltungsverfahren als nationales Kulturgut von künstlerischem, geschichtlichem oder archäologi schem Wert im Sinne des Artikels 36 des Vertrags über die Arbeitsweise der Europäischen Union eingestuft oder definiert worden ist.

§ 51 Rückgabeanspruch wegen Verstoßes gegen das Recht der Europäischen Union

Ist Kulturgut entgegen einem im Amtsblatt der Europäischen Union veröffentlichten, unmittelbar geltenden Rechtsakt der Europäischen Union unrechtmäßig eingeführt worden, so ist es an den betreffenden Staat zurück zugeben.

§ 52 Rückgabeanspruch eines Vertragsstaates

(1) Auf Ersuchen eines Vertragsstaates ist Kulturgut zurückzugeben, wenn es

1. einer der in Artikel 1 des UNESCO-Übereinkommens genannten Kategorien angehört,
2. aus dessen Hoheitsgebiet nach dem 26. April 2007 unter Verstoß gegen dortige Rechtsvorschriften verbracht worden ist,
3. vor der Ausfuhr von dem ersuchenden Vertragsstaat als bedeutsam nach Artikel 1 des UNESCO-Überein- kommens oder im Sinne des Artikels 13 Buchstabe d des UNESCO-Übereinkommens als unveräußerlich eingestuft oder erklärt worden ist und
4. hinsichtlich seiner Herkunft dem ersuchenden Vertragsstaat zuzuordnen ist, insbesondere wenn es zum Be stand einer Einrichtung im Vertragsstaat gehört oder eine Einigung nach § 60 vorliegt.

(2) Lässt sich nicht klären, ob das Kulturgut nach dem 26. April 2007 verbracht worden ist, so wird wider leglich vermutet, dass das Kulturgut nach diesem Tag aus dem Hoheitsgebiet des Vertragsstaates verbracht wor den ist. Diese Vermutung kann nur durch den Nachweis widerlegt werden, dass sich das Kulturgut schon vor diesem Tag im Bundesgebiet, im Binnenmarkt oder in einem Drittstaat befunden hat. Die Abgabe einer Versiche rung an Eides statt ist zur Erbringung des Nachweises nach Satz 2 zulässig gemäß § 27 Absatz 1 des Verwal tungsverfahrensgesetzes sowie gemäß der Verwaltungsverfahrensgesetze der Länder. Für die Abnahme zuständig sind im Rahmen des behördlichen Vermittlungsverfahrens die in § 61 Absatz 1 Nummer 7 und § 62 Absatz 2 genannten Behörden.

(3) Wird der Nachweis erbracht, dass sich das Kulturgut vor dem 6. August 2016 im Bundesgebiet oder im Binnenmarkt befunden hat, so sind abweichend von Absatz 1 für den Rückgabeanspruch des Vertragsstaates § 6 Absatz 2 und für die Entschädigung § 10 des Kulturgüterrückgabege setzes vom 18. Mai 2007 (BGBl. I S. 757, 2547) in der bis zum 5. August 2016 geltenden Fassung anzuwenden.

§ 53 Rückgabeanspruch nach der Haager Konvention

(1) Kulturgut nach Kapitel I Artikel 1 der Haager Konvention, das entgegen § 28 Nummer 3 aufgrund eines bewaffneten Konflikts eingeführt worden ist, ist nach Beendigung des bewaffneten Konflikts an die jeweils zu ständige Behörde des Herkunftsgebiets nach Abschnitt I Nummer 3 des Protokolls zur Haager Konvention zu rückzugeben, wenn

1. es nach dem 11. November 1967 verbracht worden ist und
2. die jeweils zuständige Behörde des Herkunftsgebiets um Rückgabe ersucht.

(2) Kulturgut, das im Sinne von Abschnitt II Nummer 5 des Protokolls zur Haager Konvention deponiert worden ist, ist nach Beendigung des bewaffneten Konflikts zurückzugeben, ohne dass die Voraussetzungen des Absatzes 1 Nummer 1 und 2

erfüllt sein müssen.

§ 54 Anzuwendendes Zivilrecht

(1) Wer Eigentümer des Kulturgutes ist, das nach den Bestimmungen dieses Gesetzes in das Hoheitsgebiet eines anderen Mitgliedstaates oder Vertragsstaates zurückgegeben worden ist, bestimmt sich nach den Sachvor schriften dieses Mitgliedstaates oder Vertragsstaates.

(2) Rechte, die aufgrund rechtsgeschäftlicher Verfügung oder durch Zwangsvollstreckung oder Arrestvoll ziehung erworben worden sind, stehen der Rückgabepflicht nicht entgegen.

§ 55 Befristung und Verjährung des Rückgabeanspruchs

(1) Rückgabeansprüche unterliegen nicht der Verjährung, wenn sie auf die Rückgabe von Kulturgut ge richtet sind, das

1. zu öffentlichen Sammlungen nach Artikel 2 Nummer 8 der Richtlinie 2014/60/EU gehört oder
2. in einem Bestandsverzeichnis kirchlicher oder anderer religiöser Einrichtungen in den Mitgliedstaaten auf geführt ist, in denen es nach den in diesem Mitgliedstaat geltenden Rechtsvorschriften besonderen Schutz regelungen unterliegt.

Die Ansprüche nach Satz 1 erlöschen 75 Jahre nach ihrem Entstehen. Ein Anspruch erlischt nicht nach Satz 2, wenn der ersuchende Mitgliedstaat in seinem Recht bestimmt, dass solche Rückgabeansprüche nicht erlöschen.

(2) Rückgabeansprüche verjähren außer in den Fällen des Absatzes 1 ohne Rücksicht auf die Kenntnis in 30 Jahren ab dem Zeitpunkt der unrechtmäßigen Verbringung des Kulturgutes aus dem Hoheitsgebiet des ersu chenden Mitgliedstaates oder Vertragsstaates.

(3) Alle anderen Ansprüche auf Rückgabe von Kulturgut nach diesem Abschnitt verjähren nach drei Jahren.

§ 56 Beginn der Verjährung

Die Verjährungsfrist beginnt mit dem Zeitpunkt, in dem der ersuchende Mitgliedstaat oder Vertragsstaat von dem Ort der Belegenheit des Kulturgutes und von der Identität des Rückgabeschuldners Kenntnis erlangt.

§ 57 Hemmung und Neubeginn der Verjährung und Erlöschensfristen

(1) Auf die Verjährung und auf die Frist nach § 55 Absatz 1 Satz 2 sind die

Vorschriften über die Hemmung der Verjährung nach den §§ 204, 206 und 209 des Bürgerlichen Gesetzbuches und über den Neubeginn der Ver jährung nach § 212 des Bürgerlichen Gesetzbuches entsprechend anzuwenden.

(2) Die Verjährung und die Frist nach § 55 Absatz 1 Satz 2 sind wegen höherer Gewalt insbesondere auch gehemmt, solange der ersuchende Mitgliedstaat oder Vertragsstaat durch innere Unruhen, bewaffnete Konflikte oder vergleichbare Umstände gehindert ist, seine Ansprüche geltend zu machen.

Abschnitt 2
Rückgabeverfahren

§ 58 Grundsatz der Rückgabe

Die Rückgabe kann durch eine gütliche Einigung im behördlichen Vermittlungsverfahren erreicht werden oder mit einer Klage auf Rückgabe des ersuchenden Staates verfolgt werden.

§ 59 Rückgabeersuchen

Das Rückgabeersuchen ist zu stellen für

1. den Rückgabeanspruch eines Mitgliedstaates nach § 50 bei der für Kultur und Medien zuständigen obersten Bundesbehörde oder
2. Ansprüche nach den §§ 51 bis 53 auf diplomatischem Weg beim Auswärtigen Amt.

§ 60 Kollidierende Rückgabeersuchen

Stellen zu demselben Kulturgut mehrere Mitgliedstaaten oder Vertragsstaaten Rückgabeersuchen und lässt sich nicht klären, welchem Mitgliedstaat oder Vertragsstaat das Kulturgut zuzuordnen ist, so ist es erst zurückzu geben, wenn die Einigung der betroffenen Mitgliedstaaten oder Vertragsstaaten schriftlich festgehalten und der für Kultur und Medien zuständigen obersten Bundesbehörde sowie dem Auswärtigen Amt mitgeteilt worden ist.

§ 61 Aufgaben der Länder

(1) Die zuständige Behörde eines Landes hat insbesondere folgende Aufgaben:

1. Nachforschungen nach Kulturgut, bei dem der Verdacht besteht, dass es unrechtmäßig verbracht worden ist oder unrechtmäßig in Verkehr gebracht worden ist,

2. Nachforschungen nach dem Eigentümer oder dem unmittelbaren Besitzer des betreffenden Kulturgutes,
3. Unterstützung der Nachforschungen des ersuchenden Mitgliedstaates oder Vertragsstaates, insbesondere nach dem Eigentümer oder dem unmittelbaren Besitzer des betreffenden Kulturgutes,
4. Durchführung oder Veranlassung von Maßnahmen zur Erhaltung des sichergestellten Kulturgutes,
5. Durchführung von Maßnahmen, die verhindern, dass das Kulturgut der Rückgabe entzogen wird,
6. Durchführung des behördlichen Vermittlungsverfahrens zwischen dem ersuchenden Mitgliedstaat und dem Rückgabeschuldner und
7. Unterstützung des Bundes bei der Rückgabe von Kulturgut.

(2) Zur Unterstützung nach Absatz 1 Nummer 3 ist die zuständige Behörde nur verpflichtet, wenn ein Mit gliedstaat innerhalb von sechs Monaten nach Unterrichtung nach § 62 Absatz 1 Nummer 1 der zuständigen Be hörde mitteilt, dass es sich um ein Kulturgut im Sinne des Artikels 2 Nummer 1 der Richtlinie 2014/60/EU han delt. Lässt ein Mitgliedstaat diese Frist ohne diese Mitteilung verstreichen, so ist die zuständige Behörde nicht mehr verpflichtet, Maßnahmen nach Absatz 1 Nummer 4 und 5 zu ergreifen.

§ 62 Aufgaben der obersten Bundesbehörden

(1) Die für Kultur und Medien zuständige oberste Bundesbehörde hat folgende Aufgaben:

1. Unterrichtung des betroffenen Mitgliedstaates über das Auffinden und die Sicherstellung von Kulturgut, bei dem der Verdacht besteht, dass es unrechtmäßig eingeführt worden ist,
2. Unterstützung des behördlichen Vermittlungsverfahrens zwischen dem ersuchenden Mitgliedstaat und dem Rückgabeschuldner und
3. Mitteilung an die zentralen Stellen der anderen Mitgliedstaaten, wenn der ersuchende Mitgliedstaat Klage auf Rückgabe erhoben hat.

(2) Das Auswärtige Amt hat in Zusammenarbeit mit der für Kultur und Medien zuständigen obersten Bun desbehörde folgende Aufgaben:

1. Unterrichtung des betroffenen Vertragsstaates über das Auffinden und die Sicherstellung von Kulturgut, bei dem Verdacht besteht, dass es unrechtmäßig eingeführt worden ist, und
2. Durchführung des behördlichen Vermittlungsverfahrens zwischen dem ersuchenden Vertragsstaat und dem Rückgabeschuldner.

§ 63 Zulässigkeit der Klage auf Rückgabe

(1) Die Klage eines ersuchenden Mitgliedstaates oder Vertragsstaates auf Rückgabe

ist nur dann zulässig, wenn der Klageschrift folgende Unterlagen beigefügt sind:
1. eine geeignete Beschreibung des Kulturgutes mit Angaben über
   a) die Identität und Herkunft,
   b) den tatsächlichen oder mutmaßlichen Zeitpunkt der Verbringung und
   c) den tatsächlichen oder mutmaßlichen Ort der Belegenheit im Bundesgebiet,
2. eine Erklärung, dass es sich um ein nach nationalen Rechtsvorschriften oder Verwaltungsverfahren des er suchenden Mitgliedstaates oder Vertragsstaates nationales Kulturgut handelt, und
3. eine Erklärung des ersuchenden Mitgliedstaates oder Vertragsstaates, dass das Kulturgut unrechtmäßig aus seinem Hoheitsgebiet ausgeführt worden ist.

(2) Die Klage auf Rückgabe ist unzulässig, wenn das Verbringen des Kulturgutes aus dem Hoheitsgebiet des ersuchenden Mitgliedstaates oder Vertragsstaates zu dem Zeitpunkt, zu dem die Klage erhoben wird, nicht mehr unrechtmäßig ist.

§ 64 Kosten der behördlichen Sicherstellung

Hat die zuständige Behörde das Kulturgut, über dessen Rückgabe das Gericht zu entscheiden hat, nach § 33 sichergestellt, so ist in der gerichtlichen Entscheidung über die Rückgabe auch über die Kosten zu entscheiden, die der zuständigen Behörde durch die Sicherstellung entstanden sind.

§ 65 Kosten der Rückgabe und Erhaltungsmaßnahmen

(1) Die Kosten, die sich aufgrund der Rückgabe ergeben, gehen zu Lasten des ersuchenden Mitgliedstaates oder Vertragsstaates.

(2) Die Kosten, die durch Durchführung oder Veranlassung von notwendigen Maßnahmen zur Erhaltung des sichergestellten Kulturgutes entstehen, gehen zu Lasten des ersuchenden Mitgliedstaates oder Vertragsstaates. § 64 ist entsprechend anzuwenden.

Abschnitt 3
Entschädigung und Erstattungsanspruch

§ 66 Entschädigung bei Rückgabe

(1) Ist der unmittelbare Eigenbesitzer beim Erwerb des Kulturgutes mit der erforderlichen Sorgfalt vorge gangen, so kann er die Rückgabe des Kulturgutes verweigern, bis der ersuchende Mitgliedstaat oder Vertragsstaat eine angemessene Entschädigung geleistet hat.

(2) Bei einer unentgeltlichen Rechtsnachfolge muss die erforderliche Sorgfalt

beim Erwerb sowohl vom Rechtsvorgänger als auch vom Rechtsnachfolger beachtet worden sein. Beim Erwerb durch Erbschaft muss der Erbe oder Vermächtnisnehmer die mangelnde Sorgfalt des Erblassers gegen sich gelten lassen.

(3) Bei der Entscheidung, ob der unmittelbare Eigenbesitzer mit der erforderlichen Sorgfalt vorgegangen ist, werden alle Umstände beim Erwerb des Kulturgutes berücksichtigt, insbesondere

1. die Unterlagen über die Herkunft des Kulturgutes,
2. die nach dem Recht des ersuchenden Mitgliedstaates oder Vertragsstaates erforderliche Ausfuhrgenehmi gung,
3. die jeweiligen Eigenschaften der beim Erwerb des Kulturgutes Beteiligten,
4. der Kaufpreis,
5. die Einsichtnahme des unmittelbaren Eigenbesitzers in die zugänglichen Verzeichnisse entwendeten Kultur gutes und das Einholen einschlägiger Informationen, die er mit zumutbarem Aufwand erhalten konnte, und
6. jeder andere Schritt, den eine vernünftige Person unter denselben Umständen unternommen hätte.

(4) § 52 Absatz 3 bleibt unberührt.

§ 67 Höhe der Entschädigung

(1) Die Höhe der Entschädigung bestimmt sich unter Berücksichtigung der entstandenen Aufwendungen des Rückgabeschuldners für

1. den Erwerb des Kulturgutes und
2. die notwendigen Maßnahmen zur Erhaltung des Kulturgutes.

Die Entschädigung darf die Aufwendungen nicht übersteigen. Für entgangenen Gewinn ist keine Entschädigung zu zahlen.

(2) Bleibt das Kulturgut auch nach der Rückgabe Eigentum des Rückgabeschuldners, so hat der ersuchende Mitgliedstaat oder Vertragsstaat dem Rückgabeschuldner abweichend von Absatz 1 nur die Aufwendungen zu erstatten, die dem Rückgabeschuldner daraus entstanden sind, dass er darauf vertraut hat, das Kulturgut im Bun desgebiet belassen zu dürfen.

§ 68 Erstattungsanspruch des ersuchenden Mitglied- oder Vertragsstaates

(1) Der ersuchende Mitgliedstaat oder Vertragsstaat kann von den Personen, die Kulturgut unrechtmäßig verbracht haben oder die die unrechtmäßige Verbringung von Kulturgut veranlasst haben, Erstattung der aus dem Rückgabeverfahren entstandenen Kosten fordern. § 840 Absatz 1 des Bürgerlichen Gesetzbuches ist entsprechend anzuwenden.

(2) Der Anspruch nach Absatz 1 ist vor den ordentlichen Gerichten geltend zu machen.

Kapitel 6
Rückgabe unrechtmäßig ausgeführten Kulturgutes

§ 69 Rückgabeanspruch gegenüber Mitgliedstaaten

(1) Den Anspruch auf Rückgabe von Kulturgut, das unrechtmäßig in das Hoheitsgebiet eines Mitgliedstaa- tes ausgeführt worden ist, macht im jeweiligen Mitgliedstaat nach dessen Vorschriften die für Kultur und Medien zuständige oberste Bundesbehörde im Benehmen mit der zuständigen obersten Landesbehörde des Landes, in dem sich das Kulturgut vor der unrechtmäßigen Ausfuhr dauerhaft befand, geltend. Ist der Ort der letzten dauer haften Belegenheit des Kulturgutes im Bundesgebiet nicht feststellbar, so macht die für Kultur und Medien zu ständige oberste Bundesbehörde den Anspruch geltend.

(2) Die für Kultur und Medien zuständige oberste Bundesbehörde setzt die zuständige zentrale Stelle des ersuchten Mitgliedstaates unverzüglich davon in Kenntnis, dass sie Klage auf Rückgabe des betreffenden Kultur gutes erhoben hat.

§ 70 Rückgabeanspruch gegenüber Vertragsstaaten

(1) Den Anspruch auf Rückgabe von Kulturgut, das unrechtmäßig in das Hoheitsgebiet eines Vertragsstaa tes ausgeführt worden ist, macht das Auswärtige Amt im Einvernehmen mit der für Kultur und Medien zuständi gen obersten Bundesbehörde geltend.

(2) Bevor die für Kultur und Medien zuständige oberste Bundesbehörde den Rückgabeanspruch geltend macht, stellt sie das Benehmen her mit der zuständigen obersten Landesbehörde des Landes, in dem sich das Kulturgut vor der unrechtmäßigen Ausfuhr dauerhaft befand.

§ 71 Kosten

(1) Die notwendigen Kosten und Auslagen, die durch die Geltendmachung des Rückgabeanspruchs ent standen sind, trägt derjenige, der das Kulturgut unrechtmäßig ausgeführt hat. § 840 Absatz 1 des Bürgerlichen Gesetzbuches ist entsprechend anzuwenden.

(2) Die Bundesbehörde, die den Rückgabeanspruch nach den §§ 69, 70 geltend macht, setzt den zu erstat tenden Betrag durch Bescheid fest.

§ 72 Eigentum an zurückgegebenem Kulturgut

Wer Eigentümer des Kulturgutes ist, das unrechtmäßig ausgeführt worden ist und in das Bundesgebiet zu rückgegeben worden ist, bestimmt sich nach den deutschen Sachvorschriften.

Kapitel 7
Rückgabezusage im internationalen Leihverkehr

§ 73 Rechtsverbindliche Rückgabezusage

(1) Wird Kulturgut aus dem Ausland für eine öffentliche Ausstellung oder für eine andere Form der öffent lichen Präsentation, einschließlich einer vorherigen Restaurierung für diesen Zweck, oder für Forschungszwecke an eine Kulturgut bewahrende oder wissenschaftliche Einrichtung im Bundesgebiet vorübergehend ausgeliehen, so kann die oberste Landesbehörde im Benehmen mit der für Kultur und Medien zuständigen obersten Bundes behörde eine rechtsverbindliche Rückgabezusage für die Aufenthaltsdauer des Kulturgutes im Bundesgebiet er teilen. Die Rückgabezusage darf höchstens für zwei Jahre erteilt werden.

(2) Für die Erteilung der rechtsverbindlichen Rückgabezusage ist die oberste Landesbehörde des Landes zuständig, in dem der Entleiher seinen Hauptsitz hat. Bei mehreren Leihorten ist die Behörde des ersten Leihortes zuständig.

§ 74 Erteilung der rechtsverbindlichen Rückgabezusage

(1) Auf Antrag des Entleihers kann die oberste Landesbehörde im Benehmen mit der für Kultur und Medien zuständigen obersten Bundesbehörde dem Verleiher vor der Einfuhr des Kulturgutes die Rückgabezusage erteilen. Der Antrag kann schriftlich oder elektronisch übermittelt werden.

(2) Die Rückgabezusage erfolgt schriftlich und unter Gebrauch der Worte „rechtsverbindliche Rückgabe zusage".

§ 75 Verlängerung

(1) Die rechtsverbindliche Rückgabezusage kann von der obersten Landesbehörde im Einvernehmen mit der für Kultur und Medien zuständigen obersten Bundesbehörde auf Antrag des Entleihers verlängert werden. Die Höchstdauer von zwei Jahren soll auch durch eine Verlängerung nicht überschritten werden. In begründeten Aus nahmefällen kann die Frist für einen Aufenthalt im Bundesgebiet auf bis zu vier Jahre verlängert werden.

(2) § 73 Absatz 2 ist entsprechend anzuwenden.

§ 76 Wirkung

(1) Die rechtsverbindliche Rückgabezusage bewirkt, dass
1. dem Rückgabeanspruch des Verleihers keine Rechte entgegengehalten werden können, die Dritte an dem Kulturgut geltend machen, und
2. kein Verfahren zur Eintragung in ein Verzeichnis national wertvollen Kulturgutes eingeleitet werden kann.

Die Rückgabezusage kann nicht aufgehoben, zurückgenommen oder widerrufen werden und ist für die Aufent haltsdauer des Kulturgutes im Bundesgebiet sofort vollziehbar.

(2) Bis zur Rückgabe des Kulturgutes an den Verleiher, höchstens jedoch für die Dauer der erteilten Rück gabezusage, sind gerichtliche Klagen auf Herausgabe, Arrestverfügungen, Pfändungen und Beschlagnahmen des Kulturgutes sowie behördliche Vollstreckungsmaßnahmen oder Sicherstellungen nach diesem Gesetz oder ande ren Rechtsvorschriften nicht zulässig.

(3) Die Ausfuhr nach Ablauf des Leihvertrages unterliegt nicht der Genehmigungspflicht nach § 24.

Kapitel 8
Datenschutz, gemeinsames Verfahren, Zoll

§ 77 Erhebung und Verarbeitung von Informationen einschließlich personenbezogener Daten

(1) Die für die Ausführung dieses Gesetzes zuständigen Behörden des Bundes und der Länder dürfen In formationen einschließlich personenbezogener Daten erheben, verarbeiten und nutzen, soweit dies erforderlich ist
1. zur Erfüllung ihrer Aufgaben nach diesem Gesetz, nach landesrechtlichen Regelungen zum Schutz bewegli chen Kulturgutes, nach unmittelbar geltenden Rechtsakten der Europäischen Union und der Europäischen Gemeinschaft, die Verbote und Beschränkungen enthalten, sowie
2. zur Erfüllung ihrer Aufgaben nach der aufgrund dieses Gesetzes erlassenen Rechtsverordnung.

(2) Die Vorschriften zum Schutz personenbezogener Daten bleiben unberührt.

§ 78 Übermittlung von Informationen einschließlich personenbezogener Daten an die zuständige Behörde

(1) Öffentliche Stellen im Sinne von § 2 des Bundesdatenschutzgesetzes in der Fassung der Bekanntma chung vom 14. Januar 2003 (BGBl. I S. 66), das zuletzt durch

Artikel 1 des Gesetzes vom 25. Februar 2015 (BGBl. I S. 162) geändert worden ist, dürfen Informationen einschließlich personenbezogener Daten der nach diesem Gesetz zuständigen Behörde des Bundes und der Länder übermitteln, soweit dies erforderlich ist, damit diese Behörde ihre in § 77 genannten Aufgaben erfüllen kann.

(2) Öffentliche Stellen haben unverzüglich die zuständigen Behörden des Bundes und der Länder zu unter richten, wenn sie im Zusammenhang mit der Erfüllung ihrer Aufgaben Kenntnis davon erlangen, dass Kulturgut unter Verstoß gegen die Einfuhr- und Ausfuhrbestimmungen ein oder ausgeführt worden ist oder werden soll.

(3) Die für die Einleitung und Durchführung eines Straf oder eines Bußgeldverfahrens zuständigen Stellen haben die nach diesem Gesetz zuständigen Behörden des Bundes und der Länder unverzüglich über die Einleitung und die Erledigung eines auf Kulturgut bezogenen Straf- oder Bußgeldverfahrens bei der Staatsanwaltschaft, bei Gericht oder bei der für die Verfolgung und Ahndung der Ordnungswidrigkeit zuständigen Verwaltungsbehörde unter Angabe der gesetzlichen Vorschriften zu unterrichten. Satz 1 ist nicht für Verfahren wegen einer Ordnungs widrigkeit anzuwenden, die nur mit einer Geldbuße bis zu tausend Euro geahndet werden kann.

(4) Bei Eingang eines Rechtshilfeersuchens eines anderen Mitgliedstaates oder Vertragsstaates ist Absatz 3 entsprechend anzuwenden mit der Maßgabe, dass auch die für Kultur und Medien zuständige oberste Bundesbe hörde unterrichtet wird. Diese unterrichtet in Fällen eines Rechtshilfeersuchens eines Vertragsstaates das Auswärtige Amt.

§ 79 Gemeinsames Verfahren von Bund und Ländern

(1) Zum umfassenden Schutz nationalen Kulturgutes führen Bund und Länder ein gemeinsames Verfahren im Sinne des § 11 des E-Government-Gesetzes. Sie sind befugt, Informationen einschließlich personenbezogener Daten in dem gemeinsamen Verfahren zu verarbeiten.

(2) Die am gemeinsamen Verfahren beteiligten Behörden des Bundes und der Länder sind jeweils für die Rechtmäßigkeit der von ihnen vorgenommenen Datenerhebung, Datenverarbeitung und Datennutzung verant wortlich.

(3) Die am gemeinsamen Verfahren beteiligten Behörden des Bundes und der Länder unterliegen, soweit sie an dem gemeinsamen Verfahren teilnehmen, dem Bundesdatenschutzgesetz. Die zuständige Kontrollstelle im Sinne des § 11 Absatz 5 Satz 2 des E-Government-Gesetzes für die Einhaltung der Datenschutzvorschriften mit Bezug auf das gemeinsame Verfahren ist die oder der Bundesbeauftragte für den Datenschutz und die Informati onsfreiheit. Die Zuständigkeit der oder des Bundesbeauftragten für den Datenschutz und die Informationsfreiheit lässt die Zuständigkeit der oder des Landesbeauftragten für den Datenschutz im Übrigen unberührt.

(4) Im Rahmen des gemeinsamen Verfahrens werden neben den Daten zur Identifikation des Kulturgutes auch die personenbezogenen Daten der Eigentümer und soweit erforderlich der Besitzer des nationalen Kulturgu tes verarbeitet. Dies sind

insbesondere deren Namen und Adressen.

(5) Einzelheiten des gemeinsamen Verfahrens, insbesondere die jeweils verantwortliche Stelle für die Fest legung, Änderung, Fortentwicklung und Einhaltung von fachlichen und technischen Vorgaben nach § 11 Absatz 4 Satz 1 Nummer 1 des E-Government-Gesetzes, werden durch für alle Länder verbindliche Beschlüsse des Ver- waltungsausschusses nach § 4 Absatz 4 geregelt.

§ 80 Übermittlung von Informationen einschließlich personenbezogener Daten an Mitgliedstaaten und Vertragsstaaten

(1) Die für Kultur und Medien zuständige oberste Bundesbehörde erteilt den zuständigen zentralen Stellen eines Mitgliedstaates auf begründetes Ersuchen,

1. soweit es für deren Prüfung erforderlich ist, Auskunft, ob
   a) die Voraussetzungen für ein Rückgabeersuchen oder eine Klage auf Rückgabe gegeben sind oder
   b) die Voraussetzungen für die Erteilung einer Ausfuhrgenehmigung nach der Verordnung (EG) Nr. 116/2009 gegeben sind, sowie
2. Auskünfte, die zur Auffindung und Rückgabe von gestohlenem oder unrechtmäßig in das Bundesgebiet ein geführtem Kulturgut beitragen können.

Die Auskunftserteilung nach Satz 1 Nummer 1 und 2 umfasst neben nichtpersonenbezogenen Daten den Namen und die ladungsfähige Anschrift der derzeitigen oder vorherigen Eigentümer oder Besitzer, soweit dies für die Prüfung der zuständigen Stelle des anderen Mitgliedstaates erforderlich ist.

(2) Das Auswärtige Amt erteilt einem Vertragsstaat auf begründetes Ersuchen

1. soweit es für dessen Prüfung erforderlich ist, Auskunft, ob die Voraussetzungen für ein Rückgabeersuchen oder eine Klage auf Rückgabe gegeben sind, sowie
2. Auskünfte, die zur Auffindung und Rückgabe von gestohlenem oder unrechtmäßig in das Bundesgebiet ein geführtem Kulturgut beitragen können.

(3) Personenbezogene Daten dürfen an Stellen in Mitgliedstaaten und Vertragsstaaten nur übermittelt wer den, wenn deren Kenntnis für die Rechtsverfolgung von Rückgabeansprüchen nach diesem Gesetz erforderlich ist. Die Datenübermittlung muss zusätzlich den Anforderungen der §§ 4b und 4c des Bundesdatenschutzgesetzes genügen.

§ 81 Mitwirkung der Zollbehörden, Anhaltung von Kulturgut

(1) Die Zollbehörden wirken im Rahmen ihrer Zuständigkeit bei der Überwachung der Ein und Ausfuhr von Kulturgut mit, für das Verbote oder Beschränkungen nach diesem Gesetz oder einer aufgrund dieses Gesetzes erlassenen Rechtsverordnung gelten. Soweit es zur Durchführung dieses Gesetzes und der aufgrund dieses Geset zes erlassenen Rechtsverordnungen erforderlich ist, dürfen die Zollbehörden die im Rahmen ihrer zollamtlichen Überwachung gewonnenen Informationen, auch soweit sie

dem Steuergeheimnis unterliegen, den zuständigen Behörden übermitteln.

(2) Die für Kultur und Medien zuständige oberste Bundesbehörde kann der zuständigen zentralen Stelle der Zollverwaltung konkrete länder-, waren- oder personenbezogene Risikohinweise übermitteln.

(3) Ergeben sich bei der zollamtlichen Überwachung Anhaltspunkte für einen Verstoß gegen dieses Gesetz oder gegen eine aufgrund dieses Gesetzes erlassene Rechtsverordnung, so unterrichten die Zollbehörden unver züglich die zuständige Behörde des Landes, in dem sich das Kulturgut bei der Anhaltung befindet.

(4) Im Falle des Absatzes 3 halten die Zollbehörden die Waren, deren Beförderungs- und Verpackungsmit tel sowie die beigefügten Unterlagen auf Kosten und Gefahr des Verfügungsberechtigten an. Sie können die an gehaltenen Waren sowie deren Beförderungs- und Verpackungsmittel auch durch einen Dritten verwahren lassen. § 39 ist entsprechend anzuwenden.

(5) Die Zollbehörde gibt das angehaltene Kulturgut, die Beförderungs- und Verpackungsmittel sowie die beigefügten Unterlagen frei, wenn die sonstigen Anforderungen und Förmlichkeiten für eine Freigabe erfüllt sind und

1. die zuständige Behörde mitgeteilt hat, dass sie das Kulturgut nach § 33 sichergestellt hat,
2. die zuständige Behörde mitgeteilt hat, dass das Kulturgut nicht sichergestellt wird, oder
3. nach Ablauf von drei Arbeitstagen seit der Unterrichtung nach Absatz 3 keine Mitteilung der zuständigen Behörde zum weiteren Vorgehen vorliegt oder
4. nach Ablauf von zehn Arbeitstagen seit der Unterrichtung nach Absatz 3 keine Mitteilung der zuständigen Behörde über die Sicherstellung des Kulturgutes nach § 33 vorliegt.

(6) Es ist verboten, nach Absatz 4 angehaltenes Kulturgut zu beschädigen, zu zerstören oder dessen Er- scheinungsbild nicht nur unerheblich und nicht nur vorübergehend zu verändern.

§ 82 Anmeldepflicht bei Ein- und Ausfuhr im Kulturgutverkehr mit Drittstaaten

(1) Bei der zuständigen Zollstelle ist Kulturgut anzumelden, das

1. unmittelbar aus einem Drittstaat eingeführt werden soll und zur Ausfuhr aus dem Herkunftsstaat einer Ge nehmigung durch diesen Staat bedarf oder
2. in einen Drittstaat ausgeführt werden soll und zur Ausfuhr aus dem Binnenmarkt einer Genehmigung nach diesem Gesetz oder nach einem im Amtsblatt der Europäischen Union veröffentlichten, unmittelbar gelten den Rechtsakt der Europäischen Union bedarf.

(2) Die Anmeldung hat die Person vorzunehmen, die das Kulturgut einführt oder ausführt. Bei der Anmel dung sind die für die Einfuhr oder Ausfuhr erforderlichen Genehmigungen oder sonstigen Dokumente vorzulegen.

(3) Auf Verlangen der zuständigen Zollstelle ist das anmeldepflichtige Kulturgut

vorzuführen.

Kapitel 9
Straf- und Bußgeldvorschriften

§ 83 Strafvorschriften

(1) Mit Freiheitsstrafe bis zu fünf Jahren oder mit Geldstrafe wird bestraft, wer
1. entgegen § 21 Nummer 1, 2, 4 oder 5 Kulturgut ausführt,
2. entgegen § 21 Nummer 3 Kulturgut ausführt, von dem er weiß, dass es nach § 32 Absatz 1 Nummer 1 oder 2 unrechtmäßig eingeführt wurde,
3. entgegen § 28 Kulturgut einführt, von dem er weiß, dass es unter Verstoß gegen eine dort genannte Rechts- vorschrift verbracht worden ist,
4. entgegen § 40 Absatz 1 Kulturgut in Verkehr bringt, das abhandengekommen ist oder von dem er weiß, dass es rechtswidrig ausgegraben oder nach § 32 Absatz 1 Nummer 1 oder 2 unrechtmäßig eingeführt worden ist, oder
5. entgegen § 40 Absatz 3 ein Verpflichtungs oder Verfügungsgeschäft über Kulturgut abschließt, das durch eine in Nummer 1 oder 2 bezeichnete Handlung ausgeführt worden ist.

(2) Ebenso wird bestraft, wer entgegen Artikel 2 Absatz 1 der Verordnung (EG) Nr. 116/2009 des Rates vom 18. Dezember 2008 über die Ausfuhr von Kulturgütern (ABl. L 39 vom 10.2.2009, S. 1) Kulturgut ausführt.

(3) Mit Freiheitsstrafe bis zu drei Jahren oder mit Geldstrafe wird bestraft, wer entgegen § 18 Absatz 1, auch in Verbindung mit Absatz 2, Kulturgut beschädigt, zerstört oder verändert.

(4) Der Versuch ist strafbar.

(5) Mit Freiheitsstrafe von einem Jahr bis zu zehn Jahren wird bestraft, wer in den Fällen des Absatzes 1 Nummer 4
1. gewerbsmäßig handelt oder
2. als Mitglied einer Bande handelt, die sich zur fortgesetzten Begehung solcher Taten verbunden hat.

(6) Mit Freiheitsstrafe bis zu drei Jahren oder mit Geldstrafe wird bestraft, wer in den Fällen des Absatzes 1 Nummer 1 oder des Absatzes 2 in Ausübung einer gewerblichen Tätigkeit fahrlässig handelt.

(7) Das Gericht kann in den Fällen des Absatzes 1 Nummer 1 die Strafe nach § 49 Absatz 1 des Strafge setzbuches mildern oder von Strafe absehen, wenn der Täter das Kulturgut unverzüglich in das Bundesgebiet zurückbringt.

§ 84 Bußgeldvorschriften

(1) Ordnungswidrig handelt, wer

1. entgegen § 15 Absatz 2 eine Mitteilung nicht, nicht richtig, nicht vollständig oder nicht rechtzeitig macht,
2. entgegen § 42 Absatz 1 Satz 1 Nummer 1 Name oder Anschrift einer dort genannten Person nicht oder nicht rechtzeitig feststellt,
3. entgegen § 42 Absatz 1 Satz 1 Nummer 2 eine Beschreibung oder eine Abbildung nicht oder nicht rechtzei tig anfertigt oder
4. entgegen § 42 Absatz 1 Satz 1 Nummer 7 eine dort genannte Erklärung nicht oder nicht rechtzeitig einholt.

(2) Ordnungswidrig handelt, wer vorsätzlich oder fahrlässig
1. entgegen § 30 Satz 1 bei der Einfuhr von Kulturgut, von dem er weiß oder hätte wissen müssen, dass es von einem Mitgliedstaat oder Vertragsstaat als nationales Kulturgut eingestuft oder definiert worden ist, eine dort verlangte Unterlage nicht mit sich führt oder
2. entgegen § 82 Absatz 3 Kulturgut nicht oder nicht rechtzeitig vorführt.

(3) Die Ordnungswidrigkeit kann in den Fällen des Absatzes 1 Nummer 2 bis 4 mit einer Geldbuße bis zu dreißigtausend Euro, in den übrigen Fällen mit einer Geldbuße bis zu hunderttausend Euro geahndet werden.

§ 85 Einziehung und erweiterter Verfall

(1) Ist eine Straftat nach § 83 oder eine Ordnungswidrigkeit nach § 84 Absatz 1 oder 2 begangen worden, so können folgende Gegenstände eingezogen werden:
1. Gegenstände, auf die sich die Straftat oder Ordnungswidrigkeit bezieht, oder
2. Gegenstände, die durch sie hervorgebracht oder zu ihrer Begehung oder Vorbereitung gebraucht worden oder bestimmt gewesen sind.

§ 74a des Strafgesetzbuches und § 23 des Gesetzes über Ordnungswidrigkeiten sind anzuwenden.

(2) In den Fällen des § 83 Absatz 5 Nummer 2 ist § 73d des Strafgesetzbuches anzuwenden.

§ 86 Besondere Voraussetzung der Verwertung von Kulturgut

(1) Kulturgut, das nach § 85 der Einziehung oder dem Verfall unterliegt, darf nur mit Zustimmung der zuständigen Behörde verwertet werden.

(2) Die Zustimmung kann versagt werden. Sie ist im Regelfall zu versagen für Kulturgut,
1. das der genehmigungspflichtigen Ausfuhr nach § 24 unterliegt und dessen Eintragung in ein Verzeichnis national wertvollen Kulturgutes noch nicht abschließend geprüft worden ist,
2. das einem Rückgabeanspruch nach Kapitel 5 unterliegen könnte und für das die Verjährungsfrist für den Rückgabeanspruch noch nicht abgelaufen oder der Anspruch noch nicht erloschen ist oder

3. dessen Inverkehrbringen nach § 40 verboten ist oder für dessen Inverkehrbringen eine erhöhte Sorgfalts pflicht nach § 44 besteht.

(3) Vor der Verwertung von Kulturgut ausländischer Staaten sind das Auswärtige Amt und die für Kultur und Medien zuständige oberste Bundesbehörde anzuhören.

(4) Die Absätze 1 bis 3 sind auch bei Einziehung und Verfall nach anderen Rechtsvorschriften anzuwenden.

(5) Eine Verwertung von Kulturgut, das die zuständige Behörde nach diesem Gesetz eingezogen hat, ist erst möglich, wenn die Voraussetzungen nach Absatz 2 abschließend geprüft sind.

§ 87 Aufgaben und Befugnisse der Zollbehörden

(1) Die Staatsanwaltschaft kann bei Straftaten und Ordnungswidrigkeiten nach den §§ 83 und 84 Ermitt- lungen nach § 161 Absatz 1 Satz 1 der Strafprozessordnung in den Fällen des § 83 Absatz 1 Nummer 1, 2 oder 3 in Verbindung mit den Absätzen 4 und 6 sowie im Fall des § 83 Absatz 2 in Verbindung mit Absatz 4 auch durch die Hauptzollämter oder die Zollfahndungsämter vornehmen lassen. Die nach § 36 Absatz 1 Nummer 2 oder Ab satz 2 des Gesetzes gegen Ordnungswidrigkeiten zuständige Verwaltungsbehörde kann in den Fällen des Satzes 1 Ermittlungen auch durch die Hauptzollämter oder die Zollfahndungsämter vornehmen lassen.

(2) § 21 Absatz 3 des Außenwirtschaftsgesetzes vom 6. Juni 2013 (BGBl. I S. 1482), das durch Artikel 297 der Verordnung vom 31. August 2015 (BGBl. I S. 1474) geändert worden ist, ist entsprechend anzuwenden.

§ 88 Straf-und Bußgeldverfahren

Soweit für Straftaten nach § 83 das Amtsgericht sachlich zuständig ist, liegt die örtliche Zuständigkeit bei dem Amtsgericht, in dessen Bezirk das örtlich zuständige Landgericht seinen Sitz hat. Die Landesregierung kann durch Rechtsverordnung die örtliche Zuständigkeit des Amtsgerichts abweichend regeln, soweit dies mit Rück sicht auf die Wirtschafts- oder Verkehrsverhältnisse, den Aufbau der Verwaltung oder andere örtliche Bedürfnisse zweckmäßig erscheint. Die Landesregierung kann diese Ermächtigung auf die Landesjustizverwaltung übertra gen.

Kapitel 10
Evaluierung, Übergangs- und Ausschlussvorschriften

§ 89 Evaluierung

Das für Kultur und Medien zuständige Mitglied der Bundesregierung unterrichtet den

Deutschen Bundestag und den Bundesrat über die Anwendung des Gesetzes fünf Jahre und vorab zum Umfang des Verwaltungsauf wandes zwei Jahre nach Inkrafttreten des Gesetzes.

§ 90 Fortgeltung und Befristung bisherigen Abwanderungsschutzes

(1) Bestandteil des Verzeichnisses national wertvollen Kulturgutes ist Kulturgut, das aufgrund des Gesetzes zum Schutz deutschen Kulturgutes gegen Abwanderung in der Fassung der Bekanntmachung vom 8. Juli 1999 (BGBl. I S. 1754), das zuletzt durch Artikel 2 des Gesetzes vom 18. Mai 2007 (BGBl. I S. 757) geändert worden ist, eingetragen worden ist in

1. ein Verzeichnis national wertvollen Kulturgutes oder
2. ein Verzeichnis national wertvoller Archive eines Landes.

(2) Die Ausfuhr bleibt genehmigungspflichtig, längstens bis zum Ablauf des 31. Dezember 2025

1. von Kunstwerken, die aufgrund der Verordnung über die Ausfuhr von Kunstwerken der Reichsregierung vom 11. Dezember 1919 (RGBl. S. 1961), die zuletzt durch die Verordnung vom 20. Dezember 1932 (RGBl. I S. 572) verlängert worden ist, in das Verzeichnis der national wertvollen Kunstwerke eingetragen waren und über deren Eintragung in ein Verzeichnis national wertvollen Kulturgutes noch nicht entschieden worden ist, und
2. von registriertem Kulturgut nach dem Kulturgutschutzgesetz vom 3. Juli 1980 (GBl. I Nr. 20 S. 191) und über dessen Eintragung in ein Verzeichnis national wertvollen Kulturgutes noch nicht entschieden worden ist.

(3) Für Verfahren, die bis 6. August 2016 eingeleitet und bekannt gemacht worden sind, gelten die Vorschriften des Gesetzes zum Schutz deutschen Kulturgutes gegen Abwande rung in der Fassung der Bekanntmachung vom 8. Juli 1999 (BGBl. I S. 1754), das zuletzt durch Artikel 2 des Gesetzes vom 18. Mai 2007 (BGBl. I S. 757, 2547) geändert worden ist, bis zum Abschluss des Verfahrens fort.

§ 91 Ausschluss abweichenden Landesrechts

Von den in den §§ 7 bis 17, 22 bis 27 und 73 bis 76 getroffenen Regelungen des Verwaltungsverfahrens kann durch Landesrecht nicht abgewichen werden.

Artikel 2
Änderung des Gesetzes zur Errichtung einer Stiftung „Deutsche Bundesstiftung Umwelt"

In § 2 Absatz 2 des Gesetzes zur Errichtung einer Stiftung „Deutsche

Bundesstiftung Umwelt“ vom 18. Juli 1990 (BGBl. I S. 1448) werden die Wörter „– Bewahrung und Sicherung national wertvoller Kulturgüter im Hin blick auf schädliche Umwelteinflüsse (Modellvorhaben).“ durch die Wörter „– Bewahrung und Sicherung natio nalen Kulturgutes im Hinblick auf schädliche Umwelteinflüsse (Modellvorhaben).“ ersetzt.

Artikel 3

Änderung des Gesetzes zu der Konvention vom 14. Mai 1954 zum Schutz von Kulturgut bei bewaffneten Konflikten

Artikel 2 Absatz 5 des Gesetzes zu der Konvention vom 14. Mai 1954 zum Schutz von Kulturgut bei be waffneten Konflikten vom 11. April 1967 (BGBl. 1967 II S. 1233), das zuletzt durch Artikel 4 des Gesetzes vom 27. April 2004 (BGBl. I S. 630) geändert worden ist, wird wie folgt gefasst:

„(5) Das Bundesamt für Bevölkerungsschutz und Katastrophenhilfe ist zuständig für

1. die Verbreitung des Wortlauts der Konvention und ihrer Ausführungsbestimmungen nach Artikel 25 der Konvention, soweit sie nicht nach Absatz 4 Buchstabe b erfolgt,
2. die Verpackung, Dokumentation, Einlagerung und Aufbewahrung von Sicherungsmedien an einem zentralen Bergungsort.“

Artikel 4

Änderung des Einführungsgesetzes zum Gerichtsverfassungsgesetz

In § 14 Absatz 1 Nummer 9 des Einführungsgesetzes zum Gerichtsverfassungsgesetz in der im Bundesge setzblatt Teil III, Gliederungsnummer 300-1, veröffentlichten bereinigten Fassung, das zuletzt durch Artikel 130 der Verordnung vom 31. August 2015 (BGBl. I S. 1474) geändert worden ist, werden die Wörter „Klima und Landschaft“ durch die Wörter „Klima und Landschaft sowie das kulturelle Erbe“ ersetzt.

Artikel 5

Änderung des Gesetzes über die internationale Rechtshilfe in Strafsachen

§ 56b Absatz 2 des Gesetzes über die internationale Rechtshilfe in Strafsachen in der Fassung der Bekannt machung vom 27. Juni 1994 (BGBl. I S. 1537), das zuletzt durch Artikel 163 der Verordnung vom 31. August 2015 (BGBl. I S. 1474) geändert worden ist, wird wie folgt gefasst:

„(2) Vereinbarungen, die sich auf nationales Kulturgut nach § 6 Absatz 1 Nummer 1 des Kulturgutschutz gesetzes vom 31. Juli 2016 (BGBl. IS. 1914) beziehen, bedürfen der Einwilligung der für Kultur und Medien zuständigen obersten Bundesbehörde."

Artikel 6
Änderung der FIDE-Verzeichnis-Verordnung

§ 1 Absatz 1 Nummer 8 der FIDE-Verzeichnis-Verordnung vom 5. Oktober 2011 (BGBl. I S. 2057), die zuletzt durch Artikel 6 des Gesetzes vom 10. Dezember 2015 (BGBl. I S. 22 10) geändert worden ist, wird wie folgt gefasst:

„8. Straftaten gegen Vorschriften über den Warenverkehr zum Schutz des Kulturgutes nach § 83 Absatz 1 Num mer 1 des Kulturgutschutzgesetzes vom 31. Juli 2016 (BGBl. IS. 1914)."

Artikel 7
Änderung des Einkommensteuergesetzes

In § 10g Absatz 1 Satz 2 Nummer 4 des Einkommensteuergesetzes in der Fassung der Bekanntmachung vom 8. Oktober 2009 (BGBl. I S. 3366, 3862), das zuletzt durch Artikel 3 des Gesetzes vom 19. Juli 2016 (BGBl. IS. 1730) geändert worden ist, werden die Wörter „oder in das Verzeichnis national wertvollen Kultur gutes oder das Verzeichnis national wertvoller Archive eingetragen sind" durch die Wörter „oder als nationales Kulturgut in ein Verzeichnis national wertvollen Kulturgutes nach § 7 Absatz 1 des Kulturgutschutzgesetzes 31. Juli 2016 (BGBl. IS. 1914) eingetragen ist" ersetzt.

Artikel 8
Änderung des Erbschaftsteuer- und Schenkungsteuergesetzes

Das Erbschaftsteuer- und Schenkungsteuergesetz in der Fassung der Bekanntmachung vom 27. Februar 1997 (BGBl. I S. 378), das zuletzt durch Artikel 10 des Gesetzes vom 2. November 2015 (BGBl. I S. 1834) geändert worden ist, wird wie folgt geändert:

1. § 13 Absatz 1 Nummer 2 Buchstabe b Doppelbuchstabe bb wird wie folgt gefasst:
   „bb) die Gegenstände sich seit mindestens 20 Jahren im Besitz der Familie befinden oder in ein Verzeichnis national wertvollen Kulturgutes nach § 7 Absatz 1 des Kulturgutschutzgesetzes vom 31. Juli 2016 (BGBl. I S. 1914) in der jeweils geltenden Fassung eingetragen sind."
2. Dem § 37 wird folgender Absatz 11 angefügt:
   „(11) § 13 Absatz 1 Nummer 2 Buchstabe b Doppelbuchstabe bb in der am 6. August 2016 geltenden Fassung ist auf Erwerbe anzu wenden, für die die Steuer nach dem 5. August 2016 ent standen ist."

Artikel 9
Änderung der Gewerbeordnung

§ 29 Absatz 1 Nummer 5 der Gewerbeordnung in der Fassung der Bekanntmachung vom 22. Februar 1999 (BGBl. I S. 202), die zuletzt durch Artikel 4 Absatz 58 des Gesetzes vom 18. Juli 2016 (BGBl. IS. 1666) geändert worden ist, wird wie folgt gefasst:

„5. soweit diese einer gewerblichen Tätigkeit nach § 42 Absatz 1 des Kulturgutschutzgesetzes nachgehen."

Artikel 10
Inkrafttreten, Außerkrafttreten

Dieses Gesetz tritt am Tag nach der Verkündung in Kraft. Gleichzeitig treten außer Kraft

1. das Gesetz zum Schutz deutschen Kulturgutes gegen Abwanderung in der Fassung der Bekanntmachung vom 8. Juli 1999 (BGBl. IS. 1754), das zuletzt durch Artikel 2 des Gesetzes vom 18. Mai 2007 (BGBl. IS. 757, 2547) geändert worden ist,
2. das Kulturgüterrückgabegesetz vom 18. Mai 2007 (BGBl. I S. 757, 2547; 2008 11 S. 235), das durch Artikel 2 Absatz 8 des Gesetzes vom 6. Juni 2013 (BGBl. I S. 1482) geändert worden ist,
3. die Kulturgüterverzeichnis-Verordnung vom 15. Oktober 2008 (BGBl. I S. 2002) sowie
4. das Gesetz zur Ausführung der Konvention vom 14. Mai 1954 zum Schutz von Kulturgut bei bewaffneten Konflikten vom 18. Mai 2007 (BGBl. I S. 757, 762, 2547).

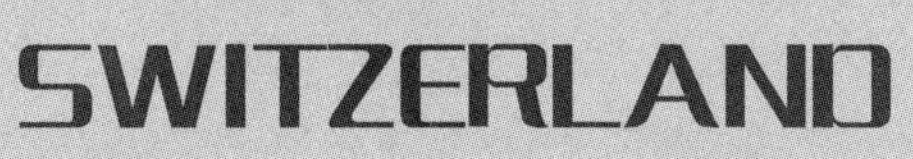
SWITZERLAND

Federal Act on the International Transfer of Cultural Property (Cultural Property Transfer Act, CPTA)

dated June 20, 2003

The Federal Assembly of the Swiss Confederation,
Pursuant to Articles 69, para. 2 and 95, para. 1, of the Swiss Federal Constitution[1], in execution of the UNESCO Convention from November 14, 1970[2] on the Means of Prohibiting and Preventing the Illicit Import, Export and Transfer of Ownership of Cultural Property (UNESCO Convention 1970), after having examined the Message of the Federal Council dated November 21, 2001[3],
decides:

Section 1: General Provisions

Article 1 Scope and Purpose
1. This Act regulates the import of cultural property into Switzerland, its transit and export as well as its repatriation from Switzerland.
2. With this Act, the Confederation desires to make a contribution to the maintenance of the cultural heritage of mankind and prevent theft, looting, and illicit import and export of cultural property.

Article 2 Terms
1. *Cultural property* is defined as significant property from a religious or universal standpoint for archeology, pre-history, history, literature, arts or sciences belonging to the categories under Article 1 of the UNESCO Convention of 1970.
2. *Cultural heritage* is considered the entirety of cultural property belonging to one of the categories under Article 4 of the UNESCO Convention 1970.
3. *Contracting states* are considered states having ratified the UNESCO Convention of 1970.
4. *Specialized body* refers to the administrative body responsible for executing the tasks outlined in Article 18.
5. *Illicit import* refers to an import in violation of an agreement in terms of Article 7 or a measure in terms of Article 8, para. 1, letter a.

AS 2005 1869
1. SR **101**
2. SR **0.444.1**
3. BBl **2002** 535

Section 2: Registries of Cultural Property

Article 3 Federal Registry

1. Cultural property of the Confederation of significant importance for the cultural heritage is registered in the Federal Registry.

2. The registration has the following effect:

- **a.** cultural property may neither be acquired by adverse possession nor acquired in good faith;
- **b.** the claim for return is not subject to a statute of limitation;
- **c.** the definitive export of the cultural property from Switzerland is prohibited.

3. The registration of cultural property in the Federal Registry may be removed, to the extent that:

- **a.** the cultural property no longer has a significant importance to the cultural heritage;
- **b.** consolidation speaks in favor of an ensemble;
- **c.** the Confederation loses its title to the cultural property or waives the same.

4. The specialized body operates the Federal Registry in the form of an electronic database and publishes the same.

Article 4 Cantonal Registries

1. To simplify checks at the borders, the Cantons, which regulate the export of cultural property within their territories, may connect to the federal database:

- **a.** registries of their cultural property;
- **b.** registries of privately-owned cultural property, to the extent approval to this end is granted by the private party.

2. The Cantons may declare that cultural property in their registries may neither be acquired through adverse possession nor in good faith and that the claim of return is not subject to a statute of limitations.

Section 3: Import and Export

Article 5 Export Permit for Cultural Property Registered in the Federal Registry

1. Whoever desires to export cultural property registered in the Federal Registry from Switzerland requires authorization of the specialized body.

2. Authorization shall be granted if:

- **a.** the cultural property is exported on a temporary basis; and
- **b.** the export occurs for reasons of research, conservation, exhibition, or similar reasons.

Article 6 Swiss Repatriation Claims

1. The Federal Council will claim the right of repatriation vis-à-vis all other contracting states should cultural property registered in the Federal Registry be illicitly exported from Switzerland. Any compensation and costs will be carried by the Confederation.

2. The Federal Council will claim the right of repatriation at the request of a Canton vis-à-vis all other contracting states should cultural property registered in a cantonal registry be illicitly exported from Switzerland. Any compensation and costs will be carried by the requesting Canton.

Article 7 Agreements

1. For the protection of cultural and foreign affairs interests and to secure cultural heritage, the Federal Council may conclude international treaties with contracting states on the import and repatriation of cultural property (Agreements).

2. The following conditions must be fulfilled:

- **a.** the scope of the agreement must be cultural property of significant importance to the cultural heritage of the contracting state in question;
- **b.** the cultural property must be subject to export provisions in the state in question for the purpose of protecting cultural heritage; and
- **c.** the contracting state must grant reciprocal rights.

Article 8 Limited Measures

1. To protect a state's cultural heritage jeopardized by exceptional events, the Federal Council may:

- **a.** enable the import, transit, and export of cultural property, tie it to conditions, limitations, or prohibitions;
- **b.** participate in common international actions in terms of Article 9 UNESCO Convention of 1970.

2. The measures must be limited in time.

Article 9 Repatriation Claims based on Agreements

1. Whoever possesses cultural property illicitly imported into Switzerland, can be sued for repatriation by the country from which the cultural property was illicitly exported. In particular, the country filing suit must show that the cultural property is of significant importance to its cultural heritage and was imported illicitly.

2. The court can suspend the execution of repatriation until such time as the cultural property is no longer in jeopardy during repatriation.

3. The country filing suit carries the costs for measures necessary for securing, maintaining, and repatriating the cultural property.

4. Claims for repatriation by a state are subject to a statute of limitation of one year after its authorities gain knowledge of where and with whom the cultural property is located, at the latest, however, 30 years after the cultural property is illicitly exported.

5. Whoever acquires cultural property in good faith and must return the same, has a claim for compensation at the time of repatriation, oriented to the purchase price as well as necessary and useful expenses for protecting and maintaining the cultural property.

6. The state filing suit must pay the compensation. The person required to return the cultural property retains a right of retention of the same until compensation is paid.

Section 4: Return Guarantee

Article 10 Request

Should cultural property of one contracting state be on temporary loan for an exhibition in a museum or another cultural institute in Switzerland, the institution borrowing the cultural property may request that the specialized body issue a return guarantee to the loaning institution for the period of the exhibition as stipulated in the loan agreement.

Article 11 Publication and Procedures for Objections

1. The request is published in the Federal Bulletin. The publication contains a precise description of the cultural property and its origin.

2. If the request clearly fails to fulfill the conditions for issuing a return guarantee, the request will be denied and not published.

3. Parties pursuant to provisions of the Federal Act on Administration Procedure from December 20,1968[4], may file an objection in writing to the specialized body within 30 days. The deadline commences with publication.

4. Failure to file an objection, precludes the parties from further action.

Article 12 Issuance

1. The specialized body decides on the request for issuing a return guarantee.

2. The return guarantee may be issued in the event that:

- **a.** no person claims ownership to the cultural property through an objection;
- **b.** the import of the cultural property is not illicit;
- **c.** the loan agreement stipulates that the cultural property will be returned to the contracting state of origin following the conclusion of the exhibition.

3. The Federal Council may establish additional requirements.

Article 13 Effect

The return guarantee means that neither private parties nor authorities may make legal claims to the cultural property as long as the cultural property is located in Switzerland.

Section 5: Financial Assistance to the Benefit of Maintaining Cultural Heritage

Article 14

1. The Confederation may grant financial assistance:

- **a.** to museums or similar institutions in Switzerland for the temporary fiduciary custody and conservatory care of cultural property that is part of the cultural heritage of another state and is in jeopardy in that state due to exceptional events;
- **b.** for projects to maintain the cultural heritage of other contracting states;
- **c.** under exceptional circumstances to ease the restitution of the cultural heritage of contracting states.

2. Financial assistance pursuant to paragraph 1, letter a, may only be paid out when the fiduciary custody:

- **a.** occurs in agreement with the authorities of the other state; or
- **b.** occurs under the auspices of UNESCO or another international organization for the protection of cultural property.

4. SR **172.021**

Section 6: Transfer of Cultural Property

Article 15 Transfer to Federal Institutions

1. Federal institutions are prohibited from acquiring or exhibiting cultural property that:

- **a.** was stolen, lost against the will of the owner or illegally excavated;
- **b.** are part of the cultural heritage of a state and have been illicitly exported from the same.

2. Federal institutions offered such property must immediately report it to the specialized body.

Article 16 Duty of Diligence

1. In the art trade and auctioning business, cultural property may only be transferred when the person transferring the property may assume, under the circumstances, that the cultural property:

- **a.** was not stolen, not lost against the will of the owner, and not illegally excavated;
- **b.** not illicitly imported.

2. Persons active in the art trade and auctioning business are obligated:

- **a.** to establish the identity of the supplier or seller and require a written declaration from the same of his or her right to dispose of the cultural property;
- **b.** to inform their customers about existing import and export regulations of the contracting states;
- **c.** to maintain written records on the acquisition of cultural property by specifically recording the origin of the cultural property, to the extent known, and the name and address of the supplier or seller, a description as well as the sales price of the cultural property;
- **d.** to provide to the specialized body all necessary information on fulfilling this duty of diligence.

3. The records and receipts must be stored for 30 years. Article 962, para. 2 Swiss Law of Obligations[5] applies accordingly.

Article 17 Inspection

1. To inspect adherence to duty of diligence, the specialized body has access to business rooms and storage areas of persons active in the art trade and auctioning business.

2. When the body has reasonable suspicion that criminal activity is present under this Act, the specialized body will file a complaint with the competent criminal prosecution authorities.

Section 7: Authorities

Article 18 Specialized body

The Confederation appoints a specialized body for the execution of this Act, specifically assuming the following tasks:

- **a.** advising and supporting the Federal Authorities on issues of the transfer of cultural property and coordinating the corresponding work;

5. SR 220

b. advising the cantonal authorities on issues of the transfer of cultural property and working together with them;
c. representing Switzerland vis-à-vis foreign authorities on issues of the transfer of cultural property;
d. working together with authorities from other states to secure their cultural heritage;
e. providing information on issues of the transfer of cultural property to persons active in the art trade and auctioning business as well as other interested circles;
f. maintaining a listing of information centers on reported stolen cultural property;
g. administering the Federal Registry in the form of an electronic database and publishing it (Art. 3);
h. issuing return guarantees (Art. 10–13);
i. inspecting compliance to the duty of diligence of persons active in the art trade and auctioning business (Art. 16 and 17).

Article 19 Customs
1. Customs authorities inspect the transfer of cultural property at the border.
2. They are authorized to withhold suspicious cultural property during import, transit, and export, and report it to criminal prosecution authorities.
3. Arrival of cultural property at customs storage facilities is considered import in terms of this Act.

Article 20 Criminal Prosecution Authorities
1. The competent criminal prosecution authorities will order the seizure of the cultural property when suspicion exists that the cultural property was stolen, lost against the will of the owner or illicitly imported into Switzerland.
2. Each seizure must be reported immediately to the specialized body.

Section 8: Official and Legal Assistance

Article 21 Official Assistance in Switzerland
The competent authorities from the Confederation, Cantons, and Municipalities provide all the data required for the execution of this Act to each other as well as the appropriate oversight authorities.

Article 22 International Official and Legal Assistance
1. The Federal Authorities responsible for the execution of this Act may cooperate with competent foreign authorities and international organizations and bodies and coordinate inquiries to the extent that:
a. it is required for the execution of this Act; and
b. the foreign authorities, international organizations or bodies are bound by official secrecy or are subject to a corresponding duty to observe secrecy.
2. They may request delivery of required data from foreign authorities. In order to receive the data, they may provide them data specifically on:
a. the quality, quantity, destination and location of use, purpose of use as well as the

recipients of cultural property;

b. the persons participating in the delivery or procurement of cultural property;

c. the financial arrangement of the transactions.

3. The Federal Authorities may provide the data pursuant to paragraph 2 on their own initiative or at the request of the foreign state, to the extent that the state in question:

a. retains reciprocal rights;

b. guarantees that data will only be processed for purposes pursuant to this Act; and

c. guarantees that the data may only be used in criminal proceedings, if legal assistance in criminal proceedings would not be precluded by the type of crime; in this case, the competent federal administrative authorities consult the Federal Office of Justice in advance on the possibility of legal assistance in criminal proceedings.

Article 23 Relationship to the Legal Assistance Act

Legal assistance may be provided to the competent foreign authorities for violations of this Act. Such violations are not considered as currency, trade, or economic crimes in terms of Article 3, para. 3 Legal Assistance Act from March 20, 1981[6]; the procedural provisions of this Act apply accordingly.

Section 9: Criminal Sanctions

Article 24 Misdemeanor

1. To the extent that the offence is not threatened with a higher sanction under another provision, punishment of imprisonment up to one year or a fine up to 100,000 Swiss Francs will be imposed on whoever intentionally:

a. imports, sells, distributes, procures, acquires, or exports cultural property stolen or otherwise lost against the will of the owner;

b. appropriates excavation finds in terms of Article 724, Swiss Civil Code[7];

c. illicitly imports cultural property or incorrectly declares the same during import or transit;

d. illicitly exports cultural goods listed in the Federal Registry or incorrectly declares the same during export;

2. If the offender acts negligently, the sanction is a fee of up to 20,000 Swiss Francs.

3. If the offender acts on a professional basis, the sanction is jail for up to two years or a fine of up to 200,000 Swiss Francs.

Article 25 Violations

1. To the extent that the offense is not threatened with a higher sanction under another provision, a person may be fined up to 20,000 Swiss Francs, who within the art trade or auctioning business:

a. disregards the duty of diligence (Art. 16);

b. frustrates inspections (Art. 17).

6. SR **351.1**
7. SR **210**

2. Attempts and aiding and abetting are punishable acts.
3. Punishment may be dispensed for lesser violations.

Article 26 Violation in Businesses
Articles 6 and 7 of the Federal Act on the Administrative Penal Code from March 22, 1974[8] apply to violations in businesses.

Article 27 Criminal Prosecution
The Cantons are responsible for prosecuting and assessing criminal activities pursuant to this Act.

Article 28 Seizure of Cultural Property and Assets
Cultural property and assets seized under Articles 58 and 59 of the Swiss Penal Code[9] are assigned to the Confederation. The Federal Council controls their application. It considers the purposes of this Act to this end.

Article 29 Disclosure Requirement
The customs authorities and the competent criminal prosecution authorities are required to disclose violations of this Act to the specialized body.

Section 10: Appeal and Data Protection

Article 30
1. The general provisions of the Federal Act on the Organization of the Federal Judiciary govern the complaint procedures against decrees pursuant this to Act.
2. Legislation on the protection of data governs the processing of personal data.

Section 11: Final Provisions

Article 31 Implementation
The Federal Council shall enact the provisions for implementation.

Article 32 Amendments to Applicable Law
The following legislation is amended as follows:
1. Swiss Civil Code[10]

*Art. 724, para. 1 and 1bis*
1 Derelict natural bodies or antiquities of scientific value are the property of the Canton where the items are found.
1bis Such items may not be sold without the permission of the competent cantonal authorities. They can neither be acquired by adverse possession nor acquired in good faith. The claim for

8. SR **313.0**
9. SR **311.0**
10. SR **210**

return is not subject to a statute of limitation.

Art. 728, para. 1ter

1bis Under the reservation of statutory exceptions, the period for adverse possession of cultural property is thirty years pursuant to Article 2, para. 1 Cultural Property Transfer Act from June 20,2003[11].

Art. 934, para. 1bis

1bis The claim for the return of cultural property lost against the will of the owner in terms of Article 2, para. 1 Cultural Property Transfer Act from June 20, 2003[12], is subject to a statute of limitations of one year after the owner gains knowledge of the locations and the ownership of the cultural property, at the latest, however, 30 years after the property is lost.

2. Swiss Law of Obligations[13]

c. For cultural-property

Art. 196a

For cultural property in terms of Article 2, para. 1 Cultural Property Transfer Act from June 20, 2003[14], the claim for guaranteeing the sold rights expires one year after the purchaser discovers the fault, in any case, however, 30 years after conclusion of the contract.

Art. 210, para. 1bis

1bis For cultural property in terms of Article 2, para. 1 Cultural Property Transfer Act from June 20, 2003[15], the claim expires one year after the purchaser discovers the fault, in any case, however, 30years after conclusion of the contract.

3. Federal Act on Private International Law from December 18, 1987[16]

3. Cultural property

Art. 98a

The court at the domicile or registered office of the defendant or at the location where the cultural property is located has jurisdiction for claims to return cultural property pursuant to Article 9 Cultural Property Transfer Act from June 20, 2003[17].

4. Federal Act on the Protection of Nature and Home Country from July 1, 1966[18]

11. SR **444.1**
12. SR **444.1**
13. SR **220**
14. SR **444.1**
15. SR **444.1**
16. SR **291**
17. SR **444.1**
18. SR **451**

Art. 24, para. 1, letter c

1. Punishment of imprisonment for up to one year or a fine of up to 100,000 Swiss Francs may be imposed on whoever intentionally and without justification:

c. destroys or seriously damages natural bodies or antiquities of scientific value contained in the ground (Art. 724, para. 1 CC[19]);

Article 33 Non-retroactivity

This Act is not applicable retroactively. In particular, it is not applicable to acquisition activities that took place prior to this Act entering into force.

Article 34 Referendum and Effective Date

1. The present Act is subject to an optional referendum.

2. The Federal Council shall set the date of entry into effect.

Date of Publication: July 1, 2003[20]

19. SR **210**

20. AS 2005 **1881** (BBl **2003** 4475)

CANADA

Cultural Property Export and Import Act
C-51

An Act respecting the export from Canada of cultural property and the import into Canada of cultural property illegally exported from foreign states

SHORT TITLE

Short title

1. This Act may be cited as the *Cultural Property Export and Import Act*.
1974-75-76, c. 50, s. 1.

INTERPRETATION

Definitions

2. In this Act,
"Control List"
《nomenclature》

"Control List" means the Canadian Cultural Property Export Control List established under section 4;

"expert examiner"
«expert-vérificateur»

"expert examiner" means a person or institution designated as an expert examiner under section 6;

"export permit"
«licence»

"export permit" means a permit to export issued by a permit officer under this Act;

"general permit"
«licence générale»

"general permit" means a permit to export issued by the Minister under section 17;

"institution"
«établissement»

"institution" means an institution that is publicly owned and is operated solely for the benefit of the public, that is established for educational or cultural purposes and that conserves objects and exhibits them or otherwise makes them available to the public;

"Minister"
«ministre»

"Minister" means such member of the Queen's Privy Council for Canada as is designated by the Governor in Council as the Minister for the purposes of this Act;

"permit officer"
«agent»

"permit officer" means a person designated as a permit officer under section 5;

"public authority"
«administration»

"public authority" means Her Majesty in right of Canada or a province, an agent of Her Majesty in either such right, a municipality in Canada, a municipal or public body performing a function of government in Canada or a corporation performing a function or duty on behalf of Her Majesty in right of Canada or a province;

"resident of Canada"
«résident»

"resident of Canada" means, in the case of a natural person, a person who ordinarily resides in Canada and, in the case of a corporation, a corporation that has its head office in Canada or maintains one or more establishments in Canada to which employees of the corporation employed in connection with the business of the corporation ordinarily report for work;

"Review Board"
«Commission»

"Review Board" means the Canadian Cultural Property Export Review Board established by section 18.
1974-75-76, c. 50, s. 2; SI/80-153; 1984, c. 40, s. 21.

HER MAJESTY

Binding on Her Majesty

3. This Act is binding on Her Majesty in right of Canada or a province.
1974-75-76, c. 50, s. 2.

CANADIAN CULTURAL PROPERTY EXPORT CONTROL LIST

Establishment of Control List

4. (1) The Governor in Council, on the recommendation of the Minister made after consultation with the Minister of Foreign Affairs, may by order establish a Canadian Cultural Property Export Control List.

Inclusions

(2) Subject to subsection (3), the Governor in Council may include in the Control List, regardless of their places of origin, any objects or classes of objects hereinafter described in this subsection, the export of which the Governor in Council deems it necessary to control in order to preserve the national heritage in Canada:

(a) objects of any value that are of archaeological, prehistorical, historical, artistic or scientific interest and that have been recovered from the soil of Canada, the territorial sea of Canada or the inland or other internal waters of Canada;

(b) objects that were made by, or objects referred to in paragraph (d) that relate to, the aboriginal peoples of Canada and that have a fair market value in Canada of more than five hundred dollars;

(c) objects of decorative art, hereinafter described in this paragraph, that were made in the territory that is now Canada and are more than one hundred years old:

(i) glassware, ceramics, textiles, woodenware and works in base metals that have a fair market value in Canada of more than five hundred dollars, and

(ii) furniture, sculptured works in wood, works in precious metals and other objects of decorative art that have a fair market value in Canada of more than two thousand dollars;

(d) books, records, documents, photographic positives and negatives, sound recordings, and collections of any of those objects that have a fair market value in Canada of more than five hundred dollars;

(e) drawings, engravings, original prints and water-colours that have a fair market value in Canada of more than one thousand dollars; and

(f) any other objects that have a fair market value in Canada of more than three thousand dollars.

Exclusions

(3) No object shall be included in the Control List if that object is less than fifty years old or was made by a natural person who is still living.

Deeming provision

(4) For the purposes of this Act, an object within a class of objects included in the Control List is deemed to be an object included in the Control List.
R.S., 1985, c. C-51, s. 4; 1995, c. 5, s. 25; 2001, c. 34, s. 37(F).

PERMIT OFFICERS

Designation of permit officers

5. The Minister, with the approval of the Minister of Public Safety and Emergency Preparedness, may designate any persons or classes of persons employed by the Canada Border Services Agency as permit officers to receive applications for export permits and to issue export permits under this Act.
R.S., 1985, c. C-51, s. 5; 1994, c. 13, s. 7; 1999, c. 17, s. 121; 2005, c. 38, ss. 59, 145.

EXPERT EXAMINERS

Designation of expert examiners

6. (1) The Minister may designate any resident of Canada or any institution in Canada as an expert examiner for the purposes of this Act.

Remuneration

(2) An expert examiner that is not an agent of Her Majesty in right of Canada or a province or is not an employee of, or an employee of an agent of, Her Majesty in right of Canada or a province shall be paid such remuneration for services performed under this Act as may be approved by the Treasury Board.

Expenses

(3) An expert examiner or, where an expert examiner is an institution, the person acting for the institution is entitled, within such limits as may be established by the Treasury Board, to be paid reasonable travel and living expenses incurred while absent from his ordinary place of residence in connection with services performed under this Act.
1974-75-76, c. 50, s. 5.

EXPORT PERMITS

Immediate issue of export permit

7. A permit officer who receives from a resident of Canada an application for an export permit shall issue the permit forthwith if the person applying for the permit establishes to the satisfaction of the permit officer that the object in respect of which the application is made

(a) was imported into Canada within the thirty-five years immediately preceding the date of the application and was not exported from Canada under a permit issued under this Act prior to that importation;

(b) was lent to an institution or public authority in Canada by a person who was not a resident of Canada at the time the loan was made; or

(c) is to be removed from Canada for a purpose prescribed by regulation for a period of time not exceeding such period of time as may be prescribed by regulation for the purposes of this paragraph.

1974-75-76, c. 50, s. 6.

Determination by permit officer

8. (1) A permit officer who receives from a resident of Canada an application for an export permit in respect of an object shall, where he does not issue an export permit under section 7, and where he is not aware of any notice of refusal sent in respect of the object under subsection 13(1) during the two years immediately preceding the date of the application, determine whether the object is included in the Control List.

Export permit where object not included in Control List

(2) Where a permit officer determines that an object in respect of which an application for an export permit is made is not included in the Control List, the permit officer shall forthwith issue an export permit in respect of the object.

Reference to expert examiner

(3) Where a permit officer determines that an object in respect of which an application for an export permit is made is or might be included in the Control List, the permit officer shall forthwith refer the application to an expert examiner for consideration.
1974-75-76, c. 50, s. 7.

Determination by expert examiner

9. Where an application for an export permit is referred to an expert examiner pursuant to subsection 8(3), the expert examiner shall forthwith determine whether the object in respect of which the application is made is included in the Control List.
1974-75-76, c. 50, s. 8.

Where object not included in Control List

10. Where an expert examiner determines that an object that is the subject of an application for an export permit that has been referred to him is not included in the Control List, the expert examiner shall forthwith in writing advise the permit officer who referred the application to issue an export permit in respect of the object and shall forthwith send a copy of that advice to the Review Board and the Minister.
1974-75-76, c. 50, s. 8.

Where object included in Control List

11. (1) Where an expert examiner determines that an object that is the subject of an application for an export permit that has been referred to him is included in the Control List, the expert examiner shall forthwith further determine

(a) whether that object is of outstanding significance by reason of its close association with Canadian history or national life, its aesthetic qualities, or its value in the study of the arts or sciences; and
(b) whether the object is of such a degree of national importance that its loss to Canada would significantly diminish the national heritage.

Export permit to be issued

(2) Where an expert examiner determines that an object that is the subject of an application for an export permit that has been referred to him is not of outstanding significance under paragraph (1)(a) or does not meet the degree of national importance referred to in paragraph (1)(b), the expert examiner shall forthwith in writing advise the permit officer who referred the application to issue an export permit in respect of the object and shall forthwith send a copy of that advice to the Review Board and the Minister.

Export permit not to be issued

(3) Where an expert examiner determines that an object that is the subject of an application for an export permit that has been referred to him is of outstanding significance under paragraph (1)(a) and meets the degree of national importance referred to in paragraph (1)(b), the expert examiner shall forthwith in writing advise the permit officer who referred the application not to issue an export permit in respect of the object and shall provide the permit officer with the reasons therefor.
1974-75-76, c. 50, s. 8; 1980-81-82-83, c. 47, s. 53.

Issue of export permit

12. Subject to sections 14 and 16, a permit officer shall issue an export permit forthwith where the permit officer is advised by an expert examiner or directed by the Review Board to do so.
1974-75-76, c. 50, s. 9.

Notice of refusal

13. (1) Where a permit officer is advised by an expert examiner pursuant to subsection 11(3) not to issue an export permit, the permit officer shall send a written notice of refusal to the applicant, which notice shall include the reasons given by the expert examiner for the refusal.

Copy to Review Board

(2) A permit officer who sends a notice of refusal under subsection (1) shall forthwith send a copy thereof to the Review Board.
1974-75-76, c. 50, s. 10.

Deposit of copy

14. No export permit shall, unless it is issued under section 7, be issued under this Act for an object within a class of objects prescribed under paragraph 39(d), where the object is included in the Control List, until a copy of that object has been deposited by the person applying for the permit in such institution as the Minister may direct.
1974-75-76, c. 50, s. 11.

Alteration of permits by Minister and notice

15. The Minister may amend, suspend, cancel or reinstate any export permit, other than an export permit issued on the direction of the Review Board, and where an export permit is amended, suspended, cancelled or reinstated, the Minister shall forthwith send a written notice to that effect to the person who applied for the permit.
1974-75-76, c. 50, s. 12.

No export permit for two years

16. No export permit shall, unless it is issued under section 7 or on the direction of the Review Board pursuant to section 29 or 30, be issued under this Act in respect of an object, where the object is included in the Control List, during a period of two years from the date on which a notice of refusal was sent in respect of that object under subsection 13(1).
1974-75-76, c. 50, s. 13.

GENERAL PERMITS

General permits to export

17. (1) The Minister may issue to any resident of Canada who applies therefor a general permit to export any objects included in the Control List subject to such terms and conditions as the Minister may require and may at any time amend, suspend, cancel or reinstate any such permit.

Open general permits to export

(2) The Minister may, with the concurrence of the Minister of Foreign Affairs, issue generally to all persons a general permit to export objects within any class of objects that is included in the Control List and that is specified in the permit subject to such terms and conditions as the Minister may require and may, with the concurrence of the Minister of Foreign Affairs, at any time amend, suspend, cancel or reinstate any such permit.
R.S., 1985, c. C-51, s. 17; 1995, c. 5, s. 25.

REVIEW BOARD

Review Board Established

Review Board established

18. (1) There is hereby established a board to be known as the Canadian Cultural Property Export Review Board, consisting of a Chairperson and not more than nine other members appointed by the Governor in Council on the recommendation of the Minister.

Members

(2) The Chairperson and one other member shall be chosen generally from among residents of Canada, and

(a) up to four other members shall be chosen from among residents of Canada who are or have been officers, members or employees of art galleries, museums, archives, libraries or other collecting institutions in Canada; and

(b) up to four other members shall be chosen from among residents of Canada who are or have been dealers in or collectors of art, antiques or other objects that form part of the national heritage.

Acting Chairperson

(3) The Review Board may authorize one of its members to act as Chairperson in the event of the absence or incapacity of the Chairperson or if the office of Chairperson is vacant.

Quorum

(4) Three members, at least one of whom is a person described in paragraph (2)(a) and one of whom is a person described in paragraph (2)(b), constitute a quorum of the Review Board.
R.S., 1985, c. C-51, s. 18; 1995, c. 29, ss. 21, 22(E); 2001, c. 34, s. 38.

Remuneration

19. (1) Each member of the Review Board who is not an employee of, or an employee of an agent of, Her Majesty in right of Canada or a province shall be paid such salary or other amount by way of remuneration as may be fixed by the Governor in Council.

Expenses

(2) Each member of the Review Board is entitled, within such limits as may be established

by the Treasury Board, to be paid reasonable travel and living expenses incurred while absent from his ordinary place of residence in connection with the work of the Review Board.
1974-75-76, c. 50, s. 16.

Duties

Duties

20. The Review Board shall, on request,
(a) pursuant to section 29, review applications for export permits;
(b) pursuant to section 30, make determinations respecting fair cash offers to purchase; and
(c) pursuant to section 32, make determinations for the purposes of subparagraph 39(1)(a)(i.1), paragraph 110.1(1)(c), the definition "total cultural gifts" in subsection 118.1(1) and subsection 118.1(10) of the *Income Tax Act*.
R.S., 1985, c. C-51, s. 20; 1991, c. 49, s. 216.

Head Office and Sittings

Head office

21. (1) The head office of the Review Board shall be at such place in Canada as the Governor in Council may by order prescribe.

Sittings

(2) The Review Board may sit at such times and places in Canada as it considers necessary or desirable for the proper conduct of its business.
1974-75-76, c. 50, s. 18.

Advisers

Expert advice

22. (1) The Review Board may call on any person who has professional, technical or other special knowledge to assist it in any matter in an advisory capacity.

Valuation experts

(2) The Minister, on the request of the Review Board, may appoint and fix the remuneration of valuation experts to assist the Review Board in making determinations pursuant to section 30 respecting fair cash offers to purchase or pursuant to section 32 respecting the fair market value of objects disposed of, or proposed to be disposed of, to institutions or public authorities.
R.S., 1985, c. C-51, s. 22; 1991, c. 49, s. 217.

ADMINISTRATION

Administrative services

23. The Minister shall provide administrative services to the Review Board.
1974-75-76, c. 50, s. 20.

RULES AND PROCEDURE

Rules

24. The Review Board may make rules not inconsistent with this Act for the conduct of its proceedings and the performance of its duties and functions under this Act.
1974-75-76, c. 50, s. 21.

Review Board may receive information

25. The Review Board may receive any information presented to it orally or in writing that it considers to be relevant to any matter before it and in so doing it is not bound by any legal or technical rules of evidence.
1974-75-76, c. 50, s. 22.

Information given to applicant

26. The Review Board shall make the substance of any information received by it in respect of a matter before it known to the person who applied for an export permit in respect of the object to which the matter relates, or to the person, institution or public authority that applied for a determination under subsection 32(1), as the case may be, and, before the Review Board decides the matter, it shall give that person, institution or public authority an opportunity to make representations in respect of that information.
1974-75-76, c. 50, s. 22.

Exclusion from hearing

27. The Review Board may exclude any person not directly interested in a matter being heard before it from the hearing unless, where the matter is in respect of an object in respect of which an application for an export permit has been made, the applicant for the permit requests that the hearing be held in public, in which case it shall be so held.
1974-75-76, c. 50, s. 22.

Review Board shall dispose of matters informally and expeditiously

28. The Review Board shall dispose of any matter before it as informally and expeditiously as, in its opinion, the circumstances and considerations of fairness will permit.
1974-75-76, c. 50, s. 22.

Review of Applications for Export permits

Request for review by Review Board

29. (1) Any person who receives a notice of refusal under section 13 or a notice under section 15 may, within thirty days after the date on which the notice was sent, by notice in writing given to the Review Board, request a review of his application for an export permit by the Review Board.

Review to be held within four months

(2) The Review Board shall review an application for an export permit and, unless the circumstances of a particular case require otherwise, render its decision within four months after the date a request is received under subsection (1).

Determination of the Review Board

(3) In reviewing an application for an export permit, the Review Board shall determine whether the object in respect of which the application was made

(a) is included in the Control List;

(b) is of outstanding significance for one or more of the reasons set out in paragraph 11(1)(a); and

(c) meets the degree of national importance referred to in paragraph 11(1)(b).

Object that does not meet criteria

(4) Where the Review Board determines that an object fails to meet one or more of the

criteria set out in subsection (3), it shall direct a permit officer to issue an export permit forthwith in respect of the object.

Object that meets criteria

(5) Where the Review Board determines that an object meets all of the criteria set out in subsection (3), it shall,

(a) if it is of the opinion that a fair offer to purchase the object might be made by an institution or public authority in Canada within six months after the date of its determination, establish a delay period of not less than two months and not more than six months during which the Review Board will not direct that an export permit be issued in respect of the object; or

(b) in any other case, direct a permit officer to issue an export permit forthwith in respect of the object.

Notification of delay period

(6) Where the Review Board establishes a delay period under paragraph (5)(a) in respect of an object, the Board shall give written notice of the delay period to the person who has applied for an export permit in respect of the object and to the Minister, which notice shall include the reasons for the determination of the Board that the object meets all of the criteria set out in subsection (3).

Idem

(7) The Minister, on receiving notice of a delay period under subsection (6), shall advise such institutions and public authorities in Canada as the Minister sees fit of the delay period and of the object in respect of which the delay period was established.
1974-75-76, c. 50, s. 23.

Request for determination of fair offer to purchase

30. (1) Subject to subsection (2), where the Review Board establishes a delay period under paragraph 29(5)(a) in respect of an object and an offer to purchase the object is made by an institution or a public authority in Canada within that period, either the person who applied for an export permit in respect of the object or the institution or public authority making the offer to purchase may, where the offer is not accepted, by notice in writing given to the Review Board, request the Review Board to determine the amount of a fair cash offer to purchase.

When request to be made

(2) No request may be made under subsection (1) less than thirty days before the end of the delay period established under paragraph 29(5)(a) in respect of the object in respect of which

the request is made.

Determination of the Review Board

(3) Where the Review Board receives a request under subsection (1), it shall determine the amount of a fair cash offer to purchase the object in respect of which the request is made and advise the person who applied for an export permit in respect of the object and the institution or public authority that offered to purchase the object of its determination.

Direction for export permit

(4) Where the Review Board establishes a delay period under paragraph 29(5)(a) in respect of an object and does not receive a request under subsection (1) in respect of the object, it shall forthwith, after the expiration of the delay period and on the request of the person who requested the review under subsection 29(1), direct a permit officer to issue an export permit forthwith in respect of the object.

Idem

(5) Where the Review Board establishes a delay period under paragraph 29(5)(a) in respect of an object and receives a request under subsection (1) in respect of the object, it shall, after the expiration of the delay period or after it has determined the amount of a fair cash offer to purchase the object under subsection (3), whichever time is the later, and on the request of the person who requested the review under subsection 29(1), direct a permit officer to issue an export permit forthwith in respect of the object unless it is satisfied that an institution or public authority has, before the request under this subsection was made, offered to purchase the object for an amount equal to or greater than the amount of the fair cash offer to purchase determined by the Review Board.
1974-75-76, c. 50, s. 24.

Limitation on export permits

31. The Review Board shall not direct that an export permit be issued except in accordance with section 29 or 30.
1974-75-76, c. 50, s. 25.

Determination Relating to Income Tax Matters

Request for determination of Review Board

32. (1) For the purposes of subparagraph 39(1)(a)(i.1), paragraph 110.1(1)(c), the definition "total cultural gifts" in subsection 118.1(1) and subsection 118.1(10) of the *Income Tax Act*, where a person disposes of or proposes to dispose of an object to an institution or a public authority designated under subsection (2), the person, institution or public authority may request, by notice in writing given to the Review Board, a determination by the Review Board as to whether the object meets the criteria set out in paragraphs 29(3)(b) and (c) and a determination by the Review Board of the fair market value of the object.

Designated authorities and institutions

(2) For the purposes of subparagraph 39(1)(a)(i.1), paragraph 110.1(1)(c), the definition "total cultural gifts" in subsection 118.1(1), subsection 118.1(10) and section 207.3 of the *Income Tax Act*, the Minister may designate any institution or public authority indefinitely or for a period of time, and generally or for a specified purpose.

Revocation of designation

(3) The Minister may at any time revoke a designation made under subsection (2).

Determination within four months

(4) The Review Board shall consider a request made under subsection (1) and, unless the circumstances of a particular case require otherwise, make a determination within four months after the date the request is received and shall give notice of the determination in writing or by electronic means to the person who has disposed of, or who proposes to dispose of, the object and, where the request was made by a designated institution or public authority, to the designated institution or public authority.

Redetermination

(5) Where the Review Board has, under subsection (4), determined the fair market value of an object in respect of its disposition or proposed disposition, the Review Board

(a) shall, on request in writing by the person who has disposed of, or who proposes to dispose of, the object to a designated institution or public authority or by an agent of such a person appointed for that purpose, made within twelve months after the day on which notice was given under that subsection, redetermine the fair market value of the object; and

(b) may, on its own initiative, at any time, redetermine the fair market value of the object.

Decision within four months and notice of redetermination

(6) In the case of a redetermination under paragraph (5)(a), the Review Board shall, unless the circumstances of a particular case require otherwise, make the redetermination within four months after it receives the request under that paragraph and shall give notice of the

redetermination in writing or by electronic means to the person who made the request.

Notice of redetermination where no request

(7) In the case of a redetermination under paragraph (5)(b), the Review Board shall give notice of the redetermination in writing or by electronic means to the person who has disposed of, or who proposes to dispose of, the object and, where the request made under subsection (1) in relation to the object was made by a designated institution or public authority, to the designated institution or public authority.

Limitation

(8) Unless the circumstances of a particular case require otherwise, the Review Board shall not redetermine the fair market value of an object more than once.

Redetermination final and conclusive

(9) A redetermination under subsection (5) in respect of a proposed disposition is not subject to appeal to or review by any court.
R.S., 1985, c. C-51, s. 32; 1991, c. 49, s. 218; 1995, c. 38, s. 1.

Income Tax Certificate

Income tax certificate

33. (1) Where the Review Board determines or redetermines the fair market value of an object in respect of which a request was made under section 32 and determines that the object meets the criteria set out in paragraphs 29(3)(b) and (c), it shall, where the object has been irrevocably disposed of to a designated institution or public authority, issue to the person who made the disposition a certificate attesting to the fair market value and to the meeting of those criteria, in such form as the Minister of National Revenue may specify.

Copy to Minister of National Revenue

(1.1) The Review Board shall send a copy of a certificate referred to in subsection (1) to the Minister of National Revenue.

Where more than one certificate

(1.2) Where the Review Board has issued more than one certificate referred to in subsection

(1) in relation to an object, the last certificate is deemed to be the only certificate issued by the Review Board in relation to that object.

Communication of information

(2) An official of the Department of Canadian Heritage or a member of the Review Board may communicate to an official of the Canada Revenue Agency, solely for the purposes of administering the *Income Tax Act*, information obtained under this Act for the purposes of administering this section and sections 32, 33.1 and 33.2.
R.S., 1985, c. C-51, s. 33; 1991, c. 49, s. 219; 1995, c. 11, s. 45, c. 38, s. 2; 1999, c. 17, s. 122; 2005, c. 38, s. 138.

APPEALS BEFORE THE TAX COURT OF CANADA

Appeal of redetermination of fair market value

33.1 (1) Any person who has irrevocably disposed of an object, the fair market value of which has been redetermined under subsection 32(5), to a designated institution or public authority may, within ninety days after the day on which a certificate referred to in subsection 33(1) is issued in relation to that object, appeal the redetermination to the Tax Court of Canada.

Decision of Court

(2) On an appeal under subsection (1), the Tax Court of Canada may confirm or vary the fair market value and, for the purposes of the *Income Tax Act*, the value fixed by the Court is deemed to be the fair market value of the object determined by the Review Board in respect of its disposition.
1995, c. 38, s. 2.

Extension of time for appeal

33.2 (1) Where an appeal has not been instituted by a person under section 33.1 within the time limited by that section, the person may make an application to the Tax Court of Canada for an order extending the time within which the appeal may be instituted and the Court may make an order extending the time for appealing and may impose such terms as it considers just.

Contents of application

(2) An application made under subsection (1) shall set out the reasons why the appeal was

not instituted within the time limited by section 33.1.

How application made

(3) An application made under subsection (1) shall be made by filing in the Registry of the Tax Court of Canada, in accordance with the provisions of the *Tax Court of Canada Act*, three copies of the application accompanied by three copies of the notice of appeal.

Copy to Deputy Attorney General

(4) The Tax Court of Canada shall send a copy of each application made under this section to the office of the Deputy Attorney General of Canada.

When order to be made

(5) No order shall be made under this section unless
(a) the application is made within one year after the expiration of the time limited by section 33.1 for appealing; and
(b) the person making the application demonstrates that
(i) within the time limited by section 33.1 for appealing, the person
(A) was unable to act or to instruct another to act in the person's name, or
(B) had a *bona fide intention* to appeal,
(ii) given the reasons set out in the application and the circumstances of the case, it would be just and equitable to grant the application,
(iii) the application was made as soon as circumstances permitted, and
(iv) there are reasonable grounds for the appeal.

1995, c. 38, s. 2; 2000, c. 30, s. 159.

Report to Minister

Report to Minister

34. The Chairperson of the Review Board shall, as soon as possible after March 31 in each year, submit to the Minister a report of the operations of the Review Board for the previous fiscal year and its recommendations, if any.

R.S., 1985, c. C-51, s. 34; 1995, c. 29, s. 22(E).

FINANCIAL

Grants and loans from moneys appropriated

35. The Minister may, out of moneys appropriated by Parliament for such purposes, make grants and loans to institutions and public authorities in Canada for the purchase of objects in respect of which export permits have been refused under this Act or for the purchase of cultural property situated outside Canada that is related to the national heritage.
1974-75-76, c. 50, s. 29.

Canadian Heritage Preservation Endowment Account established

36. (1) There shall be established in the accounts of Canada a special account to be known as the Canadian Heritage Preservation Endowment Account.

Amounts to be credited to the Canadian Heritage Preservation Endowment Account

(2) There shall be credited to the Canadian Heritage Preservation Endowment Account

(a) all moneys received by Her Majesty by gift, bequest or otherwise for the purpose of making grants to institutions and public authorities in Canada for the purchase of objects in respect of which export permits have been refused under this Act, or for the purchase of cultural property situated outside Canada that is related to the national heritage;

(b) all moneys received by Her Majesty as income on or as proceeds from the sale of any securities received by Her Majesty for a purpose referred to in paragraph (a); and

(c) an amount representing interest on the balance from time to time to the credit of the account at such rates and calculated in such manner as the Governor in Council may, on the recommendation of the Minister of Finance, prescribe.

Amounts that may be charged to the Canadian Heritage Preservation Endowment Account

(3) There may be charged to the Canadian Heritage Preservation Endowment Account such amounts as the Minister may expend otherwise than under section 35 for grants to institutions and public authorities in Canada for the purchase of objects in respect of which export permits have been refused under this Act or for the purchase of cultural property situated outside Canada that is related to the national heritage.
1974-75-76, c. 50, s. 30.

CONVENTION FOR THE PROTECTION OF CULTURAL PROPERTY IN THE EVENT OF ARMED CONFLICT AND ITS PROTOCOLS

Definitions

36.1 (1) The following definitions apply in this section. "Convention"
«convention»
"Convention" means the Convention for the Protection of Cultural Property in the Event of Armed Conflict, done at The Hague on May 14, 1954. Article 1 of the Convention is set out in the schedule.

"First Protocol"
«premier protocole»
"First Protocol" means the first protocol, done at The Hague on May 14, 1954, to the Convention.

"Second Protocol"
«deuxième protocole»
"Second Protocol" means the second protocol, done at The Hague on March 26, 1999, to the Convention.

"State Party"
«État partie»
"State Party" means a state that is a party to the Convention and the First or Second Protocol.

Export or removal of cultural property

(2) No person shall knowingly export or otherwise remove cultural property as defined in subparagraph (a) of Article 1 of the Convention from an occupied territory of a State Party to the Second Protocol, unless the export or removal conforms with the applicable laws of that territory or is necessary for the property's protection or preservation.

Offence outside Canada deemed in Canada

(3) Despite anything in this Act or any other Act, a person who commits an act or omission outside Canada that if committed in Canada would constitute an offence under subsection (2), or a conspiracy or an attempt to commit such an offence, or being an accessory after the fact or counselling in relation to such an offence, is deemed to have committed that act or omission in Canada if the person

(a) is a Canadian citizen;
(b) is not a citizen of any state and ordinarily resides in Canada; or
(c) is a permanent resident within the meaning of subsection 2(1) of the *Immigration and Refugee Protection Act* and is, after the commission of the act or omission, present in Canada.

Action for recovery of cultural property

(4) If the government of a State Party submits a request in writing to the Minister for the recovery and return of any cultural property that has been exported from an occupied territory of that State Party and that is in Canada in the possession of or under the control of any person, institution or public authority, the Attorney General of Canada may institute an action in the Federal Court or in a superior court of a province for the recovery of the property by the State Party.

Notice

(5) Notice of the commencement of an action under this section on behalf of a State Party shall be served by the Attorney General of Canada on such persons and given in such manner as is provided by the rules of the court in which the action is taken, or, if the rules do not so provide, served on such persons and given in such manner as is directed by a judge of the court.

Order for recovery of cultural property

(6) The court in which an action has been taken under this section may, after affording all persons that it considers to have an interest in the action a reasonable opportunity to be heard, make an order for the recovery of the property in respect of which the action has been taken or any other order sufficient to ensure the return of the property to the State Party, if the court is satisfied that the property was exported in contravention of the applicable laws of the occupied territory of the State Party or was imported into Canada for its protection or preservation and that the amount fixed under subsection (7), if any, has been paid.

Compensation

(7) The court in which an action has been taken under this section may fix any amount that it considers just in the circumstances to be paid as compensation by the State Party to a person, institution or public authority that establishes to the satisfaction of the court that the person, institution or public authority is a *bona fide purchaser* for value or has a valid title to the property in respect of which the action has been taken and had no knowledge at the time the property was purchased or the title to the property was acquired that the property
(a) had been exported in contravention of the applicable laws of the occupied territory of

the State Party; or
(b) had been imported into Canada for its protection or preservation.

Safe-keeping

(8) The court may, at any time in the course of an action under this section, order that the property in respect of which the action has been taken be turned over to the Minister for safe-keeping and conservation pending final disposition of the action.

Permit to export

(9) The Minister shall, on receipt of a copy of a court order made under subsection (6), issue a permit authorizing any person authorized by the State Party on behalf of which the action was taken to export the property in respect of which the order was made to that State.

Limitations inapplicable

(10) Section 39 of the *Federal Courts Act* does not apply in respect of any action taken under this section.
2005, c. 40, s. 4.

FOREIGN CULTURAL PROPERTY

Definitions

37. (1) In this section, "cultural property agreement"
《accord》

"cultural property agreement", in relation to a foreign State, means an agreement between Canada and the foreign State or an international agreement to which Canada and the foreign State are both parties, relating to the prevention of illicit international traffic in cultural property;

"foreign cultural property"
《biens culturels étrangers》

"foreign cultural property", in relation to a reciprocating State, means any object that is specifically designated by that State as being of importance for archaeology, prehistory, history, literature, art or science;

"reciprocating State"
«État contractant»

"reciprocating State" means a foreign State that is a party to a cultural property agreement.

Illegal imports

(2) From and after the coming into force of a cultural property agreement in Canada and a reciprocating State, it is illegal to import into Canada any foreign cultural property that has been illegally exported from that reciprocating State.

Action for recovery of foreign cultural property

(3) Where the government of a reciprocating State submits a request in writing to the Minister for the recovery and return of any foreign cultural property that has been imported into Canada illegally by virtue of subsection (2) and that is in Canada in the possession of or under the control of any person, institution or public authority, the Attorney General of Canada may institute an action in the Federal Court or in a superior court of a province for the recovery of the property by the reciprocating State.

Notice

(4) Notice of the commencement of an action under this section shall be served by the Attorney General of Canada on such persons and given in such manner as is provided by the rules of the court in which the action is taken, or, where the rules do not so provide, served on such persons and given in such manner as is directed by a judge of the court.

Order for recovery of designated property

(5) A court in which an action has been taken under this section on behalf of a reciprocating State may, after affording all persons that it considers to have an interest in the action a reasonable opportunity to be heard, make an order for the recovery of the property in respect of which the action has been taken or any other order sufficient to ensure the return of the property to the reciprocating State, where the court is satisfied that the property has been illegally imported into Canada by virtue of subsection (2) and that the amount fixed under subsection (6), if any, has been paid to or for the benefit of the person, institution or public authority referred to in that subsection.

Compensation

(6) Where any person, institution or public authority establishes to the satisfaction of the court in which an action under this section is being considered that the person, institution or public authority

(a) is a bona fide purchaser for value of the property in respect of which the action has been taken and had no knowledge at the time the property was purchased by him or it that the property had been illegally exported from the reciprocating State on whose behalf the action has been taken, or

(b) has a valid title to the property in respect of which the action has been taken and had no knowledge at the time such title was acquired that the property had been illegally exported from the reciprocating State on whose behalf the action has been taken,

the court may fix such amount to be paid as compensation by the reciprocating State to that person, institution or public authority as the court considers just in the circumstances.

Safe-keeping

(7) The court may, at any time in the course of an action under this section, order that the property in respect of which the action has been taken be turned over to the Minister for safe-keeping and conservation pending final disposition of the action.

Permit to export

(8) The Minister shall, on receipt of a copy of an order of a court made under subsection (5), issue a permit authorizing any person authorized by the reciprocating State on behalf of which the action was taken to export the property in respect of which the order was made to that State.

Limitations inapplicable

(9) Section 39 of the *Federal Courts Act* does not apply in respect of any action taken under this section.

R.S., 1985, c. C-51, s. 37; 2002, c. 8, s. 182.

DESIGNATION OF CULTURAL PROPERTY

Designation of cultural property

38. For the purposes of article 1 of the *Convention on the means of prohibiting and preventing the illicit import, export and transfer of ownership of cultural property,* any object included in the Control List is hereby designated by Canada as being of importance for archaeology, prehistory, history, literature, art or science.

1974-75-76, c. 50, s. 32.

REGULATIONS

Regulations

39. The Governor in Council, on the recommendation of the Minister and the Minister of Foreign Affairs, may make regulations

(a) prescribing the information, documentation and undertakings to be furnished by applicants for permits and certificates under this Act, the procedures to be followed in applying for and in issuing those permits and certificates, the terms and conditions applicable to them and the duration of the permits;

(b) prescribing the circumstances in which information may be required from persons to whom permits have been issued under this Act and the type of information that may be so required;

(c) prescribing the purposes for which an object may be removed from Canada for a limited period of time for the purpose of paragraph 7(c) and the length of time for which it may be so removed; and

(d) prescribing classes of manuscripts, original documents, archives, photographic positives and negatives, films and sound recordings for the purpose of section 14.

R.S., 1985, c. C-51, s. 39; 1995, c. 5, s. 25; 1998, c. 19, s. 261.

OFFENCES AND PUNISHMENT

Export or attempt to export

40. No person shall export or attempt to export from Canada any object included in the Control List except under the authority of and in accordance with a permit issued under this Act.
1974-75-76, c. 50, s. 34.

No transfer of permits

41. No person who is authorized under a permit issued under this Act to export an object from Canada shall transfer the permit to or allow it to be used by a person who is not so authorized.
1974-75-76, c. 50, s. 35.

False information

42. No person shall wilfully furnish any false or misleading information or knowingly make any misrepresentation

(a) in an application for a permit under this Act;
(b) for the purpose of procuring the issue of a permit under this Act; or
(c) in connection with the use of a permit issued under this Act or the disposition of any object to which such permit relates.

1974-75-76, c. 50, s. 36.

Import or attempt to import foreign cultural property

43. No person shall import or attempt to import into Canada any property that it is illegal to import into Canada under subsection 37(2).

1974-75-76, c. 50, s. 37.

Export or attempt to export

44. (1) No person shall export or attempt to export from Canada any property in respect of which an action has been instituted under subsection 37(3) while the action is being considered.

Idem

(2) No person shall export or attempt to export from Canada any property in respect of which an order has been made under subsection 37(5) except under the authority of and in accordance with a permit issued by the Minister under subsection 37(8).

1974-75-76, c. 50, s. 38.

Offences and punishment

45. (1) Every person who contravenes any of the provisions of subsection 36.1(2) and sections 40 to 44 is guilty of an offence and liable

(a) on summary conviction to a fine not exceeding five thousand dollars or to imprisonment for a term not exceeding twelve months or to both; or
(b) on conviction on indictment to a fine not exceeding twenty-five thousand dollars or to imprisonment for a term not exceeding five years or to both.

Limitation period

(2) A prosecution under paragraph (1)(a) may be instituted at any time within but not later than three years after the time when the subject-matter of the complaint arose.

R.S., 1985, c. C-51, s. 45; 2005, c. 40, s. 5.

Officers, etc., of corporations

46. Where a corporation commits an offence under this Act, any officer, director or agent of the corporation who directed, authorized, assented to, acquiesced in or participated in the

commission of the offence is a party to and guilty of the offence and is liable on summary conviction or on conviction on indictment to the punishment provided for the offence whether or not the corporation has been prosecuted or convicted.
1974-75-76, c. 50, s. 40.

Venue

47. Any proceedings in respect of an offence under this Act may be instituted, tried or determined at the place in Canada where the offence was committed or at the place in Canada in which the person charged with the offence is, resides or has an office or place of business at the time of institution of the proceedings.
1974-75-76, c. 50, s. 41.

Evidence

48. (1) The original or a copy of a bill of lading, customs document, commercial invoice or other document (in this section called a "shipping document") is admissible in evidence in any prosecution under this Act in relation to the sending or shipping of an object where it appears from the shipping document that

(a) the object was sent or shipped from Canada or came into Canada;

(b) a person, as shipper, consignor or consignee, sent or shipped the object from Canada or brought the object into Canada; or

(c) the object was sent or shipped to a particular destination or person.

Proof of the facts

(2) In the absence of evidence to the contrary, a shipping document that is admissible in evidence under subsection (1) is proof of any of the facts set out in paragraph (1)(a), (b) or (c) that appear from the shipping document.
1974-75-76, c. 50, s. 42.

GENERAL

Other lawful obligations

49. An export permit or other permit to export issued under this Act does not affect the obligation of any person to obtain any licence, permit or certificate to export that may be required under any other law or to pay any tax, duty, toll or other sum required by any law to be paid in respect of the export of any goods.
1974-75-76, c. 50, s. 43.

Customs officers' duties

50. An officer, as defined in the Customs Act, before permitting the export or import of any object that the officer has reason to suspect is being exported or imported in contravention of any of the provisions of this Act or the regulations, shall satisfy himself that the exporter or importer has not contravened any of the provisions of this Act or the regulations and that all requirements thereof have been complied with in respect of that object.
R.S., 1985, c. C-51, s. 50; R.S., 1985, c. 1 (2nd Supp.), s. 213.

Application of powers under the Customs Act

51. All officers, as defined in the *Customs Act*, have, with respect to any object to which this Act applies, all the powers they have under the *Customs Act* with respect to the export or import of goods and all the provisions of the *Customs Act* and regulations thereunder respecting search, detention, forfeiture and condemnation apply, with such modifications as the circumstances require,

(a) to any objects tendered for export or import, exported or imported, or otherwise dealt with contrary to the provisions of this Act and the regulations; and

(b) to all documents relating to objects described in paragraph (a).

R.S., 1985, c. C-51, s. 51; R.S., 1985, c. 1 (2nd Supp.), s. 213.

Report to Parliament

52. As soon as practicable after receiving, pursuant to section 34, the report of the Chairperson of the Review Board, the Minister shall prepare and lay before Parliament a report of the operations under this Act for the fiscal year to which the report of the Chairperson relates and shall include therewith the report of the Chairperson.
R.S., 1985, c. C-51, s. 52; 1995, c. 29, s. 22(E).

SCHEDULE

(Subsection 36.1(1))

ARTICLE 1 OF THE CONVENTION FOR THE PROTECTION OF CULTURAL PROPERTY IN THE EVENT OF ARMED CONFLICT DONE AT THE HAGUE ON MAY 14, 1954

Article 1 Definition of Cultural Property

For the purposes of the present Convention, the term "cultural property" shall cover, irrespective of origin or ownership:

(a) movable or immovable property of great importance to the cultural heritage of every people, such as monuments of architecture, art or history, whether religious or secular; archaeological sites; groups of buildings which, as a whole, are of historical or artistic interest; works of art; manuscripts, books and other objects of artistic, historical or archaeological interest; as well as scientific collections and important collections of books or archives or of reproductions of the property defined above;

(b) buildings whose main and effective purpose is to preserve or exhibit the movable cultural property defined in subparagraph (a) such as museums, large libraries and depositories of archives, and refuges intended to shelter, in the event of armed conflict, the movable cultural property defined in subparagraph (a);

(c) centres containing a large amount of cultural property as defined in subparagraphs (a) and (b), to be known as "centres containing monuments".

2005, c. 40, s. 6.

RELATED PROVISIONS

-- 1991, c. 49, s. 216(2): (2) Subsection (1) is applicable after December 11, 1988, except that, in respect of gifts made before February 21, 1990, paragraph 20(c) of the said Act, as enacted by subsection (1), shall be read without reference to the expression "and subsection 118.1(10)".

-- 1991, c. 49, s. 217(2): (2) Subsection (1) is applicable after February 20, 1990.

-- 1991, c. 49, ss. 218(3), (4): (3) Subsection (1) is applicable after December 11, 1988, except that, in respect of gifts made before February 21, 1990, subsection 32(1) of the said Act, as enacted by subsection (1), shall be read without reference to the expression "and a determination by the Review Board of the fair market value of the object".

-- 1991, c. 49, ss. 218(3), (4): (4) Subsection (2) is applicable with respect to gifts made after February 20, 1990.

-- 1991, c. 49, s. 219(2): (2) Subsection 33(1) of the said Act, as enacted by subsection (1), is applicable after February 20, 1990.

-- 1995, c. 38, ss. 8(1) to (3):

Transitional

8. (1) A person who, before the day on which this section comes into force, has irrevocably disposed of, to a designated institution or public authority, an object, the fair market value of which was determined or redetermined by the Canadian Cultural Property Export Review Board pursuant to section 32 of the *Cultural Property Export and Import Act* between January 1, 1992 and the day on which this section comes into force, may, within six months after the day on which this section comes into force, appeal the determination or redetermination to the

Tax Court of Canada.

Transitional

(2) A person who, within six months after the day on which this section comes into force, irrevocably disposes of, to a designated institution or public authority, an object, the fair market value of which was determined or redetermined by the Canadian Cultural Property Export Review Board pursuant to section 32 of the *Cultural Property Export and Import Act* between January 1, 1992 and the day on which this section comes into force, may, within six months after the day of the disposition, appeal the determination or redetermination to the Tax Court of Canada.

Application of certain provisions

(3) Subsections 33(2) and 33.1(2) and section 33.2 of the *Cultural Property Export and Import Act*, as enacted by section 2 of this Act, apply, with such modifications as the circumstances require, in respect of an appeal under subsection (1) or (2).

AUSTRALIA

Protection of Movable Cultural Heritage Act 1986

No. 11, 1986 as amended

Compilation start date:	1 July 2014
Includes amendments up to:	Act No. 62, 2014

Prepared by the Office of Parliamentary Counsel, Canberra

About this compilation

This compilation

This is a compilation of the *Protection of Movable Cultural Heritage Act 1986* as in force on 1 July 2014. It includes any commenced amendment affecting the legislation to that date.

This compilation was prepared on 13 August 2014.

The notes at the end of this compilation (the *endnotes*) include information about amending laws and the amendment history of each amended provision.

Uncommenced amendments

The effect of uncommenced amendments is not reflected in the text of the compiled law but the text of the amendments is included in the endnotes.

Application, saving and transitional provisions for provisions and amendments

If the operation of a provision or amendment is affected by an application, saving or transitional provision that is not included in this compilation, details are included in the endnotes.

Modifications

If a provision of the compiled law is affected by a modification that is in force, details are included in the endnotes.

Provisions ceasing to have effect

If a provision of the compiled law has expired or otherwise ceased to have effect in accordance with a provision of the law, details are included in the endnotes.

An Act to protect Australia's heritage of movable cultural objects, to support the protection by foreign countries of their heritage of movable cultural objects, and for related purposes

Part I—Preliminary

1. Short title

This Act may be cited as the *Protection of Movable Cultural Heritage Act 1986.*

2. Commencement

This Act shall come into operation on a day to be fixed by Proclamation.

3. Interpretation

(1) In this Act, unless the contrary intention appears:

aircraft means a machine or apparatus that can derive support in the atmosphere from the reactions of the air or from buoyancy.

appoint includes re-appoint.

Australia includes the external Territories other than Norfolk Island.

Australian protected object means a Class A object or a Class B object.

certificate means a certificate in force under section 12.

Chairperson means the Chairperson of the Committee.

Class A object means an object included in the class of Class A objects in the Control List.

Class B object means an object included in the class of Class B objects in the Control List.

coastal sea, in relation to Australia, means:

(a) the territorial sea of Australia; and

(b) the sea on the landward side of the territorial sea of Australia.

Committee means the National Cultural Heritage Committee established under section 15.

condition, in relation to a permit, means a condition to which the permit is subject.

Control List means the National Cultural Heritage Control List in force under section 8.

expert examiner means a person whose name is in the register kept under section 22.

export means export from Australia.

import means import into Australia.

inland waters of Australia includes all waters on the landward side of the coastal sea of Australia.

inspector means a person who is an inspector by virtue of section 28.

member means a member of the Committee.

National Cultural Heritage Account means the Account established by section 25.

permit means a permit in force under section 11.

principal collecting institution means:

(a) a public art gallery; or
(b) a public museum; or
(c) a public library; or
(d) public archives;

established under a law of the Commonwealth, a State or a Territory.

protected object means an Australian protected object or a protected object of a foreign country.

protected object of a foreign country means an object forming part of the movable cultural heritage of a foreign country.

structure includes a platform fixed to the seabed or otherwise operating in the sea.

vessel means anything capable of carrying persons or goods through or on water, and includes an air-cushion vehicle or similar craft.

(2) A power conferred on a person by this Act may be exercised in the discretion of the person.

(3) A reference in this Act to an offence against a particular provision of this Act, or against this Act, includes a reference to an offence against:

(a) section 6 of the *Crimes Act 1914*; or
(b) an ancillary offence (within the meaning of the *Criminal Code*);

being an offence that relates to an offence against that provision of this Act, or against this Act, as the case may be.

(3A) A reference in this Act to an offence against this Act includes a reference to an offence against section 148.1, 148.2, 147.1 or 149.1 of the Criminal Code that relates to this Act.

(4) For the purposes of the application of this Act in relation to a body corporate, but without prejudice to the liability of any person other than the body corporate:

(a) a statement made, or document furnished, by a person acting on behalf of the body corporate shall be deemed to be made or furnished by the body corporate; and
(b) the knowledge of any person employed by, or concerned in the management of, the body corporate shall be deemed to be knowledge of the body corporate.

(5) A reference in this Act to the movable cultural heritage, in relation to a foreign country, is a reference to objects that are of importance to that country, or to a particular part of that country, for:

(a) ethnological, archaeological, historical, literary, artistic, scientific or technological reasons; or

(b) any other prescribed reasons.

(6) The provisions of this Act relating to the exportation or importation of an object apply notwithstanding that the object may have been brought into Australia from a country for the purpose of transportation to another country or as part of the stores or equipment of a vessel or aircraft.

4. Act to bind Crown

This Act binds the Crown in right of the Commonwealth, of each of the States, of the Northern Territory and of Norfolk Island.

5. Application

This Act applies both within and outside Australia.

6. Extension to Territories

This Act extends to every external Territory other than Norfolk Island.

6A. Application of the *Criminal Code*

Chapter 2 of the *Criminal Code* applies to all offences against this Act.

Note: Chapter 2 of the *Criminal Code* sets out the general principles of criminal responsibility.

Part II—Control of Exports and Imports

Division 1—Exports

7. Movable cultural heritage of Australia

(1) A reference in section 8 to the movable cultural heritage of Australia is a reference to objects that are of importance to Australia, or to a particular part of Australia, for ethnological, archaeological, historical, literary, artistic, scientific or technological reasons, being objects falling within one or more of the following categories:

(a) objects recovered from:

(i) the soil or inland waters of Australia;

(ii) the coastal sea of Australia or the waters above the continental shelf of Australia; or

(iii) the seabed or subsoil beneath the sea or waters referred to in subparagraph (ii);

(b) objects relating to members of the Aboriginal race of Australia and descendants of the indigenous inhabitants of the Torres Strait Islands;

(c) objects of ethnographic art or ethnography;

(d) military objects;

(e) objects of decorative art;

(f) objects of fine art;

(g) objects of scientific or technological interest;

(h) books, records, documents or photographs, graphic, film or television material or sound recordings;

(j) any other prescribed categories.

(2) The generality of paragraph (1)(j) is not limited by any of the other paragraphs of subsection (1).

8. National Cultural Heritage Control List

(1) Subject to subsection (2), the regulations shall prescribe a list, to be known as the National Cultural Heritage Control List, of categories of objects that constitute the movable cultural heritage of Australia and are to be subject to export control.

(2) The Control List shall divide such objects into 2 classes, namely:

(a) Class A objects, being objects that are not to be exported otherwise than in accordance with a certificate; and

(b) Class B objects, being objects that are not to be exported otherwise than in accordance with a permit or certificate.

(3) Subsection (2) does not prevent the division of Class A objects and Class B objects into sub-classes and other divisions or categories.

(4) Nothing in this section shall be taken to limit the application of subsection 33(3A) of the *Acts Interpretation Act 1901*.

9. Unlawful exports

(1) Where a person exports an Australian protected object otherwise than in accordance with a permit or certificate, the object is forfeited.

(2) Where a person attempts to export an Australian protected object otherwise than in accordance with a permit or certificate, the object is liable to forfeiture.

(3) A person is guilty of an offence if:

(a) the person exports, or attempts to export, an object; and

(b) the object is an Australian protected object; and

(c) the person's conduct referred to in paragraph (a) is otherwise than in accordance with a permit or certificate.

(3A) A person is guilty of an offence if:

(a) a permit or certificate relates to an Australian protected object; and

(b) the person engages in conduct; and

(c) the conduct contravenes a condition of the permit or certificate.

(3B) A person who is convicted of an offence against subsection (3) or (3A) is punishable by:

(a) if the person is an individual—a fine not exceeding 1,000 penalty units or imprisonment for a period not exceeding 5 years, or both; or

(b) if the person is a body corporate—a fine not exceeding 2,000 penalty units.

Note: See subsection 46(4) for penalties that may be imposed by a court of summary jurisdiction.

(4) For the purposes of this section, an object shall be taken to be exported at the time when:

(a) the object has been placed on board a ship or aircraft at a particular place in Australia with the intention that it be taken out of Australia by that ship or aircraft and the departure of the ship or aircraft from that place has commenced; or

(b) the object has been delivered as a postal article into the control of the Australian Postal Corporation at a particular place in Australia with the intention that it be sent out of Australia by post and the movement of the postal article from that place has commenced.

(5) Without limiting the meaning of references in this section to a person attempting to export an object, a person shall be taken to attempt to export an object if the person conveys, or has possession of, the object with intent to export it or knowing that it is intended to be exported.

(6) For the purposes of this section, a person who exports or attempts to export an Australian protected object shall be taken to export, or attempt to export, the object otherwise than in accordance with a permit or certificate unless, before exporting or attempting to export the object, the person produces a permit or certificate authorising the export:

(a) where the export is not from an external Territory to an officer of Customs; or

(b) where the export is from an external Territory—to an inspector performing duties in relation to the export of Australian protected objects.

(7) In this section:

engage in conduct means:

(a) do an act; or

(b) omit to perform an act.

10. Grant of permits in respect of particular objects

(1) A person may apply to the Minister for a permit to export a Class B object.

(2) An application shall be made in writing in the prescribed form, or, if no form is prescribed, the form approved by the Minister.

(3) On receipt of an application, the Minister shall refer it to the Committee and the Committee shall refer it to one or more expert examiners.

(4) The expert examiner or examiners shall submit to the Committee a written report on the application, and the Committee shall forward the report to the Minister together with the written recommendations (if any) made by the Committee.

(5) The Minister shall consider the report and recommendations (if any) and:

(a) grant a permit to export the Class B object concerned, subject to such conditions (if any) as the Minister specifies; or

(b) refuse to grant a permit.

(6) In considering the application, an expert examiner, the Committee and the Minister:

(a) shall have regard, among other things, to the reasons referred to in subsection 7(1) that are relevant to the object to which the application relates; and

(b) if satisfied that the object is of such importance to Australia, or a part of Australia, for those reasons, that its loss to Australia would significantly diminish the cultural heritage of Australia—shall not recommend the grant of a permit, or grant a permit, as the case may be, to export the object permanently.

(7) If the Minister refuses to grant the permit, the Minister shall, within the prescribed period after the decision is made, cause to be served on the applicant notice in writing of the refusal, setting out the reasons for the refusal.

10A. Grant of general permits for certain institutions

(1) A principal collecting institution may apply to the Minister for a permit to export a Class B object that is accessioned into the collection for which the institution is responsible.

(2) If a principal collecting institution is not a body corporate, the person responsible for the institution's operations may make an application under subsection (1).

(3) An application is to be made in writing in the prescribed form, or, if no form is prescribed, the form approved by the Minister.

(4) On receipt of an application, the Minister must refer it to the Committee.

(5) The Committee must submit to the Minister a written report on the application.

(6) The Minister must consider the report and:

(a) grant to the applicant a permit to export any Class B object that is accessioned into the collection for which the institution is responsible; or

(b) refuse to grant a permit.

(7) A permit is subject to:

(a) a condition that an exportation of a Class B object is not in accordance with the permit unless it is exported on loan for the purposes of research, public exhibition or a similar purpose; and

(b) such other conditions (if any) as the Minister specifies in the permit.

(8) If the Minister refuses to grant a permit, the Minister must, within the prescribed period after the decision is made, cause to be served on the applicant written notice of the refusal, setting out the reasons for the refusal.

11. Permits

(1) A permit granted under section 10 or 10A shall be in writing in the prescribed form, or if no form is prescribed, the form approved by the Minister.

(2) A permit granted under section 10 or 10A comes into force on the date on which it is granted and remains in force for an indefinite period or for a period specified in the permit.

12. Certificates of exemption

(1) Where a person intends to import an Australian protected object:

(a) for temporary purposes; or

(b) in circumstances in which the person may wish subsequently to export the object;

the person may apply to the Minister for a certificate authorising the exportation of the object.

(2) An application shall be made in writing in the prescribed form or, if no form is prescribed, the form approved by the Minister.

(3) On receipt of an application, the Minister shall:

(a) grant a certificate, subject to such conditions (if any) as the Minister specifies; or

(b) refuse to grant a certificate.

(4) A certificate shall be in writing in the prescribed form or, if no form is prescribed, the form approved by the Minister.

(5) A certificate comes into force on the date on which it is granted and remains in force for the period specified in the certificate.

(6) If the Minister refuses to grant a certificate, the Minister shall, within the prescribed period after the decision is made, cause to be served on the applicant notice in writing of the refusal, setting out the reasons for the refusal.

13. Variation etc. of conditions and period of permit or certificate

(1) At any time while a permit or certificate is in force, the Minister may, by notice in writing served on the holder of the permit or certificate:

(a) impose a condition to which the permit or certificate is to be subject;

(b) vary or revoke a condition of the permit or certificate;

(c) vary the period of effect of the permit or certificate; or

(d) revoke the permit or certificate.

(2) A notice under subsection (1) takes effect when it is served on the holder of the permit or certificate or on such later date (if any) as is specified in the notice.

(3) The Minister shall not exercise a power under subsection (1) in relation to a permit or certificate except upon an application by the holder of the permit or certificate made in writing in the prescribed form, or, if no form is prescribed, the form approved by the Minister.

13A. Address for service of notices

(1) A person applying for a permit under section 10 or 10A or a certificate under section 12 must specify, as the person's address for the purposes of this Part, an address in Australia.

(2) A person who has specified an address, under subsection (1) or through a previous application of this subsection, may, at any time, give to the Minister a written

notice specifying, as the person's address for the purposes of this Part, an address in Australia that is different from the address last specified.

(3) The last address specified by a person under this section is taken to be the person's place of residence or business for the purpose of serving notices on the person under this Part.

Division 2—Imports

14. Unlawful imports

(1) Where:

(a) a protected object of a foreign country has been exported from that country;

(b) the export was prohibited by a law of that country relating to cultural property; and

(c) the object is imported;

the object is liable to forfeiture.

(2) Where a person imports an object, knowing that:

(a) the object is a protected object of a foreign country that has been exported from that country; and

(b) the export was prohibited by a law of that country relating to cultural property;

the person is guilty of an offence punishable, on conviction, by:

(a) if the person is a natural person—a fine not exceeding $100,000 or imprisonment for a period not exceeding 5 years, or both; or

(b) if the person is a body corporate—a fine not exceeding $200,000.

(3) This section does not apply in relation to the importation of an object if:

(a) the importation takes place under an agreement between:

(i) the Commonwealth, a State, a Territory, a principal collecting institution or an exhibition co-ordinator; and

(ii) any other person or body (including a government); and

(b) the agreement provides for the object to be loaned, for a period not exceeding 2 years, to the Commonwealth, State, Territory, principal collecting institution or exhibition co-ordinator, as the case may be, for the purpose of its public exhibition within Australia.

(4) In subsection (3):

exhibition co-ordinator means a body that arranges for the conducting in Australia of public exhibitions of objects from collections outside Australia, and that achieves this by, from time to time:

(a) entering into an agreement with a person or body (including a government) for the importation of such objects on loan; and

(b) entering into an agreement with the Commonwealth, a State or a Territory under which the Commonwealth, State or Territory agrees to compensate the person or body referred to in paragraph (a) for any loss of or damage to the objects arising from, or connected with, the carrying out of the agreement referred to in that paragraph or the public exhibition of the objects in Australia.

Part III—Administration

15. National Cultural Heritage Committee

There shall be a committee, to be known as the National Cultural Heritage Committee.

16. Functions of Committee

The functions of the Committee are:

(a) to furnish advice to the Minister, either of its own motion or on request made to it by the Minister:

(i) in relation to the operation of this Act;

(ii) in relation to objects that should be included in, or removed from, the Control List;

(iii) in relation to the classification and re-classification of objects so included; and

(iv) in relation to the operation of the National Cultural Heritage Account;

(b) to furnish advice to the Minister pursuant to subsections 10(4) and 10A (5);

(c) to establish and maintain the register referred to in section 22; and

(d) to consult and co-operate with appropriate authorities of the Commonwealth, of the States and of the Territories, and with other organisations, associations and persons, on matters related to its functions.

17. Constitution of Committee

(1) The Committee shall consist of:

(a) 4 persons, each of whom represents a different collecting institution;

(b) a member of The Australian Vice-Chancellors' Committee;

(c) a nominee of the Minister administering the *Aboriginal Land Grant (Jervis Bay Territory) Act 1986*; and

(d) 4 persons having experience relevant to the cultural heritage of Australia.

(1A) The member referred to in paragraph (1)(c) must be:

(a) a person of the Aboriginal race of Australia; or

(b) a descendant of an indigenous inhabitant of the Torres Strait Islands.

(2) A member of the Committee:

(a) shall be appointed by the Minister;

(b) holds office on a part-time basis;

(c) holds office for such period, not exceeding 4 years, as is specified in the

instrument of appointment; and
(d) is eligible for re-appointment.

(3) The Minister shall designate, in writing, one of the members to be the Chairperson.

(5) The exercise of a power or the performance of a function by the Committee is not invalidated by reason only that:
(a) there is a vacancy for a period of not more than 3 months in an office of a member referred to in paragraph (1)(b) or (c); or
(b) the number of members referred to in paragraph (1)(a) or (d) falls below 4 for a period of not more than 3 months.

(6) For the purposes of this section, a person shall be taken to represent a collecting institution if the person holds a senior position in connection with the collecting functions of that institution.

(7) In this section, *collecting institution* means:
(a) a public art gallery;
(b) a public museum;
(c) a public library; or
(d) public archives.

18. Removal and resignation

(1) The Minister may terminate the appointment of a member for misbehaviour or physical or mental incapacity.

(2) The Minister may terminate the appointment of a member referred to in paragraph 17(1)(c) on the request of the Minister administering the *Aboriginal Land Grant (Jervis Bay Territory) Act 1986.*

(3) If a member fails, without reasonable excuse, to comply with section 20, the Minister shall terminate the appointment of the member.

(4) A member may resign the office of member by writing signed by the member and delivered to the Minister.

19. Remuneration and allowances

(1) A member shall be paid such remuneration as is determined by the Remuneration Tribunal.

(2) A member shall be paid such allowances as are prescribed.

(3) Subsections (1) and (2) have effect subject to the *Remuneration Tribunal Act 1973.*

20. Disclosure of interests

(1) A member who has a direct or indirect pecuniary interest in a matter being considered or about to be considered by the Committee shall, as soon as possible after the relevant facts have come to the knowledge of the member, disclose the nature of the interest at a meeting of the Committee.

(2) A disclosure under subsection (1) shall be recorded in the minutes of the meeting of the Committee and the member shall not, unless the Minister or the Committee otherwise determines:

(a) be present during any deliberation of the Committee with respect to that matter; or

(b) take part in any decision of the Committee with respect to that matter.

(3) For the purpose of the making of a determination by the Committee under subsection (2) in relation to a member who has made a disclosure under subsection (1), a member who has a direct or indirect pecuniary interest in the matter to which the disclosure relates shall not:

(a) be present during any deliberation of the Committee for the purpose of making the determination; or

(b) take part in the making by the Committee of the determination.

21. Meetings

(1) Meetings of the Committee shall be held at such times and places as the Committee from time to time determines.

(2) The Chairperson may at any time convene a meeting.

(3) At a meeting, 5 members constitute a quorum.

(4) Subject to subsection (5), the Chairperson shall preside at all meetings.

(5) If the Chairperson is absent from a meeting, the members present shall elect one of their number to preside at the meeting.

(6) Questions arising at a meeting shall be determined by a majority of the members present and voting.

(7) The member presiding at a meeting has a deliberative vote and, in the event of an equality of votes, also has a casting vote.

21A. Conduct of meetings

(1) The Committee may regulate the conduct of proceedings at its meetings as it considers appropriate.

(2) Without limiting subsection (1), the Committee may permit members to participate in, and form part of the quorum at, a particular meeting, or at all meetings, of the Committee by any of the following methods of communication:

(a) telephone;

(b) closed-circuit television;

(c) any other method of communication determined by the Committee.

(3) A member who is permitted to participate in a meeting under subsection (2) is regarded as being present at that meeting.

21B. Certain resolutions may be made without meetings

(1) If all the members of the Committee (other than any member to whom subsection

(3) applies) sign a document containing a statement that they support a recommendation or report made, in the terms set out in the document, in relation to an application made under section 10 or 10A, a recommendation or report in those terms is taken to have been adopted by a duly constituted meeting of the Committee held on the day the document was signed, or if the members sign the document on different days, on the last of those days.

(2) For the purposes of subsection (1), 2 or more separate documents containing statements in identical terms, each of which is signed by one or more members, are together taken to constitute one document containing a statement in those terms signed by those members on the respective days on which they signed the separate documents.

(3) A member must not sign a document containing a statement in favour of the recommendation or report if it is in respect of a matter in which the member would, for the purposes of section 20, be taken to have a direct or indirect pecuniary interest.

(4) This section does not apply to a document that less than 5 members of the Committee are eligible to sign.

22. Register of expert examiners

(1) The Committee shall, in accordance with the regulations, maintain a register of the names of persons determined by the Committee to be expert examiners for the purposes of this Act.

(2) In subsection (1), *person* includes:

(a) a body or association of persons, whether incorporated or not; and

(b) a person resident or domiciled outside Australia.

23. Expert examiners

It is the function of an expert examiner to give advice to the Committee on a matter referred by the Committee.

24. Delegation

(1) The Minister may, either generally or as otherwise provided by the instrument of delegation, by instrument in writing, delegate to:

(a) the person holding or performing the duties of the office of Secretary of the Department; or

(b) an SES employee, or acting SES employee, in the Department;

all or any of the Minister's powers under this Act, other than this power of delegation or a power conferred by section 17 or 18, subsection 28(3), (4) or (5) or section 38 or 47.

(2) A power so delegated, when exercised by the delegate, shall, for the purposes of this Act, be deemed to have been exercised by the Minister.

(3) A delegation under this section does not prevent the exercise of a power by the Minister.

Part IV—National Cultural Heritage Account

25. Establishment of National Cultural Heritage Account

(1) There is hereby established the National Cultural Heritage Account.

(2) The Account is a special account for the purposes of the *Public Governance, Performance and Accountability Act 2013*.

25A. Credits to Account

There must be credited to the National Cultural Heritage Account:

(a) amounts equal to all money received from a State or Territory, or from an authority of a State or Territory, for the purposes of the Account; and

(b) amounts equal to all money received, whether by way of gift, bequest or otherwise, for the purposes of the Account; and

(c) if amounts are debited from the Account for the purpose of investment—amounts equal to the interest generated by the investment.

Note: An Appropriation Act provides for amounts to be credited to a special account if any of the purposes of the special account is a purpose that is covered by an item in the Appropriation Act.

25B. Purpose of Account

Amounts standing to the credit of the National Cultural Heritage Account may be expended for the purpose of facilitating the acquisition of Australian protected objects for display or safe-keeping.

26. Taxation

The income and transactions of the National Cultural Heritage Account are not subject to taxation under any law of the Commonwealth or of a State or Territory.

Part V—Enforcement of Act

27. Interpretation

(1) In this Part (except sections 35, 36, 37 and 38), *forfeited* includes liable to forfeiture.

(2) Where, at a particular time, an object is delivered by a Customs officer to an inspector under section 203T of the *Customs Act 1901* or voluntarily surrendered to an inspector by the owner or person having possession, custody or control of the object, the object shall, for the purposes of this Part, be taken to be seized under this Act by the inspector at that time.

28. Inspectors

(1) The Minister may, by instrument in writing, appoint a person as an inspector.

(2) By force of this subsection:

(a) a member or special member of the Australian Federal Police; and

(b) a member of a police force of a State or Territory;

is an inspector.

(3) The Minister may make an arrangement with a Minister of a State for and in relation to the exercise of powers, and the performance of duties, of inspectors under this Act by officers of the State.

(4) An arrangement may contain such incidental or supplementary provisions as the Minister and the Minister of the State think necessary.

(5) The Minister may arrange with the Minister of a State with whom an arrangement is in force for the variation or revocation of the arrangement.

(6) An arrangement, or the variation or revocation of an arrangement, shall be in writing and a copy of each instrument by which an arrangement has been made, varied or revoked shall be published in the *Gazette*.

29. Identity cards

(1) The Minister may cause to be issued to an inspector, other than a member of a police force, an identity card in a form approved by the Minister by instrument in writing.

(2) A person who ceases to be an inspector shall forthwith return his or her identity card to the Minister.

(3) A person who contravenes subsection (2) is guilty of an offence punishable on conviction by a fine not exceeding $100.

(4) Subsection (3) is an offence of strict liability.

Note: For *strict liability*, see section 6.1 of the *Criminal Code*.

30. Search warrants

(1) Where an information on oath is laid before a Magistrate alleging that there are reasonable grounds for suspecting that there may be, at that time or within the next following 24 hours, upon any land or upon or in any premises, structure, vessel, aircraft or vehicle, a thing or things of a particular kind that is or are forfeited or connected with a particular offence against this Act, and the information sets out those grounds, the Magistrate may issue a search warrant authorising an inspector named in the warrant, with such assistance as he or she thinks necessary and if necessary by force:

(a) to enter upon the land or upon or into the premises, structure, vessel, aircraft or vehicle;

(b) to search the land, premises, structure, vessel, aircraft or vehicle for things of that kind; and

(c) to seize any thing of that kind found there that he or she believes on reasonable grounds to be forfeited or connected with that offence.

(2) A Magistrate shall not issue a warrant under subsection (1) unless:

(a) the informant or some other person has given to the Magistrate, either orally or by affidavit, such further information (if any) as the Magistrate requires concerning the grounds on which the issue of the warrant is being sought; and

(b) the Magistrate is satisfied that there are reasonable grounds for issuing the warrant.

(3) There shall be stated in a warrant issued under this section:

(a) a statement of the purpose for which the warrant is issued, which shall include a reference to the nature of the forfeited thing or things, or the offence, in relation to which the entry and search are authorised;

(b) whether entry is authorised to be made at any time of the day or night or during specified hours of the day or night;

(c) a description of the kind of things authorised to be seized; and

(d) a date, not being later than one month after the date of issue of the warrant, upon which the warrant ceases to have effect.

(4) If, in the course of searching, in accordance with a warrant issued under this section, for things that are forfeited or connected with a particular offence, being things of a kind specified in the warrant, an inspector finds any thing that he or she believes on reasonable grounds to be forfeited or connected with the offence, although not of a kind specified in the warrant, or to be connected with another offence against this Act, and he or she believes on reasonable grounds that there is a compelling need for the immediate seizure of the thing in order to prevent its exportation, importation, concealment, loss or destruction, or its use in committing, continuing or repeating the offence or in committing the other offence, the inspector may seize that thing.

(5) For the purposes of this section, a thing is connected with a particular offence if it is:

(a) a thing in respect of which the offence was committed;

(b) a thing that will afford evidence of the offence; or

(c) a thing that was used, or is intended to be used, for the purpose of the offence.

(6) A reference in this section to an offence includes a reference to an offence that there are reasonable grounds for believing has been, or will be, committed.

31. Search warrants granted by telephone

(1) Where, by reason of circumstances of urgency, an inspector considers it necessary to do so, the inspector may make application for a search warrant to a Magistrate, by telephone, in accordance with this section.

(2) Before so making application, an inspector shall prepare an information of a kind referred to in subsection 30(1) that sets out the grounds on which the issue of the warrant is being sought, but may, if it is necessary to do so, make the application before the information has been sworn.

(3) Where a Magistrate is, upon application made under subsection (1), satisfied:

(a) after having considered the terms of the information prepared in accordance with subsection (1); and

(b) after having received such further information (if any) as the Magistrate requires concerning the grounds on which the issuc of the warrant is being sought;

that there are reasonable grounds for issuing the warrant, the Magistrate shall complete and sign such a search warrant as the Magistrate would issue under section 30 if the application had been made to the Magistrate in accordance with that section.

(4) Where a Magistrate signs a warrant under subsection (3):

(a) the Magistrate shall inform the inspector of the terms of the warrant and the date on which and the time at which it was signed, and record on the warrant the reasons for granting the warrant; and

(b) the inspector shall complete a form of warrant in the terms furnished by the Magistrate and write on it the name of the Magistrate and the date on which and the time at which the warrant was signed.

(5) Where an inspector completes a form of warrant in accordance with subsection (4), the inspector shall, not later than the day next following the date of expiry of the warrant, forward to the Magistrate who signed the warrant the form of warrant completed by the inspector and the information duly sworn in connection with the warrant.

(6) Upon receipt of the documents referred to in subsection (5), the Magistrate shall attach to them the warrant signed by the Magistrate and deal with the documents in the manner in which the Magistrate would have dealt with the information if the application for the warrant had been made in accordance with section 30.

(7) A form of warrant duly completed by an inspector in accordance with subsection (4) is, if it is in accordance with the terms of the warrant signed by the Magistrate, authority for any search, entry or seizure that the warrant so signed authorises.

(8) Where it is material, in any proceedings, for a court to be satisfied that a search, entry or seizure was authorised in accordance with this section, and the warrant signed by a Magistrate in accordance with this section authorising the search, entry or seizure is not produced in evidence, the court shall assume, unless the contrary is proved, that the search, entry or seizure was not authorised by such a warrant.

32. Searches in emergencies

(1) An inspector may:

(a) search a person, or the clothing that is being worn by, and property in the immediate control of, a person, suspected by the inspector to be carrying any thing that is forfeited or connected with an offence against this Act; or

(b) enter upon any land, or upon or into any premises, structure, vessel, aircraft or vehicle, on or in which the inspector believes on reasonable grounds that any thing forfeited or connected with an offence against this Act is situated;

and may seize any such thing found in the course of that search, or upon the land or in the premises, structure, vessel, aircraft or vehicle, as the case may be, if:

(c) the inspector believes on reasonable grounds that it is necessary to do so in order to prevent the exportation or importation of that thing or the concealment, loss or destruction of any thing forfeited or connected with an offence against this Act; and

(d) the search or entry is made in circumstances of such seriousness and urgency as to require and justify immediate search or entry without the authority or an order of a court or of a warrant issued under this Act.

(2) An inspector may stop a person, vessel, aircraft or vehicle for the purposes of subsection (1).

(3) Subsections 30(5) and (6) apply in relation to this section as they apply in relation to section 30.

33. Powers of arrest

(1) An inspector may, without warrant, arrest any person if the inspector believes on reasonable grounds:

(a) that the person is committing or has committed a n offence against this Act; and

(b) that proceedings against the person by summons would not be effective.

(2) Where a person is arrested under subsection (1), an inspector shall forthwith bring the person, or cause the person to be brought, before a Magistrate or other proper authority to be dealt with in accordance with law.

(3) Without limiting the generality of the meaning of any expression in subsection (1), where:

(a) an inspector requests a person whom the inspector finds committing, or whom the inspector believes on reasonable grounds to have committed, an offence against this Act, being a person whose full name or usual place of residence are unknown to the inspector, to state his or her full name or usual place of residence, as the case may be; and

(b) the person:

(i) refuses or fails to comply with the request; or

(ii) whether or not in compliance, or purported compliance, with the request, states as his or her full name or usual place of residence a name or a place, as the case may be, that the inspector believes on reasonable grounds to be false or misleading in a material particular;

the inspector shall be taken, for the purposes of paragraph (1)(b), to have reasonable grounds for believing that proceedings against the person by summons in respect of the offence will not be effective.

(4) Nothing in this section prevents the arrest of a person in accordance with any other law.

34. Seizure of protected objects

An inspector may seize a protected object that the inspector believes on reasonable grounds to be forfeited.

35. Power of retention

(1) A thing seized under this Act may be retained:

(a) in the case of a protected object seized on the grounds that it is forfeited by virtue of subsection 9(1)—until a court orders the return of the object or the object is disposed of under section 38;

(b) in the case of any other protected object—until a court orders the return of the object or the object is forfeited; or

(c) in the case of any other thing—until the end of the period of 60 days after the seizure or, if proceedings involving the thing are instituted within that period, until those proceedings (including any appeal to a court in relation to those proceedings) are terminated.

(2) The Minister may, by instrument in writing, authorise any thing seized under this Act (other than a protected object that is forfeited) to be released to the owner, or the person who had the possession, custody or control of the thing immediately before it was seized, and thereupon sections 36 and 37 do not apply, or cease to apply, as the case requires, in relation to the thing.

36. Notice of seizure

(1) In this section, *appropriate person* means the Minister or a person designated by the Minister in writing for the purposes of this section.

(2) Subject to this section, as soon as practicable after a protected object has been seized by an inspector under this Act, the inspector shall serve on the owner, or the person who had the possession, custody or control of the object immediately before it was seized, a notice in writing:

(a) identifying the object and the date of the seizure;

(b) setting out the reasons for the seizure;

(c) setting out the terms of the provisions of subsection 37(1); and

(d) where subsection (5) applies—setting out the terms of the provisions of that subsection and specifying, and setting out the address of, an appropriate person and stating that any notice under that subsection is to be given to that person.

(3) An inspector is not required to serve a notice under subsection (2) if, after making such inquiries as the inspector thinks appropriate, the inspector does not have sufficient information to do so.

(4) Where:

(a) a notice under subsection (2) has not been served in respect of an object seized by an inspector under this Act; and

(b) within 30 days after the day on which the object was seized, a person who claims to be a person entitled to be served with such a notice gives an appropriate person sufficient information, in writing, to enable the notice to be served;

the appropriate person shall forthwith convey that information to the inspector.

(5) Where a protected object has been seized on the grounds that it is liable to forfeiture by virtue of subsection 9(2) or 14(1) and a notice under subsection (2) is served in respect of the object, the object is forfeited unless, within 30 days after the service of the notice, the owner, or the person who had possession, custody or control of the object immediately before it was seized:

(a) gives notice, in writing, to the appropriate person specified in the notice under subsection (2) claiming the object; or

(b) brings an action for recovery of the object.

(6) Where, at the end of the period of 30 days after the day on which a protected object was seized under this Act:

(a) a notice has not been served in respect of the object under subsection (2); and

(b) a person claiming to be a person entitled to be served with such a notice has not given an appropriate person sufficient information to enable the notice to be served;

the object is forfeited.

(7) Where notice is given under subsection (5) to the appropriate person, the appropriate person shall serve on the person who gave the notice a notice, in writing, setting out the terms of the provisions of subsection (8).

(8) Where:

(a) a notice is given to a person under subsection (7) in relation to an object; and

(b) the person does not, within 4 months after the service of the notice, bring an action for recovery of the object;

the object is forfeited.

37. Court proceedings

(1) Where:

(a) a protected object has been seized under this Act; and

(b) the object is not forfeited by section 36 or by or under this section;

the owner, or the person who had the possession, custody or control of the object immediately before it was seized, may bring an action against the Commonwealth in a court of competent jurisdiction for the recovery of the object on the ground that the object is not forfeited or liable to be forfeited.

(2) Where:

(a) a protected object has been seized on the grounds that it is liable to forfeiture by virtue of subsection 9(2) or 14(1);

(b) a person brings an action for recovery of the object; and

(c) the person discontinues the action;

the object is forfeited.

(3) Where an action is brought for recovery of a protected object, the court shall determine, on a balance of probabilities, whether:

(a) the object is forfeited by virtue of subsection 9(1); or

(b) the object is liable to forfeiture by virtue of subsection 9(2) or 14(1);

and the court:

(c) where paragraph (a) applies—shall reject the claim for recovery;

(d) where paragraph (b) applies—shall order that the object is forfeited; or

(e) in any other case—may order the return of the object.

(4) Where a person is convicted of attempting to export a protected object in contravention of subsection 9(3) or of an offence against subsection 14(2) in relation to a protected object, the court shall order that the object is forfeited.

38. Result of forfeiture

Where a protected object is forfeited by or under this Act:

(a) all title and interest in the object is vested in the Commonwealth without further proceedings;

(b) the object shall be dealt with and disposed of in accordance with the directions of the Minister; and

(c) any costs incurred by the Commonwealth in transporting or disposing of the object are a debt due to the Commonwealth by the person who was the owner of the object immediately before it was forfeited and may be recovered by the Commonwealth in a court of competent jurisdiction.

39. Production of permit

(1) An inspector may require any person whom the inspector suspects on reasonable grounds of intending to export, of exporting, or of having exported, an Australian protected object to produce a permit or certificate authorising the export or to produce evidence of the existence and contents of such a permit or certificate.

(2) A person who fails to comply with a requirement made under subsection (1) is guilty of an offence punishable on conviction by a fine not exceeding $1,000.

(3) Subsection (2) does not apply if the person has a reasonable excuse.

Note: A defendant bears an evidential burden in relation to the matter in subsection (3) (see subsection 13.3(3) of the *Criminal Code*).

(4) Subsection (2) is an offence of strict liability.

Note: For *strict liability*, see section 6.1 of the *Criminal Code*.

40. Proof of authority

An inspector (other than a member of a police force who is in uniform) is not entitled to exercise any powers under section 32, 33, 34, 39 or 43 in relation to a person unless:

(a) if the inspector is a member of a police force—the inspector produces, for inspection by the person, written evidence of the fact that the inspector is a member of that police force; or

(b) in any other case—the inspector produces his or her identity card for inspection by the person.

41. Foreign country to request return of objects

(1) A power conferred by this Part shall not be exercised by an inspector in relation to

a protected object of a foreign country unless the inspector believes on reasonable grounds that the Commonwealth has received from the Government of the country a request for the return of the object.

(2) Proceedings for a contravention of section 14 in relation to a protected object of a foreign country shall not be instituted unless the Commonwealth has received from the Government of the country a request for the return of the object.

(3) In any proceedings, the mere production of a document purporting to be signed by the Secretary of the Department and stating that the Commonwealth has received a request from the Government of a specified foreign country for the return of a specified protected object is *prima facie* evidence of the facts stated.

43. Assistance of inspectors

An inspector exercising or proposing to exercise powers pursuant to this Part in relation to property, being any premises, structure, vessel, aircraft or vehicle, may require the owner or person in charge of the property to provide reasonable assistance to the inspector in the exercise of those powers in relation to the property, and the person shall comply with the request.

Penalty: $2,000 or imprisonment for 12 months, or both.

46. Indictable offences

(1) An offence against subsection 9(3), 9(3A) or 14(2) is an indictable offence.

(2) An offence against section 43 is punishable on summary conviction.

(3) Notwithstanding that an offence referred to in subsection (1) is an indictable offence, a court of summary jurisdiction may hear and determine proceedings in respect of the offence if the court is satisfied that it is proper to do so and the defendant and the prosecutor consent.

(4) If, in accordance with subsection (3), a court of summary jurisdiction convicts a person of an offence referred to in subsection (1), the penalty that the court may impose is:

(a) if the person is an individual—a fine not exceeding 50 penalty units or imprisonment for a period not exceeding 2 years, or both; or

(b) if the person is a body corporate—a fine not exceeding 200 penalty units.

Part VI—Miscellaneous

47. Annual report

(1) The Minister shall, as soon as practicable after 30 June in each year, cause to be prepared a report on the working of this Act during the year that ended on that 30 June.

(2) The Minister must cause a copy of the report to be laid before each House of the Parliament within 15 sitting days of that House after the Minister receives it.

48. Administrative Appeals Tribunal

(1) Application may be made to the Administrative Appeals Tribunal for review of:

(a) a decision by the Minister to refuse to grant a permit or certificate;

(b) a decision by the Minister to impose a condition under paragraph 10(5)(a), 10A(7)(b) or 12(3)(a); or

(c) a decision by the Minister under subsection 11(2), 12(5) or 13(1).

(2) Where a person is notified of a decision referred to in subsection (1), the Minister shall cause to be served on the person a notice stating that, subject to the *Administrative Appeals Tribunal Act 1975*, application may be made to the Administrative Appeals Tribunal for review of the decision.

(3) A failure to comply with subsection (2) in relation to a decision does not affect the validity of the decision.

49. Regulations

The Governor-General may make regulations, not inconsistent with this Act, prescribing matters:

(a) required or permitted by this Act to be prescribed; or

(b) necessary or convenient to be prescribed for carrying out or giving effect to this Act.

Endnotes

Endnote 1—About the endnotes

The endnotes provide details of the history of this legislation and its provisions.
The following endnotes are included in each compilation:

Endnote 1—About the endnotes
Endnote 2—Abbreviation key
Endnote 3—Legislation history
Endnote 4—Amendment history
Endnote 5—Uncommenced amendments
Endnote 6—Modifications
Endnote 7—Misdescribed amendments
Endnote 8—Miscellaneous

If there is no information under a particular endnote, the word "none" will appear in square brackets after the endnote heading.

Abbreviation key—Endnote 2
The abbreviation key in this endnote sets out abbreviations that may be used in the endnotes.

Legislation history and amendment history—Endnotes 3 and 4
Amending laws are annotated in the legislation history and amendment history.
The legislation history in endnote 3 provides information about each law that has amended the compiled law. The information includes commencement information for amending laws and details of application, saving or transitional provisions that are not included in this compilation.
The amendment history in endnote 4 provides information about amendments at the provision level. It also includes information about any provisions that have expired or otherwise ceased to have effect in accordance with a provision of the compiled law.

Uncommenced amendments—Endnote 5
The effect of uncommenced amendments is not reflected in the text of the compiled law but the text of the amendments is included in endnote 5.

Modifications—Endnote 6
If the compiled law is affected by a modification that is in force, details of the modification are included in endnote 6.

Misdescribed amendments—Endnote 7
An amendment is a misdescribed amendment if the effect of the amendment cannot be incorporated into the text of the compilation. Any misdescribed amendment is included in endnote 7.

Miscellaneous—Endnote 8
Endnote 8 includes any additional information that may be helpful for a reader of the compilation.

Endnote 2—Abbreviation key

ad = added or inserted
am = amended
c = clause(s)
Ch = Chapter(s)
def = definition(s)
Dict = Dictionary
disallowed = disallowed by Parliament
Div = Division(s)
exp = expired or ceased to have effect
hdg = heading(s)
LI = Legislative Instrument
LIA = *Legislative Instruments Act 2003*
mod = modified/modification
No = Number(s)
o = order(s)
Ord = Ordinance
orig = original
par = paragraph(s)/subparagraph(s) /sub-subparagraph(s)
pres = present
prev = previous
(prev) = previously
Pt = Part(s)
r = regulation(s)/rule(s)
Reg = Regulation/Regulations
reloc = relocated
renum = renumbered
rep = repealed
rs = repealed and substituted
s = section(s)
Sch = Schedule(s)
Sdiv = Subdivision(s)
SLI = Select Legislative Instrument
SR = Statutory Rules
Sub-Ch = Sub -Chapter(s)
SubPt = Subpart(s)

Endnote 3—Legislation history

Act	Number and year	Assent	Commencement	Application, saving and transitional provisions
Protection of Movable Cultural Heritage Act 1986	11, 1986	13 May 1986	1 July 1987 (*see Gazette* 1987, No. S138)	
Postal Services Amendment Act 1988	126, 1988	14 Dec 1988	ss. 4, 5, 9–11, 21(2) and 22(1): 1 Jan 1989 (*see Gazette* 1988, No. S402) ss. 12, 21(3) and 22(2): 30 June 1989 (*see Gazette* 1989, No. S216) Remainder: Royal Assent	—

Act	Number and year	Assent	Commencement	Application, saving and transitional provisions
Arts, Environment, Tourism and Territories Legislation Amendment Act 1990	88, 1990	20 Nov 1992	Part 7 (ss. 14–23): Royal Assent (a)	—
Arts, Sport, Environment, Tourism And Territories Legislation Amendment Act (No.2) 1991	179,1991	25 Nov 1991	25 Nov 1991	
Arts, Sport, Environment and Territories Legislation Amendment Act 1992	21,1992	10 Apr 1992	8 May 1992	
Statute Law Revision Act 1996	43,1996	25 Oct 1996	Schedule 4 (item 123): Royal Assent (b)	—
Protection of Movable Cultural Heritage Amendment Act 1999	101,1999	16, July 1999	16, July 1999	Sch.1(item 9)
Public Employment (Consequential and Transitional) Amendment Act 1999	146, 1999	11 Nov 1999	Schedule 1 (item 752): 5 Dec 1999 (*see Gazette* 1999, No. S584) (c)	—
Criminal Code Amendment (Theft, Fraud, Bribery and Related Offences) Act 2000	137, 2000	24 Nov 2000	ss. 1–3, Schedule 1 (items 1, 4, 6, 7, 9–11, 32): Royal Assent Remainder: 24 May 2001	Sch. 2 (items 418, 419)
Communications and the Arts Legislation Amendment (Application of Criminal Code) Act 2001	5, 2001	20 Mar 2001	s. 4 and Schedule 1 (items 40–49): (d)	s. 4

Act	Number and year	Assent	Commencement	Application, saving and transitional provisions
Financial Framework Legislation Amendment Act 2005	8, 2005	22 Feb 2005	s. 4 and Schedule 1 (items 313, 314, 496): Royal Assent	S. 4 and Sch 1 (item 496)
Statute Law Revision Act 2011	5,2011	22 Mar 2011	Schedule 7 (items 113, 114): 19 Apr 2011	—
Acts Interpretation Amendment Act 2011	46,2011	27 June 2011	Schedule 2 (items 937, 938) and Schedule 3 (items 10, 11): 27 Dec 2011	Sch. 3 (items 10, 11)
Statute Law Revision Act 2012	136, 2012	22 Sept 2012	Schedule 1 (item 108): Royal Assent	—
Statute Law Revision Act (No. 1) 2014	31, 2014	27 May 2014	Sch 3 (items 2, 3) and Sch 7 (item 8): 24 June 2014	—
Public Governance, Performance and Accountability (Consequential and Transitional Provisions) Act 2014	62, 2014	30 June 2014	Sch 11 (items 79–81) and Sch 14 (items 1–4): 1 July 2014 (s 2(1) items 6, 14)	Sch 14 (items 1–4)

(a) The *Protection of Movable Cultural Heritage Act 1986* was amended by Part 7 (sections14–23) only of the *Arts, Environment, Tourism and Territories Legislation Amendment Act 1990*, subsection 2(1) of which provides as follows:

(1) Parts 1, 4, 5, 6, 7 and 8 commence on the day on which this Act receives the Royal Assent.

(b) The *Protection of Movable Cultural Heritage Act 1986* was amended by Schedule 4 (item 123) only of the *Statute Law Revision Act 1996*, subsection 2(1) of which provides as follows:

(1) Subject to subsections (2) and (3), this Act commences on the day on which it receives the Royal Assent.

(c) The *Protection of Movable Cultural Heritage Act 1986* was amended by Schedule 1 (item 752) only of the *Public Employment (Consequential and Transitional) Amendment Act 1999*, subsections 2(1) and (2) of which provide as follows:

(1) In this Act, *commencing time* means the time when the *Public Service Act 1999* commences.

(2) Subject to this section, this Act commences at the commencing time.

(d) The *Protection of Movable Cultural Heritage Act 1986* was amended by Schedule 1 (items 4 0–49) only of the *Communications and the Arts Legislation Amendment (Application of Criminal Code) Act 2001*, subsection 2(1)(a) of which provides as follows:

(1) Subject to this section, this Act commences at the latest of the following times:

(a) immediately after the commencement of item 15 of Schedule 1 to the *Criminal Code Amendment (Theft, Fraud, Bribery and Related Offences) Act 2000*;

Item 15 commenced on 24 May 2001.

Endnote 4—Amendment history

Provision affected	How affected
Part I	
s. 3	am. No. 88, 1990; No. 101, 1999; No. 137, 2000; No. 5, 2001; No. 46, 2011
s. 6A	ad. No. 5, 2001
Part II	
Division 1	
s. 9	am. No. 126, 1988; No. 5, 2001
s. 10	am. No. 88, 1990
s. 10A	ad. No. 88, 1990
s. 11	am. No. 88, 1990
s. 13A	ad. No. 88, 1990
Division 2	
s. 14	am. No. 88, 1990
Part III	
s. 16	am. No. 88, 1990; No. 101, 1999
s. 17	am. No. 88, 1990; No 31, 2014
s 18	am. No 31, 2014
s. 19	am. No. 43, 1996

Provision affected	How affected
s. 21A	ad. No. 179, 1991
s. 21B	ad. No. 21, 1992
s. 24	am. No. 146, 1999; No. 5, 2011
Part IV	
Heading to Part IV	rs. No. 101, 1999
s. 25	rs. No. 101, 1999
	am No 62, 2014
s. 25A	ad. No. 101, 1999
	am. No. 8, 2005; No 62, 2014
Note to s. 25A	ad. No. 8, 2005
	am No 62, 2014
s. 25B	ad. No. 101, 1999
s. 6	am. No. 101, 1999
Part V	
s. 27	am. No. 136, 2012
s. 29	am. No. 5, 2001
s. 39	am. No. 5, 2001
s. 41	am. No. 5, 2001
s. 42	rep. No. 5, 2001
ss. 44, 45	rep. No. 137, 2000
s. 46	am. No. 137, 2000; No. 5, 2001
Part VI	
s. 47	am. No. 101, 1999
s. 48	am. No. 88, 1990

Endnote 5—Uncommenced amendments [none]

Endnote 6—Modifications

A.C.T. Self-Government (Consequential Provisions) Regulations (1989 No. 3)

Endnote 7—Misdescribed amendments [none]

Endnote 8—Miscellaneous [none]

THE ARAB REPUBLIC OF EGYPT

MINISTRY OF CULTURE SUPREME
COUNCIL OF ANTIQUITIES

LAW NO. 117 OF 1983

AS AMENDED
BY LAW NO.3 OF 2010

PROMULGATING THE ANTIQUITIES' PROTECTION LAW

(Published in the Official Gazette on February 14, 2010)

INTRODUCTION

The progress of countries is measured by their success in keeping hold of their culture and heritage, and I think Egypt is one of the very few countries in the world maintaining her cultural patrimony. We have been able, through a great effort led by Farouk Hosni, the Minister of Culture, to preserve and offer this heritage to the world as evidence of the magnificence of this great country, on whose land the most important civilization in existence was born. This civilization is in the heart of every human being on earth. The French newspaper, Le Figaro, published an article some time ago commending the quality of restoration and maintenance of Egyptian monuments, as well as new discoveries made by an Egyptian team.

The world is following our efforts in building museums, managing archaeological sites, conducting archaeological awareness programs and repatriating smuggled antiquities.

I think the most important issue for us all is to protect Egypt's cultural heritage, which previously was unsecured and at the mercy of looters and thieves. This spurred the construction of more than 36 warehouses with world-class maintenance, restoration and electronic guarding, and which are equipped with conservation and photography labs that make the objects within them available for scholarly use. Moreover, we started registering this heritage through a national project led by trained, conscientious youths at the Antiquities Registration Center. We created more than 29 units at airports, seaports and border crossings in order to prevent the smuggling of antiquities from within the country after we found that most of the antiquities that leave Egypt are being smuggled through ports near Cairo and Alexandria. We also employed about 8000 new guards and for the first time they are well paid, so they will ensure the protection of Egyptian cultural heritage.

Mr. Farouk Hosni. Minister of Culture, formed a committee in 2003 with top archeologists, legal experts and public figures to change the antiquities law. We have held meetings and discussions for the last 8 years until finally we completed the preparation of this law. It was then sent to the State Council and the Council of Ministers, and then to the People's Assembly, which seek to modify the terms of law and not the law as a whole.

Among the most important of the terms under discussion is the abolishment of the agreement that foreign missions could keep 10% of their discoveries, as well as more extensive efforts to prevent and criminalize trading in antiquities and the need for citizens to register the antiquities they possess within six months of the law's promulgation. We established a new department to address this and to receive registration requests from citizens, in addition to a media campaign to make citizens aware of their responsibility to record and examine what they have. Now, the executive regulation of this law is being prepared, through which the new terms can be implemented at a high level. Some antiquities have also now been copy written for use commercially and only the Supreme Council of

Antiquities is allowed to reproduce antiquities at a 1:1 scale.

I, like many archaeologists, wish that the penalty for theft and smuggling antiquities was more severe because the theft of antiquities is also theft of the honor of Egypt and Egyptian history. Regrettably, the current penalty will not deter the bleeding of antiquities out of this country. In general, however, we have taken a serious step in order to preserve the heritage of Egypt. Here I thank all the members of the People's Assembly from the opposition, independents, and the National Party for their great interest in discussing the antiquities law and for its approval. I hope that all citizens help to maintain this heritage and guide us to any antiquities that are still at large. There will be a remunerative reward for those who preserve the heritage of their country. The memory of the homeland is the right of future generations, and our duty to them is to keep this memory alive and vibrant.

Zahi Hawass

NOTIFICATION

FROM THE LEGAL COUNSELLOR OF THE SUPREME COUNCIL OF ANTIQUITIES

This is to notify that in accordance with the provisions of the Egyptian laws. The attached translation will be a mere guiding translation

Therefore, In case of the occurrence of any difference between the Arabic text and the translated one, reliance will be on the Arabic text.

June 2010 **ACHRAF EI-ACHMAWI**

LAW NO. 117 OF 1983, AS AMENDED BY LAW NO. 3 OF 2010 PROMULGATING THE ANTIQUTTIES' PROTECTION LAW

In the Name of the People

The President of the Republic

After having reviewed the Constitution,

The Civil Code,

The Penal Code,

Law No. 529 for 1953 on Organization of Antiquities' Service, amended by Law No. 192 of 1955 and Law No. 27 of 1970,

Law No. 86 for 1956 concerning mines and quarries,

Law on Customs Promulgated by Law No. 66 of 1963,

Law No. 93 of 1973 concerning the General Budget of the State, Antiquities' Protection Law No. 117 of 1983,

Law No. 10 of 1990 concerning Expropriation of property for the public benefit,

Law of the General Sales Tax Promulgated by Law No. 11 of 1990, Environmental Law No. 4 of 1994,

Law on the Protection of Intellectual Property Rights Promulgated by Law No. 82 of 2002,

Law of the Demolition of Ramshackle Buildings and Facilities and Preservation of Architectural Heritage No. 144 of 2006,

Law of Unified Building No. 119 of 2008,

and Presidential Decree No. 82 of 1994 to establish the Supreme Council of Antiquities,

and after the approval of the Council of Ministers,

and based on the view of the Council of State.

Decreed

The People's Assembly has approved the following Law and we have issued it.

ARTICLE I

Provisions of ARTICLE I, II and III of the promulgation Law and ARTICLES: 1,4,5,6,7,8, 10,16, 17,25,32, paragraph c of ARTICLE 34, and ARTICLES 35, 36, 39,41,42,43,44 and 45 of Antiquities' Protection Law No. 117 of the Year 1983 shall be replaced by the following provisions.

The words "Authority" and "to the Authority" shall be replaced by "the Council" and "to the Council" as well as the term "Head of the Authority" and "Antiquities' Authority" shall be replaced by "Head of the Council" and "Supreme Council of Antiquities" wherever they mentioned in the referred-to antiquities' law.

ARTICLE II

In the application of the provisions of this Law, the capitalized words and terms shall have the following meanings:

- **"Minister"** means competent Minister in culture affairs.

- **"The Council"** means Supreme Council of Antiquities.

- **"Head of the Council"** means Minister of Culture, Chairman of the Supreme Council of Antiquities' Board of Directors.

- **"Board of Directors"** means the Supreme Council of Antiquities' Board of Directors.

- **"Secretary General"** means the secretary general of the Supreme Council of Antiquities.

- **"Competent Permanent Committee"** means, according to the conditions set forth in the law, either the permanent committee concerned with the ancient Egyptian, Greek and Roman Antiquities or the permanent committee concerned with Islamic and Coptic monuments.

- **"Antiquity Sacrum"** means places or lands adjacent to the antiquity determined by the Competent Permanent Committee to ensure protection for the antiquity.

- **"Antiquities Public Utilities Lands"** means the State-owned lands, which are proved to be archaeological lands according to archaeological evidences existing in the same.

- **"Adjacent Places or lands"** means the places or lands lying outside the range of the archaeological sites, places or lands, and it extends to any distance determined by the Council which are considered as such by a decree to be issued by the Supreme Council for Planning and Urban Development whether for inhabited areas or any other areas to ensure protection for the antiquity.

- **"Approved Beautifying Lines of the Antiquity"** means the area surrounding the antiquity and extends to a distance determined by the Council to ensure the aesthetic aspect of the antiquity. Said lands shall be treated as archaeological lands.

ARTICLE III

The Minister is entitled to issue the executive regulation and the necessary decrees to enforce Said Law.

ARTICLE IV

The following shall be added to Antiquities' Protection Law No. 117 of 1983:

-Article 5 bis,

-The sentence: "Without prejudice to the right of the owner of such real antiquity to have a fair compensation" at the beginning of Article 13,

-The sentence: "in accordance with terms and conditions set by Supreme Council for Planning and Urban Development upon recommendation from the Minister" at the beginning of Article 20,

-The sentence: "in accordance with terms and conditions set by Supreme Council for Planning and Urban" at the beginning of Article 22,

-Articles 36 bis, 44 bis, 45 bis and 52.

ARTICLE V

The provisions of Article (9) of Antiquities' Protection Law No. 117 of 1983 shall be deleted.

ARTICLE VI

This Decree shall be published in the official Gazette, and shall enter into force as from the day following the date of publication.

This Law shall be stamped with the State Seal and shall be executed as one of its laws.

Issued at the Presidency of the Republic on February 14, 2010.

President of the Republic
Hosni Mubarak

CHAPTER ONE GENERAL REGULATIONS

ARTICLE 1

In application of the provisions of this Law any real-estate or chattel is considered an antiquity whenever it meets the following conditions:

1. To be the product of Egyptian civilization or the successive civilizations or the creation of art, sciences, literature. or religions that took place on the Egyptian lands since the pre-historic ages and during the successive historic ages till before 100 years.

2. To be of archaeological or artistic value or of historical importance as an aspect of the different aspects of Egyptian civilization or any other civilization that took place on the Egyptian lands.

3. To be produced and grown up on the Egyptian lands and of a historical relation thereto and also the mummies of human races and beings contemporary to them are considered like any antiquity which is being registered in accordance with this Law.

ARTICLE 2

Any real-estate or chattel of a historic, scientific, religious, artistic, or literal value may be considered an antiquity by a decree from the Prime Minister upon recommendation of the competent Minister in cultural affairs, whenever the Stale finds a national interest in keeping and preserving such real-estate or chattel, this without being bound with the time limit specified in the hereinbefore article. Said estate or chattel shall hereby be registered in accordance with the provisions of said law, and in this case the owner of the antiquity shall be deemed liable for the preservation of such and has no right to make any change therein as from the date such owner is notified of said decree by a registered letter attached with a receipt.

ARTICLE 3

Lands owned by the State which were considered archaeological in pursuance to decrees or decisions prior to effecting said law or lands which are considered as such by a decree to be issued by the Prime Minister upon recommendation of the competent Minister in cultural affairs are deemed archaeological lands. By a decree from the Prime Minister upon recommendation of the competent Minister in cultural affairs. any land may be excluded from being one among the archaeological lands or public service facilities, lands set for antiquities on condition that the Council attested that such lands is free from antiquities or lies out of the lands of the beautifying line authorized for the antiquity.

ARTICLE 4

Archaeological Buildings are the buildings which were registered in pursuance to decrees and decisions prior to effecting said law or which are registered as archaeological buildings by a decree in accordance with the provisions of this law. The Council -whenever the State finds such a national interest- may adjust the status of the tenants of historic buildings or archaeological places. The expropriation of which was not determined, and related rent relationships shall be ended within one year as from the date of the procedure of status adjustment by finding suitable alternative places or giving them a fair compensation.

ARTICLE 5

Taking into consideration the provision of ARTICLE 32 of this law, the Council is the exclusive authority concerned with all that is related to antiquities' affairs at its museums and stores. at archaeological sites and areas, over or under earth's surface, at the local waters and the Egyptian regional waters and any antiquity discovered by accident. The Council undertakes exploration and excavation in lands even if owned by others as well as any cultural, tourist, commercial or promotional activities relating to antiquities to be exercised at the archaeological sites or inside the antiquity sacrum. The executive regulation of this Law regulates the exercise of these activities realizing rehabilitation and security of the archaeological site.

ARTICLE 5 bis

The SCA has the right to terminate any contractual relationship of any occupancy, whether residential, commercial. industrial or any other occupancy at archaeological sites and areas, whoever the relationship parties are, against a fair compensation.

Presence of any type of street vendors or any type of animals in the archaeological sites is prohibited except in places and in accordance with terms and conditions stipulated in the executive regulation of this law.

ARTICLE 6

All real-estate and movable antiquities and lands which are considered archaeological lands are considered public property except the wakfs and private properties. The ownership, possession or disposal of is not permitted except in the terms and conditions stipulated in said law and its executive regulation.

ARTICLE 7

Two permanent committees are set up in the SCA, one of which is concerned with the ancient Egyptian, Greek and Roman Antiquities and the other is concerned with Islamic, Coptic and Jewish monuments. The executive regulation shall specify the formation and competences of each committee.

ARTICLE 8

Trade, sale or commerce in antiquities including all antiquities held as private property shall be prohibited in accordance with the provisions of this law or legal existing possession at the time of implementation of said law or such which originates in accordance with its provisions. The owner or the possessor of any antiquity may not dispose of, allow deterioration of or leave such except after getting a written consent from the Council within 60 (sixty) days at least in accordance with the procedures, terms and conditions, of which a resolution from the Minister is issued, otherwise such act shall be illegal.

In all cases it is provided that such trade, sale, commerce in, or disposal of any antiquity shall transferring said antiquity outside the country by any means.

The Council in all cases has the priority of having the antiquity from its owner or possessor in return for a fair compensation.

Any one owns any archaeological object in accordance with the provisions of this Law must notify the Council of such object within six months starting from the beginning of March 2010 provided that such persons are required to preserve such objects until the Council registers it.

Moreover, the Council may restitute, from its owners or possessors, antiquities taken of architectural elements whenever the Board of Directors finds a national interest and upon recommendation from the competent Permanent Committee which possessors have in return for a valuable consideration.

ARTICLE 10

By a Presidential resolution some antiquities- except the unique ones and that determined by the competent committees- may be exhibited abroad for a specific period and some of the duplicate movable antiquities may be exchanged with states. museums or educational institutes whether Arab or foreign After taking necessary procedures to secure them adequately.

ARTICLE 11

The SCA is entitled to accept cession of corporations or individuals for their ownership of historic real-estate through donation or sale for a symbolic price or through laying such under the Council's disposal for no less than 50 (fifty) years, whenever the State finds such a national interest.

ARTICLE 12

Any antiquity is registered due to a ministerial resolution from the competent Minister in culture affairs upon recommendations of the Board of Directors. The Decree issued for the registration of the real-estate antiquity is announced to its owner or the person in charge through administrative means and is published in the Egyptian Official Gazette. and is marked as such on the margin of the real-estate register at the Real -Estate Publicity Administration.

ARTICLE 13

Without prejudice to the right of the owner of such real antiquity to have a fair compensation, registration of the such real antiquity and notifying the owner of such in accordance with the provisions of Article 11 of this law shall result in the hereinafter provisions:

1. Pulling down all or part of the real-estate or taking part of the same outside the Arab Republic of Egypt is not permitted.

2. Expropriation of land or real-estate for the interest of any other party is not permitted, while such expropriation is permitted with regards to adjacent lands after the approval of the competent Minister in cultural affairs upon recommendations of the SCA Board of Directors.

3. Any easement of title for a third party on the real estate is thereupon not permitted.

4. Renovation of the real-estate or changing its characteristics by any means is not permitted except with a license from the Head of Council after the approval of the Competent Permanent Committee and the execution of the work he licensed be under the direct supervision of the Council representative. If the party concerned executed any work without the referred-to license. the Council undertakes returning the case to its previous state on the expense of the transgressor without prejudice to the right of having compensation and without prejudice to the penalties stipulated in this law.

5. The owner is obliged to have a written consent from the Council as to every disposal that may occur to the real-estate together with mentioning the name of the person disposed to and his place of residence. On disposal of such, the owner must notify the party disposed to that the said real-estate is registered. The Council must thereto declare its opinion within a period of 30 (thirty) days as of date of notifying the Council with the application for disposal and expiration of this time without reply from the Council is deemed a refusal from SCA.

6. The Council is entitled, at any time, to carry out on its expense whatever it deems necessary for the conservation of the antiquity.

The provisions of this Article shall remain applicable even if what in the real-estate of antiquity became movable.

ARTICLE 14

By a decree from the competent Minister in Culture affairs upon recommendation of the Council's Board of Directors and after consulting the Competent Permanent Committee registration of the immovable antiquity or part of it may be cancelled, and the decree of cancellation shall hereupon be published in the Egyptian Official Gazette, and shall be informed to individuals and bodies that notified before of its registration. The same shall be recorded on the margin of the antiquity's register at the Council and on the margin of the real-estate register at Real-Estate Publicity Administration.

ARTICLE 15

Any existing exploitation by individuals or corporations to any archaeological site shall not result in any statue of ownership by prescription, and the Council is entitled to evacuate the same whenever it deemed such evacuation necessary against a valuable consideration.

ARTICLE 16

Upon recommendation of the competent Minister in cultural affairs and against a fair compensation, Supreme Council for Planning and Urban Development is entitled to arrange easement on real-estates adjacent to the archaeological sites and historic buildings within the Antiquity Sacrum to ensure the conservation of the aesthetic characteristics or the general appearance of said estate. The resolution issued thereto identifies the real-estate properties or parts of such resulting in one or more easements and scope of such right and constraints which consequently originate on the right of the owner or the possessor.

ARTICLE 17

Without prejudice to penalties stipulated in present law or other laws, Head of the Council or the Secretary General- exclusively- after approval of the competent Permanent Committee is entitled to remove any infringement on any archaeological site or real-estate through the administrative means, provided that notifying the Governorate of such resolution. The competent local authorities undertake executing the resolutions of violations removal in police custody in a period not exceeding 10 (ten) days, otherwise the Council shall execute the resolution through its own authorities or other bodies upon the Council's request in police custody on the transgressor's expenses.

ARTICLE 18

Lands owned by individuals may be expropriated for their archaeological importance. It also may. By a resolution from the President of the Republic, temporarily seized until procedures of expropriation are completed. Such land shall thereby be considered in the governance of antiquity as of the date of the provisional seizure, and all this against fair compensation. The possibility of the presence of antiquity in the expropriated land is not observed in the compensation.

ARTICLE 19

Upon a request of the Board of Directors, the competent Minister in cultural affairs may issue a resolution to determine the beautifying lines of public antiquities and archeological sites. Lands lying within said lines shall be considered archaeological lands and provisions of present law shall be applicable thereupon.

ARTICLE 20

In accordance with special conditions set by Supreme Council for Planning and Urban Development upon recommendation from the Minister, granting buildings licenses at archaeological sites or lands shall not be permitted.

Other parties shall be prohibited from establishing foundations or cemeteries or digging canals or constructing roads or cultivating in the same or in the public-service facilities set for antiquities or lands lying within the approved beautifying lines. Implanting trees or the cutting of such or carrying rubble or taking soil or fertilizers or sand or the execution of any other work which result in changing the characteristics of said sites and Lands shall be prohibited except with a license from the Council and under its supervision.

Provision of the previous paragraph shall be applicable on adjacent lands lying outside the scope of the sites referred to in the previous paragraph which extend to 3 (three) kilometers distance in uninhabited places or to the distance the Council determines in a way that realizes protecting the environment of the antiquity at other sites.

By a resolution of the competent Minister in culture affairs, provisions of present article may be applicable on lands of which the Council becomes evident, on the basis of studies it undertakes, of the possibility of the presence of antiquities in such. Provisions of this article shall thereto be applicable on the desert areas and places where operation of store quarries is licensed.

ARTICLE 21

Archaeological sites and lands, and buildings and places of historical importance must be observed when the lying out of cities, districts and villages where the same are found is being changed. Implementation of modernized planning or expansion or amendment in archaeological and historical areas and what belongs to it shall not be permitted except after the approval of the Council in writing with deference to easement of title arranged by the Council.

The Council must declare its opinion concerning the planning within a period of 3(three) months as of date of submission. In case the Council does not declare its opinion within said period, the matter may be submitted to the competent Minister in culture affairs to issue a resolution thereto.

ARTICLE 22

Building in places adjacent to archaeological sites inside the inhabited area shall not be licensed except in accordance with special terms set by Supreme Council for Planning and Urban Development to the competent organ after taking the Council's approval. The competent organ must include in the license provisions which the Council sees guaranteeing the establishment of the building is in a proper way that does not predominate over the antiquity or spoil its appearance and ensure for such a suitable sanctum together with taking appropriate of the archaeological and historical environment and specifications guaranteeing protection of stated antiquity. The Council must declare its opinion in the application within a period of 60 (sixty) days as of date of submission of such otherwise the lapse of the period referred to is considered a refusal.

ARTICLE 23

Any individual who finds an unregistered real-estate antiquity must notify the Supreme Council of Antiquities of such. This antiquity is considered the ownership of the State and the Council must undertake the necessary procedures to take care of such antiquity. Within a period of 3 (three) months, the Council is entitled either to take stated immovable present in the property of individuals or undertake procedures of expropriation of the land wherein the same was found or to leave said antiquity at its place together with registering it in accordance with provisions of present law. In estimating the value of the expropriated land, the value of antiquities found at said land is not observed. The Council may grant whoever guided to the antiquity a recompense which is determined by the Competent Permanent Committee.

ARTICLE 24

Whoever accidentally finds a movable antiquity or part or parts of an immovable monument, must give notice of such to the nearest administrative power within 48 (forty-eight) hours as of time of finding the same. Moreover, he must take good care of such antiquity till handing it over to the competent authority otherwise he is considered possessor of antiquity without license, and the authority referred to must immediately notify the Council of such.

The antiquity becomes the property of the State and the Council is thereby entitled to grant whoever found the antiquity and notified of such a recompense which is determined by the Competent Permanent Committee.

ARTICLE 25

A committee formed by a decree from the Minister, wherein the Board of Directors is represented, undertakes estimating the compensation stipulated in ARTICLE 4, 5 bis,8,13,15,16 and 18 of present law.

State Treasury shall pay referred to compensations, and those concerned may raise a complaint to the competent Minister in cultural affairs from the committee's estimation within a period of 60 (sixty) days as of date of notifying them of the compensation estimated by the committee by a registered letter with a receipt otherwise the estimation is considered final

In all cases the action for compensation falls if such is not raised within a three years period as of date of its becoming a final estimation.

CHAPTER TWO REGISTRATION, PRESERVATION AND DISCOVERY OF ANTIQUITIES

ARTICLE 26

The Council undertakes enumerating, photographing, drawing and registering immovable and movable antiquities together with gathering information pertaining to said antiquities in registers prepared for such uses. Registration is effected in accordance with terms and conditions of which a decree by the Board of Directors is issued. The registered antiquities are those registered at the date of effecting present law at the registers set for it.

The Council aims at generalizing archaeological survey for archaeological sites and lands and defining places and characteristics of the said and recording them on maps together with sending photocopies of such to both the competent local department and the General Authority for Urban Planning for the observance of such at the preparation of the general planning.

The Council shall prepare a register for environmental and urban data and factors affecting every archaeological site according to its importance.

ARTICLE 27

The Council undertakes preparing the registered archaeological places and sites and historical buildings for visit or study in a way that is not incompatible with their security and preservation. The Council also aims at revealing the aesthetic and historic characteristics and distinguishing features of the same.

The Council thereto employs the capabilities of archaeological sites and museums in developing archaeological awareness by all means.

ARTICLE 28

Movable antiquities shall be kept together with what entails its transference for objective considerations of architectural antiquities and all shall be put at the Council's museums and stores. The Council undertakes organizing the exhibition therein and in its departments with scientific methods, together with preserving its contents and holding temporary internal exhibitions that are affiliated with such.

The Council is entitled to entrust the Egyptian universities with organizing and managing museums therein located or at its faculties together with ensuring the registration and security of such.

In all these cases, antiquities' museums and stores are considered among the public property of the State.

ARTICLE 29

The Council is charged with taking care of antiquities, museums, stores, and archaeological sites and areas and historical buildings besides the guarding of such through the competent police, and special watchmen and guards commissioned by the stated Council in accordance with the rules regulating such. The Council shall put a maximum limit for the extension of every inspection of antiquities in a way guaranteeing the case of movement of such inspection in their area and enabling it to supervise its antiquities.

By a decree from the Board of Directors, the border of every archaeological site guarded by the Council shall he defined. Said may include, after consulting Ministry of Tourism, imposing admission fees to said sites provided that it does not exceed 5 (five) Egyptian pounds for Egyptians or 100 (one hundred) Egyptian pounds or what equals it of free currency in respect to foreigners. Stated fee does not detriment any that are imposed as stipulated in ARTICLE 39 of this Law.

ARTICLE 30

The Council and no other shall be concerned with the execution of maintenance and restoration work necessary for all registered antiquities and archaeological sites and areas and historical buildings.

Ministry of Religious Endowment "the Wakf Ministry", Egyptian Wakf Authority and Christian Wakf Authority shall bear expenses of restoration and conservation of archaeological and historical real-estate affiliated with and registered to such Ministry and authorities.

The Council shall bear the expenses of restoring registered historical buildings in the possession of individuals and other authorities unless the reason for restoration originating from the bad use of the possessor according to what the Competent Permanent Committee decides and in this case the possessors shall bear the expenses of restoration.

After the approval of the Competent Permanent Committee, Chairman of Council's Board of Directors may license competent authorities and scientific missions to undertake operations of restoration and conservation under the Council's supervision. Also specialized individuals may be given the license in writing to undertake such operations.

ARTICLE 31

The Council shall arrange priorities of permission for missions and authorities to excavate antiquities starting with places that are more subject to the environmental dangers and more affected by the State's projects of urban extension in accordance with an objective timetable that is decided by the Board of Directors.

ARTICLE 32

The Council undertakes discovery of antiquities located over earth surface and excavations for antiquities underground and in the local and territorial waters. According to terms and conditions stipulated in the executive regulation of this Law and after the approval of the Competent Permanent Committee, the Board of Directors may license any specialized scientific institutions and universities, whether national or foreign, to excavate and search for antiquities in specified sites and for limited period of time due to a special license, which can not be assigned to any other party. Such license is granted only after verification of the availability of sufficient scientific, technical, financial and archaeological practical experience of the institution or the university demanding this license.

The above-mentioned provision is applicable even if the search and exploration were in a non-archaeological land.

The licensee are licensed to study, draw, photograph antiquities discovered by the same within the license period, and the right in the scientific publication about its excavations is preserved for five years as of date of its first discovery at the site.

ARTICLE 33

The Council's Board of Directors shall issue a decree with the terms and conditions which must be observed and executed at the excavation licenses so that the license includes an illustration of the boundaries of the area the search takes place, the time licensed, the minimum rate for working in such, and the insurances that must be deposited to the Council and terms for the execution of excavation together with the confinement to a special area until work in such area is completed, and the obligation to successive registration and undertaking guard and conservation of such and provide the Council with a complete registration and a comprehensive scientific report about the work to be licensed.

ARTICLE 34

License for foreign missions to search and excavate antiquities shall be subject to the following rules:

a) Each mission is obliged to restore and preserve whatever it undertakes discovering of architectural and movable antiquities, one after the other and before the end of its working season, this under the supervision of the competent organs at the Council and with their cooperation.

b) The association of the plan of every foreign mission for archaeological excavation work in Egypt with a complementary one wherein the mission undertakes any restoration work to present antiquities which were previously discovered, or whatever suits its capabilities of archaeological survey, enumeration, and registration of areas wherein it works or those nearby. This is executed with the approval of the Council or in cooperation with it.

c) The Competent Permanent Committee is entitled to estimate the work of any licensed authority.

ARTICLE 35

All discovered antiquities found by any of the foreign or Egyptian scientific excavation mission are the property of the State.

ARTICLE 36

All rights of intellectual property and trademark and the exploitation of such for the Council's benefit provided by Act No. 82 of 2002 are applicable to archaeological replica produced by the Council and photos of archaeological objects and sites owned by the Council. Rules set forth in this regard are stipulated by the executive regulation of the present law.

ARTICLE 36 bis

For achievement of its objectives, the Council is entitled to establish production units of a special nature. Rules for establishment and work system of such production unites are stipulated by the executive regulation of the present law.

ARTICLE 37

By a decree from the Council's Board of Directors, working licenses granted to any authority or mission for work in excavations may be terminated for transgressions made during their work without prejudice to penalties stipulated for the appropriation of antiquities without a right, or the smuggling of such. The Council may prevent any archeological mission or any foreign antiquities museum from practicing archaeological excavations at the Arab Republic of Egypt for a period not less that 5 (five) years if participation or assistance of any of its members in committing any crime of those referred to in this law was proved.

ARTICLE 38

The Supreme Council of Antiquities and missions of Egyptian Universities shall be exempted from custom duties on instruments, equipments and sets imported from abroad for work of excavations, restoration of archaeological and historical buildings and preparation of museums, antiquities centers affiliated with the same and artistic and archaeological exhibitions. The Customs Administration shall thereto release on provisional bases instruments and sets imported to the country by foreign missions for excavations, restoration and natural studies pertaining to antiquities for using the same in their set uses. These missions shall be completely exempted from custom duties in case they dispose of or transfer these instruments or sets to the Council or to archaeological missions at Egyptian Universities. The mission shall bear the value of stipulated customs duties if it disposed of said instruments or sets after the termination of its work to other than these organs.

ARTICLE 39

By a resolution from the Minster after the approval of the Council's Board of Directors, admission fees shall be defined for visiting museums and archaeological sites for Egyptians and foreigners. Said fees shall not exceed 1000 Egyptian Pounds for Egyptians and 5000 Egyptian pounds or what equals it of free currency in respect to foreigners.

CHAPTER THREE PENALTIES

ARTICLE 40

Without prejudice to any severer penalty stipulated by the penal law or any other law punishing, for the violation of the provisions of present law, by the penalties stated in the hereinafter articles.

ARTICLE 41

Whoever smuggles an antiquity outside the republic of Egypt, together with his knowledge of such act shall be punished by intensive imprisonment and by a mulct not less than 100,000 (one hundred thousand) Egyptian Pounds and not more than one million Egyptian Pounds. In this case the antiquity, object of the crime, shall be confiscated together with sets, instruments, machinery, and cars used in said crime for the benefit of the Council.

ARTICLE 42

Whoever steals an antiquity or part of such, whether this antiquity is a registered antiquity owned by the State, under registration or discovered through archaeological excavations of the Council or licensed missions, bodies or universities work for the purpose of smuggling such shall be punished by imprisonment and by a mulct not less than 50,000 (fifty thousand) Egyptian Pounds and not than 500,000 (five hundred thousand) Egyptian Pounds. Whoever hide an antiquity or part of such for the purpose of smuggling it shall be punished by imprisonment for not less than 7 (seven) years. In all cases the antiquity, object of the crime, shall be confiscated together with sets, instruments, machinery, and cars used in said crime for the benefit of the Council.

The following shall be punished by imprisonment for not less than one year and not more than 7 (seven) years and by a mulct not less than 50,000 (fifty thousand) Egyptian Pounds and not more than 100,000(one hundred thousand) Egyptian Pounds:

1. Whoever intentionally pulls down or damages or spoils or changes the distinguishing features of a movable or immovable antiquity or intentionally separates part of the same.

2. Whoever executes archaeological excavation for the purpose of finding antiquities without license.

Penalty in the above-mentioned cases shall be by imprisonment and by a mulct not less than 100,000 (one hundred thousand) Egyptian Pounds and not more than 250,000 (two hundred fifty thousand) Egyptian Pounds if the doer is one of those working in the Supreme Council of Antiquities or officials or workers of excavation missions or of the contractors having a contract with the Council or their workers.

ARTICLE 42 bis

Whoever steals an antiquity or part of such that is owned by the State shall be punished by imprisonment for a period not exceeding 7 (seven) years and by a mulct not less than 50,000 (fifty thousand) Egyptian Pounds and not more than 250,000 (two hundred and fifty thousand) Egyptian Pounds. Except for the mulct penalty, whoever hide an antiquity or part of such if obtained from any crime shall be punished by imprisonment for a period not exceeding 5 (five) years. In all cases the antiquity, object of the crime, shall be confiscated together with sets, instruments, machinery and cars used in said crime for the benefit of the Council.

ARTICLE 43

The following shall be punished by imprisonment for a period not less that one year and not more than 5 (five) years and by a mulct not less than 10,000(ten thousand) Egyptian Pounds and not more than 100,000(one hundred thousand) Egyptian Pounds:

1. Whoever transfers, without a written permission from the Council, an antiquity owned by the State or a registered antiquity or intentionally tears the same off its place.

2. Whoever transfers archaeological buildings or lands or parts of such to a residence or yard or store or factory or cultivates the same or prepares it for cultivation or implants trees therein or makes a barn or digs drainage or irrigation canals or sets in the same by any other such work or infringes upon the same by any other means without license in accordance of the provisions of this law.

3. Whoever counterfeits one of the ancient antiquities with the aim of deception or fraud.

ARTICLE 44

Whoever violates provisions of ARTICLES 6, 8, 13, 17 and 20 of this law shall be punished by penalties stated in ARTICLE 43 of this law. In all cases the antiquity, object of the crime, shall be confiscated together with sets, instruments, machinery, and cars used in said crime for the benefit of the Council.

ARTICLE 44 bis

Whoever violates provisions of ARTICLE 5 bis,24 and 36 of this law shall he punished by imprisonment for a period not more than one year and by a mulct not less than 5,000 (five thousand) Egyptian Pounds and not more than 20,000 (twenty thousand) Egyptian Pounds or one of either above-mentioned penalties. In all cases the antiquity, object of the crime, shall be confiscated together with sets, instruments, machinery, and cars used in said crime for the benefit of the Council.

ARTICLE 45

The following shall be punished by imprisonment for a period not more than one year and by a mulct not less than 1,000 (one thousand) Egyptian Pounds and not more than 50,000 (fifty thousand) Egyptian Pounds or one of either above-mentioned penalties:

1. Whoever puts advertisements or propaganda posters on the antiquities.

2. Whoever writes or inscribes on the antiquity or puts paints on such.

3. Whoever spoils or damages an immovable or a movable antiquity or separates part of such.

4. Whoever appropriates rubble or fertilizers or soil or sand or other materials from an archaeological site or land without license from the Council or exceeds terms in the license granted to him in quarries or brings to the site or archaeological place fertilizers or soil or waste or other materials.

In all cases the guilty is obliged to pay a compensation for the damages originating from the violation.

ARTICLE 45 bis

Whoever notified the competent authorities or investigation bodies of his crime before proceeding to investigate shall be exempted from the penalty stated in ARTCLES 41 and 42 of this law. The court may exempt the guilty from the penalty if the said admitted his guilty of the crime that leads to confiscation of the antiquities, subject of the crime, or helps to repatriate such antiquity whether locally or abroad.

ARTICLE 46

Whoever violates provisions of ARTICLE 18,19 and 20 of this law from those working in the State shall be punished by imprisonment for a period not less than two years and by a mulct not less than 100 (one hundred) Egyptian Pounds and not more than 500 (five hundreds) Egyptian Pounds together with obliging him to pay a compensation for the damages originating from the violation.

ARTICLE 47

In case of violation of ARTICLES 7, 21 and 22, the antiquities shall be confiscated for the benefit of the Supreme Council of Antiquities.

CHAPTER FOUR FINAL REGULATIONS

ARTICLE 48

Head of the Council's Board of Directors, antiquities directors, museums directors, assistant curators, superintendents, directors of archeological areas, antiquities inspectors and assistant inspectors are entitled to enjoy the quality of judicial arrests with regards to impounding crimes and violations stipulated in this law and decrees issued in implementation of said law.

ARTICLE 49

Mulcts stipulated in accordance with provisions of present law and fees prescribed in ARTICLES 29 and 39 of this law shall go to the fund financing antiquities and museums projects at the Council. The Council may grant recompenses from revenues of these sums, which the Head of the Board of Directors decides to whoever participates in guiding or impounding violations, this is in pursuance to terms and conditions of which a decree from the Council's Board of Directors is issued.

ARTICLE 50

All sums payable to the Council in the application of present law may be collected through administrative confiscation.

ARTICLE 51

The Council undertakes coordinating work among authorities and bodies concerned with planning, housing, tourism, public utilities, security and councils of governorates in a way guaranteeing the protection of antiquities, museums, and historical buildings from shakes, shocks and reasons for leak and pollution, industrial danger and its historical and archaeological environment in a way realizing the balance between urban needs and the necessity of preserving antiquities and heritage.

ARTICLE 52

The Council is the authority entitled to form technical and archaeological committees which shall examine the archaeological objects, subject of the crimes. Said committees shall prepare technical and archaeological reports on the results of such examination and shall submit the same to the courts and investigation bodies. Procedures to form said committees are regulated by the executive regulation of the present law.

JAPAN

文化財保護法[①]

昭和 25 年 5 月 30 日法律第 214 号
昭和 26 年 12 月 24 日法律第 318 号〔第一次改正〕
昭和 27 年 7 月 31 日号外法律第 272 号〔第二次改正〕
昭和 28 年 8 月 10 日法律第 194 号〔改正〕
昭和 28 年 8 月 15 日法律第 213 号〔改正〕
昭和 29 年 5 月 29 日法律第 131 号〔第三次改正〕
昭和 31 年 6 月 12 日法律第 148 号〔改正〕
昭和 31 年 6 月 30 日法律第 163 号〔改正〕
昭和 33 年 4 月 25 日号外法律第 86 号〔改正〕
昭和 34 年 4 月 20 日号外法律第 148 号〔改正〕
昭和 36 年 6 月 2 日法律第 111 号〔改正〕
昭和 37 年 5 月 16 日法律第 140 号〔改正〕
昭和 37 年 9 月 15 日号外法律第 161 号〔改正〕
昭和 40 年 3 月 31 日号外法律第 36 号〔改正〕
昭和 43 年 6 月 15 日号外法律第 99 号〔改正〕
昭和 46 年 5 月 31 日法律第 88 号〔改正〕
昭和 46 年 6 月 1 日号外法律第 96 号〔改正〕
昭和 47 年 6 月 3 日法律第 53 号〔改正〕
昭和 50 年 7 月 1 日法律第 49 号〔第四次改正〕
昭和 58 年 12 月 2 日号外法律第 78 号〔改正〕
平成 5 年 11 月 12 日号外法律第 89 号〔改正〕
平成 6 年 6 月 29 日号外法律第 49 号〔改正〕

① 本版本为日本《文化财保护法》2014 年版本。2018 年的最新修改部分详见本书第 251 页。

平成6年11月11日号外法律第97号〔改正〕
平成8年6月12日号外法律第66号〔第五次改正〕
平成11年7月16日号外法律第87号〔改正〕
平成11年7月16日号外法律第102号〔改正〕
平成11年12月22日号外法律第160号〔改正〕
平成11年12月22日号外法律第178号〔改正〕
平成11年12月22日号外法律第179号〔改正〕
平成12年5月19日号外法律第73号〔改正〕
平成14年2月8日号外法律第1号〔改正〕
平成14年7月3日号外法律第82号〔第六次改正〕
平成16年5月28日号外法律第61号〔第七次改正〕
平成16年6月9日号外法律第84号〔改正〕
平成18年5月31日号外法律第46号〔改正〕
平成18年6月15日号外法律第73号〔改正〕
平成19年3月31日号外法律第7号〔改正〕
平成23年5月2日号外法律第37号〔改正〕
平成26年6月4日号外法律第51号〔改正〕
平成26年6月13日号外法律第69号〔改正〕
平成30年6月8日号外法律第42号〔改正〕

目　次

第一章　総則

（この法律の目的）

第一条　この法律は、文化財を保存し、且つ、その活用を図り、もつて国民の文化的向上に資するとともに、世界文化の進歩に貢献することを目的とする。

（文化財の定義）

第二条　この法律で「文化財」とは、次に掲げるものをいう。

一　建造物、絵画、彫刻、工芸品、書跡、典籍、古文書その他の有形の文化的所産で我が国にとつて歴史上又は芸術上価値の高いもの（これらのものと一体をなしてその価値を形成している土地その他の物件を含む。）並びに考古資料及びその他の学術上価値の高い歴史資料（以下「有形文化財」という。）

二　演劇、音楽、工芸技術その他の無形の文化的所産で我が国にとつて歴史上又は芸術上価値の高いもの（以下「無形文化財」という。）

三　衣食住、生業、信仰、年中行事等に関する風俗慣習、民俗芸能、民俗技術及びこれらに用いられる衣服、器具、家屋その他の物件で我が国民の生活の推移の理解のため欠くことのできないもの（以下「民俗文化財」という。）

四　貝づか、古墳、都城跡、城跡、旧宅その他の遺跡で我が国にとつて歴史上又は学術上価値の高いもの、庭園、橋梁（りよう）、峡谷、海浜、山岳その他の名勝地で我が国にとつて芸術上又は観賞上価値の高いもの並びに動物（生息地、繁殖地及び渡来地を含む。）、植物（自生地を含む。）及び地質鉱物（特異な自然の現象の生じている土地を含む。）で我が国にとつて学術上価値の高いもの（以下「記念物」という。）

五　地域における人々の生活又は生業及び当該地域の風土により形成された景観地で我が国民の生活又は生業の理解のため欠くことのできないもの（以下「文化的景観」という。）

六　周囲の環境と一体をなして歴史的風致を形成している伝統的な建造物群で価値の高いもの（以下「伝統的建造物群」という。）

2　この法律の規定（第二十七条から第二十九条まで、第三十七条、第五十五条第一項第四号、第百五十三条第一項第一号、第百六十五条、第百七十一条及び附則第三条の規定を除く。）中「重要文化財」には、国宝を含むものとする。

3　この法律の規定（第百九条、第百十条、第百十二条、第百二十二条、第百三十一条第一項第四号、第百五十三条第一項第七号及び第八号、第百六十五条並びに第百七十一条の規定を除く。）中「史跡名勝天然記念物」には、特別史跡名勝天然記念物を含むものとする。

（政府及び地方公共団体の任務）

第三条　政府及び地方公共団体は、文化財がわが国の歴史、文化等の正しい理解のため欠くことのできないものであり、且つ、将来の文化の向上発展の基礎をなすものであることを認識し、その保存が適切に行われるように、周到の注意をもつてこの法律の趣旨の徹底に努めなければならない。

（国民、所有者等の心構）

第四条　一般国民は、政府及び地方公共団体がこの法律の目的を達成するために行う措置に誠実に協力しなければならない。

2　文化財の所有者その他の関係者は、文化財が貴重な国民的財産であることを自覚し、これを公共のために大切に保存するとともに、できるだけこれを公開する等その文化的活用に努めなければならない。

3　政府及び地方公共団体は、この法律の執行に当つて関係者の所有権その他の財産権を尊重しなければならない。

第二章　削除（第五条から第二十六条まで）削除

第三章　有形文化財

第一節　重要文化財

第一款　指定

（指定）

第二十七条　文部科学大臣は、有形文化財のうち重要なものを重要文化財に指定することができる。

2　文部科学大臣は、重要文化財のうち世界文化の見地から価値の高いもので、たぐいない国民の宝たるものを国宝に指定することができる。

（告示、通知及び指定書の交付）

第二十八条　前条の規定による指定は、その旨を官報で告示するとともに、当該国宝又は重要文化財の所有者に通知してする。

2　前条の規定による指定は、前項の規定による官報の告示があつた日からその効力を生ずる。但し、当該国宝又は重要文化財の所有者に対しては、同項の規定による通知が当該所有者に到達した時からその効力を生ずる。

3　前条の規定による指定をしたときは、文部科学大臣は、当該国宝又は重要文化財の所有者に指定書を交付しなければならない。

4　指定書に記載すべき事項その他指定書に関し必要な事項は、文部科学省令で定める。

5　第三項の規定により国宝の指定書の交付を受けたときは、所有者は、三十日以内に国宝に指定された重要文化財の指定書を文部科学大臣に返付しなければならない。

（解除）

第二十九条　国宝又は重要文化財が国宝又は重要文化財としての価値を失つた場合その他特殊の事由があるときは、文部科学大臣は、国宝又は重要文化財の指定を解除することができる。

2　前項の規定による指定の解除は、その旨を官報で告示するとともに、当該国宝又は重要文化財の所有者に通知してする。

3　第一項の規定による指定の解除には、前条第二項の規定を準用する。

4　第二項の通知を受けたときは、所有者は、三十日以内に指定書を文部科学大臣に返付しなければならない。

5　第一項の規定により国宝の指定を解除した場合において当該有形文化財につき重要文化財の指定を解除しないときは、文部科学大臣は、直ちに重要文化財の指定書を所有者に交付しなければならない。

第二款　管理

（管理方法の指示）

第三十条　文化庁長官は、重要文化財の所有者に対し、重要文化財の管理に関し必要な指示をすることができる。

（所有者の管理義務及び管理責任者）

第三十一条　重要文化財の所有者は、この法律並びにこれに基いて発する文部科学省令及び文化庁長官の指示に従い、重要文化財を管理しなければならない。

2　重要文化財の所有者は、特別の事情があるときは、適当な者をもつぱら自己に代り当該重要文化財の管理の責に任ずべき者（以下この節及び第十二章において「管理責任者」という。）に選任することができる。

3　前項の規定により管理責任者を選任したときは、重要文化財の所有者は、文部科学省令の定める事項を記載した書面をもつて、当該管理責任者と連署の上二十日以内に文化庁長官に届け出なければならない。管理責任者を解任した場合も同様とする。

4　管理責任者には、前条及び第一項の規定を準用する。

（所有者又は管理責任者の変更）

第三十二条　重要文化財の所有者が変更したときは、新所有者は、文部科学省令の定める事項を記載した書面をもつて、且つ、旧所有者に対し交付された指定書を添えて、二十日以内に文化庁長官に届け出なければならない。

2　重要文化財の所有者は、管理責任者を変更したときは、文部科学省令の定める事項を記載した書面をもつて、新管理責任者と連署の上二十日以内に文化庁長官に届け出なければならない。この場合には、前条第三項の規定は、適用しない。

3　重要文化財の所有者又は管理責任者は、その氏名若しくは名称又は住所を変更したときは、文部科学省令の定める事項を記載した書面をもつて、二十日以内に文化庁長官に届け出なければならない。氏名若しくは名称又は住所の変更が重要文化財の所有者に係るときは、届出の際指定書を添えなければならない。

（管理団体による管理）

第三十二条の二　重要文化財につき、所有者が判明しない場合又は所有者若しくは管理責任者による管理が著しく困難若しくは不適当であると明らかに認められる場合には、文化庁長官は、適当な地方公共団体その他の法人を指定して、当該重要文化財の保存のため必要な管理（当該重要文化財の保存のため必要な施設、設備その他の物件で当該重要文化財の所有者の所有又は管理に属するものの管理を含む。）を行わせることができる。

2　前項の規定による指定をするには、文化庁長官は、あらかじめ、当該重要文化財の所有者（所有者が判明しない場合を除く。）及び権原に基く占有者並びに指定しようとする地方公共団体その他の法人の同意を得なければならない。

3　第一項の規定による指定は、その旨を官報で告示するとともに、前項に規定する所有者、占有者及び地方公共団体その他の法人に通知してする。

4　第一項の規定による指定には、第二十八条第二項の規定を準用する。

5　重要文化財の所有者又は占有者は、正当な理由がなくて、第一項の規定による指定を受けた地方公共団体その他の法人（以下この節及び第十二章において「管理団体」という。）が行う管理又はその管理のため必要な措置を拒み、妨げ、又は忌避してはならない。

6　管理団体には、第三十条及び第三十一条第一項の規定を準用する。

第三十二条の三　前条第一項に規定する事由が消滅した場合その他特殊の事由があるときは、文化庁長官は、管理団体の指定を解除することができる。

２　前項の規定による解除には、前条第三項及び第二十八条第二項の規定を準用する。

第三十二条の四　管理団体が行う管理に要する費用は、この法律に特別の定のある場合を除いて、管理団体の負担とする。

２　前項の規定は、管理団体と所有者との協議により、管理団体が行う管理により所有者の受ける利益の限度において、管理に要する費用の一部を所有者の負担とすることを妨げるものではない。

（滅失、き損等）

第三十三条　重要文化財の全部又は一部が滅失し、若しくはき損し、又はこれを亡失し、若しくは盗み取られたときは、所有者（管理責任者又は管理団体がある場合は、その者）は、文部科学省令の定める事項を記載した書面をもつて、その事実を知つた日から十日以内に文化庁長官に届け出なければならない。

（所在の変更）

第三十四条　重要文化財の所在の場所を変更しようとするときは、重要文化財の所有者（管理責任者又は管理団体がある場合は、その者）は、文部科学省令の定める事項を記載した書面をもつて、且つ、指定書を添えて、所在の場所を変更しようとする日の二十日前までに文化庁長官に届け出なければならない。但し、文部科学省令の定める場合には、届出を要せず、若しくは届出の際指定書の添附を要せず、又は文部科学省令の定めるところにより所在の場所を変更した後届け出ることをもつて足りる。

第三款　保護

（修理）

第三十四条の二　重要文化財の修理は、所有者が行うものとする。但し、管理団体がある場合は、管理団体が行うものとする。

（管理団体による修理）

第三十四条の三　管理団体が修理を行う場合は、管理団体は、あらかじめ、その修理の方法及び時期について当該重要文化財の所有者（所有者が判明しない場合を除く。）及び権原に基く占有者の意見を聞かなければならない。

２　管理団体が修理を行う場合には、第三十二条の二第五項及び第三十二条の四の規定を準用する。

（管理又は修理の補助）

第三十五条　重要文化財の管理又は修理につき多額の経費を要し、重要文化財の所有者又は管理団体がその負担に堪えない場合その他特別の事情がある場合には、政府は、その経費の一部に充てさせるため、重要文化財の所有者又は管理団体に対し補助金を交付することができる。

２　前項の補助金を交付する場合には、文化庁長官は、その補助の条件として管理又は修理に関し必要な事項を指示することができる。

3　文化庁長官は、必要があると認めるときは、第一項の補助金を交付する重要文化財の管理又は修理について指揮監督することができる。

（管理に関する命令又は勧告）

第三十六条　重要文化財を管理する者が不適任なため又は管理が適当でないため重要文化財が滅失し、き損し、又は盗み取られる虞があると認めるときは、文化庁長官は、所有者、管理責任者又は管理団体に対し、重要文化財の管理をする者の選任又は変更、管理方法の改善、防火施設その他の保存施設の設置その他管理に関し必要な措置を命じ、又は勧告することができる。

2　前項の規定による命令又は勧告に基いてする措置のために要する費用は、文部科学省令の定めるところにより、その全部又は一部を国庫の負担とすることができる。

3　前項の規定により国庫が費用の全部又は一部を負担する場合には、前条第三項の規定を準用する。

（修理に関する命令又は勧告）

第三十七条　文化庁長官は、国宝がき損している場合において、その保存のため必要があると認めるときは、所有者又は管理団体に対し、その修理について必要な命令又は勧告をすることができる。

2　文化庁長官は、国宝以外の重要文化財がき損している場合において、その保存のため必要があると認めるときは、所有者又は管理団体に対し、その修理について必要な勧告をすることができる。

3　前二項の規定による命令又は勧告に基いてする修理のために要する費用は、文部科学省令の定めるところにより、その全部又は一部を国庫の負担とすることができる。

4　前項の規定により国庫が費用の全部又は一部を負担する場合には、第三十五条第三項の規定を準用する。

（文化庁長官による国宝の修理等の施行）

第三十八条　文化庁長官は、左の各号の一に該当する場合においては、国宝につき自ら修理を行い、又は滅失、き損若しくは盗難の防止の措置をすることができる。

一　所有者、管理責任者又は管理団体が前二条の規定による命令に従わないとき。

二　国宝がき損している場合又は滅失し、き損し、若しくは盗み取られる虞がある場合において、所有者、管理責任者又は管理団体に修理又は滅失、き損若しくは盗難の防止の措置をさせることが適当でないと認められるとき。

2　前項の規定による修理又は措置をしようとするときは、文化庁長官は、あらかじめ、所有者、管理責任者又は管理団体に対し、当該国宝の名称、修理又は措置の内容、着手の時期その他必要と認める事項を記載した令書を交付するとともに、権原に基く占有者にこれらの事項を通知しなければならない。

第三十九条　文化庁長官は、前条第一項の規定による修理又は措置をするときは、文化庁の職員のうちから、当該修理又は措置の施行及び当該国宝の管理の責に任ずべき者を定めなければならない。

2　前項の規定により責に任ずべき者と定められた者は、当該修理又は措置の施行に当るときは、その身分を証明する証票を携帯し、関係者の請求があつたときは、これを示し、且つ、その正当な意見を十分に尊重しなければならない。

3　前条第一項の規定による修理又は措置の施行には、第三十二条の二第五項の規定を準用する。

第四十条　第三十八条第一項の規定による修理又は措置のために要する費用は、国庫の負担とする。

2　文化庁長官は、文部科学省令の定めるところにより、第三十八条第一項の規定による修理又は措置のために要した費用の一部を所有者（管理団体がある場合は、その者）から徴収することができる。但し、同条第一項第二号の場合には、修理又は措置を要するに至つた事由が所有者、管理責任者若しくは管理団体の責に帰すべきとき、又は所有者若しくは管理団体がその費用の一部を負担する能力があるときに限る。

3　前項の規定による徴収については、行政代執行法（昭和二十三年法律第四十三号）第五条及び第六条の規定を準用する。

第四十一条　第三十八条第一項の規定による修理又は措置によつて損失を受けた者に対しては、国は、その通常生ずべき損失を補償する。

2　前項の補償の額は、文化庁長官が決定する。

3　前項の規定による補償額に不服のある者は、訴えをもつてその増額を請求することができる。ただし、前項の補償の決定の通知を受けた日から六箇月を経過したときは、この限りでない。

4　前項の訴えにおいては、国を被告とする。

（補助等に係る重要文化財譲渡の場合の納付金）

第四十二条　国が修理又は滅失、き損若しくは盗難の防止の措置（以下この条において、「修理等」という。）につき第三十五条第一項の規定により補助金を交付し、又は第三十六条第二項、第三十七条第三項若しくは第四十条第一項の規定により費用を負担した重要文化財のその当時における所有者又はその相続人、受遺者若しくは受贈者（第二次以下の相続人、受遺者又は受贈者を含む。以下この条において同じ。）（以下この条において、「所有者等」という。）は、補助又は費用負担に係る修理等が行われた後当該重要文化財を有償で譲り渡した場合においては、当該補助金又は負担金の額（第四十条第一項の規定による負担金については、同条第二項の規定により所有者から徴収した部分を控除した額をいう。以下この条において同じ。）の合計額から当該修理等が行われた後重要文化財の修理等のため自己の費した金額を控除して得た金額（以下この条において、「納付金額」という。）を、文部科学省令の定めるところにより国庫に納付しなければならない。

2　前項に規定する「補助金又は負担金の額」とは、補助金又は負担金の額を、補助又は費用負担に係る修理等を施した重要文化財又はその部分につき文化庁長官が個別的に定める耐用年数で除して得た金額に、更に当該耐用年数から修理等を行つた時以後重要文化財の譲渡の時までの年数を控除した残余の年数（一年に満たない部分があるときは、これを切り捨てる。）を乗じて得た金額に相当する金額とする。

3　補助又は費用負担に係る修理等が行われた後、当該重要文化財が所有者等の責に帰することのできない事由により著しくその価値を減じた場合又は当該重要文化財を国に譲り渡した場合には、文化庁長官は、納付金額の全部又は一部の納付を免除することができる。

4　文化庁長官の指定する期限までに納付金額を完納しないときは、国税滞納処分の例により、これを徴収することができる。この場合における徴収金の先取特権の順位は、国税及び地方税に次ぐものとする。

5　納付金額を納付する者が相続人、受遺者又は受贈者であるときは、第一号に定める相続税額又は贈与税額と第二号に定める額との差額に相当する金額を第三号に定める年数で除して得た金額に第四号に定める年数を乗じて得た金額をその者が納付すべき納付金額から控除するものとする。

一　当該重要文化財の取得につきその者が納付した、又は納付すべき相続税額又は贈与税額

二　前号の相続税額又は贈与税額の計算の基礎となつた課税価格に算入された当該重要文化財又はその部分につき当該相続、遺贈又は贈与の時までに行つた修理等に係る第一項の補助金又は負担金の額の合計額を当該課税価格から控除して得た金額を課税価格として計算した場合に当該重要文化財又はその部分につき納付すべきこととなる相続税額又は贈与税額に相当する額

三　第二項の規定により当該重要文化財又はその部分につき文化庁長官が定めた耐用年数から当該重要文化財又はその部分の修理等を行つた時以後当該重要文化財の相続、遺贈又は贈与の時までの年数を控除した残余の年数（一年に満たない部分があるときは、これを切り捨てる。）

四　第二項に規定する当該重要文化財又はその部分についての残余の耐用年数

6　前項第二号に掲げる第一項の補助金又は負担金の額については、第二項の規定を準用する。この場合において、同項中「譲渡の時」とあるのは、「相続、遺贈又は贈与の時」と読み替えるものとする。

7　第一項の規定により納付金額を納付する者の同項に規定する譲渡に係る所得税法（昭和四十年法律第三十三号）第三十三条第一項に規定する譲渡所得の金額の計算については、第一項の規定により納付する金額は、同条第三項に規定する資産の譲渡に要した費用とする。

（現状変更等の制限）

第四十三条　重要文化財に関しその現状を変更し、又はその保存に影響を及ぼす行為を

しようとするときは、文化庁長官の許可を受けなければならない。ただし、現状の変更については維持の措置又は非常災害のために必要な応急措置を執る場合、保存に影響を及ぼす行為については影響の軽微である場合は、この限りでない。

2　前項但書に規定する維持の措置の範囲は、文部科学省令で定める。

3　文化庁長官は、第一項の許可を与える場合において、その許可の条件として同項の現状の変更又は保存に影響を及ぼす行為に関し必要な指示をすることができる。

4　第一項の許可を受けた者が前項の許可の条件に従わなかつたときは、文化庁長官は、許可に係る現状の変更若しくは保存に影響を及ぼす行為の停止を命じ、又は許可を取り消すことができる。

5　第一項の許可を受けることができなかつたことにより、又は第三項の許可の条件を付せられたことによつて損失を受けた者に対しては、国は、その通常生ずべき損失を補償する。

6　前項の場合には、第四十一条第二項から第四項までの規定を準用する。

（修理の届出等）

第四十三条の二　重要文化財を修理しようとするときは、所有者又は管理団体は、修理に着手しようとする日の三十日前までに、文部科学省令の定めるところにより、文化庁長官にその旨を届け出なければならない。但し、前条第一項の規定により許可を受けなければならない場合その他文部科学省令の定める場合は、この限りでない。

2　重要文化財の保護上必要があると認めるときは、文化庁長官は、前項の届出に係る重要文化財の修理に関し技術的な指導と助言を与えることができる。

（輸出の禁止）

第四十四条　重要文化財は、輸出してはならない。但し、文化庁長官が文化の国際的交流その他の事由により特に必要と認めて許可した場合は、この限りでない。

（環境保全）

第四十五条　文化庁長官は、重要文化財の保存のため必要があると認めるときは、地域を定めて一定の行為を制限し、若しくは禁止し、又は必要な施設をすることを命ずることができる。

2　前項の規定による処分によつて損失を受けた者に対しては、国は、その通常生ずべき損失を補償する。

3　前項の場合には、第四十一条第二項から第四項までの規定を準用する。

（国に対する売渡しの申出）

第四十六条　重要文化財を有償で譲り渡そうとする者は、譲渡の相手方、予定対価の額（予定対価が金銭以外のものであるときは、これを時価を基準として金銭に見積つた額。以下同じ。）その他文部科学省令で定める事項を記載した書面をもつて、まず文化庁長官に国に対する売渡しの申出をしなければならない。

2　前項の書面においては、当該相手方に対して譲り渡したい事情を記載することができる。
3　文化庁長官は、前項の規定により記載された事情を相当と認めるときは、当該申出のあつた後三十日以内に当該重要文化財を買い取らない旨の通知をするものとする。
4　第一項の規定による売渡しの申出のあつた後三十日以内に文化庁長官が当該重要文化財を国において買い取るべき旨の通知をしたときは、第一項の規定による申出書に記載された予定対価の額に相当する代金で、売買が成立したものとみなす。
5　第一項に規定する者は、前項の期間（その期間内に文化庁長官が当該重要文化財を買い取らない旨の通知をしたときは、その時までの期間）内は、当該重要文化財を譲り渡してはならない。
（管理団体による買取りの補助）
第四十六条の二　国は、管理団体である地方公共団体その他の法人が、その管理に係る重要文化財（建造物その他の土地の定着物及びこれと一体のものとして当該重要文化財に指定された土地に限る。）で、その保存のため特に買い取る必要があると認められるものを買い取る場合には、その買取りに要する経費の一部を補助することができる。
2　前項の場合には、第三十五条第二項及び第三項並びに第四十二条の規定を準用する。
（管理又は修理の受託又は技術的指導）
第四十七条　重要文化財の所有者（管理団体がある場合は、その者）は、文化庁長官の定める条件により、文化庁長官に重要文化財の管理（管理団体がある場合を除く。）又は修理を委託することができる。
2　文化庁長官は、重要文化財の保存上必要があると認めるときは、所有者（管理団体がある場合は、その者）に対し、条件を示して、文化庁長官にその管理（管理団体がある場合を除く。）又は修理を委託するように勧告することができる。
3　前二項の規定により文化庁長官が管理又は修理の委託を受けた場合には、第三十九条第一項及び第二項の規定を準用する。
4　重要文化財の所有者、管理責任者又は管理団体は、文部科学省令の定めるところにより、文化庁長官に重要文化財の管理又は修理に関し技術的指導を求めることができる。

第四款　公開

（公開）
第四十七条の二　重要文化財の公開は、所有者が行うものとする。但し、管理団体がある場合は、管理団体が行うものとする。
2　前項の規定は、所有者又は管理団体の出品に係る重要文化財を、所有者及び管理団体以外の者が、この法律の規定により行う公開の用に供することを妨げるものではない。
3　管理団体は、その管理する重要文化財を公開する場合には、当該重要文化財につき観覧料を徴収することができる。
（文化庁長官による公開）

第四十八条　文化庁長官は、重要文化財の所有者（管理団体がある場合は、その者）に対し、一年以内の期間を限つて、国立博物館（独立行政法人国立文化財機構が設置する博物館をいう。以下この条において同じ。）その他の施設において文化庁長官の行う公開の用に供するため重要文化財を出品することを勧告することができる。

2　文化庁長官は、国庫が管理又は修理につき、その費用の全部若しくは一部を負担し、又は補助金を交付した重要文化財の所有者（管理団体がある場合は、その者）に対し、一年以内の期間を限つて、国立博物館その他の施設において文化庁長官の行う公開の用に供するため当該重要文化財を出品することを命ずることができる。

3　文化庁長官は、前項の場合において必要があると認めるときは、一年以内の期間を限つて、出品の期間を更新することができる。但し、引き続き五年をこえてはならない。

4　第二項の命令又は前項の更新があつたときは、重要文化財の所有者又は管理団体は、その重要文化財を出品しなければならない。

5　前四項に規定する場合の外、文化庁長官は、重要文化財の所有者（管理団体がある場合は、その者）から国立博物館その他の施設において文化庁長官の行う公開の用に供するため重要文化財を出品したい旨の申出があつた場合において適当と認めるときは、その出品を承認することができる。

第四十九条　文化庁長官は、前条の規定により重要文化財が出品されたときは、第百八十五条に規定する場合を除いて、文化庁の職員のうちから、その重要文化財の管理の責に任ずべき者を定めなければならない。

第五十条　第四十八条の規定による出品のために要する費用は、文部科学省令の定める基準により、国庫の負担とする。

2　政府は、第四十八条の規定により出品した所有者又は管理団体に対し、文部科学省令の定める基準により、給与金を支給する。

（所有者等による公開）

第五十一条　文化庁長官は、重要文化財の所有者又は管理団体に対し、三箇月以内の期間を限つて、重要文化財の公開を勧告することができる。

2　文化庁長官は、国庫が管理、修理又は買取りにつき、その費用の全部若しくは一部を負担し、又は補助金を交付した重要文化財の所有者又は管理団体に対し、三箇月以内の期間を限つて、その公開を命ずることができる。

3　前項の場合には、第四十八条第四項の規定を準用する。

4　文化庁長官は、重要文化財の所有者又は管理団体に対し、前三項の規定による公開及び当該公開に係る重要文化財の管理に関し必要な指示をすることができる。

5　重要文化財の所有者、管理責任者又は管理団体が前項の指示に従わない場合には、文化庁長官は、公開の停止又は中止を命ずることができる。

6　第二項及び第三項の規定による公開のために要する費用は、文部科学省令の定めるところにより、その全部又は一部を国庫の負担とすることができる。

7　前項に規定する場合のほか、重要文化財の所有者又は管理団体がその所有又は管理に係る重要文化財を公開するために要する費用は、文部科学省令で定めるところにより、その全部又は一部を国庫の負担とすることができる。

第五十一条の二　前条の規定による公開の場合を除き、重要文化財の所在の場所を変更してこれを公衆の観覧に供するため第三十四条の規定による届出があつた場合には、前条第四項及び第五項の規定を準用する。

（損失の補償）

第五十二条　第四十八条又は第五十一条第一項、第二項若しくは第三項の規定により出品し、又は公開したことに起因して当該重要文化財が滅失し、又はき損したときは、国は、その重要文化財の所有者に対し、その通常生ずべき損失を補償する。ただし、重要文化財が所有者、管理責任者又は管理団体の責に帰すべき事由によつて滅失し、又はき損した場合は、この限りでない。

2　前項の場合には、第四十一条第二項から第四項までの規定を準用する。

（所有者等以外の者による公開）

第五十三条　重要文化財の所有者及び管理団体以外の者がその主催する展覧会その他の催しにおいて重要文化財を公衆の観覧に供しようとするときは、文化庁長官の許可を受けなければならない。ただし、文化庁長官以外の国の機関若しくは地方公共団体があらかじめ文化庁長官の承認を受けた博物館その他の施設（以下この項において「公開承認施設」という。）において展覧会その他の催しを主催する場合又は公開承認施設の設置者が当該公開承認施設においてこれらを主催する場合は、この限りでない。

2　前項ただし書の場合においては、同項に規定する催しを主催した者（文化庁長官を除く。）は、重要文化財を公衆の観覧に供した期間の最終日の翌日から起算して二十日以内に、文部科学省令で定める事項を記載した書面をもつて、文化庁長官に届け出るものとする。

3　文化庁長官は、第一項の許可を与える場合において、その許可の条件として、許可に係る公開及び当該公開に係る重要文化財の管理に関し必要な指示をすることができる。

4　第一項の許可を受けた者が前項の許可の条件に従わなかつたときは、文化庁長官は、許可に係る公開の停止を命じ、又は許可を取り消すことができる。

第五款　調査

（保存のための調査）

第五十四条　文化庁長官は、必要があると認めるときは、重要文化財の所有者、管理責任者又は管理団体に対し、重要文化財の現状又は管理、修理若しくは環境保全の状況につき報告を求めることができる。

第五十五条　文化庁長官は、次の各号の一に該当する場合において、前条の報告によつてもなお重要文化財に関する状況を確認することができず、かつ、その確認のため他に方法がないと認めるときは、調査に当たる者を定め、その所在する場所に立ち入つてその現状又は管理、修理若しくは環境保全の状況につき実地調査をさせることができる。

一　重要文化財に関し現状の変更又は保存に影響を及ぼす行為につき許可の申請があつたとき。

二　重要文化財がき損しているとき又はその現状若しくは所在の場所につき変更があつたとき。

三　重要文化財が滅失し、き損し、又は盗み取られる虞のあるとき。

四　特別の事情によりあらためて国宝又は重要文化財としての価値を鑑査する必要があるとき。

2　前項の規定により立ち入り、調査する場合においては、当該調査に当る者は、その身分を証明する証票を携帯し、関係者の請求があつたときは、これを示し、且つ、その正当な意見を十分に尊重しなければならない。

3　第一項の規定による調査によつて損失を受けた者に対しては、国は、その通常生ずべき損失を補償する。

4　前項の場合には、第四十一条第二項から第四項までの規定を準用する。

第六款　雑則

（所有者変更等に伴う権利義務の承継）

第五十六条　重要文化財の所有者が変更したときは、新所有者は、当該重要文化財に関しこの法律に基いてする文化庁長官の命令、勧告、指示その他の処分による旧所有者の権利義務を承継する。

2　前項の場合には、旧所有者は、当該重要文化財の引渡と同時にその指定書を新所有者に引き渡さなければならない。

3　管理団体が指定され、又はその指定が解除された場合には、第一項の規定を準用する。但し、管理団体が指定された場合には、もつぱら所有者に属すべき権利義務については、この限りでない。

第二節　登録有形文化財

（有形文化財の登録）

第五十七条　文部科学大臣は、重要文化財以外の有形文化財（第百八十二条第二項に規定する指定を地方公共団体が行つているものを除く。）のうち、その文化財としての価値にかんがみ保存及び活用のための措置が特に必要とされるものを文化財登録原簿に登録することができる。

2　文部科学大臣は、前項の規定による登録をしようとするときは、あらかじめ、関係地方公共団体の意見を聴くものとする。

3　文化財登録原簿に記載すべき事項その他文化財登録原簿に関し必要な事項は、文部科学省令で定める。

（告示、通知及び登録証の交付）

第五十八条　前条第一項の規定による登録をしたときは、速やかに、その旨を官報で告示するとともに、当該登録をされた有形文化財（以下「登録有形文化財」という。）の所有者に通知する。

2　前条第一項の規定による登録は、前項の規定による官報の告示があつた日からその効力を生ずる。ただし、当該登録有形文化財の所有者に対しては、同項の規定による通知が当該所有者に到達した時からその効力を生ずる。

3　前条第一項の規定による登録をしたときは、文部科学大臣は、当該登録有形文化財の所有者に登録証を交付しなければならない。

4　登録証に記載すべき事項その他登録証に関し必要な事項は、文部科学省令で定める。

（登録有形文化財の登録の抹消）

第五十九条　文部科学大臣は、登録有形文化財について、第二十七条第一項の規定により重要文化財に指定したときは、その登録を抹消するものとする。

2　文部科学大臣は、登録有形文化財について、第百八十二条第二項に規定する指定を地方公共団体が行つたときは、その登録を抹消するものとする。ただし、当該登録有形文化財について、その保存及び活用のための措置を講ずる必要があり、かつ、その所有者の同意がある場合は、この限りでない。

3　文部科学大臣は、登録有形文化財についてその保存及び活用のための措置を講ずる必要がなくなつた場合その他特殊の事由があるときは、その登録を抹消することができる。

4　前三項の規定により登録の抹消をしたときは、速やかに、その旨を官報で告示するとともに、当該登録有形文化財の所有者に通知する。

5　第一項から第三項までの規定による登録の抹消には、前条第二項の規定を準用する。

6　第四項の通知を受けたときは、所有者は、三十日以内に登録証を文部科学大臣に返付しなければならない。

（登録有形文化財の管理）

第六十条　登録有形文化財の所有者は、この法律及びこれに基づく文部科学省令に従い、登録有形文化財を管理しなければならない。

2　登録有形文化財の所有者は、特別の事情があるときは、適当な者を専ら自己に代わり当該登録有形文化財の管理の責めに任ずべき者（以下この節において「管理責任者」という。）に選任することができる。

3　文化庁長官は、登録有形文化財について、所有者が判明せず、又は所有者若しくは管理責任者による管理が著しく困難若しくは不適当であることが明らかである旨の関係地方公共団体の申出があつた場合には、関係地方公共団体の意見を聴いて、適当な地方公共団体その他の法人を、当該登録有形文化財の保存のため必要な管理（当該登録有形文化財の保存のため必要な施設、設備その他の物件で当該登録有形文化財の所有者の所有又は管理に属するものの管理を含む。）を行う団体（以下この節において「管理団体」という。）に指定することができる。

4　登録有形文化財の管理には、第三十一条第三項、第三十二条、第三十二条の二第二項から第五項まで、第三十二条の三及び第三十二条の四の規定を準用する。

5　登録有形文化財の管理責任者及び管理団体には、第一項の規定を準用する。

（登録有形文化財の滅失、き損等）

第六十一条　登録有形文化財の全部又は一部が滅失し、若しくはき損し、又はこれを亡失し、若しくは盗み取られたときは、所有者（管理責任者又は管理団体がある場合は、その者）は、文部科学省令で定める事項を記載した書面をもつて、その事実を知つた日から十日以内に文化庁長官に届け出なければならない。

（登録有形文化財の所在の変更）

第六十二条　登録有形文化財の所在の場所を変更しようとするときは、登録有形文化財の所有者（管理責任者又は管理団体がある場合は、その者）は、文部科学省令の定める事項を記載した書面をもつて、所在の場所を変更しようとする日の二十日前までに、登録証を添えて、文化庁長官に届け出なければならない。ただし、文部科学省令で定める場合には、届出を要せず、若しくは届出の際登録証の添付を要せず、又は文部科学省令で定めるところにより所在の場所を変更した後届け出ることをもつて足りる。

（登録有形文化財の修理）

第六十三条　登録有形文化財の修理は、所有者が行うものとする。ただし、管理団体がある場合は、管理団体が行うものとする。

2　管理団体が修理を行う場合には、第三十二条の二第五項、第三十二条の四及び第三十四条の三第一項の規定を準用する。

（登録有形文化財の現状変更の届出等）

第六十四条　登録有形文化財に関しその現状を変更しようとする者は、現状を変更しようとする日の三十日前までに、文部科学省令で定めるところにより、文化庁長官にその旨を届け出なければならない。ただし、維持の措置若しくは非常災害のために必要な応急措置又は他の法令の規定による現状の変更を内容とする命令に基づく措置を執る場合は、この限りでない。

2　前項ただし書に規定する維持の措置の範囲は、文部科学省令で定める。

3

（登録有形文化財の輸出の届出）

第六十五条　登録有形文化財を輸出しようとする者は、輸出しようとする日の三十日前までに、文部科学省令で定めるところにより、文化庁長官にその旨を届け出なければならない。

２　登録有形文化財の保護上必要があると認めるときは、文化庁長官は、前項の届出に係る登録有形文化財の輸出に関し必要な指導、助言又は勧告をすることができる。

（登録有形文化財の管理又は修理に関する技術的指導）

第六十六条　登録有形文化財の所有者、管理責任者又は管理団体は、文部科学省令で定めるところにより、文化庁長官に登録有形文化財の管理又は修理に関し技術的指導を求めることができる。

（登録有形文化財の公開）

第六十七条　登録有形文化財の公開は、所有者が行うものとする。ただし、管理団体がある場合は、管理団体が行うものとする。

２　前項の規定は、登録有形文化財の所有者及び管理団体以外の者が、所有者（管理団体がある場合は、その者）の同意を得て、登録有形文化財を公開の用に供することを妨げるものではない。

３　管理団体が行う登録有形文化財の公開には、第四十七条の二第三項の規定を準用する。

４　登録有形文化財の活用上必要があると認めるときは、文化庁長官は、登録有形文化財の所有者又は管理団体に対し、登録有形文化財の公開及び当該公開に係る登録有形文化財の管理に関し、必要な指導又は助言をすることができる。

（登録有形文化財の現状等の報告）

第六十八条　文化庁長官は、必要があると認めるときは、登録有形文化財の所有者、管理責任者又は管理団体に対し、登録有形文化財の現状又は管理若しくは修理の状況につき報告を求めることができる。

（所有者変更に伴う登録証の引渡し）

第六十九条　登録有形文化財の所有者が変更したときは、旧所有者は、当該登録有形文化財の引渡しと同時にその登録証を新所有者に引き渡さなければならない。

第三節　重要文化財及び登録有形文化財以外の有形文化財

（技術的指導）

第七十条　重要文化財及び登録有形文化財以外の有形文化財の所有者は、文部科学省令の定めるところにより、文化庁長官に有形文化財の管理又は修理に関し技術的指導を求めることができる。

第四章　無形文化財

（重要無形文化財の指定等）

第七十一条　文部科学大臣は、無形文化財のうち重要なものを重要無形文化財に指定することができる。

２　文部科学大臣は、前項の規定による指定をするに当たつては、当該重要無形文化財の保持者又は保持団体（無形文化財を保持する者が主たる構成員となつている団体で代表者の定めのあるものをいう。以下同じ。）を認定しなければならない。

3　第一項の規定による指定は、その旨を官報で告示するとともに、当該重要無形文化財の保持者又は保持団体として認定しようとするもの（保持団体にあつては、その代表者）に通知してする。

4　文部科学大臣は、第一項の規定による指定をした後においても、当該重要無形文化財の保持者又は保持団体として認定するに足りるものがあると認めるときは、そのものを保持者又は保持団体として追加認定することができる。

5　前項の規定による追加認定には、第三項の規定を準用する。

（重要無形文化財の指定等の解除）

第七十二条　重要無形文化財が重要無形文化財としての価値を失つた場合その他特殊の事由があるときは、文部科学大臣は、重要無形文化財の指定を解除することができる。

2　保持者が心身の故障のため保持者として適当でなくなつたと認められる場合、保持団体がその構成員の異動のため保持団体として適当でなくなつたと認められる場合その他特殊の事由があるときは、文部科学大臣は、保持者又は保持団体の認定を解除することができる。

3　第一項の規定による指定の解除又は前項の規定による認定の解除は、その旨を官報で告示するとともに、当該重要無形文化財の保持者又は保持団体の代表者に通知してする。

4　保持者が死亡したとき、又は保持団体が解散したとき（消滅したときを含む。以下この条及び次条において同じ。）は、当該保持者又は保持団体の認定は解除されたものとし、保持者のすべてが死亡したとき、又は保持団体のすべてが解散したときは、重要無形文化財の指定は解除されたものとする。この場合には、文部科学大臣は、その旨を官報で告示しなければならない。

（保持者の氏名変更等）

第七十三条　保持者が氏名若しくは住所を変更し、又は死亡したとき、その他文部科学省令の定める事由があるときは、保持者又はその相続人は、文部科学省令の定める事項を記載した書面をもつて、その事由の生じた日（保持者の死亡に係る場合は、相続人がその事実を知つた日）から二十日以内に文化庁長官に届け出なければならない。保持団体が名称、事務所の所在地若しくは代表者を変更し、構成員に異動を生じ、又は解散したときも、代表者（保持団体が解散した場合にあつては、代表者であつた者）について、同様とする。

（重要無形文化財の保存）

第七十四条　文化庁長官は、重要無形文化財の保存のため必要があると認めるときは、重要無形文化財について自ら記録の作成、伝承者の養成その他その保存のため適当な措置を執ることができるものとし、国は、保持者、保持団体又は地方公共団体その他その保存に当たることを適当と認める者に対し、その保存に要する経費の一部を補助することができる。

2　前項の規定により補助金を交付する場合には、第三十五条第二項及び第三項の規定を準用する。

（重要無形文化財の公開）

第七十五条　文化庁長官は、重要無形文化財の保持者又は保持団体に対し重要無形文化財の公開を、重要無形文化財の記録の所有者に対しその記録の公開を勧告することができる。

2　重要無形文化財の保持者又は保持団体が重要無形文化財を公開する場合には、第五十一条第七項の規定を準用する。

3　重要無形文化財の記録の所有者がその記録を公開する場合には、国は、その公開に要する経費の一部を補助することができる。

（重要無形文化財の保存に関する助言又は勧告）

第七十六条　文化庁長官は、重要無形文化財の保持者若しくは保持団体又は地方公共団体その他その保存に当たることを適当と認める者に対し、重要無形文化財の保存のため必要な助言又は勧告をすることができる。

（重要無形文化財以外の無形文化財の記録の作成等）

第七十七条　文化庁長官は、重要無形文化財以外の無形文化財のうち特に必要のあるものを選択して、自らその記録を作成し、保存し、又は公開することができるものとし、国は、適当な者に対し、当該無形文化財の公開又はその記録の作成、保存若しくは公開に要する経費の一部を補助することができる。

2　前項の規定により補助金を交付する場合には、第三十五条第二項及び第三項の規定を準用する。

第五章　民俗文化財

（重要有形民俗文化財及び重要無形民俗文化財の指定）

第七十八条　文部科学大臣は、有形の民俗文化財のうち特に重要なものを重要有形民俗文化財に、無形の民俗文化財のうち特に重要なものを重要無形民俗文化財に指定することができる。

2　前項の規定による重要有形民俗文化財の指定には、第二十八条第一項から第四項までの規定を準用する。

3　第一項の規定による重要無形民俗文化財の指定は、その旨を官報に告示してする。

（重要有形民俗文化財及び重要無形民俗文化財の指定の解除）

第七十九条　重要有形民俗文化財又は重要無形民俗文化財が重要有形民俗文化財又は重要無形民俗文化財としての価値を失つた場合その他特殊の事由があるときは、文部科学大臣は、重要有形民俗文化財又は重要無形民俗文化財の指定を解除することができる。

2　前項の規定による重要有形民俗文化財の指定の解除には、第二十九条第二項から第四項までの規定を準用する。

3　第一項の規定による重要無形民俗文化財の指定の解除は、その旨を官報に告示してする。

（重要有形民俗文化財の管理）

第八十条　重要有形民俗文化財の管理には、第三十条から第三十四条までの規定を準用する。

（重要有形民俗文化財の保護）

第八十一条　重要有形民俗文化財に関しその現状を変更し、又はその保存に影響を及ぼす行為をしようとする者は、現状を変更し、又は保存に影響を及ぼす行為をしようとする日の二十日前までに、文部科学省令の定めるところにより、文化庁長官にその旨を届け出なければならない。ただし、文部科学省令の定める場合は、この限りでない。

2　重要有形民俗文化財の保護上必要があると認めるときは、文化庁長官は、前項の届出に係る重要有形民俗文化財の現状変更又は保存に影響を及ぼす行為に関し必要な事項を指示することができる。

第八十二条　重要有形民俗文化財を輸出しようとする者は、文化庁長官の許可を受けなければならない。

第八十三条　重要有形民俗文化財の保護には、第三十四条の二から第三十六条まで、第三十七条第二項から第四項まで、第四十二条、第四十六条及び第四十七条の規定を準用する。

（重要有形民俗文化財の公開）

第八十四条　重要有形民俗文化財の所有者及び管理団体（第八十条で準用する第三十二条の二第一項の規定による指定を受けた地方公共団体その他の法人をいう。以下この章及び第十二章において同じ。）以外の者がその主催する展覧会その他の催しにおいて重要有形民俗文化財を公衆の観覧に供しようとするときは、文部科学省令の定める事項を記載した書面をもつて、観覧に供しようとする最初の日の三十日前までに、文化庁長官に届け出なければならない。ただし、文化庁長官以外の国の機関若しくは地方公共団体があらかじめ文化庁長官から事前の届出の免除を受けた博物館その他の施設（以下この項において「公開事前届出免除施設」という。）において展覧会その他の催しを主催する場合又は公開事前届出免除施設の設置者が当該公開事前届出免除施設においてこれらを主催する場合には、重要有形民俗文化財を公衆の観覧に供した期間の最終日の翌日から起算して二十日以内に、文化庁長官に届け出ることをもつて足りる。

2　前項本文の届出に係る公開には、第五十一条第四項及び第五項の規定を準用する。

第八十五条　重要有形民俗文化財の公開には、第四十七条の二から第五十二条までの規定を準用する。

（重要有形民俗文化財の保存のための調査及び所有者変更等に伴う権利義務の承継）

第八十六条　重要有形民俗文化財の保存のための調査には、第五十四条の規定を、重要有形民俗文化財の所有者が変更し、又は重要有形民俗文化財の管理団体が指定され、若しくはその指定が解除された場合には、第五十六条の規定を準用する。

（重要無形民俗文化財の保存）

第八十七条　文化庁長官は、重要無形民俗文化財の保存のため必要があると認めるときは、重要無形民俗文化財について自ら記録の作成その他その保存のため適当な措置を執ることができるものとし、国は、地方公共団体その他その保存に当たることを適当と認める者に対し、その保存に要する経費の一部を補助することができる。

2　前項の規定により補助金を交付する場合には、第三十五条第二項及び第三項の規定を準用する。

（重要無形民俗文化財の記録の公開）

第八十八条　文化庁長官は、重要無形民俗文化財の記録の所有者に対し、その記録の公開を勧告することができる。

2　重要無形民俗文化財の記録の所有者がその記録を公開する場合には、第七十五条第三項の規定を準用する。

（重要無形民俗文化財の保存に関する助言又は勧告）

第八十九条　文化庁長官は、地方公共団体その他重要無形民俗文化財の保存に当たることを適当と認める者に対し、その保存のため必要な助言又は勧告をすることができる。

（登録有形民俗文化財）

第九十条　文部科学大臣は、重要有形民俗文化財以外の有形の民俗文化財（第百八十二条第二項に規定する指定を地方公共団体が行つているものを除く。）のうち、その文化財としての価値にかんがみ保存及び活用のための措置が特に必要とされるものを文化財登録原簿に登録することができる。

2　前項の規定による登録には、第五十七条第二項及び第三項の規定を準用する。

3　前二項の規定により登録された有形の民俗文化財（以下「登録有形民俗文化財」という。）については、第三章第二節（第五十七条の規定を除く。）の規定を準用する。この場合において、第六十四条第一項及び第六十五条第一項中「三十日前」とあるのは「二十日前」と、第六十四条第一項ただし書中「維持の措置若しくは非常災害のために必要な応急措置又は他の法令の規定による現状の変更を内容とする命令に基づく措置を執る場合」とあるのは「文部科学省令で定める場合」と読み替えるものとする。

（重要無形民俗文化財以外の無形の民俗文化財の記録の作成等）

第九十一条　重要無形民俗文化財以外の無形の民俗文化財には、第七十七条の規定を準用する。

第六章　埋蔵文化財

（調査のための発掘に関する届出、指示及び命令）

第九十二条　土地に埋蔵されている文化財（以下「埋蔵文化財」という。）について、その調査のため土地を発掘しようとする者は、文部科学省令の定める事項を記載した書面をもつて、発掘に着手しようとする日の三十日前までに文化庁長官に届け出なければならない。ただし、文部科学省令の定める場合は、この限りでない。

２　埋蔵文化財の保護上特に必要があると認めるときは、文化庁長官は、前項の届出に係る発掘に関し必要な事項及び報告書の提出を指示し、又はその発掘の禁止、停止若しくは中止を命ずることができる。

（土木工事等のための発掘に関する届出及び指示）

第九十三条　土木工事その他埋蔵文化財の調査以外の目的で、貝づか、古墳その他埋蔵文化財を包蔵する土地として周知されている土地（以下「周知の埋蔵文化財包蔵地」という。）を発掘しようとする場合には、前条第一項の規定を準用する。この場合において、同項中「三十日前」とあるのは、「六十日前」と読み替えるものとする。

２　埋蔵文化財の保護上特に必要があると認めるときは、文化庁長官は、前項で準用する前条第一項の届出に係る発掘に関し、当該発掘前における埋蔵文化財の記録の作成のための発掘調査の実施その他の必要な事項を指示することができる。

（国の機関等が行う発掘に関する特例）

第九十四条　国の機関、地方公共団体又は国若しくは地方公共団体の設立に係る法人で政令の定めるもの（以下この条及び第九十七条において「国の機関等」と総称する。）が、前条第一項に規定する目的で周知の埋蔵文化財包蔵地を発掘しようとする場合においては、同条の規定を適用しないものとし、当該国の機関等は、当該発掘に係る事業計画の策定に当たつて、あらかじめ、文化庁長官にその旨を通知しなければならない。

２　文化庁長官は、前項の通知を受けた場合において、埋蔵文化財の保護上特に必要があると認めるときは、当該国の機関等に対し、当該事業計画の策定及びその実施について協議を求めるべき旨の通知をすることができる。

３　前項の通知を受けた国の機関等は、当該事業計画の策定及びその実施について、文化庁長官に協議しなければならない。

４　文化庁長官は、前二項の場合を除き、第一項の通知があつた場合において、当該通知に係る事業計画の実施に関し、埋蔵文化財の保護上必要な勧告をすることができる。

５　前各項の場合において、当該国の機関等が各省各庁の長（国有財産法（昭和二十三年法律第七十三号）第四条第二項に規定する各省各庁の長をいう。以下同じ。）であるときは、これらの規定に規定する通知、協議又は勧告は、文部科学大臣を通じて行うものとする。

（埋蔵文化財包蔵地の周知）

第九十五条　国及び地方公共団体は、周知の埋蔵文化財包蔵地について、資料の整備その他その周知の徹底を図るために必要な措置の実施に努めなければならない。

2　国は、地方公共団体が行う前項の措置に関し、指導、助言その他の必要と認められる援助をすることができる。

（遺跡の発見に関する届出、停止命令等）

第九十六条　土地の所有者又は占有者が出土品の出土等により貝づか、住居跡、古墳その他遺跡と認められるものを発見したときは、第九十二条第一項の規定による調査に当たつて発見した場合を除き、その現状を変更することなく、遅滞なく、文部科学省令の定める事項を記載した書面をもつて、その旨を文化庁長官に届け出なければならない。ただし、非常災害のために必要な応急措置を執る場合は、その限度において、その現状を変更することを妨げない。

2　文化庁長官は、前項の届出があつた場合において、当該届出に係る遺跡が重要なものであり、かつ、その保護のため調査を行う必要があると認めるときは、その土地の所有者又は占有者に対し、期間及び区域を定めて、その現状を変更することとなるような行為の停止又は禁止を命ずることができる。ただし、その期間は、三月を超えることができない。

3　文化庁長官は、前項の命令をしようとするときは、あらかじめ、関係地方公共団体の意見を聴かなければならない。

4　第二項の命令は、第一項の届出があつた日から起算して一月以内にしなければならない。

5　第二項の場合において、同項の期間内に調査が完了せず、引き続き調査を行う必要があるときは、文化庁長官は、一回に限り、当該命令に係る区域の全部又は一部について、その期間を延長することができる。ただし、当該命令の期間が、同項の期間と通算して六月を超えることとなつてはならない。

6　第二項及び前項の期間を計算する場合においては、第一項の届出があつた日から起算して第二項の命令を発した日までの期間が含まれるものとする。

7　文化庁長官は、第一項の届出がなされなかつた場合においても、第二項及び第五項に規定する措置を執ることができる。

8　文化庁長官は、第二項の措置を執つた場合を除き、第一項の届出がなされた場合には、当該遺跡の保護上必要な指示をすることができる。前項の規定により第二項の措置を執つた場合を除き、第一項の届出がなされなかつたときも、同様とする。

9　第二項の命令によつて損失を受けた者に対しては、国は、その通常生ずべき損失を補償する。

10　前項の場合には、第四十一条第二項から第四項までの規定を準用する。

（国の機関等の遺跡の発見に関する特例）

第九十七条　国の機関等が前条第一項に規定する発見をしたときは、同条の規定を適用しないものとし、第九十二条第一項又は第九十九条第一項の規定による調査に当たつて発見した場合を除き、その現状を変更することなく、遅滞なく、その旨を文化庁長官に通知しなければならない。ただし、非常災害のために必要な応急措置を執る場合は、その限度において、その現状を変更することを妨げない。

2　文化庁長官は、前項の通知を受けた場合において、当該通知に係る遺跡が重要なものであり、かつ、その保護のため調査を行う必要があると認めるときは、当該国の機関等に対し、その調査、保存等について協議を求めるべき旨の通知をすることができる。

3　前項の通知を受けた国の機関等は、文化庁長官に協議しなければならない。

4　文化庁長官は、前二項の場合を除き、第一項の通知があつた場合において、当該遺跡の保護上必要な勧告をすることができる。

5　前各項の場合には、第九十四条第五項の規定を準用する。

（文化庁長官による発掘の施行）

第九十八条　文化庁長官は、歴史上又は学術上の価値が特に高く、かつ、その調査が技術的に困難なため国において調査する必要があると認められる埋蔵文化財については、その調査のため土地の発掘を施行することができる。

2　前項の規定により発掘を施行しようとするときは、文化庁長官は、あらかじめ、当該土地の所有者及び権原に基づく占有者に対し、発掘の目的、方法、着手の時期その他必要と認める事項を記載した令書を交付しなければならない。

3　第一項の場合には、第三十九条（同条第三項において準用する第三十二条の二第五項の規定を含む。）及び第四十一条の規定を準用する。

（地方公共団体による発掘の施行）

第九十九条　地方公共団体は、文化庁長官が前条第一項の規定により発掘を施行するものを除き、埋蔵文化財について調査する必要があると認めるときは、埋蔵文化財を包蔵すると認められる土地の発掘を施行することができる。

2　地方公共団体は、前項の発掘に関し、事業者に対し協力を求めることができる。

3　文化庁長官は、地方公共団体に対し、第一項の発掘に関し必要な指導及び助言をすることができる。

4　国は、地方公共団体に対し、第一項の発掘に要する経費の一部を補助することができる。

（返還又は通知等）

第百条　第九十八条第一項の規定による発掘により文化財を発見した場合において、文化庁長官は、当該文化財の所有者が判明しているときはこれを所有者に返還し、所有者が判明しないときは、遺失物法（平成十八年法律第七十三号）第四条第一項の規定にかかわらず、警察署長にその旨を通知することをもつて足りる。

2　前項の規定は、前条第一項の規定による発掘により都道府県又は地方自治法（昭和二十二年法律第六十七号）第二百五十二条の十九第一項の指定都市（以下「指定都市」

という。）若しくは同法第二百五十二条の二十二第一項の中核市（以下「指定都市等」という。）の教育委員会が文化財を発見した場合における当該教育委員会について準用する。

3　第一項（前項において準用する場合を含む。）の通知を受けたときは、警察署長は、直ちに当該文化財につき遺失物法第七条第一項の規定による公告をしなければならない。

（提出）

第百一条　遺失物法第四条第一項の規定により、埋蔵物として提出された物件が文化財と認められるときは、警察署長は、直ちに当該物件を当該物件の発見された土地を管轄する都道府県の教育委員会（当該土地が指定都市等の区域内に存する場合にあつては、当該指定都市等の教育委員会。次条において同じ。）に提出しなければならない。ただし、所有者の判明している場合は、この限りでない。

（鑑査）

第百二条　前条の規定により物件が提出されたときは、都道府県の教育委員会は、当該物件が文化財であるかどうかを鑑査しなければならない。

2　都道府県の教育委員会は、前項の鑑査の結果当該物件を文化財と認めたときは、その旨を警察署長に通知し、文化財でないと認めたときは、当該物件を警察署長に差し戻さなければならない。

（引渡し）

第百三条　第百条第一項に規定する文化財又は同条第二項若しくは前条第二項に規定する文化財の所有者から、警察署長に対し、その文化財の返還の請求があつたときは、文化庁長官又は都道府県若しくは指定都市等の教育委員会は、当該警察署長にこれを引き渡さなければならない。

（国庫帰属及び報償金）

第百四条　第百条第一項に規定する文化財又は第百二条第二項に規定する文化財（国の機関又は独立行政法人国立文化財機構が埋蔵文化財の調査のための土地の発掘により発見したものに限る。）で、その所有者が判明しないものの所有権は、国庫に帰属する。この場合においては、文化庁長官は、当該文化財の発見された土地の所有者にその旨を通知し、かつ、その価格の二分の一に相当する額の報償金を支給する。

2　前項の場合には、第四十一条第二項から第四項までの規定を準用する。

（都道府県帰属及び報償金）

第百五条　第百条第二項に規定する文化財又は第百二条第二項に規定する文化財（前条第一項に規定するものを除く。）で、その所有者が判明しないものの所有権は、当該文化財の発見された土地を管轄する都道府県に帰属する。この場合においては、当該都道府県の教育委員会は、当該文化財の発見者及びその発見された土地の所有者にその旨を通知し、かつ、その価格に相当する額の報償金を支給する。

2　前項に規定する発見者と土地所有者とが異なるときは、前項の報償金は、折半して支給する。

3　第一項の報償金の額は、当該都道府県の教育委員会が決定する。

4　前項の規定による報償金の額については、第四十一条第三項の規定を準用する。

5　前項において準用する第四十一条第三項の規定による訴えにおいては、都道府県を被告とする。

（譲与等）

第百六条　政府は、第百四条第一項の規定により国庫に帰属した文化財の保存のため又はその効用から見て国が保有する必要がある場合を除いて、当該文化財の発見された土地の所有者に、その者が同条の規定により受けるべき報償金の額に相当するものの範囲内でこれを譲与することができる。

2　前項の場合には、その譲与した文化財の価格に相当する金額は、第百四条に規定する報償金の額から控除するものとする。

3　政府は、第百四条第一項の規定により国庫に帰属した文化財の保存のため又はその効用から見て国が保有する必要がある場合を除いて、独立行政法人国立文化財機構又は当該文化財の発見された土地を管轄する地方公共団体に対し、その申請に基づき、当該文化財を譲与し、又は時価よりも低い対価で譲渡することができる。

第百七条　都道府県の教育委員会は、第百五条第一項の規定により当該都道府県に帰属した文化財の保存のため又はその効用から見て当該都道府県が保有する必要がある場合を除いて、当該文化財の発見者又はその発見された土地の所有者に、その者が同条の規定により受けるべき報償金の額に相当するものの範囲内でこれを譲与することができる。

2　前項の場合には、その譲与した文化財の価格に相当する金額は、第百五条に規定する報償金の額から控除するものとする。

（遺失物法の適用）

第百八条　埋蔵文化財に関しては、この法律に特別の定めのある場合のほか、遺失物法の適用があるものとする。

第七章　史跡名勝天然記念物

（指定）

第百九条　文部科学大臣は、記念物のうち重要なものを史跡、名勝又は天然記念物（以下「史跡名勝天然記念物」と総称する。）に指定することができる。

2　文部科学大臣は、前項の規定により指定された史跡名勝天然記念物のうち特に重要なものを特別史跡、特別名勝又は特別天然記念物（以下「特別史跡名勝天然記念物」と総称する。）に指定することができる。

3　前二項の規定による指定は、その旨を官報で告示するとともに、当該特別史跡名勝天然記念物又は史跡名勝天然記念物の所有者及び権原に基づく占有者に通知してする。

4　前項の規定により通知すべき相手方が著しく多数で個別に通知し難い事情がある場合には、文部科学大臣は、同項の規定による通知に代えて、その通知すべき事項を当該特別史跡名勝天然記念物又は史跡名勝天然記念物の所在地の市（特別区を含む。以下同じ。）町村の事務所又はこれに準ずる施設の掲示場に掲示することができる。この場合においては、その掲示を始めた日から二週間を経過した時に前項の規定による通知が相手方に到達したものとみなす。

5　第一項又は第二項の規定による指定は、第三項の規定による官報の告示があつた日からその効力を生ずる。ただし、当該特別史跡名勝天然記念物又は史跡名勝天然記念物の所有者又は権原に基づく占有者に対しては、第三項の規定による通知が到達した時又は前項の規定によりその通知が到達したものとみなされる時からその効力を生ずる。

6　文部科学大臣は、第一項の規定により名勝又は天然記念物の指定をしようとする場合において、その指定に係る記念物が自然環境の保護の見地から価値の高いものであるときは、環境大臣と協議しなければならない。

（仮指定）

第百十条　前条第一項の規定による指定前において緊急の必要があると認めるときは、都道府県の教育委員会（当該記念物が指定都市の区域内に存する場合にあつては、当該指定都市の教育委員会。第百三十三条を除き、以下この章において同じ。）は、史跡名勝天然記念物の仮指定を行うことができる。

2　前項の規定により仮指定を行つたときは、都道府県の教育委員会は、直ちにその旨を文部科学大臣に報告しなければならない。

3　第一項の規定による仮指定には、前条第三項から第五項までの規定を準用する。

（所有権等の尊重及び他の公益との調整）

第百十一条　文部科学大臣又は都道府県の教育委員会は、第百九条第一項若しくは第二項の規定による指定又は前条第一項の規定による仮指定を行うに当たつては、特に、関係者の所有権、鉱業権その他の財産権を尊重するとともに、国土の開発その他の公益との調整に留意しなければならない。

2　文部科学大臣又は文化庁長官は、名勝又は天然記念物に係る自然環境の保護及び整備に関し必要があると認めるときは、環境大臣に対し、意見を述べることができる。この場合において、文化庁長官が意見を述べるときは、文部科学大臣を通じて行うものとする。

3　環境大臣は、自然環境の保護の見地から価値の高い名勝又は天然記念物の保存及び活用に関し必要があると認めるときは、文部科学大臣に対し、又は文部科学大臣を通じ文化庁長官に対して意見を述べることができる。

（解除）

第百十二条　特別史跡名勝天然記念物又は史跡名勝天然記念物がその価値を失つた場合

その他特殊の事由のあるときは、文部科学大臣又は都道府県の教育委員会は、その指定又は仮指定を解除することができる。

2　第百十条第一項の規定により仮指定された史跡名勝天然記念物につき第百九条第一項の規定による指定があつたとき、又は仮指定があつた日から二年以内に同項の規定による指定がなかつたときは、仮指定は、その効力を失う。

3　第百十条第一項の規定による仮指定が適当でないと認めるときは、文部科学大臣は、これを解除することができる。

4　第一項又は前項の規定による指定又は仮指定の解除には、第百九条第三項から第五項までの規定を準用する。

（管理団体による管理及び復旧）

第百十三条　史跡名勝天然記念物につき、所有者がないか若しくは判明しない場合又は所有者若しくは第百十九条第二項の規定により選任された管理の責めに任ずべき者による管理が著しく困難若しくは不適当であると明らかに認められる場合には、文化庁長官は、適当な地方公共団体その他の法人を指定して、当該史跡名勝天然記念物の保存のため必要な管理及び復旧（当該史跡名勝天然記念物の保存のため必要な施設、設備その他の物件で当該史跡名勝天然記念物の所有者の所有又は管理に属するものの管理及び復旧を含む。）を行わせることができる。

2　前項の規定による指定をするには、文化庁長官は、あらかじめ、指定しようとする地方公共団体その他の法人の同意を得なければならない。

3　第一項の規定による指定は、その旨を官報で告示するとともに、当該史跡名勝天然記念物の所有者及び権原に基づく占有者並びに指定しようとする地方公共団体その他の法人に通知してする。

4　第一項の規定による指定には、第百九条第四項及び第五項の規定を準用する。

第百十四条　前条第一項に規定する事由が消滅した場合その他特殊の事由があるときは、文化庁長官は、管理団体の指定を解除することができる。

2　前項の規定による解除には、前条第三項並びに第百九条第四項及び第五項の規定を準用する。

第百十五条　第百十三条第一項の規定による指定を受けた地方公共団体その他の法人（以下この章及び第十二章において「管理団体」という。）は、文部科学省令の定める基準により、史跡名勝天然記念物の管理に必要な標識、説明板、境界標、囲いその他の施設を設置しなければならない。

2　史跡名勝天然記念物の指定地域内の土地について、その土地の所在、地番、地目又は地積に異動があつたときは、管理団体は、文部科学省令の定めるところにより、文化庁長官にその旨を届け出なければならない。

3　管理団体が復旧を行う場合は、管理団体は、あらかじめ、その復旧の方法及び時期について当該史跡名勝天然記念物の所有者（所有者が判明しない場合を除く。）及び権原に基づく占有者の意見を聞かなければならない。

4　史跡名勝天然記念物の所有者又は占有者は、正当な理由がなくて、管理団体が行う管理若しくは復旧又はその管理若しくは復旧のため必要な措置を拒み、妨げ、又は忌避してはならない。

第百十六条　管理団体が行う管理及び復旧に要する費用は、この法律に特別の定めのある場合を除いて、管理団体の負担とする。

2　前項の規定は、管理団体と所有者との協議により、管理団体が行う管理又は復旧により所有者の受ける利益の限度において、管理又は復旧に要する費用の一部を所有者の負担とすることを妨げるものではない。

3　管理団体は、その管理する史跡名勝天然記念物につき観覧料を徴収することができる。

第百十七条　管理団体が行う管理又は復旧によつて損失を受けた者に対しては、当該管理団体は、その通常生ずべき損失を補償しなければならない。

2　前項の補償の額は、管理団体（管理団体が地方公共団体であるときは、当該地方公共団体の教育委員会）が決定する。

3　前項の規定による補償額については、第四十一条第三項の規定を準用する。

4　前項で準用する第四十一条第三項の規定による訴えにおいては、管理団体を被告とする。

第百十八条　管理団体が行う管理には、第三十条、第三十一条第一項及び第三十三条の規定を、管理団体が行う管理及び復旧には、第三十五条及び第四十七条の規定を、管理団体が指定され、又はその指定が解除された場合には、第五十六条第三項の規定を準用する。

（所有者による管理及び復旧）

第百十九条　管理団体がある場合を除いて、史跡名勝天然記念物の所有者は、当該史跡名勝天然記念物の管理及び復旧に当たるものとする。

2　前項の規定により史跡名勝天然記念物の管理に当たる所有者は、特別の事情があるときは、適当な者を専ら自己に代わり当該史跡名勝天然記念物の管理の責めに任ずべき者（以下この章及び第十二章において「管理責任者」という。）に選任することができる。この場合には、第三十一条第三項の規定を準用する。

第百二十条　所有者が行う管理には、第三十条、第三十一条第一項、第三十二条、第三十三条並びに第百十五条第一項及び第二項（同条第二項については、管理責任者がある場合を除く。）の規定を、所有者が行う管理及び復旧には、第三十五条及び第四十七条の規定を、所有者が変更した場合の権利義務の承継には、第五十六条第一項の規定を、管理責任者が行う管理には、第三十条、第三十一条第一項、第三十二条第三項、第三十三条、第四十七条第四項及び第百十五条第二項の規定を準用する。

（管理に関する命令又は勧告）

第百二十一条　管理が適当でないため史跡名勝天然記念物が滅失し、き損し、衰亡し、又は盗み取られるおそれがあると認めるときは、文化庁長官は、管理団体、所有者又は管理責任者に対し、管理方法の改善、保存施設の設置その他管理に関し必要な措置を命じ、又は勧告することができる。

2　前項の場合には、第三十六条第二項及び第三項の規定を準用する。

（復旧に関する命令又は勧告）

第百二十二条　文化庁長官は、特別史跡名勝天然記念物がき損し、又は衰亡している場合において、その保存のため必要があると認めるときは、管理団体又は所有者に対し、その復旧について必要な命令又は勧告をすることができる。

2　文化庁長官は、特別史跡名勝天然記念物以外の史跡名勝天然記念物が、き損し、又は衰亡している場合において、その保存のため必要があると認めるときは、管理団体又は所有者に対し、その復旧について必要な勧告をすることができる。

3　前二項の場合には、第三十七条第三項及び第四項の規定を準用する。

（文化庁長官による特別史跡名勝天然記念物の復旧等の施行）

第百二十三条　文化庁長官は、次の各号のいずれかに該当する場合においては、特別史跡名勝天然記念物につき自ら復旧を行い、又は滅失、き損、衰亡若しくは盗難の防止の措置をすることができる。

一　管理団体、所有者又は管理責任者が前二条の規定による命令に従わないとき。

二　特別史跡名勝天然記念物がき損し、若しくは衰亡している場合又は滅失し、き損し、衰亡し、若しくは盗み取られるおそれのある場合において、管理団体、所有者又は管理責任者に復旧又は滅失、き損、衰亡若しくは盗難の防止の措置をさせることが適当でないと認められるとき。

2　前項の場合には、第三十八条第二項及び第三十九条から第四十一条までの規定を準用する。

（補助等に係る史跡名勝天然記念物譲渡の場合の納付金）

第百二十四条　国が復旧又は滅失、き損、衰亡若しくは盗難の防止の措置につき第百十八条及び第百二十条で準用する第三十五条第一項の規定により補助金を交付し、又は第百二十一条第二項で準用する第三十六条第二項、第百二十二条第三項で準用する第三十七条第三項若しくは前条第二項で準用する第四十条第一項の規定により費用を負担した史跡名勝天然記念物については、第四十二条の規定を準用する。

（現状変更等の制限及び原状回復の命令）

第百二十五条　史跡名勝天然記念物に関しその現状を変更し、又はその保存に影響を及ぼす行為をしようとするときは、文化庁長官の許可を受けなければならない。ただし、現状変更については維持の措置又は非常災害のために必要な応急措置を執る場合、保存に影響を及ぼす行為については影響の軽微である場合は、この限りでない。

2　前項ただし書に規定する維持の措置の範囲は、文部科学省令で定める。

3　第一項の規定による許可を与える場合には、第四十三条第三項の規定を、第一項の規定による許可を受けた者には、同条第四項の規定を準用する。
4　第一項の規定による処分には、第百十一条第一項の規定を準用する。
5　第一項の許可を受けることができなかつたことにより、又は第三項で準用する第四十三条第三項の許可の条件を付せられたことによつて損失を受けた者に対しては、国は、その通常生ずべき損失を補償する。
6　前項の場合には、第四十一条第二項から第四項までの規定を準用する。
7　第一項の規定による許可を受けず、又は第三項で準用する第四十三条第三項の規定による許可の条件に従わないで、史跡名勝天然記念物の現状を変更し、又はその保存に影響を及ぼす行為をした者に対しては、文化庁長官は、原状回復を命ずることができる。この場合には、文化庁長官は、原状回復に関し必要な指示をすることができる。
（関係行政庁による通知）
第百二十六条　前条第一項の規定により許可を受けなければならないこととされている行為であつてその行為をするについて、他の法令の規定により許可、認可その他の処分で政令に定めるものを受けなければならないこととされている場合において、当該他の法令において当該処分の権限を有する行政庁又はその委任を受けた者は、当該処分をするときは、政令の定めるところにより、文化庁長官（第百八十四条第一項の規定により前条第一項の規定による許可を都道府県又は市の教育委員会が行う場合には、当該都道府県又は市の教育委員会）に対し、その旨を通知するものとする。
（復旧の届出等）
第百二十七条　史跡名勝天然記念物を復旧しようとするときは、管理団体又は所有者は、復旧に着手しようとする日の三十日前までに、文部科学省令の定めるところにより、文化庁長官にその旨を届け出なければならない。ただし、第百二十五条第一項の規定により許可を受けなければならない場合その他文部科学省令の定める場合は、この限りでない。
2　史跡名勝天然記念物の保護上必要があると認めるときは、文化庁長官は、前項の届出に係る史跡名勝天然記念物の復旧に関し技術的な指導と助言を与えることができる。
（環境保全）
第百二十八条　文化庁長官は、史跡名勝天然記念物の保存のため必要があると認めるときは、地域を定めて一定の行為を制限し、若しくは禁止し、又は必要な施設をすることを命ずることができる。
2　前項の規定による処分によつて損失を受けた者に対しては、国は、その通常生ずべき損失を補償する。
3　第一項の規定による制限又は禁止に違反した者には、第百二十五条第七項の規定を、前項の場合には、第四十一条第二項から第四項までの規定を準用する。
（管理団体による買取りの補助）

第百二十九条　管理団体である地方公共団体その他の法人が、史跡名勝天然記念物の指定に係る土地又は建造物その他の土地の定着物で、その管理に係る史跡名勝天然記念物の保存のため特に買い取る必要があると認められるものを買い取る場合には、国は、その買取りに要する経費の一部を補助することができる。

2　前項の場合には、第三十五条第二項及び第三項並びに第四十二条の規定を準用する。

（保存のための調査）

第百三十条　文化庁長官は、必要があると認めるときは、管理団体、所有者又は管理責任者に対し、史跡名勝天然記念物の現状又は管理、復旧若しくは環境保全の状況につき報告を求めることができる。

第百三十一条　文化庁長官は、次の各号のいずれかに該当する場合において、前条の報告によつてもなお史跡名勝天然記念物に関する状況を確認することができず、かつ、その確認のため他に方法がないと認めるときは、調査に当たる者を定め、その所在する土地又はその隣接地に立ち入つてその現状又は管理、復旧若しくは環境保全の状況につき実地調査及び土地の発掘、障害物の除却その他調査のため必要な措置をさせることができる。ただし、当該土地の所有者、占有者その他の関係者に対し、著しい損害を及ぼすおそれのある措置は、させてはならない。

一　史跡名勝天然記念物に関する現状変更又は保存に影響を及ぼす行為の許可の申請があつたとき。

二　史跡名勝天然記念物がき損し、又は衰亡しているとき。

三　史跡名勝天然記念物が滅失し、き損し、衰亡し、又は盗み取られるおそれのあるとき。

四　特別の事情によりあらためて特別史跡名勝天然記念物又は史跡名勝天然記念物としての価値を調査する必要があるとき。

2　前項の規定による調査又は措置によつて損失を受けた者に対しては、国は、その通常生ずべき損失を補償する。

3　第一項の規定により立ち入り、調査する場合には、第五十五条第二項の規定を、前項の場合には、第四十一条第二項から第四項までの規定を準用する。

（登録記念物）

第百三十二条　文部科学大臣は、史跡名勝天然記念物（第百十条第一項に規定する仮指定を都道府県の教育委員会が行つたものを含む。）以外の記念物（第百八十二条第二項に規定する指定を地方公共団体が行つているものを除く。）のうち、その文化財としての価値にかんがみ保存及び活用のための措置が特に必要とされるものを文化財登録原簿に登録することができる。

2　前項の規定による登録には、第五十七条第二項及び第三項、第百九条第三項から第五項まで並びに第百十一条第一項の規定を準用する。

第百三十三条　前条の規定により登録された記念物（以下「登録記念物」という。）については、第五十九条第一項から第五項まで、第六十四条、第六十八条、第百十一条第二項及び第三項並びに第百十三条から第百二十条までの規定を準用する。この場合において、第五十九条第一項中「第二十七条第一項の規定により重要文化財に指定したとき」とあるのは「第百九条第一項の規定により史跡名勝天然記念物に指定したとき（第百十条第一項に規定する仮指定を都道府県の教育委員会（当該記念物が指定都市の区域内に存する場合にあつては、当該指定都市の教育委員会）が行つたときを含む。）」と、同条第四項中「所有者に通知する」とあるのは「所有者及び権原に基づく占有者に通知する。ただし、通知すべき相手方が著しく多数で個別に通知し難い事情がある場合には、文部科学大臣は、当該通知に代えて、その通知すべき事項を当該登録記念物の所在地の市町村の事務所又はこれに準ずる施設の掲示場に掲示することができる。この場合においては、その掲示を始めた日から二週間を経過した時に当該通知が相手方に到達したものとみなす」と、同条第五項中「抹消には、前条第二項の規定を準用する」とあるのは「抹消は、前項の規定による官報の告示があつた日からその効力を生ずる。ただし、当該登録記念物の所有者又は権原に基づく占有者に対しては、前項の規定による通知が到達した時又は同項の規定によりその通知が到達したものとみなされる時からその効力を生ずる」と、第百十三条第一項中「不適当であると明らかに認められる場合には」とあるのは「不適当であることが明らかである旨の関係地方公共団体の申出があつた場合には、関係地方公共団体の意見を聴いて」と、第百十八条及び第百二十条中「第三十条、第三十一条第一項」とあるのは「第三十一条第一項」と、「準用する」とあるのは「準用する。この場合において、第三十一条第一項中「並びにこれに基いて発する文部科学省令及び文化庁長官の指示に従い」とあるのは「及びこれに基づく文部科学省令に従い」と読み替えるものとする」と、第百十八条中「第三十五条及び第四十七条の規定を、管理団体が指定され、又はその指定が解除された場合には、第五十六条第三項」とあるのは「第四十七条第四項」と、第百二十条中「第三十五条及び第四十七条の規定を、所有者が変更した場合の権利義務の承継には、第五十六条第一項」とあるのは「第四十七条第四項」と読み替えるものとする。

第八章　重要文化的景観

（重要文化的景観の選定）

第百三十四条　文部科学大臣は、都道府県又は市町村の申出に基づき、当該都道府県又は市町村が定める景観法（平成十六年法律第百十号）第八条第二項第一号に規定する景観計画区域又は同法第六十一条第一項に規定する景観地区内にある文化的景観であつて、文部科学省令で定める基準に照らして当該都道府県又は市町村がその保存のため必要な措置を講じているもののうち特に重要なものを重要文化的景観として選定することができる。

2　前項の規定による選定には、第百九条第三項から第五項までの規定を準用する。この場合において、同条第三項中「権原に基づく占有者」とあるのは、「権原に基づく占有者並びに第百三十四条第一項に規定する申出を行つた都道府県又は市町村」と読み替えるものとする。

（重要文化的景観の選定の解除）

第百三十五条　重要文化的景観がその価値を失つた場合その他特殊の事由があるときは、文部科学大臣は、その選定を解除することができる。

2　前項の場合には、前条第二項の規定を準用する。

（滅失又はき損）

第百三十六条　重要文化的景観の全部又は一部が滅失し、又はき損したときは、所有者又は権原に基づく占有者（以下この章において「所有者等」という。）は、文部科学省令の定める事項を記載した書面をもつて、その事実を知つた日から十日以内に文化庁長官に届け出なければならない。ただし、重要文化的景観の保存に著しい支障を及ぼすおそれがない場合として文部科学省令で定める場合は、この限りでない。

（管理に関する勧告又は命令）

第百三十七条　管理が適当でないため重要文化的景観が滅失し、又はき損するおそれがあると認めるときは、文化庁長官は、所有者等に対し、管理方法の改善その他管理に関し必要な措置を勧告することができる。

2　文化庁長官は、前項に規定する勧告を受けた所有者等が、正当な理由がなくてその勧告に係る措置を執らなかつた場合において、特に必要があると認めるときは、当該所有者等に対し、その勧告に係る措置を執るべきことを命ずることができる。

3　文化庁長官は、第一項の規定による勧告又は前項の規定による命令をしようとするときは、あらかじめ、当該重要文化的景観について第百三十四条第一項に規定する申出を行つた都道府県又は市町村の意見を聴くものとする。

4　第一項及び第二項の場合には、第三十六条第二項及び第三項の規定を準用する。

（費用負担に係る重要文化的景観譲渡の場合の納付金）

第百三十八条　国が滅失又はき損の防止の措置につき前条第四項で準用する第三十六条第二項の規定により費用を負担した重要文化的景観については、第四十二条の規定を準用する。

（現状変更等の届出等）

第百三十九条　重要文化的景観に関しその現状を変更し、又はその保存に影響を及ぼす行為をしようとする者は、現状を変更し、又は保存に影響を及ぼす行為をしようとする日の三十日前までに、文部科学省令で定めるところにより、文化庁長官にその旨を届け出なければならない。ただし、現状変更については維持の措置若しくは非常災害のために必要な応急措置又は他の法令の規定による現状の変更を内容とする命令に基づく措置を執る場合、保存に影響を及ぼす行為については影響の軽微である場合は、この限りでない。
2　前項ただし書に規定する維持の措置の範囲は、文部科学省令で定める。
3　重要文化的景観の保護上必要があると認めるときは、文化庁長官は、第一項の届出に係る重要文化的景観の現状の変更又は保存に影響を及ぼす行為に関し必要な指導、助言又は勧告をすることができる。

（現状等の報告）

第百四十条　文化庁長官は、必要があると認めるときは、所有者等に対し、重要文化的景観の現状又は管理若しくは復旧の状況につき報告を求めることができる。

（他の公益との調整等）

第百四十一条　文部科学大臣は、第百三十四条第一項の規定による選定を行うに当たつては、特に、関係者の所有権、鉱業権その他の財産権を尊重するとともに、国土の開発その他の公益との調整及び農林水産業その他の地域における産業との調和に留意しなければならない。
2　文化庁長官は、第百三十七条第一項の規定による勧告若しくは同条第二項の規定による命令又は第百三十九条第三項の規定による勧告をしようとするときは、重要文化的景観の特性にかんがみ、国土の開発その他の公益との調整及び農林水産業その他の地域における産業との調和を図る観点から、政令で定めるところにより、あらかじめ、関係各省各庁の長と協議しなければならない。
3　国は、重要文化的景観の保存のため特に必要と認められる物件の管理、修理、修景又は復旧について都道府県又は市町村が行う措置について、その経費の一部を補助することができる。

第九章　伝統的建造物群保存地区

（伝統的建造物群保存地区）

第百四十二条　この章において「伝統的建造物群保存地区」とは、伝統的建造物群及びこれと一体をなしてその価値を形成している環境を保存するため、次条第一項又は第二項の定めるところにより市町村が定める地区をいう。

（伝統的建造物群保存地区の決定及びその保護）

第百四十三条　市町村は、都市計画法（昭和四十三年法律第百号）第五条又は第五条の二の規定により指定された都市計画区域又は準都市計画区域内においては、都市計画に伝統的建造物群保存地区を定めることができる。この場合においては、市町村は、条例で、当該地区の保存のため、政令の定める基準に従い必要な現状変更の規制について定めるほか、その保存のため必要な措置を定めるものとする。
2　市町村は、前項の都市計画区域又は準都市計画区域以外の区域においては、条例の定めるところにより、伝統的建造物群保存地区を定めることができる。この場合においては、前項後段の規定を準用する。

3　都道府県知事は、第一項の伝統的建造物群保存地区に関する都市計画についての都市計画法第十九条第三項の規定による同意に当たつては、あらかじめ、当該都道府県の教育委員会の意見を聴かなければならない。

4　市町村は、伝統的建造物群保存地区に関し、地区の決定若しくはその取消し又は条例の制定若しくはその改廃を行つた場合は、文化庁長官に対し、その旨を報告しなければならない。

5　文化庁長官又は都道府県の教育委員会は、市町村に対し、伝統的建造物群保存地区の保存に関し、必要な指導又は助言をすることができる。

（重要伝統的建造物群保存地区の選定）

第百四十四条　文部科学大臣は、市町村の申出に基づき、伝統的建造物群保存地区の区域の全部又は一部で我が国にとつてその価値が特に高いものを、重要伝統的建造物群保存地区として選定することができる。

2　前項の規定による選定は、その旨を官報で告示するとともに、当該申出に係る市町村に通知してする。

（選定の解除）

第百四十五条　文部科学大臣は、重要伝統的建造物群保存地区がその価値を失つた場合その他特殊の事由があるときは、その選定を解除することができる。

2　前項の場合には、前条第二項の規定を準用する。

（管理等に関する補助）

第百四十六条　国は、重要伝統的建造物群保存地区の保存のための当該地区内における建造物及び伝統的建造物群と一体をなす環境を保存するため特に必要と認められる物件の管理、修理、修景又は復旧について市町村が行う措置について、その経費の一部を補助することができる。

第十章　文化財の保存技術の保護

（選定保存技術の選定等）

第百四十七条　文部科学大臣は、文化財の保存のために欠くことのできない伝統的な技術又は技能で保存の措置を講ずる必要があるものを選定保存技術として選定することができる。

2　文部科学大臣は、前項の規定による選定をするに当たつては、選定保存技術の保持者又は保存団体（選定保存技術を保存することを主たる目的とする団体（財団を含む。）で代表者又は管理人の定めのあるものをいう。以下同じ。）を認定しなければならない。

3　一の選定保存技術についての前項の認定は、保持者と保存団体とを併せてすることができる。

4　第一項の規定による選定及び前二項の規定による認定には、第七十一条第三項から第五項までの規定を準用する。

（選定等の解除）

第百四十八条　文部科学大臣は、選定保存技術について保存の措置を講ずる必要がなくなつた場合その他特殊の事由があるときは、その選定を解除することができる。

2　文部科学大臣は、保持者が心身の故障のため保持者として適当でなくなつたと認められる場合、保存団体が保存団体として適当でなくなつたと認められる場合その他特殊の事由があるときは、保持者又は保存団体の認定を解除することができる。

3　前二項の場合には、第七十二条第三項の規定を準用する。

4　前条第二項の認定が保持者のみについてなされた場合にあつてはそのすべてが死亡したとき、同項の認定が保存団体のみについてなされた場合にあつてはそのすべてが解散したとき（消滅したときを含む。以下この項において同じ。）、同項の認定が保持者と保存団体とを併せてなされた場合にあつては保持者のすべてが死亡しかつ保存団体のすべてが解散したときは、選定保存技術の選定は、解除されたものとする。この場合には、文部科学大臣は、その旨を官報で告示しなければならない。

（保持者の氏名変更等）

第百四十九条　保持者及び保存団体には、第七十三条の規定を準用する。この場合において、同条後段中「代表者」とあるのは、「代表者又は管理人」と読み替えるものとする。

（選定保存技術の保存）

第百五十条　文化庁長官は、選定保存技術の保存のため必要があると認めるときは、選定保存技術について自ら記録を作成し、又は伝承者の養成その他選定保存技術の保存のために必要と認められるものについて適当な措置を執ることができる。

（選定保存技術の記録の公開）

第百五十一条　選定保存技術の記録の所有者には、第八十八条の規定を準用する。

（選定保存技術の保存に関する援助）

第百五十二条　国は、選定保存技術の保持者若しくは保存団体又は地方公共団体その他その保存に当たることを適当と認める者に対し、指導、助言その他の必要と認められる援助をすることができる。

第十一章　文化審議会への諮問

第百五十三条　文部科学大臣は、次に掲げる事項については、あらかじめ、文化審議会に諮問しなければならない。

一　国宝又は重要文化財の指定及びその指定の解除

二　登録有形文化財の登録及びその登録の抹消（第五十九条第一項又は第二項の規定による登録の抹消を除く。）

三　重要無形文化財の指定及びその指定の解除

四　重要無形文化財の保持者又は保持団体の認定及びその認定の解除

五　重要有形民俗文化財又は重要無形民俗文化財の指定及びその指定の解除
六　登録有形民俗文化財の登録及びその登録の抹消（第九十条第三項で準用する第五十九条第一項又は第二項の規定による登録の抹消を除く。）
七　特別史跡名勝天然記念物又は史跡名勝天然記念物の指定及びその指定の解除
八　史跡名勝天然記念物の仮指定の解除
九　登録記念物の登録及びその登録の抹消（第百三十三条で準用する第五十九条第一項又は第二項の規定による登録の抹消を除く。）
十　重要文化的景観の選定及びその選定の解除
十一　重要伝統的建造物群保存地区の選定及びその選定の解除
十二　選定保存技術の選定及びその選定の解除
十三　選定保存技術の保持者又は保存団体の認定及びその認定の解除
2　文化庁長官は、次に掲げる事項については、あらかじめ、文化審議会に諮問しなければならない。
一　重要文化財の管理又は国宝の修理に関する命令
二　文化庁長官による国宝の修理又は滅失、き損若しくは盗難の防止の措置の施行
三　重要文化財の現状変更又は保存に影響を及ぼす行為の許可
四　重要文化財の環境保全のための制限若しくは禁止又は必要な施設の命令
五　国による重要文化財の買取り
六　重要無形文化財以外の無形文化財のうち文化庁長官が記録を作成すべきもの又は記録の作成等につき補助すべきものの選択
七　重要有形民俗文化財の管理に関する命令
八　重要有形民俗文化財の買取り
九　重要無形民俗文化財以外の無形の民俗文化財のうち文化庁長官が記録を作成すべきもの又は記録の作成等につき補助すべきものの選択
十　遺跡の現状変更となる行為についての停止命令又は禁止命令の期間の延長
十一　文化庁長官による埋蔵文化財の調査のための発掘の施行
十二　史跡名勝天然記念物の管理又は特別史跡名勝天然記念物の復旧に関する命令
十三　文化庁長官による特別史跡名勝天然記念物の復旧又は滅失、き損、衰亡若しくは盗難の防止の措置の施行
十四　史跡名勝天然記念物の現状変更又は保存に影響を及ぼす行為の許可
十五　史跡名勝天然記念物の環境保全のための制限若しくは禁止又は必要な施設の命令
十六　史跡名勝天然記念物の現状変更若しくは保存に影響を及ぼす行為の許可を受けず、若しくはその許可の条件に従わない場合又は史跡名勝天然記念物の環境保全のための制限若しくは禁止に違反した場合の原状回復の命令
十七　重要文化的景観の管理に関する命令
十八　第百八十四条第一項の政令（同項第二号に掲げる事務に係るものに限る。）の

制定又は改廃の立案

第十二章　補則

第一節　聴聞、意見の聴取及び審査請求

（聴聞の特例）

第百五十四条　文化庁長官（第百八十四条第一項の規定により文化庁長官の権限に属する事務を都道府県又は市の教育委員会が行う場合には、当該都道府県又は市の教育委員会。次項及び次条において同じ。）は、次に掲げる処分を行おうとするときは、行政手続法（平成五年法律第八十八号）第十三条第一項の規定による意見陳述のための手続の区分にかかわらず、聴聞を行わなければならない。

一　第四十五条第一項又は第百二十八条第一項の規定による制限、禁止又は命令で特定の者に対して行われるもの

二　第五十一条第五項（第五十一条の二（第八十五条で準用する場合を含む。）、第八十四条第二項及び第八十五条で準用する場合を含む。）の規定による公開の中止命令

三　第九十二条第二項の規定による発掘の禁止又は中止命令

四　第九十六条第二項の規定による同項の調査のための停止命令若しくは禁止命令又は同条第五項の規定によるこれらの命令の期間の延長

五　第百二十五条第七項（第百二十八条第三項で準用する場合を含む。）の規定による原状回復の命令

2　文化庁長官は、前項の聴聞又は第四十三条第四項（第百二十五条第三項で準用する場合を含む。）若しくは第五十三条第四項の規定による許可の取消しに係る聴聞をしようとするときは、当該聴聞の期日の十日前までに、行政手続法第十五条第一項の規定による通知をし、かつ、当該処分の内容並びに当該聴聞の期日及び場所を公示しなければならない。

3　前項の聴聞の期日における審理は、公開により行わなければならない。

（意見の聴取）

第百五十五条　文化庁長官は、次に掲げる措置を行おうとするときは、関係者又はその代理人の出頭を求めて、公開による意見の聴取を行わなければならない。

一　第三十八条第一項又は第百二十三条第一項の規定による修理若しくは復旧又は措置の施行

二　第五十五条第一項又は第百三十一条第一項の規定による立入調査又は調査のため必要な措置の施行

三　第九十八条第一項の規定による発掘の施行

2　文化庁長官は、前項の意見の聴取を行おうとするときは、その期日の十日前までに、同項各号に掲げる措置を行おうとする理由、その措置の内容並びに当該意見の聴取の期日及び場所を当該関係者に通告し、かつ、その措置の内容並びに当該意見の聴取の

期日及び場所を公示しなければならない。

3　第一項の意見の聴取においては、当該関係者又はその代理人は、自己又は本人のために意見を述べ、又は釈明し、かつ、証拠を提出することができる。

4　当該関係者又はその代理人が正当な理由がなくて第一項の意見の聴取に応じなかつたときは、文化庁長官は、当該意見の聴取を行わないで同項各号に掲げる措置をすることができる。

（審査請求の手続における意見の聴取）

第百五十六条　第一号に掲げる処分若しくはその不作為又は第二号に掲げる処分についての審査請求に対する裁決は、行政不服審査法（平成二十六年法律第六十八号）第二十四条の規定により当該審査請求を却下する場合を除き、当該審査請求がされた日（同法第二十三条の規定により不備を補正すべきことを命じた場合にあつては、当該不備が補正された日）から三十日以内に、審査請求人及び参加人（同法第十三条第四項に規定する参加人をいう。以下同じ。）又はこれらの者の代理人の出頭を求めて、審理員（同法第十一条第二項に規定する審理員をいい、審査庁（同法第九条第一項に規定する審査庁をいう。以下この条において同じ。）が都道府県又は市の教育委員会である場合にあつては、審査庁とする。次項及び次条において同じ。）が公開による意見の聴取をした後でなければ、してはならない。

一　第四十三条第一項又は第百二十五条第一項の規定による現状変更又は保存に影響を及ぼす行為の許可又は不許可

二　第百十三条第一項（第百三十三条で準用する場合を含む。）の規定による管理団体の指定

2　審理員は、前項の意見の聴取の期日及び場所をその期日の十日前までに全ての審理関係人（行政不服審査法第二十八条に規定する審理関係人をいい、審査庁が都道府県又は市の教育委員会である場合にあつては、審査請求人及び参加人とする。）に通告し、かつ、事案の要旨並びに当該意見の聴取の期日及び場所を公示しなければならない。

3　第一項に規定する審査請求については、行政不服審査法第三十一条の規定は適用せず、同項の意見の聴取については、同条第二項から第五項まで（同法第九条第三項の規定により読み替えて適用する場合を含む。）の規定を準用する。

（参加）

第百五十七条　審査請求人、参加人及び代理人のほか、当該処分について利害関係を有する者で前条第一項の意見の聴取に参加して意見を述べようとするものは、文部科学省令の定める事項を記載した書面をもつて、審理員にその旨を申し出て、その許可を受けなければならない。

（証拠の提示等）

第百五十八条　第百五十六条第一項の意見の聴取においては、審査請求人、参加人及び前条の規定により意見の聴取に参加した者又はこれらの者の代理人に対して、当該事

案について、証拠を提示し、かつ、意見を述べる機会を与えなければならない。

（裁決前の協議等）

第百五十九条　鉱業又は採石業との調整に関する事案に係る審査請求に対する裁決（却下の裁決を除く。）は、あらかじめ公害等調整委員会に協議した後にしなければならない。

2　関係各行政機関の長は、審査請求に係る事案について意見を述べることができる。

（手続）

第百六十条　第百五十六条から前条まで及び行政不服審査法に定めるもののほか、審査請求に関する手続は、文部科学省令で定める。

第百六十一条　削除

第二節　国に関する特例

（国に関する特例）

第百六十二条　国又は国の機関に対しこの法律の規定を適用する場合において、この節に特別の規定のあるときは、その規定による。

（重要文化財等についての国に関する特例）

第百六十三条　重要文化財、重要有形民俗文化財、史跡名勝天然記念物又は重要文化的景観が国有財産法に規定する国有財産であるときは、そのものは、文部科学大臣が管理する。ただし、そのものが文部科学大臣以外の者が管理している同法第三条第二項に規定する行政財産であるときその他文部科学大臣以外の者が管理すべき特別の必要のあるものであるときは、そのものを関係各省各庁の長が管理するか、又は文部科学大臣が管理するかは、文部科学大臣、関係各省各庁の長及び財務大臣が協議して定める。

第百六十四条　前条の規定により重要文化財、重要有形民俗文化財、史跡名勝天然記念物又は重要文化的景観を文部科学大臣が管理するため、所属を異にする会計の間において所管換え又は所属替えをするときは、国有財産法第十五条の規定にかかわらず、無償として整理することができる。

第百六十五条　国の所有に属する有形文化財又は有形の民俗文化財を国宝若しくは重要文化財又は重要有形民俗文化財に指定したときは、第二十八条第一項又は第三項（第七十八条第二項で準用する場合を含む。）の規定により所有者に対し行うべき通知又は指定書の交付は、当該有形文化財又は有形の民俗文化財を管理する各省各庁の長に対し行うものとする。この場合においては、国宝の指定書を受けた各省各庁の長は、直ちに国宝に指定された重要文化財の指定書を文部科学大臣に返付しなければならない。

2　国の所有に属する国宝若しくは重要文化財又は重要有形民俗文化財の指定を解除したときは、第二十九条第二項（第七十九条第二項で準用する場合を含む。）又は第五項の規定により所有者に対し行うべき通知又は指定書の交付は、当該国宝若しくは重要文化財又は重要有形民俗文化財を管理する各省各庁の長に対し行うものとする。この場合においては、当該各省各庁の長は、直ちに指定書を文部科学大臣に返付しなければならない。

3　国の所有又は占有に属するものを特別史跡名勝天然記念物若しくは史跡名勝天然記念物に指定し、若しくは仮指定し、又はその指定若しくは仮指定を解除したときは、第百九条第三項（第百十条第三項及び第百十二条第四項で準用する場合を含む。）の規定により所有者又は占有者に対し行うべき通知は、その指定若しくは仮指定又は指定若しくは仮指定の解除に係るものを管理する各省各庁の長に対し行うものとする。

4　国の所有又は占有に属するものを重要文化的景観に選定し、又はその選定を解除したときは、第百三十四条第二項（第百三十五条第二項で準用する場合を含む。）で準用する第百九条第三項の規定により所有者又は占有者に対し行うべき通知は、当該重要文化的景観を管理する各省各庁の長に対し行うものとする。

第百六十六条　重要文化財、重要有形民俗文化財、史跡名勝天然記念物又は重要文化的景観を管理する各省各庁の長は、この法律並びにこれに基づいて発する文部科学省令及び文化庁長官の勧告に従い、重要文化財、重要有形民俗文化財、史跡名勝天然記念物又は重要文化的景観を管理しなければならない。

第百六十七条　次に掲げる場合には、関係各省各庁の長は、文部科学大臣を通じ文化庁長官に通知しなければならない。

一　重要文化財、重要有形民俗文化財又は史跡名勝天然記念物を取得したとき。

二　重要文化財、重要有形民俗文化財又は史跡名勝天然記念物の所管換えを受け、又は所属替えをしたとき。

三　所管に属する重要文化財、重要有形民俗文化財、史跡名勝天然記念物又は重要文化的景観の全部又は一部が滅失し、き損し、若しくは衰亡し、又はこれを亡失し、若しくは盗み取られたとき。

四　所管に属する重要文化財又は重要有形民俗文化財の所在の場所を変更しようとするとき。

五　所管に属する重要文化財又は史跡名勝天然記念物を修理し、又は復旧しようとするとき（次条第一項第一号の規定により文化庁長官の同意を求めなければならない場合その他文部科学省令の定める場合を除く。）。

六　所管に属する重要有形民俗文化財又は重要文化的景観の現状を変更し、又はその保存に影響を及ぼす行為をしようとするとき。

七　所管に属する史跡名勝天然記念物の指定地域内の土地について、その土地の所在、地番、地目又は地積に異動があつたとき。

2　前項第一号及び第二号の場合に係る通知には、第三十二条第一項（第八十条及び第百二十条で準用する場合を含む。）の規定を、前項第三号の場合に係る通知には、第三十三条（第八十条及び第百二十条で準用する場合を含む。）及び第百三十六条の規定を、前項第四号の場合に係る通知には、第三十四条（第八十条で準用する場合を含む。）の規定を、前項第五号の場合に係る通知には、第四十三条の二第一項及び第百二十七条第一項の規定を、前項第六号の場合に係る通知には、第八十一条第一項及び第百三十九条第一項の規定を、前項第七号の場合に係る通知には、第百十五条第二項の規定を準用する。

3　文化庁長官は、第一項第五号又は第六号の通知に係る事項に関し必要な勧告をすることができる。

第百六十八条　次に掲げる場合には、関係各省各庁の長は、あらかじめ、文部科学大臣を通じ文化庁長官の同意を求めなければならない。

一　重要文化財又は史跡名勝天然記念物の現状を変更し、又はその保存に影響を及ぼす行為をしようとするとき。

二　所管に属する重要文化財又は重要有形民俗文化財を輸出しようとするとき。

三　所管に属する重要文化財、重要有形民俗文化財又は史跡名勝天然記念物の貸付、交換、売払、譲与その他の処分をしようとするとき。

2　各省各庁の長以外の国の機関が、重要文化財又は史跡名勝天然記念物の現状を変更し、又はその保存に影響を及ぼす行為をしようとするときは、あらかじめ、文化庁長官の同意を求めなければならない。

3　第一項第一号及び前項の場合には、第四十三条第一項ただし書及び同条第二項並びに第百二十五条第一項ただし書及び同条第二項の規定を準用する。

4　文化庁長官は、第一項第一号又は第二項に規定する措置につき同意を与える場合においては、その条件としてその措置に関し必要な勧告をすることができる。

5　関係各省各庁の長その他の国の機関は、前項の規定による文化庁長官の勧告を十分に尊重しなければならない。

第百六十九条　文化庁長官は、必要があると認めるときは、文部科学大臣を通じ各省各庁の長に対し、次に掲げる事項につき必要な勧告をすることができる。

一　所管に属する重要文化財、重要有形民俗文化財又は史跡名勝天然記念物の管理方法

二　所管に属する重要文化財、重要有形民俗文化財、史跡名勝天然記念物又は重要文化的景観の修理若しくは復旧又は滅失、き損、衰亡若しくは盗難の防止の措置

三　重要文化財又は史跡名勝天然記念物の環境保全のため必要な施設

四　所管に属する重要文化財又は重要有形民俗文化財の出品又は公開

2　前項の勧告については、前条第五項の規定を準用する。

3　第一項の規定による文化庁長官の勧告に基づいて施行する同項第二号に規定する修理、復旧若しくは措置又は同項第三号に規定する施設に要する経費の分担については、文部科学大臣と各省各庁の長が協議して定める。

第百七十条　文化庁長官は、次の各号のいずれかに該当する場合においては、国の所有

に属する国宝又は特別史跡名勝天然記念物につき、自ら修理若しくは復旧を行い、又は滅失、き損、衰亡若しくは盗難の防止の措置をすることができる。この場合においては、文化庁長官は、当該文化財が文部科学大臣以外の各省各庁の長の所管に属するものであるときは、あらかじめ、修理若しくは復旧又は措置の内容、着手の時期その他必要な事項につき、文部科学大臣を通じ当該文化財を管理する各省各庁の長と協議し、当該文化財が文部科学大臣の所管に属するものであるときは、文部科学大臣の定める場合を除いて、その承認を受けなければならない。

一　関係各省各庁の長が前条第一項第二号に規定する修理若しくは復旧又は措置についての文化庁長官の勧告に応じないとき。

二　国宝又は特別史跡名勝天然記念物がき損し、若しくは衰亡している場合又は滅失し、き損し、衰亡し、若しくは盗み取られるおそれのある場合において、関係各省各庁の長に当該修理若しくは復旧又は措置をさせることが適当でないと認められるとき。

第百七十一条　文部科学大臣は、国の所有に属するものを国宝、重要文化財、重要有形民俗文化財、特別史跡名勝天然記念物若しくは史跡名勝天然記念物に指定し、若しくは重要文化的景観に選定するに当たり、又は国の所有に属する国宝、重要文化財、重要有形民俗文化財、特別史跡名勝天然記念物、史跡名勝天然記念物若しくは重要文化的景観に関する状況を確認するため必要があると認めるときは、関係各省各庁の長に対し調査のため必要な報告を求め、又は、重要有形民俗文化財及び重要文化的景観に係る場合を除き、調査に当たる者を定めて実地調査をさせることができる。

第百七十二条　文化庁長官は、国の所有に属する重要文化財、重要有形民俗文化財又は史跡名勝天然記念物の保存のため特に必要があると認めるときは、適当な地方公共団体その他の法人を指定して当該文化財の保存のため必要な管理（当該文化財の保存のため必要な施設、設備その他の物件で国の所有又は管理に属するものの管理を含む。）を行わせることができる。

2　前項の規定による指定をするには、文化庁長官は、あらかじめ、文部科学大臣を通じ当該文化財を管理する各省各庁の長の同意を求めるとともに、指定しようとする地方公共団体その他の法人の同意を得なければならない。

3　第一項の規定による指定には、第三十二条の二第三項及び第四項の規定を準用する。

4　第一項の規定による管理によつて生ずる収益は、当該地方公共団体その他の法人の収入とする。

5　地方公共団体その他の法人が第一項の規定による管理を行う場合には、重要文化財又は重要有形民俗文化財の管理に係るときは、第三十条、第三十一条第一項、第三十二条の四第一項、第三十三条、第三十四条、第三十五条、第三十六条、第四十七条の二第三項及び第五十四条の規定を、史跡名勝天然記念物に係るときは、第三十条、第三十一条第一項、第三十三条、第三十五条、第百十五条第一項及び第二項、第百十六条第一項及び第三項、第百二十一条並びに第百三十条の規定を準用する。

第百七十三条　前条第一項の規定による指定の解除については、第三十二条の三の規定を準用する。

第百七十四条　文化庁長官は、重要文化財、重要有形民俗文化財又は史跡名勝天然記念物の保護のため特に必要があると認めるときは、第百七十二条第一項の規定による指定を受けた地方公共団体その他の法人に当該文化財の修理又は復旧を行わせることができる。

2　前項の規定による修理又は復旧を行わせる場合には、第百七十二条第二項の規定を準用する。

3　地方公共団体その他の法人が第一項の規定による修理又は復旧を行う場合には、重要文化財又は重要有形民俗文化財に係るときは、第三十二条の四第一項及び第三十五条の規定を、史跡名勝天然記念物に係るときは、第三十五条、第百十六条第一項及び第百十七条の規定を準用する。

第百七十五条　第百七十二条第一項の規定による指定を受けた地方公共団体は、その管理する国の所有に属する重要文化財、重要有形民俗文化財又は史跡名勝天然記念物でその指定に係る土地及び建造物を、その管理のため必要な限度において、無償で使用することができる。

2　国有財産法第二十二条第二項及び第三項の規定は、前項の規定により土地及び建造物を使用させる場合について準用する。

第百七十六条　文化庁長官は、第九十八条第一項の規定により発掘を施行しようとする場合において、その発掘を施行しようとする土地が国の所有に属し、又は国の機関の占有するものであるときは、あらかじめ、発掘の目的、方法、着手の時期その他必要と認める事項につき、文部科学大臣を通じ関係各省各庁の長と協議しなければならない。ただし、当該各省各庁の長が文部科学大臣であるときは、その承認を受けるべきものとする。

第百七十七条　第百四条第一項の規定により国庫に帰属した文化財は、文化庁長官が管理する。ただし、その保存のため又はその効用から見て他の機関に管理させることが適当であるときは、これを当該機関の管理に移さなければならない。

（登録有形文化財等についての国に関する特例）

第百七十八条　国の所有に属する有形文化財又は有形の民俗文化財について第五十七条第一項又は第九十条第一項の規定による登録をしたときは、第五十八条第一項又は第三項（これらの規定を第九十条第三項で準用する場合を含む。）の規定により所有者に対して行うべき通知又は登録証の交付は、当該登録有形文化財又は登録有形民俗文化財を管理する各省各庁の長に対して行うものとする。

2　国の所有に属する登録有形文化財又は登録有形民俗文化財について、第五十九条第一項から第三項まで（これらの規定を第九十条第三項で準用する場合を含む。）の規定による登録の抹消をしたときは、第五十九条第四項（第九十条第三項で準用する場合を含む。）の規定により所有者に対して行うべき通知は、当該登録有形文化財又は登録有形民俗文化財を管理する各省各庁の長に対して行うものとする。この場合においては、当該各省各庁の長は、直ちに登録証を文部科学大臣に返付しなければならない。

3　国の所有又は占有に属する記念物について第百三十二条第一項の規定による登録をし、又は第百三十三条で準用する第五十九条第一項から第三項までの規定による登録の抹消をしたときは、第百三十二条第二項で準用する第百九条第三項又は第百三十三条で読み替えて準用する第五十九条第四項の規定により所有者又は占有者に対して行うべき通知は、当該登録記念物を管理する各省各庁の長に対して行うものとする。

第百七十九条　次に掲げる場合には、関係各省各庁の長は、文部科学大臣を通じ文化庁長官に通知しなければならない。

一　登録有形文化財、登録有形民俗文化財又は登録記念物を取得したとき。

二　登録有形文化財、登録有形民俗文化財又は登録記念物の所管換えを受け、又は所属替えをしたとき。

三　所管に属する登録有形文化財、登録有形民俗文化財又は登録記念物の全部又は一部が滅失し、き損し、若しくは衰亡し、又はこれを亡失し、若しくは盗み取られたとき。

四　所管に属する登録有形文化財又は登録有形民俗文化財の所在の場所を変更しようとするとき。

五　登録有形文化財、登録有形民俗文化財又は登録記念物の現状を変更しようとするとき。

六　所管に属する登録有形文化財又は登録有形民俗文化財を輸出しようとするとき。

七　所管に属する登録記念物の所在する土地について、その土地の所在、地番、地目又は地積に異動があつたとき。

2　各省各庁の長以外の国の機関が登録有形文化財、登録有形民俗文化財又は登録記念物の現状を変更しようとするときは、文化庁長官に通知しなければならない。

3　第一項第一号及び第二号に掲げる場合に係る通知には第三十二条第一項の規定を、第一項第三号に掲げる場合に係る通知には第三十三条又は第六十一条（第九十条第三項で準用する場合を含む。）の規定を、第一項第四号に掲げる場合に係る通知には第六十二条（第九十条第三項で準用する場合を含む。）の規定を、第一項第五号及び前項に規定する場合に係る通知には第六十四条第一項（第九十条第三項及び第百三十三条で準用する場合を含む。）の規定を、第一項第六号に掲げる場合に係る通知には第六十五条第一項（第九十条第三項で準用する場合を含む。）の規定を、第一項第七号に掲げる場合に係る通知には第百十五条第二項の規定を準用する。

4　第一項第五号及び第二項に規定する現状の変更には、第六十四条第一項ただし書及び第二項の規定を準用する。

5　登録有形文化財、登録有形民俗文化財又は登録記念物の保護上必要があると認めるときは、文化庁長官は、第一項第五号又は第二項に規定する現状の変更に関し、文部科学大臣を通じ関係各省各庁の長に対し、又は各省各庁の長以外の国の機関に対して意見を述べることができる。

第百八十条　文部科学大臣は、国の所有に属する登録有形文化財、登録有形民俗文化財又は登録記念物に関する状況を確認するため必要があると認めるときは、関係各省各庁の長に対し調査のため必要な報告を求めることができる。

第百八十一条　国の所有に属する登録有形文化財又は登録有形民俗文化財については、第六十条第三項から第五項まで、第六十三条第二項及び第六十七条第三項（これらの規定を第九十条第三項で準用する場合を含む。）の規定は、適用しない。

2　国の所有に属する登録記念物については、第百三十三条で準用する第百十三条から第百十八条までの規定は、適用しない。

第三節　地方公共団体及び教育委員会

（地方公共団体の事務）

第百八十二条　地方公共団体は、文化財の管理、修理、復旧、公開その他その保存及び活用に要する経費につき補助することができる。

2　地方公共団体は、条例の定めるところにより、重要文化財、重要無形文化財、重要有形民俗文化財、重要無形民俗文化財及び史跡名勝天然記念物以外の文化財で当該地方公共団体の区域内に存するもののうち重要なものを指定して、その保存及び活用のため必要な措置を講ずることができる。

3　前項に規定する条例の制定若しくはその改廃又は同項に規定する文化財の指定若しくはその解除を行つた場合には、教育委員会は、文部科学省令の定めるところにより、文化庁長官にその旨を報告しなければならない。

（地方債についての配慮）

第百八十三条　地方公共団体が文化財の保存及び活用を図るために行う事業に要する経費に充てるために起こす地方債については、法令の範囲内において、資金事情及び当該地方公共団体の財政状況が許す限り、適切な配慮をするものとする。

（都道府県又は市の教育委員会が処理する事務）

第百八十四条　次に掲げる文化庁長官の権限に属する事務の全部又は一部は、政令で定めるところにより、都道府県又は市の教育委員会が行うこととすることができる。

一　第三十五条第三項（第三十六条第三項（第八十三条、第百二十一条第二項（第百七十二条第五項で準用する場合を含む。）及び第百七十二条第五項で準用する場合を含む。）、第三十七条第四項（第八十三条及び第百二十二条第三項で準用する場合を含む。）、第四十六条の二第二項、第七十四条第二項、第七十七条第二項（第九十一条で準用する場合を含む。）、第八十三条、第八十七条第二項、第百十八条、第百二十条、第百二十九条第二項、第百七十二条第五項及び第百七十四条第三項で

準用する場合を含む。）の規定による指揮監督

二　第四十三条又は第百二十五条の規定による現状変更又は保存に影響を及ぼす行為の許可及びその取消し並びにその停止命令（重大な現状変更又は保存に重大な影響を及ぼす行為の許可及びその取消しを除く。）

三　第五十一条第五項（第五十一条の二（第八十五条で準用する場合を含む。）、第八十四条第二項及び第八十五条で準用する場合を含む。）の規定による公開の停止命令

四　第五十三条第一項、第三項及び第四項の規定による公開の許可及びその取消し並びに公開の停止命令

五　第五十四条（第八十六条及び第百七十二条第五項で準用する場合を含む。）、第五十五条、第百三十条（第百七十二条第五項で準用する場合を含む。）又は第百三十一条の規定による調査又は調査のため必要な措置の施行

六　第九十二条第一項（第九十三条第一項において準用する場合を含む。）の規定による届出の受理、第九十二条第二項の規定による指示及び命令、第九十三条第二項の規定による指示、第九十四条第一項の規定による通知の受理、同条第二項の規定による通知、同条第三項の規定による協議、同条第四項の規定による勧告、第九十六条第一項の規定による届出の受理、同条第二項又は第七項の規定による命令、同条第三項の規定による意見の聴取、同条第五項又は第七項の規定による期間の延長、同条第八項の規定による指示、第九十七条第一項の規定による通知の受理、同条第二項の規定による通知、同条第三項の規定による協議並びに同条第四項の規定による勧告

2　都道府県又は市の教育委員会が前項の規定によつてした同項第五号に掲げる第五十五条又は第百三十一条の規定による立入調査又は調査のための必要な措置の施行については、審査請求をすることができない。

3　都道府県又は市の教育委員会が、第一項の規定により、同項第六号に掲げる事務のうち第九十四条第一項から第四項まで又は第九十七条第一項から第四項までの規定によるものを行う場合には、第九十四条第五項又は第九十七条第五項の規定は適用しない。

4　都道府県又は市の教育委員会が第一項の規定によつてした次の各号に掲げる事務（当該事務が地方自治法第二条第八項に規定する自治事務である場合に限る。）により損失を受け た者に対しては、当該各号に定める規定にかかわらず、当該都道府県又は市が、その通常生ずべき損失を補償する。

一　第一項第二号に掲げる第四十三条又は第百二十五条の規定による現状変更又は保存に影響を及ぼす行為の許可　第四十三条第五項又は第百二十五条第五項

二　第一項第五号に掲げる第五十五条又は第百三十一条の規定による調査又は調査のため必要な措置の施行　第五十五条第三項又は第百三十一条第二項

三　第一項第六号に掲げる第九十六条第二項の規定による命令　同条第九項

5　前項の補償の額は、当該都道府県又は市の教育委員会が決定する。
6　前項の規定による補償額については、第四十一条第三項の規定を準用する。
7　前項において準用する第四十一条第三項の規定による訴えにおいては、都道府県又は市を被告とする。
8　都道府県又は市の教育委員会が第一項の規定によつてした処分その他公権力の行使に当たる行為のうち地方自治法第二条第九項第一号に規定する第一号法定受託事務に係るものについての審査請求は、文化庁長官に対してするものとする。

（出品された重要文化財等の管理）

第百八十五条　文化庁長官は、政令で定めるところにより、第四十八条（第八十五条で準用する場合を含む。）の規定により出品された重要文化財又は重要有形民俗文化財の管理の事務の全部又は一部を、都道府県又は指定都市等の教育委員会が行うこととすることができる。
2　前項の規定により、都道府県又は指定都市等の教育委員会が同項の管理の事務を行う場合には、都道府県又は指定都市等の教育委員会は、その職員のうちから、当該重要文化財又は重要有形民俗文化財の管理の責めに任ずべき者を定めなければならない。

（修理等の施行の委託）

第百八十六条　文化庁長官は、必要があると認めるときは、第三十八条第一項又は第百七十条の規定による国宝の修理又は滅失、き損若しくは盗難の防止の措置の施行、第九十八条第一項の規定による発掘の施行及び第百二十三条第一項又は第百七十条の規定による特別史跡名勝天然記念物の復旧又は滅失、き損、衰亡若しくは盗難の防止の措置の施行につき、都道府県の教育委員会に対し、その全部又は一部を委託することができる。
2　都道府県の教育委員会が前項の規定による委託に基づき、第三十八条第一項の規定による修理又は措置の施行の全部又は一部を行う場合には、第三十九条の規定を、第九十八条第一項の規定による発掘の施行の全部又は一部を行う場合には、同条第三項で準用する第三十九条の規定を、第百二十三条第一項の規定による復旧又は措置の施行の全部又は一部を行う場合には、同条第二項で準用する第三十九条の規定を準用する。

（重要文化財等の管理等の受託又は技術的指導）

第百八十七条　都道府県又は指定都市の教育委員会は、所有者（管理団体がある場合は、その者）又は管理責任者の求めに応じ、重要文化財、重要有形民俗文化財又は史跡名勝天然記念物の管理（管理団体がある場合を除く。）、修理若しくは復旧につき委託を受け、又は技術的指導をすることができる。
2　都道府県又は指定都市の教育委員会が前項の規定により管理、修理又は復旧の委託を受ける場合には、第三十九条第一項及び第二項の規定を準用する。

（書類等の経由）

第百八十八条　この法律の規定により文化財に関し文部科学大臣又は文化庁長官に提出

すべき届書その他の書類及び物件の提出は、都道府県の教育委員会（当該文化財が指定都市の区域内に存する場合にあつては、当該指定都市の教育委員会。以下この条において同じ。）を経由すべきものとする。

2　都道府県の教育委員会は、前項に規定する書類及び物件を受理したときは、意見を具してこれを文部科学大臣又は文化庁長官に送付しなければならない。

3　この法律の規定により文化財に関し文部科学大臣又は文化庁長官が発する命令、勧告、指示その他の処分の告知は、都道府県の教育委員会を経由すべきものとする。ただし、特に緊急な場合は、この限りでない。

（文部科学大臣又は文化庁長官に対する意見具申）

第百八十九条　都道府県及び市町村の教育委員会は、当該都道府県又は市町村の区域内に存する文化財の保存及び活用に関し、文部科学大臣又は文化庁長官に対して意見を具申することができる。

（地方文化財保護審議会）

第百九十条　都道府県及び市町村の教育委員会に、条例の定めるところにより、地方文化財保護審議会を置くことができる。

2　地方文化財保護審議会は、都道府県又は市町村の教育委員会の諮問に応じて、文化財の保存及び活用に関する重要事項について調査審議し、並びにこれらの事項に関して当該都道府県又は市町村の教育委員会に建議する。

3　地方文化財保護審議会の組織及び運営に関し必要な事項は、条例で定める。

（文化財保護指導委員）

第百九十一条　都道府県の教育委員会に、文化財保護指導委員を置くことができる。

2　文化財保護指導委員は、文化財について、随時、巡視を行い、並びに所有者その他の関係者に対し、文化財の保護に関する指導及び助言をするとともに、地域住民に対し、文化財保護思想について普及活動を行うものとする。

3　文化財保護指導委員は、非常勤とする。

（事務の区分）

第百九十二条　第百十条第一項及び第二項、第百十二条第一項並びに第百十条第三項及び第百十二条第四項において準用する第百九条第三項及び第四項の規定により都道府県又は指定都市が処理することとされている事務は、地方自治法第二条第九項第一号に規定する第一号法定受託事務とする。

第十三章　罰則

第百九十三条　第四十四条の規定に違反し、文化庁長官の許可を受けないで重要文化財を輸出した者は、五年以下の懲役若しくは禁錮（こ）又は百万円以下の罰金に処する。

第百九十四条　第八十二条の規定に違反し、文化庁長官の許可を受けないで重要有形民俗文化財を輸出した者は、三年以下の懲役若しくは禁錮（こ）又は五十万円以下の罰金に処する。

第百九十五条　重要文化財を損壊し、き棄し、又は隠匿した者は、五年以下の懲役若しくは禁錮（こ）又は三十万円以下の罰金に処する。

2　前項に規定する者が当該重要文化財の所有者であるときは、二年以下の懲役若しくは禁錮（こ）又は二十万円以下の罰金若しくは科料に処する。

第百九十六条　史跡名勝天然記念物の現状を変更し、又はその保存に影響を及ぼす行為をして、これを滅失し、き損し、又は衰亡するに至らしめた者は、五年以下の懲役若しくは禁錮（こ）又は三十万円以下の罰金に処する。

2　前項に規定する者が当該史跡名勝天然記念物の所有者であるときは、二年以下の懲役若しくは禁錮（こ）又は二十万円以下の罰金若しくは科料に処する。

第百九十七条　次の各号のいずれかに該当する者は、二十万円以下の罰金に処する。

一　第四十三条又は第百二十五条の規定に違反して、許可を受けず、若しくはその許可の条件に従わないで、重要文化財若しくは史跡名勝天然記念物の現状を変更し、若しくはその保存に影響を及ぼす行為をし、又は現状の変更若しくは保存に影響を及ぼす行為の停止の命令に従わなかつた者

二　第九十六条第二項の規定に違反して、現状を変更することとなるような行為の停止又は禁止の命令に従わなかつた者

第百九十八条　次の各号のいずれかに該当する者は、十万円以下の罰金に処する。

一　第三十九条第三項（第百八十六条第二項で準用する場合を含む。）で準用する第三十二条の二第五項の規定に違反して、国宝の修理又は滅失、き損若しくは盗難の防止の措置の施行を拒み、又は妨げた者

二　第九十八条第三項（第百八十六条第二項で準用する場合を含む。）で準用する第三十九条第三項で準用する第三十二条の二第五項の規定に違反して、発掘の施行を拒み、又は妨げた者

三　第百二十三条第二項（第百八十六条第二項で準用する場合を含む。）で準用する第三十九条第三項で準用する第三十二条の二第五項の規定に違反して、特別史跡名勝天然記念物の復旧又は滅失、き損、衰亡若しくは盗難の防止の措置の施行を拒み、又は妨げた者

第百九十九条　法人の代表者又は法人若しくは人の代理人、使用人その他の従業者がその法人又は人の業務又は財産の管理に関して第百九十三条から前条までの違反行為をしたときは、その行為者を罰するほか、その法人又は人に対し、各本条の罰金刑を科する。

第二百条　第三十九条第一項（第四十七条第三項（第八十三条で準用する場合を含む。）、第百二十三条第二項、第百八十六条第二項又は第百八十七条第二項で準用する場合を含む。）、第四十九条（第八十五条で準用する場合を含む。）又は第百八十五条第二項に規定する重要文化財、重要有形民俗文化財又は史跡名勝天然記念物の管理、修理

又は復旧の施行の責めに任ずべき者が怠慢又は重大な過失によりその管理、修理又は復旧に係る重要文化財、重要有形民俗文化財又は史跡名勝天然記念物を滅失し、き損し、衰亡し、又は盗み取られるに至らしめたときは、三十万円以下の過料に処する。

第二百一条　次の各号のいずれかに該当する者は、三十万円以下の過料に処する。

一　正当な理由がなくて、第三十六条第一項（第八十三条及び第百七十二条第五項で準用する場合を含む。）又は第三十七条第一項の規定による重要文化財若しくは重要有形民俗文化財の管理又は国宝の修理に関する文化庁長官の命令に従わなかつた者

二　正当な理由がなくて、第百二十一条第一項（第百七十二条第五項で準用する場合を含む。）又は第百二十二条第一項の規定による史跡名勝天然記念物の管理又は特別史跡名勝天然記念物の復旧に関する文化庁長官の命令に従わなかつた者

三　正当な理由がなくて、第百三十七条第二項の規定による重要文化的景観の管理に関する勧告に係る措置を執るべき旨の文化庁長官の命令に従わなかつた者

第二百二条　次の各号のいずれかに該当する者は、十万円以下の過料に処する。

一　正当な理由がなくて、第四十五条第一項の規定による制限若しくは禁止又は施設の命令に違反した者

二　第四十六条（第八十三条で準用する場合を含む。）の規定に違反して、文化庁長官に国に対する売渡しの申出をせず、若しくは申出をした後第四十六条第五項（第八十三条で準用する場合を含む。）に規定する期間内に、国以外の者に重要文化財又は重要有形民俗文化財を譲り渡し、又は第四十六条第一項（第八十三条で準用する場合を含む。）の規定による売渡しの申出につき、虚偽の事実を申し立てた者

三　第四十八条第四項（第五十一条第三項（第八十五条で準用する場合を含む。）及び第八十五条で準用する場合を含む。）の規定に違反して、出品若しくは公開をせず、又は第五十一条第五項（第五十一条の二（第八十五条で準用する場合を含む。）、第八十四条第二項及び第八十五条で準用する場合を含む。）の規定に違反して、公開の停止若しくは中止の命令に従わなかつた者

四　第五十三条第一項、第三項又は第四項の規定に違反して、許可を受けず、若しくはその許可の条件に従わないで重要文化財を公開し、又は公開の停止の命令に従わなかつた者

五　第五十四条（第八十六条及び第百七十二条第五項で準用する場合を含む。）、第五十五条、第六十八条（第九十条第三項及び第百三十三条で準用する場合を含む。）、第百三十条（第百七十二条第五項で準用する場合を含む。）、第百三十一条又は第百四十条の規定に違反して、報告をせず、若しくは虚偽の報告をし、又は当該公務員の立入調査若しくは調査のための必要な措置の施行を拒み、妨げ、若しくは忌避した者

六　第九十二条第二項の規定に違反して、発掘の禁止、停止又は中止の命令に従わな

かつた者

七　正当な理由がなくて、第百二十八条第一項の規定による制限若しくは禁止又は施設の命令に違反した者

第二百三条　次の各号のいずれかに該当する者は、五万円以下の過料に処する。

一　第二十八条第五項、第二十九条第四項（第七十九条第二項で準用する場合を含む。）、第五十六条第二項（第八十六条で準用する場合を含む。）又は第五十九条第六項若しくは第六十九条（これらの規定を第九十条第三項で準用する場合を含む。）の規定に違反して、重要文化財若しくは重要有形民俗文化財の指定書又は登録有形文化財若しくは登録有形民俗文化財の登録証を文部科学大臣に返付せず、又は新所有者に引き渡さなかつた者

二　第三十一条第三項（第六十条第四項（第九十条第三項で準用する場合を含む。）、第八十条及び第百十九条第二項（第百三十三条で準用する場合を含む。）で準用する場合を含む。）、第三十二条（第六十条第四項（第九十条第三項で準用する場合を含む。）、第八十条及び第百二十条（第百三十三条で準用する場合を含む。）で準用する場合を含む。）、第三十三条（第八十条、第百十八条及び第百二十条（これらの規定を第百三十三条で準用する場合を含む。）並びに第百七十二条第五項で準用する場合を含む。）、第三十四条（第八十条及び第百七十二条第五項で準用する場合を含む。）、第四十三条の二第一項、第六十一条若しくは第六十二条（これらの規定を第九十条第三項で準用する場合を含む。）、第六十四条第一項（第九十条第三項及び第百三十三条で準用する場合を含む。）、第六十五条第一項（第九十条第三項で準用する場合を含む。）、第七十三条、第八十一条第一項、第八十四条第一項本文、第九十二条第一項、第九十六条第一項、第百十五条第二項（第百二十条、第百三十三条及び第百七十二条第五項で準用する場合を含む。）、第百二十七条第一項、第百三十六条又は第百三十九条第一項の規定に違反して、届出をせず、又は虚偽の届出をした者

三　第三十二条の二第五項（第三十四条の三第二項（第八十三条で準用する場合を含む。）、第六十条第四項及び第六十三条第二項（これらの規定を第九十条第三項で準用する場合を含む。）並びに第八十条で準用する場合を含む。）又は第百十五条第四項（第百三十三条で準用する場合を含む。）の規定に違反して、管理、修理若しくは復旧又は管理、修理若しくは復旧のため必要な措置を拒み、妨げ、又は忌避した者

附　則

（施行期日）

第一条　この法律施行の期日は、公布の日から起算して三月を超えない期間内において、政令で定める。

（関係法令の廃止）

第二条　左に掲げる法律、勅令及び政令は、廃止する。
国宝保存法（昭和四年法律第十七号）
重要美術品等の保存に関する法律（昭和八年法律第四十三号）
史跡名勝天然紀念物保存法（大正八年法律第四十四号）
国宝保存法施行令（昭和四年勅令第二百十号）
史跡名勝天然紀念物保存法施行令（大正八年勅令第四百九十九号）
国宝保存会官制（昭和四年勅令第二百十一号）
重要美術品等調査審議会令（昭和二十四年政令第二百五十一号）
史跡名勝天然記念物調査会令（昭和二十四年政令第二百五十二号）

（法令廃止に伴う経過規定）

第三条　この法律施行前に行つた国宝保存法第一条の規定による国宝の指定（同法第十一条第一項の規定により解除された場合を除く。）は、第二十七条第一項の規定による重要文化財の指定とみなし、同法第三条又は第四条の規定による許可は、第四十三条又は第四十四条の規定による許可とみなす。

2　この法律施行前の国宝の滅失又はき損並びにこの法律施行前に行つた国宝保存法第七条第一項の規定による命令及び同法第十五条前段の規定により交付した補助金については、同法第七条から第十条まで、第十五条後段及び第二十四条の規定は、なおその効力を有する。この場合において同法第九条第二項中「主務大臣」とあるのは、「文化財保護委員会」と読み替えるものとする。

3　この法律施行前にした行為の処罰については、国宝保存法は、第六条及び第二十三条の規定を除くほか、なおその効力を有する。

4　この法律施行の際現に国宝保存法第一条の規定による国宝を所有している者は、委員会規則の定める事項を記載した書面をもつて、この法律施行後三箇月以内に委員会に届け出なければならない。

5　前項の規定による届出があつたときは、委員会は、当該所有者に第二十八条に規定する重要文化財の指定書を交付しなければならない。

6　第四項の規定に違反して、届出をせず、又は虚偽の届出をした者は、五千円以下の過料に処する。

7　この法律施行の際現に国宝保存法第一条の規定による国宝で国の所有に属するものを管理する各省各庁の長は、委員会規則の定める事項を記載した書面をもつて、この法律施行後三箇月以内に委員会に通知しなければならない。ただし、委員会規則で定める場合は、この限りでない。

8　前項の規定による通知があつたときは、委員会は、当該各省各庁の長に第二十八条に規定する重要文化財の指定書を交付するものとする。

第四条　この法律施行の際現に重要美術品等の保存に関する法律第二条第一項の規定により認定されている物件については、同法は当分の間、なおその効力を有する。この場合において、同法の施行に関する事務は、文化庁長官が行うものとし、同法中「国宝」とあるのは、「文化財保護法ノ規定ニ依ル重要文化財」と、「主務大臣」とあるのは、「文化庁長官」と、「当該物件ヲ国宝保存法第一条ノ規定ニ依リテ国宝トシテ指定シ又ハ前条」とあるのは、「前条」と読み替えるものとする。

2　文化審議会は、当分の間、文化庁長官の諮問に応じて重要美術品等の保存に関する法律第二条第一項の規定による認定の取消しに関する事項を調査審議し、及びこれに関し必要と認める事項を文化庁長官に建議する。

3　重要美術品等の保存に関する法律の施行に関しては、当分の間、第百八十八条の規定を準用する。

第五条　この法律施行前に行つた史跡名勝天然紀念物保存法第一条第一項の規定による指定（解除された場合を除く。）は、第百九条第一項の規定による指定、同法第一条第二項の規定による仮指定（解除された場合を除く。）は、第百十条第一項の規定による仮指定とみなし、同法第三条の規定による許可は、第百二十五条第一項の規定による許可とみなす。

2　この法律施行前に行つた史跡名勝天然紀念物保存法第四条第一項の規定による命令又は処分については、同法第四条及び史跡名勝天然紀念物保存法施行令第四条の規定は、なおその効力を有する。この場合において同令第四条中「文部大臣」とあるのは、「文化財保護委員会」と読み替えるものとする。

3　この法律施行前にした行為の処罰については、史跡名勝天然紀念物保存法は、なおその効力を有する。

（従前の国立博物館）

第六条　法律（これに基づく命令を含む。）に特別の定めのある場合を除くほか、従前の国立博物館及びその職員（美術研究所及びこれに所属する職員を除く。）は、この法律に基づく国立博物館及びその職員となり、従前の国立博物館附置の美術研究所及びこれに所属する職員は、この法律に基づく研究所及びその職員となり、同一性をもつて存続するものとする。

2　この法律に基づく東京国立文化財研究所は、従前の国立博物館附置の美術研究所の所掌した調査研究と同一のものについては、「美術研究所」の名称を用いることができる。

（国の無利子貸付け等）

第七条　国は、当分の間、重要文化財の所有者又は管理団体に対し、第三十五条第一項の規定により国がその経費について補助することができる重要文化財の管理で日本電信電話株式会社の株式の売払収入の活用による社会資本の整備の促進に関する特別措置法（昭和六十二年法律第八十六号）第二条第一項第二号に該当するものに要する費用に充てる資金の一部を、予算の範囲内において、無利子で貸し付けることができる。

2　前項の国の貸付金の償還期間は、五年（二年以内の据置期間を含む。）以内で政令で定める期間とする。

3　前項に定めるもののほか、第一項の規定による貸付金の償還方法、償還期限の繰上げその他償還に関し必要な事項は、政令で定める。

4　国は、第一項の規定により重要文化財の所有者又は管理団体に対し貸付けを行つた場合には、当該貸付けの対象である重要文化財の管理について、当該貸付金に相当する金額の補助を行うものとし、当該補助については、当該貸付金の償還時において、当該貸付金の償還金に相当する金額を交付することにより行うものとする。

5　重要文化財の所有者又は管理団体が、第一項の規定による貸付けを受けた無利子貸付金について、第二項及び第三項の規定に基づき定められる償還期限を繰り上げて償還を行つた場合（政令で定める場合を除く。）における前項の規定の適用については、当該償還は、当該償還期限の到来時に行われたものとみなす。

6　国が第一項の規定により無利子貸付金の貸付けを行う場合においては、第三十五条第二項中「交付する」とあるのは「貸し付ける」と、「補助の」とあるのは「貸付けの」と、「管理又は修理」とあるのは「管理」と、同条第三項中「交付する」とあるのは「貸し付ける」と、「管理又は修理」とあるのは「管理」として、これらの規定を適用する。

附　則　（昭和二六年一二月二四日法律第三一八号）　抄

1　この法律は、公布の日から施行する。但し、第二十条、第二十二条、第二十三条及び第百二十四条第二項の改正規定並びに附則第三項の規定は、昭和二十七年四月一日から施行する。

2　この法律施行前にした行為に対する罰則の適用については、改正前の文化財保護法第三十四条の規定は、なおその効力を有する。

附　則　（昭和二七年七月三一日法律第二七二号）　抄

（施行期日）

1　この法律は、昭和二十七年八月一日から施行する。但し、附則第三項の規定は、公布の日から施行する。

（東京国立博物館の分館の職員に関する経過規定）

2　この法律施行の際現に東京国立博物館の分館の職員である者は、別に辞令を発せられない限り、同一の勤務条件をもつて、奈良国立博物館の職員となるものとする。

附　則　（昭和二八年八月一〇日法律第一九四号）　抄

1　この法律は、公布の日から施行する。

附　則　（昭和二八年八月一五日法律第二一三号）　抄

1　この法律は、昭和二十八年九月一日から施行する。

2　この法律施行前従前の法令の規定によりなされた許可、認可その他の処分又は申請、届出その他の手続は、それぞれ改正後の相当規定に基いてなされた処分又は手続とみなす。

附　則　（昭和二九年五月二九日法律第一三一号）　抄

1　この法律は、昭和二十九年七月一日から施行する。

2　この法律の施行前にした史跡名勝天然記念物の仮指定は、この法律による改正後の文化財保護法（以下「新法」という。）第七十一条第二項の規定にかかわらず、新法第六十九条第一項の規定による指定があつた場合の外、この法律の施行の日から三年以内に同条同項の規定による指定がなかつたときは、その効力を失う。

3　この法律の施行前六月以内にこの法律による改正前の文化財保護法第四十三条第一項若しくは第八十条第一項の規定によつてした現状変更等の許可若しくは不許可の処分又は同法第四十五条第一項若しくは第八十一条第一項の規定によつてした制限、禁止又は命令で特定の者に対して行われたものに不服のある者は、この法律の施行の日から三十日以内に委員会に対して異議の申立をすることができる。この場合には、第八十五条の二第二項及び第三項並びに第八十五条の三から第八十五条の九までの規定を準用する。

4　この法律の施行前にした行為に対する罰則の適用については、なお従前の例による。

5　史跡名勝天然記念物を管理すべき団体の指定等に関する政令（昭和二十八年政令第二百八十九号）は、廃止する。

6　旧史跡名勝天然記念物を管理すべき団体の指定等に関する政令第一条第一項の規定により指定を受けた地方公共団体その他の団体及び同令附則第二項の規定により同令第一条第一項の規定により指定を受けた地方公共団体その他の団体とみなされたもので法人であるものは、新法第七十一条の二第一項又は第九十五条第一項の規定により指定を受けた地方公共団体その他の法人とみなす。

7　前項に規定する団体で法人でないものには、新法第七十一条の二、第九十五条又は第九十五条の三の規定にかかわらず、この法律の施行の日から一年間は、新法第七十一条の二第一項、第九十五条第一項又は第九十五条の三第一項に規定する管理及び復旧を行わせることができる。この場合には、新法中第七十一条の二第一項又は第九十五条第一項の規定による指定を受けた法人に関する規定を準用する。

附　則　（昭和三一年六月一二日法律第一四八号）　抄

1　この法律は、地方自治法の一部を改正する法律（昭和三十一年法律第百四十七号）の施行の日から施行する。

附　則　（昭和三一年六月三〇日法律第一六三号）　抄

（施行期日）

1　この法律は、昭和三十一年十月一日から施行する。

附　則　（昭和三三年四月二五日法律第八六号）　抄

1　この法律は、公布の日から施行し、特別職の職員の給与に関する法律第四条、第九条及び第十四条第一項の改正規定、文化財保護法第十三条の次に一条を加える改正規定、自治庁設置法第十六条の次に一条を加える改正規定並びに附則第二項の規定を除くほか、昭和三十三年四月一日から適用する。

附　則　（昭和三四年四月二〇日法律第一四八号）　抄

（施行期日）

1　この法律は、国税徴収法（昭和三十四年法律第百四十七号）の施行の日から施行する。

（公課の先取特権の順位の改正に関する経過措置）

7　第二章の規定による改正後の各法令（徴収金の先取特権の順位に係る部分に限る。）の規定は、この法律の施行後に国税徴収法第二条第十二号に規定する強制換価手続による配当手続が開始される場合について適用し、この法律の施行前に当該配当手続が開始されている場合における当該法令の規定に規定する徴収金の先取特権の順位については、なお従前の例による。

附　則　（昭和三六年六月二日法律第一一一号）　抄

（施行期日）

1　この法律は、公布の日から施行し、昭和三十六年四月一日から適用する。

（行政機関職員定員法の廃止）

2　行政機関職員定員法（昭和二十四年法律第百二十六号）は、廃止する。

（常勤の職員に対する暫定措置）

3　昭和三十六年四月一日において、現に二月以内の期間を定めて雇用されている職員のうち常勤の職員は、当分の間、国家行政組織法第十九条第一項若しくは第二項又は第二十一条第二項の規定に基づいて定められる定員の外に置くことができる。

附　則　（昭和三七年五月一六日法律第一四〇号）　抄

1　この法律は、昭和三十七年十月一日から施行する。

2　この法律による改正後の規定は、この附則に特別の定めがある場合を除き、この法律の施行前に生じた事項にも適用する。ただし、この法律による改正前の規定によつて生じた効力を妨げない。

3　この法律の施行の際現に係属している訴訟については、当該訴訟を提起することができない旨を定めるこの法律による改正後の規定にかかわらず、なお従前の例による。

4　この法律の施行の際現に係属している訴訟の管轄については、当該管轄を専属管轄とする旨のこの法律による改正後の規定にかかわらず、なお従前の例による。

5　この法律の施行の際現にこの法律による改正前の規定による出訴期間が進行している処分又は裁決に関する訴訟の出訴期間については、なお従前の例による。ただし、この法律による改正後の規定による出訴期間がこの法律による改正前の規定による出訴期間より短い場合に限る。

6　この法律の施行前にされた処分又は裁決に関する当事者訴訟で、この法律による改正により出訴期間が定められることとなつたものについての出訴期間は、この法律の施行の日から起算する。

7　この法律の施行の際現に係属している処分又は裁決の取消しの訴えについては、当該法律関係の当事者の一方を被告とする旨のこの法律による改正後の規定にかかわらず、なお従前の例による。ただし、裁判所は、原告の申立てにより、決定をもつて、当該訴訟を当事者訴訟に変更することを許すことができる。

8　前項ただし書の場合には、行政事件訴訟法第十八条後段及び第二十一条第二項から第五項までの規定を準用する。

附　則　（昭和三七年九月一五日法律第一六一号）　抄

1　この法律は、昭和三十七年十月一日から施行する。

2　この法律による改正後の規定は、この附則に特別の定めがある場合を除き、この法律の施行前にされた行政庁の処分、この法律の施行前にされた申請に係る行政庁の不作為その他この法律の施行前に生じた事項についても適用する。ただし、この法律による改正前の規定によつて生じた効力を妨げない。

3　この法律の施行前に提起された訴願、審査の請求、異議の申立てその他の不服申立て（以下「訴願等」という。）については、この法律の施行後も、なお従前の例による。この法律の施行前にされた訴願等の裁決、決定その他の処分（以下「裁決等」という。）又はこの法律の施行前に提起された訴願等につきこの法律の施行後にされる裁決等にさらに不服がある場合の訴願等についても、同様とする。

4　前項に規定する訴願等で、この法律の施行後は行政不服審査法による不服申立てをすることができることとなる処分に係るものは、同法以外の法律の適用については、行政不服審査法による不服申立てとみなす。

5　第三項の規定によりこの法律の施行後にされる審査の請求、異議の申立てその他の不服申立ての裁決等については、行政不服審査法による不服申立てをすることができない。

6　この法律の施行前にされた行政庁の処分で、この法律による改正前の規定により訴願等をすることができるものとされ、かつ、その提起期間が定められていなかつたものについて、行政不服審査法による不服申立てをすることができる期間は、この法律の施行の日から起算する。

8　この法律の施行前にした行為に対する罰則の適用については、なお従前の例による。

9　前八項に定めるもののほか、この法律の施行に関して必要な経過措置は、政令で定める。

10　この法律及び行政事件訴訟法の施行に伴う関係法律の整理等に関する法律（昭和三十七年法律第百四十号）に同一の法律についての改正規定がある場合においては、当該法律は、この法律によつてまず改正され、次いで行政事件訴訟法の施行に伴う関係法律の整理等に関する法律によつて改正されるものとする。

附　則　（昭和四〇年三月三一日法律第三六号）　抄

（施行期日）

第一条　この法律は、昭和四十年四月一日から施行する。

（その他の法令の一部改正に伴う経過規定の原則）

第五条　第二章の規定による改正後の法令の規定は、別段の定めがあるものを除き、昭和四十年分以後の所得税又はこれらの法令の規定に規定する法人の施行日以後に終了する事業年度分の法人税について適用し、昭和三十九年分以前の所得税又は当該法人の同日前に終了した事業年度分の法人税については、なお従前の例による。

附　則　（昭和四三年六月一五日法律第九九号）　抄

（施行期日）

1　この法律は、公布の日から施行する。

（経過規定）

2　この法律の施行の際現に文部省文化局、文化財保護委員会事務局、文部省の附属機関（この法律の規定により文化庁の相当の附属機関となるものに限る。）又は文化財保護委員会の附属機関（文化財専門審議会を除く。）の職員である者は、別に辞令の発せられない限り、同一の勤務条件をもつて文化庁の相当の職員となるものとする。

3　この法律の施行の際現にこの法律による改正前の文化財保護法、著作権法、著作権に関する仲介業務に関する法律、万国著作権条約の実施に伴う著作権法の特例に関する法律、銃砲刀剣類所持等取締法又は国立劇場法の規定により文化財保護委員会又は文部大臣がした許可、認可、指定その他の処分又は通知その他の手続は、この法律による改正後のこれらの法律の相当規定に基づいて、文部大臣又は文化庁長官がした処分又は手続とみなす。

4　この法律の施行の際現にこの法律による改正前の文化財保護法、著作権法、著作権に関する仲介業務に関する法律、万国著作権条約の実施に伴う著作権法の特例に関する法律、銃砲刀剣類所持等取締法又は国立劇場法の規定により文化財保護委員会又は文部大臣に対してされている申請、届出その他の手続は、この法律による改正後のこれらの法律の相当規定に基づいて、文部大臣又は文化庁長官に対してされた手続とみなす。

5　この法律の施行の際現に効力を有する文化財保護委員会規則は、文部省令としての効力を有するものとする。

附　則　（昭和四六年五月三一日法律第八八号）　抄

（施行期日）

第一条　この法律は、昭和四十六年七月一日から施行する。

附　則　（昭和四六年六月一日法律第九六号）　抄

（施行期日等）

1　この法律は、公布の日から施行する。

附　則　（昭和四七年六月三日法律第五二号）　抄

（施行期日等）

第一条　この法律は、公布の日から起算して三十日をこえない範囲内において政令で定める日から施行する。

（土地調整委員会又は中央公害審査委員会がした処分等に関する経過措置）

第十六条　この法律の施行前にこの法律による改正前の法律の規定により土地調整委員会又は中央公害審査委員会がした処分その他の行為は、政令で別段の定めをするものを除き、この法律又はこの法律による改正後の法律の相当規定により、公害等調整委員会がした処分その他の行為とみなす。

附　則　（昭和五〇年七月一日法律第四九号）　抄

（施行期日）

1　この法律は、公布の日から起算して三箇月を経過した日から施行する。

（遺跡発見の場合の停止命令等の特例）

2　この法律の施行の日から起算して五年間は、この法律による改正後の文化財保護法（以下「新法」という。）第五十七条の五の規定の適用については、同条第二項ただし書中「三箇月」とあるのは「六箇月」と、同条第五項ただし書中「六箇月」とあるのは「九箇月」とする。この場合において、この法律の施行の日から起算して五年を経過する日前に執つた同条第二項に規定する措置については、同日以後も、なお、同日前の同条の例によるものとする。

（経過措置）

3　文部大臣は、この法律の施行の際現にこの法律による改正前の文化財保護法（以下「旧法」という。）第五十六条の三第一項の規定により指定されている重要無形文化財のうち、旧法第五十六条の三第二項の規定による保持者の認定に代えて新法第五十六条の三第二項の保持団体の認定をする必要があると認められるものについては、この法律の施行後一年以内に、旧法第五十六条の三第二項の規定によつてしたすべての保持者の認定を解除するとともに、新法第五十六条の三第二項の規定により保持団体の認定をしなければならない。この場合においては、新法第五十六条の三第三項及び第五十六条の四第三項の規定を準用する。

4　この法律の施行の際現に旧法第五十六条の十第一項の規定により指定されている重要民俗資料は、新法の規定の適用については、新法第五十六条の十第一項の規定により指定された重要有形民俗文化財とみなす。この場合において、旧法第五十六条の十第二項において準用する旧法第二十八条第三項の規定により交付された重要民俗資料の指定書は、新法第五十六条の十第二項において準用する新法第二十八条第三項の規定により交付された重要有形民俗文化財の指定書とみなす。

5　この法律の施行前に旧法第五十七条の二第一項の規定によりした届出に係る発掘については、新法第五十七条の二及び第五十七条の三の規定にかかわらず、旧法第五十七条の二の規定の例による。

6　この法律の施行前に新法第五十七条の三第一項に規定する事業計画を策定した同項に規定する国の機関等（当該事業計画の実施につき旧法第五十七条の二第一項の規定による届出をしたものを除く。）に対する新法第五十七条の三の規定の適用については、同条第一項中「当該発掘に係る事業計画の策定に当たつて、あらかじめ」とあるのは、「この法律の施行後遅滞なく」とする。

7　この法律の施行前に旧法第八十四条第一項の規定によりした届出に係る遺跡と認められるものについては、新法第五十七条の五（旧法第八十七条に規定する各省各庁の長に該当しない新法第五十七条の三第一項に規定する国の機関等にあつては、新法第五十七条の六）の規定にかかわらず、旧法第八十四条の規定は、なお、その効力を有する。

8　この法律の施行前に旧法第八十七条に規定する各省各庁の長が旧法第九十条第一項第八号の規定によりした通知に係る遺跡と認められるものについては、新法第五十七条の六の規定にかかわらず、旧法第九十条第一項第八号の通知に係る旧法第九十条第三項の規定は、なお、その効力を有する。

9　この法律の施行前にした行為に対する罰則の適用については、なお、従前の例による。

10　前七項に規定するもののほか、この法律の施行に関し必要な経過措置は、政令で定める。

附　則　（昭和五八年一二月二日法律第七八号）

1　この法律（第一条を除く。）は、昭和五十九年七月一日から施行する。

2　この法律の施行の日の前日において法律の規定により置かれている機関等で、この法律の施行の日以後は国家行政組織法又はこの法律による改正後の関係法律の規定に基づく政令（以下「関係政令」という。）の規定により置かれることとなるものに関し必要となる経過措置その他この法律の施行に伴う関係政令の制定又は改廃に関し必要となる経過措置は、政令で定めることができる。

附　則　（平成五年一一月一二日法律第八九号）　抄

（施行期日）

第一条　この法律は、行政手続法（平成五年法律第八十八号）の施行の日から施行する。

（諮問等がされた不利益処分に関する経過措置）

第二条　この法律の施行前に法令に基づき審議会その他の合議制の機関に対し行政手続法第十三条に規定する聴聞又は弁明の機会の付与の手続その他の意見陳述のための手続に相当する手続を執るべきことの諮問その他の求めがされた場合においては、当該諮問その他の求めに係る不利益処分の手続に関しては、この法律による改正後の関係法律の規定にかかわらず、なお従前の例による。

（罰則に関する経過措置）

第十三条　この法律の施行前にした行為に対する罰則の適用については、なお従前の例による。

（聴聞に関する規定の整理に伴う経過措置）

第十四条　この法律の施行前に法律の規定により行われた聴聞、聴問若しくは聴聞会（不利益処分に係るものを除く。）又はこれらのための手続は、この法律による改正後の関係法律の相当規定により行われたものとみなす。

（政令への委任）

第十五条　附則第二条から前条までに定めるもののほか、この法律の施行に関して必要な経過措置は、政令で定める。

附　則　（平成六年六月二九日法律第四九号）　抄

（施行期日）

1　この法律中、第一章の規定及び次項の規定は地方自治法の一部を改正する法律（平成六年法律第四十八号）中地方自治法（昭和二十二年法律第六十七号）第二編第十二章の改正規定の施行の日から、第二章の規定は地方自治法の一部を改正する法律中地方自治法第三編第三章の改正規定の施行の日から施行する。

附　則　（平成六年一一月一一日法律第九七号）　抄

（施行期日）

第一条　この法律は、公布の日から施行する。

（文化財保護法の一部改正に伴う経過措置）

第四条　第四条の規定の施行前にされた同条の規定による改正前の文化財保護法第四十六条第一項（同法第五十六条の十四において準用する場合を含む。）の規定による売渡しの申出又は第四条の規定による改正前の文化財保護法第四十六条第一項ただし書（同法第五十六条の十四において準用する場合を含む。）の規定による承認の申請については、第四条の規定による改正後の文化財保護法の規定にかかわらず、なお従前の例による。

（罰則に関する経過措置）

第二十条　この法律（附則第一条各号に掲げる規定については、当該各規定）の施行前にした行為並びに附則第二条、第四条、第七条第二項、第八条、第十一条、第十二条第二項、第十三条及び第十五条第四項の規定によりなお従前の例によることとされる場合における第一条、第四条、第八条、第九条、第十三条、第二十七条、第二十八条及び第三十条の規定の施行後にした行為に対する罰則の適用については、なお従前の例による。

（政令への委任）

第二十一条　附則第二条から前条までに定めるもののほか、この法律の施行に関して必要となる経過措置（罰則に関する経過措置を含む。）は、政令で定める。

附　則　（平成八年六月一二日法律第六六号）

（施行期日）

1　この法律は、公布の日から起算して九月を超えない範囲内において政令で定める日から施行する。

（重要文化財等の公開の届出に関する経過措置）

2　この法律の施行の際現に改正前の文化財保護法（以下「旧法」という。）第五十三条第一項の規定による許可を受け、又はその申請を行っている改正後の文化財保護法（以下「新法」という。）第五十三条第一項ただし書に規定する公開承認施設の設置者であって当該公開承認施設において展覧会その他の催しを主催するものは、同条第二項の規定による届出を行ったものとみなす。

3　この法律の施行前に旧法第五十三条第一項ただし書の規定による届出を行った文化庁長官以外の国の機関又は地方公共団体であって、新法第五十三条第一項ただし書に規定する公開承認施設において展覧会その他の催しを主催するものは、同条第二項の規定による届出を行ったものとみなす。

4　文化庁長官以外の国の機関若しくは地方公共団体であって新法第五十六条の十五第一項ただし書に規定する公開事前届出免除施設において展覧会その他の催しを主催するもの又は公開事前届出免除施設の設置者であって当該公開事前届出免除施設においてこれらを主催するもののうち、この法律の施行前に旧法第五十六条の十五第一項の規定による届出を行ったものは、新法第五十六条の十五第一項ただし書の規定による届出を行ったものとみなす。

（罰則に関する経過措置）

5　この法律の施行前にした行為に対する罰則の適用については、なお従前の例による。

（検討）

6　政府は、この法律の施行後十年を経過した場合において、この法律の実施状況、保護すべき文化財の状況等を勘案し、有形文化財の登録に係る制度について検討を加え、その結果に基づいて所要の措置を講ずるものとする。

附　則　（平成一一年七月一六日法律第八七号）　抄

（施行期日）

第一条　この法律は、平成十二年四月一日から施行する。ただし、次の各号に掲げる規定は、当該各号に定める日から施行する。

一　第一条中地方自治法第二百五十条の次に五条、節名並びに二款及び款名を加える改正規定（同法第二百五十条の九第一項に係る部分（両議院の同意を得ることに係る部分に限る。）に限る。）、第四十条中自然公園法附則第九項及び第十項の改正規定（同法附則第十項に係る部分に限る。）、第二百四十四条の規定（農業改良助長法第十四条の三の改正規定に係る部分を除く。）並びに第四百七十二条の規定（市町村の合併の特例に関する法律第六条、第八条及び第十七条の改正規定に係る部分を除く。）並びに附則第七条、第十条、第十二条、第五十九条ただし書、第六十条第四項及び第五項、第七十三条、第七十七条、第百五十七条第四項から第六項まで、

第百六十条、第百六十三条、第百六十四条並びに第二百二条の規定　公布の日

（文化財保護法の一部改正に伴う経過措置）

第五十八条　施行日前に発見された文化財でこの法律の施行の際現にその所有者が判明しないものの所有権の帰属及び報償金については、第百三十五条の規定による改正前の文化財保護法（以下この条及び次条において「旧文化財保護法」という。）第五十九条第一項に規定する文化財及び旧文化財保護法第六十一条第二項に規定する文化財のうち国の機関が埋蔵文化財の調査のための土地の発掘により発見したものについては第百三十五条の規定による改正後の文化財保護法（以下この条において「新文化財保護法」という。）第六十三条の規定を適用し、その他のものについては新文化財保護法第六十三条の二の規定を適用する。

第五十九条　旧文化財保護法第六十三条第一項の規定により国庫に帰属した文化財のうち、この法律の施行の際現に地方公共団体において保管しているもの（物品管理法第八条第三項又は第六項に規定する物品管理官又は分任物品管理官の管理に係るものを除く。）の所有権は、施行日において、当該文化財を保管している地方公共団体に帰属するものとする。ただし、施行日の前日までに、文部省令で定めるところにより、当該地方公共団体から別段の申出があった場合は、この限りでない。

（国等の事務）

第百五十九条　この法律による改正前のそれぞれの法律に規定するもののほか、この法律の施行前において、地方公共団体の機関が法律又はこれに基づく政令により管理し又は執行する国、他の地方公共団体その他公共団体の事務（附則第百六十一条において「国等の事務」という。）は、この法律の施行後は、地方公共団体が法律又はこれに基づく政令により当該地方公共団体の事務として処理するものとする。

（処分、申請等に関する経過措置）

第百六十条　この法律（附則第一条各号に掲げる規定については、当該各規定。以下この条及び附則第百六十三条において同じ。）の施行前に改正前のそれぞれの法律の規定によりされた許可等の処分その他の行為（以下この条において「処分等の行為」という。）又はこの法律の施行の際現に改正前のそれぞれの法律の規定によりされている許可等の申請その他の行為（以下この条において「申請等の行為」という。）で、この法律の施行の日においてこれらの行為に係る行政事務を行うべき者が異なることとなるものは、附則第二条から前条までの規定又は改正後のそれぞれの法律（これに基づく命令を含む。）の経過措置に関する規定に定めるものを除き、この法律の施行の日以後における改正後のそれぞれの法律の適用については、改正後のそれぞれの法律の相当規定によりされた処分等の行為又は申請等の行為とみなす。

2　この法律の施行前に改正前のそれぞれの法律の規定により国又は地方公共団体の機関に対し報告、届出、提出その他の手続をしなければならない事項で、この法律の施行の日前にその手続がされていないものについては、この法律及びこれに基づく政令

に別段の定めがあるもののほか、これを、改正後のそれぞれの法律の相当規定により国又は地方公共団体の相当の機関に対して報告、届出、提出その他の手続をしなければならない事項についてその手続がされていないものとみなして、この法律による改正後のそれぞれの法律の規定を適用する。

（不服申立てに関する経過措置）

第百六十一条　施行日前にされた国等の事務に係る処分であって、当該処分をした行政庁（以下この条において「処分庁」という。）に施行日前に行政不服審査法に規定する上級行政庁（以下この条において「上級行政庁」という。）があったものについての同法による不服申立てについては、施行日以後においても、当該処分庁に引き続き上級行政庁があるものとみなして、行政不服審査法の規定を適用する。この場合において、当該処分庁の上級行政庁とみなされる行政庁は、施行日前に当該処分庁の上級行政庁であった行政庁とする。

2　前項の場合において、上級行政庁とみなされる行政庁が地方公共団体の機関であるときは、当該機関が行政不服審査法の規定により処理することとされる事務は、新地方自治法第二条第九項第一号に規定する第一号法定受託事務とする。

（手数料に関する経過措置）

第百六十二条　施行日前においてこの法律による改正前のそれぞれの法律（これに基づく命令を含む。）の規定により納付すべきであった手数料については、この法律及びこれに基づく政令に別段の定めがあるもののほか、なお従前の例による。

（罰則に関する経過措置）

第百六十三条　この法律の施行前にした行為に対する罰則の適用については、なお従前の例による。

（その他の経過措置の政令への委任）

第百六十四条　この附則に規定するもののほか、この法律の施行に伴い必要な経過措置（罰則に関する経過措置を含む。）は、政令で定める。

（検討）

第二百五十条　新地方自治法第二条第九項第一号に規定する第一号法定受託事務については、できる限り新たに設けることのないようにするとともに、新地方自治法別表第一に掲げるもの及び新地方自治法に基づく政令に示すものについては、地方分権を推進する観点から検討を加え、適宜、適切な見直しを行うものとする。

第二百五十一条　政府は、地方公共団体が事務及び事業を自主的かつ自立的に執行できるよう、国と地方公共団体との役割分担に応じた地方税財源の充実確保の方途について、経済情勢の推移等を勘案しつつ検討し、その結果に基づいて必要な措置を講ずるものとする。

附　則　（平成一一年七月一六日法律第一〇二号）　抄

（施行期日）

第一条　この法律は、内閣法の一部を改正する法律（平成十一年法律第八十八号）の施行の日から施行する。ただし、次の各号に掲げる規定は、当該各号に定める日から施行する。

一　略

二　附則第十条第一項及び第五項、第十四条第三項、第二十三条、第二十八条並びに第三十条の規定　公布の日

（別に定める経過措置）

第三十条　第二条から前条までに規定するもののほか、この法律の施行に伴い必要となる経過措置は、別に法律で定める。

附　則　（平成一一年一二月二二日法律第一六〇号）　抄

（施行期日）

第一条　この法律（第二条及び第三条を除く。）は、平成十三年一月六日から施行する。ただし、次の各号に掲げる規定は、当該各号に定める日から施行する。

一　第九百九十五条（核原料物質、核燃料物質及び原子炉の規制に関する法律の一部を改正する法律附則の改正規定に係る部分に限る。）、第千三百五条、第千三百六条、第千三百二十四条第二項、第千三百二十六条第二項及び第千三百四十四条の規定　公布の日

附　則　（平成一一年一二月二二日法律第一七八号）　抄

（施行期日）

第一条　この法律は、平成十三年一月六日から施行する。ただし、附則第九条の規定は、同日から起算して六月を超えない範囲内において政令で定める日から施行する。

附　則　（平成一一年一二月二二日法律第一七九号）　抄

（施行期日）

第一条　この法律は、平成十三年一月六日から施行する。ただし、附則第八条の規定は、同日から起算して六月を超えない範囲内において政令で定める日から施行する。

附　則　（平成一二年五月一九日法律第七三号）　抄

（施行期日）

第一条　この法律は、公布の日から起算して一年を超えない範囲内において政令で定める日から施行する。

附　則　（平成一四年二月八日法律第一号）　抄

（施行期日）

第一条　この法律は、公布の日から施行する。

附　則　（平成一四年七月三日法律第八二号）

この法律は、文化財の不法な輸入、輸出及び所有権移転を禁止し及び防止する手段に関する条約が日本国について効力を生ずる日から施行する。

附　則　（平成一六年五月二八日法律第六一号）　抄

（施行期日）

第一条　この法律は、平成十七年四月一日から施行する。

附　則　（平成一六年六月九日法律第八四号）　抄

（施行期日）

第一条　この法律は、公布の日から起算して一年を超えない範囲内において政令で定める日から施行する。

附　則　（平成一八年五月三一日法律第四六号）　抄

（施行期日）

第一条　この法律は、公布の日から起算して一年六月を超えない範囲内において政令で定める日から施行する。ただし、次の各号に掲げる規定は、当該各号に定める日から施行する。

一・二　略

三　第一条中都市計画法第五条の二第一項及び第二項、第六条、第八条第二項及び第三項、第十三条第三項、第十五条第一項並びに第十九条第三項及び第五項の改正規定、同条第六項を削る改正規定並びに同法第二十一条、第二十二条第一項及び第八十七条の二の改正規定、第二条中建築基準法第六条第一項の改正規定、第三条、第六条、第七条中都市再生特別措置法第五十一条第四項の改正規定並びに附則第三条、第四条第一項、第五条、第八条及び第十三条の規定　公布の日から起算して六月を超えない範囲内において政令で定める日

附　則　（平成一八年六月一五日法律第七三号）　抄

（施行期日）

第一条　この法律は、公布の日から起算して一年六月を超えない範囲内において政令で定める日から施行する。

附　則　（平成一九年三月三〇日法律第七号）　抄

（施行期日）

第一条　この法律は、平成十九年四月一日から施行する。

（文化財保護法の一部改正に伴う経過措置）

第十一条　前条の規定による改正後の文化財保護法第百四条第一項の規定の適用については、施行日前に研究所が埋蔵文化財（同法第九十二条第一項に規定する埋蔵文化財をいう。）の調査のための土地の発掘により発見した同法第百二条第二項に規定する文化財は、機構が発見したものとみなす。

附　則　（平成二三年五月二日法律第三七号）　抄

（施行期日）

第一条　この法律は、公布の日から施行する。

（罰則に関する経過措置）

第二十三条　この法律（附則第一条各号に掲げる規定にあっては、当該規定）の施行前

にした行為に対する罰則の適用については、なお従前の例による。

（政令への委任）

第二十四条　附則第二条から前条まで及び附則第三十六条に規定するもののほか、この法律の施行に関し必要な経過措置は、政令で定める。

附　則　（平成二六年六月四日法律第五一号）　抄

（施行期日）

第一条　この法律は、平成二十七年四月一日から施行する。

（処分、申請等に関する経過措置）

第七条　この法律（附則第一条各号に掲げる規定については、当該各規定。以下この条及び次条において同じ。）の施行前にこの法律による改正前のそれぞれの法律の規定によりされた許可等の処分その他の行為（以下この項において「処分等の行為」という。）又はこの法律の施行の際現にこの法律による改正前のそれぞれの法律の規定によりされている許可等の申請その他の行為（以下この項において「申請等の行為」という。）で、この法律の施行の日においてこれらの行為に係る行政事務を行うべき者が異なることとなるものは、附則第二条から前条までの規定又はこの法律による改正後のそれぞれの法律（これに基づく命令を含む。）の経過措置に関する規定に定めるものを除き、この法律の施行の日以後におけるこの法律による改正後のそれぞれの法律の適用については、この法律による改正後のそれぞれの法律の相当規定によりされた処分等の行為又は申請等の行為とみなす。

2　この法律の施行前にこの法律による改正前のそれぞれの法律の規定により国又は地方公共団体の機関に対し報告、届出、提出その他の手続をしなければならない事項で、この法律の施行の日前にその手続がされていないものについては、この法律及びこれに基づく政令に別段の定めがあるもののほか、これを、この法律による改正後のそれぞれの法律の相当規定により国又は地方公共団体の相当の機関に対して報告、届出、提出その他の手続をしなければならない事項についてその手続がされていないものとみなして、この法律による改正後のそれぞれの法律の規定を適用する。

（罰則に関する経過措置）

第八条　この法律の施行前にした行為に対する罰則の適用については、なお従前の例による。

（政令への委任）

第九条　附則第二条から前条までに規定するもののほか、この法律の施行に関し必要な経過措置（罰則に関する経過措置を含む。）は、政令で定める。

附　則　（平成二六年六月一三日法律第六九号）　抄

（施行期日）

第一条　この法律は、行政不服審査法（平成二十六年法律第六十八号）の施行の日から施行する。

（経過措置の原則）

第五条　行政庁の処分その他の行為又は不作為についての不服申立てであってこの法律の施行前にされた行政庁の処分その他の行為又はこの法律の施行前にされた申請に係る行政庁の不作為に係るものについては、この附則に特別の定めがある場合を除き、なお従前の例による。

（訴訟に関する経過措置）

第六条　この法律による改正前の法律の規定により不服申立てに対する行政庁の裁決、決定その他の行為を経た後でなければ訴えを提起できないこととされる事項であって、当該不服申立てを提起しないでこの法律の施行前にこれを提起すべき期間を経過したもの（当該不服申立てが他の不服申立てに対する行政庁の裁決、決定その他の行為を経た後でなければ提起できないとされる場合にあっては、当該他の不服申立てを提起しないでこの法律の施行前にこれを提起すべき期間を経過したものを含む。）の訴えの提起については、なお従前の例による。

2　この法律の規定による改正前の法律の規定（前条の規定によりなお従前の例によることとされる場合を含む。）により異議申立てが提起された処分その他の行為であって、この法律の規定による改正後の法律の規定により審査請求に対する裁決を経た後でなければ取消しの訴えを提起することができないこととされるものの取消しの訴えの提起については、なお従前の例による。

3　不服申立てに対する行政庁の裁決、決定その他の行為の取消しの訴えであって、この法律の施行前に提起されたものについては、なお従前の例による。

（罰則に関する経過措置）

第九条　この法律の施行前にした行為並びに附則第五条及び前二条の規定によりなお従前の例によることとされる場合におけるこの法律の施行後にした行為に対する罰則の適用については、なお従前の例による。

（その他の経過措置の政令への委任）

第十条　附則第五条から前条までに定めるもののほか、この法律の施行に関し必要な経過措置（罰則に関する経過措置を含む。）は、政令で定める。

文化財保護法及び地方教育行政の組織及び運営に関する法律の一部を改正する法律

法律第四十二号（平三〇・六・八）[①]

（文化財保護法の一部改正）

第一条　文化財保護法（昭和二十五年法律第二百十四号）の一部を次のように改正する。

目次中「第四款公開（第四十七条の二－第五十三条）」を「第四款公開（第四十七条の二－第五十三条）第五款重要文化財保存活用計画（第五十三条の二－第五十三条の八）」に、

「第五款」を「第六款」に、

「第六款」を「第七款」に、

「第百三十三条」を「第百三十三条の四」に、

「第三節　地方公共団体及び教育委員会（第百八十二条－第百九十二条）」を「第三節地方公共団体及び教育委員会（第百八十二条－第百九十二条）第四節文化財保存活用支援団体（第百九十二条の二－第百九十二条の六）に改める。」

第三十一条第二項中「特別の事情」を「当該重要文化財の適切な管理のため必要」に、「適当な者をもつぱら自己に代り」を「第百九十二条の二第一項に規定する文化財保存活用支援団体その他の適当な者を専ら自己に代わり」に、「責に」を「責めに」に、「第十二章」を「第百八十七条第一項第一号」に改める。

第三十二条の二第五項中「第十二章」を「第百八十七条第一項第一号」に改める。

第四十三条第一項ただし書、第三項及び第四項中「現状の変更」を「現状変更」に改める。

第三章第一節第六款を同節第七款とする。

第五十五条　第一項中「一に」を「いずれかに」に改め、同項第一号中「現状の変更」を「現状変更」に改め、同項第二号中「き損して」を「毀損して」に改め、同項第三号中「き損し」を「毀損し」に、「虞」を「おそれ」に改め、同項第四号中「あらためて」を「改めて」に改める。

第三章第一節中第五款を第六款とし、第四款の次に次の一款を加える。

第五款　重要文化財保存活用計画

（重要文化財保存活用計画の認定）

第五十三条の二　重要文化財の所有者（管理団体がある場合は、その者）は、文部科学省令で定めるところにより、重要文化財の保存及び活用に関する計画（以下「重要文化財保存活用計画」という。）を作成し、文化庁長官の認定を申請することができる。

2　重要文化財保存活用計画には、次に掲げる事項を記載するものとする。

一　当該重要文化財の名称及び所在の場所

二　当該重要文化財の保存及び活用のために行う具体的な措置の内容

三　計画期間

四　その他文部科学省令で定める事項

---

① 2018年6月8日公布的修改稿，是《日本文化财保护法》截至本书出版之前最新、也是最大一次修改，但并未与之前2014年版本合并公布。因此本书单独纳入修改部分。

3　前項第二号に掲げる事項には、次に掲げる事項を記載することができる。

一　当該重要文化財の現状変更又は保存に影響を及ぼす行為に関する事項

二　当該重要文化財の修理に関する事項

三　当該重要文化財（建造物であるものを除く。次項第六号において同じ。）の公開を目的とする寄託契約に関する事項

4　文化庁長官は、第一項の規定による認定の申請があつた場合において、その重要文化財保存活用計画が次の各号のいずれにも適合するものであると認めるときは、その認定をするものとする。

一　当該重要文化財保存活用計画の実施が当該重要文化財の保存及び活用に寄与するものであると認められること。

二　円滑かつ確実に実施されると見込まれるものであること。

三　第百八十三条の二第一項に規定する文化財保存活用大綱又は第百八十三条の五第一項に規定する認定文化財保存活用地域計画が定められているときは、これらに照らし適切なものであること。

四　当該重要文化財保存活用計画に前項第一号に掲げる事項が記載されている場合には、その内容が重要文化財の現状変更又は保存に影響を及ぼす行為を適切に行うために必要なものとして文部科学省令で定める基準に適合するものであること。

五　当該重要文化財保存活用計画に前項第二号に掲げる事項が記載されている場合には、その内容が重要文化財の修理を適切に行うために必要なものとして文部科学省令で定める基準に適合するものであること。

六　当該重要文化財保存活用計画に前項第三号に掲げる事項が記載されている場合には、当該寄託契約の内容が重要文化財の公開を適切かつ確実に行うために必要なものとして文部科学省令で定める基準に適合するものであること。

5　文化庁長官は、前項の認定をしたときは、遅滞なく、その旨を当該認定を申請した者に通知しなければならない。

（認定を受けた重要文化財保存活用計画の変更）

第五十三条の三　前条第四項の認定を受けた重要文化財の所有者又は管理団体は、当該認定を受けた重要文化財保存活用計画の変更（文部科学省令で定める軽微な変更を除く。）をしようとするときは、文化庁長官の認定を受けなければならない。

2　前条第四項及び第五項の規定は、前項の認定について準用する。

（現状変更等の許可の特例）

第五十三条の四　第五十三条の二第三項第一号に掲げる事項が記載された重要文化財保存活用計画が同条第四項の認定（前条第一項の変更の認定を含む。以下この款及び第百五十三条第二項第六号において同じ。）を受けた場合において、当該重要文化財の現状変更又は保存に影響を及ぼす行為をその記載された事項の内容に即して行うに当たり、第四十三条第一項の許可を受けなければならないときは、同項の規定にかかわらず、

当該現状変更又は保存に影響を及ぼす行為が終了した後遅滞なく、文部科学省令で定めるところにより、その旨を文化庁長官に届け出ることをもつて足りる。

（修理の届出の特例）

第五十三条の五　第五十三条の二第三項第二号に掲げる事項が記載された重要文化財保存活用計画が同条第四項の認定を受けた場合において、当該重要文化財の修理をその記載された事項の内容に即して行うに当たり、第四十三条の二第一項の規定による届出を行わなければならないときは、同項の規定にかかわらず、当該修理が終了した後遅滞なく、文部科学省令で定めるところにより、その旨を文化庁長官に届け出ることをもつて足りる。

（認定重要文化財保存活用計画の実施状況に関する報告の徴収）

第五十三条の六　文化庁長官は、第五十三条の二第四項の認定を受けた重要文化財の所有者又は管理団体に対し、当該認定を受けた重要文化財保存活用計画（変更があつたときは、その変更後のもの。次条第一項及び第五十三条の八において「認定重要文化財保存活用計画」という。）の実施の状況について報告を求めることができる。

（認定の取消し）

第五十三条の七　文化庁長官は、認定重要文化財保存活用計画が第五十三条の二第四項各号のいずれかに適合しなくなつたと認めるときは、その認定を取り消すことができる。

2　文化庁長官は、前項の規定により認定を取り消したときは、遅滞なく、その旨を当該認定を受けていた者に通知しなければならない。

（所有者等への指導又は助言）

第五十三条の八　都道府県及び市（特別区を含む。以下同じ。）町村の教育委員会（地方教育行政の組織及び運営に関する法律（昭和三十一年法律第百六十二号）第二十三条第一項の条例の定めるところによりその長が文化財の保護に関する事務を管理し、及び執行することとされた地方公共団体（以下「特定地方公共団体」という。）にあつては、その長。第百四十三条第三項、第百八十三条の八第四項、第百九十条第一項及び第百九十一条第一項を除き、以下同じ。）は、重要文化財の所有者又は管理団体の求めに応じ、重要文化財保存活用計画の作成及び認定重要文化財保存活用計画の円滑かつ確実な実施に関し必要な指導又は助言をすることができる。

2　文化庁長官は、重要文化財の所有者又は管理団体の求めに応じ、重要文化財保存活用計画の作成及び認定重要文化財保存活用計画の円滑かつ確実な実施に関し必要な指導又は助言をするように努めなければならない。

第五十七条　第二項に次のただし書を加える。

ただし、当該登録をしようとする有形文化財が第百八十三条の五第一項の規定による登録の提案に係るものであるときは、この限りでない。

第六十条　第二項中「特別の事情」を「当該登録有形文化財の適切な管理のため必要」

に、「適当な」を「第百九十二条の二第一項に規定する文化財保存活用支援団体その他の適当な」に改める。

第六十四条　第一項ただし書及び第三項中「現状の変更」を「現状変更」に改める。

第六十七条　の次に次の六条を加える。

（登録有形文化財保存活用計画の認定）

第六十七条の二　登録有形文化財の所有者（管理団体がある場合は、その者）は、文部科学省令で定めるところにより、登録有形文化財の保存及び活用に関する計画（以下「登録有形文化財保存活用計画」という。）を作成し、文化庁長官の認定を申請することができる。

2　登録有形文化財保存活用計画には、次に掲げる事項を記載するものとする。

一　当該登録有形文化財の名称及び所在の場所

二　当該登録有形文化財の保存及び活用のために行う具体的な措置の内容

三　計画期間

四　その他文部科学省令で定める事項

3　前項第二号に掲げる事項には、次に掲げる事項を記載することができる。

一　当該登録有形文化財の現状変更に関する事項

二　当該登録有形文化財（建造物であるものを除く。次項第五号において同じ。）のうち世界文化の見地から歴史上、芸術上又は学術上特に優れた価値を有するものの公開を目的とする寄託契約に関する事項

4　文化庁長官は、第一項の規定による認定の申請があつた場合において、その登録有形文化財保存活用計画が次の各号のいずれにも適合するものであると認めるときは、その認定をするものとする。

一　当該登録有形文化財保存活用計画の実施が当該登録有形文化財の保存及び活用に寄与するものであると認められること。

二　円滑かつ確実に実施されると見込まれるものであること。

三　第百八十三条の二第一項に規定する文化財保存活用大綱又は第百八十三条の五第一項に規定する認定文化財保存活用地域計画が定められているときは、これらに照らし適切なものであること。

四　当該登録有形文化財保存活用計画に前項第一号に掲げる事項が記載されている場合には、その内容が登録有形文化財の現状変更を適切に行うために必要なものとして文部科学省令で定める基準に適合するものであること。

五　当該登録有形文化財保存活用計画に前項第二号に掲げる事項が記載されている場合には、当該寄託契約の内容が登録有形文化財の公開を適切かつ確実に行うために必要なものとして文部科学省令で定める基準に適合するものであること。

5　文化庁長官は、前項の認定をしたときは、遅滞なく、その旨を当該認定を申請した者に通知しなければならない。

（認定を受けた登録有形文化財保存活用計画の変更）

第六十七条の三　前条第四項の認定を受けた登録有形文化財の所有者又は管理団体は、当該認定を受けた登録有形文化財保存活用計画の変更（文部科学省令で定める軽微な変更を除く。）をしようとするときは、文化庁長官の認定を受けなければならない。

2　前条第四項及び第五項の規定は、前項の認定について準用する。

（現状変更の届出の特例）

第六十七条の四　第六十七条の二第三項第一号に掲げる事項が記載された登録有形文化財保存活用計画が同条第四項の認定（前条第一項の変更の認定を含む。以下この節及び第百五十三条第二項第七号において同じ。）を受けた場合において、当該登録有形文化財の現状変更をその記載された事項の内容に即して行うに当たり、第六十四条第一項の規定による届出を行わなければならないときは、同項の規定にかかわらず、当該現状変更が終了した後遅滞なく、文部科学省令で定めるところにより、その旨を文化庁長官に届け出ることをもつて足りる。

（認定登録有形文化財保存活用計画の実施状況に関する報告の徴収）

第六十七条の五　文化庁長官は、第六十七条の二第四項の認定を受けた登録有形文化財の所有者又は管理団体に対し、当該認定を受けた登録有形文化財保存活用計画（変更があつたときは、その変更後のもの。次条第一項及び第六十七条の七において「認定登録有形文化財保存活用計画」という。）の実施の状況について報告を求めることができる。

（認定の取消し）

第六十七条の六　文化庁長官は、認定登録有形文化財保存活用計画が第六十七条の二第四項各号のいずれかに適合しなくなつたと認めるときは、その認定を取り消すことができる。

2　文化庁長官は、前項の規定により認定を取り消したときは、遅滞なく、その旨を当該認定を受けていた者に通知しなければならない。

（所有者等への指導又は助言）

第六十七条の七　都道府県及び市町村の教育委員会は、登録有形文化財の所有者又は管理団体の求めに応じ、登録有形文化財保存活用計画の作成及び認定登録有形文化財保存活用計画の円滑かつ確実な実施に関し必要な指導又は助言をすることができる。

2　文化庁長官は、登録有形文化財の所有者又は管理団体の求めに応じ、登録有形文化財保存活用計画の作成及び認定登録有形文化財保存活用計画の円滑かつ確実な実施に関し必要な指導又は助言をするように努めなければならない。

第七十四条　第一項中「を適当と認める者」を「が適当と認められる者（以下この章において「保持者等」という。）」に改める。

第七十六条　中「保持者若しくは保持団体又は地方公共団体その他その保存に当たることを適当と認める者」を「保持者等」に改め、同条の次に次の五条を加える。

（重要無形文化財保存活用計画の認定）

第七十六条の二　重要無形文化財の保持者等は、文部科学省令で定めるところにより、重要無形文化財の保存及び活用に関する計画（以下この章及び第百五十三条第二項第八号において「重要無形文化財保存活用計画」という。）を作成し、文化庁長官の認定を申請することができる。

2　重要無形文化財保存活用計画には、次に掲げる事項を記載するものとする。

一　当該重要無形文化財の名称及び保持者又は保持団体

二　当該重要無形文化財の保存及び活用のために行う具体的な措置の内容

三　計画期間

四　その他文部科学省令で定める事項

3　文化庁長官は、第一項の規定による認定の申請があつた場合において、その重要無形文化財保存活用計画が次の各号のいずれにも適合するものであると認めるときは、その認定をするものとする。

一　当該重要無形文化財保存活用計画の実施が当該重要無形文化財の保存及び活用に寄与するものであると認められること。

二　円滑かつ確実に実施されると見込まれるものであること。

三　第百八十三条の二第一項に規定する文化財保存活用大綱又は第百八十三条の五第一項に規定する認定文化財保存活用地域計画が定められているときは、これらに照らし適切なものであること。

4　文化庁長官は、前項の認定をしたときは、遅滞なく、その旨を当該認定を申請した者に通知しなければならない。

（認定を受けた重要無形文化財保存活用計画の変更）

第七十六条の三　前条第三項の認定を受けた重要無形文化財の保持者等は、当該認定を受けた重要無形文化財保存活用計画の変更（文部科学省令で定める軽微な変更を除く。）をしようとするときは、文化庁長官の認定を受けなければならない。

2　前条第三項及び第四項の規定は、前項の認定について準用する。

（認定重要無形文化財保存活用計画の実施状況に関する報告の徴収）

第七十六条の四　文化庁長官は、第七十六条の二第三項の認定を受けた重要無形文化財の保持者等に対し、当該認定（前条第一項の変更の認定を含む。次条及び第百五十三条第二項第八号において同じ。）を受けた重要無形文化財保存活用計画（変更があつたときは、その変更後のもの。次条第一項及び第七十六条の六において「認定重要無形文化財保存活用計画」という。）の実施の状況について報告を求めることができる。

（認定の取消し）

第七十六条の五　文化庁長官は、認定重要無形文化財保存活用計画が第七十六条の二第三項各号のいずれかに適合しなくなつたと認めるときは、その認定を取り消すことができる。

2　文化庁長官は、前項の規定により認定を取り消したときは、遅滞なく、その旨を当該認定を受けていた者に通知しなければならない。

（保持者等への指導又は助言）

第七十六条の六　都道府県及び市町村の教育委員会は、重要無形文化財の保持者等の求めに応じ、重要無形文化財保存活用計画の作成及び認定重要無形文化財保存活用計画の円滑かつ確実な実施に関し必要な指導又は助言をすることができる。

2　文化庁長官は、重要無形文化財の保持者等の求めに応じ、重要無形文化財保存活用計画の作成及び認定重要無形文化財保存活用計画の円滑かつ確実な実施に関し必要な指導又は助言をするように努めなければならない。

第八十四条　第一項中「で準用する」を「において準用する」に、「及び第十二章」を「（第九十条の二第一項を除く。）及び第百八十七条第一項第二号」に改める。

第八十五条の次に次の三条を加える。

（重要有形民俗文化財保存活用計画の認定）

第八十五条　の二　重要有形民俗文化財の所有者（管理団体がある場合は、その者）は、文部科学省令で定めるところにより、重要有形民俗文化財の保存及び活用に関する計画（以下「重要有形民俗文化財保存活用計画」という。）を作成し、文化庁長官の認定を申請することができる。

2　重要有形民俗文化財保存活用計画には、次に掲げる事項を記載するものとする。

一　当該重要有形民俗文化財の名称及び所在の場所

二　当該重要有形民俗文化財の保存及び活用のために行う具体的な措置の内容

三　計画期間

四　その他文部科学省令で定める事項

3　前項第二号に掲げる事項には、当該重要有形民俗文化財の現状変更又は保存に影響を及ぼす行為に関する事項を記載することができる。

4　文化庁長官は、第一項の規定による認定の申請があつた場合において、その重要有形民俗文化財保存活用計画が次の各号のいずれにも適合するものであると認めるときは、その認定をするものとする。

一　当該重要有形民俗文化財保存活用計画の実施が当該重要有形民俗文化財の保存及び活用に寄与するものであると認められること。

二　円滑かつ確実に実施されると見込まれるものであること。

三　第百八十三条の二第一項に規定する文化財保存活用大綱又は第百八十三条の五第一項に規定する認定文化財保存活用地域計画が定められているときは、これらに照らし適切なものであること。

四　当該重要有形民俗文化財保存活用計画に前項に規定する事項が記載されている場合には、その内容が重要有形民俗文化財の現状変更又は保存に影響を及ぼす行為を適切に行うために必要なものとして文部科学省令で定める基準に適合するものであること。

5　文化庁長官は、前項の認定をしたときは、遅滞なく、その旨を当該認定を申請した者に通知しなければならない。

（現状変更等の届出の特例）

第八十五条の三　前条第三項に規定する事項が記載された重要有形民俗文化財保存活用計画が同条第四項の認定（次条において準用する第五十三条の三第一項の変更の認定を含む。第百五十三条第二項第十二号において同じ。）を受けた場合において、当該重要有形民俗文化財の現状変更又は保存に影響を及ぼす行為をその記載された事項の内容に即して行うに当たり、第八十一条第一項の規定による届出を行わなければならないときは、同項の規定にかかわらず、当該現状変更又は保存に影響を及ぼす行為が終了した後遅滞なく、文部科学省令で定めるところにより、その旨を文化庁長官に届け出ることをもつて足りる。

（準用）

第八十五条の四　重要有形民俗文化財保存活用計画については、第五十三条の三及び第五十三条の六から第五十三条の八までの規定を準用する。この場合において、第五十三条の三第一項中「前条第四項」とあるのは「第八十五条の二第四項」と、同条第二項中「前条第四項及び第五項」とあるのは「第八十五条の二第四項及び第五項」と、第五十三条の六中「第五十三条の二第四項」とあるのは「第八十五条の二第四項」と、第五十三条の七第一項中「第五十三条の二第四項各号」とあるのは「第八十五条の二第四項各号」と読み替えるものとする。

第八十七条　第一項中「を適当と認める者」を「が適当と認められる者（第八十九条及び第八十九条の二第一項において「保存地方公共団体等」という。）」に改める。

第八十九条　中「地方公共団体その他重要無形民俗文化財の保存に当たることを適当と認める者」を「保存地方公共団体等」に改め、同条の次に次の二条を加える。

（重要無形民俗文化財保存活用計画の認定）

第八十九条の二　保存地方公共団体等は、文部科学省令で定めるところにより、重要無形民俗文化財の保存及び活用に関する計画（以下この章及び第百五十三条第二項第十三号において「重要無形民俗文化財保存活用計画」という。）を作成し、文化庁長官の認定を申請することができる。

2　重要無形民俗文化財保存活用計画には、次に掲げる事項を記載するものとする。

一　当該重要無形民俗文化財の名称

二　当該重要無形民俗文化財の保存及び活用のために行う具体的な措置の内容

三　計画期間

四　その他文部科学省令で定める事項

3　文化庁長官は、第一項の規定による認定の申請があつた場合において、その重要無形民俗文化財保存活用計画が次の各号のいずれにも適合するものであると認めるときは、その認定をするものとする。

一　当該重要無形民俗文化財保存活用計画の実施が当該重要無形民俗文化財の保存

及び活用に寄与するものであると認められること。

二　円滑かつ確実に実施されると見込まれるものであること。

三　第百八十三条の二第一項に規定する文化財保存活用大綱又は第百八十三条の五第一項に規定する認定文化財保存活用地域計画が定められているときは、これらに照らし適切なものであること。

4　文化庁長官は、前項の認定をしたときは、遅滞なく、その旨を当該認定を申請した者に通知しなければならない。

（準用）

第八十九条の三　重要無形民俗文化財保存活用計画については、第七十六条の三から第七十六条の六までの規定を準用する。この場合において、第七十六条の三第一項中「前条第三項」とあるのは「第八十九条の二第三項」と、同条第二項中「前条第三項及び第四項」とあるのは「第八十九条の二第三項及び第四項」と、第七十六条の四中「第七十六条の二第三項」とあるのは「第八十九条の二第三項」と、「次条及び第百五十三条第二項第八号」とあるのは「次条」と、第七十六条の五第一項中「第七十六条の二第三項各号」とあるのは「第八十九条の二第三項各号」と読み替えるものとする。

第九十条　第三項中「第五十七条」の下に「及び第六十七条の二から第六十七条の七まで」を加え、「現状の変更」を「現状変更」に改め、同条の次に次の三条を加える。

（登録有形民俗文化財保存活用計画の認定）

の二　登録有形民俗文化財の所有者（管理団体（前条第三項において準用する第六十条第三項の規定による指定を受けた地方公共団体その他の法人をいう。）がある場合は、その者）は、文部科学省令で定めるところにより、登録有形民俗文化財の保存及び活用に関する計画（以下「登録有形民俗文化財保存活用計画」という。）を作成し、文化庁長官の認定を申請することができる。

2　登録有形民俗文化財保存活用計画には、次に掲げる事項を記載するものとする。

一　当該登録有形民俗文化財の名称及び所在の場所

二　当該登録有形民俗文化財の保存及び活用のために行う具体的な措置の内容

三　計画期間

四　その他文部科学省令で定める事項

3　前項第二号に掲げる事項には、当該登録有形民俗文化財の現状変更に関する事項を記載することができる。

4　文化庁長官は、第一項の規定による認定の申請があつた場合において、その登録有形民俗文化財保存活用計画が次の各号のいずれにも適合するものであると認めるときは、その認定をするものとする。

一　当該登録有形民俗文化財保存活用計画の実施が当該登録有形民俗文化財の保存及び活用に寄与するものであると認められること。

二　円滑かつ確実に実施されると見込まれるものであること。

三　第百八十三条の二第一項に規定する文化財保存活用大綱又は第百八十三条の五第一項に規定する認定文化財保存活用地域計画が定められているときは、これらに照らし適切なものであること。

四　当該登録有形民俗文化財保存活用計画に前項に規定する事項が記載されている場合には、登録有形民俗文化財の現状変更を適切に行うために必要なものとして文部科学省令で定める基準に適合するものであること。

5　文化庁長官は、前項の認定をしたときは、遅滞なく、その旨を当該認定を申請した者に通知しなければならない。

（現状変更の届出の特例）

第九十条の三　前条第三項に規定する事項が記載された登録有形民俗文化財保存活用計画が同条第四項の認定（次条において準用する第六十七条の三第一項の変更の認定を含む。第百五十三条第二項第十四号において同じ。）を受けた場合において、当該登録有形民俗文化財の現状変更をその記載された事項の内容に即して行うに当たり、第九十条第三項において準用する第六十四条第一項の規定による届出を行わなければならないときは、同項の規定にかかわらず、当該現状変更が終了した後遅滞なく、文部科学省令で定めるところにより、その旨を文化庁長官に届け出ることをもつて足りる。

（準用）

第九十条の四　登録有形民俗文化財保存活用計画については、第六十七条の三及び第六十七条の五から第六十七条の七までの規定を準用する。この場合において、第六十七条の三第一項中「前条第四項」とあるのは「第九十条の二第四項」と、同条第二項中「前条第四項及び第五項」とあるのは「第九十条の二第四項及び第五項」と、第六十七条の五中「第六十七条の二第四項」とあるのは「第九十条の二第四項」と、第六十七条の六第一項中「第六十七条の二第四項各号」とあるのは「第九十条の二第四項各号」と読み替えるものとする。

第百九条第四項中「（特別区を含む。以下同じ。）」を削り、「に前項」を「に同項」に改める。

第百十五条第一項中「及び第十二章」を「（第百三十三条の二第一項を除く。）及び第百八十七条第一項第三号」に改める。

第百十九条第二項中「特別の事情」を「当該史跡名勝天然記念物の適切な管理のため必要」に、「適当な」を「第百九十二条の二第一項に規定する文化財保存活用支援団体その他の適当な」に、「第十二章」を「第百八十七条第一項第三号」に改める。

第百二十六条中「第百八十四条第一項」の下に「又は第百八十四条の二第一項」を加え、「市の」を「市町村の」に改める。

第百二十九条の次に次の六条を加える。

（史跡名勝天然記念物保存活用計画の認定）

第百二十九条の二　史跡名勝天然記念物の管理団体又は所有者は、文部科学省令で定めるところにより、史跡名勝天然記念物の保存及び活用に関する計画（以下「史跡名勝天然記念物保存活用計画」という。）を作成し、文化庁長官の認定を申請することができる。

2　史跡名勝天然記念物保存活用計画には、次に掲げる事項を記載するものとする。

一　当該史跡名勝天然記念物の名称及び所在地

二　当該史跡名勝天然記念物の保存及び活用のために行う具体的な措置の内容

三　計画期間

四　その他文部科学省令で定める事項

3　前項第二号に掲げる事項には、当該史跡名勝天然記念物の現状変更又は保存に影響を及ぼす行為に関する事項を記載することができる。

4　文化庁長官は、第一項の規定による認定の申請があつた場合において、その史跡名勝天然記念物保存活用計画が次の各号のいずれにも適合するものであると認めるときは、その認定をするものとする。

一　当該史跡名勝天然記念物保存活用計画の実施が当該史跡名勝天然記念物の保存及び活用に寄与するものであると認められること。

二　円滑かつ確実に実施されると見込まれるものであること。

三　第百八十三条の二第一項に規定する文化財保存活用大綱又は第百八十三条の五第一項に規定する認定文化財保存活用地域計画が定められているときは、これらに照らし適切なものであること。

四　当該史跡名勝天然記念物保存活用計画に前項に規定する事項が記載されている場合には、その内容が史跡名勝天然記念物の現状変更又は保存に影響を及ぼす行為を適切に行うために必要なものとして文部科学省令で定める基準に適合するものであること。

5　文化庁長官は、前項の認定をしたときは、遅滞なく、その旨を当該認定を申請した者に通知しなければならない。

（認定を受けた史跡名勝天然記念物保存活用計画の変更）

第百二十九条の三　前条第四項の認定を受けた史跡名勝天然記念物の管理団体又は所有者は、当該認定を受けた史跡名勝天然記念物保存活用計画の変更（文部科学省令で定める軽微な変更を除く。）をしようとするときは、文化庁長官の認定を受けなければならない。

2　前条第四項及び第五項の規定は、前項の認定について準用する。

（現状変更等の許可の特例）

第百二十九条の四　第百二十九条の二第三項に規定する事項が記載された史跡名勝天然記念物保存活用計画が同条第四項の認定（前条第一項の変更の認定を含む。以下この章及び第百五十三条第二項第二十三号において同じ。）を受けた場合において、当該史跡名勝天然記念物の現状変更又は保存に影響を及ぼす行為をその記載された事項の内容に即して行うに当たり、第百二十五条第一項の許可を受けなければならないときは、同項の規定にかかわらず、当該現状変更又は保存に影響を及ぼす行為が終了した後遅滞なく、文部科学省令で定めるところにより、その旨を文化庁長官に届け出ることをもつて足りる。

（認定史跡名勝天然記念物保存活用計画の実施状況に関する報告の徴収）

第百二十九条の五　文化庁長官は、第百二十九条の二第四項の認定を受けた史跡名勝天然記念物の管理団体又は所有者に対し、当該認定を受けた史跡名勝天然記念物保存活用計画（変更があつたときは、その変更後のもの。次条第一項及び第百二十九条の七において「認定史跡名勝天然記念物保存活用計画」という。）の実施の状況について報告を求めることができる。

（認定の取消し）

第百二十九条の六　文化庁長官は、認定史跡名勝天然記念物保存活用計画が第百二十九条の二第四項各号のいずれかに適合しなくなつたと認めるときは、その認定を取り消すことができる。

2　文化庁長官は、前項の規定により認定を取り消したときは、遅滞なく、その旨を当該認定を受けていた者に通知しなければならない。

（管理団体等への指導又は助言）

第百二十九条の七　都道府県及び市町村の教育委員会は、史跡名勝天然記念物の管理団体又は所有者の求めに応じ、史跡名勝天然記念物保存活用計画の作成及び認定史跡名勝天然記念物保存活用計画の円滑かつ確実な実施に関し必要な指導又は助言をすることができる。

2　文化庁長官は、史跡名勝天然記念物の管理団体又は所有者の求めに応じ、史跡名勝天然記念物保存活用計画の作成及び認定史跡名勝天然記念物保存活用計画の円滑かつ確実な実施に関し必要な指導又は助言をするように努めなければならない。

第七章中第百三十三条の次に次の三条を加える。

（登録記念物保存活用計画の認定）

第百三十三条の二　登録記念物の管理団体（前条において準用する第百十三条第一項の規定による指定を受けた地方公共団体その他の法人をいう。）又は所有者は、文部科学省令で定めるところにより、登録記念物の保存及び活用に関する計画（以下「登録記念物保存活用計画」という。）を作成し、文化庁長官の認定を申請することができる。

2　登録記念物保存活用計画には、次に掲げる事項を記載するものとする。

一　当該登録記念物の名称及び所在地

二　当該登録記念物の保存及び活用のために行う具体的な措置の内容

三　計画期間

四　その他文部科学省令で定める事項

3　前項第二号に掲げる事項には、当該登録記念物の現状変更に関する事項を記載することができる。

4　文化庁長官は、第一項の規定による認定の申請があつた場合において、その登録記念物保存活用計画が次の各号のいずれにも適合するものであると認めるときは、その認定をするものとする。

一　当該登録記念物保存活用計画の実施が当該登録記念物の保存及び活用に寄与するものであると認められること。

二　円滑かつ確実に実施されると見込まれるものであること。

三　第百八十三条の二第一項に規定する文化財保存活用大綱又は第百八十三条の五第一項に規定する認定文化財保存活用地域計画が定められているときは、これらに照らし適切なものであること。

四　当該登録記念物保存活用計画に前項に規定する事項が記載されている場合には、その内容が登録記念物の現状変更を適切に行うために必要なものとして文部科学省令で定める基準に適合するものであること。

5　文化庁長官は、前項の認定をしたときは、遅滞なく、その旨を当該認定を申請した者に通知しなければならない。

（現状変更の届出の特例）

第百三十三条の三　前条第三項に規定する事項が記載された登録記念物保存活用計画が同条第四項の認定（次条において準用する第六十七条の三第一項の変更の認定を含む。第百五十三条第二項第二十四号において同じ。）を受けた場合において、当該登録記念物の現状変更をその記載された事項の内容に即して行うに当たり、第百三十三条において準用する第六十四条第一項の規定による届出を行わなければならないときは、同項の規定にかかわらず、当該現状変更が終了した後遅滞なく、文部科学省令で定めるところにより、その旨を文化庁長官に届け出ることをもつて足りる。

（準用）

第百三十三条の四　登録記念物保存活用計画については、第六十七条の三及び第六十七条の五から第六十七条の七までの規定を準用する。この場合において、第六十七条の三第一項中「前条第四項」とあるのは「第百三十三条の二第四項」と、同条第二項中「前条第四項及び第五項」とあるのは「第百三十三条の二第四項及び第五項」と、第六十七条の五中「第六十七条の二第四項」とあるのは「第百三十三条の二第四項」と、第六十七条の六第一項中「第六十七条の二第四項各号」とあるのは「第百三十三条の二第四項各号」と読み替えるものとする。

第百三十九条第一項ただし書及び第三項中「現状の変更」を「現状変更」に改める。

第百四十三条第三項に次のただし書を加える。

ただし、当該都道府県が特定地方公共団体である場合は、この限りでない。

第百五十三条第二項第二号中「き損」を「毀損」に改め、同項第十八号中「限る。）」の下に「又は第百八十四条の二第一項の政令（第百八十四条第一項第二号に掲げる事務に係るものに限る。）」を加え、同号を同項第二十七号とし、同項中第十七号を第二十五号とし、同号の次に次の一号を加える。

二十六　第百八十三条の三第一項に規定する文化財保存活用地域計画の同条第五項の認定（第百八十三条の四第一項の変更の認定を含む。）

第百五十三条第二項中第十六号を第二十二号とし、同号の次に次の二号を加える。

二十三　史跡名勝天然記念物保存活用計画の第百二十九条の二第四項の認定

二十四　登録記念物保存活用計画の第百三十三条の二第四項の認定

第百五十三条第二項中第十五号を第二十一号とし、第十四号を第二十号とし、同項第十三号中「き損」を「毀損」に改め、同号を同項第十九号とし、同項中第十二号を第十八号とし、第九号から第十一号までを六号ずつ繰り下げ、第八号を第十一号とし、同号の次に次の三号を加える。

十二　重要有形民俗文化財保存活用計画の第八十五条の二第四項の認定

十三　重要無形民俗文化財保存活用計画の第八十九条の二第三項の認定（第八十九条の三において準用する第七十六条の三第一項の変更の認定を含む。）

十四　登録有形民俗文化財保存活用計画の第九十条の二第四項の認定

第百五十三条第二項中第七号を第十号とし、第六号を第九号とし、第五号の次に次の三号を加える。

六　重要文化財保存活用計画の第五十三条の二第四項の認定

七　登録有形文化財保存活用計画の第六十七条の二第四項の認定

八　重要無形文化財保存活用計画の第七十六条の二第三項の認定

第百五十四条第一項中「。次項及び次条において同じ。」を削り、同項第二号及び第五号中「で準用する」を「において準用する」に改め、同条第二項中「文化庁長官」の下に「（第百八十四条第一項又は第百八十四条の二第一項の規定により文化庁長官の権限に属する事務を都道府県又は市町村の教育委員会が行う場合には、当該都道府県又は市町村の教育委員会。次条において同じ。）」を加え、「で準用する」を「において準用する」に改める。

第百五十六条第一項中「市の」を「市町村の」に改め、同項第二号中「で準用する」を「において準用する」に、「管理団体」を「地方公共団体その他の法人」に改め、同条第二項中「市の」を「市町村の」に改める。

第百七十条の次に次の五条を加える。

第百七十条の二　国の所有に属する重要文化財、重要有形民俗文化財又は史跡名勝天然記念物を管理する各省各庁の長は、文部科学省令で定めるところにより、重要文化財保存活用計画、重要有形民俗文化財保存活用計画又は史跡名勝天然記念物保存活用計画を作成し、文部科学大臣を通じ文化庁長官の同意を求めることができる。

2　文化庁長官は、前項の規定による同意の求めがあつた場合において、その重要文化財保存活用計画、重要有形民俗文化財保存活用計画又は史跡名勝天然記念物保存活用計画がそれぞれ第五十三条の二第四項各号、第八十五条の二第四項各号又は第百二十九条の二第四項各号のいずれにも適合するものであると認めるときは、その同意をするものとする。

第百七十条の三　前条第二項の同意を得た各省各庁の長は、当該同意を得た重要文化財保存活用計画、重要有形民俗文化財保存活用計画又は史跡名勝天然記念物保存活用計画の変更（文部科学省令で定める軽微な変更を除く。）をしようとするときは、文部科学大臣を通じ文化庁長官の同意を求めなければならない。

2　前条第二項の規定は、前項の同意について準用する。

第百七十条の四　第五十三条の二第三項第一号に掲げる事項が記載された重要文化財保存活用計画、第八十五条の二第三項に規定する事項が記載された重要有形民俗文化財保存活用計画又は第百二十九条の二第三項に規定する事項が記載された史跡名勝天然記念物保存活用計画について第百七十条の二第二項の同意（前条第一項の変更の同意を含む。次条及び第百七十条の六において同じ。）を得た場合において、当該重要文化財、重要有形民俗文化財又は史跡名勝天然記念物の現状変更又は保存に影響を及ぼす行為をその記載された事項の内容に即して行うに当たり、第百六十七条第一項（第六号に係る部分に限る。）の規定による通知をし、又は第百六十八条第一項（第一号に係る部分に限る。）の規定による同意を求めなければならないときは、これらの規定にかかわらず、当該現状変更又は保存に影響を及ぼす行為が終了した後遅滞なく、文部科学省令で定めるところにより、その旨を文部科学大臣を通じ文化庁長官に通知することをもつて足りる。

第百七十条の五　第五十三条の二第三項第二号に掲げる事項が記載された重要文化財保存活用計画について第百七十条の二第二項の同意を得た場合において、当該重要文化財の修理をその記載された事項の内容に即して行うに当たり、第百六十七条第一項（第五号に係る部分に限る。）の規定による通知をしなければならないときは、同項の規定にかかわらず、当該修理が終了した後遅滞なく、文部科学省令で定めるところにより、その旨を文部科学大臣を通じ文化庁長官に通知することをもつて足りる。

第百七十条の六　文部科学大臣は、第百七十条の二第二項の同意を得た各省各庁の長に対し、当該同意を得た重要文化財保存活用計画、重要有形民俗文化財保存活用計画又は史跡名勝天然記念物保存活用計画（いずれも変更があつたときは、その変更後のもの）の実施の状況について報告を求めることができる。

第百七十四条の次に次の一条を加える。

第百七十四条の二　第百七十二条第一項の規定による指定を受けた地方公共団体その他の法人が作成する重要文化財保存活用計画、重要有形民俗文化財保存活用計画又は史跡名勝天然記念物保存活用計画については、それぞれ第五十三条の二から第五十三条の八までの規定、第八十五条の二から第八十五条の四までの規定又は第百二十九条の二から第百二十九条の七までの規定を準用する。

2　文化庁長官は、前項において準用する第五十三条の二第四項、第八十五条の二第四項又は第百二十九条の二第四項の認定（前項において準用する第五十三条の三第一項（前項において準用する第八十五条の四において準用する場合を含む。）又は第百二十九条の三第一項の変更の認定を含む。）をしようとするときは、あらかじめ、文部科学大臣を通じ当該重要文化財、重要有形民俗文化財又は史跡名勝天然記念物を管理する各省各庁の長と協議しなければならない。ただし、当該各省各庁の長が文部科学大臣であるときは、その承認を受けるべきものとする。

　第百七十九条第四項中「現状の変更に」を「現状変更について」に改め、同条第五項中「現状の変更」を「現状変更」に改め、同条の次に次の四条を加える。

第百七十九条の二　国の所有に属する登録有形文化財、登録有形民俗文化財又は登録記念物を管理する各省各庁の長は、文部科学省令で定めるところにより、登録有形文化財保存活用計画、登録有形民俗文化財保存活用計画又は登録記念物保存活用計画を作成し、文部科学大臣を通じ文化庁長官の同意を求めることができる。

2　文化庁長官は、前項の規定による同意の求めがあつた場合において、その登録有形文化財保存活用計画、登録有形民俗文化財保存活用計画又は登録記念物保存活用計画がそれぞれ第六十七条の二第四項各号、第九十条の二第四項各号又は第百三十三条の二第四項各号のいずれにも適合するものであると認めるときは、その同意をするものとする。

第百七十九条の三　前条第二項の同意を得た各省各庁の長は、当該同意を得た登録有形文化財保存活用計画、登録有形民俗文化財保存活用計画又は登録記念物保存活用計画の変更（文部科学省令で定める軽微な変更を除く。）をしようとするときは、文部科学大臣を通じ文化庁長官の同意を求めなければならない。

2　前条第二項の規定は、前項の同意について準用する。

第百七十九条の四　第六十七条の二第三項第一号に掲げる事項が記載された登録有形文化財保存活用計画、第九十条の二第三項に規定する事項が記載された登録有形民俗文化財保存活用計画又は第百三十三条の二第三項に規定する事項が記載された登録記念物保存活用計画について第百七十九条の二第二項の同意（前条第一項の変更の同意を含む。次条において同じ。）を得た場合において、当該登録有形文化財、登録有形民俗文化財又は登録記念物の現状変更をその記載された事項の内容に即して行うに当たり、第百七十九条第一項（第五号に係る部分に限る。）の規定による通知をしなければならないときは、同項の規定にかかわらず、当該現状変更が終了した後遅滞なく、文部科学省令で定めるところにより、その旨を文部科学大臣を通じ文化庁長官に通知することをもつて足りる。

第百七十九条の五　文部科学大臣は、第百七十九条の二第二項の同意を得た各省各庁の長に対し、当該同意を得た登録有形文化財保存活用計画、登録有形民俗文化財保存活用計画又は登録記念物保存活用計画（いずれも変更があつたときは、その変更後のもの）の実施の状況について報告を求めることができる。

　第百八十三条の次に次の八条を加える。

（文化財保存活用大綱）

第百八十三条の二　都道府県の教育委員会は、当該都道府県の区域における文化財の保存及び活用に関する総合的な施策の大綱（次項及び次条において「文化財保存活用大綱」という。）を定めることができる。

2　都道府県の教育委員会は、文化財保存活用大綱を定め、又は変更したときは、遅滞なく、これを公表するよう努めるとともに、文化庁長官及び関係市町村に送付しなければならない。

（文化財保存活用地域計画の認定）

第百八十三条の三　市町村の教育委員会（地方文化財保護審議会を置くものに限る。）は、文部科学省令で定めるところにより、単独で又は共同して、文化財保存活用大綱が定められているときは当該文化財保存活用大綱を勘案して、当該市町村の区域における文化財の保存及び活用に関する総合的な計画（以下この節及び第百九十二条の六第一項において「文化財保存活用地域計画」という。）を作成し、文化庁長官の認定を申請することができる。

2　文化財保存活用地域計画には、次に掲げる事項を記載するものとする。

一　当該市町村の区域における文化財の保存及び活用に関する基本的な方針

二　当該市町村の区域における文化財の保存及び活用を図るために当該市町村が講ずる措置の内容

三　当該市町村の区域における文化財を把握するための調査に関する事項

四　計画期間

五　その他文部科学省令で定める事項

3　市町村の教育委員会は、文化財保存活用地域計画を作成しようとするときは、あらかじめ、公聴会の開催その他の住民の意見を反映させるために必要な措置を講ずるよう努めるとともに、地方文化財保護審議会（第百八十三条の九第一項に規定する協議会が組織されている場合にあつては、地方文化財保護審議会及び当該協議会。第百八十三条の五第二項において同じ。）の意見を聴かなければならない。

4　文化財保存活用地域計画は、地域における歴史的風致の維持及び向上に関する法律（平成二十年法律第四十号）第五条第一項に規定する歴史的風致維持向上計画が定められているときは、当該歴史的風致維持向上計画との調和が保たれたものでなければならない。

5　文化庁長官は、第一項の規定による認定の申請があつた場合において、その文化財保存活用地域計画が次の各号のいずれにも適合するものであると認めるときは、その認定をするものとする。

一　当該文化財保存活用地域計画の実施が当該市町村の区域における文化財の保存及び活用に寄与するものであると認められること。

二　円滑かつ確実に実施されると見込まれるものであること。

三　文化財保存活用大綱が定められているときは、当該文化財保存活用大綱に照らし適切なものであること。

6　文化庁長官は、前項の認定をしようとするときは、あらかじめ、文部科学大臣を通じ関係行政機関の長に協議しなければならない。

7　文化庁長官は、第五項の認定をしたときは、遅滞なく、その旨を当該認定を申請した市町村の教育委員会に通知しなければならない。

8　市町村の教育委員会は、前項の通知を受けたときは、遅滞なく、当該通知に係る文化財保存活用地域計画を公表するよう努めなければならない。

（認定を受けた文化財保存活用地域計画の変更）

第百八十三条の四　前条第五項の認定を受けた市町村（以下この節及び第百九十二条の六第二項において「認定市町村」という。）の教育委員会は、当該認定を受けた文化財保存活用地域計画の変更（文部科学省令で定める軽微な変更を除く。）をしようとするときは、文化庁長官の認定を受けなければならない。

2　前条第三項から第八項までの規定は、前項の認定について準用する。

（文化財の登録の提案）

第百八十三条の五　認定市町村の教育委員会は、第百八十三条の三第五項の認定（前条第一項の変更の認定を含む。第百八十三条の七第一項及び第二項において同じ。）を受けた文化財保存活用地域計画（変更があつたときは、その変更後のもの。以下この節及び第百九十二条の六において「認定文化財保存活用地域計画」という。）の計画期間内に限り、当該認定市町村の区域内に存する文化財であつて第五十七条第一項、第九十条第一項又は第百三十二条第一項の規定により登録されることが適当であると思料するものがあるときは、文部科学省令で定めるところにより、文部科学大臣に対し、当該文化財を文化財登録原簿に登録することを提案することができる。

2　認定市町村の教育委員会は、前項の規定による提案をしようとするときは、あらかじめ、地方文化財保護審議会の意見を聴かなければならない。

3　文部科学大臣は、第一項の規定による提案が行われた場合において、当該提案に係る文化財について第五十七条第一項、第九十条第一項又は第百三十二条第一項の規定による登録をしないこととしたときは、遅滞なく、その旨及びその理由を当該提案をした認定市町村の教育委員会に通知しなければならない。

（認定文化財保存活用地域計画の実施状況に関する報告の徴収）

第百八十三条の六　文化庁長官は、認定市町村の教育委員会に対し、認定文化財保存活用地域計画の実施の状況について報告を求めることができる。

（認定の取消し）

第百八十三条の七　文化庁長官は、認定文化財保存活用地域計画が第百八十三条の三第五項各号のいずれかに適合しなくなつたと認めるときは、その認定を取り消すことができる。

2　文化庁長官は、前項の規定により認定を取り消したときは、遅滞なく、その旨を当該認定を受けていた市町村の教育委員会に通知しなければならない。

3　市町村の教育委員会は、前項の通知を受けたときは、遅滞なく、その旨を公表するよう努めなければならない。

（市町村への助言等）

第百八十三条の八　都道府県の教育委員会は、市町村に対し、文化財保存活用地域計画の作成及び認定文化財保存活用地域計画の円滑かつ確実な実施に関し必要な助言をすることができる。

2　国は、市町村に対し、文化財保存活用地域計画の作成及び認定文化財保存活用地域計画の円滑かつ確実な実施に関し必要な情報の提供又は指導若しくは助言をするように努めなければならない。

3　前二項に定めるもののほか、国、都道府県及び市町村は、文化財保存活用地域計画の作成及び認定文化財保存活用地域計画の円滑かつ確実な実施が促進されるよう、相互に連携を図りながら協力しなければならない。

4　市町村の長及び教育委員会は、文化財保存活用地域計画の作成及び認定文化財保存活用地域計画の円滑かつ確実な実施が促進されるよう、相互に緊密な連携を図りながら協力しなければならない。

（協議会）

第百八十三条の九　市町村の教育委員会は、単独で又は共同して、文化財保存活用地域計画の作成及び変更に関する協議並びに認定文化財保存活用地域計画の実施に係る連絡調整を行うための協議会（以下この条において「協議会」という。）を組織することができる。

2　協議会は、次に掲げる者をもつて構成する。

一　当該市町村

二　当該市町村の区域をその区域に含む都道府県

三　第百九十二条の二第一項の規定により当該市町村の教育委員会が指定した文化財保存活用支援団体

四　文化財の所有者、学識経験者、商工関係団体、観光関係団体その他の市町村の教育委員会が必要と認める者

3　協議会は、必要があると認めるときは、関係行政機関に対して、資料の提供、意見の表明、説明その他必要な協力を求めることができる。

4　協議会において協議が調つた事項については、協議会の構成員は、その協議の結果を尊重しなければならない。

5　前各項に定めるもののほか、協議会の運営に関し必要な事項は、協議会が定める。

第百八十四条の次に次の一条を加える。

（認定市町村の教育委員会が処理する事務）

第百八十四条の二　前条第一項第二号、第四号又は第五号に掲げる文化庁長官の権限

に属する事務であつて認定市町村の区域内に係るものの全部又は一部は、認定文化財保存活用地域計画の計画期間内に限り、政令で定めるところにより、当該認定文化財保存活用地域計画の実施に必要な範囲内において、当該認定市町村の教育委員会が行うこととすることができる。

2　前項の規定により認定市町村の教育委員会が同項に規定する事務を行う場合には、前条第二項、第四項（第三号に係る部分を除く。）及び第五項から第八項までの規定を準用する。

3　第一項の規定により認定市町村の教育委員会が同項に規定する事務を開始する日前になされた当該事務に係る許可等の処分その他の行為（以下この条において「処分等の行為」という。）又は許可の申請その他の行為（以下この条において「申請等の行為」という。）は、同日以後においては、当該認定市町村の教育委員会のした処分等の行為又は当該認定市町村の教育委員会に対して行つた申請等の行為とみなす。

4　認定文化財保存活用地域計画の計画期間の終了その他の事情により認定市町村の教育委員会が第一項に規定する事務を終了する日以前になされた当該事務に係る処分等の行為又は申請等の行為は、同日の翌日以後においては、その終了後に当該事務を行うこととなる者のした処分等の行為又は当該者に対して行つた申請等の行為とみなす。

第百八十七条第一項中「所有者（管理団体がある場合は、その者）又は管理責任者」を「次の各号に掲げる者」に、「重要文化財、重要有形民俗文化財又は史跡名勝天然記念物の管理（管理団体がある場合を除く。）、修理若しくは」を「当該各号に定める管理、修理又は」に改め、同項に次の各号を加える。

一　重要文化財の所有者（管理団体がある場合は、その者）又は管理責任者　当該重要文化財の管理（管理団体がある場合を除く。）又は修理

二　重要有形民俗文化財の所有者（管理団体がある場合は、その者）又は管理責任者（第八十条において準用する第三十一条第二項の規定により選任された管理の責めに任ずべき者をいう。）　当該重要有形民俗文化財の管理（管理団体がある場合を除く。）又は修理

三　史跡名勝天然記念物の所有者（管理団体がある場合は、その者）又は管理責任者当該史跡名勝天然記念物の管理（管理団体がある場合を除く。）又は復旧

第百九十条第一項中「市町村」の下に「（いずれも特定地方公共団体であるものを除く。）」を、「より、」の下に「文化財に関して優れた識見を有する者により構成される」を加え、同条中第三項を第四項とし、第二項を第三項とし、第一項の次に次の一項を加える。

2　特定地方公共団体に、条例の定めるところにより、地方文化財保護審議会を置くものとする。

第百九十一条第一項中「都道府県」の下に「及び市町村」を、「教育委員会」の下に「（当該都道府県及び市町村が特定地方公共団体である場合には、当該特定地方公共団体）」

を加える。

第十二章に次の一節を加える。

第四節　文化財保存活用支援団体

（文化財保存活用支援団体の指定）

第百九十二条の二　市町村の教育委員会は、法人その他これに準ずるものとして文部科学省令で定める団体であつて、次条に規定する業務を適正かつ確実に行うことができると認められるものを、その申請により、文化財保存活用支援団体（以下この節において「支援団体」という。）として指定することができる。

2　市町村の教育委員会は、前項の規定による指定をしたときは、当該支援団体の名称、住所及び事務所の所在地を公示しなければならない。

3　支援団体は、その名称、住所又は事務所の所在地を変更しようとするときは、あらかじめ、その旨を市町村の教育委員会に届け出なければならない。

4　市町村の教育委員会は、前項の規定による届出があつたときは、当該届出に係る事項を公示しなければならない。

（支援団体の業務）

第百九十二条の三　支援団体は、次に掲げる業務を行うものとする。

一　当該市町村の区域内に存する文化財の保存及び活用を行うこと。

二　当該市町村の区域内に存する文化財の保存及び活用を図るための事業を行う者に対し、情報の提供、相談その他の援助を行うこと。

三　文化財の所有者の求めに応じ、当該文化財の管理、修理又は復旧その他その保存及び活用のため必要な措置につき委託を受けること。

四　文化財の保存及び活用に関する調査研究を行うこと。

五　前各号に掲げるもののほか、当該市町村の区域における文化財の保存及び活用を図るために必要な業務を行うこと。

（監督等）

第百九十二条の四　市町村の教育委員会は、前条各号に掲げる業務の適正かつ確実な実施を確保するため必要があると認めるときは、支援団体に対し、その業務に関し報告をさせることができる。

2　市町村の教育委員会は、支援団体が前条各号に掲げる業務を適正かつ確実に実施していないと認めるときは、支援団体に対し、その業務の運営の改善に関し必要な措置を講ずべきことを命ずることができる。

3　市町村の教育委員会は、支援団体が前項の規定による命令に違反したときは、第百九十二条の二第一項の規定による指定を取り消すことができる。

4　市町村の教育委員会は、前項の規定により指定を取り消したときは、その旨を公示しなければならない。

（情報の提供等）

第百九十二条の五　国及び関係地方公共団体は、支援団体に対し、その業務の実施に関し必要な情報の提供又は指導若しくは助言をするものとする。

（文化財保存活用地域計画の作成の提案等）

第百九十二条の六　支援団体は、市町村の教育委員会に対し、文化財保存活用地域計画の作成又は認定文化財保存活用地域計画の変更をすることを提案することができる。

2　支援団体は、認定市町村の教育委員会に対し、認定文化財保存活用地域計画の計画期間内に限り、当該認定市町村の区域内に存する文化財であつて第五十七条第一項、第九十条第一項又は第百三十二条第一項の規定により登録されることが適当であると思料するものがあるときは、文部科学省令で定めるところにより、当該文化財について第百八十三条の五第一項の規定による提案をするよう要請することができる。

第百九十五条第一項中「き棄し」を「毀棄し」に、「禁錮（こ）」を「禁錮」に、「三十万円」を「百万円」に改め、同条第二項中「禁錮（こ）」を「禁錮」に、「二十万円」を「五十万円」に改める。

第百九十六条第一項中「き損し」を「毀損し」に、「禁錮（こ）」を「禁錮」に、「三十万円」を「百万円」に改め、同条第二項中「禁錮（こ）」を「禁錮」に、「二十万円」を「五十万円」に改める。

第百九十七条中「二十万円」を「五十万円」に改め、同条第一号中「現状の変更」を「現状変更」に改める。

第百九十八条中「十万円」を「三十万円」に改め、同条第一号中「で準用する」を「において準用する」に、「き損」を「毀損」に改め、同条第二号中「で準用する」を「において準用する」に改め、同条第三号中「で準用する」を「において準用する」に、「き損」を「毀損」に改める。

第二百二条第二号及び第三号中「で準用する」を「において準用する」に改め、同条第五号中「第五十四条」を「第五十三条の六（第八十五条の四（第百七十四条の二第一項において準用する場合を含む。）及び第百七十四条の二第一項において準用する場合を含む。）、第五十四条」に、「で準用する」を「において準用する」に改め、「第五十五条」の下に「、第六十七条の五（第九十条の四及び第百三十三条の四において準用する場合を含む。）」を加え、「第百三十条」を「第七十六条の四（第八十九条の三において準用する場合を含む。）、第百二十九条の五（第百七十四条の二第一項において準用する場合を含む。）、第百三十条」に改める。

第二百三条第一号中「で準用する」を「において準用する」に改め、同条第二号中「で準用する」を「において準用する」に改め、「第四十三条の二第一項」の下に「、第五十三条の四若しくは第五十三条の五（これらの規定を第百七十四条の二第一項において準用する場合を含む。）」を加え、「第七十三条」を「第六十七条の四、第七十三条」に改め、「第八十四条第一項本文」の下に「、第八十五条の三（第百七十四条の二第一項において準用する場合を含む。）、第九十条の三」を、「第百二十七条第一項」の下に「、第百二十九条の四（第百七十四条の二第一項において準用する場合を含む。）、第百三十三条の三」を加え、同条第三号中「で準用する」を「において準用する」に改める。

（地方教育行政の組織及び運営に関する法律の一部改正）

第二条　地方教育行政の組織及び運営に関する法律（昭和三十一年法律第百六十二号）の一部を次のように改正する。

第二十三条　第一項第二号中「文化財の保護に関すること」を「次号に掲げるもの」に改め、同項に次の一号を加える。

三　文化財の保護に関すること。

附　則

（施行期日）

第一条　この法律は、平成三十一年四月一日から施行する。

（罰則に関する経過措置）

第二条　この法律の施行前にした行為に対する罰則の適用については、なお従前の例による。

（政令への委任）

第三条　前条に定めるもののほか、この法律の施行に関し必要な経過措置は、政令で定める。

（銃砲刀剣類所持等取締法の一部改正）

第四条　銃砲刀剣類所持等取締法（昭和三十三年法律第六号）の一部を次のように改正する。

第十四条第一項中「教育委員会」の下に「（地方教育行政の組織及び運営に関する法律（昭和三十一年法律第百六十二号）第二十三条第一項の条例の定めるところによりその長が文化財の保護に関する事務を管理し、及び執行することとされた都道府県にあつては、当該都道府県の知事。以下同じ。）」を加える。

（文化芸術基本法の一部改正）

第五条　文化芸術基本法（平成十三年法律第百四十八号）の一部を次のように改正する。

第七条の二第一項中「文化に関する事務（文化財の保護に関する事務を除く。）」を「同項第二号に掲げる事務」に改める。

（武力攻撃事態等における国民の保護のための措置に関する法律の一部改正）

第六条　武力攻撃事態等における国民の保護のための措置に関する法律（平成十六年法律第百十二号）の一部を次のように改正する。

第百二十五条第六項中「教育委員会」の下に「（地方教育行政の組織及び運営に関する法律（昭和三十一年法律第百六十二号）第二十三条第一項の条例の定めるところによりその長が文化財の保護に関する事務を管理し、及び執行することとされた都道府県にあっては、当該都道府県の知事。次項において同じ。）」を加え、「同法」を「文化財保護法」に改める。

（地域における歴史的風致の維持及び向上に関する法律の一部改正）

第七条　地域における歴史的風致の維持及び向上に関する法律（平成二十年法律第四十号）の一部を次のように改正する。

第五条第六項中「第百九十条第一項」の下に「若しくは第二項」を、「教育委員会」の下に「若しくは当該市町村」を加える。

第十二条　第二項に次のただし書を加える。

ただし、当該市町村が文化財保護法第五十三条の八第一項に規定する特定地方公共団体（以下単に「特定地方公共団体」という。）であるときは、当該市町村の教育委員会の意見を聴くことを要しない。

第十三条　第四項及び第十五条第四項に次のただし書を加える。

ただし、当該市町村が特定地方公共団体であるときは、この限りでない。

第十七条　第二項に次のただし書を加える。

ただし、当該市町村が特定地方公共団体であるときは、当該市町村の教育委員会の意見を聴くことを要しない。

第二十四条　第一項中「教育委員会」の下に「（当該認定町村が特定地方公共団体である場合にあっては、当該認定町村の長。次項から第四項までにおいて同じ。）」を加え、同条第五項中「教育委員会」の下に「（当該認定市町村が特定地方公共団体である場合にあっては、当該認定市町村の長）」を加え、同条第六項に次のただし書を加える。

ただし、当該認定市町村が特定地方公共団体であるときは、この限りでない。

文化財の不法な輸出入等の規制等に関する法律

〔通称: 文化財不法輸出入等規制法〕
平成 14 年 7 月 3 日法律第 81 号
平成 16 年 5 月 28 日法律第 61 号

〔文化財保護法の一部を改正する法律附則 13 条による改正〕

（目的）
第一条　この法律は、文化財の不法な輸入、輸出及び所有権移転を禁止し及び防止する手段に関する条約（以下「条約」という。）の適確な実施を確保するため、盗取された文化財の輸入、輸出及び回復に関する所要の措置を講ずることを目的とする。

（定義）
第二条　この法律において「文化財」とは、国内文化財及び条約の締約国である外国（以下「外国」という。）が条約第一条の規定に基づき指定した物件をいう。

2　この法律において「国内文化財」とは、条約第一条（a）から（k）までに掲げる分類に属する物件のうち、文化財保護法 （昭和二十五年法律第二百十四号）第二十七条第一項 の規定に基づき指定された重要文化財、同法第七十八条第一項 の規定に基づき指定された重要有形民俗文化財及び同法第百九条第一項 の規定に基づき指定された史跡名勝天然記念物をいう。

（特定外国文化財）
第三条　外務大臣は、外国から、条約第七条（ｂ）（ｉ）に規定する施設から文化財が盗取された旨の通知を受けたときは、遅滞なく、その内容を文部科学大臣に通知するものとする。

２　文部科学大臣は、前項の規定により外務大臣から通知を受けたときは、当該通知に係る文化財を、文部科学省令で定めるところにより、特定外国文化財として指定する。

３　文部科学大臣は、前項の規定による指定をしようとするときは、経済産業大臣に協議しなければならない。

（輸入の承認）
第四条　特定外国文化財を輸入しようとする者は、外国為替及び外国貿易法（昭和二十四年法律第二百二十八号）第五十二条 の規定により、輸入の承認を受ける義務を課せられるものとする。

（届出の公示等）
第五条　文化庁長官は、国内文化財について文化財保護法第三十三条（同法第八十条、第百十八条及び第百二十条で準用する場合を含む。）の規定による届出（亡失又は盗難に係るものに限る。）があったときは、その旨を官報で公示するとともに、当該国内文化財が条約第七条（ｂ）（ｉ）に規定する施設から盗取されたものであるときは、外務大臣に通知するものとする。

２　外務大臣は、前項の通知を受けたときは、その内容を遅滞なく外国に通知するものとする。

（特定外国文化財に係る善意取得の特則）
第六条　特定外国文化財の占有者が民法（明治二十九年法律第八十九号）第百九十二条 の条件を具備している場合であっても、第三条第一項の盗難の被害者は、同法第百九十三条 の規定による回復の請求に加え、盗難の時から二年を経過した後十年を経過するまでの期間にあっては、当該占有者に対してこれを回復することを求めることができる。ただし、当該特定外国文化財が本邦に輸入された後に第三条第二項の規定により指定されたものであるときは、この限りでない。

２　前項本文の場合においては、被害者は、占有者が支払った代価を弁償しなければならない。

（国民の理解を深める等のための措置）
第七条　国は、教育活動、広報活動等を通じて、文化財の不法な輸入、輸出及び所有権移転の防止に関し、国民の理解を深め、かつ、その協力を得るよう努めなければならない。

附　則

（施行期日）
1　この法律は、条約が日本国について効力を生ずる日から施行する。

（経過措置）
2　第三条の規定は、この法律の施行前に盗取された文化財については、適用しない。
3　第五条の規定は、この法律の施行前に亡失し又は盗取された文化財については、適用しない。

附　則　（平成16年5月28日法律第61号）　抄

（施行期日）
第一条　この法律は、平成十七年四月一日から施行する。

国宝又は重要文化財の現状変更等及び輸出並びに重要有形民俗文化財の輸出の許可申請等に関する規則

【制定題名：国宝又は重要文化財の現状変更等の許可申請等に関する規則】

昭和 29 年 6 月 29 日文化財保護委員会規則第 3 号
昭和 43 年 12 月 26 日文部省令第 31 号〔改正〕
昭和 50 年 9 月 30 日文部省令第 33 号〔改正〕
昭和 53 年 9 月 12 日文部省令第 34 号〔改正〕
平成 12 年 3 月 8 日号外文部省令第 8 号〔改正〕
平成 14 年 10 月 30 日文部科学省令第 43 号〔改正〕
平成 17 年 3 月 28 日号外文部科学省令第 11 号〔改正〕
平成 31 年 3 月 29 日号外文部科学省令第 7 号〔改正〕

文化財保護法（昭和二十五年法律第二百十四号）第十五条第一項 及び第四十三条第二項（同法第九十一条第三項で準用する場合を含む。）の規定に基き、国宝又は重要文化財の現状変更の許可申請等に関する規則を次のように定める。

（国宝又は重要文化財の現状変更等の許可の申請）

第一条　文化財保護法（昭和二十五年法律第二百十四号。以下「法」という。）第四十三条第一項 の規定による許可を受けようとする者（以下「現状変更等許可申請者」という。）は、次に掲げる事項を記載した許可申請書を文化庁長官（法第百八十四条第

一項第二号 及び文化財保護法施行令 （昭和五十年政令第二百六十七号。以下「令」という。）第五条第三項第一号 の規定により当該許可を都道府県又は指定都市等（地方自治法 （昭和二十二年法律第六十七号）第二百五十二条の十九第一項 の指定都市又は同法第二百五十二条の二十二第一項 の中核市をいう。以下同じ。）の教育委員会が行う場合には、当該都道府県又は指定都市等の教育委員会）に提出しなければならない。

一　国宝又は重要文化財の名称及び員数

二　指定年月日及び指定書の記号番号

三　国宝又は重要文化財の指定書記載の所在の場所

四　所有者の氏名又は名称及び住所

五　管理責任者がある場合は、その氏名及び住所

六　管理団体がある場合は、その名称及び事務所の所在地

七　現状変更等許可申請者の氏名及び住所又は名称及び代表者の氏名並びに事務所の所在地

八　現状変更又は保存に影響を及ぼす行為（以下「現状変更等」という。）を必要とする理由

九　現状変更等の内容及び実施の方法

十　現在の所在の場所が指定書記載の所在の場所と異なるときは、現在の所在の場所

十一　現状変更等のために所在の場所を変更するときは、変更後の所在の場所並びに現状変更等の終了後復すべき所在の場所及びその時期

十二　現状変更等の着手及び終了の予定時期

十三　現状変更等に係る工事その他の行為の施行者の氏名及び住所又は名称及び代表者の氏名並びに事務所の所在地

十四　その他参考となるべき事項

（国宝又は重要文化財の現状変更等の許可申請書の添附書類等）

第二条　前条の許可申請書には、次に掲げる書類、図面及び写真を添えなければならない。

一　現状変更等の設計仕様書及び設計図

二　現状変更等をしようとする箇所の写真又は見取図

三　現状変更等を必要とする理由を証するに足りる資料があるときは、その資料

四　現状変更等許可申請者が所有者以外の者であるときは、所有者の承諾書

五　管理責任者がある場合において、現状変更等許可申請者が管理責任者以外の者であるときは、管理責任者の承諾書

六　管理団体がある場合において、現状変更等許可申請者が管理団体以外の者であるときは、管理団体の承諾書

（国宝又は重要文化財の輸出の許可の申請）

第三条　法第四十四条 但書の規定による許可を受けようとする者（以下「重要文化財等

輸出許可申請者」という。）は、次に掲げる事項を記載した許可申請書を文化庁長官に提出しなければならない。

一　国宝又は重要文化財の名称及び員数

二　指定年月日及び指定書の番号

三　管理団体がある場合は、その名称及び住所並びに代表者の氏名

四　重要文化財等輸出許可申請者の氏名又は名称及び住所並びに法人にあつては、その代表者の氏名

五　輸出を必要とする理由

六　輸出の時期又は期間

七　輸出における輸送方法

八　輸出後の展覧会等の主催者、名称、会場及び会期

九　輸出後の展覧会等における管理方法

十　輸出及び展覧会等における保険に関する事項

十一　輸出後の展覧会等における警備方法

十二　その他参考となるべき事項

（国宝又は重要文化財の輸出の許可申請書の添付書類等）

第四条　前条の許可申請書には、次に掲げる書類を添えなければならない。

一　国宝又は重要文化財の写真

二　輸出後の展覧会等の概要及び会場図面

三　輸出後の展覧会等の主催者との協定書

四　輸出を必要とする理由を証するに足りる資料があるときは、その資料

五　重要文化財等輸出許可申請者が所有者以外の者であるときは、所有者の承諾書

六　管理団体がある場合において、重要文化財等輸出許可申請者が管理団体以外の者であるときは、管理団体の承諾書

七　その他参考となるべき資料

（重要有形民俗文化財の輸出の許可の申請）

第五条　法第八十二条の規定による許可を受けようとする者（以下「重要有形民俗文化財輸出許可申請者」という。）は、次に掲げる事項を記載した許可申請書を文化庁長官に提出しなければならない。

一　重要有形民俗文化財の名称及び員数

二　指定年月日及び指定書の番号

三　管理団体がある場合は、その名称及び住所並びに代表者の氏名

四　重要有形民俗文化財輸出許可申請者の氏名又は名称及び住所並びに法人にあつては、その代表者の氏名

五　輸出を必要とする理由

六　輸出の時期又は期間

七　仕向地並びに受取人の氏名又は名称及び住所並びに法人にあつては、その代表者の氏名
八　輸出後における取扱いの予定の概要
九　その他参考となるべき事項
（重要有形民俗文化財の輸出の許可申請書の添付書類等）
第六条　前条の許可申請書には、次に掲げる書類を添えなければならない。
一　重要有形民俗文化財の写真
二　輸出を必要とする理由を証するに足りる資料があるときは、その資料
三　重要有形民俗文化財輸出許可申請者が所有者以外の者であるときは、所有者の承諾書
四　管理団体がある場合において、重要有形民俗文化財輸出許可申請者が管理団体以外の者であるときは、管理団体の承諾書
五　その他参考となるべき資料
（終了の報告）
第七条　法第四十三条第一項 の規定による許可を受けた者は、当該許可に係る現状変更等を終了したときは、遅滞なくその旨を文化庁長官（法第百八十四条第一項第二号 及び令第五条第三項第一号 の規定により当該許可を都道府県又は指定都市等の教育委員会が行つた場合には、当該都道府県又は指定都市等の教育委員会）に報告するものとする。
２　前項の終了の報告には、その結果を示す写真又は見取図を添えるものとする。
３　法第四十四条 ただし書又は第八十二条 の規定による許可を受けた者は、当該許可に係る輸出を終了したときは、遅滞なくその旨を文化庁長官に報告するものとする。
（維持の措置の範囲）
第八条　法第四十三条第二項 の維持の措置の範囲は、次の各号に掲げる場合とする。
一　国宝又は重要文化財がき損している場合において、その価値に影響を及ぼすことなく当該国宝又は重要文化財をその指定当時の原状（指定後において現状変更等の許可を受けたものについては、当該現状変更等後の原状）に復するとき。
二　国宝又は重要文化財がき損している場合において、当該き損の拡大を防止するため応急の措置をするとき。
（国の機関による現状変更等）
第九条　各省各庁の長その他の国の機関が、国宝、重要文化財又は重要有形民俗文化財の現状変更等又は輸出について、法第百六十八条第一項第一号若しくは第二号又は第二項 の規定による同意を求めようとする場合には第一条から第六条までの規定を、法第百六十八条第一項第一号 若しくは第二号又は第二項の規定による同意を受けた場合には第七条の規定を準用する。
２　法第百六十八条第三項 において準用する法第四十三条第二項の維持の措置の範囲は、前条各号に掲げる場合とする。

附　則
この規則は、昭和二十九年七月一日から施行する。

附　則　（昭和四三年一二月二六日文部省令第三一号）　抄
1　この省令は、公布の日から施行する。

附　則　（昭和五〇年九月三〇日文部省令第三三号）　抄
1　この省令は、文化財保護法の一部を改正する法律の施行の日（昭和五十年十月一日）から施行する。

附　則　（昭和五三年九月一二日文部省令第三四号）
この省令は、公布の日から施行する。

附　則　（平成一二年三月八日文部省令第八号）
この省令は、平成十二年四月一日から施行する。

附　則　（平成一四年一〇月三〇日文部科学省令第四三号）
1　この省令は、文化財保護法の一部を改正する法律（平成十四年法律第八十二号）の施行の日（平成十四年十二月九日）から施行する。
2　この省令の施行の際現に文化財保護法（昭和二十五年法律第二百十四号）第四十四条但書の規定によりされている許可の申請については、なお従前の例による。

附　則　（平成一七年三月二八日文部科学省令第一一号）
この省令は、平成十七年四月一日から施行する。

REPUBLIC OF KOREA

문화재보호법

[시행 2019.4.17.][법률 제 15827 호 , 2018.10.16., 일부개정]

문화재청 (법무감사담당관) 1600-0064
문화재청 (천연기념물과) 042-481-4981
문화재청 (근대문화재과) 042-481-4882
문화재청 (안전기준과) 042-481-4972

제 1 장 총칙

제 1 조 (목적) 이 법은 문화재를 보존하여 민족문화를 계승하고 , 이를 활용할 수 있도록 함으로써 국민의 문화적 향상을 도모함과 아울러 인류문화의 발전에 기여함을 목적으로 한다 .

제 2 조 (정의) ① 이 법에서 " 문화재 " 란 인위적이거나 자연적으로 형성된 국가적 · 민족적 또는 세계적 유산으로서 역사 적 · 예술적 · 학술적 또는 경관적 가치가 큰 다음 각 호의 것을 말한다 . < 개정 2015. 3. 27.>

1. 유형문화재 : 건조물 , 전적 (典籍), 서적 (書跡), 고문서 , 회화 , 조각 , 공예품 등 형의 문화적 소산으로서 역사적 · 예술적 또는 학술적 가치가 큰 것과 이에 준하는 고고자료 (考古資料)

2. 무형문화재 : 여러 세대에 걸쳐 전승되어 온 무형의 문화적 유산 중 다음 각 목의 어느 하나에 해당하는 것을 말한 다 .

가 . 전통적 공연 · 예술
나 . 공예 , 미술 등에 관한 전통기술
다 . 한의약 , 농경 · 어로 등에 관한 전통지식
라 . 구전 전통 및 표현
마 . 의식주 등 전통적 생활관습

바 . 민간신앙 등 사회적 의식 (儀式)
사 . 전통적 놀이 · 축제및 기예 · 무예
3. 기념물 : 다음 각 목에서 정하는 것
가 . 절터 , 옛무덤 , 조개무덤 , 성터 , 궁터 , 가마터 , 유물포함층 등의 사적지 (史蹟地) 와 특별히 기념이 될 만한 시설 물로서 역사적 · 학술적 가치가 큰 것
나 . 경치 좋은 곳으로서 예술적 가치가 크고 경관이 뛰어난 것
다 . 동물 (그 서식지 , 번식지 , 도래지를 포함한다), 식물 (그 자생지를 포함한다), 지형 , 지질 , 광물 , 동굴 , 생물학적 생성물 또는 특별한 자연현상으로서 역사적 · 경관적 또는 학술적 가치가 큰 것
4. 민속문화재 : 의식주 , 생업 , 신앙 , 연중행사 등에 관한 풍속이나 관습에 사용되는 의복 , 기구 , 가옥 등으로서 국민 생활의 변화를 이해하는 데 반드시 필요한 것
② 이 법에서 " 지정문화재 " 란 다음 각 호의 것을 말한다 . < 개정 2014. 1. 28.>
1. 국가지정문화재 : 문화재청장이 제 23 조부터 제 26 조까지의 규정에 따라 지정한 문화재
2. 시 · 도지정문화재 : 특별시장 · 광역시장 · 특별자치시장 · 도지사 또는 특별자치도지사 (이하 " 시 · 도지사 " 라 한 다) 가 제 70 조제 1 항에 따라 지정한 문화재
3. 문화재자료 : 제 1 호나 제 2 호에 따라 지정되지 아니한 문화재 중 시 · 도지사가 제 70 조제 2 항에 따라 지정한 문화 재
③ 이 법에서 " 등록문화재 " 란 지정문화재가 아닌 문화재 중에서 문화재청장이 제 53 조에 따라 등록한 문화재를 말한 다 .
④ 이 법에서 " 보호구역 " 이란 지상에 고정되어 있는 유형물이나 일정한 지역이 문화재로 지정된 경우에 해당 지정문 화재의 점유 면적을 제외한 지역으로서 그 지정문화재를 보호하기 위하여 지정된 구역을 말한다 .
⑤ 이 법에서 " 보호물 " 이란 문화재를 보호하기 위하여 지정한 건물이나 시설물을 말한다 .
⑥ 이 법에서 " 역사문화환경 " 이란 문화재 주변의 자연경관이나 역사적 · 문화적인 가치가 뛰어난 공간으로서 문화재 와 함께 보호할 필요성이 있는 주변 환경을 말한다 .
⑦ 이 법에서 " 건설공사 " 란 토목공사 , 건축공사 , 조경공사 또는 토지나 해저의 원형 변경이 수반되는 공사로서 대통 령령으로 정하는 공사를 말한다 .
⑧ 이 법에서 " 국외소재문화재 " 란 외국에 소재하는 문화재 (제 39 조제 1 항 단서 또는 제 60 조제 1 항 단서에 따라 반출 된 문화재는 제외한다) 로서 대한민국과 역사적 · 문화적으로 직접적 관련이 있는 것을 말한다 . < 개정 2017. 3. 21.>
제 3 조 (문화재보호의 기본원칙) 문화재의 보존 · 관리 및 활용은 원형유지를 기본원칙으로 한다 .
제 4 조 (국가와 지방자치단체 등의 책무) ①국가는 문화재의 보존 · 관리 및 활용을 위

한 종합적인 시책을 수립·추진하 여야 한다.

②지방자치단체는 국가의 시책과 지역적 특색을 고려하여 문화재의 보존·관리 및 활용을 위한 시책을 수립·추진 하여야 한다.

③국가와 지방자치단체는 각종 개발사업을 계획하고 시행하는 경우 문화재나 문화재의 보호물·보호구역 및 역사 문화환경이 훼손되지 아니하도록 노력하여야 한다.

④국민은 문화재의 보존·관리를 위하여 국가와 지방자치단체의 시책에 적극 협조하여야 한다.

제 5 조 (다른 법률과의 관계) ① 문화재의 보존·관리 및 활용에 관하여 다른 법률에 특별한 규정이 있는 경우를 제외하 고는 이 법에서 정하는 바에 따른다.

② 지정문화재 (제 32 조에 따른 가지정문화재를 포함한다) 의 수리·실측·설계·감리와 매장문화재의 보호 및 조사, 무형문화재 보전 및 진흥에 관하여는 따로 법률로 정한다. < 개정 2015. 3. 27.>

제 2 장 문화재 보호 정책의 수립 및 추진

제 6 조 (문화재기본계획의 수립) ① 문화재청장은 시·도지사와의 협의를 거쳐 문화재의 보존·관리 및 활용을 위하여 다음 각 호의 사항이 포함된 종합적인 기본계획 (이하 " 문화재기본계획 " 이라 한다) 을 5 년마다 수립하여야 한다. < 개 정 2012. 1. 26., 2015. 3. 27., 2017. 3. 21.>

1. 문화재 보존에 관한 기본방향 및 목표

2. 이전의 문화재기본계획에 관한 분석 평가

3. 문화재 보수·정비 및 복원에 관한 사항

4. 문화재의 역사문화환경 보호에 관한 사항

5. 문화재 안전관리에 관한 사항

6. 문화재 기록정보화에 관한 사항

7. 문화재 보존에 사용되는 재원의 조달에 관한 사항

7 의 2. 국외소재문화재 환수 및 활용에 관한 사항

7 의 3. 남북한 간 문화재 교류 협력에 관한 사항

8. 문화재의 보존·관리 및 활용 등을 위한 연구개발에 관한 사항

9. 그 밖에 문화재의 보존·관리 및 활용에 필요한 사항

② 문화재청장은 문화재기본계획을 수립하는 경우 대통령령으로 정하는 소유자, 관리자 또는 관리단체 및 관련 전 문가의 의견을 들어야 한다.

③ 문화재청장은 문화재기본계획을 수립하면 이를 시·도지사에게 알리고, 관보 (官報) 등에 고시하여야 한다.

④ 문화재청장은 문화재기본계획을 수립하기 위하여 필요하면 시 · 도지사에게 관할 구역의 문화재에 대한 자료를 제출하도록 요청할 수 있다 .

제 6 조의 2 (문화재의 연구개발) ① 문화재청장은 문화재의 보존 · 관리 및 활용 등의 연구개발을 효율적으로 추진하기 위하여 고유연구 외에 공동연구 등을 실시할 수 있다 .

② 제 1 항에 따른 공동연구는 분야별 연구과제를 선정하여 대학 , 산업체 , 지방자치단체 , 정부출연연구기관 등과 협약 을 맺어 실시한다 .

③ 문화재청장은 제 2 항에 따른 공동연구의 수행에 필요한 비용의 전부 또는 일부를 예산의 범위에서 출연하거나 지 원할 수 있다 .

④ 제 2 항에 따른 공동연구의 대상 사업이나 그 밖에 공동연구 수행에 필요한 사항은 대통령령으로 정한다 .

[본조신설 2017. 3. 21.]

제 7 조 (문화재 보존 시행계획 수립) ① 문화재청장 및 시 · 도지사는 문화재기본계획에 관한 연도별 시행계획을 수립 · 시행하여야 한다 .

② 시 · 도지사는 제 1 항에 따라 연도별 시행계획을 수립하거나 시행을 완료한 때에는 그 결과를 문화재청장에게 제 출하여야 한다 .

③ 문화재청장 및 시 · 도지사는 연도별 시행계획을 수립한 때에는 이를 공표하여야 한다 .

④ 제 2 항에 따른 연도별 시행계획과 그 시행 결과의 제출대상 , 시기 및 절차와 제 3 항에 따른 공표방법 등에 관하여 필요한 사항은 대통령령으로 정한다 .

제 8 조 (문화재위원회의 설치) ① 문화재의 보존 · 관리 및 활용에 관한 다음 각 호의 사항을 조사 · 심의하기 위하여 문 화재청에 문화재위원회를 둔다 .

1. 문화재기본계획에 관한 사항
2. 국가지정문화재의 지정과 그 해제에 관한 사항
3. 국가지정문화재의 보호물 또는 보호구역 지정과 그 해제에 관한 사항
4. 삭제 <2015. 3. 27.>
5. 국가지정문화재의 현상변경에 관한 사항
6. 국가지정문화재의 국외 반출에 관한 사항
7. 국가지정문화재의 역사문화환경 보호에 관한 사항
8. 문화재의 등록 및 등록 말소에 관한 사항
9. 매장문화재 발굴 및 평가에 관한 사항
10. 국가지정문화재의 보존 · 관리에 관한 전문적 또는 기술적 사항으로서 중요하다고 인정되는 사항
11. 그 밖에 문화재의 보존 · 관리 및 활용 등에 관하여 문화재청장이 심의에 부치는 사항

② 문화재위원회 위원은 다음 각 호의 어느 하나에 해당하는 자 중에서 문화재청장이 위촉한다 .

1. 「고등교육법」에 따른 대학에서 문화재의 보존 · 관리 및 활용과 관련된 학과의 부교수 이상에 재직하거나 재직 하였던 사람

2. 문화재의 보존 · 관리 및 활용과 관련된 업무에 10 년 이상 종사한 사람

3. 인류학 · 사회학 · 건축 · 도시계획 · 관광 · 환경 · 법률 · 종교 · 언론분야의 업무에 10 년 이상 종사한 사람으로서 문화재에 관한 지식과 경험이 풍부한 전문가

③ 제 1 항 각 호의 사항에 관하여 문화재 종류별로 업무를 나누어 조사 · 심의하기 위하여 문화재위원회에 분과위원 회를 둘 수 있다 .

④ 제 3 항에 따른 분과위원회는 조사 · 심의 등을 위하여 필요한 경우 다른 분과위원회와 함께 위원회 (이하 " 합동분 과위원회 " 라 한다) 를 열 수 있다 .

⑤ 분과위원회 또는 합동분과위원회에서 제 1 항제 2 호부터 제 11 호까지에 관하여 조사 · 심의한 사항은 문화재위원회 에서 조사 · 심의한 것으로 본다 . < 신설 2017. 11. 28.>

⑥ 문화재위원회 , 분과위원회 및 합동분과위원회는 다음 각 호의 사항을 적은 회의록을 작성하여야 한다 . 이 경우 필요하다고 인정되면 속기나 녹음 또는 녹화를 할 수 있다 . < 개정 2017. 11. 28.>

1. 회의일시 및 장소

2. 출석위원

3. 심의내용 및 의결사항

⑦ 제 6 항에 따라 작성된 회의록은 공개하여야 한다 . 다만 , 특정인의 재산상의 이익에 영향을 미치거나 사생활의 비 밀을 침해하는 등 대통령령으로 정하는 경우에는 해당 위원회의 의결로 공개하지 아니할 수 있다 . < 개정 2017. 11. 28.>

⑧ 문화재위원회 , 분과위원회 및 합동분과위원회의 조직 , 분장사항 및 운영 등에 필요한 사항은 대통령령으로 정한 다 . < 개정 2017. 11. 28.>

⑨ 문화재위원회에는 문화재청장이나 각 분과위원회 위원장의 명을 받아 문화재위원회의 심의사항에 관한 자료수 집 · 조사 및 연구 등의 업무를 수행하는 비상근 전문위원을 둘 수 있다 . < 신설 2011. 7. 14., 2017. 11. 28.>

⑩ 문화재위원회 위원 및 전문위원의 수와 임기 , 전문위원의 자격 등에 필요한 사항은 대통령령으로 정한다 . < 신설 2011. 7. 14., 2017. 11. 28.>

제 9 조 (한국문화재재단의 설치) ① 문화재의 보호 · 보존 · 보급 및 활용과 전통생활문화의 계발을 위하여 문화재청 산 하에 한국문화재재단 (이하 " 재단 " 이라 한다) 을 설립한다 . < 개정 2014. 5. 28.>

② 재단은 법인으로 한다 . < 개정 2014. 5. 28.>

③ 재단은 설립목적을 달성하기 위하여 다음 각 호의 사업을 수행한다 . < 신설 2014. 5. 28.>

1. 공연 · 전시 등 무형문화재 활동 지원 및 진흥

2. 문화재 관련 교육 , 출판 , 학술조사 · 연구 및 콘텐츠 개발 · 활용

3. 「매장문화재 보호 및 조사에 관한 법률」 제 11 조제 1 항 및 같은 조 제 3 항 단서에 따른 매장문화재 발굴
4. 전통 문화상품 · 음식 · 혼례 등의 개발 · 보급 및 편의시설 등의 운영
5. 문화재 공적개발원조 등 국제교류
6. 문화재 보호운동의 지원
7. 전통문화행사의 복원 및 재현
8. 국가 · 지방자치단체 또는 공공기관 등으로부터 위탁받은 사업
9. 재단의 설립목적을 달성하기 위한 수익사업과 그 밖에 정관으로 정하는 사업

④ 재단에는 정관으로 정하는 바에 따라 임원과 필요한 직원을 둔다 . < 개정 2014. 5. 28.>

⑤ 재단에 관하여 이 법에 규정한 것 외에는 「민법」 중 재단법인에 관한 규정을 준용한다 . < 개정 2014. 5. 28.>

⑥ 재단 운영에 필요한 경비는 국고에서 지원할 수 있다 . < 개정 2014. 5. 28.>

⑦ 국가나 지방자치단체는 재단의 업무 수행을 위하여 필요하다고 인정하면 국유재산이나 공유재산을 무상으로 사 용 · 수익하게 할 수 있다 . < 개정 2014. 5. 28.>

[제목개정 2014. 5. 28.]

제 3 장　문화재 보호의 기반 조성

제 10 조 (문화재 기초조사) ① 국가 및 지방자치단체는 문화재의 멸실 방지 등을 위하여 현존하는 문화재의 현황 , 관리 실태 등에 대하여 조사하고 그 기록을 작성할 수 있다 .

②문화재청장 및 지방자치단체의 장은 제 1 항에 따른 조사를 위하여 필요한 경우 직접 조사하거나 문화재의 소유자 , 관리자 또는 조사 · 발굴과 관련된 단체 등에 대하여 관련 자료의 제출을 요구할 수 있다 .

③ 문화재청장 및 지방자치단체의 장은 지정문화재가 아닌 문화재에 대하여 조사를 할 경우에는 해당 문화재의 소 유자 또는 관리자의 사전 동의를 받아야 한다 .

④ 문화재 조사의 구체적인 절차와 방법 등에 관하여 필요한 사항은 대통령령으로 정한다 .

제 11 조 (문화재 정보화의 촉진) ①문화재청장은 제 10 조에 따른 조사 자료와 그 밖의 문화재 보존 · 관리에 필요한 자료 를 효율적으로 활용하고 , 국민이 문화재 정보에 쉽게 접근하고 이용할 수 있도록 문화재정보체계를 구축 · 운영하여 야 한다 .

②문화재청장은 제 1 항에 따른 문화재정보체계 구축을 위하여 관계 중앙행정기관의 장 및 지방자치단체의 장과 박 물관 · 연구소 등 관련 법인 및 단체의 장에게 필요한 자료의 제출을 요청할 수 있다 . 이 경우 요청을 받은 자는 특별 한 사유가 없으면 이

에 따라야 한다 . < 개정 2017. 11. 28.>

③ 문화재청장은 제 2 항에 따라 필요한 자료의 제출을 요청하는 경우 관계 중앙행정기관의 장 및 지방자치단체의 장 외의 자에 대하여는 정당한 대가를 지급할 수 있다 . < 신설 2017. 11. 28.>

④ 제 1 항에 따른 문화재정보체계의 구축 범위 · 운영절차 및 그 밖에 필요한 사항은 대통령령으로 정한다 . < 개정 2017. 11. 28.>

제 12 조 (건설공사 시의 문화재 보호) 건설공사로 인하여 문화재가 훼손 , 멸실 또는 수몰 (水沒) 될 우려가 있거나 그 밖 에 문화재의 역사문화환경 보호를 위하여 필요한 때에는 그 건설공사의 시행자는 문화재청장의 지시에 따라 필요한 조치를 하여야 한다 . 이 경우 그 조치에 필요한 경비는 그 건설공사의 시행자가 부담한다 .

제 13 조 (역사문화환경 보존지역의 보호) ① 시 · 도지사는 지정문화재 (동산에 속하는 문화재와 무형문화재를 제외한다 . 이하 이 조에서 같다) 의 역사문화환경 보호를 위하여 문화재청장과 협의하여 조례로 역사문화환경 보존지역을 정하 여야 한다 .

② 건설공사의 인가 · 허가 등을 담당하는 행정기관은 지정문화재의 외곽경계 (보호구역이 지정되어 있는 경우에는 보호구역의 경계를 말한다) 의 외부 지역에서 시행하려는 건설공사로서 제 1 항에 따라 시 · 도지사가 정한 역사문화 환경 보존지역에서 시행하는 건설공사에 관하여는 그 공사에 관한 인가 · 허가 등을 하기 전에 해당 건설공사의 시 행이 지정문화재의 보존에 영향을 미칠 우려가 있는 행위에 해당하는지 여부를 검토하여야 한다 . 이 경우 해당 행정 기관은 대통령령으로 정하는 바에 따라 관계 전문가의 의견을 들어야 한다 . < 개정 2014. 1. 28.>

③ 역사문화환경 보존지역의 범위는 해당 지정문화재의 역사적 · 예술적 · 학문적 · 경관적 가치와 그 주변 환경 및 그 밖에 문화재 보호에 필요한 사항 등을 고려하여 그 외곽 경계로부터 500 미터 안으로 한다 . 다만 , 문화재의 특성 및 입지여건 등으로 인하여 지정문화재의 외곽 경계로부터 500 미터 밖에서 건설공사를 하게 되는 경우에 해당 공 사가 문화재에 영향을 미칠 것이 확실하다고 인정되면 500 미터를 초과하여 범위를 정할 수 있다 .

④ 문화재청장 또는 시 · 도지사는 문화재를 지정하면 그 지정 고시가 있는 날부터 6 개월 안에 역사문화환경 보존지 역에서 지정문화재의 보존에 영향을 미칠 우려가 있는 행위에 관한 구체적인 행위기준을 정하여 고시하여야 한다 .

⑤ 제 4 항에 따른 구체적인 행위기준을 정하려는 경우 문화재청장은 시 · 도지사 또는 시장 · 군수 · 구청장 (자치구의 구청장을 말한다 . 이하 같다) 에게 , 시 · 도지사는 시장 · 군수 · 구청장에게 필요한 자료 또는 의견을 제출하도록 요 구할 수 있다 . < 신설 2014. 1. 28.>

⑥ 제 4 항에 따른 구체적인 행위기준이 고시된 지역에서 그 행위기준의 범위 안에서 행하여지는 건설공사에 관하여 는 제 2 항에 따른 검토는 생략한다 . < 개정 2014. 1. 28.>

⑦ 제 5 항에 따른 자료 또는 의견 제출절차 등에 필요한 세부 사항은 문화체육관광부

령으로 정한다 . < 신설 2014. 1. 28.>

제 14 조 (화재등 방지 시책 수립과 교육훈련 · 홍보 실시) ① 문화재청장과 시 · 도지사는 지정문화재 및 등록문화재의 화재 , 재난 및 도난 (이하 " 화재등 " 이라 한다) 방지를 위하여 필요한 시책을 수립하고 이를 시행하여야 한다 .

② 문화재청장과 지방자치단체의 장은 문화재 소유자 , 관리자 및 관리단체 등을 대상으로 문화재 화재등에 대한 초 기대응과 평상시 예방관리를 위한 교육훈련을 실시하여야 한다 .

③ 문화재청장과 지방자치단체의 장은 문화재 화재등의 방지를 위한 대국민 홍보를 실시하여야 한다 .

[전문개정 2017. 3. 21.]

제 14 조의 2 (화재등 대응매뉴얼 마련 등) ① 문화재청장 및 시 · 도지사는 지정문화재 및 등록문화재의 특성에 따른 화재 등 대응매뉴얼을 마련하고 , 이를 그 소유자 , 관리자 또는 관리단체가 사용할 수 있도록 조치하여야 한다 .

② 제 1 항에 따른 매뉴얼에 포함되어야 할 사항 , 매뉴얼을 마련하여야 하는 문화재의 범위 및 매뉴얼의 정기적 점검 · 보완 등에 필요한 사항은 대통령령으로 정한다 .

[본조신설 2017. 3. 21.]

제 14 조의 3 (화재등 방지 시설 설치 등) ① 지정문화재의 소유자 , 관리자 및 관리단체는 지정문화재의 화재예방 및 진화 를 위하여 「화재예방 , 소방시설 설치 · 유지 및 안전관리에 관한 법률」에서 정하는 기준에 따른 소방시설과 재난방 지를 위한 시설을 설치하고 유지 · 관리하여야 하며 , 지정문화재의 도난방지를 위하여 문화체육관광부령으로 정하는 기준에 따라 도난방지장치를 설치하고 유지 · 관리하도록 노력하여야 한다 .

② 제 1 항의 시설을 설치하고 유지 · 관리하는 자는 해당 시설과 역사문화환경보존지역이 조화를 이루도록 하여야 한다 .

③ 문화재청장 또는 지방자치단체의 장은 다음 각 호의 어느 하나에 해당하는 시설을 설치 또는 유지 · 관리하는 자 에게 예산의 범위에서 그 소요비용의 전부나 일부를 보조할 수 있다 .

1. 제 1 항에 따른 소방시설 , 재난방지 시설 또는 도난방지장치

2. 제 14 조의 4 제 2 항에 따른 금연구역과 흡연구역의 표지

[본조신설 2017. 3. 21.]

제 14 조의 4(금연구역의 지정 등) ① 지정문화재 및 등록문화재와 그 보호물 · 보호구역 및 보관시설 (이하 이 조에서 " 지 정문화재등 " 이라 한다) 의 소유자 , 관리자 또는 관리단체는 지정문화재등 해당 시설 또는 지역 전체를 금연구역으로 지정하여야 한다 . 다만 , 주거용 건축물은 화재의 우려가 없는 경우에 한정하여 금연구역과 흡연구역을 구분하여 지 정할 수 있다 .

② 지정문화재등의 소유자 , 관리자 또는 관리단체는 제 1 항에 따른 금연구역과 흡연

구역을 알리는 표지를 설치하여 야 한다.

③ 시·도지사는 제 2 항을 위반한 자에 대하여 일정한 기간을 정하여 그 시정을 명할 수 있다.

④ 제 2 항에 따른 금연구역과 흡연구역을 알리는 표지의 설치 기준 및 방법 등은 문화체육관광부령 또는 시·도조례 로 정한다.

⑤ 누구든지 제 1 항에 따른 금연구역에서 흡연을 하여서는 아니 된다.

[본조신설 2017. 3. 21.]

제 14 조의 5 (관계 기관 협조 요청) 문화재청장 또는 지방자치단체의 장은 화재등 방지 시설을 점검하거나, 화재등에 대비 한 훈련을 하는 경우 또는 화재등에 대한 긴급대응이 필요한 경우에 다음 각 호의 어느 하나에 해당하는 기관 또는 단체의 장에게 필요한 장비 및 인력의 협조를 요청할 수 있으며, 요청을 받은 기관 및 단체의 장은 특별한 사유가 없 으면 이에 협조하여야 한다.

1. 소방관서

2. 경찰관서

3. 「재난 및 안전관리 기본법」 제 3 조제 5 호의 재난관리책임기관

4. 그 밖에 대통령령으로 정하는 문화재 보호 관련 기관 및 단체

[본조신설 2017. 3. 21.]

제 14 조의 6 (정보의 구축 및 관리) ① 문화재청장은 화재등 문화재 피해에 대하여 효과적으로 대응하기 위하여 문화재 방재 관련 정보를 정기적으로 수집하여 이를 데이터베이스화하여 구축·관리하여야 한다. 이 경우 문화재청장은 구축된 정보가 항상 최신으로 유지될 수 있도록 하여야 한다.

② 제 1 항에 따른 정보의 구축범위 및 운영절차 등 세부사항은 대통령령으로 정한다.

[본조신설 2017. 3. 21.]

제 15 조 (문화재보호활동의 지원 등) 문화재청장은 문화재의 보호·보존·보급 또는 선양을 위하여 필요하다고 인정하 면 관련 단체를 지원·육성할 수 있다.

제 16 조 (문화재 전문인력의 양성) ① 문화재청장은 문화재의 보호·관리 및 수리 등을 위한 전문인력을 양성할 수 있다.

② 문화재청장은 제 1 항의 전문인력 양성을 위하여 필요하다고 인정하면 장학금을 지급할 수 있다.

③ 문화재청장은 제 2 항의 장학금 (이하 "장학금" 이라 한다) 을 지급받고 있는 자의 교육이나 연구 상황을 확인하기 위하여 필요하다고 인정하면 성적증명서나 연구실적보고서를 제출하도록 명할 수 있다.

④ 장학금을 지급받고 있는 자 또는 받은 자는 수학이나 연구의 중단, 내용 변경 등 문화체육관광부령으로 정하는 사유가 발생하면 지체 없이 문화재청장에게 신고하여야 한다.

⑤ 문화재청장은 수학이나 연구의 중단, 내용변경, 실적저조 등 문화체육관광부령으

로 정하는 사유가 발생하면 장 학금 지급을 중지하거나 반환을 명할 수 있다.

⑥ 제 1 항부터 제 5 항까지의 규정에 따른 장학금 지급 대상자, 장학금 지급 신청, 장학금 지급 중지 또는 반환 등에 필 요한 사항은 문화체육관광부령으로 정한다.

제 17 조 (문화재 국제교류협력의 촉진 등)

① 국가는 문화재 관련 국제기구 및 다른 국가와의 협력을 통하여 문화재에 관한 정보와 기술교환, 인력교류, 공동조사·연구 등을 적극 추진하여야 한다.

② 문화재청장은 예산의 범위에서 제 1 항에 따른 문화재분야 협력에 관한 시책을 추진하는 데 필요한 비용의 전부 또는 일부를 지원할 수 있다.

제 17 조의 2 삭제 <2015. 3. 27.>

제 18 조 (남북한 간 문화재 교류 협력) ① 국가는 남북한 간 문화재분야의 상호교류 및 협력을 증진할 수 있도록 노력하 여야 한다.

② 문화재청장은 남북한 간 문화재분야의 상호교류 및 협력증진을 위하여 북한의 문화재 관련 정책·제도 및 현황 등에 관하여 조사·연구하여야 한다.

③ 문화재청장은 대통령령으로 정하는 바에 따라 제 1 항 및 제 2 항에 따른 교류 협력사업과 조사·연구 등을 위하여 필요한 경우 관련 단체 등에 협력을 요청할 수 있으며, 이에 사용되는 경비의 전부 또는 일부를 지원할 수 있다.

제 19 조 (세계유산등의 등재 및 보호) ① 문화재청장은 「세계문화유산 및 자연유산의 보호에 관한 협약」, 「무형문화 유산의 보호를 위한 협약」 또는 유네스코의 프로그램에 따라 국내의 우수한 문화재를 유네스코에 세계유산, 인류무 형문화유산 또는 세계기록유산으로 등재 신청할 수 있다. 이 경우 등재 신청 대상 선정절차 등에 관하여는 유네스코 의 규정을 참작하여 문화재청장이 정한다. <개정 2011. 4. 6.>

② 문화재청장은 유네스코에 세계유산, 인류무형문화유산 또는 세계기록유산으로 등재된 문화재(이하 이 조에서 "세계유산등"이라 한다)를 비롯한 인류 문화재의 보존과 문화재의 국외 선양을 위하여 적극 노력하여야 한다. <개정 2011. 4. 6.>

③ 국가와 지방자치단체는 세계유산등에 대하여는 등재된 날부터 국가지정문화재에 준하여 유지·관리 및 지원하 여야 하며, 문화재청장은 대통령령으로 정하는 바에 따라 세계유산과 그 역사문화환경에 영향을 미칠 우려가 있는 행위를 하는 자에 대하여 세계유산과 그 역사문화환경의 보호에 필요한 조치를 할 것을 명할 수 있다.

제 20 조 (외국문화재의 보호) ① 인류의 문화유산을 보존하고 국가 간의 우의를 증진하기 위하여 대한민국이 가입한 문 화재 보호에 관한 국제조약(이하 "조약"이라 한다)에 가입된 외국의 법령에 따라 문화재로 지정·보호되는 문화재(이하 "외국문화재"라 한다)는 조약과 이 법에서 정하는 바에 따라 보호되어야 한다.

② 문화재청장은 국내로 반입하려 하거나 이미 반입된 외국문화재가 해당 반출국으로부터 불법반출된 것으로 인정 할 만한 상당한 이유가 있으면 그 문화재를 유치할 수 있다.

③ 문화재청장은 제 2 항에 따라 외국문화재를 유치하면 그 외국문화재를 박물관 등

에 보관·관리하여야 한다.

④ 문화재청장은 제 3 항에 따라 보관 중인 외국문화재가 그 반출국으로부터 적법하게 반출된 것임이 확인되면 지체 없이 이를 그 소유자나 점유자에게 반환하여야 한다. 그 외국문화재가 불법반출된 것임이 확인되었으나 해당 반출 국이 그 문화재를 회수하려는 의사가 없는 것이 분명한 경우에도 또한 같다.

⑤ 문화재청장은 외국문화재의 반출국으로부터 대한민국에 반입된 외국문화재가 자국에서 불법반출된 것임을 증명 하고 조약에 따른 정당한 절차에 따라 그 반환을 요청하는 경우 또는 조약에 따른 반환 의무를 이행하는 경우에는 관계 기관의 협조를 받아 조약에서 정하는 바에 따라 해당 문화재가 반출국에 반환될 수 있도록 필요한 조치를 하여 야 한다.

제 21 조 (비상시의 문화재보호) ① 문화재청장은 전시·사변 또는 이에 준하는 비상사태 시 문화재의 보호에 필요하다 고 인정하면 국유문화재와 국유 외의 지정문화재 및 제 32 조에 따른 가지정문화재를 안전한 지역으로 이동·매몰 또 는 그 밖에 필요한 조치를 하거나 해당 문화재의 소유자, 보유자, 점유자, 관리자 또는 관리단체에 대하여 그 문화재 를 안전한 지역으로 이동·매몰 또는 그 밖에 필요한 조치를 하도록 명할 수 있다.

② 문화재청장은 전시·사변 또는 이에 준하는 비상사태 시 문화재 보호를 위하여 필요하면 제 39 조에도 불구하고 이를 국외로 반출할 수 있다. 이 경우에는 미리 국무회의의 심의를 거쳐야 한다.

③ 제 1 항에 따른 조치 또는 명령의 이행으로 인하여 손실을 받은 자에 대한 보상에 관하여는 제 46 조를 준용한다. 다 만, 전화 (戰禍) 등 불가항력으로 인한 경우에는 예외로 한다.

제 22 조 (지원 요청) 문화재청장이나 그 명령을 받은 공무원은 제 21 조제 1 항의 조치를 위하여 필요하면 관계 기관의 장 에게 필요한 지원을 요청할 수 있다.

제 4 장　국가지정문화재

제 1 절 지정

제 23 조 (보물 및 국보의 지정) ① 문화재청장은 문화재위원회의 심의를 거쳐 유형문화재 중 중요한 것을 보물로 지정할 수 있다.

② 문화재청장은 제 1 항의 보물에 해당하는 문화재 중 인류문화의 관점에서 볼 때 그 가치가 크고 유례가 드문 것을 문화재위원회의 심의를 거쳐 국보로 지정할 수 있다.

③ 제 1 항과 제 2 항에 따른 보물과 국보의 지정기준과 절차 등에 필요한 사항은 대통령령으로 정한다.

제 24 조 (국가무형문화재의 지정) ① 문화재청장은 「무형문화재 보전 및 진흥에 관한 법률」 제 9 조에 따른 무형문화재 위원회의 심의를 거쳐 무형문화재 중 중요한 것을 국가무형문화재로 지정할 수 있다 . < 개정 2015. 3. 27.>

② 삭제 <2015. 3. 27.>

③ 삭제 <2015. 3. 27.>

④ 삭제 <2015. 3. 27.>

⑤ 삭제 <2015. 3. 27.>

[제목개정 2015. 3. 27.]

제 25 조 (사적 , 명승 , 천연기념물의 지정) ① 문화재청장은 문화재위원회의 심의를 거쳐 기념물 중 중요한 것을 사적 , 명 승 또는 천연기념물로 지정할 수 있다 .

② 제 1 항에 따른 사적 , 명승 , 천연기념물의 지정기준과 절차 등에 필요한 사항은 대통령령으로 정한다 .

제 26 조 (국가민속문화재 지정) ① 문화재청장은 문화재위원회의 심의를 거쳐 민속문화재 중 중요한 것을 국가민속문화 재로 지정할 수 있다 . < 개정 2017. 3. 21.>

② 제 1 항에 따른 국가민속문화재의 지정기준과 절차 등에 필요한 사항은 대통령령으로 정한다 . < 개정 2017. 3. 21.>

[제목개정 2017. 3. 21.]

제 27 조 (보호물 또는 보호구역의 지정) ① 문화재청장은 제 23 조 · 제 25 조 또는 제 26 조에 따른 지정을 할 때 문화재 보 호를 위하여 특히 필요하면 이를 위한 보호물 또는 보호구역을 지정할 수 있다 .

② 문화재청장은 인위적 또는 자연적 조건의 변화 등으로 인하여 조정이 필요하다고 인정하면 제 1 항에 따라 지정된 보호물 또는 보호구역을 조정할 수 있다 .

③ 문화재청장은 제 1 항 및 제 2 항에 따라 보호물 또는 보호구역을 지정하거나 조정한 때에는 지정 또는 조정 후 매 10 년이 되는 날 이전에 다음 각 호의 사항을 고려하여 그 지정 및 조정의 적정성을 검토하여야 한다 . 다만 , 특별한 사정으로 인하여 적정성을 검토하여야 할 시기에 이를 할 수 없는 경우에는 대통령령으로 정하는 기간까지 그 검토 시기를 연기할 수 있다 .

1. 해당 문화재의 보존가치

2. 보호물 또는 보호구역의 지정이 재산권 행사에 미치는 영향

3. 보호물 또는 보호구역의 주변 환경

④ 제 1 항부터 제 3 항까지의 규정에 따른 지정 , 조정 및 적정성 검토 등에 필요한 사항은 대통령령으로 정한다 .

제 28 조 (지정의 고시 및 통지) ① 문화재청장이 제 23 조 , 제 25 조부터 제 27 조까지의 규정에 따라 국가지정문화재 (보호 물과 보호구역을 포함한다) 를 지정하면 그 취지를 관보에 고시하고 , 지체 없이 해당 문화재의 소유자에게 알려야 한 다 . < 개정 2015. 3. 27.>

② 제 1 항의 경우 그 문화재의 소유자가 없거나 분명하지 아니하면 그 점유자 또는 관리자에게 이를 알려야 한다.

[제목개정 2015. 3. 27.]

제 29 조 (지정서의 교부) ① 문화재청장은 제 23 조나 제 26 조에 따라 국보, 보물 또는 국가민속문화재를 지정하면 그 소 유자에게 해당 문화재의 지정서를 내주어야 한다. < 개정 2017. 3. 21.>

② 삭제 <2015. 3. 27.>

[제목개정 2015. 3. 27.]

제 30 조 (지정의 효력 발생 시기) 제 23 조, 제 25 조부터 제 27 조까지의 규정에 따른 지정은 그 문화재의 소유자, 점유자 또는 관리자에 대하여는 관보에 고시한 날부터 그 효력을 발생한다. < 개정 2015. 3. 27.>

[제목개정 2015. 3. 27.]

제 31 조 (지정의 해제) ① 문화재청장은 제 23 조 · 제 25 조 또는 제 26 조에 따라 지정된 문화재가 국가지정문화재로서의 가치를 상실하거나 가치평가를 통하여 지정을 해제할 필요가 있을 때에는 문화재위원회의 심의를 거쳐 그 지정을 해 제할 수 있다.

② 삭제 <2015. 3. 27.>

③ 삭제 <2015. 3. 27.>

④ 문화재청장은 제 27 조제 3 항에 따른 검토 결과 보호물 또는 보호구역 지정이 적정하지 아니하거나 그 밖에 특별 한 사유가 있으면 보호물 또는 보호구역 지정을 해제하거나 그 범위를 조정하여야 한다. 국가지정문화재 지정이 해 제된 경우에는 지체 없이 해당 문화재의 보호물 또는 보호구역 지정을 해제하여야 한다.

⑤ 제 1 항 및 제 4 항에 따른 문화재 지정의 해제에 관한 고시 및 통지와 그 효력 발생시기에 관하여는 제 28 조 및 제 30 조를 준용한다. < 개정 2015. 3. 27.>

⑥ 국보, 보물 또는 국가민속문화재의 소유자가 제 5 항과 제 28 조에 따른 해제 통지를 받으면 그 통지를 받은 날부터 30 일 이내에 해당 문화재 지정서를 문화재청장에게 반납하여야 한다. < 개정 2017. 3. 21.>

⑦ 삭제 <2015. 3. 27.>

[제목개정 2015. 3. 27.]

제 32 조 (가지정) ① 문화재청장은 제 23 조 · 제 25 조 또는 제 26 조에 따라 지정할 만한 가치가 있다고 인정되는 문화재가 지정 전에 원형보존을 위한 긴급한 필요가 있고 문화재위원회의 심의를 거칠 시간적 여유가 없으면 중요문화재로 가 지정 (假指定) 할 수 있다.

② 제 1 항에 따른 가지정의 효력은 가지정된 문화재 (이하 " 가지정문화재 " 라 한다) 의 소유자, 점유자 또는 관리자에 게 통지한 날부터 발생한다.

③ 제 1 항에 따른 가지정은 가지정한 날부터 6 개월 이내에 제 23 조 · 제 25 조 또는 제 26 조에 따른 지정이 없으면 해 제된 것으로 본다.

④ 제 1 항에 따른 가지정의 통지와 가지정서의 교부에 관하여는 제 28 조와 제 29 조 제 1 항을 준용하되, 제 28 조제 1 항 에 따른 관보 고시는 하지 아니한다.

제 2 절 관리 및 보호

제 33 조 (소유자관리의 원칙) ① 국가지정문화재의 소유자는 선량한 관리자의 주의로써 해당 문화재를 관리ㆍ보호하여 야 한다.

② 국가지정문화재의 소유자는 필요에 따라 그에 대리하여 그 문화재를 관리ㆍ보호할 관리자를 선임할 수 있다.

제 34 조 (관리단체에 의한 관리) ① 문화재청장은 국가지정문화재의 소유자가 분명하지 아니하거나 그 소유자 또는 관 리자에 의한 관리가 곤란하거나 적당하지 아니하다고 인정하면 해당 국가지정문화재 관리를 위하여 지방자치단체나 그 문화재를 관리하기에 적당한 법인 또는 단체를 관리단체로 지정할 수 있다. 이 경우 국유에 속하는 국가지정문화 재 중 국가가 직접 관리하지 아니하는 문화재의 관리단체는 관할 특별자치시, 특별자치도 또는 시ㆍ군ㆍ구 (자치구를 말한다. 이하 같다) 가 된다. 다만, 문화재가 2 개 이상의 시ㆍ군ㆍ구에 걸쳐 있는 경우에는 관할 특별시ㆍ광역시ㆍ도 (특별자치시와 특별자치도는 제외한다) 가 관리단체가 된다. < 개정 2014. 1. 28.>

② 관리단체로 지정된 지방자치단체는 문화재청장과 협의하여 그 문화재를 관리하기에 적당한 법인 또는 단체에 해 당 문화재의 관리 업무를 위탁할 수 있다.

③ 문화재청장은 제 1 항 전단에 따라 관리단체를 지정할 경우에 그 문화재의 소유자나 지정하려는 지방자치단체, 법 인 또는 단체의 의견을 들어야 한다.

④ 문화재청장이 제 1 항에 따라 관리단체를 지정하면 지체 없이 그 취지를 관보에 고시하고, 국가지정문화재의 소유 자 또는 관리자와 해당 관리단체에 이를 알려야 한다.

⑤ 누구든지 제 1 항에 따라 지정된 관리단체의 관리행위를 방해하여서는 아니 된다. < 개정 2014. 1. 28.>

⑥ 관리단체가 국가지정문화재를 관리할 때 필요한 운영비 등 경비는 이 법에 특별한 규정이 없으면 해당 관리단체 의 부담으로 하되, 관리단체가 부담능력이 없으면 국가나 지방자치단체가 예산의 범위에서 이를 지원할 수 있다. < 개정 2016. 2. 3.>

⑦ 제 1 항에 따른 관리단체 지정의 효력 발생 시기에 관하여는 제 30 조를 준용한다.

제 34 조의 2 (국가에 의한 특별관리) ① 문화재청장은 국가지정문화재에 대하여 제 34 조제 1 항에도 불구하고 소유자ㆍ관 리자 또는 관리단체에 의한 관리가 곤란하거나 적당하지 아니하다고 인정하면 문화재위원회의 심의를 거쳐 해당 문 화재를 특별히 직접 관리ㆍ보호할 수 있다.

② 제 1 항에 따른 국가지정문화재의 관리ㆍ보호에 필요한 경비는 국가가 부담한다.

[본조신설 2014. 1. 28.]

제 35 조 (허가사항) ① 국가지정문화재 (국가무형문화재는 제외한다 . 이하 이 조에서 같다) 에 대하여 다음 각 호의 어느 하나에 해당하는 행위를 하려는 자는 대통령령으로 정하는 바에 따라 문화재청장의 허가를 받아야 하며 , 허가사항을 변경하려는 경우에도 문화재청장의 허가를 받아야 한다 . 다만 , 국가지정문화재 보호구역에 안내판 및 경고판을 설치 하는 행위 등 대통령령으로 정하는 경미한 행위에 대해서는 특별자치시장 , 특별자치도지사 , 시장 · 군수 또는 구청장 의 허가 (변경허가를 포함한다) 를 받아야 한다 . < 개정 2014. 1. 28., 2015. 3. 27., 2017. 11. 28.>

1. 국가지정문화재 (보호물 · 보호구역과 천연기념물 중 죽은 것 및 제 41 조제 1 항에 따라 수입 · 반입 신고된 것을 포 함한다) 의 현상을 변경하는 행위로서 대통령령으로 정하는 행위

2. 국가지정문화재 (동산에 속하는 문화재는 제외한다) 의 보존에 영향을 미칠 우려가 있는 행위로서 대통령령으로 정하는 행위

3. 국가지정문화재를 탁본 또는 영인 (影印) 하거나 그 보존에 영향을 미칠 우려가 있는 촬영을 하는 행위

4. 명승이나 천연기념물로 지정되거나 가지정된 구역 또는 그 보호구역에서 동물 , 식물 , 광물을 포획 (捕獲) · 채취 (採取) 하거나 이를 그 구역 밖으로 반출하는 행위

② 국가지정문화재와 시 · 도지정문화재의 역사문화환경 보존지역이 중복되는 지역에서 제 1 항제 2 호에 따라 문화재 청장이나 특별자치시장 , 특별자치도지사 , 시장 · 군수 또는 구청장의 허가를 받은 경우에는 제 74 조제 2 항에 따른 시 · 도지사의 허가를 받은 것으로 본다 . < 개정 2014. 1. 28.>

③ 문화재청장은 제 1 항제 2 호에 따른 국가지정문화재의 보존에 영향을 미칠 우려가 있는 행위에 관하여 허가한 사 항 중 대통령령으로 정하는 경미한 사항의 변경허가에 관하여는 시 · 도지사에게 위임할 수 있다 . < 개정 2014. 1. 28.>

④ 문화재청장과 특별자치시장 , 특별자치도지사 , 시장 · 군수 또는 구청장은 제 1 항에 따른 허가 또는 변경허가의 신 청을 받은 날부터 30 일 이내에 허가 여부를 신청인에게 통지하여야 한다 . < 신설 2018. 6. 12.>

⑤ 문화재청장과 특별자치시장 , 특별자치도지사 , 시장 · 군수 또는 구청장이 제 4 항에서 정한 기간 내에 허가 또는 변경허가 여부나 민원 처리 관련 법령에 따른 처리기간의 연장을 신청인에게 통지하지 아니하면 그 기간 (민원 처리 관련 법령에 따라 처리기간이 연장 또는 재연장된 경우에는 해당 처리기간을 말한다) 이 끝난 날의 다음 날에 허가 또는 변경허가를 한 것으로 본다 . < 신설 2018. 6. 12.>

제 36 조 (허가기준) ①문화재청장과 특별자치시장 , 특별자치도지사 , 시장 · 군수 또는 구청장은 제 35 조제 1 항에 따라 허 가신청을 받으면 그 허가신청 대상 행위가 다음 각 호의 기준에 맞는 경우에만 허가하여야 한다 . < 개정 2014. 1.28.>

1. 문화재의 보존과 관리에 영향을 미치지 아니할 것

2. 문화재의 역사문화환경을 훼손하지 아니할 것

3. 문화재기본계획과 제 7 조에 따른 연도별 시행계획에 들어맞을 것

② 문화재청장과 특별자치시장 , 특별자치도지사 , 시장 · 군수 또는 구청장은 제 1 항에 따른 허가를 위하여 필요한 경 우 대통령령으로 정하는 바에 따라 관계 전문가에게 조사를 하게 할 수 있다 . < 신설 2014. 1. 28.>

제 37 조 (허가사항의 취소) ① 문화재청장은 제 35 조제 1 항 본문 , 같은 조 제 3 항 , 제 39 조제 1 항 단서 , 같은 조 제 3 항 및 제 48 조제 5 항에 따라 허가를 받은 자가 다음 각 호의 어느 하나에 해당하는 경우에는 허가를 취소할 수 있다 . < 개정 2014. 1. 28., 2016. 2. 3., 2018. 6. 12.>

1. 허가사항이나 허가조건을 위반한 때

2. 속임수나 그 밖의 부정한 방법으로 허가를 받은 때

3. 허가사항의 이행이 불가능하거나 현저히 공익을 해할 우려가 있다고 인정되는 때

② 특별자치시장 , 특별자치도지사 , 시장 · 군수 또는 구청장은 제 35 조제 1 항 단서에 따라 허가를 받은 자가 제 1 항 각 호의 어느 하나에 해당하는 경우에는 허가를 취소할 수 있다 . < 신설 2014. 1. 28.>

③ 제 35 조제 1 항에 따라 허가를 받은 자가 착수신고를 하지 아니하고 허가기간이 지난 때에는 그 허가가 취소된 것 으로 본다 . < 개정 2014. 1. 28.>

제 38 조 (천연기념물 동물의 치료 등) ① 천연기념물 동물이 조난당하면 구조를 위한 운반 , 약물 투여 , 수술 , 사육 및 야 생 적응훈련 등 (이하 " 치료 " 라 한다) 은 시 · 도지사가 지정하는 동물치료소에서 하게 할 수 있다 .

② 시 · 도지사는 제 1 항에 따른 동물치료소를 지정하는 경우에 문화재에 관한 전문지식을 가지고 있거나 천연기념 물 보호활동 또는 야생동물의 치료경험이 있는 다음 각 호의 어느 하나에 해당하는 기관 중에서 지정하여야 하며 , 지정절차 및 그 밖에 필요한 사항은 지방자치단체의 조례로 정한다 .

1. 「수의사법」 에 따른 수의사 면허를 받은 자가 개설하고 있는 동물병원

2. 「수의사법」 에 따른 수의사 면허를 받은 자를 소속 직원으로 두고 있는 지방자치단체의 축산 관련 기관

3. 「수의사법」 에 따른 수의사 면허를 받은 자를 소속 회원으로 두고 있는 관리단체 또는 동물 보호단체

③ 문화재청장과 특별자치시장 , 특별자치도지사 , 시장 · 군수 또는 구청장은 천연기념물 동물의 조난으로 긴급한 보 호가 필요하면 제 35 조제 1 항에도 불구하고 동물치료소에 현상변경허가 없이 먼저 치료한 후 그 결과를 보고하게 할 수 있다 . < 개정 2014. 1. 28.>

④ 국가나 지방자치단체는 천연기념물 동물을 치료한 동물치료소에 예산의 범위에서 치료에 드는 경비를 지급할 수 있다 . 이 경우 천연기념물 동물 치료 경비 지급에 관한 업무는 문화체육관광부령으로 정하는 천연기념물의 치료와 보호 관련 단체에 위탁할

수 있으며, 치료 경비 지급절차 및 그 밖에 필요한 사항은 문화체육관광부령으로 정한다.

⑤ 시·도지사는 동물치료소가 다음 각 호의 어느 하나에 해당하면 그 지정을 취소할 수 있다. < 개정 2016. 2. 3.>

1. 거짓이나 그 밖의 부정한 방법으로 지정을 받은 경우

2. 제 2 항에 따른 지정 요건에 미달하게 된 경우

3. 고의나 중대한 과실로 치료 중인 천연기념물 동물을 죽게 하거나 장애를 입힌 경우

4. 제 3 항에 따른 치료 결과를 보고하지 아니하거나 거짓으로 보고한 경우

5. 제 4 항에 따른 치료 경비를 거짓으로 청구한 경우

6. 제 42 조제 1 항에 따른 문화재청장이나 지방자치단체의 장의 명령을 위반한 경우

⑥ 시·도지사는 제 2 항 및 제 5 항에 따라 동물치료소를 지정하거나 그 지정을 취소하는 경우에는 문화재청장에게 보고하여야 한다.

제 39 조 (수출 등의 금지) ① 국보, 보물, 천연기념물 또는 국가민속문화재는 국외로 수출하거나 반출할 수 없다. 다만, 문화재의 국외 전시 등 국제적 문화교류를 목적으로 반출하되, 그 반출한 날부터 2 년 이내에 다시 반입할 것을 조건 으로 문화재청장의 허가를 받으면 그러하지 아니하다. < 개정 2017. 3. 21.>

② 제 1 항 단서에 따라 문화재의 국외 반출을 허가받으려는 자는 반출 예정일 5 개월 전에 문화체육관광부령으로 정 하는 바에 따라 반출허가신청서를 문화재청장에게 제출하여야 한다. < 신설 2016. 2. 3.>

③ 문화재청장은 제 1 항 단서에 따라 반출을 허가받은 자가 그 반출 기간의 연장을 신청하면 당초 반출목적 달성이 나 문화재의 안전 등을 위하여 필요하다고 인정되는 경우 제 4 항에 따른 심사기준에 부합하는 경우에 한정하여 2 년 의 범위에서 그 반출 기간의 연장을 허가할 수 있다. < 개정 2016. 2. 3.>

④ 제 1 항 단서 및 제 3 항에 따른 국외 반출 또는 반출 기간의 연장을 허가하기 위한 구체적 심사기준은 문화체육관 광부령으로 정한다. < 신설 2016. 2. 3.>

⑤ 문화재청장은 제 1 항 단서에 따라 국외 반출을 허가받은 자에게 해당 문화재의 현황 및 보존·관리 실태 등의 자 료를 제출하도록 요구할 수 있다. 이 경우 요구를 받은 자는 특별한 사유가 없으면 이에 따라야 한다. < 신설 2017. 11. 28.>

⑥ 제 1 항에도 불구하고 다음 각 호의 어느 하나에 해당하는 경우에는 문화재청장의 허가를 받아 수출할 수 있다. < 개정 2016. 2. 3., 2017. 11. 28.>

1. 제 35 조제 1 항제 1 호에 따른 허가를 받아 천연기념물을 표본·박제 등으로 제작한 경우

2. 특정한 시설에서 연구 또는 관람목적으로 증식된 천연기념물의 경우

⑦ 문화재청장은 제 6 항에 따른 허가의 신청을 받은 날부터 30 일 이내에 허가 여부를 신청인에게 통지하여야 한다. < 신설 2018. 6. 12.>

⑧ 문화재청장이 제 7 항에서 정한 기간 내에 허가 여부 또는 민원 처리 관련 법령에

따른 처리기간의 연장을 신청인 에게 통지하지 아니하면 그 기간 (민원 처리 관련 법령에 따라 처리기간이 연장 또는 재연장된 경우에는 해당 처리기 간을 말한다) 이 끝난 날의 다음 날에 허가를 한 것으로 본다 . < 신설 2018. 6. 12.>

제 40 조 (신고 사항) ① 국가지정문화재 (보호물과 보호구역을 포함한다 . 이하 이 조에서 같다) 의 소유자 , 관리자 또는 관 리단체는 해당 문화재에 다음 각 호의 어느 하나에 해당하는 사유가 발생하면 대통령령으로 정하는 바에 따라 그 사 실과 경위를 문화재청장에게 신고하여야 한다 . 다만 , 제 35 조제 1 항 단서에 따라 허가를 받고 그 행위를 착수하거나 완료한 경우에는 특별자치시장 , 특별자치도지사 , 시장 · 군수 또는 구청장에게 신고하여야 한다 . < 개정 2014. 1. 28., 2015. 3. 27., 2017. 11. 28.>

1. 관리자를 선임하거나 해임한 경우

2. 국가지정문화재의 소유자가 변경된 경우

3. 소유자 또는 관리자의 성명이나 주소가 변경된 경우

4. 국가지정문화재의 소재지의 지명 , 지번 , 지목 (地目), 면적 등이 변경된 경우

5. 보관 장소가 변경된 경우

6. 국가지정문화재의 전부 또는 일부가 멸실 , 유실 , 도난 또는 훼손된 경우

7. 제 35 조제 1 항제 1 호에 따라 허가 (변경허가를 포함한다) 를 받고 그 문화재의 현상변경을 착수하거나 완료한 경우

8. 제 35 조제 1 항제 4 호 또는 제 39 조제 1 항에 따라 허가받은 문화재를 반출한 후 이를 다시 반입한 경우

9. 동식물의 종 (種) 이 천연기념물로 지정되는 경우 그 지정일 이전에 표본이나 박제를 소유하고 있는 경우

9 의 2. 폐사한 천연기념물 동물을 부검하는 경우

9 의 3. 천연기념물로 지정된 동물에 대하여 질병 등 기타 위험의 방지 , 보존 및 생존을 위하여 필요한 조치 등 대통령 령으로 정하는 행위를 한 경우

② 제 1 항에 따른 신고를 하는 때에는 같은 항 제 1 호의 경우 소유자와 관리자가 , 같은 항 제 2 호의 경우에는 신 · 구 소유자가 각각 신고서에 함께 서명하여야 한다 . < 신설 2014. 1. 28.>

③ 역사문화환경 보존지역에서 건설공사를 시행하는 자는 해당 역사문화환경 보존지역에서 제 35 조제 1 항제 2 호에 따라 허가 (변경허가를 포함한다) 를 받고 허가받은 사항을 착수 또는 완료한 경우에는 대통령령으로 정하는 바에 따 라 그 사실과 경위를 문화재청장에게 신고하여야 한다 . 다만 , 제 35 조제 1 항 단서에 따라 허가를 받고 그 행위를 착수 하거나 완료한 경우에는 특별자치시장 , 특별자치도지사 , 시장 · 군수 또는 구청장에게 신고하여야 한다 . < 개정 2014. 1. 28.>

제 41 조 (동물의 수입 · 반입 신고) ① 천연기념물로 지정된 동물의 종 (種)[아종 (亞種) 을 포함한다] 을 국외로부터 수입 · 반입하는 경우에는 대통령령으로 정하는 바에 따라 문화재청장에게 신고하여야 한다 .

② 문화재청장은 제 1 항에 따른 신고사항과 관련하여 관계 중앙행정기관, 공공기관 등 관련 기관의 장에게 필요한 자료 또는 정보의 제공을 요청할 수 있다. 이 경우 자료 또는 정보의 제공을 요청받은 기관의 장은 특별한 사유가 없 으면 이에 따라야 한다.
[본조신설 2017. 11. 28.]

제 42 조 (행정명령) ① 문화재청장이나 지방자치단체의 장은 국가지정문화재 (보호물과 보호구역을 포함한다. 이하 이 조에서 같다) 와 그 역사문화환경 보존지역의 관리·보호를 위하여 필요하다고 인정하면 다음 각 호의 사항을 명할 수 있다. < 개정 2015. 3. 27.>

1. 국가지정문화재의 관리 상황이 그 문화재의 보존상 적당하지 아니하거나 특히 필요하다고 인정되는 경우 그 소 유자, 관리자 또는 관리단체에 대한 일정한 행위의 금지나 제한

2. 국가지정문화재의 소유자, 관리자 또는 관리단체에 대한 수리, 그 밖에 필요한 시설의 설치나 장애물의 제거

3. 국가지정문화재의 소유자, 관리자 또는 관리단체에 대한 문화재 보존에 필요한 긴급한 조치

4. 제 35 조제 1 항 각 호에 따른 허가를 받지 아니하고 국가지정문화재의 현상을 변경하거나 보존에 영향을 미칠 우려 가 있는 행위 등을 한 자에 대한 행위의 중지 또는 원상회복 조치

② 문화재청장 또는 지방자치단체의 장은 국가지정문화재의 소유자, 관리자 또는 관리단체가 제 1 항제 1 호부터 제 3 호까지의 규정에 따른 명령을 이행하지 아니하거나 그 소유자, 관리자, 관리단체에 제 1 항제 1 호부터 제 3 호까지의 조치를 하게 하는 것이 적당하지 아니하다고 인정되면 국가의 부담으로 직접 제 1 항제 1 호부터 제 3 호까지의 조치를 할 수 있다. < 개정 2015. 3. 27.>

③ 문화재청장 또는 지방자치단체의 장은 제 1 항제 4 호에 따른 명령을 받은 자가 명령을 이행하지 아니하는 경우 「 행정대집행법」에서 정하는 바에 따라 대집행하고, 그 비용을 명령 위반자로부터 징수할 수 있다.

④ 지방자치단체의 장은 제 1 항에 따른 명령을 하면 문화재청장에게 보고하여야 한다.

제 43 조 (기록의 작성·보존) ① 문화재청장과 해당 특별자치시장, 특별자치도지사, 시장·군수 또는 구청장 및 관리단 체의 장은 국가지정문화재의 보존·관리 및 변경사항 등에 관한 기록을 작성·보존하여야 한다. < 개정 2014. 1. 28.>

② 문화재청장은 국가지정문화재의 보존·관리를 위하여 필요하다고 인정하면 문화재에 관한 전문적 지식이 있는 자나 연구기관에 국가지정문화재의 기록을 작성하게 할 수 있다.

제 44 조 (정기조사) ① 문화재청장은 국가지정문화재의 현상, 관리, 수리, 그 밖의 환경보전상황 등에 관하여 정기적으로 조사하여야 한다. < 개정 2015. 3. 27.>

② 문화재청장은 제 1 항에 따른 정기조사 후 보다 깊이 있는 조사가 필요하다고 인정하면 그 소속 공무원에게 해당 국가지정문화재에 대하여 재조사하게 할 수 있다 .

③ 제 1 항과 제 2 항에 따라 조사하는 경우에는 미리 그 문화재의 소유자 , 관리자 , 관리단체에 대하여 그 뜻을 알려야 한다 . 다만 , 긴급한 경우에는 사후에 그 취지를 알릴 수 있다 . < 개정 2015. 3. 27.>

④ 제 1 항과 제 2 항에 따라 조사를 하는 공무원은 소유자 , 관리자 , 관리단체에 문화재의 공개 , 현황자료의 제출 , 문화 재 소재장소 출입 등 조사에 필요한 범위에서 협조를 요구할 수 있으며 , 그 문화재의 현상을 훼손하지 아니하는 범 위에서 측량 , 발굴 , 장애물의 제거 , 그 밖에 조사에 필요한 행위를 할 수 있다 . 다만 , 해 뜨기 전이나 해진 뒤에는 소 유자 , 관리자 , 관리단체의 동의를 받아야 한다 . < 개정 2015. 3. 27.>

⑤ 제 4 항에 따라 조사를 하는 공무원은 그 권한을 표시하는 증표를 지니고 이를 관계인에게 내보여야 한다 .

⑥ 문화재청장은 제 1 항과 제 2 항에 따른 정기조사와 재조사의 전부 또는 일부를 대통령령으로 정하는 바에 따라 지 방자치단체에 위임하거나 전문기관 또는 단체에 위탁할 수 있다 .

⑦ 문화재청장은 제 1 항 및 제 2 항에 따른 정기조사 · 재조사의 결과를 다음 각 호의 국가지정문화재의 관리에 반영 하여야 한다 .

1. 문화재의 지정과 그 해제

2. 보호물 또는 보호구역의 지정과 그 해제

3. 삭제 <2015. 3. 27.>

4. 문화재의 수리 및 복구

5. 문화재 보존을 위한 행위의 제한 · 금지 또는 시설의 설치 · 제거 및 이전

6. 그 밖에 관리에 필요한 사항

제 45 조 (직권에 의한 조사) ① 문화재청장은 필요하다고 인정하면 그 소속 공무원에게 국가지정문화재의 현상 , 관리 , 수 리 , 그 밖의 환경보전상황에 관하여 조사하게 할 수 있다 . < 개정 2015. 3. 27.>

② 제 1 항에 따라 직권에 의한 조사를 하는 경우 조사통지 , 조사의 협조요구 및 조사상 필요한 행위범위 , 조사 증표 휴대 및 제시 등에 관하여는 제 44 조제 3 항부터 제 5 항까지의 규정을 준용한다 .

제 46 조 (손실의 보상) 국가는 다음 각 호의 어느 하나에 해당하는 자에 대하여는 그 손실을 보상하여야 한다 .

1. 제 42 조제 1 항제 1 호부터 제 3 호까지의 규정에 따른 명령을 이행하여 손실을 받은 자

2. 제 42 조제 2 항에 따른 조치로 인하여 손실을 받은 자

3. 제 44 조제 4 항 (제 45 조제 2 항에 따라 준용되는 경우를 포함한다) 에 따른 조사행위로 인하여 손실을 받은 자

제 47 조 (가지정문화재에 관한 허가사항 등의 준용) 가지정문화재의 관리와 보호에 관하여는 제 35 조제 1 항 , 제 37 조 , 제 39 조 , 제 40 조제 1 항 (같은 항 제 2 호부터 제 4 호까지 및 제 6 호부터 제 8 호까지에 한한다), 제 40 조제 2 항 , 제 42 조제 1 항 제 1 호 · 제 3 호 및 제 46 조를 준용한다 . < 개정 2014. 1. 28.>

제 3 절 공개 및 관람료

제 48 조 (국가지정문화재의 공개 등) ① 국가지정문화재 (국가무형문화재는 제외한다 . 이하 이 조에서 같다) 는 제 2 항에 따라 해당 문화재의 공개를 제한하는 경우 외에는 특별한 사유가 없으면 이를 공개하여야 한다 . < 개정 2015. 3. 27.>

② 문화재청장은 국가지정문화재의 보존과 훼손 방지를 위하여 필요하면 해당 문화재의 전부나 일부에 대하여 공개 를 제한할 수 있다 . 이 경우 문화재청장은 해당 문화재의 소유자 (관리단체가 지정되어 있으면 그 관리단체를 말한다) 의 의견을 들어야 한다 .

③ 문화재청장은 제 2 항에 따라 국가지정문화재의 공개를 제한하면 해당 문화재가 있는 지역의 위치 , 공개가 제한되 는 기간 및 지역 등을 문화체육관광부령으로 정하는 바에 따라 고시하고 , 해당 문화재의 소유자 · 관리자 또는 관리 단체 , 관할 시 · 도지사와 시장 · 군수 또는 구청장에게 알려야 한다 .

④ 문화재청장은 제 2 항에 따른 공개 제한의 사유가 소멸하면 지체 없이 제한 조치를 해제하여야 한다 . 이 경우 문화 재청장은 문화체육관광부령으로 정하는 바에 따라 이를 고시하고 해당 문화재의 소유자 · 관리자 또는 관리단체 , 관 할 시 · 도지사와 시장 · 군수 또는 구청장에게 알려야 한다 .

⑤ 제 2 항과 제 3 항에 따라 공개가 제한되는 지역에 출입하려는 자는 그 사유를 명시하여 문화재청장의 허가를 받아 야 한다 .

⑥ 문화재청장은 제 5 항에 따른 허가의 신청을 받은 날부터 30 일 이내에 허가 여부를 신청인에게 통지하여야 한다 . < 신설 2018. 6. 12.>

⑦ 문화재청장이 제 6 항에서 정한 기간 내에 허가 여부 또는 민원 처리 관련 법령에 따른 처리기간의 연장을 신청인 에게 통지하지 아니하면 그 기간 (민원 처리 관련 법령에 따라 처리기간이 연장 또는 재연장된 경우에는 해당 처리기 간을 말한다) 이 끝난 날의 다음 날에 허가를 한 것으로 본다 . < 신설 2018. 6. 12.>

제 49 조 (관람료의 징수 및 감면) ① 국가지정문화재의 소유자는 그 문화재를 공개하는 경우 관람자로부터 관람료를 징 수할 수 있다 . 다만 , 관리단체가 지정된 경우에는 관리단체가 징수권자가 된다 . < 개정 2015. 3. 27.>

② 제 1 항에 따른 관람료는 해당 국가지정문화재의 소유자 또는 관리단체가 정한다 . < 개정 2015. 3. 27.>

③ 국가 또는 지방자치단체는 제 1 항에도 불구하고 국가가 관리하는 국가지정문화재

의 경우 문화체육관광부령으로, 지방자치단체가 관리하는 국가지정문화재의 경우 조례로 각각 정하는 바에 따라 지역주민 등에 대하여 관람료를 감 면할 수 있다. <신설 2014. 1. 28.>

[제목개정 2014. 1. 28.]

제 50 조 삭제 <2015. 3. 27.>

제 4 절 보조금 및 경비 지원

제 51 조 (보조금) ① 국가는 다음 각 호의 경비의 전부나 일부를 보조할 수 있다.

1. 제 34 조제 1 항에 따른 관리단체가 그 문화재를 관리할 때 필요한 경비

2. 제 42 조제 1 항제 1 호부터 제 3 호까지에 따른 조치에 필요한 경비

3. 제 1 호와 제 2 호의 경우 외에 국가지정문화재의 관리·보호·수리·활용 또는 기록 작성을 위하여 필요한 경비

4. 삭제 <2015. 3. 27.>

② 문화재청장은 제 1 항에 따른 보조를 하는 경우 그 문화재의 수리나 그 밖의 공사를 감독할 수 있다.

③ 제 1 항제 2 호 및 제 3 호의 경비에 대한 보조금은 시·도지사를 통하여 교부하고, 그 지시에 따라 관리·사용하게 한다. 다만, 문화재청장이 필요하다고 인정하면 소유자, 관리자, 관리단체에게 직접 교부하고, 그 지시에 따라 관리 ·사용하게 할 수 있다. <개정 2015. 3. 27.>

제 52 조 (지방자치단체의 경비 부담) 지방자치단체는 그 관할구역에 있는 국가지정문화재로서 지방자치단체가 소유하 거나 관리하지 아니하는 문화재에 대한 관리·보호·수리 또는 활용 등에 필요한 경비를 부담하거나 보조할 수 있다.

제 5 장 등록문화재

제 53 조 (문화재의 등록) ① 문화재청장은 문화재위원회의 심의를 거쳐 지정문화재가 아닌 유형문화재, 기념물(제 2 조제 1 항제 3 호나목 및 다목은 제외한다) 및 민속문화재 중에서 보존과 활용을 위한 조치가 특별히 필요한 것을 등록문화 재로 등록할 수 있다. <개정 2017. 3. 21.>

② 등록문화재의 등록기준, 절차 및 등록 사항 등은 문화체육관광부령으로 정한다.

제 54 조 (등록문화재의 관리) ① 등록문화재의 소유자 또는 관리자 등 등록문화재를 관리하는 자는 등록문화재의 원형 보존에 노력하여야 한다.

② 문화재청장은 등록문화재의 소유자가 분명하지 아니하거나 그 소유자나 관리자

가 등록문화재를 관리할 수 없으 면 지방자치단체나 그 문화재를 관리하기에 적당한 법인이나 단체 중에서 해당 등록문화재를 관리할 자를 지정하여 이를 관리하게 할 수 있다 .

③ 등록문화재의 소유자나 관리자 또는 제 2 항에 따라 지정을 받은 자 (이하 " 등록문화재관리단체 " 라 한다) 는 문화체 육관광부령으로 정하는 바에 따라 문화재청장에게 등록문화재의 관리 및 수리와 관련된 기술 지도를 요청할 수 있 다 .

제 55 조 (등록문화재의 신고 사항) 등록문화재의 소유자나 관리자 또는 등록문화재관리단체는 해당 문화재에 관하여 다 음 각 호의 어느 하나에 해당하는 사유가 발생하면 대통령령으로 정하는 바에 따라 그 사실과 경위를 문화재청장에 게 신고하여야 한다 . 다만 , 제 1 호의 경우에는 소유자와 관리자가 , 제 2 호의 경우에는 신 · 구 소유자가 각각 신고서에 함께 서명하여야 한다 . < 개정 2014. 1. 28.>

1. 관리자를 선임하거나 해임한 경우

2. 소유자가 변경된 경우

3. 소유자 또는 관리자의 주소가 변경된 경우

4. 소재지의 지명 , 지번 , 지목 (地目), 면적 등이 변경된 경우

5. 보관 장소가 변경된 경우

6. 전부 또는 일부가 멸실 , 유실 , 도난 또는 훼손된 경우

7. 제 56 조제 2 항에 따라 허가 (변경허가를 포함한다) 를 받고 그 문화재의 현상변경 행위에 착수하거나 완료한 경우

8. 제 59 조제 2 항에서 준용하는 제 39 조제 1 항 단서에 따라 허가된 문화재를 반출하였다가 반입한 경우

제 56 조 (등록문화재의 현상변경) ① 등록문화재에 관하여 다음 각 호의 어느 하나에 해당하는 행위를 하려는 자는 변경 하려는 날의 30 일 전까지 관할 특별자치시장 , 특별자치도지사 , 시장 · 군수 또는 구청장에게 신고하여야 한다 . < 개 정 2014. 1. 28.>

1. 해당 문화재 (동산에 속하는 문화재는 제외한다) 의 외관을 변경하는 행위로서 대통령령으로 정하는 행위

2. 해당 문화재 (동산에 속하는 문화재는 제외한다) 를 다른 곳으로 이전하거나 철거하는 행위

3. 동산에 속하는 문화재를 수리하거나 보존처리하는 행위

② 제 1 항에도 불구하고 다음 각 호의 어느 하나에 해당하는 등록문화재의 현상을 변경하려는 자는 대통령령으로 정 하는 바에 따라 문화재청장의 허가를 받아야 한다 . 허가사항을 변경하는 경우에도 또한 같다 .

1. 제 57 조에 따라 건축물의 건폐율이나 용적률에 관한 특례적용을 받은 등록문화재

2. 제 59 조제 2 항에서 준용하는 제 51 조에 따라 국가로부터 보조금을 지원받은 등록문화재

3. 등록문화재의 소유자가 국가 또는 지방자치단체인 등록문화재

③ 제 1 항에 따른 신고를 받은 특별자치시장, 특별자치도지사, 시장·군수 또는 구청장은 그 사실을 시·도지사(특 별자치시장과 특별자치도지사는 제외한다)를 거쳐 문화재청장에게 보고하여야 한다. <개정 2014. 1. 28.>

④ 문화재청장은 등록문화재의 보호를 위하여 필요하면 제 1 항에 따라 신고된 등록문화재의 현상변경에 관하여 지 도·조언 및 권고 등을 할 수 있다.

제 57 조 (등록문화재의 건폐율과 용적률에 관한 특례) 등록문화재인 건축물이 있는 대지 안에서의 건폐율과 용적률은 「국토의 계획 및 이용에 관한 법률」 제 77 조부터 제 79 조까지의 규정에도 불구하고 해당 용도지역 등에 적용되는 건폐율 및 용적률의 150 퍼센트 이내에서 대통령령으로 정하는 기준에 따라 완화하여 적용할 수 있다.

제 58 조 (등록의 말소) ① 문화재청장은 등록문화재에 대하여 보존과 활용의 필요가 없거나 그 밖에 특별한 사유가 있으 면 문화재위원회의 심의를 거쳐 그 등록을 말소할 수 있다.

② 등록문화재가 지정문화재로 지정되면 그 등록은 효력을 상실한다.

③ 등록문화재의 소유자는 등록말소의 통지를 받은 때에는 그 통지를 받은 날부터 30 일 이내에 해당 문화재의 등록 증을 문화재청장에게 반납하여야 한다.

제 59 조 (준용 규정) ① 등록문화재의 등록·등록말소의 고시 및 통지, 등록증의 교부, 등록·등록말소의 효력 발생 시기 에 관하여는 제 28 조부터 제 30 조까지의 규정을 준용한다. 이 경우 "국가지정문화재"는 "등록문화재"로, "지정"은 "등 록"으로, "문화재의 지정서"는 "등록증"으로 본다.

② 등록문화재 소유자관리의 원칙, 등록문화재관리단체에 의한 관리, 등록문화재의 허가취소 및 수출 등의 금지, 등 록문화재에 관한 기록의 작성과 보존, 정기조사, 직권에 의한 등록문화재 현상 등의 조사, 정기조사로 인한 손실의 보상, 등록문화재의 관람료 징수, 국가에 의한 보조금의 지원, 지방자치단체의 경비 부담, 소유자 변경 시 권리·의 무의 승계에 관하여는 제33조, 제34조제2항부터 제7항까지, 제37조, 제 39 조, 제 43 조부터 제 45 조까지, 제 46 조제 3 호, 제 49 조, 제 51 조제 1 항제 1 호·제 3 호 및 제 2 항·제 3 항, 제 52 조 및 제 81 조를 준용한다. 이 경우 "국가지정문화 재"는 "등록문화재"로, "관리단체"는 "등록문화재관리단체"로 본다. <개정 2014. 1. 28., 2017. 3. 21.>

제 6 장 일반동산문화재

제 60 조 (일반동산문화재 수출 등의 금지) ① 이 법에 따라 지정 또는 등록되지 아니한 문화재 중 동산에 속하는 문화재 (이하 "일반동산문화재"라 한다)에 관하여는 제 39 조제 1 항과 제 3 항을 준용한다. 다만, 일반동산문화재의 국외전시 등 국제적 문

화교류를 목적으로 다음 각 호의 어느 하나에 해당하는 사항으로서 문화재청장의 허가를 받은 경우에는 그러하지 아니하다. < 개정 2016. 2. 3.>

1. 「박물관 및 미술관 진흥법」에 따라 설립된 박물관 등이 외국의 박물관 등에 일반동산문화재를 반출한 날부터 10 년 이내에 다시 반입하는 경우

2. 외국 정부가 인증하는 박물관이나 문화재 관련 단체가 자국의 박물관 등에서 전시할 목적으로 국내에서 일반동 산문화재를 구입 또는 기증받아 반출하는 경우

② 문화재청장은 제 1 항 단서에 따라 허가를 받은 자가 제 37 조제 1 항 각 호의 어느 하나에 해당하는 경우에는 허가를 취소할 수 있다.

③ 제 1 항제 2 호에 따른 일반동산문화재의 수출이나 반출에 관한 절차 등에 필요한 사항은 문화체육관광부령으로 정 한다.

④ 제 1 항 단서에 따라 허가받은 자는 허가된 일반동산문화재를 반출한 후 이를 다시 반입한 경우 문화재청장에게 신고하여야 한다.

⑤ 일반동산문화재로 오인될 우려가 있는 동산을 국외로 수출하거나 반출하려면 미리 문화재청장의 확인을 받아야 한다.

⑥ 제 1 항 및 제 5 항에 따른 일반동산문화재의 범위와 확인 등에 필요한 사항은 대통령령으로 정한다.

제 60 조의 2 (문화재감정위원의 배치 등) ① 문화재청장은 문화재의 불법반출 방지 및 국외 반출 동산에 대한 감정 등에 관한 업무를 수행하기 위하여 「공항시설법」 제 2 조제 3 호에 따른 공항, 「항만법」 제 2 조제 2 호의 무역항, 「관세법」 제 256 조제 2 항의 통관우체국 등에 문화재감정위원을 배치할 수 있다. < 개정 2016. 3. 29.>

② 제 1 항에 따른 문화재감정위원의 배치·운영 등에 필요한 사항은 대통령령으로 정한다.

[본조신설 2015. 3. 27.]

제 61 조 (일반동산문화재에 관한 조사) ① 문화재청장은 필요하다고 인정하면 그 소속 공무원으로 하여금 국가기관 또 는 지방자치단체가 소장하고 있는 일반동산문화재에 관한 현상, 관리, 수리, 그 밖의 보전상황에 관하여 조사하게 할 수 있다. 이 경우 해당 국가기관 또는 지방자치단체의 장은 조사에 협조하여야 한다.

② 문화재청장은 제 1 항에 따라 조사한 결과 문화재의 보존·관리가 적절하지 아니하다고 인정되면 해당 기관의 장 에게 문화재에 관한 보존·관리 방안을 마련하도록 요청할 수 있다.

③ 제 2 항에 따라 문화재청장의 요청을 받은 국가기관 또는 지방자치단체의 장은 해당 문화재에 관한 보존·관리 방 안을 마련하여 대통령령으로 정하는 바에 따라 문화재청장에게 보고하여야 한다.

④ 제 1 항에 따라 문화재청장이 조사를 하는 경우 조사의 통지, 조사의 협조요구, 그 밖에 조사에 필요한 사항 등에 관하여는 제 44 조제 3 항부터 제 5 항까지의 규정을 준용한다.

제 7 장 국유문화재에 관한 특례

제62조 (관리청과 총괄청) ① 국유에 속하는 문화재(이하 "국유문화재"라 한다)는「국유재산법」 제 8 조와 「물품관리 법」 제 7 조에도 불구하고 문화재청장이 관리·총괄한다. 다만, 국유문화재가 문화재청장 외의 중앙관서의 장(「국 가재정법」에 따른 중앙행정기관의 장을 말한다. 이하 같다)이 관리하고 있는 행정재산(行政財産)인 경우 또는 문화 재청장 외의 중앙관서의 장이 관리하여야 할 특별한 필요가 있는 것인 경우에는 문화재청장은 관계 기관의 장 및 기 획재정부장관과 협의하여 그 관리청을 정한다.

② 문화재청장은 제 1 항 단서에 따라 관리청을 정할 때에는 문화재위원회의 의견을 들어야 한다.

③ 문화재청장은 제 1 항 단서에 해당하지 아니하는 국유문화재의 관리를 지방자치단체에 위임하거나 비영리법인 또 는 법인 아닌 비영리단체에 위탁할 수 있다. 이 경우 국유문화재의 관리로 인하여 생긴 수익은 관리를 위임받거나 위탁받은 자의 수입으로 한다.

제 63 조 (회계 간의 무상관리전환) 국유문화재를 문화재청장이 관리하기 위하여 소속을 달리하는 회계로부터 관리전환 을 받을 때에는「국유재산법」제 17 조에도 불구하고 무상으로 할 수 있다.

제 64 조 (절차 및 방법의 특례) ① 문화재청장이 제 62 조제 1 항 단서에 따라 그 관리청이 따로 정하여진 국유문화재를 국 가지정문화재로 지정 또는 가지정하거나 그 지정이나 가지정을 해제하는 경우 이 법에 따라 행하는 해당 문화재의 소유자나 점유자에 대한 통지는 그 문화재의 관리청에 대하여 하여야 한다.

② 제 62 조제 1 항 단서에 따라 그 관리청이 따로 정하여진 국유문화재에 관하여 제 40 조·제 42 조·제 45 조 및 제 49 조를 적용하는 경우 그 문화재의 소유자란 그 문화재의 관리청을 말한다.

제 65 조 (처분의 제한) 제 62 조제 1 항 단서에 따른 관리청이 그 관리에 속하는 국가지정문화재 또는 가지정문화재에 관하 여 제 35 조제 1 항 각 호에 정하여진 행위 외의 행위를 하려면 미리 문화재청장의 동의를 받아야 한다.

제 66 조 (양도 및 사권설정의 금지) 국유문화재(그 부지를 포함한다)는 이 법에 특별한 규정이 없으면 이를 양도하거나 사권(私權)을 설정할 수 없다. 다만, 그 관리·보호에 지장이 없다고 인정되면 공공용, 공용 또는 공익사업에 필요한 경우에 한정하여 일정한 조건을 붙여 그 사용을 허가할 수 있다.

제 8 장　국외소재문화재

제 67 条 (국외소재문화재의 보호) 국가는 국외소재문화재의 보호・환수 및 활용 등을 위하여 노력하여야 하며 , 이에 필 요한 조직과 예산을 확보하여야 한다 .

제 68 条 (국외소재문화재의 조사・연구) ① 문화재청장 또는 지방자치단체의 장은 국외소재문화재의 현황 , 보존・관리 실태 , 반출 경위 등에 관하여 조사・연구를 실시할 수 있다 . < 개정 2016. 2. 3.>

② 문화재청장 또는 지방자치단체의 장은 제 1 항에 따른 조사・연구의 효율적 수행을 위하여 박물관 , 한국국제교류 재단 , 국사편찬위원회 및 각 대학 등 관련 기관에 필요한 자료의 제출과 정보제공 등을 요청할 수 있으며 , 요청을 받 은 관련 기관은 이에 협조하여야 한다 . < 개정 2016. 2. 3.>

제 69 条 (국외소재문화재 보호 및 환수 활동의 지원) ①문화재청장 또는 지방자치단체의 장은 국외소재문화재 보호 및 환수를 위하여 필요하면 관련 기관 또는 단체를 지원・육성할 수 있다 . < 개정 2016. 2. 3.>

② 제 1 항에 따라 지방자치단체의 장이 지원・육성하는 기관 또는 단체의 선정 및 재정지원 등에 필요한 사항은 해 당 지방자치단체의 조례로 정한다 . < 신설 2016. 2. 3.>

제 69 条의 2 (국외소재문화재 환수 및 활용에 대한 의견 청취) 문화재청장은 국외소재문화재 환수 및 활용 관련 중요 정 책 등에 대하여 관계 전문가 또는 관계 기관의 의견을 들을 수 있다 .

[전문개정 2016. 2. 3.]

제 69 条의 3 (국외소재문화재재단의 설립) ① 국외소재문화재의 현황 및 반출 경위 등에 대한 조사・연구 , 국외소재문화 재 환수・활용과 관련한 각종 전략・정책 연구 등 국외소재문화재와 관련한 제반 사업을 종합적・체계적으로 수행 하기 위하여 문화재청 산하에 국외소재문화재재단 (이하 " 국외문화재재단 " 이라 한다) 을 설립한다 .

② 국외문화재재단은 법인으로 한다 .

③ 국외문화재재단에는 정관으로 정하는 바에 따라 임원과 필요한 직원을 둔다 .

④ 국외문화재재단에 관하여 이 법에 규정한 것 외에는「민법 중 재단법인에 관한 규정을 준용한다 .

⑤ 국가는 국외문화재재단의 설립과 운영에 소요되는 경비를 예산의 범위에서 또는「문화재보호기금법」에 따른 문화재보호기금에서 출연 또는 보조할 수 있다 .

⑥ 국외문화재재단은 설립목적을 달성하기 위하여 다음 각 호의 사업을 행한다 .

1. 국외소재문화재의 현황 , 반출 경위 등에 대한 조사・연구

2. 국외소재문화재 환수 및 보호・활용에 관한 연구

3. 국외소재문화재의 취득 및 보전・관리

4. 국외소재문화재의 환수 및 활용 관련 단체에 대한 지원・교류 및 국제연대 강화

5. 국외소재문화재 환수 및 활용 관련 홍보 · 교육 · 출판 및 보급
6. 외국박물관 한국실 운영 지원
7. 한국담당 학예사의 파견 및 교육 훈련
8. 국외소재문화재의 보존처리 및 홍보 지원
9. 국외문화재재단의 설립목적을 달성하기 위한 수익사업 . 이 경우 수익사업은 문화재청장의 사전승인을 받아야 한 다 .
10. 그 밖에 국외문화재재단의 설립 목적을 달성하는 데 필요한 사업
⑦ 국외문화재재단은 문화재청장을 거쳐 관계 행정기관이나 국외소재문화재 환수 및 활용과 관련된 법인 또는 단체 의 장에게 사업수행에 필요한 자료의 제공을 요청할 수 있다 .
[본조신설 2012. 1. 26.]

제 9 장 시 · 도지정문화재

제 70 조 (시 · 도지정문화재의 지정 등) ① 시 · 도지사는 그 관할구역에 있는 문화재로서 국가지정문화재로 지정되지 아 니한 문화재 중 보존가치가 있다고 인정되는 것을 시 · 도지정문화재로 지정할 수 있다 . < 개정 2015. 3. 27.>
② 시 · 도지사는 제 1 항에 따라 지정되지 아니한 문화재 중 향토문화보존상 필요하다고 인정하는 것을 문화재자료 로 지정할 수 있다 .
③ 문화재청장은 문화재위원회의 심의를 거쳐 필요하다고 인정되는 문화재에 대하여 시 · 도지사에게 시 · 도지정문 화재나 문화재자료 (보호물이나 보호구역을 포함한다 . 이하 같다) 로 지정 · 보존할 것을 권고할 수 있다 . 이 경우 시 · 도지사는 특별한 사유가 있는 경우를 제외하고는 문화재 지정절차를 이행하고 그 결과를 문화재청장에게 보고하 여야 한다 .
④ 제 1 항부터 제 3 항까지의 규정에 따라 시 · 도지정문화재와 문화재자료를 지정할 때에는 해당 특별시 · 광역시 · 특별자치시 · 도 또는 특별자치도가 지정하였다는 것을 알 수 있도록 " 지정 " 앞에 해당 특별시 · 광역시 · 특별자치시 · 도 또는 특별자치도의 명칭을 표시하여야 한다 . < 개정 2014. 1. 28.>
⑤ 시 · 도지정문화재와 문화재자료의 지정 및 해제절차 , 관리 , 보호 · 육성 , 공개 등에 필요한 사항은 해당 지방자치 단체의 조례로 정한다 .
⑥ 삭제 <2015. 3. 27.>

제 71 조 (시 · 도문화재위원회의 설치) ① 시 · 도지사의 관할구역에 있는 문화재의 보존 · 관리와 활용에 관한 사항을 조 사 · 심의하기 위하여 시 · 도에 문화재위원회 (이하 " 시 · 도문화재위원회 " 라 한다) 를 둔다 .

② 시 · 도문화재위원회의 조직과 운영 등에 관한 사항은 조례로 정하되, 다음 각 호의 사항을 포함하여야 한다.

1. 문화재의 보존 · 관리 및 활용과 관련된 조사 · 심의에 관한 사항

2. 위원의 위촉과 해촉에 관한 사항

3. 분과위원회의 설치와 운영에 관한 사항

4. 전문위원의 위촉과 활용에 관한 사항

③ 시 · 도지사가 그 관할구역에 있는 문화재의 국가지정문화재(보호물과 보호구역을 포함한다) 지정 또는 해제를 문화재청장에게 요청하려면 시 · 도문화재위원회의 사전 심의를 거쳐야 한다.

제 72 조 (경비부담) ① 제 70 조제 1 항과 제 2 항에 따라 지정된 시 · 도지정문화재나 문화재자료가 국유 또는 공유재산이면 그 보존상 필요한 경비는 국가나 해당 지방자치단체가 부담한다.

② 국가나 지방자치단체는 국유 또는 공유재산이 아닌 시 · 도지정문화재나 문화재자료의 보존 · 관리 · 수리 · 활용 또는 기록 작성을 위한 경비의 전부 또는 일부를 보조할 수 있다. <개정 2015. 3. 27.>

제 73 조 (보고 등) ① 시 · 도지사는 다음 각 호의 어느 하나에 해당하는 사유가 있으면 대통령령으로 정하는 바에 따라 이를 문화재청장에게 보고하여야 한다.

1. 시 · 도지정문화재나 문화재자료를 지정하거나 그 지정을 해제한 경우

2. 시 · 도지정문화재 또는 문화재자료의 소재지나 보관 장소가 변경된 경우

3. 시 · 도지정문화재나 문화재자료의 전부 또는 일부가 멸실, 유실, 도난 또는 훼손된 경우

② 문화재청장은 제 1 항제 1 호와 제 2 호의 행위가 적합하지 아니하다고 인정되면 시정이나 필요한 조치를 명할 수 있 다.

제 74 조 (준용규정) ① 시 · 도지정문화재와 문화재자료의 수출 또는 반출에 관하여는 제 39 조제 1 항부터 제 5 항까지를 준 용한다. <개정 2016. 2. 3., 2017. 11. 28.>

② 시 · 도지정문화재와 문화재자료의 지정과 지정해제 및 관리 등에 관하여는 제 27 조, 제 31 조제 1 항 · 제 4 항, 제 32 조부터 제 34 조까지, 제 35 조제 1 항, 제 36 조, 제 37 조, 제 40 조, 제 42 조부터 제 45 조까지, 제 48 조, 제 49 조 및 제 81 조를 준용한다. 이 경우 "문화재청장"은 "시 · 도지사"로, "대통령령"은 "시 · 도조례"로, "국가"는 "지방자치단체"로 본다. <개정 2015. 3. 27., 2018. 10. 16.>

제 10 장 문화재매매업 등

제 75 조 (매매 등 영업의 허가) ① 동산에 속하는 유형문화재나 유형의 민속문화재를

매매 또는 교환하는 것을 업으로 하려는 자 (위탁을 받아 매매 또는 교환하는 것을 업으로 하는 자를 포함한다) 는 대통령령으로 정하는 바에 따라 특 별자치시장 , 특별자치도지사 , 시장 · 군수 또는 구청장의 문화재매매업 허가를 받아야 한다 . < 개정 2014. 1. 28.>

② 제 1 항에 따라 허가를 받은 자 (이하 " 문화재매매업자 " 라 한다) 는 특별자치시장 , 특별자치도지사 , 시장 · 군수 또 는 구청장에게 대통령령으로 정하는 바에 따라 문화재의 보존 상황 , 매매 또는 교환의 실태를 신고하여야 한다 . < 개 정 2014. 1. 28.>

③ 제 2 항에 따라 신고를 받은 특별자치시장 , 특별자치도지사 , 시장 · 군수 또는 구청장은 신고받은 사항을 대통령령 으로 정하는 바에 따라 문화재청장에게 정기적으로 보고하여야 한다 . < 개정 2014. 1. 28.>

④ 제 1 항에 따라 허가를 받은 자는 다음 각 호의 어느 하나에 해당하는 사항이 변경된 때에는 문화체육관광부령으 로 정하는 바에 따라 특별자치시장 , 특별자치도지사 , 시장 · 군수 또는 구청장에게 변경신고를 하여야 한다 . < 신설 2018. 6. 12.>

1. 상호 변경

2. 영업장 주소지의 변경

제 76 조 (자격 요건) ① 제 75 조제 1 항에 따라 문화재매매업의 허가를 받으려는 자는 다음 각 호의 어느 하나에 해당하는 자이어야 한다 .

1. 국가 , 지방자치단체 , 박물관 또는 미술관에서 2 년 이상 문화재를 취급한 자

2. 전문대학 이상의 대학 (대학원을 포함한다) 에서 역사학 · 고고학 · 인류학 · 미술사학 · 민속학 · 서지학 · 전통공 예학 또는 문화재관리학 계통의 학문을 1 년 이상 전공한 자

3. 문화재매매업자에게 고용되어 3 년 이상 문화재를 취급한 자

② 제 1 항에 따른 박물관 · 미술관의 범위 , 전공과목 등에 관하여 필요한 사항은 문화체육관광부령으로 정한다 .

제 77 조 (결격사유) 다음 각 호의 어느 하나에 해당하는 자는 문화재매매업자가 될 수 없다 . < 개정 2017. 3. 21.>

1. 피성년후견인 또는 피한정후견인

2. 이 법과 「형법」 제 347 조 또는 제 362 조를 위반하여 금고 이상의 실형을 선고받고 그 집행이 끝나거나 집행을 받지 아니하기로 확정된 후 3 년이 지나지 아니한 자

3. 제 80 조에 따라 허가가 취소된 날부터 3 년이 지나지 아니한 자

제 78 조 (준수 사항) ①문화재매매업자는 문화체육관광부령으로 정하는 바에 따라 매매 · 교환 등에 관한 장부를 갖추어 두고 그 거래 내용을 기록하며 , 해당 문화재를 확인할 수 있도록 실물 사진을 촬영하여 붙여 놓아야 한다 . < 개정 2014. 1. 28.>

② 문화재매매업자는 문화체육관광부령으로 정하는 바에 따라 해마다 제 1 항에 따른 매매 · 교환 등에 관한 장부에 대하여 검인을 받아야 한다 . 문화재매매업을 폐업하려는 경우에도 또한 같다 . < 신설 2014. 1. 28.>

제 79 조 (폐업신고의 의무) 제 75 조제 1 항에 따라 허가를 받은 자는 문화재매매업을 폐업하면 3 개월 이내에 문화체육관 광부령으로 정하는 바에 따라 폐업신고서를 특별자치시장 , 특별자치도지사 , 시장 · 군수 또는 구청장에게 제출하여 야 한다 . < 개정 2014. 1. 28.>

제 80 조 (허가취소 등) ① 특별자치시장 , 특별자치도지사 , 시장 · 군수 또는 구청장은 문화재매매업자가 다음 각 호의 어 느 하나에 해당하면 그 허가를 취소하거나 1 년 이내의 기간을 정하여 그 영업의 전부 또는 일부의 정지를 명할 수 있 다 . 다만 , 제 1 호부터 제 3 호까지의 규정에 해당하면 그 허가를 취소하여야 한다 . < 개정 2014. 1. 28.>

1. 거짓이나 그 밖의 부정한 방법으로 허가를 받은 경우

2. 제 90 조 · 제 92 조 및 「매장문화재 보호 및 조사에 관한 법률」 제 31 조를 위반하여 벌금 이상의 처벌을 받은 경 우

3. 영업정지 기간 중에 영업을 한 경우

4. 제 78 조에 따른 준수 사항을 위반한 경우

② 제 1 항에 따른 행정처분의 세부 기준은 문화체육관광부령으로 정한다 .

제 11 장　보칙

제 81 조 (권리 · 의무의 승계) ① 국가지정문화재 (보호물과 보호구역 및 가지정문화재를 포함한다) 의 소유자가 변경된 때에는 새 소유자는 이 법 또는 이 법에 따라 문화재청장이 행하는 명령 · 지시 , 그 밖의 처분으로 인한 전소유자 (前 所有者) 의 권리 · 의무를 승계한다 .

② 제 34 조에 따라 관리단체가 지정되거나 그 지정이 해제된 경우에 관리단체와 소유자에 대하여는 제 1 항을 준용한 다 . 다만 , 소유자에게 전속 (專屬) 하는 권리 · 의무는 그러하지 아니하다 .

제 82 조 (권한의 위임 · 위탁) 이 법에 따른 문화재청장의 권한은 대통령령으로 정하는 바에 따라 그 일부를 시 · 도지사 나 시장 · 군수 · 구청장에게 위임하거나 문화재의 보호 · 보존 · 보급 또는 활용 등을 목적으로 설립된 기관이나 법인 또는 단체 등에 위탁할 수 있다 .

제 82 조의 2 (유사명칭의 사용금지) 이 법에 따른 재단이 아닌 자는 한국문화재재단 또는 이와 유사한 명칭을 사용하지 못한다 .

[본조신설 2014. 5. 28.]

제 83 조 (토지의 수용 또는 사용) ① 문화재청장이나 지방자치단체의 장은 문화재의 보존 · 관리를 위하여 필요하면 지 정문화재나 그 보호구역에 있는 토지 , 건물 , 입목 (立木), 죽 (竹), 그 밖의 공작물을 「공익사업을 위한 토지 등의 취 득 및 보상에 관한

법률」에 따라 수용(收用)하거나 사용할 수 있다.

② 삭제 <2014. 1. 28.>

제84조(국·공유재산의 대부·사용 등) ① 국가 또는 지방자치단체는 문화재의 보존·관리·활용 또는 전승을 위하여 필요하다고 인정하면 「국유재산법」 또는 「공유재산 및 물품 관리법」에도 불구하고 국유 또는 공유재산을 수의 계약으로 대부·사용·수익하게 하거나 매각할 수 있다.

② 제1항에 따른 국유 또는 공유재산의 대부·사용·수익·매각 등의 내용 및 조건에 관하여는 「국유재산법」 또 는 「공유재산 및 물품 관리법」에서 정하는 바에 따른다.

제85조(문화재 방재의 날) ① 문화재를 화재 등의 재해로부터 안전하게 보존하고 국민의 문화재에 대한 안전관리의식 을 높이기 위하여 매년 2월 10일을 문화재 방재의 날로 정한다.

② 국가 및 지방자치단체는 문화재 방재의 날 취지에 맞도록 문화재에 대한 안전점검, 방재훈련 등의 사업 및 행사 를 실시한다.

③ 문화재 방재의 날 행사에 관하여 필요한 사항은 문화재청장 또는 시·도지사가 따로 정할 수 있다.

제86조(포상금) ① 문화재청장은 제90조부터 제92조까지와 「매장문화재 보호 및 조사에 관한 법률」 제31조의 죄를 범한 자나 그 미수범(未遂犯)이 기소유예 처분을 받거나 유죄판결이 확정된 경우 그 자를 수사기관에 제보(提報)한 자와 체포에 공로가 있는 자에게 예산의 범위에서 포상금을 지급하여야 한다.

② 수사기관의 범위, 제보의 처리, 포상금의 지급기준 등 포상금 지급에 필요한 사항은 대통령령으로 정한다.

제87조(다른 법률과의 관계) ① 문화재청장이 「자연공원법」에 따른 공원구역에서 대통령령으로 정하는 면적 이상의 지역을 대상으로 다음 각 호의 어느 하나에 해당하는 행위를 하려면 해당 공원관리청과 협의하여야 한다. <개정 2014. 1. 28.>

1. 제25조에 따라 일정한 지역을 사적, 명승, 천연기념물로 지정하는 경우

2. 제27조에 따라 보호구역을 지정하는 경우

3. 제35조제1항 본문에 따라 허가나 변경허가를 하는 경우

② 특별자치시장, 특별자치도지사, 시장·군수 또는 구청장이 「자연공원법」에 따른 공원구역에서 대통령령으로 정하는 면적 이상의 지역을 대상으로 제35조제1항 단서에 따라 허가나 변경허가를 하려면 해당 공원관리청과 협의 하여야 한다. <신설 2014. 1. 28.>

③ 제35조제1항(제74조제2항에 따라 준용되는 경우를 포함한다)에 따라 허가를 받은 때에는 다음 각 호의 허가를 받은 것으로 본다. <개정 2014. 1. 28.>

1. 「자연공원법」 제23조에 따른 공원구역에서의 행위 허가

2. 「도시공원 및 녹지 등에 관한 법률」 제24조·제27조 및 제38조에 따른 도시

공원 · 도시자연공원구역 · 녹지의 점용 및 사용 허가

④ 제 23 조, 제 25 조부터 제 27 조까지 또는 제 70 조제 1 항에 따라 국가지정문화재 또는 시 · 도지정문화재로 지정되거 나 그의 보호물 또는 보호구역으로 지정 · 고시된 지역이 「국토의 계획 및 이용에 관한 법률」 제 6 조제 1 호에 따른 도시지역에 속하는 경우에는 같은 법 제 37 조제 1 항제 5 호에 따른 보호지구로 지정 · 고시된 것으로 본다. < 개정 2014. 1. 28., 2017. 4. 18.>

⑤ 다음 각 호의 어느 하나에 해당하는 문화재의 매매 등 거래행위에 관하여는 「민법」 제 249 조의 선의취득에 관 한 규정을 적용하지 아니한다. 다만, 양수인이 경매나 문화재매매업자 등으로부터 선의로 이를 매수한 경우에는 피 해자 또는 유실자(遺失者)는 양수인이 지급한 대가를 변상하고 반환을 청구할 수 있다. < 개정 2014. 1. 28.>

1. 문화재청장이나 시 · 도지사가 지정한 문화재

2. 도난물품 또는 유실물(遺失物)인 사실이 공고된 문화재

3. 그 출처를 알 수 있는 중요한 부분이나 기록을 인위적으로 훼손한 문화재

⑥ 제 5 항제 2 호에 따른 공고에 필요한 사항은 문화체육관광부령으로 정한다. < 개정 2014. 1. 28.>

제 88 조 (청문) 문화재청장, 시 · 도지사, 시장 · 군수 또는 구청장은 다음 각 호의 어느 하나에 해당하는 처분을 하려면 청문을 하여야 한다.

1. 제 35 조제 1 항, 제 39 조, 제 56 조제 2 항 또는 제 60 조제 1 항 단서에 따라 허가받은 자가 그 허가 사항이나 허가 조건 을 위반한 경우의 허가취소

2. 제 38 조제 5 항에 따른 동물치료소의 지정 취소

3. 제 80 조에 따른 문화재매매업자의 허가취소 또는 영업정지

제 89 조 (벌칙 적용에서의 공무원 의제) 다음 각 호의 어느 하나에 해당하는 자는 「형법」 제 129 조부터 제 132 조까지 의 규정을 적용할 때에는 공무원으로 본다. < 개정 2014. 1. 28.>

1. 제 8 조제 1 항에 따라 문화재 보존 · 관리에 관한 사항을 조사 · 심의하는 문화재위원회 위원(제 71 조제 1 항에 따른 시 · 도문화재위원회의 위원을 포함한다)

1 의 2. 제 13 조제 2 항 후단에 따라 지정문화재 보존 영향 검토에 대한 의견을 제출하는 자

1 의 3. 제 36 조제 2 항에 따라 현상변경허가 조사 의견을 제출하는 자

2. 제 38 조제 4 항에 따라 천연기념물 동물 치료경비 지급업무를 위탁받아 수행하는 자

3. 제 44 조제 6 항에 따라 문화재조사를 위탁받아 수행하는 자

4. 제 82 조에 따라 문화재청장의 권한을 위탁받은 사무에 종사하는 자

제 12 장 벌칙

제 90 조 (무허가수출 등의 죄) ① 제 39 조제 1 항 본문 (제 59 조제 2 항과 제 74 조제 1 항에 따라 준용하는 경우를 포함한다) 을 위반하여 지정문화재 또는 가지정문화재를 국외로 수출 또는 반출하거나 제 39 조제 1 항 단서 및 제 2 항부터 제 4 항까지 (제 59 조제 2 항과 제 74 조제 1 항에 따라 준용하는 경우를 포함한다) 에 따라 반출한 문화재를 기한 내에 다시 반입하지 아니한 자는 5 년 이상의 유기징역에 처하고 그 문화재는 몰수한다 . < 개정 2016. 2. 3.>

② 제 60 조제 1 항을 위반하여 문화재를 국외로 수출 또는 반출하거나 반출한 문화재를 다시 반입하지 아니한 자는 3 년 이상의 유기징역에 처하고 그 문화재는 몰수한다 .

③ 제 1 항 또는 제 2 항을 위반하여 국외로 수출 또는 반출하는 정 (情) 을 알고 해당 문화재를 양도 · 양수 또는 중개한 자는 3 년 이상의 유기징역에 처하고 그 문화재는 몰수한다 .

제 91 조 (허위 지정 등 유도죄) 거짓이나 그 밖의 부정한 방법으로 지정문화재 또는 가지정문화재로 지정하게 한 자는 5 년 이상의 유기징역에 처한다 .

제 92 조 (손상 또는 은닉 등의 죄) ① 국가지정문화재 (국가무형문화재는 제외한다) 를 손상 , 절취 또는 은닉하거나 그 밖 의 방법으로 그 효용을 해한 자는 3 년 이상의 유기징역에 처한다 . < 개정 2015. 3. 27.>

② 다음 각 호의 어느 하나에 해당하는 자는 2 년 이상의 유기징역에 처한다 .

1. 제 1 항에 규정된 것 외의 지정문화재 또는 가지정문화재 (건조물은 제외한다) 를 손상 , 절취 또는 은닉하거나 그 밖 의 방법으로 그 효용을 해한 자

2. 일반동산문화재인 것을 알고 일반동산문화재를 손상 , 절취 또는 은닉하거나 그 밖의 방법으로 그 효용을 해한 자

③ 다음 각 호의 어느 하나에 해당하는 자는 2 년 이상의 유기징역이나 2 천만원 이상 1 억 5 천만원 이하의 벌금에 처 한다 .

1. 제 35 조제 1 항제 1 호에 따른 현상변경의 허가나 변경허가를 받지 아니하고 천연기념물을 박제 또는 표본으로 제작 한 자

2. 제 1 항 · 제 2 항 또는 제 1 호를 위반한 행위를 알고 해당 문화재를 취득 , 양도 , 양수 또는 운반한 자

3. 제 2 호에 따른 행위를 알선한 자

④ 제 1 항과 제 2 항에 규정된 은닉 행위 이전에 타인에 의하여 행하여진 같은 항에 따른 손상 , 절취 , 은닉 , 그 밖의 방 법으로 그 지정문화재 , 가지정문화재 또는 일반동산문화재의 효용을 해하는 행위가 처벌되지 아니한 경우에도 해당 은닉 행위자는 같은 항에 정한 형으로 처벌한다 .

⑤ 제 1 항부터 제 4 항까지의 경우에 해당하는 문화재는 몰수하되 , 몰수하기가 불가능하면 해당 문화재의 감정가격을 추징한다 . 다만 , 제 4 항에 따른 은닉 행위자가 선

의로 해당 문화재를 취득한 경우에는 그러하지 아니하다 .

제 93 조 (가중죄) ① 단체나 다중 (多衆) 의 위력 (威力) 을 보이거나 위험한 물건을 몸에 지녀서 제 90 조부터 제 92 조까지 의 죄를 범하면 각 해당 조에 정한 형의 2 분의 1 까지 가중한다 .

② 제 1 항의 죄를 범하여 지정문화재나 가지정문화재를 관리 또는 보호하는 사람을 상해에 이르게 한 때에는 무기 또는 5 년 이상의 징역에 처한다 . 사망에 이르게 한 때에는 사형 , 무기 또는 5 년 이상의 징역에 처한다 .

제 94 조 (「형법」 의 준용) 다음 각 호의 건조물에 대하여 방화 , 일수 (溢水) 또는 파괴의 죄를 범한 자는 「형법」 제 165 조 · 제 178 조 또는 제 367 조와 같은 법 중 이들 조항에 관계되는 법조 (法條) 의 규정을 준용하여 처벌하되 , 각 해 당 조에 정한 형의 2 분의 1 까지 가중한다 .

1. 지정문화재나 가지정문화재인 건조물

2. 지정문화재나 가지정문화재를 보호하기 위한 건조물

제 95 조 (사적 등에의 일수죄) 물을 넘겨 문화재청장이 지정 또는 가지정한 사적 , 명승 또는 천연기념물이나 보호구역을 침해한 자는 2 년 이상 10 년 이하의 징역에 처한다 .

제 96 조 (그 밖의 일수죄) 물을 넘겨 제 95 조에 규정한 것 외의 지정문화재 또는 가지정문화재나 그 보호구역을 침해한 자는 10 년 이하의 징역이나 1 억원 이하의 벌금에 처한다 .

제 97 조 (미수범 등) ① 제 90 조부터 제 92 조까지 , 제 93 조제 1 항 , 제 95 조 및 제 96 조의 미수범은 처벌한다 .

② 제 90 조부터 제 92 조까지 , 제 93 조제 1 항 , 제 95 조 및 제 96 조의 죄를 범할 목적으로 예비 또는 음모한 자는 2 년 이 하의 징역이나 2 천만원 이하의 벌금에 처한다 .

제 98 조 (과실범) ① 과실로 인하여 제 95 조 또는 제 96 조의 죄를 범한 자는 1 천만원 이하의 벌금에 처한다 .

② 업무상 과실이나 중대한 과실로 인하여 제 95 조 또는 제 96 조의 죄를 범한 자는 3 년 이하의 금고나 3 천만원 이하 의 벌금에 처한다 .

제 99 조 (무허가 행위 등의 죄) ① 다음 각 호의 어느 하나에 해당하는 자는 5 년 이하의 징역이나 5 천만원 이하의 벌금에 처한다 .

1. 제 35 조제 1 항제 1 호 또는 제 2 호 (제 47 조와 제 74 조제 2 항에 따라 준용되는 경우를 포함한다) 를 위반하여 지정문화 재 (보호물 , 보호구역과 천연기념물 중 죽은 것을 포함한다) 나 가지정문화재의 현상을 변경하거나 그 보존에 영향 을 미칠 우려가 있는 행위를 한 자

2. 제 35 조제 1 항제 4 호 (제 74 조제 2 항에 따라 준용되는 경우를 포함한다) 를 위반하여 허가 없이 명승 , 천연기념물로 지정 또는 가지정된 구역 또는 보호구역에서 동물 , 식물 , 광물을 포획 · 채취하거나 이를 그 구역 밖으로 반출한 자

3. 제 75 조제 1 항을 위반하여 허가를 받지 아니하고 영업행위를 한 자

② 다음 각 호의 어느 하나에 해당하는 자는 2 년 이하의 징역이나 2 천만원 이하의 벌금에 처한다 .

1. 제 1 항 각 호의 경우 그 문화재가 자기 소유인 자
2. 제 56 조제 2 항을 위반하여 허가나 변경허가를 받지 아니하고 등록문화재의 현상을 변경하는 행위를 한 자

제 100 조 (행정명령 위반 등의 죄) 다음 각 호의 어느 하나에 해당하는 자는 3 년 이하의 징역이나 3 천만원 이하의 벌금 에 처하고 , 제 2 호의 경우에는 그 물건을 몰수한다 .

1. 정당한 사유 없이 제 21 조제 1 항이나 제 42 조제 1 항 (제 74 조제 2 항에 따라 준용되는 경우를 포함한다) 에 따른 명령 을 위반한 자
2. 천연기념물 (시 · 도지정문화재 중 기념물을 포함한다) 로 지정 또는 가지정된 동물의 서식지 , 번식지 , 도래지 등에 그 생장에 해로운 물질을 유입하거나 살포한 자

제 101 조 (관리행위 방해 등의 죄) 다음 각 호의 어느 하나에 해당하는 자는 2 년 이하의 징역이나 2 천만원 이하의 벌금 에 처한다 .

1. 정당한 사유 없이 제 12 조에 따른 지시에 불응하는 자
2. 제 34 조제 5 항 (제 74 조제 2 항에 따라 준용되는 경우를 포함한다) 을 위반하여 관리단체의 관리행위를 방해하거나 그 밖에 정당한 사유 없이 지정문화재나 가지정문화재의 관리권자의 관리행위를 방해한 자
3. 허가 없이 제 35 조제 1 항제 3 호 (제 74 조제 2 항에 따라 준용되는 경우를 포함한다) 에 규정된 행위를 한 자
4. 제 44 조제 4 항 본문 (제 45 조제 2 항과 제 74 조제 2 항에 따라 준용되는 경우를 포함한다) 에 따른 협조를 거부하거나 필요한 행위를 방해한 자
5. 지정문화재나 가지정문화재의 관리 · 보존에 책임이 있는 자 중 중대한 과실로 인하여 해당 문화재를 멸실 또는 훼손하게 한 자
6. 거짓의 신고 또는 보고를 한 자
7. 지정문화재로 지정된 구역이나 그 보호구역의 경계 표시를 고의로 손괴 , 이동 , 제거 , 그 밖의 방법으로 그 구역의 경계를 식별할 수 없게 한 자
8. 제 48 조제 2 항에 따른 문화재청장의 공개 제한을 위반하여 문화재를 공개하거나 같은 조 제 5 항에 따른 허가를 받 지 아니하고 출입한 자 (제 74 조제 2 항에 따라 준용되는 경우를 포함한다)

제 102 조 (양벌규정) 법인의 대표자나 법인 또는 개인의 대리인 , 사용인 , 그 밖의 종업원이 그 법인 또는 개인의 업무에 관하여 제 94 조부터 제 96 조까지 또는 제 98 조부터 제 101 조까지의 어느 하나에 해당하는 위반행위를 하면 그 행위자 를 벌하는 외에 그 법인 또는 개인에게도 해당 조문의 벌금형을 과 (科) 하고 벌금형이 없는 경우에는 3 억원 이하의 벌금에 처한다 . 다만 , 법인 또는 개인이 그 위반행위를 방지하기 위

하여 해당 업무에 관하여 상당한 주의와 감독을 게을리하지 아니한 경우에는 그러하지 아니하다 .

제 103 조 (과태료) ① 다음 각 호의 어느 하나에 해당하는 자에게는 500 만원 이하의 과태료를 부과한다 . < 개정 2012. 1. 26., 2014. 5. 28., 2017. 3. 21., 2017. 11. 28.>

1. 제 14 조의 4 제 3 항에 따른 시정명령을 따르지 아니한 자

2. 제 40 조제 1 항제 6 호 · 제 9 호 · 제 9 호의 2 또는 제 9 호의 3(제 74 조제 2 항에 따라 준용되는 경우를 포함한다) 에 따른 신고를 하지 아니한 자

2 의 2. 제 41 조제 1 항에 따른 수입 · 반입 신고를 하지 아니한 자

3. 제 55 조제 6 호에 따른 신고를 하지 아니한 자

4. 제 56 조제 1 항에 따른 신고를 하지 아니한 자

5. 제 78 조에 따른 준수 사항을 이행하지 아니한 자

6. 제 79 조에 따른 폐업신고를 하지 아니한 자

7. 제 82 조의 2 를 위반하여 한국문화재재단 또는 이와 유사한 명칭을 사용한 자

② 제 40 조제 1 항제 5 호 (제 74 조제 2 항에 따라 준용되는 경우를 포함한다) 에 따른 신고를 하지 아니한 자에게는 400 만원 이하의 과태료를 부과한다 .

③ 제 40 조제 1 항제 7 호나 같은 조 제 3 항 (제 74 조제 2 항에 따라 준용되는 경우를 포함한다) 에 따른 신고를 하지 아니 한 자에게는 300 만원 이하의 과태료를 부과한다 . < 개정 2014. 1. 28.>

④ 다음 각 호의 어느 하나에 해당하는 자에게는 200 만원 이하의 과태료를 부과한다 . < 개정 2018. 6. 12.>

1. 제 40 조제 1 항제 1 호부터 제 4 호까지 또는 제 8 호 (제 74 조제 2 항에 따라 준용되는 경우를 포함한다) 에 따른 신고를 하지 아니한 자

2. 제 55 조제 1 호부터 제 5 호까지 , 제 7 호 또는 제 8 호에 따른 신고를 하지 아니한 자

3. 제 60 조제 4 항에 따른 신고를 하지 아니한 자

4. 제 75 조제 4 항에 따른 변경신고를 하지 아니한 자

⑤ 제 14 조의 4 제 5 항을 위반하여 금연구역에서 흡연을 한 사람에게는 10 만원 이하의 과태료를 부과한다 . < 신설 2012. 1. 26., 2017. 3. 21.>

제 104 조 (과태료의 부과 · 징수) 제 103 조에 따른 과태료는 대통령령으로 정하는 바에 따라 문화재청장 , 시 · 도지사 또 는 시장 · 군수 · 구청장이 부과 · 징수한다 .

부칙 < 제 15827 호 ,2018. 10. 16.>

제 1 조 (시행일) 이 법은 공포 후 6 개월이 경과한 날부터 시행한다 .

제 2 조 (권리 · 의무 승계의 준용에 관한 적용례) 제 74 조제 2 항의 개정규정은 이 법 시행 후 시 · 도지정문화재와 문화재 자료의 소유자가 변경된 경우 또는 관리단체가 지정되거나 그 지정이 해제된 경우부터 적용한다 .

EUROPEAN UNION

COUNCIL REGULATION (EC) No 116/2009 of 18 December 2008 on the export of cultural goods

(Codified version)

THE COUNCIL OF THE EUROPEAN UNION,
Having regard to the Treaty establishing the European Community, and in particular Article 133 thereof,
Having regard to the proposal from the Commission,

Whereas:

(1) Council Regulation (EEC) No 3911/92 of 9 December 1992 on the export of cultural goods [1] has been substantially amended several times [2]. In the interests of clarity and rationality the said Regulation should be codified.

(2) In order to maintain the internal market, rules on trade with third countries are needed for the protection of cultural goods.

(3) It seems necessary to take measures in particular to ensure that exports of cultural goods are subject to uniform controls at the Community's external borders.

(4) Such a system should require the presentation of a licence issued by the competent

(1) OJ L 395, 31.12.1992, p. 1.
(2) See Annex II.

Member State prior to the export of cultural goods covered by this Regulation. This necessitates a clear definition of the scope of such measures and the procedures for their implementation. The implementation of the system should be as simple and efficient as possible.

(5) The measures necessary for the implementation of this Regulation should be adopted in accordance with Council Decision 1999/468/EC of 28 June 1999 laying down the procedures for the exercise of implementing powers conferred on the Commission [(1)].

(6) In view of the considerable experience of the Member States' authorities in the application of Council Regulation (EC) No 515/97 of 13 March 1997 on mutual assistance between the administrative authorities of the Member States and cooperation between the latter and the Commission to ensure the correct application of the law on customs and agricultural matters [(2)], the said Regulation should be applied to this matter.

(7) Annex I to this Regulation is aimed at making clear the categories of cultural goods which should be given particular protection in trade with third countries, but is not intended to prejudice the definition, by Member States, of national treasures within the meaning of Article 30 of the Treaty,

HAS ADOPTED THIS REGULATION:

Article 1 Definition

Without prejudice to Member States' powers under Article 30 of the Treaty, the term "cultural goods" shall refer, for the purposes of this Regulation, to the items listed in Annex I.

Article 2 Export licence

1. The export of cultural goods outside the customs territory of the Community shall be subject to the presentation of an export licence.

2. The export licence shall be issued at the request of the person concerned:

(a) by a competent authority of the Member State in whose territory the cultural object in question was lawfully and definitively located on 1 January1993;

(b) or, thereafter, by a competent authority of the Member State in whose territory it is located following either lawful and definitive dispatch from another Member State, or importation from a third country, or re-importation from a third country after lawful dispatch from a Member State to that country.

However, without prejudice to paragraph 4, the Member State which is competent in accordance with points (a) or (b) of the first subparagraph is authorised not to require export licences for the cultural goods specified in the first and second indents of category A.1 of

(1) OJ L 184, 17.7.1999, p. 23.
(2) OJ L 82, 22.3.1997, p. 1.

Annex I where they are of limited archaeological or scientific interest, and provided that they are not the direct product of excavations, finds or archaeological sites within a Member State, and that their presence on the market is lawful.
The export licence may be refused, for the purposes of this Regulation, where the cultural goods in question are covered by legislation protecting national treasures of artistic, historical or archaeological value in the Member State concerned.
Where necessary, the authority referred to in point (b) of the first subparagraph shall enter into contact with the competent authorities of the Member State from which the cultural object in question came, and in particular the competent authorities within the meaning of Council Directive93/7/EEC of 15 March 1993 on the return of cultural objects unlawfully removed from the territory of a Member State [(1)].

3. The export licence shall be valid throughout the Community.

4. Without prejudice to the provisions of paragraphs 1, 2 and 3, direct export from the customs territory of the Community of national treasures having artistic, historic or archaeological value which are not cultural goods within the meaning of this Regulation is subject to the national law of the Member State of export.

Article 3 Competent authorities

1. Member States shall furnish the Commission with a list of the authorities empowered to issue export licences for cultural goods.

2. The Commission shall publish a list of the authorities and any amendment to that list in the "C" series of the Official Journal of the European Union.

Article 4 Presentation of licence

The export licence shall be presented, in support of the export declaration, when the customs export formalities are carried out, at the customs office which is competent to accept that declaration.

Article 5 Limitation of competent customs offices

1. Member States may restrict the number of customs offices empowered to handle formalities for the export of cultural goods.

2. Member States availing themselves of the option afforded by paragraph 1shall inform the Commission of the customs offices duly empowered.
The Commission shall publish this information in the "C" series of the Official Journal of the European Union.

(1) OJ L 74, 27.3.1993, p. 74.

Article 6 Administrative cooperation

For the purposes of implementing this Regulation, the provisions of Regulation (EC) No 515/97, and in particular the provisions on the confidentiality of information, shall apply mutatis mutandis.
In addition to the cooperation provided for under the first paragraph, Member States shall take all necessary steps to establish, in the context of their mutual relations, cooperation between the customs authorities and the competent authorities referred to in Article 4 of Directive 93/7/EEC.

Article 7 Implementing measures

The measures necessary for the implementation of this Regulation, in particular those concerning the form to be used (for example, the model and technical properties) shall be adopted in accordance with the procedure referred to in Article 8(2).

Article 8 Committee

1. The Commission shall be assisted by a committee.

2. Where reference is made to this paragraph, Articles 3 and 7 of Decision1999/468/EC shall apply.

Article 9 Penalties

The Member States shall lay down the rules on penalties applicable to infringements of the provisions of this Regulation and shall take all measures necessary to ensure that they are implemented. The penalties provided for must be effective, proportionate and dissuasive.

Article 10 Reporting

1. Each Member State shall inform the Commission of the measures taken pursuant to this Regulation.

The Commission shall pass on this information to the other Member States.

2. Every three years the Commission shall present a report to the European Parliament, the Council and the European Economic and Social Committee on the implementation of this Regulation.

The Council, acting on a proposal from the Commission, shall examine every three years and, where appropriate, update the amounts indicated in Annex I, on the basis of economic and monetary indicators in the Community.

Article 11 Repeal

Regulation (EEC) No 3911/92, as amended by the Regulations listed in Annex II, is repealed. References to the repealed Regulation shall be construed as references to this Regulation and shall be read in accordance with the correlation table in Annex III.

Article 12 Entry into force

This Regulation shall enter into force on the 20th day following its publication in the *Official Journal of the European Union.*

This Regulation shall be binding in its entirety and directly applicable in all Member States.

Done at Brussels, 18 December 2008.

For the Council
The President
M. BARNIER

ANNEX I

Categories of cultural objects covered by Article 1

A.	1.	Archaeological objects more than 100 years old which are the products of:	
		— excavations and finds on land or under water	9705 00 00
		— archaeological sites	9706 00 00
		— archaeological collections	
	2.	Elements forming an integral part of artistic, historical or religious monuments which have been dismembered, of an age exceeding 100 years	9705 00 00 9706 00 00
	3.	Pictures and paintings, other than those included in categories 4 or 5, executed entirely by hand in any medium and on any material (1)	9701
	4.	Watercolours, gouaches and pastels executed entirely by hand on any material (1)	9701
	5.	Mosaics in any material executed entirely by hand, other than those falling in categories 1 or 2, and drawings in any medium executed entirely by hand on any material (1)	6914 9701
	6.	Original engravings, prints, serigraphs and lithographs with their respective plates and original posters (1)	Chapter 49 9702 00 00 8442 50 99
	7.	Original sculptures or statuary and copies produced by the same process as the original (1), other than those in category 1	9703 00 00

(1) Which are more than 50 years old and do not belong to their originators.

8. Photographs, films and negatives thereof [1]	3704 3705 3706 4911 91 80
9. Incunabula and manuscripts, including maps and musical scores, singly or in collections [1]	9702 00 00 9706 00 00 4901 10 00 4901 99 00 4904 00 00 4905 91 00 4905 99 00 4906 00 00
10. Books more than 100 years old, singly or in collections	9705 00 00 9706 00 00
11. Printed maps more than 200 years old	9706 00 00
12. Archives, and any elements thereof, of any kind or any medium which are more than 50 years old	3704 3705 3706 4901 4906 9705 00 00 9706 00 00
13. (a) Collections [2] and specimens from zoological, botanical, mineralogical or anatomical collections;	9705 00 00
(b) Collections [2] of historical, palaeontological, ethnographic or numismatic interest	9705 00 00
14. Means of transport more than 75 years old	9705 00 00 Chapters 86-89
15. Any other antique items not included in categories A.1 to A.14	
(a) between 50 and 100 years old	
toys, games	Chapter 95
glassware	7013
articles of goldsmiths' or silversmiths' wares	7114
furniture	Chapter 94
optical, photographic or cinematographic apparatus	Chapter 90
musical instruments	Chapter 92
clocks and watches and parts thereof	Chapter 91
articles of wood	Chapter 44
pottery	Chapter 69
tapestries	5805 00 00
carpets	Chapter 57

(1) Which are more than 50 years old and do not belong to their originators.

(2) As defined by the Court of Justice in its judgment in Case 252/84, as follows: 'Collectors' pieces within the meaning of heading No 97.05 of the Common Customs Tariff are articles which possess the requisite characteristics for inclusion in a collection, that is to say, articles which are relatively rare, are not normally used for their original purpose, are the subject of special transactions outside the normal trade in similar utility articles and are of high value'.

wallpaper	4814
arms	Chapter 93
(b) more than 100 years old	9706 00 00

The cultural objects in categories A.1 to A.15 are covered by this Regulation only if their value corresponds to, or exceeds, the financial thresholds under B.

B. Financial thresholds applicable to certain categories under A (in euro)

Value:

Whatever the value

— 1 (Archaeological objects)

— 2 (Dismembered monuments)

— 9 (Incunabula and manuscripts)

— 12 (Archives)

15 000

— 5 (Mosaics and drawings)

— 6 (Engravings)

— 8 (Photographs)

— 11 (Printed maps)

30 000

— 4 (Watercolours, gouaches and pastels)

10.2.2009 EN Official Journal of the European Union L 39/5

50 000

— 7 (Statuary)

— 10 (Books)

— 13 (Collections)

— 14 (Means of transport)

— 15 (Any other object)

150 000

— 3 (Pictures)

The assessment of whether or not the conditions relating to financial value are fulfilled must be made when an application for an export licence is submitted. The financial value is that of the cultural object in the Member State referred to in Article 2(2).

For the Member States which do not have the euro as their currency, the values expressed in euro in Annex I shall be converted and expressed in national currencies at the rate of exchange on 31 December 2001 published in the *Official Journal of the European Communities*. This countervalue in national currencies shall be reviewed every two years with effect from 31 December 2001. Calculation of this countervalue shall be based on the average daily value of those currencies, expressed in euro, during the 24 months ending on the last day of August preceding the revision which takes effect on 31 December. This method of calculation shall be reviewed, on a proposal from the Commission, by the Advisory Committee on Cultural Goods, in principle two years after the first application. For each revision, the values expressed in euro and their countervalues in national currency shall be published periodically in the *Official Journal of the European Union* in the first days of the month of November preceding the date on which the revision takes effect.

ANNEX II

Repealed Regulation with its successive amendments

Council Regulation (EEC) No 3911/92 (OJ L 395, 31.12.1992, p. 1)	
Council Regulation (EC) No 2469/96 (OJ L 335, 24.12.1996, p. 9)	
Council Regulation (EC) No 974/2001 (OJ L 137, 19.5.2001, p. 10)	
Council Regulation (EC) No 806/2003 (OJ L 122, 16.5.2003, p. 1)	Annex I, point 2 only

ANNEX III

Correlation Table

Regulation (EEC) No 3911/92	This Regulation
Article 1	Article 1
Article 2(1)	Article 2(1)
Article 2(2), first subparagraph, introductory wording	Article 2(2), first subparagraph, introductory wording
Article 2(2), first subparagraph, first indent	Article 2(2), first subparagraph, point (a)
Article 2(2), first subparagraph, second indent	Article 2(2), first subparagraph, point (b)
Article 2(2), second subparagraph	Article 2(2), second subparagraph
Article 2(2), third subparagraph	Article 2(2), third subparagraph
Article 2(2), fourth subparagraph	Article 2(2), fourth subparagraph
Article 2(3)	Article 2(3)
Article 2(4)	Article 2(4)
Articles 3 to 9	Articles 3 to 9
Articles 10, first paragraph	Article 10(1), first subparagraph
Article 10, second paragraph	Article 10(1), second subparagraph

Article 10, third paragraph	Article 10(2), first subparagraph
Article 10, fourth paragraph	—
Article 10, fifth paragraph	Article 10(2), second subparagraph
—	Article 11
Article 11	Article 12
Annex, points A.1, A.2 and A.3	Annex I, points A.1, A.2 and A.3
Annex, point A.3A	Annex I, point A.4
Annex, point A.4	Annex I, point A.5
Annex, point A.5	Annex I, point A.6
Annex, point A.6	Annex I, point A.7
Annex, point A.7	Annex I, point A.8
Annex, point A.8	Annex I, point A.9
Annex, point A.9	Annex I, point A.10
Annex, point A.10	Annex I, point A.11
Annex, point A.11	Annex I, point A.12
Annex, point A.12	Annex I, point A.13
Annex, point A.13	Annex I, point A.14
Annex, point A.14	Annex I, point A.15
Annex, point B	Annex I, point B
—	Annex II
—	Annex III

DIRECTIVE 2014/60/EU OF THE EUROPEAN PARLIAMENT AND OF THE COUNCIL of 15 May 2014

on the return of cultural objects unlawfully removed from the territory of a Member State and amending Regulation (EU) No 1024/2012 (Recast)

THE EUROPEAN PARLIAMENT AND THE COUNCIL OF THE EUROPEAN UNION,

Having regard to the Treaty on the Functioning of the European Union, and in particular Article 114 thereof,

Having regard to the proposal from the European Commission,

After transmission of the draft legislative act to the national parliaments,

Acting in accordance with the ordinary legislative procedure [1],

Whereas:

(1) Council Directive 93/7/EEC [2] has been substantially amended by Directives 96/100/

(1) Position of the European Parliament of 16 April 2014 (not yet published in the Official Journal) and decision of the Council of 8 May 2014.

(2) Council Directive 93/7/EEC of 15 March 1993 on the return of cultural objects unlawfully removed from the territory of a Member State (OJ L 74, 27.3.1993, p. 74).

EC [1] and 2001/38/EC [2] of the European Parliament and of the Council. Since further amendments are to be made, it should be recast in the interests of clarity.

(2) The internal market comprises an area without internal frontiers in which the free movement of goods, persons, services and capital is ensured in accordance with the Treaty on the Functioning of the European Union (TFEU). According to Article 36 TFEU, the relevant provisions on free movement of goods do not preclude prohibitions or restrictions on imports, exports or goods in transit, justified on grounds of the protection of national treasures possessing artistic, historic or archaeological value.

(3) Under the terms and within the limits of Article 36 TFEU, Member States retain the right to define their national treasures and to take the necessary measures to protect them. Nevertheless, the Union plays a valuable role in encouraging cooperation between Member States with a view to protecting cultural heritage of European significance, to which such national treasures belong.

(4) Directive 93/7/EEC introduced arrangements enabling Member States to secure the return to their territory of cultural objects which are classified as national treasures within the meaning of Article 36 TFEU, which fall within the common categories of cultural objects referred to in the Annex to that Directive, and which have been removed from their territory in breach of the national measures or of Council Regulation (EC) No 116/2009 [3]. That Directive also covered cultural objects classified as national treasures and forming an integral part of public collections or inventories of ecclesiastical institutions which did not fall within those common categories.

(5) Directive 93/7/EEC established administrative cooperation between Member States as regards their national treasures, closely linked to their cooperation with Interpol and other competent bodies in the field of stolen works of art and involving, in particular, the recording of lost, stolen or illegally removed cultural objects forming part of their national treasures and their public collections.

(6) The procedure provided for in Directive 93/7/EEC was a first step in establishing cooperation between Member States in this field in the context of the internal market, with the aim of further mutual recognition of relevant national laws.

(7) Regulation (EC) No 116/2009, together with Directive 93/7/EEC, introduced a Union system for the protection of Member States' cultural objects.

(8) The objective of Directive 93/7/EEC was to ensure the physical return of the cultural objects to the Member State from whose territory those objects have been unlawfully removed, irrespective of the property rights applying to such objects. The application

(1) Directive 96/100/EC of the European Parliament and of the Council of 17 February 1997 amending the Annex to Directive 93/7/EEC on the return of cultural objects unlawfully removed from the territory of a Member State (OJ L 60, 1.3.1997, p. 59).

(2) Directive 2001/38/EC of the European Parliament and of the Council of 5 June 2001 amending Council Directive 93/7/EEC on the return of cultural objects unlawfully removed from the territory of a Member State (OJ L 187, 10.7.2001, p. 43).

(3) Council Regulation (EC) No 116/2009 of 18 December 2008 on the export of cultural goods (OJ L 39, 10.2.2009, p. 1).

of that Directive, however, has shown the limitations of the arrangements for securing the return of such cultural objects. The reports on the application of that Directive have pointed out its infrequent application due in particular to the limitation of its scope, which resulted from the conditions set out in the Annex to that Directive, the short period of time allowed to initiate return proceedings and the costs associated with return proceedings.

(9) The scope of this Directive should be extended to any cultural object classified or defined by a Member State under national legislation or administrative procedures as a national treasure possessing artistic, historic or archaeological value within the meaning of Article 36 TFEU. This Directive should thus cover objects of historical, paleontological, ethnographic, numismatic interest or scientific value, whether or not they form part of public or other collections or are single items, and whether they originate from regular or clandestine excavations, provided that they are classified or defined as national treasures. Furthermore, cultural objects classified or defined as national treasures should no longer have to belong to categories or comply with thresholds related to their age and/or financial value in order to qualify for return under this Directive.

(10) The diversity of national arrangements for protecting national treasures is recognised in Article 36 TFEU. In order to foster mutual trust, a willingness to cooperate and mutual understanding between Member States, the scope of the term 'national treasure' should be determined, in the framework of Article 36 TFEU. Member States should also facilitate the return of cultural objects to the Member State from whose territory those objects have been unlawfully removed regardless of the date of accession of that Member State, and should ensure that the return of such objects does not give rise to unreasonable costs. It should be possible for Member States to return cultural objects other than those classified or defined as national treasures provided that they respect the relevant provisions of the TFEU, as well as cultural objects unlawfully removed before 1 January 1993.

(11) The administrative cooperation between Member States needs to be increased so that this Directive can be applied more effectively and uniformly. Therefore, the central authorities should be required to cooperate efficiently with each other and to exchange information relating to unlawfully removed cultural objects through the use of the Internal Market Information System ('IMI') provided for by Regulation (EU) No 1024/2012 of the European Parliament and of the Council [(1)]. In order to improve the implementation of this Directive, a module of the IMI system specifically customised for cultural objects should be established. It is also desirable for other competent authorities of the Member States to use the same system, where appropriate.

(12) In order to ensure the protection of personal data, administrative cooperation and the

(1) Regulation (EU) No 1024/2012 of the European Parliament and of the Council of 25 October 2012 on administrative cooperation through the Internal Market Information System and repealing Commission Decision 2008/49/EC ('the IMI Regulation') (OJ L 316, 14.11.2012, p. 1).

exchange of information between the competent authorities should comply with the rules set out in Directive 95/46/EC of the European Parliament and of the Council (1), and, in so far as the IMI is used, in Regulation (EU) No 1024/2012. The definitions used in Directive 95/46/EC and in Regulation (EC) No 45/2001 of the European Parliament and of the Council (2) should also apply for the purposes of this Directive.

(13) The time-limit for checking whether the cultural object found in another Member State is a cultural object within the meaning of Directive 93/7/EEC was identified as being too short in practice. Therefore, it should be extended to six months. A longer period should allow Member States to take the necessary measures to preserve the cultural object and, where appropriate, prevent any action to evade the return procedure.

(14) The time-limit for bringing return proceedings should also be extended to three years after the Member State from whose territory the cultural object was unlawfully removed became aware of the location of the cultural object and of the identity of its possessor or holder. The extension of this period should facilitate the return and discourage the illegal removal of national treasures. In the interest of clarity, it should be stipulated that the time-limit for bringing proceedings begins on the date on which the information came to the knowledge of the central authority of the Member State from whose territory the cultural object was unlawfully removed.

(15) Directive 93/7/EEC provided that return proceedings may not be brought more than 30 years after the object was unlawfully removed from the territory of the Member State. However, in the case of objects forming part of public collections and of objects belonging to inventories of ecclesiastical institutions in the Member States where they are subject to special protection arrangements under national law, return proceedings are subject to a longer time-limit under certain circumstances. Due to the fact that Member States may have special protection arrangements under national law with religious institutions other than ecclesiastical ones, this Directive should also extend to those other religious institutions.

(16) In its Conclusions on preventing and combating crime against cultural goods adopted on 13 and 14 December 2011, the Council recognised the need to take measures in order to make preventing and combating crime concerning cultural objects more effective. It recommended that the Commission support Member States in the effective protection of cultural objects with a view to preventing and combating trafficking and promoting complementary measures where appropriate. In addition, the Council recommended that the Member States consider the ratification of the Unesco Convention on the Means of Prohibiting and Preventing the Illicit Import, Export and Transfer of Ownership of Cultural Property signed in Paris on 17 November 1970, and the UNIDROIT Convention on Stolen or Illegally Exported Cultural Objects signed in Rome on 24 June 1995.

---

(1) Directive 95/46/EC of the European Parliament and of the Council of 24 October 1995 on the protection of individuals with regard to the processing of personal data and on the free movement of such data (OJ L 281, 23.11.1995, p. 74).

(2) Regulation (EC) No 45/2001 of the European Parliament and of the Council of 18 December 2000 on the protection of individuals with regard to the processing of personal data by the Community institutions and bodies and on the free movement of such data (OJ L 8, 12.1.2001, p. 1).

(17) It is desirable to ensure that all those involved in the market exercise due care and attention in transactions involving cultural objects. The consequences of acquiring a cultural object of unlawful origin will only be genuinely dissuasive if the payment of compensation is coupled with an obligation on the possessor to prove the exercise of due care and attention. Therefore, in order to achieve the Union's objectives of preventing and combating unlawful trafficking in cultural objects, this Directive should stipulate that the possessor must provide proof that he exercised due care and attention in acquiring the object, for the purpose of compensation.

(18) It would also be useful for any person, and in particular those who are involved in the market, to have easy access to public information on cultural objects classified or defined as national treasures by the Member States. Member States should try to facilitate access to this public information.

(19) In order to facilitate a uniform interpretation of the concept of due care and attention, this Directive should set out non-exhaustive criteria to be taken into account to determine whether the possessor exercised due care and attention when acquiring the cultural object.

(20) Since the objective of this Directive, namely to enable the return of cultural objects classified or defined as national treasures which have been unlawfully removed from the territory of Member States, cannot be sufficiently achieved by the Member States, but can, by reason of its scale and effects, be better achieved at Union level, the Union may adopt measures, in accordance with the principle of subsidiarity as set out in Article 5 of the Treaty on European Union. In accordance with the principle of proportionality as set out in that Article, this Directive does not go beyond what is necessary in order to achieve that objective.

(21) Since the tasks of the committee set up by Regulation (EC) No 116/2009 are rendered obsolete by the deletion of the Annex to Directive 93/7/EEC, references to that committee should be deleted accordingly. However, in order to maintain the platform for the exchange of experience and good practices on the implementation of this Directive among Member States, the Commission should set up an expert group, composed of experts from the Member States' central authorities responsible for the implementation of this Directive, which should be involved, inter alia, in the process of customising a module of the IMI system for cultural objects.

(22) Since the Annex to Regulation (EU) No 1024/2012 contains a list of provisions on administrative cooperation in Union acts which are implemented by means of the IMI, that Annex should be amended to include this Directive.

(23) The obligation to transpose this Directive into national law should be confined to those provisions which represent a substantive amendment as compared to the earlier Directives. The obligation to transpose the provisions which are unchanged arises from the earlier Directives.

(24) This Directive should be without prejudice to the obligations of the Member States relating to the time-limits for the transposition into national law of the Directives set out in Annex I, Part B,

HAVE ADOPTED THIS DIRECTIVE:

Article 1

This Directive applies to the return of cultural objects classified or defined by a Member State as being among national treasures, as referred to in point (1) of Article 2, which have been unlawfully removed from the territory of that Member State.

Article 2

For the purposes of this Directive, the following definitions apply:

(1) 'cultural object' means an object which is classified or defined by a Member State, before or after its unlawful removal from the territory of that Member State, as being among the 'national treasures possessing artistic, historic or archaeological value' under national legislation or administrative procedures within the meaning of Article 36 TFEU;

(2) 'unlawfully removed from the territory of a Member State' means:

(a) removed from the territory of a Member State in breach of its rules on the protection of national treasures or in breach of Regulation (EC) No 116/2009; or

(b) not returned at the end of a period of lawful temporary removal or any breach of another condition governing such temporary removal;

(3) 'requesting Member State' means the Member State from whose territory the cultural object has been unlawfully removed;

(4) 'requested Member State' means the Member State in whose territory a cultural object, which was unlawfully removed from the territory of another Member State, is located;

(5) 'return' means the physical return of the cultural object to the territory of the requesting Member State;

(6) 'possessor' means the person physically holding the cultural object on his own account;

(7) 'holder' means the person physically holding the cultural object for third parties;

(8) 'public collections' means collections, defined as public in accordance with the legislation of a Member State, which are the property of that Member State, of a local or regional authority within that Member State or of an institution situated in the territory of that Member State, such institution being the property of, or significantly financed by, that Member State or local or regional authority.

Article 3

Cultural objects which have been unlawfully removed from the territory of a Member State shall be returned in accordance with the procedure and in the circumstances provided for in this Directive.

Article 4

Each Member State shall appoint one or more central authorities to carry out the tasks provided for in this Directive.

Member States shall inform the Commission of all the central authorities they appoint pursuant to this Article.

The Commission shall publish a list of those central authorities and any changes concerning them in the C series of the *Official Journal of the European Union*.

Article 5

Member States' central authorities shall cooperate and promote consultation between the Member States' competent national authorities. The latter shall in particular:

(1) upon application by the requesting Member State, seek a specified cultural object which has been unlawfully removed from its territory, identifying the possessor and/or holder. The application must include all information needed to facilitate the search, with particular reference to the actual or presumed location of the object;

(2) notify the Member States concerned, where a cultural object is found in their own territory and there are reasonable grounds for believing that it has been unlawfully removed from the territory of another Member State;

(3) enable the competent authorities of the requesting Member State to check that the object in question is a cultural object, provided that the check is made within six months of the notification provided for in point (2). If it is not made within the stipulated period, points (4) and (5) shall cease to apply;

(4) take any necessary measures, in cooperation with the Member State concerned, for the physical preservation of the cultural object;

(5) prevent, by the necessary interim measures, any action to evade the return procedure;

(6) act as intermediary between the possessor and/or holder and the requesting Member State with regard to return. To that end, the competent authorities of the requested Member State may, without prejudice to Article 6, first facilitate the implementation of an arbitration procedure, in accordance with the national legislation of the requested Member State and provided that the requesting Member State and the possessor or holder give their formal approval.

In order to cooperate and consult with each other, the central authorities of the Member States shall use a module of the Internal Market Information System ('IMI') established by Regulation (EU) No 1024/2012 specifically customised for cultural objects. They may also use the IMI to disseminate relevant case-related information concerning cultural objects which have been stolen or unlawfully removed from their territory. The Member States shall decide on the use of the IMI by other competent authorities for the purposes of this Directive.

Article 6

The requesting Member State may initiate, before the competent court in the requested Member State, proceedings against the possessor or, failing him, the holder, with the aim of securing the return of a cultural object which has been unlawfully removed from its territory.

Proceedings may be brought only where the document initiating them is accompanied by:

(a) a document describing the object covered by the request and stating that it is a cultural object;

(b) a declaration by the competent authorities of the requesting Member State that the cultural object has been unlawfully removed from its territory.

Article 7

The competent central authority of the requesting Member State shall forthwith inform the competent central authority of the requested Member State that proceedings have been initiated with the aim of securing the return of the object in question.

The competent central authority of the requested Member State shall forthwith inform the central authorities of the other Member States.

The exchange of information shall be conducted using the IMI in accordance with the applicable legal provisions on the protection of personal data and privacy, without prejudice to the possibility for the competent central authorities to use other means of communication in addition to the IMI.

Article 8

1. Member States shall provide in their legislation that return proceedings under this Directive may not be brought more than three years after the competent central authority of the requesting Member State became aware of the location of the cultural object and of the identity of its possessor or holder.

Such proceedings may, in any event, not be brought more than 30 years after the object was unlawfully removed from the territory of the requesting Member State.

However, in the case of objects forming part of public collections, defined in point (8) of Article 2, and objects belonging to inventories of ecclesiastical or other religious institutions in the Member States where they are subject to special protection arrangements under national law, return proceedings shall be subject to a time-limit of 75 years, except in Member States where proceedings are not subject to a time-limit or in the case of bilateral agreements between Member States providing for a period exceeding 75 years.

2. Return proceedings may not be brought if removal of the cultural object from the national territory of the requesting Member State is no longer unlawful at the time when they are to be initiated.

Article 9

Save as otherwise provided in Articles 8 and 14, the competent court shall order the return of the cultural object in question where it is found to be a cultural object within the meaning of point (1) of Article 2 and to have been removed unlawfully from national territory.

Article 10

Where return of the object is ordered, the competent court in the requested Member State shall award the possessor fair compensation according to the circumstances of the case, provided that the possessor demonstrates that he exercised due care and attention in acquiring the object.

In determining whether the possessor exercised due care and attention, consideration shall be given to all the circumstances of the acquisition, in particular the documentation on the object's provenance, the authorisations for removal required under the law of the requesting Member State, the character of the parties, the price paid, whether the possessor consulted any accessible register of stolen cultural objects and any relevant information which he could reasonably have obtained, or took any other step which a reasonable person would have taken in the circumstances.

In the case of a donation or succession, the possessor shall not be in a more favourable position than the person from whom he acquired the object by those means.
The requesting Member State shall pay that compensation upon return of the object.

Article 11

Expenses incurred in implementing a decision ordering the return of a cultural object shall be borne by the requesting Member State. The same applies to the costs of the measures referred to in point (4) of Article 5.

Article 12

Payment of the fair compensation and of the expenses referred to in Articles 10 and 11 respectively shall be without prejudice to the requesting Member State's right to take action with a view to recovering those amounts from the persons responsible for the unlawful removal of the cultural object from its territory.

Article 13

Ownership of the cultural object after return shall be governed by the law of the requesting Member State.

Article 14

This Directive shall apply only to cultural objects unlawfully removed from the territory of a Member State on or after 1 January 1993.

Article 15

1. Each Member State may apply the arrangements provided for in this Directive to the return of cultural objects other than those defined in point (1) of Article 2.

2. Each Member State may apply the arrangements provided for in this Directive to requests for the return of cultural objects unlawfully removed from the territory of other Member States prior to 1 January 1993.

Article 16

This Directive shall be without prejudice to any civil or criminal proceedings that may be brought, under the national laws of the Member States, by the requesting Member State and/or the owner of a cultural object that has been stolen.

Article 17

1. By 18 December 2015 and every five years thereafter, Member States shall submit to the Commission a report on the application of this Directive.

2. Every five years the Commission shall present a report to the European Parliament, the Council and the European Economic and Social Committee, reviewing the application and effectiveness of this Directive. The report shall be accompanied, if necessary, by appropriate proposals.

Article 18

The following point shall be added to the Annex to Regulation (EU) No 1024/2012:

'8. Directive 2014/60/EU of the European Parliament and the Council of 15 May 2014 on the return of cultural objects unlawfully removed from the territory of a Member State and amending Regulation (EU) No 1024/2012 (*): Articles 5 and 7.

(*) OJ L 159 28.5.2014, p. 1'.

Article 19

1. By 18 December 2015, Member States shall bring into force the laws, regulations and administrative provisions necessary to comply with point (1) of Article 2, point (3) of the first paragraph of Article 5, the second paragraph of Article 5, the third paragraph of Article

7, Article 8(1), the first and the second paragraphs of Article 10 and Article 17(1) of this Directive.

They shall forthwith communicate the text of those measures to the Commission.

When Member States adopt those measures, they shall contain a reference to this Directive or shall be accompanied by such reference on the occasion of their official publication. They shall also include a statement that references in existing laws, regulations and administrative provisions to the Directive repealed by this Directive shall be construed as references to this Directive. Member States shall determine how such reference is to be made and how that statement is to be formulated.

2. Member States shall communicate to the Commission the text of the main provisions of national law which they adopt in the field covered by this Directive.

Article 20

Directive 93/7/EEC, as amended by the Directives listed in Annex I, Part A, is repealed with effect from 19 December 2015, without prejudice to the obligations of Member States relating to the time-limits for transposition into national law of the Directives set out in Annex I, Part B.

References to the repealed Directive shall be construed as references to this Directive and shall be read in accordance with the correlation table in Annex II.

Article 21

This Directive shall enter into force on the twentieth day following that of its publication in the Official Journal of the European Union.
Points (2) to (8) of Article 2, Articles 3 and 4, points (1), (2) and (4) to (6) of the first paragraph of Article 5, Article 6, the first and second paragraphs of Article 7, Article 8(2), Article 9, the third and fourth paragraphs of Article 10, and Articles 11 to 16 shall apply from 19 December 2015.

Article 22

The Directive is addressed to the Member States.

Done at Brussels, 15 May 2014.

For the European Parliament	*For the Council*
The President	*The President*
M. SCHULZ	D. KOURKOULAS

ANNEX I

PART A

Repealed Directive with list of its successive amendments

(referred to in Article 20)

Council Directive 93/7/EEC (OJ L 74, 27.3.1993, p. 74).
Directive 96/100/EC of the European Parliament and of the Council (OJ L 60, 1.3.1997, p. 59).
Directive 2001/38/EC of the European Parliament and of the Council (OJ L 187, 10.7.2001, p. 43).

PART B

List of time-limits for transposition into national law

(referred to in Article 20)

Directive	Time-limit for transposition
93/7/EEC	15.12.1993 (15.3.1994 for Belgium, Germany and the Netherlands)
96/100/EC	1.9.1997
2001/38/EC	31.12.2001

ANNEX II

Correlation table

Directive 93/7/EEC	This Directive
—	Article1
Article 1, point (1), firstindent	Article 2, point (1)
Article 1, point (1), second indent, introductorypart	—
Article 1, point (1), second indent, first sub-indent, first phrase	—
Article 1, point (1), second indent, first sub-indent, second phrase	Article 2, point (8)
Article 1, point (1), second indent, second sub-indent	—
Article 1, point (2), firs tindent	Article 2, point (2) (a)

Directive 93/7/EEC	This Directive
Article 1, point (2), second indent	Article 2, point (2) (b)
Article 1, points (3) to (7)	Article 2, points (3) to (7)
Article 2	Article 3
Article 3	Article 4
Article 4, introductory part	Article 5, first paragraph, introductory part
Article 4, points (1) and (2)	Article 5, first paragraph, points (1) and (2)
Article 4, point (3)	Article 5, first paragraph, point (3)
Article 4, points (4) to (6)	Article 5, first paragraph, points (4) to (6)
—	Article 5, second paragraph
Article 5, first paragraph	Article 6, first paragraph
Article 5, second paragraph, first indent	Article 6, second paragraph, point (a)
Article 5, second paragraph, second indent	Article 6, second paragraph, point (b)
Article 6, first paragraph	Article 7, first paragraph
Article 6, second paragraph	Article 7, second paragraph
—	Article 7, third paragraph
Article 7(1) and (2)	Article 8(1) and (2)
Article 8	Article 9
Article 9, first paragraph	Article 10, first paragraph
Article 9, second paragraph	—
—	Article 10, second paragraph
Article 9, third and fourth paragraphs	Article 10, third and fourth paragraphs
Articles 10 to15	Articles 11 to16
Article 16(1) and (2)	Article 17(1) and (2)
Article 16(3)	—
Article 16(4)	—
Article 17	—
—	Article 18
Article 18	Article 19
—	Article 20
—	Article 21
Article 19	Article 22
Annex	—
—	Annex I
—	Annex II

一、美　国

述 评

1906 年，美国《古迹法》(The Antiquities Act) 颁布，规定凡属联邦所有或归联邦管辖土地上的所有历史性纪念地（包括考古遗址），均属国家古迹，严禁任何人对联邦考古资源进行非法挖掘、损害和破坏。1979 年颁布的《考古资源保护法》(Archaeological Resources Protection Act) 进一步明确考古资源范围，即所有具有考古价值，过去人类生活或活动而形成的 100 年以上历史的文化遗存，并规定未经许可在联邦土地上发掘文物者都将受到法律严惩。此法的主要目的之一便是遏制文物走私。

1982 年颁布的《国家被盗财产法》规定：明知是被盗的外国物品而运输、收受、隐匿或买卖的，构成联邦刑事犯罪。此项规定常被用来返还非法进境文化财产。美国联邦检察官适用该法起诉相关行为人，扣押文化财产并归还原合法所有人。并且，根据美国法律，进口到美国的艺术品必须在海关申报，否则，将被认为是走私品而由美国海关扣押。

1972 年，美国签署了联合国教科文组织《关于禁止和防止非法进出口文化财产和非法转让其所有权的方法的公约》(United Nations Educational, Scientific and Cultural Organization Convention on the Means of Prohibiting and Preventing the Illicit Import , Export and Transfer of Ownership of Cultural Property)(以下简称《1970 年公约》)，经过十余年的实践，又于 1983 年通过《文化财产公约执行法》(Convention on Cultural Property Implementation Act, CPIA)，目的是防止对文化财产的考古掠夺和非法贩运，保护那些无论对原主国还是对全世界都有重要意义的文化财产，并加强与其他国家在这方面的合作。

该执行法规定的“文化财产”的范围与《1970 年公约》保持一致，同时也作出了进一步限制，在 302 节中对“缔约国的考古或人种学资料”术语进行界定。即，如果缔约国如能证明其文化财产正处于被掠夺的危险境地，并且已经按照《1970 年公约》采取了相应的保护措施，可向美国提出限制进口该财产的请求。美国总统拥有是否施加进口限制的决定权。进口限制一般只适用于与美国签订双边或多边协议的国家。其中，双边协议国家同时也应是缔约国，而多边协议国家，并不要求一定是缔约国，但要求其他协议国家也应对该文化财产采取对等的限制措施。但是在特定危急情况下，美国可采取紧急措施限制文化财产进口，而不要求对方一定是其双边协议国家。申请进口限制的缔约国首先要证明存在危急情况，同时总统在听取文化财产咨询委员会（Cultural Property Advisory Committee, CPAC）建议的前提下，决定是否采取进口限制措施。

该法生效后，或是《1970 年公约》对缔约国生效后（以较后生效的日期为准），任何业已列入缔约国博物馆、宗教或世俗的公共纪念馆或类似机构财产清册中的文化财产被盗后，一律禁止向美国进口。在美国签订的双边或多边协议中，或危急情况下采取的进口限制措施中都附上限制进口的文化财产清单，并公布。清单中的文化财产只有在出示出口国颁发的出口证明的情况下才允许进口到美国。

根据该法，自 1987 年开始，美国先后同玻利维亚、柬埔寨、加拿大、哥伦比亚、塞浦路斯、萨尔瓦多、危地马拉、洪都拉斯、意大利、马里、尼加拉瓜、秘鲁和中国等国家签订了文化财产协定或采取紧急措施保护来自上述国家的考古或人种学物品。但是由于该法规定只能在紧急情况下才能将保护扩大到非协议国家，并且未给私人提供救济途径，其作用还是有限的。

美国有关文物进出境管理的其他法规还有 1990 年国会通过的《美国原住民墓葬保护及返还法》（Native American Graves Protection and Repatriation Act, NAGPRA）。该法提出联邦机构或博物馆应将本属原住民的人体遗骸、相关陪葬物和非相关陪葬物、圣物、文化遗物等返还给被认可的印第安部落或夏威夷原住民。上述文物的返还必须在具有共同族群特征的文物相关方的要求下做出。该法案限制买卖在 1990 年 11 月 16 日以后从政府或部落土地上发掘的物品，并进一步限制进入印第安人遗址；限制获取和出售在联邦土地或部落土地上非法发掘的印第安人物品，除非取得其后裔或所属部落的同意，否则禁止购买或出售人体遗骸或相关陪葬物，违反该法将受到罚金或 / 和监禁的处罚。

美国的《海关法》也有关于文物进出境限制的规定。在美国法典第19编第11章的第2091—2095条对前哥伦布时期纪念物或建筑雕塑或壁画的进境作出规定。这一章涉及哥伦布到达美洲以前的纪念物、建筑雕塑或者壁画的进口。该章首先提出以规章的形式颁布一份前哥伦布时期的纪念物、建筑雕塑或者壁画的清单，规章生效后清单中的文物从原产国出口的，都不得被进口到美国，除非收货人能够提供原产国政府证书。非法进口到美国的上述文物将被扣押并没收，在其原产国承担由于归还造成的附加费以及遵守有关归还的其他要求的情况下，文物首选归还原产国。

《文化财产公约执行法》

（另请参阅 19 U.S.C. 2601 及后续条文）

文化财产公约执行法

（王鈊平　初校）

公法 97-446【众议院法案 4566】（1983 年 1 月 12 日批准，联邦法律汇编第 96 卷 2329 页）的部分内容；由公法 100-204【众议院法案 1777】（1987 年 12 月 22 日批准，联邦法律汇编第 101 卷 1331 页）修正

本法案旨在减轻某些义务、暂缓某些义务、延长某些义务的暂缓期限，以及其他。

由美利坚合众国参议院和众议院代表在国会颁布

第三卷　文化财产公约执行法

第 301 节　简称

援引本法案时，可以称为“文化财产公约执行法”。【1】

第 302 节　定义

就本法案而言，

（1）术语“协议”包括任何依据本法且对美国生效的协议的修改或延期。

（2）术语“缔约国的考古或人种学资料”系指：

（A）任何具有考古价值的物品；

（B）任何具有人种学价值的物品；

（C）（A）项或（B）项所指物品如在缔约国境内首次发现，其任何组成部分都将受到缔约国的出口管制。就本款而言，

（i）符合下列情况的物品属于具有考古价值的物品：

（I）具有重要的文化价值；

（II）至少有二百五十年历史；

（III）通常因科学挖掘、私自挖掘或偶然发现，或者陆地或水下探险发现；

（ii）符合下列情况的属于具有人种学价值的物品：

（I）部落社会或非工业社会的产物，以及

（II）因为其显著的特征、相对稀缺或有助于了解某民族的起源、发展或历史而对该民族的文化遗产具有重要性。

（3）术语“委员会”系指根据第206节成立的文化财产咨询委员会。【2】

（4）术语“受托人”系指《美国1930年关税法》（《美国法典》第19卷第1483节）第483节所定义之受托人。

（5）术语“公约”系指联合国教育、科学及文化组织第十六届大会通过的《关于禁止和防止非法进出口文化财产和非法转让其所有权的方法的公约》。

（6）术语“文化财产”包括公约第1条（a）至（k）中所述物品，且无论这些物品是否被缔约国特别指定为符合本条的物品。

（7）术语“指定考古或人种学资料”系指缔约国符合下述条件的任何考古或人种学的资料：

（A）即：

（i）在任何依据本法且对美国生效的协议范围内，或

（ii）符合第304节规定的紧急措施的情况，和

（B）根据第305节规定列示。

（8）术语“部长”系指财政部长或其代表。

（9）术语“缔约国”系指凡批准、认可或加入本公约的国家。

（10）术语“美国”包括部分州、哥伦比亚特区以及由美国负责外交关系的任何领地或区域。

（11）术语“美国公民”系指：

（A）任何美国公民（citizen）或国民（national）①；

（B）根据美国法律或州法律组建或存续的公司、合伙企业、团体或其他企业法人；或

（C）联邦政府或州政府的部门、机构或实体。

第303节【3】有关执行公约第9条的协议

（a）协议授权。-

（1）【4】一般性规定 - 缔约国根据公约第9条向美国发出请求后，总统确定 -

（A）该缔约国的文化遗产因考古或人种学资料遭受掠夺而面临危险；

（B）该缔约国已根据公约采取了相应措施保护本国文化遗产；

（C）那么 -

（i）第307节规定的缔约国考古或人种学资料的进口限制，如果其他从事此类考古或人种学资料重要进口贸易的国家（无论是否缔约国）也采取一致行动（包括施以类似限制或合理期间内限制），将有效遏制严峻的掠夺现状，

（ii）没有比进口限制更为温和的措施；

（D）在特殊情况下，在执行第307节规定的进口限制时，应符合国家间因科学、文化和教育等目的而进行文化财产交流的基本利益；总统可根据本章规定采取第（2）款所述行动。

（2）【5】总统的权力。- 依据第（1）款，总统 -

（A）可与缔约国签订双边协议，以便根据第307节对该国考古或人

① citizen（公民）和national（国民）在包括我国在内的大多数国家没有区分意义，但是对于有海外领地的国家，如美国、英国，就有区分意义。比如，美国公民肯定是美国国民，但美国国民不一定是美国公民。目前，不是美国公民的美国国民只有斯温斯岛和美属萨摩亚的居民。

种学资料采取进口限制，这些考古或人种学资料正因遭受掠夺而导致该国文化遗产处境危急（如第（1）款（A）项所述）；或

（B）与缔约国和一个或多个其他国家（无论是否缔约国）签订多边协议后，根据该协议，美国将对上述资料采取上述限制，而其他协议国家也应采取类似限制。

（3）请求。- 缔约国根据公约第 9 条向美国发送的请求必须附有该国已知事实的书面报告，这些事实关系到应作出第（1）款中（A）项至（D）项的哪些决定。

（4）执行。- 在执行中，总统应当尽力获得相关缔约国的承诺，即：在不损害其文化遗产的情况下，允许交换它的考古与人种学资料。

（b）**有效期**。- 根据第（a）小节的规定，总统不可签订任何有效期超过 5 年（自协议在美国生效之日起）的协议。

（c）**签订协议限制**。-

（1）一般性规定。- 缔约国根据公约第 9 条向美国提出请求后，根据第 307 节对该缔约国考古或人种学资料采取的进口限制，若那些从事此类考古或人种学资料重要进口贸易的国家（无论是否缔约国）也采取或即将采取类似措施，总统方可签订第（a）小节授权的双边或多边协议。

（2）例外情况。- 尽管第（1）款如此规定，但若总统确定从事此类考古或人种学资料重要进口贸易的国家未采取或不太可能采取类似限制，总统也可签订协议，条件是 -

（A）此类限制并非遏制严峻掠夺状态所必需，并且

（B）其他从事此类考古或人种学资料重要进口贸易的国家（无论是否缔约国）也采取与第 307 节规定的类似进口限制，有效遏制严峻的掠夺现状。

（d）【6】**暂停协议项下的进口限制**。

协议对美国生效后，如果总统确定进行协议所涉及的考古和人种学资料的重要进口贸易的多个协议相关方（而非第（c）（2）小节中所述各方）-

（1）未在合理的期间内执行与第 307 节规定的限制相似的进口限制，或

（2）未按要求执行上述限制，导致未能遏制相关缔约国的掠夺状态，那

么总统应暂停执行第 307 节规定的进口限制，直至该国采取合理的纠正措施。

（e）【7】**延长协议期限**。

总统可延长对美国生效的任何协议的期限，但每次延长的时间不得超过 5 年，但前提是总统需确定 -

（1）本节第（a）（1）小节中所述情形（协议签订条件）依然存在，且

（2）不存在第（d）小节规定的暂停理由。

（f）【8】**程序**。- 如果缔约国作出第（a）小节所述的任何请求或总统提议延长本节第（e）小节所述任何协议的期限，那么总统应 -

（1）在联邦公告上发布有关该请求或提议的通知；

（2）将请求或提议的相关信息（如果可以，也包括缔约国根据第 304 节采取紧急行动的信息）提交给委员会，以使委员会能履行第 306（f）节规定的职责；以及

（3）在就请求或提议采取行动时，考虑任何委员会报告中所含的观点和建议 -

（A）本卷第 306 节的（f）小节第（1）款或第（2）款中规定的报告，和

（B）自总统按照第（2）款规定将相关信息提交至委员会之日起，至 150 天前，委员会在此期限内向总统提交的报告。

（g）【9】**总统行动信息**。-

（1）一般性规定。- 在任何情况下，即：

（A）总统根据第（a）或（e）小节规定签订协议或延长协议期限，或

（B）【10】实行第 304 节规定的进口限制，总统应在采取行动后立即将报告提交至国会。

（2）报告。- 第（1）款规定的“报告”应包含 -

（A）行动说明（包括任何已签订协议的正文），

（B）此次行动与委员会报告中观点与建议的差异（若有的话），和

（C）出现上述差异的原因。

（3）委员会建议信息。- 如果委员会报告建议总统考虑签订协议，但协议

最终未能签订，那么总统须向国会提交报告解释未能签订协议的原因。

第 304 节 【11】紧急进口限制

（a）**紧急情况定义**。- 根据本节规定，对于任何缔约国的任何考古或人种学资料，术语“紧急情况”系指这些材料 -

（1）对了解人类历史具有重大意义的新发现的种类，且这些资料正面临被掠夺、拆毁、消失或分裂的危险；

（2）可以确认来自极具文化价值的遗址，而该遗址正面临被掠夺、拆毁、消失或分裂的危险，或受此威胁；

（3）是某种独特文化或文明的部分遗存，而该遗存正面临被掠夺、拆毁、消失或分裂的危险；作为部分特殊文化或文明的遗迹，其记录面临或将面临被掠夺、拆毁、消失或破碎的危险；暂时采取第 307 节规定的进口限制将会减少上述被掠夺、拆毁、消失或分裂的全部或部分诱因。

（b）【12】**总统的行动**。- 根据第（c）小节规定，如果总统确定紧急情况适用于任何缔约国的任何考古或人种学资料，那么总统可实行第 307 节中针对这些资料的进口限制。

（c）**限制**。-

（1）除非缔约国已向美国发出第 303（a）节所述的请求并提供了能够确定存在紧急情况的信息，否则总统不能对任何缔约国的考古或人种学资料适用本节规定。

（2）在应缔约国请求（根据第 303（a）节）依本节（b）小节采取行动之际，如果委员会编制的报告（根据第 306（f）（3）节）在总统根据第 303（f）（2）节向委员会提交信息之日起 90 天内提交给总统，总统就应当考虑报告中提出的观点和建议。

（3）【13】自缔约国按照第 303（a）节的规定向美国提出请求之日起 5 年后，本卷第 307 节规定的进口限制便不再适用于任何缔约国的考古或人种学资料。如果总统确定紧急情况依然存在，可将该期限再延长 3 年。但是，如果总统在 90 天内收到包括建议及理由的委员会报告，在采取上述行动前，总统应慎重考虑是否将进口限制延期。

（4）【14】如果在第（3）款所述期限到期前，已根据第203【15】节签署了有关考古或人种学资料的协议或与缔约国（参议院已给出建议并同意批准）签订了协议，那么可在协议存续期间继续实行本节规定的全部或部分的进口限制。

第305节 【16】指定协议或紧急措施涉及的资料

第303节项下签订的任何协议生效后或采取第304节规定的紧急措施后，经与美国新闻署署长商议，部长应依据规则发布协议或措施涉及的缔约国考古或人种学资料清单（必要时可修改）。部长可按类型或其它合理分类列示上述资料，但是应确保其针对性和精确性，以便

（1）第307节规定的进口限制仅适用于协议或紧急措施涉及的考古和人种学资料；且

（2）就受限资料向进口商和其他人发出诚实的通知。

第306节【17】文化财产咨询委员会

（a）**成立**。- 成立文化财产咨询委员会。

（b）**成员**。-

（1）委员会应由总统任命的11名成员组成，如下所示：

（A）2名代表博物馆利益的成员。

（B）3名考古学、人类学、人种学或相关领域的专家成员。

（C）3名熟悉考古的、人种的或其他文化财产国际交易的成员。

（D）3名代表公共利益的成员。

（2）为实现第（1）款所述任命，应确保 -

（A）确保公允列示考古和人种学资料国际交流中国有和私营部门的各种利益，以及

（B）确保在这些部门中，公允列示区域和当地的机构及博物馆的利益。

（3）

（A）【18】委员会成员任期 3 年且可连任一个或多个任期。对于首次任命，总统应尽最大可能选择最具代表性的成员，包括 4 名任期为 3 年的成员、4 名任期为 2 年的成员以及 3 名任期为 1 年的成员。其后的每次任命的任期均应为 3 年。

（B）

（i）【19】如果在任职期间出现空缺，那么应使用与首次任命相同的方式填补委员会的空缺以完成剩余的任期。凡委员会成员在其任期结束后均可继续担任委员会的成员，直至重新任命或指定其继任者。

（ii）总统应从委员会成员中选出委员会主席。

（c）**费用**。- 应报销委员会成员在履行委员会职责时实际产生的费用。

（d）**事务处理**。- 委员会法定人数为 6 名成员。出席成员多数投赞成票方可通过委员会决定。

（e）**员工和管理**。-

（1）美国新闻署署长应向委员会提供其开展活动所需的合理的行政和技术支持与协助。根据委员会的请求，任何其它联邦机构的负责人可向委员会有偿提供其机构任一人员的详细信息，以助委员会履行职责，并提供委员会认为开展活动所需的合理信息和帮助。

（2）委员会应在美国新闻署署长的号召下召开会议，或在委员会大多数成员书面请求的情况下召开会议。

（f）**委员会报告**。-

（1）对于缔约国根据第 303（a）节提出的每一个请求，委员会应根据第 303（a）（1）节就缔约国相关问题进行调查和评估，并编制报告，报告中应载明 -

（A）调查和评估的结果；

（B）关于独立从事相关资料重要进口贸易国家的调查结果；和

（C）关于是否应当根据第 303（a）节的规定与缔约国签订协议的建议及其原因。

（2）若总统欲根据第 303（e）节的规定延长协议期限，委员会应编制一份报告，建议是否应当延期并阐明原因。

（3）若委员会发现存在第 304 节规定的紧急情况，应编制一份报告，建议是否应当执行第 304 节规定的紧急措施并说明原因。如果任何缔约国在其根据第 303（a）节所提出的请求中表示存在紧急情况但委员会发现并未出现紧急情况，那么委员会应在报告中说明原因。

（4）委员会编制的任何有关建议签署协议、延长协议期限或采取紧急措施的报告应说明 -

（A）为了执行公约，该协议必须包含的或执行上述措施所需的合理条款和条件；和

（B）上述协议或措施中涉及的缔约国的考古或人种学资料，委员会应将这些资料按照类型或是其他认为合理的方法进行分类。

（5）如果委员会成员不同意根据本小节编制的任何报告中所涉事宜，该成员可提交一份声明，说明不同意的原因，该声明应附于报告之后并视作报告的组成部分。

（6）【20】委员会应将根据本小节编制的每份报告的副本提交国会和总统。

（g）【21】**委员会审查**。-

（1）一般性规定。- 委员会应负责持续审查根据第 303 节签署的对美国生效的协议的有效性，以及审查根据第 304 节采取的紧急措施的有效性。

（2）委员会的行动。- 如果委员在审查中发现 -

（A）存在根据第 303（d）节暂停协议项下进口限制的情形；

（B）协议或紧急措施都未能实现签订协议或采取措施应达到的目的；或

（C）为了充分履行美国的公约义务，可变更本条款；委员会可向国会和总统提交报告，阐明其暂停进口限制或提高上述任何协议或紧急措施有效性的建议。

（h）【22】**联邦咨询委员会法**。-《联邦咨询委员会法》（公法 92-463；《美国

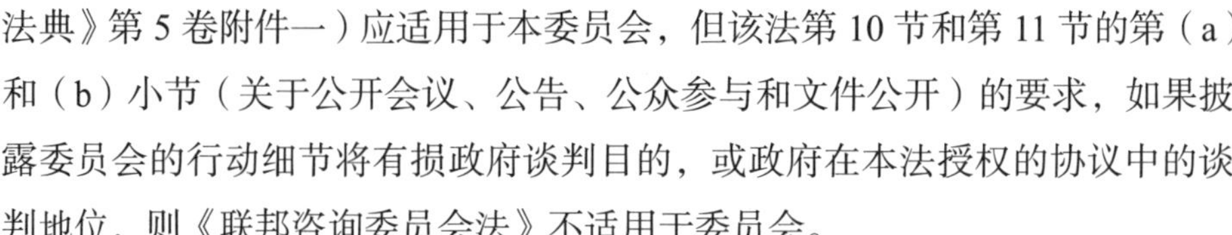

法典》第5卷附件一）应适用于本委员会，但该法第10节和第11节的第（a）和（b）小节（关于公开会议、公告、公众参与和文件公开）的要求，如果披露委员会的行动细节将有损政府谈判目的，或政府在本法授权的协议中的谈判地位，则《联邦咨询委员会法》不适用于委员会。

（i）**保密信息**。-

（1）一般性规定 - 私营机构以保密方式向美国官员、雇员或委员会相关负责人员提交的任何资料（包括商业秘密、商业或财务保密信息），除了以下人士不得向他人披露— -

（A）美国新闻署署长任命的美国官员和雇员；

（B）由委员会主席任命的美国众议院筹款委员会成员和参议院财政委员会成员，以及由委员会主席任命的负责协议谈判和本法授权其他事宜的工作人员；以及

（C）根据本法成立的委员会。

（2）政府信息。- 不得泄露美国官员或雇员秘密提交给委员会的信息，除非根据美国新闻署署长在咨询委员会后颁布的规定。这些规范应考虑上述信息向公众披露的程度以防美国的利益受到损害，并规定需要委员会限制或保密的信息类别。这些规范应在最大的可行范围内允许委员会成员与拟定协议（由本法授权）相关人员展开有效协商。

（j）**无谈判授权**。- 不得根据本节规定授权或允许任何个人（非其他授权或允许）直接参与本法授权的任何协议的谈判。

第307节【23】进口限制

（a）**合法出口文件**。- 根据第305节指定的缔约国考古或人种学资料，不得从缔约国出口（无论是否出口至美国），除非缔约国颁发出口许可证或其他可以证明出口未违反该缔约国法律的文件。

（b）**缺乏证明文件时的海关行动**。- 如果收货人在进口指定考古或人种学资料时，无法向海关官员提供上述证明文件 -

（1）根据第（a）小节应当提供缔约国出口许可证或其他证明文件；或

（2）充分证据证明 -

（A）此类资料进入美国前已从缔约国出口 10 年以上，负责资料进口的人员（或任何相关人员）在资料进口前超过 1 年的时间内未直接取得或间接约定取得这些资料或这些资料带来的利益，或

（B）此类资料在根据第 305 节指定资料当日或之前从缔约国出口，相关海关人员应拒绝资料通关并应将资料送往其持有的保税仓库或关栈，风险和费用均由收货人承担，直至相关文件或证据提交给上述海关人员，法律另有规定的除外。如果在拒绝通关后的 90 天内或秘书长因正当理由允许的更长期限内，未能提交上述文件或证据，这些资料将被充公没收。这些文件或证据的提交不应妨碍第 310 节规定的后续行动计划。

（c）**充分证据的定义**。- 术语“充分证据”系指 -

（1）根据第（b）（2）（A）小节规定 -

（A）进口商或负责资料进口的人员作出宣誓声明，表示据他所知

（i）在进口美国前，这些资料已从缔约国出口至少 10 年。

（ii）在资料进口前超过 1 年的时间内，上述进口商或人员（或任何相关人员）未直接取得或间接约定取得这些资料或这些资料带来的利益；并且

（B）收货人或向进口商出售此类资料的人员作出陈述，说明出口日期，如果不知道日期，则要说明其确信这些资料在进口美国之前已从缔约国出口至少 10 年的原因；以及

（2）根据第（b）（2）（B）小节规定 -

（A）进口商或负责资料进口的人员作出宣誓声明，表示据他所知，该资料在根据第 305 节指定资料当日或之前从缔约国出口，和

（B）收货人或向进口商出售此类资料的人员作出陈述，发货人或将资料销售给进口商的人员提供的陈述，说明出口日期，如果不知道日期则要说明其确信这些资料在根据第 305 节指定资料当日或之前从缔约国出口的原因。

（d）**相关人员**。- 根据本节第（b）和（c）小节的规定，符合下面条件的，可

认为是与进口商或负责资料进口的人员相关的人员 -

（1）与进口商或同等重要的人属同一个家族的成员，包括但不限于兄弟姐妹（无论是纯血亲关系还是同父异母或同母异父的关系）、配偶、被继承人或直系后代；

（2）进口商或重要人员在合伙企业、协会或其他合资公司中的合作伙伴或合股人；或

（3）由进口商或重要人员直接或间接所有、控制或持有 20% 或以上流通的有投票权股票的公司或其他法律实体。

第 308 节 【24】被盗文化财产

本法生效后或公约对缔约国生效后（以较晚日期为准），从缔约国的博物馆、宗教或世俗的公共纪念馆或任类似机构中窃取的文化财产，如果该文化财产已用文件形式列入该机构的财产清册，一律不得进口至美国。

第 309 节 【25】根据本法资料和物品的临时处理

在最终确定任何考古、人种学资料或任何文化财产进口至美国是否违反第 307 节和第 308 节之前，秘书长应根据美国的博物馆或其他文化、科学机构（对公众开放）的申请，允许将此类资料或文化财产在上述机构保存，如果他确信 -

（1）该机构将采取充分的安保措施保护上述资料或文化财产；且

（2）机构向秘书长缴纳足额保证金，以确保能完璧归还。

第 310 节 【26】扣押和没收

（a）**一般性规定**。- 若违反第 307 节或第 308 节规定将任何指定的考古或人种学资料或文化财产进口至美国（视情况而定），则应扣押及没收。所有关于因

违反海关法而扣押、没收的法律条款均应适用于已发生的或疑似的扣押和没收物品，以便这些规定适用于且不违反本法。

（b）**考古和人种学资料**。- 若任何指定考古和人种学资料违反第 307 节规定被进口至美国且被美国根据本法没收，则 -

（1）首先应被提交并返还缔约国；

（2）如果未返还缔约国，则应将其返还没收资料相关的请求人，但前提是该请求人 -

（A）享有该资料的有效所有权，

（B）是这些资料的善意购买人；或

（3）如果未根据第（1）款规定返还缔约国，或未根据第（2）款规定归还给原告，那么应按照因违反海关法而没收物品的处理方式依法处置。只有缔约国或原告（视情况而定）承担因返还或运输产生的费用，并满足部长提出的有关返还的其他要求，方可根据第（1）款或第（2）款归还资料。

（c）**文化财产**。-

（1）违反第 308 节规定将文化财产进口美国，根据本节规定应予以没收。按照现行法律，请求人享有这些被盗物品的有效所有权，则不应判定没收，除非主张返还被盗物品的缔约国向请求人支付合理补偿。如果请求人虽不享有该物品的有效所有权但能证明其购买该物品时支付了合理对价并确信不知晓其是被盗物品，也不应根据本节规定判定采取没收措施，除非 -

（A）主张返还被盗物品的缔约国向请求人支付与其购买价格相等的金额，或

（B）美国确定按照法律或互惠原则，该缔约国将在相似条件下返还从美国机构盗窃的物品，无需支付赔偿金。

（2）若违反第 308 节规定将任何文化财产进口至美国且被美国依法没收，则 -

（A）应首先提交该物品以便归还给被盗机构所在缔约国，如果缔约国承担归还和运输产生的费用并遵循部长提出的有关返还的其它要求，就应归还该物品；或

（B）如果未归还给缔约国，那么应按照因违反海关法而没收物品的处理方式依法处置。

第 311 节 【27】证明要求

尽管《美国 1930 年关税法》(《美国法典》第 19 卷第 1615 节）第 615 节有所规定，但在任何人就本法所涉资料或物品提起的没收之诉中，美国

（1）对于第 307 节规定的任何资料，应确定部长已经根据第 305 节列示；和

（2）对于第 308 节规定的任何物品，确定 -

（A）该物品已由缔约国的博物馆、宗教或世俗的公共纪念馆或任类似机构以文件形式列入该机构的财产清册，且

（B）该物品是在本法生效后或公约对缔约国生效后（以较晚日期为准）从上述机构盗窃而来。

第 312 节 【28】不受本法约束的资料或物品

本法规定不适用于 -

（1）进口至美国供临时展览展示的任何考古或人种学资料或任何文化财产，根据 1965 年 10 月 19 日批准的《因临时展览展示或其它用途进口美国的具有文化价值的物品司法免扣押法案》(《美国法典》第 22 卷第 2459 节）不得扣押上述资料或物品；或

（2）进口至美国的任何指定考古及人种学资料或任何文化财产，前提是上述资料或物品 -

（A）由美国的（政府）认证博物馆[①]、宗教或世俗纪念馆、类似机构持续持有达 3 年以上，且该机构在不知上述资料或物品系违法进口

① recognized museum，是指被政府授予一种水平证明的博物馆。详见：https://www.museums.ab.ca/what-we-do/recognized-museum-program.aspx.

的情况下善意购买，且 -

（i）在该机构的出版物、任何定期发行的报纸或期刊（发行量至少为 5 万份），或者在与不受本法约束的资料或物品相关的期刊或展览目录上刊登上述资料或物品的购买情况。

（ii）上述资料或物品已向公众持续展出一段时间，或 3 年内累计展出时间至少 1 年，或

（iii）上述物品或资料的编目可接受公众申请对外开放，3 年期内开放时间至少 2 年；

（B）如果第（A）项不适用，上述资料或物品在美国的时间达到连续 10 年以上，而且在此期间，该资料或物品在美国的（政府）认证博物馆、宗教或世俗公共纪念馆及类似机构向公众开放展览的时间达 5 年以上；或

（C）如果第（A）项和第（B）项不适用，那么上述资料或物品在美国的时间达到连续 10 年以上，而且在此期间，相关缔约国已收到或应当收到该资料或物品在美国境内位置的合理通知（通过发行量较大的、易获得的出版物或其它方式，具体方式依部长的规定）；

（D）如果前述各项均不适用，那么上述资料或物品在美国的时间达到连续 20 年以上，并且申请人在不知上述资料或物品系违法进口的情况下善意购买。

第 313 节　【29】规定

部长应制定履行本法所需的合理规则与规定。

第 314 节　【30】执行

在美国关税区和维尔京群岛内，应由相关的海关人员执行本法规定。在美国的任何其它领域或区域内（不属于上述关税区或维尔京群岛），应由总统任命海关人员执行上述规定。

第315节　生效日期

（a）**一般性规定**。-本法自颁布之日起90日生效，或在总统确定并发布在联邦公报上的日期生效，只要该日期-

（1）早于上述第90天且晚于颁布日期；和

（2）在任命委员会的创始成员之后。

（b）**例外情况**。-尽管有第（a）小节的规定，也可在本法颁布之日后的任何时间，采用第306节规定的方式任命委员会成员。

注释：

【1】《美国法典》第19卷第2601节。

【2】第206节的参考很可能实际是第306节的参考。

【3】《美国法典》第19卷第2602节。

【4】第303（a）（1）节授予总统的双边或多边协议谈判的启动权由美国新闻署署长代为行使，并按照1986年3月10日第12555号总统行政令51 F.R. 8475经与国务卿和财政部长协商行事。

【5】第303（a）（2）节和第303（a）（4）节授予总统的职权由国务卿代为行使，并按照1986年3月10日第12555号总统行政令51 F.R. 8475与美国新闻署署长（需亲身参与）和财政部长协商。

【6】第303（d）节授予总统的判断其他协议方是否未能执行或有效执行协议的权能由美国新闻署署长代为行使，并按照1986年3月10日第12555号总统行政令51 F.R. 8475经与国务卿和财政部长协商行事。根据该总统行政令，国务卿负责协议的解释。若涉及暂停进口限制，则应将此决定权委托给财政部长。

【7】第303（e）节授予总统的协议延期决定权由美国新闻署署长代为行使，并按照1986年3月10日第12555号总统行政令51 F.R. 8475经与国务卿和财政部长协商行事。若仅为谈判并签署延期协议，该职能将委托给国

务卿，并与美国新闻署署长（需亲身参与）和财政部长协商。

【8】第 303（f）节授予总统的在收到缔约国请求后采取措施的权能由美国新闻署署长代为行使，并按照 1986 年 3 月 10 日第 12555 号总统行政令 51 F.R. 8475 经与国务卿和财政部长协商行事。

【9】第 303（g）节授予总统的权能由国务卿代为行使，并按照 1986 年 3 月 10 日第 12555 号总统行政令 51 F.R. 8475 与美国新闻署署长（需亲身参与）和财政部长协商，第 303（g）（1）（B）小节除外。

【10】第 303（1）（b）节[①]授予总统的行动计划通知和向国会提交报告权能由美国新闻署署长代为行使，并按照 1986 年 3 月 10 日第 12555 号总统行政令 51 F.R. 8475 经与国务卿和财政部长协商行事。

【11】《美国法典》第 19 卷第 2603 节。本节授予总统的进口限制权（第 307 节）和进口限制延期权（第 304（c）（3）节）由财政部长代为行使，并按照 1986 年 3 月 10 日第 12555 号总统行政令 51 F.R. 8475 与美国新闻署署长和财政部长协商。

【12】第 304（b）节授予总统的在公约缔约国的考古或人种学资料面临紧急情况时，依据第 304（c）（1）节、第 304（c）（2）节和第 304（c）（3）节作出限制决定的权能由美国新闻署署长代为行使，并按照 1986 年 3 月 10 日第 12555 号总统行政令 51 F.R. 8475 与国务卿和财政部长协商。

【13】第 304（c）（3）节授予总统的考量文化财产咨询委员会咨询报告并决定延长紧急进口限制的权能是否由美国新闻署署长代为行使，并按照 1986 年 3 月 10 日第 12555 号总统行政令 51 F.R. 8475 经与国务卿和财政部长协商行事。

【14】第 303（c）（4）节授予总统的根据参议院建议和批准同意书进行谈判和签订协议的权能由国务卿代为行使，并按照 1986 年 3 月 10 日第 12555 号总统行政令 51 F.R. 8475 与美国新闻署署长（需亲身参与）和财政部长协商。

【15】第 203 节注释应当是第 303 节的。

---

① 法律原文中注释 10 在第 303（g）（1）（B）小节，本项总统权力疑为该小节授权。

【16】《美国法典》第 19 卷第 2604 节。

【17】《美国法典》第 19 卷第 2605 节。

【18】由 1988 财年和 1989 财年《外交关系授权法》(公法 100–204；101 法令 . 1380）第 307（a）节修正和重述第（3)(A）小节。《外交关系授权法》第 307（c）节的第（3)(A）小节适用于在颁布公法 100–204 后首次任命的文化财产咨询委员会成员。

【19】由 1988 财年《外交关系授权法》(公法 100–204；101 Stat. 1380)第 307(b)节修正和重述第（3)(B）小节。

【20】第 306（f)(6）节授予总统的权能由美国新闻署署长代为行使，并按照 1986 年 3 月 10 日第 12555 号总统行政令 51 F.R. 8475 经与国务卿和财政部长协商行事。

【21】本小节授予总统的接收报告权能由美国新闻署署长代为行使，并按照 1986 年 3 月 10 日第 12555 号总统行政令 51 F.R. 8475 经与国务卿和财政部长协商行事。

【22】本节授予总统的披露委员会议事程序的决定权由美国新闻署署长代为行使，并按照 1986 年 3 月 10 日第 12555 号总统行政令 51 F.R. 8475 经与国务卿和财政部长协商行事。

【23】《美国法典》第 19 卷第 2606 节。

【24】《美国法典》第 19 卷第 2607 节。

【25】《美国法典》第 19 卷第 2608 节。

【26】《美国法典》第 19 卷第 2609 节。

【27】《美国法典》第 19 卷第 2610 节。

【28】《美国法典》第 19 卷第 2611 节。

【29】《美国法典》第 19 卷第 2612 节。

【30】《美国法典》第 19 卷第 2613 节。

二、英　国

述 评

1939 年 9 月 1 日第二次世界大战爆发之际，英国国会当天颁布《进出境海关权利法令 1939》[Import, Export and Customs Powers（Defence）Act 1939]，旨在限制包括文物、艺术品在内的物资流转至敌国，确保出境物品可获得相应外汇。为确保欧盟第 3911/92 号理事会条例的实施，英国制定《商品出境（管制）命令 1992》[The Export of Goods（Control）Order 1992]，其中对于“文物”的界定沿用欧盟第 3911/92 号理事会条例内容，并规定此类物品的出境必须申请出境许可证。

根据《出境管理法 2002》（Export Control Act 2002），英国文化、媒体及体育部于 2003 年 11 月 17 日制定《文物出境管控令》[The Export of Objects of Cultural Interest（Control）Order 2003]，共 8 条，明确了相关概念，规定了文物出口许可证明的申发、海关的权力以及法律适用。该命令规定任何文物出境都须依法进行适用许可证申请，否则，相关人员即构成犯罪并应承担相应法律责任。该命令将制作时间距出境日期超过 50 年的物品定义为文物，并规定了除外条款，并对出境许可管理和海关权力作出明确规定。该命令于 2009 年 8 月 5 日修订，当月 28 日生效。

2003 年 10 月 31 日英国加入《1970 年公约》，为了履行条约义务，制定《文物交易（犯罪）法 2003》[Dealing in Cultural Objects（Offences）Act 2003]，并于 2003 年 12 月 30 日正式生效。本法共 6 条，明确规定“文物”是具有历史、建筑或考古意义的物品，并将“非法挖掘物；从具有历史、建筑或考古意义的建筑物或构造物中被移除的物件，或从具有历史、建筑或考古意义的遗址遗迹中的被移除物”等定义为污点文物（tainted cultural object），任何在明知或认为某物是污点文物的情况下，进行不诚实交易，包括进出口污点文物的行为，都被认为是犯罪，行为人将会受到相应刑事处罚。涉及文物进出境的，由海关部门进行调查，并视情况扣押该文物。在此之前对此类文物的保护仅适用 1968 年《盗窃法》(The Theft Act 1968),《文物交易(犯罪)法》显然扩大了文物的保护范围，更有利于遏制非法文物交易。根据本法可通过认定“污点文物”在特殊情况下限制某地文物进境，以保障文物流失国家的权益。2003 年通过的《伊拉克(联合国制裁)命令》[The Iraq (United Nations Sanctions) Order 2003] 的第 8 条规定，禁止进境非法转移的伊拉克文化财产，其中非法转移文化财产特指自 1990 年 8 月 6 日起从伊拉克非法转移的历史、文化及考古学类文化财产。2014 年通过的《出口管制(叙利亚制裁)命令》[The Export Control (Syria Sanctions) (Amendment) Order 2014] 的第 11c 条规定，执行与叙利亚文化财产相关物品的贸易制裁，对违约行为制定了新的罪行和处罚，禁止整个欧盟进境非法转移的叙利亚考古、历史、文化及宗教性质的文化财产，除非提供有效证据证明文化财产是在 2011 年 3 月 15 日之前从叙利亚合法出境。此外，命令还规定了“交易”的含义以及税务与海关检控署的职责。

英国文物进出境管理机构主要是文化、媒体及体育部(Department for Culture, Media and Sport)及其下设的英格兰艺术理事会(Arts Council England)，英格兰艺术理事会下设的出境许可处(Export Licensing Unit)代表英国国务大臣负责发放文物艺术品出境许可证[①]。相关机构还有 1952 年成立的文物艺术品出境审议委员会(Reviewing Committee on the Export of Works of Art and Objects of Cultural Interest)，这是非政府部门咨询机构，主要职责是依据《出境管理法 2002》，为财政部提供有关文物艺术品出境方面的政策建议。

---

① 出境许可证由文化、媒体及体育部大臣签发，任何文物从英国出境到欧盟其他成员国或非欧盟地区，无论临时还是永久出境，都需要申请对应的出境许可证，文化、媒体及体育部大臣会根据文物艺术品出境审议委员会建议决定是否准许出境。出境许可证分为开放许可证(Open Licence)(低于特定年限及价格的文物出境时申请)和特定出境许可证(Individual Export Licence)。

（一）《文物出境管控令》

《文物出境管控令 2003》

2003 No.2759

海关

（李睿琦　翻译　　徐书林　初校）

制定：2003 年 11 月 17 日

提交至议会：2003 年 11 月 18 日

生效：2004 年 5 月 1 日

国务大臣根据《出境管理法 2002》第 1、5、7 章节授权作出以下命令：

引用，实施及注释

1.（1）本命令可引称为《文物出境管控令 2003》，2004 年 5 月 1 日起生效。

（2）在本命令中，除另有规定：

"该法"指《出境管理法 2002》；

"关长"指海关关长；

"通用许可证"指国务大臣依据条例所作的授权证书（无论这一证书是在本命令生效前或者生效后做出）；

"文物"与条例中定义相同；

"出口"包括仓储货物在内，除文中另有规定外，指从英国出口至除英属地曼岛以外的任何地方；

"物品"指符合本命令附表指定描述并包含在内的文物；

“规定数额”与《海关和国内税管理法 1979》中定义一致；

“条例”指 1992 年 12 月 9 日欧盟《关于文物出口的第 3911/92 号理事会条例》。

文物出口管制

2. 依据本命令条款，除非持有国务大臣书面签署的许可证并且符合许可证中附带的所有条件，否则一切文物禁止出境。

许可证

3.（1）通用许可证或者是由国务大臣根据第 2 条授予的许可证分为：

（a）普通许可证与特定许可证；

（b）无限期许可证与需重新申请的有期限许可证；

（c）附条件许可证与无条件许可证，此处的条件是指文物凭许可证出境前后要作出某项行为或完成某项任务

（2）任何许可证都可以被国务大臣在任何认为合适的时间、情况以及期限内修改、暂停或者废除，只需通知许可证持有人。

错误的许可证申请等

4.（1）任何人想要获得第 2 条的许可证或者是通用许可证 -

（a）故意在重要事项上作出本人明知虚假的陈述或者提供本人明知虚假的文件及信息，或者

（b）在重要事项上过失作出虚假陈述或者提供虚假文件及信息，

即构成犯罪。

（2）依第（1）款被控有罪者应承担以下责任：

（a）依照简易程序定罪的，判处规定数额的罚金，

（b）依照公诉程序定罪的，判处无上限的罚金，或 / 并处 2 年以下监禁。

任何通过虚假陈述，虚假文件或信息申请到的许可证，自始无效。

未遵守许可证规定

5.（1）任何人依据下述第（2）款规定 -

（a）根据第 2 条取得的许可证或通用许可证授权行事；

（b）没有遵守许可证所附条件，

即构成犯罪。

（2）依第（1）款被控有罪者应承担以下责任：

（a）依照简易程序定罪的，判处规定数额的罚金，

（b）依照公诉程序定罪的，判处无上限的罚金，或 / 并处 2 年以下监禁。

（3）依第（1）款被控有罪者的免责情况：

（a）许可证中存在问题的附带条件已先由国务大臣修改；且

（b）如果许可证未作相应的修改，所谓的不遵守不是真正的不遵守；以及

（c）许可证持有人已经完成许可证授权行为后，只有经他同意，国务大臣才能修改此人未遵守的条件。

海关目的地证明查询权

6.（1）依照海关与货物税务署的要求，出口或者运送本命令或条例中规定的文物的行为人需在规定时间内提供货物运送目的地证明，如无法提供即构成犯罪。

（2）任何依第（1）款被控有罪者应依照简易程序定罪，判处四级标准等级以下罚金①。

1979 年**《海关和国内税管理法》的适用**

7.（1）海关关长应采取适当行动保证本命令实施。

---

① 英国 1982 年《刑事审判法》（Criminal Justice Act 1982）第 37 条规定了适用简易罪的罚款标准等级（the standard scale），共分五级，一级罚金 200 英镑，二级罚金 500 英镑，三级罚金 1000 英镑，四级罚金 2500 英镑，五级罚金 5000 英镑。

（2）海关关长应采取适当行动保证有关文物出境条例的实施。

信息使用与公开

8. （1）本条适用于由：

（a）国务大臣，或者

（b）海关关长，

掌握的与本命令或者可直接适用的欧洲共同体关于文物出口条款的规定中有关管控实施的信息。

（2）本条所涉信息可用于下列目的，或者与之相关的目的：

（a）行使本命令或者《出境管理法 2002》规定的管控职能；

（b）对欧共体或是英国应承担的其他国际义务产生效力；

（c）便利英国以外的权威机构或国际组织使用根据本命令或《出境管理法 2002》授权的或者与之有关的行动信息。

并且可以为了上述目的向任何人披露。

（3）国务大臣或者海关关长不得根据本条对外披露信息，除非认为有必要这样做。

（4）就本条而言，“信息”是指与个人从事的特定业务或其他活动有关的任何信息。

（5）本条任何规定均不得损害本条之外规定的信息披露权利。

（6）经本条可以披露的信息包括本命令实施之前获得的信息。

Tessa Jowell

文化媒体及体育部大臣

文化媒体及体育部

2003 年 11 月 17 日

附件 1：文物的定义

1. 任何在出口之前制作的超过 50 年的文物，以下物品除外：

（a）邮票以及其他与集邮相关的物品；

（b）出口人或其配偶出生、婚姻、死亡证明或与其个人事务相关的其他文件；

（c）出口人或其配偶收到或寄出的信件或其他书面文件；

（d）制造者、生产者或其配偶、遗孀、鳏夫携带出境的所有私人物品。

2009 修订案：

《文物出境管控令（修订）2009》

制定：2009 年 08 月 05 日

提交至议会：2009 年 08 月 06 日

生效：2009 年 08 月 28 日

国务大臣根据《出境管理法 2002》第 1、5、7 章节授权作出以下命令：

引用和实施

1. 本命令可引称为《文物出境管控令（修订）2009》，2009 年 8 月 28 日起生效。

对于《文物出境（管理）命令 2003》的修改

2. 对于第 1（2）条中关于文物出境规定中“条例”的界定，替换为“2008 年 10 月 18 日欧盟《关于文物出口的第 116/2009 号理事会条例》”。

Gerry Sutcliffe

国务部长

文化媒体及体育部

2009 年 8 月 5 日

（二）《文物交易（犯罪）法》

《文物交易（犯罪）法2003》

2003年

第27章

（徐书林　初校）

本法对购买、处置、进出口污点文物或者商定、安排上述行为的罪行，以及相关事项作出了规定。

【2003年10月30日】

经本届议会的上议院和下议院同意并遵其建议，女王陛下根据议会授权颁布本法，具体如下：

1. 交易污点文物罪

（1）明知或认为某件文物有污点的情况下依然进行不诚实交易的行为人构成此罪。

（2）是否知道或了解涉案物品为文物与定罪无关。

（3）构成本罪应承担以下责任：

（a）依照公诉程序定罪的，判处7年以下有期徒刑或/并处罚金；

（b）依照简易程序定罪的，判处6个月以下监禁，或/并处以不超过法定最高限额的罚金。

2.“污点文物”的含义

（1）“文物”是指具有历史、建筑或考古意义的物品。

（2）本法生效后，如符合下列情况之一的，文物即为有污点的：

（a）物品是在第（4）款所述情形下被拆除，或被发掘；且

（b）拆除或发掘行为本身构成犯罪。

（3）以下因素与定罪无关：

（a）拆除或发掘行为是发生在英国境内还是境外，

（b）拆除与发掘构成犯罪，是依据英国法律或是其他国家或地区的法律。

（4）符合下列情况即认定物品被拆除：

（a）从具有历史、建筑或考古意义的建筑物或构造物上被拆除，且该物品已构成该建筑物或构造物的一部分；

（b）从具有历史、建筑或考古意义的古迹上拆除的。

（5）“古迹”包括：

（a）工事、洞穴或发掘遗迹；

（b）包含建筑物或构造物遗迹，或者工事、洞穴或发掘遗迹的遗址，

（c）包含车、船、飞行器或其他可移动物（或其一部分）遗迹的遗址。

（6）“遗迹”包括以上物品存在的任何痕迹或迹象。

（7）以下因素无关——

（a）建筑物、构造物或工事是在地上还是地下，

（b）遗址是在水面还是水下。

（8）本条规定适用于第 1 条。

3.“交易”的含义

（1）以下情形下，方可认定为“交易”：

（a）取得、处置、进口或出口该物品；

（b）同意他人实施（a）项所列行为；或

（c）安排他人实施上述行为，或协助他人同意第三人实施上述行为。

（2）“处置”是指购买、租用、借用或收受。

（3）“处分”是指出售、出租、出借或赠与。

（4）判断是否构成同意或协助实施上述行为，与发生地点是在英国还是他国无关。

（5）本条规定适用于第 1 条。

4. 海关起诉

（1）如果涉嫌进出口污点文物，由海关关长签发命令，启动交易有污点文物罪的调查程序。

（2）下列情形涉嫌交易污点文物罪：

（a）本法第 1 条规定的犯罪；

（b）煽动、企图或密谋实施此罪的行为。

（3）依据本条第 1 款启动的调查程序将以一位公职人员名义进行，但是可以由其他公职人员接替。

（4）当海关关长调查或提议调查：

（a）是否确信某人涉嫌与交易污点文物或进出口污点文物相关罪行，或

（b）是否应以此罪起诉某人，

有关事项应依据 1979 年《海关和国内税管理法》第 2 条的规定加以处置。

（5）本条规定不影响任何人（包括公职人员）依其他法律享有的权力。

（6）“公职人员”是指海关关长依据 1979 年《海关和国内税管理法》第 6（3）条由任命的人员。（已废除）

5. 法人犯罪

（1）如果法人实施了本法第 1 条规定的罪行，并被证明：

（a）系经高级职员同意或默许；或

（b）归咎于该高级职员的任何过失，

那么，该高级职员与法人均犯有此罪，须接受相应调查、承担相应责任。

（2）与法人相关的“公职人员”包括：

（a）法人的董事、经理、秘书或担任类似职位的人员；

（b）宣称行使上述职权的人。

（3）如果法人事务由其成员负责管理，那么第（1）款应适用于成员在履行属于法人董事职责时发生的违法行为。

6. 简称、开始实施日期及效力范围

（1）本法可引称为“《文物交易（犯罪）法2003》”。

（2）本法自通过之日起两个月后生效。

（3）本法不适用于苏格兰。

三、德　国

述 评

第二次世界大战后，联邦德国于1955年8月6日通过了《文化财产保护法》(又被称为《保护德国文化财产以防其出口法》[①])，该法沿革了1919年法律精神，确认以制定财产清单的形式防止文物外流。根据该法，应将那些一旦被运出德国就会“给德国文化财带来实质性损失”的艺术品和其他文化财产，列入其所在州的“国家珍贵文化财产清单”，清单将根据需要不断增补。清单中文化财产的转移、损坏、丢失都应通知有关当局，并且经批准才能出口这类文化财产。2007年，德国加入《1970年公约》，并于同年制定《文化财产归还法》，但是该法执行效果并不理想。为了更有效地保护德国的文化财产，2013年4月，德国联邦政府向国会提出修改现行文化财产保护法的建议，并提交了新法草案(以下简称新法案)。经过专业讨论和社会听证，2015年11月4日，德国联邦内阁正式批准了新法草案，并向德国立法机构提出修改法律的议案。联邦议会在2016年6月23日以绝对多数通过了新法草案，联邦参议院也于7月8日表决批准。新法草案最终于2016年8月5日的《联邦法律公报》第一部分第39项(第1914页至1936页)公布，并于2016年8月6日生效。

新法案融合早先颁布的《文化财产保护法》和《文化财产归还法》两部法律，旨在更有效地保护德国乃至世界各国的珍贵文化财产，严格监管本国文物艺术品市场，打击盗掘、盗窃文物的非法交易。尤为引人注意的是，新法案对文物进出境作出了严格的限制，即使在欧盟内部文物艺术品也不能再自由流动，交易文物艺术品的年代、价值、价格、来源等都成为是否获得出口许可的条件。新法案还详细规定了非法进出境文物的返还机制，以及相应的处罚。新法案被认为是当时世界范围内史上最严文物进出境法案，没有

① 国家文物局法制处：《外国保护文化财法律文件选编》，紫禁城出版社，1995年8月。

之一。

事实上新法案甫一公布，便遭到来自文物艺术品经销商、收藏家、艺术家甚至博物馆等多方面的强烈抵制与反对。国际古代艺术品经销商协会（International Association of Dealers in Ancient Art，IADAA）主席认为，新法案会成为“非欧洲艺术品交易的终结”。11 位德国主要博物馆馆长曾以公开信的形式明确反对新法案执行，信中表示“大批文物正因此而远离德国，损失巨大且无法挽回”。尽管如此，新法案终获通过，在维护文物安全与促进文物艺术品市场所谓繁荣的博弈中，德国政府和立法机构显然选择了前者，他们无疑意识到肩上那份沉甸甸的责任。

根据新法案，国家文化财产受法律保护，避免流失。其中“文化财产”是指具有文化、历史或考古价值，或者是与文化遗产相关、具有古生物学、人类学、钱币学或科学价值的物品或物品总和。而国家文化财产是指有如下特征的文化财产：登记于国家珍贵文化财产名录中的；保存在一个公共法定的文化财产保管机构中，属于大众资产的；保存在一家公共资助的文化财产保管机构中，属于该机构的资产；联邦或州艺术收藏品的一部分。

那些对于德国、各州，或其历史地区的文化财产有着特别重要的意义，是德国文化的标志，以及它的外流会对德国文化财产造成巨大损失，因此让其留在德国境内才能确保公共文化的利益，这样的国家文化财产将被最高州立机关登记于国家珍贵文化财产名录，如果该文化财产的创作者或生产者仍在世，只有在征得本人同意的情况下才能登录。同时，如果某件文化财产存在部分毁坏、保存在国内的不同地方，或部分保存在国外等情况，登录也不具有强制性。

德国的文物保护机构包括：（1）州最高主管机关，由各州通过法律或法规指定，负责文化财产保护，管理文化财产交易的主管部门。（2）联邦文化和媒体最高管理局，负责欧盟成员国之间联系和协作的中央机构。（3）管理委员会，联邦和各州共同成立，由两名联邦文化和媒体最高管理局的代表和每个州各一名代表组成，便于新法案执行以及确保各州的统一管理进行协调，尤其是决定国家珍贵文化财产名录公布的基本原则，决定共同程序的基本原则，以及联邦与各州之间的协作。此外，管理委员会还为联邦文化和媒体最高管理局提供门户网站运营方面的咨询。海关部门也在其权限范围对文化财产的进出境进行监管，并将其在监管职责范围内所收集信息提交给主管部门。关于德国文物进出境法规及管理制度的规定详见条文。

《保护文化财产法案》①*

自 2016 年 7 月 31 日始

联邦议会在经联邦参议院同意后通过下列法案：

（余建立　翻译校对）

第一项
保护文化财产法案
（文化财产保护法－KGSG）

第一章　总　则

第 1 条　适用范围

本法规定了

1. 保护国家文化财产免于外流，
2. 文化财产的进口和出口，
3. 文化财产的流通，
4. 非法进口的文化财产的返还，
5. 非法出口的文化财产的返还，以及
6. 国际借用中的返还承诺。

① 本法律的第 1 项用于落实欧洲议会和理事会于 2014 年 5 月 15 日颁布的关于返还从成员国境内非法转移的文物的 2014/60/EU 指令和第 1024/2012 号条例（修订版）（2014 年 5 月 28 日的 ABl. L 159，S. 1）。

* 编者注：关于序号设置，尊重原文，即“（1）”为第一序位，即为“款”；“1”为第二序位，即为“项”；“a）”为第三序位，即为“目”。

第 2 条　定义

（1）本法所指

1. “考古文物”是指历史上由人类所创造或加工的，或者能说明历史上人类生活情况的物品或物品总和，它们目前或曾经位于地下或水域中，或者根据整体情况推测其位于此处，

2. “出口”是指将文化财产带出德国，

3. “第三国”是指非欧盟成员国，

4. “自主占有人”是指实际占有自己的文化财产的人，

5. “进口”是指将文化财产带入德国境内，

6. “他主占有人”是指实际占有他人的文化财产的人，

7. “海牙公约”是指 1954 年 5 月 14 日颁布的《关于在武装冲突情况下保护文化财产的海牙公约》（见《联邦法律公报》，第二部分，第 1233、1235 页），

8. “来源国”是指文化财产的产生地，或与文化财产有着十分密切关系，以至于在文化财产被送出其领土之时将其作为国家文化财产列入保护的成员国或缔约国，

9. 文化财产的“流通”是指以自身或他人名义出于商业目的供应、出售、中介介绍、销售、无偿转让或出让文化财产，或以其他方式进行的商业利用。

10. “文化财产”是指具有文化、历史或考古价值，或者是与文化遗产相关、具有古生物学、人类学、钱币学或科学价值的物品或物品总和，

11. “文化财产保管机构”是指联邦境内以保管和留存文化财产，以及为大众与文化财产的接触提供保障为主要目的的机构，尤其指博物馆、图书馆和档案馆，

12. “成员国”是指除了德意志联邦共和国以外的任何欧盟成员国，

13. “海牙公约议定书”是指 1954 年 5 月 14 日颁布的《武装冲突情况下保护文化财产公约议定书》（海牙）（见《联邦法律公报》，第二

部分，第 1233、1300 页），

14.“非法盗掘”是指违反国内外考古或古生物保护法的规定，尤其是在没有获得这些法律所规定的许可的情况下进行的挖掘，

15.“返还”是指将文化财产送还提出返还要求的国家境内，

16.“物品总和”是指多个属于同一整体的文化财产，尤其是档案馆馆藏，图书馆馆藏，遗产，收藏品或其中的部分，

17.“联合国教科文组织公约”是指《关于禁止和防止非法进出口文化财产和非法转让其所有权的方法的公约》（见《联邦法律公报》，第二部分，第 626、627 页），

18. 文化财产的转移

a）“暂时的”是指从一开始就定好的，最长为 5 年的期限，

b）“长期的”是指长于 5 年的期限，

19.“缔约国”是指除德意志联邦共和国以外的，受联合国教科文组织公约约束的国家，

20.“国家珍贵文化财产名录”是指一个登记国家珍贵文化财产的名录。

（2）本法范畴内不属于进出口的情况

1. 根据 1994 年 6 月 27 日颁布的《刑事案件中国际法律援助法》第 66 条的规定通过法律援助返还文化财产的情况，该法律最近一次在 2015 年 8 月 31 日修改了第 163 条规定（见《联邦法律公报》，第一部分，第 1474 页），

2. 按照第 5 章规定返还非法转移的文化财产，以及

3. 基于双边协定将文化财产返还给另一个国家，或从另一个国家返还。

第 3 条　主管部门

（1）除非本法另有规定，本法所指的主管部门是指各州的主管部门。由各州通过法律或法规指定主管部门。

（2）根据欧洲议会和理事会于 2014 年 5 月 15 日颁布的关于返还从成员国境内非法转移的文物的 2014/60/EU 指令第 4 条和对第 1024/2012 号条

例（修订版）（2014 年 5 月 28 日的 ABl. L 159，S. 1）的修订，以及欧洲议会和理事会于 2014 年 5 月 15 日颁布的关于返还从成员国境内非法转移的文物的 2014/60/EU 指令和对第 1024/2012 号条例（修订版）（2015 年 6 月 12 日的 ABl. L 147，S. 24）的修订，德意志联邦共和国负责成员国之间联系和协作的中央机构是联邦文化和媒体最高管理局。

第 4 条　文化财产保护门户网站

（1）联邦文化和媒体最高管理局负责建设和维护一个关于文化财产保护的中央门户网站。该门户网站主要用于大众教育并确立文化财产保护的透明度，主要通过下列方式：

1. 阐述文化财产保护的任务和目标，
2. 阐述国内和国际文化财产保护法律的基本原则，
3. 通过准备表格和说明手册对管理流程等提供支持，
4. 受保护文化财产的档案数据库，以及
5. 主管部门和联系人的信息。

（2）由联邦文化和媒体最高管理局以及各州的最高主管机关负责提供网络数据。

（3）联邦和各州成立一个管理委员会以便本法执行以及确保各州管理统一协调，尤其是

1. 按照第 16 条，决定国家珍贵文化财产名录公布的基本原则，
2. 按照第 79 条，决定共同程序的基本原则，以及
3. 联邦与各州之间的协作。

此外，管理委员会还为联邦文化和媒体最高管理局提供门户网站运营方面的咨询。委员会由两名联邦文化和媒体最高管理局的代表和每个州各一名代表组成。

（4）管理委员会做决定时采取多数票制。若决定与本法规定的各州任务无关的问题，可不考虑联邦文化和媒体最高管理局代表的投票。若某决定获得的票数大于总票数的四分之三，那么该决定就对所有州都有约束力。若管理委员会成员中不到四分之三的人反对某决定，则可开展书面

形式的决定流程。

（5）管理委员会将出具一份议程用以对更多流程问题和各项任务的详细规定进行说明。

第二章　保护文化财产免于外流

第一节　将国家文化财产纳入保护

第 5 条　基本原则

国家文化财产作为德国的文化财产受本法保护，免于其流出国境。

第 6 条　国家文化财产

（1）国家文化财产是指有如下特征的文化财产，

1. 登记于国家珍贵文化财产名录中，
2. 保存在一个公共法定的文化财产保管机构中，属于大众资产，
3. 保存在一家公共资助的文化财产保管机构中，属于该机构的资产，或
4. 是联邦或州艺术收藏品的一部分。

（2）只有在出借方或寄存者对主管机关表示同意的情况下，保存于公共法定文化财产保管机构或主要由公共资助的机构的文化财产在出借和寄存合约期限内同样被视为国家文化财产。出借方或寄存者可随时撤销其许可。按照第 69 和 70 条，机构须告知出借方或寄存者关于放弃作为国家文化财产进行保护的法律后果。在出借或寄存合约终止或到期之时保护也同时终止。

第 7 条　国家珍贵文化财产的登录

（1）在下列情况下，由州最高主管机关将某个文化财产登记于国家珍贵文化财产名录，

1. 它对于德国的、各州的，或其历史地区的文化财产有着特别重要

的意义，是德国文化的标志，以及

2. 它的外流会对德国文化财产造成巨大损失，因此让其留在德国境内才能确保公共文化的利益。

在世创作者或生产者的作品只有在征得本人同意的情况下才能登录。

（2）根据第 1 款所述，若某物品的某些部分满足第 1 款列出的标准，则可将其登记于国家珍贵文化财产名录。在下列情况时，其登录不具有强制性，

1. 部分毁坏，

2. 保存在国内的不同地方，或

3. 部分保存在国外。

（3）州最高主管机关负责国家珍贵文化财产的登录，在启动该文化财产登录程序之际介入直到确定登录。

（4）对属于教会和宗教团体法人的文化财产进行登录，须遵照第 9 条规定。

第 8 条　事后登录

（1）若违反第 24 条的规定已将文化财产出口，当满足第 7 条第 1、2 款的前提条件时，则在出口之后也可由州最高主管机关将其录到进国家珍贵文化财产名录中。

（2）登录的管辖权取决于其在德国境内最后长期存放地。若无法确定该地点，则由联邦文化和媒体最高管理局决定由哪个州的最高机关来负责。同时也要从历史或其他方面的因素考虑该文化财产与管辖地的关系。

（3）若州最高主管机关在文化财产被非法出口并知道其新的存放地 1 年以内没有启动登录程序，则事后登录国家珍贵文化财产的权限将被终止。

（4）按照第 1 款所述，登录程序一旦启动，该文化财产就视同为国家文化财产，直至登录决定的确立。

第 9 条　属于教会和宗教团体资产的文化财产

（1）教会和宗教团体法人可向州最高主管机关提出申请，将其资产中的

文化财产登录到国家珍贵文化财产名录。对此适用第 7 条第 1 款和第 2 款。

（2）若按第 8 条规定进行事后登录，只能在第 8 条第 3 款所述的期限内提出申请。若州最高主管机关确定可提出第 1 款所述申请，须立即告知教会或宗教团体法人。

（3）教会和宗教团体法人可向州最高主管机关提出申请，针对文化财产保管机构的物品以及其礼拜仪式室的库存清单，只有在将教会或宗教团体法人的资助转为公共资助的情况下，才适用第6条第1款第3项的规定。

第 10 条　对于从国外借入和返还至德国境内的文化财产进行登录的例外情况

（1）对于曾经位于德国境内，并且在 2016 年 8 月 6 日之前有 5 年以上留存于德国境外并在 2016 年 8 月 6 日之后重新进入德国境内的文化财产，若按照第 7 条规定将其登录，那么在文化财产保管机构申请的情况下，州最高主管机关可在进口之前向文化财产的所有者保证不会按照第 7 条规定将该文化财产登录到国家珍贵文化财产名录中，前提是所有者保证该文化财产至少有 5 年

1. 不间断地留存在德国境内，以及

2. 提出申请的机构以出借的形式公开展出或提供研究。

（2）州最高主管机关可对其保证附加条件，即文化财产保管机构按照第 1 款的规定与文化财产所有者签订一份潜在购买该文化财产的合约。

（3）按照第 1 款所述由州最高主管机关提出的保证可附加条款，即确保遵守第 1 款第 1 和 2 项所述的前提条件。也允许有其他附加条款。

（4）州最高主管机关针对第 1 款所述的保证可与所有者签订一份公共法律的合约。

（5）若在第 1 款所述的约定期限到期后将文化财产出口，须遵守第 24 条第 1 款第 2 项所述的保密义务。

（6）若违反第 1 款规定的针对保证的附加条款，或违反按照第 4 款签订的公共法律合约将文化财产出口，即视为非法出口文化财产。若所有者在出口时违反第 1 款所述的与主管机关或文化财产保管机构签订的协议，

也同样视为非法出口。

（7）暂住或住址在国外的出借方与国内文化财产保管机构之间签订出借合约，除非出现文化财产按照第 1 款返还的情况，则州最高主管机关可在借入方申请的情况下在文化财产进口之前向出借方作出保证，在出借合约终止后的 6 个月内不会启动国家珍贵文化财产的登录程序。针对在 2016 年 8 月 6 日之前因上述出借合约而位于国内的文化财产，在出借合约到期后的 6 个月内，第 7 条的第 1 和 2 款不适用。依照本款第 1 和 2 句所述，出借合约终止后的 6 个月内的出口不受第 24 条第 1 款第 2 项规定的保密义务的约束。

第 11 条　已登录文化财产的地点变更

（1）若列入国家珍贵文化财产名录的文化财产从一个州转移至另一个州的时间短于 1 年，仍保留其列入国家珍贵文化财产名录的效力。

（2）若列入国家珍贵文化财产名录的文化财产转移至另一个州的时间超过 1 年，则将列入转入州的国家珍贵文化财产名录。直接占有人须及时以书面或电子的形式通知现今州最高主管机关文化财产变更地点和变更时间。

第 12 条　国家珍贵文化财产的税收优惠，因经济困境而出售的补偿

（1）列入国家珍贵文化财产名录的文化财产可按照下列规定获得征税优惠

1. 在 2016 年 7 月 31 日（见《联邦法律公报》，第一部分，第 1914 页）的法律第 8 项中关于继承和赠与税法第 13 条第 1 款第 2 项 b 目 bb 的规定，以及

2. 在 2016 年 7 月 31 日（见《联邦法律公报》，第一部分，第 1914 页）的法律第 7 项中关于所得税法第 10g 条的规定。

（2）依照第 23 条的规定属于禁止长期性出口的国家珍贵文化财产，若被所有者因经济困境而被迫出售，则该文化财产所在州的最高主管机关须在与联邦文化和媒体最高管理局意见一致的前提下按照第 1 款的规定给

予税收优惠补偿。

第 13 条 撤销登记

（1）若登录国家珍贵文化财产名录的文化财产相关状态发生了重大改变，州最高主管机关可依据职权或在占有人申请的情况下撤销其登录。

（2）若在法律上或经相关当事人确认，属于 1933 年 1 月 30 日至 1945 年 5 月 8 日期间被纳粹从其原所有者手中夺走并且可能会出口到德国境外的文化财产，可依照第 1 款所述认定其状态发生了重大改变，以便能将其返还给在德国境外生活的在世原所有者或其继承者。

（3）若依照第 11 条第 2 款将文化财产转入另一个州的名录内，则该州最高主管机关应在作出撤销决定之前给予原登录州最高主管机关发表意见的机会。

（4）撤销登录的程序适用第 14 条第 1 至 5 款的规定。

第二节 程序和合作义务；公布

第 14 条 登录程序

（1）依据职权或在所有者提出申请的情况下可启动国家珍贵财产的登录程序。向州最高主管机关提出的申请须包括

1. 文化财产的名称，
2. 所有者和占有人的姓名和地址，
3. 提出申请时的保存地点，
4. 满足第 7 条第 1 款第 1 和 2 项登录条件的理由。

（2）州最高主管机关召集一个独立的专家委员会。委员会由 5 名专家组成，任期 5 年，并可重复委任。委员会成员主要考虑文化财产保管机构、科学界、艺术交易和古董界以及私人收藏家界的专业人员。这些领域的机构和组织可对委员会成员的委任提出建议。其中一名专业人员由联邦文化和媒体最高管理局推荐。依照第 4 条规定，州专家委员会的组成情况须在门户网站上公布。委员会在作出决定之前也可听取外部专业人员的意见。

（3）只有在与专家委员会协商的情况下才能对文化财产进行登录。州最高主管机关在与专家委员会协商一致后，在作出决定之前，还须听取文化财产所有者的意见。

（4）若文化财产出于历史原因还与其他州有着特殊的联系，那么负责的州最高主管机关在作出将其登录到国家珍贵文化财产名录的决定之前应给予其他州发表意见的机会。

（5）为了确保国家的整体利益，联邦文化和媒体最高管理局也可提出国家珍贵财产的登录申请。

（6）在州最高主管机关作出登录决定之时登录程序即行终止。若在启动程序之后的 6 个月内未作出决定，则视为在没有登录的情况下终止程序。若所有者与州最高主管机关进行谈判，所有者诉诸法律程序，以及按照第 2 款第 7 句征求外部专业人员意见的特殊情况，那么该期限将被取消。此外若所有者没有按照第 15 条规定履行其合作义务或程序被拖延，该期限也将取消。若程序在未登录的情况下被终止并且按照第 17 条规定对终止做了公布，则只有在导致程序终止的情况发生重大变化时才可重启新的登录程序，在其他州也一样。

（7）若所有者能证明文化财产不在第 24 条第 1 款第 1 项规定的年限和价值范围内，可根据第 1 款的规定在阐述其合法权益并确保叙述完整性和真实性的情况下提出申请，由主管机关认定该文化财产不具备登录到国家珍贵文化财产名录的条件。主管机关可按照第 2 款的规定召集专家委员会介入。第 4 款和第 6 款第 5 句也同样适用。对于有此认定的文化财产，在出口时不受第 24 条第 1 款第 2 项规定的保密义务的约束。

第 15 条　登录过程中的合作义务

（1）在国家珍贵文化财产登录过程中，所有者，或直接占有人对州最高主管机关有如下义务

1. 告知州最高主管机关用于鉴定文化财产所需的资料、所有权状况和保存地点，
2. 提供文化财产的图片或由州最高主管机关或其委托人拍摄照片，

以及

3. 授予或委托州最高主管机关非独有的、无时间限定的对用于国家珍贵文化财产登录的鉴定资料和图片进行复制和公开的国际权利。

著作权法规定的效力不受影响。

（2）所有者，或直接占有人在登录过程中有义务按照第 1 款第 1 项的规定向州最高主管机关及时告知其所提供信息出现的任何更改。

第 16 条　国家珍贵文化财产名录的维护和公布

（1）各州按照第 79 条第 1 款第 1 句规定的通用程序维护国家珍贵文化财产名录并按照第 4 条在门户网站集中和跨州公布。

（2）所有者或占有人的个人信息以及已登录文化财产的地点位置不得公开。若文化财产定名需要这些信息，则无此限定。

（3）联邦文化和媒体最高管理局在公布时须通过有组织的技术措施，确保公布期间的登录工作不受影响，保持完整性和即时性，并可随时对其来源进行归类。

（4）公布途径适用《电子政务法》第 15 条第 2 款第 1 至 3 项。

（5）依照第 4 条第 4 款对所有州均有约束力的管理委员会决议规定名录维护和公布的具体细节。

第 17 条　公布

（1）州最高主管机关须在联邦司法部公报上公布每一次国家珍贵文化财产登录流程的启动和终止、登录的撤销和变更，并通知有关当事人。

（2）适用第 16 条第 2 款。

第三节　禁止损坏和通知义务

第 18 条　禁止损坏

（1）禁止对登录到国家珍贵文化财产名录的文化财产进行破坏、损坏，或是明显及长期改变其外观，除非是按照经过认证的科学标准进行专业的保养和修复或进行研究。《刑法典》第 304 条第 1 和第 2 款的效力不受影响。

（2）若针对某文化财产启动国家珍贵文化财产登录程序，则第 1 款的规定也同样适用。

第 19 条　通知义务

（1）已登录的国家珍贵文化财产直接占有人有义务在文化财产出现遗失、破坏、损坏或外观出现了明显和长期的改变时及时通知当地州最高主管机关。在占有权变更时，新的直接占有人代替之前的占有人承担通知义务。

（2）若文化财产的所有者和直接占有人并非同一人，则按照第 1 款规定的通知义务同样适用于所有者。

（3）在所有权变更时，由新的文化财产所有者代替之前的所有者承担及时通知州最高主管机关所有权变更的义务。

（4）若对文化财产启动国家珍贵文化财产登录程序，适用第 1 至 3 款的规定。

第三章　文化财产的流通

第一节　基本原则

第 20 条　文化财产流通自由

若本法律或其他法规，尤其是欧盟的有效法律文件中没有禁止或限制的情况下，文化财产可进行进出口和流通。

第二节　出口

第 21 条　出口禁令

禁止出口文化财产的情况有：

1. 已启动国家珍贵文化财产登录程序但尚未作出最终决定的文化财产，
2. 该文化财产没有获得第 22、23、24、27 条第 1 至 3 款规定的许可或按照第 25、26 或 27 条第 4 款授予的许可，
3. 按照第 32 条第 1 款所述非法进口的文化财产，
4. 按照第 33 条第 1 款作了保证的文化财产，或
5. 按照第 81 条第 4 款被截获的文化财产。

第 22 条　国家文化财产暂时性出口许可

（1）按照第 6 条规定，将国家文化财产暂时性出口至成员国或第三国须获得许可。

（2）只有在申请人能提供保证出口的文化财产完好无损且在规定期限内返回德国境内的情况下才会授予许可。

（3）按照第 6 条第 1 款第 1 项规定登记国家珍贵文化财产名录的州或按照第 6 条第 1 款第 2 至 3 项规定提出申请之时由文化财产所在州的最高主管机关负责授予许可。若申请人为拥有多个地址的法人，则其位于德国境内的主要地址即为受理地。州最高主管机关可根据州在法律将管辖权转交给另一个州的最高主管机关。

（4）所有者或委托的第三方可申请出口许可。

（5）通过胁迫、贿赂或舞弊手段，或通过错误或不完整的信息骗取的许可无效。

第 23 条　国家文化财产长期性出口许可

（1）按照第 6 条规定，将国家文化财产长期性出口至成员国或第三国须获得许可。

（2）若判断个别情况下会对德国文化财所有权益产生重大影响，将拒绝其许可。

（3）若在法律上或经相关当事人确认，属于 1933 年 1 月 30 日至 1945 年 5 月 8 日期间被纳粹从其原所有者手中夺走并且可能会出口到德国境外的

文化财产，则将对其授予许可，以便能将其归还给在德国境外生活的在世原所有者或其继承者。

（4）联邦文化和媒体最高管理局负责许可的授予。在决定之前须听取州最高主管机关和专家委员会的意见。关于专家委员会的组成适用第 14 条第 2 款的规定。若出现地点变更，按照第 11 条第 2 款规定还须听取原先负责登录的州最高主管机关的意见。

（5）在授予长期出口许可时，按照第 6 条第 1 款规定对其保护也随之终止。登录的文化财产在出口之后由当前所在州的最高主管机关将其从国家珍贵文化财产名录中撤销。

（6）若拒绝对登录的文化财产授予长期出口许可，联邦文化和媒体最高管理局按照第 4 款规定通知负责的州最高主管机关。在所有者提出申请时，联邦文化和媒体最高管理局和按照本款第 1 句规定通知的主管机关在州文化基金会的组织管理下，权衡各方利益，12 个月内公开说明德国境内有购买意向或适合保存该文化财产的文化财产保管机构的条件。这些条件主要有：

1. 说明该文化财产适合由哪个文化财产保管机构保存，
2. 在考虑所有者按照第 11 条第 1 款规定的税收优惠或其他利益的情况下确定一个合适的价格，
3. 说明文化财产保管机构按照第 1 项规定是否可以以及在何时可以因购入文化财产而获得来自公共和私人基金多大额度的资助，
4. 关于购买意向的其他安排。

在按照第 2 项规定确定合适的价格时，各州的文化基金会可邀请外部专业机构介入。

（7）若按照第 6 款规定说明了购买的条件，则文化财产保管机构可按照第 6 款第 1 项规定并在资金到位的情况下向所有者发出购买报价。若所有者证明他因经济困境而提出出口申请，则参与的联邦和州立机关将设法确保购置资金的到位，文化财产保管机构将提交一份购买报价。第 12 条第 2 款的效力不受影响。

（8）所有者可按照第 7 款规定在 6 个月内接受报价。若购买不成立，可在上一次出口申请提出 5 年后重新提交出口申请。

（9）特殊情况下向州提出申请时，联邦文化和媒体最高管理局按照第 1 款规定基于所有者和州最高主管机关之间的公共合约对未来才会发生的出口行为授予许可，前提是满足第 10 条第 1 款第 1 和 2 项关于至少 15 年的前提条件。联邦文化和媒体最高管理局应授予的许可并不取决于德国境内的机构与文化财产所有者之间是否拥有关于文化财产购买意向的合约。允许订立其他附加条款。

（10）适用第 22 条第 4 和第 5 款。

第 24 条　文化财产获得出口许可的义务；规定授权

（1）下列情况下文化财产的出口须获得许可

1. 出口至欧盟第 116/2009 号理事会条例所规定的第三国，

2. 出口至某成员国，该文化财产不符合第 2 款关于出口至（欧盟）内部市场的标准并且其所有权不属于创作者或生产者。

（2）对面向（欧盟）内部市场的出口适用第 116/2009 号理事会条例附件 I 中关于年份最低限定和价值最低限定翻倍的规定，在下列分类下文化财产的最低年份适用附录 I 的分类 A：

1. 编号 3：75 年和 300000 欧元;

2. 编号 4 和 7：75 年和 100000 欧元;

3. 编号 5，6，8 和 9：75 年和 50000 欧元;

4. 编号 12：50 年和 500000 欧元;

5. 编号 14：150 年和 100000 欧元;

6. 编号 15：100 年和 100000 欧元。

当硬币数量较大，对于考古学不具有重要价值且没有被成员国列入单独保护对象时，就不属于第 116/2009 号理事会条例附录 I 类别 1 规定的考古物品。此外还适用按照第 2 款第 1 项第 116/2009 号理事会条例附录 I 中列出的分类。

（3）联邦政府负责文化和媒体的成员有权在联邦参议院许可的情况下按法律规定提高价值限定，以适应第 2 款第 1 句所述类别市场价格的变化。

（4）按照第 1 款规定，文化财产须获得许可的认证价值为其最近 3 年内进行购买和出售时的支付价格，其他情况下则为提出申请时的国内估算价值。

（5）在对申请作出决定之时若不存在按照第 21 条第 1、3、4 和 5 项的出口禁令，则可授予许可。

（6）若按照第 1 款第 1 项所述，第 116/2009 号理事会条例附录 I 第 2 条中没有其他的管辖权规定，则按照第 1 款规定由提出申请之时文化财产所在州的最高主管机关授予许可。将申请人的住址或地址认定为文化财产非确定留存地点。适用第 22 条第 3 款第 2 句。

（7）由州最高主管机关在收到完整申请材料后的 10 个工作日内作出是否授予许可的决定。该州立机关可按照州法律规定将管辖权转移给另一个州的机关。

（8）若证明该文化财产只是暂时在德国境内留存最多 2 年，则无须按照第 1 款第 2 项获取许可。但不适用于下列情况的文化财产

1. 非法进口的（第 28 条）

2. 之前没有按照第 1 款规定获得许可就出口的。

（9）适用第 22 条第 4 和 5 款。

第 25 条　一般性公开许可

（1）对于文化财产的暂时性出口，州最高主管机关可在文化财产保管单位提出申请的情况下授予其有时间限定的一般许可（一般性公开许可），前提是该机构定期将其部分藏品进行临时性公开展出、修复或研究。对一般性公开许可可附加条款。

（2）在出口至成员国或第三国时可授予一般性公开许可。可在一次决定中授予两份许可。

（3）申请人必须提供保证，出口的文化财产完好无损且在规定的期限内重新进口。

（4）一般性公开许可的有效期不得超过 5 年。州最高主管立机关按照第 4 条规定在文化财产保护门户网站上公布获得一般性公开许可的文化财产

保管机构。

（5）文化财产保管机构藏品中的某些部分可不受最高州立机关授予的一般性公开许可的管辖。

第 26 条　特殊公开许可

（1）对于文化财产定期的暂时性出口，州最高主管机关可在所有者或法定直接占有人申请的情况下授予其有时间限定的、针对特定文化财产的许可（特殊公开许可），前提是该文化财产会在国外被反复利用或展出。

（2）在出口至成员国或第三国时可授予特殊公开许可。可在一次决定中授予两份许可。

（3）只有在申请人提供保证，出口的文化财产完好无损且在规定的期限内重新进口的情况下才会授予许可。

（4）特殊公开许可的有效期不得超过 5 年。

第 27 条　教会文化财产的出口许可

（1）对于属于教会或宗教团体法人的国家文化财产的暂时性出口，按照第 22 条的规定由教会或宗教团体在州最高主管机关同意的情况下授予许可。

（2）在按照第 23 条规定开展符合第 6 条第 1 款第 1 项以及第 9 条第 1 款规定的国家文化财产长期性出口许可程序时，对属于教会或宗教团体法人资产的文化财产，不受第 23 条第 4 款第 2 句的制约，仅需听取相关教会或宗教团体法人的意见。若与第 9 条第 3 款规定的国家文化财产相关，则教会或宗教团体法人在州最高主管机关同意的情况下授予许可。

（3）教会或宗教团体法人可提出申请，让属于其资产的文化财产按第 24 条第 1 款第 2 项规定在出口至成员国时须获得许可。在此情况下可不按照第 8 条规定在事后列入国家珍贵文化财产名录。

（4）第 25 和 26 条适用于教会或宗教团体法人及其委托的机构和组织，只有在相关教会或宗教团体同意的情况下才能授予许可。

第三节　进口

第 28 条　进口禁令

禁止进口具有以下情形的文化财产

1. 被成员国或缔约国归类或定义为国家文化财产，并在违反其国家文化财产保护法规的情况下被带出境的文化财产，

2. 违反欧盟已公布生效的关于限制和禁止文化财产跨境转移的法案而被带出境的文化财产，或

3. 违反海牙公约议定书第 1 节第 1 项规定在武装冲突情况下被带出境的文化财产。

第 29 条　进口禁令的豁免

下列文化财产不适用进口禁令

1. 在 2016 年 8 月 6 日之前合法留存在德国境内，并且没有违背欧盟相关法案的规定，或

2. 按照海牙公约议定书第 2 节第 5 项为了在武装冲突情况下免受威胁而暂时寄存德国境内保管的文化财产。

第 30 条　进口合法性的证明

若文化财产被成员国或缔约国归入或定义为国家文化财产，则在进口该文化财产时须按照第 28 条第 1 项出具其从来源国合法出口期证明文件。该证明可以是来源国的出口许可，或者是其他能够证明该文化财产从来源国合法出口的文件。

第四节　文化财产的非法流通

第 31 条　文化财产的非法出口

（1）违反第 21 至 27 条的规定或违反欧盟关于限制或禁止文化财产跨境

转移的规定出口文化财产即为非法出口。

（2）在合法的暂时性出口期限到期后未返还，以及违反暂时性出口许可附加条款的情况均视为非法出口。

第 32 条　文化财产的非法进口

（1）下列文化财产进口行为视为非法：

1. 在违反其他国家文化财产保护法规的情况下将文化财产带出境

a）在 1992 年 12 月 31 日之后带出另一个成员国的国境，或

b）在 2007 年 4 月 26 日之后带出一个缔约国的国境，

2. 进口行为违反了第 28 条的规定，或

3. 进口行为违反了德意志联邦共和国的其他相关法规。

（2）若文化财产的来源地属于现今的多个国家并且没有明确其归属，按照其中任何一个相关国家的法律属于无出口许可的情况下被出口，即视为非法出口。

第 33 条　文化财产的扣留

（1）主管机关可在下列情况下扣留文化财产，

1. 若有足够证据证明该文化财产

a）违反了第 21 条的禁令被出口，或

b）违反了第 28 条的禁令被进口，或

2. 在进口时不能出具第 30 条规定的文件。

（2）文化财产被扣留后，目前的保证受托人须出具证明对被扣留的文化财产以及被扣留的原因进行说明。若无法出具证明，（主管机关）会提供一份扣留记录，同样要注明为何无法出具证明。

（3）对文化财产扣留的异议和撤销请求不具备延迟效力。根据民法典第 136 条的规定，扣留的效力禁止转让；该禁令还包含其他的转让指令。

（4）按第 62 条的规定，主管机关在扣留文化财产后须立即通知联邦文化和媒体最高管理局。

（5）禁止破坏、损坏扣留的文化财产，或明显的、长期的改变其外观。

第 34 条　被扣留文化财产的保管

（1）被扣留的文化财产由主管机关进行保管。在扣留目的不受影响的情况下，可以让被撤销支配权的人员，或第三方对其进行保管。在此情况下，只有在获得主管机关书面或电子许可的情况下才能将文化财产转交给其他人或机构。

（2）在保管开始和结束时，主管机关或由其委托的第三方须记录文化财产被扣留时的状况。

（3）由主管机关下达或采取保管文化财产所需的措施。

第 35 条　撤销扣留

（1）在下列情况下由主管机关撤销文化财产的扣留，

1. 排除第 33 条第 1 款第 1 项所述的嫌疑，

2. 排除第 33 条第 1 款第 1 项 a 目所述的前提条件，

3. 若属于第 33 条第 1 款第 1 项 b 目所述的情况

a）明显不满足本法律第 5 章规定的返还要求的前提条件，或

b）达到本法律第 5 章规定的返还要求的时效，

4. 在第 33 条第 1 款第 1 项 b 目中所述的情况下兼顾第 50 条或 52 条的规定，以及

a）按照第 62 条第 1 款第 1 项或第 2 款第 1 项进行告知后的 6 个日历月内按照第 50 或 52 条提出了返还请求，

b）提出请求的成员国或缔约国与返还债务人之间协商一致，或

c）关于返还申诉的决定已具有法律效力，

5. 在第 33 条第 1 款第 1 项 b 目所述的情况下，若按第 51 条提出了返还要求，则应进行返还，

6. 在第 33 条第 1 款第 1 项 b 目所述的情况下，若按第 53 条提出了返还要求，则应进行返还，或

7. 在第 33 条第 1 款第 2 项所述的情况下排除了文化财产非法进口的嫌疑。

（2）若成员国或缔约国已按照第 59 条提出了返还请求，或明确了哪个成员国或缔约国可提出该请求，则只有在获得该成员国或缔约国同意的情况下才能撤销扣留，除非在此期间扣留的理由已不存在。

第 36 条　被扣留的文化财产的归还

（1）若撤销了扣留，须归还文化财产

1. 在第 35 条第 1 款第 1 至 3、4 项 a 目以及第 7 项的情况下归还给自主占有人，

2. 在第 35 条第 1 款第 4 项 b 和 c 目的情况下归还给权利人，

3. 在第 35 条第 1 款第 5 项的情况下归还给相关的成员国或缔约国，或

4. 在第 35 条第 1 款第 6 项的情况下归还给来源地的主管机关。

（2）若是归还给自主占有人，则向其发出一个关于取件期限的通知。该期限将安排足够长的时间。通知应提示：若未在该期限内取回，将没收该文化财产。

第 37 条　被扣留文化财产的没收

（1）下列情况下，主管机关可将被扣留的文化财产没收，而不按照第 36 条第 1 款第 1 项的规定将文化财产归还给自主占有人，

1. 自主占有人不明并且无法以合理的开支查明，或

2. 自主占有人未在第 36 条第 2 款第 2 句规定的期限内取回文化财产。

按照州法律没收文化财产须公开，按照第 4 条规定在门户网站上公布。并且须按照第 62 条规定的职责立即通知联邦文化和媒体最高管理局。

（2）主管机关可将没收的文化财产交给一个文化财产保管机构保管。

第 38 条　没收的后果；补偿

（1）若文化财产被没收，意味着随着没收指令的下达，对该文化财产的占有和所有权转移给了国家。第三方的权利随着指令的下达而被撤销。

（2）因没收决定而被撤销了权利的所有者将因文化财产所有权转移给国家而获得与流通价格相当的合理货币补偿，除非发生第 3 款所述的情况将潜在的补偿转让给第三方。

（3）若文化财产的权利转让给了第三方，而该权利又随着没收被撤销，则第三方也将因文化财产所有权转移给国家而获得与流通价格相当的货币补偿。

（4）在第 2 款所述情况下，若出现下列情况则不再给予补偿

1. 所有者自己的草率行为致使触犯了文化财产被扣留和没收的条件，

2. 所有者在明知会被扣留的情况下获得文化财产，或

3. 扣留和没收的理由成立以及根据其他法律的规定，可在无补偿的情况下将文化财产从所有者处没收。

若不进行补偿的情况达到了不合理的程度，则第 1 句就不适用。

（5）在第 3 款所述情况下，若出现下列情况则不再给予补偿

1. 第三方自己的草率行为致使触犯了文化财产扣留和没收的条件，

2. 第三方在明知会被扣留的情况下获得文化财产，或

3. 扣留和没收的理由成立以及根据其他法律的规定，可在无补偿的情况下将文化财产从第三方处没收。

若不进行补偿的情况达到了不合理的程度，则第 1 句就不适用。

（6）按照第 2 或 3 款所述的补偿权在公布没收 30 年后失效。

第 39 条　扣留、保管、维护和返还的费用

因文化财产扣留、保管、维护和返还产生的必要费用和开支由被撤销支配权的人员承担。第 66 和 68 条的效力不受影响。具体金额由主管机关告知。

第四章　文化财产流通时的义务

第 40 条　流通禁令

（1）属于遗失、非法盗掘或非法进口的文化财产禁止流通。

（2）对按照第 1 款规定被禁止流通的文化财产进行义务和支配权的交易是无效的。

（3）禁止违反第 21 条的出口禁令对文化财产进行义务和支配权的交易。

（4）违反第 1 款所述禁令将文化财产带入流通领域的行为人有义务赔偿购买方因购买和维护文化财产产生的损失。若将文化财产带入流通领域的行为人可证明其并非故意违规，则上述规定不成立。

第 41 条　一般注意义务

（1）将文化财产带入流通领域的行为人有义务提前认真审查文化财产是否为如下情况

1. 遗失的，
2. 非法进口的，或
3. 非法盗掘的。

（2）第 1 款所述的一般注意义务适用于将文化财产带入流通领域的行为人，作为一个完全行为能力人不容许假定存在第 1 款中所述的行为。尤其是较早购买流通的文化财产的人，在如下情况时须特别考虑假定的情况是否属实，

1. 在没有充足理由的情况下，价格异乎寻常的低，或
2. 卖方在出售价格高于 5000 欧元时要求现金支付。

（3）必要的注意义务还包括审查用高昂费用获得的相关信息，或行为人在文化财产流通的同等状况下做其他审查。

第 42 条　商业流通时的注意义务

（1）在进行商业行为时将文化财产带入流通领域的行为人有义务按照第 41 条规定提前额外做到：

1. 明确转让人、交付人、买家或委托人的姓名和住址，
2. 制作一份能确定文化财产特征的说明和图片，
3. 审查文化财产的来历，
4. 审查能证明进出口合法的文件，

5. 审查关于进出口和交易的禁令和限制，

6. 审查文化财产是否被录入了公开的名录及数据库中，以及

7. 获得一份交付人或转让人的书面或电子声明，说明其合法拥有该文化财产。

第 1 款第 2 项规定的义务不影响著作权法规定的效力。根据合理的费用，尤其是按照经济合理性履行第 1 款第 3 至 6 项所规定的义务。

（2）第 1 款所述的额外注意义务在下列情况下不适用，

1. 除旧书买卖之外的商业性书籍贸易，以及

2. 图像和声音载体的商业贸易。

（3）第 1 款所述的额外注意义务对下列文化财产也不适用，

1. 非考古文物，以及

2. 价值不超过 2500 欧元。

若硬币数量较大且对考古学不具有重要价值时，按照第 1 项属于非考古文物。

标准价值即为购买时的支付价格，其他情况下则为有依据的国内估算价值。

第 43 条　商业流通时减轻注意义务

下列情况下会减轻注意义务，

1. 由文化财产的创作者或生产者将其投入流通，或

2. 直接从创作者或生产者处购买文化财产并将其带入流通领域，或

3. 替创作者或生产者将其创作的文化财产投入流通领域。

减轻注意义务包括第 41 条，以及第 42 条第 1 款第 1 和 2 项所述的义务。第 42 条第 2 和 3 款也适用。

第 44 条　商业流通时增加注意义务

商业流通中，在下列情况下第 42 条第 1 款第 3 句所述的文化财产合理费用标准不再适用，

1. 若可证明或假定文化财产是在 1933 年 1 月 30 日到 1945 年 5 月 8

日期间被纳粹从其原所有者手中夺走，除非将其归给其原所有者或其继承人或由其他重要法规对所有权的撤销做了规定，

2. 该文化财产来自于一个被国际博物馆委员会公布于文化财产破坏红名单上的成员国或缔约国，或

3. 涉及欧盟规定的进出口和流通禁令。

属于第 1 句中的文化财产不适用第 42 条第 3 款的规定。

第 45 条　记录和保存义务

（1）通过商业行为将文化财产带入流通领域的行为人有义务按照第 42 条的规定对其审查和论断进行记录。可以电子版的形式记录和保存相关文件。

（2）按照第 1 款所述的记录和相关文件以及记录人的证明须保存 30 年。适用第 1 款第 2 句的规定。

（3）若记录与第 42 条规定的审查和论断相符，并且按照第 42 条第 1 款第 2 项所述达到了本法规定的文化财产识别标准，则其他法律规定的记录也可用作第 1 款规定的记录。适用第 2 款第 1 句规定的保存期限。

第 46 条　告知义务

（1）通过商业行为将文化财产带入流通领域的行为人有义务在主管机关要求的情况下，

1. 出示第 45 条规定的记录，或

2. 告知第 41 条第 1 款所述的关于文化财产的信息。

按照第 1 款所述出示的记录和提供的信息仅限于主管机关按照法律规定履行其职责所需的信息。

（2）《工商业管理条例》第 29 条的效力不受影响。

第 47 条　违反的法律后果

若主管机关获知第 45 和 46 条第 1 款规定的记录保存义务和告知义务被屡次违反，将通知工商业监督机构根据《工商业管理条例》第 35 条对其信用进行审查。

第 48 条　买家的查看权

（1）若根据本法或基于民法的规定对买家提出了文化财产的返还要求，若是在 2016 年 8 月 6 日之后购买的文化财产，则其有权对按第 42 至 44 条规定进入流通领域的文化财产提出查看第 45 条所述记录的要求。

（2）在非司法要求的情况下也适用第 1 款的规定

1. 成员国或缔约国的返还要求，或

2. 因受纳粹迫害而被掠夺的文化财产。

第五章　非法进口的文化财产的返还

第一节　返还要求

第 49 条　公共法律范畴的返还要求

（1）按照本节规定提出的文化财产的返还要求属于公共法定的要求。民法要求的效力不受影响。

（2）返还债务人为直接自主占有人，非直接的他主占有人。

第 50 条　成员国提出的返还要求

在下列情况，若成员国提出请求将会返还，

1.1992 年 12 月 31 日之后违反成员国法律规定被带出其国境的文化财产，

2. 在被带出该成员国国境之前或之后，通过国际法或管理程序或欧盟工作基础协定（AEUV, 也称《里斯本条约》）第 36 条的规定被归入或定义为有艺术、历史或考古价值的国家文化财产。

第 51 条　因违反欧盟法律提出的返还要求

违反欧盟公报上公布的已生效法案而被非法进口的文化财产须返还给相关国家。

第 52 条　缔约国的返还要求

（1）下列情况下，若缔约国提出请求将会返还，

1. 属于联合国教科文组织公约第 1 条所规定的类别，

2. 2007 年 4 月 26 日之后违反缔约国的法律规定被带出其国境的文化财产，

3. 在被带出该缔约国国境之前，按照联合国教科文组织公约第 1 条或联合国教科文组织公约第 13 条 d 目的规定被归入或声明为不可转让的文化财产，以及

4. 因其来源于该缔约国，尤其是属于缔约国某家机构的藏品或符合第 60 条规定的情况。

（2）若未明确该文化财产是否在 2007 年 4 月 26 日之后被转移，则其具有在这一天之后被非法带出缔约国国境的嫌疑。只有在证明该文化财产在这一天之前就已位于德国境内、在国内市场或在第三国的情况下才能消除嫌疑。按照第 2 句，以及《管理程序法》第 27 条第 1 款，以及各州的管理程序法，须为此提交一份证明。由第 61 条第 1 款第 7 项以及第 62 条第 2 款中所述的主管机关在行政调解程序的范围内负责验收。

（3）若出具了关于文化财产在 2016 年 8 月 6 日之前位于德国境内或国内市场的证明，则不再适用本条第 1 款关于缔约国返还要求的规定，赔偿则适用 2007 年 5 月 18 日的文化财产返还法（见《联邦法律公报》，第一部分，第 757、2547 页）第 10 条在 2016 年 8 月 5 日之前的内容。

第 53 条　依照海牙公约的返还要求

（1）依照海牙公约第 1 章第 1 条，对于违反第 28 条第 3 项的规定在武装冲突情况下进口的文化财产，下列情况下须在武装冲突结束后按照海牙公约议定书第 1 节第 3 条的规定返还给来源地的主管当局，

1.1967 年 11 月 11 日之后被带出来源地，以及

2. 来源地的主管当局提出返还请求。

（2）依照海牙公约议定书第 2 节第 5 条被寄放的文化财产应在武装冲突

结束后返还，无需满足第 1 款第 1 和 2 项所述的前提条件。

第 54 条　适用的民法

（1）遵照本法规定返还至另一个成员国或缔约国境内的文化财产的所有者可按照该成员国或缔约国的规定自主决定。

（2）基于合法支配或通过强制执行或拘押执行而获得的权利与返还义务不冲突。

第 55 条　返还要求的期限和时效

（1）针对下列情况的文化财产提出的返还要求没有时效，

1. 按照 2014/60/EU 指令第 2 条第 8 款规定属于公共藏品的文化财产，或

2. 在成员国的教会或其他宗教机构的收藏名录中，受到该成员国相关法律规定，尤其是保护法规的约束。

第 1 项所述的返还要求 75 年后失效。按照第 2 项所述，若提出请求的成员国在其相关法律中规定返还要求不失效的话，该要求就不会失效。

（2）除了第 1 款所述的情况外，返还要求将在文化财产被非法带出请求成员国或缔约国国境的 30 年后失效。

（3）本节所述其他关于文化财产的返还要求都是 3 年后失效。

第 56 条　时效的开始

在提出请求的成员国或缔约国获知文化财产的存留地和确认返还债务人之时即为时效开始之时。

第 57 条　时效与失效期限的延滞和重启

（1）关于第 55 条第 1 款第 2 项所述的时效和期限适用民法典第 204、206 和 209 条关于时效延滞的规定，以及民法典第 212 条关于时效重启的规定。

（2）若请求成员国或缔约国由于国内动乱、武装冲突或其他类似情况而

无法提出有效要求，那么按照第 55 条第 1 款第 2 项所述的时效和期限将因不可抗力而被延滞。

第二节　返还程序

第 58 条　返还原则

返还可以通过行政调解程序协商达成，或者由申请国家进行返还诉讼实现。

第 59 条　返还申请

返还申请的提出：

1. 成员国根据第 50 条通过联邦文化和媒体最高管理局提出返还要求，或者
2. 根据第 51 至 53 条通过外交部的外交途径提出请求。

第 60 条　冲突的返还申请

如果多个成员国或者缔约国对同一个文化财产提出返还申请，并且无法查明，文化财产应归属于哪个成员国或缔约国，则只有当相关成员国或缔约国以书面形式取得一致意见，并已通知联邦文化和媒体最高管理局或外交部时，才能返还。

第 61 条　州的职责

（1）州最高主管机关的主要职责：

1. 对有非法嫌疑或者非法流通的文化财产进行调查，
2. 对相关文化财产的所有人或直接占有人进行调查，
3. 为申请返还的成员国或缔约国的调查提供支持，尤其是相关文化财产的所有人或直接占有人，
4. 对被扣留的文化财产采取维护措施，
5. 采取措施以防止文化财产的返还被撤销，

6. 在申请返还的成员国和返还债务人之间实施行政调解程序，以及

7. 返还文化财产时为联邦提供支持。

（2）关于第 1 款第 3 项规定的支持，只有当成员国根据第 62 条第 1 款第 3 项收到告知后 6 个月内通知主管机关，涉及 2014/60/EU 指令第 2 条第 1 项意义上的文化财产时，主管机关才有此义务。如果成员国在此期限内没有通知，则主管机关不再有义务，采取第 1 款第 4、5 项规定的措施。

第 62 条　最高联邦当局的职责

（1）联邦文化和媒体最高管理局有以下职责：

1. 告知相关成员国关于发现和扣留有非法进口嫌疑的文化财产，

2. 为申请返还的成员国和返还债务人之间的行政调解程序提供支持，以及

3. 当申请成员国提起返还诉讼时，通知其他成员国的中央机构。

（2）外交部与联邦文化和媒体最高管理局合作，有下列职责：

1. 告知相关成员国关于发现和扣留有非法进口嫌疑的文化财产，以及

2. 实施申请成员国和返还债务人之间的行政调解程序。

第 63 条　返还诉讼的准许

（1）只有在诉状中附有下列文件时，才允许申请成员国或缔约国对返还提出诉讼：

1. 文化财产的适当描述，包括下列信息

a）身份和来源，

b）入境的实际或推测时间，以及

c）联邦境内实际或推测的留存地点，

2. 一份关于该文化财产根据申请成员国或缔约国的法律规定或行政管理程序属于其国家文化财产的声明，以及

3. 一份关于该文化财产非法从申请成员国或缔约国的领土出口的声明。

（2）当将文化财产带出申请成员国或缔约国的领土在提起诉讼时不再是非法时，不允许提出返还诉讼。

第64条　行政扣留的费用

如果主管机关根据第33条的规定扣留了必须由法庭裁决返还的文化财产，则必须在法庭判决中裁定因返还和由主管机关扣留而产生的费用。

第65条　返还和维护措施的费用

（1）因返还而产生的费用由申请的成员国或缔约国承担。

（2）因对被扣留的文化财产采取维护措施而产生的费用由申请的成员国或缔约国承担。适用第64条的规定。

第三节　补偿和赔偿要求

第66条　返还的补偿

（1）如果直接自主占有人在取得文化财产时已采取必要注意，则其可以拒绝返还文化财产，直到申请的成员国或缔约国给予适当的补偿。

（2）无偿权利转让时，无论是权利转让人还是权利受让人都必须遵守取得时的必要注意。通过遗产继承获得时，继承人或受赠人必须同意承担被继承人未尽到的注意义务。

（3）在决定直接自主占有人在取得文化财产时是否已采取必要注意时，要考虑到所有情况，尤其是

1. 有关文化财产来源的文件，
2. 根据申请成员国或缔约国要求的出口许可，
3. 取得文化财产时各当事人的资格，
4. 购买价格，
5. 直接自主占有人查阅被偷窃的文化财产目录和通过合理费用能够获取的相关信息，以及
6. 作为一个完全行为能力人在同样情况下可能采取的任何其他

步骤。

（4）第 52 条第 3 款不受影响。

第 67 条　补偿金额

（1）补偿金额在考虑返还债务人的下列开支后确定：

1. 取得文化财产以及

2. 维护文化财产的必要措施。

补偿不得超过支出的费用。对错过的收益，不支付补偿。

（2）如果文化财产即使在返还后仍然为返还债务人所有，则申请的成员国或缔约国可以违背第 1 款的规定仅需偿还返还债务人因相信文化财产允许留在联邦境内而产生的费用。

第 68 条　申请成员国或缔约国的赔偿要求

（1）申请成员国或缔约国可以要求非法带入或者安排非法带入文化财产的人，赔偿返还程序中产生的费用。适用民法典第 840 条第 1 款。

（2）根据第 1 款的要求须在普通民事法院进行索赔。

第六章　返还非法出口的文化财产

第 69 条　对成员国的返还要求

（1）联邦文化和媒体最高管理局在与文化财产非法出口前长期所在州的最高主管机关协商后，根据相应成员国的规定对非法出口到该成员国领土的文化财产提出返还要求。如果无法确认文化财产在联邦领域内的最后长期存留地点，则由联邦文化和媒体最高管理局提出要求。

（2）主管文化和媒体的最高联邦当局对文化财产提起返还诉讼后应立即知会相关成员国的中央主管机构。

第 70 条　对缔约国的返还要求

（1）外交部在与联邦文化和媒体最高管理局取得一致后提出对非法出口

到缔约国领土的文化财产的返还要求。

（2）在联邦文化和媒体最高管理局提出返还要求之前，应与文化财产被非法出口前长期所在州的最高主管机关进行协商。

第 71 条　费用

（1）提出返还要求所产生的必要费用和垫款由非法出口文化财产的一方承担。适用民法典第 840 条第 1 款。

（2）由根据第 69、70 条提出返还要求的联邦当局来通知确定应该偿还的具体金额。

第 72 条　返还的文化财产的所有权

被非法出口并返回联邦境内的文化财产的所有人，根据德国实体法的规定确定。

第七章　国际租用往来中的返还承诺

第 73 条　具有法律约束力的返还承诺

（1）如果从国外临时借用文化财产用于联邦境内的公共展览或者其他形式的公共展示，包括为该目的所做的事先修复，或者出于文化财产的保存或科研机构的研究目的，则州最高主管机关可以在与联邦文化和媒体最高管理局协商后，就文化财产在联邦境内的停留期间作出具有法律约束力的返还承诺。返还承诺最长不应超过 2 年。

（2）借用人总部所在地的州最高主管机关负责给予具有法律约束力的返还承诺。若有多个借用地点，则由第一个借用地点的主管机关负责。

第 74 条　给予具有法律约束力的返还承诺

（1）根据借用人的申请，州最高主管机关可以与联邦文化和媒体最高管理局协商，在文化财产进口之前给予出借人返还承诺。申请可以书面或电子形式递交。

（2）返还承诺以书面形式进行的，使用术语“具有法律约束力的返还承诺”。

第 75 条　延长

（1）具有法律约束力的返还承诺可以根据借用人的申请在取得联邦文化和媒体最高管理局同意的情况下由州最高主管机关延长。即使通过延长申请一般也不应超过 2 年的最长期限。在合理的特殊情况下，在联邦境内停留的期限最多可以延长到 4 年。

（2）适用第 73 条第 2 款。

第 76 条　效力

（1）具有法律约束力的返还承诺使得，

1. 不能对出借人的返还要求提出第三方对文化财产主张权利的异议，以及

2. 不能引入国家珍贵文化财产登录程序。

返还承诺不能废除、退回或撤销，并且文化财产在联邦境内停留时间内可立即执行。

（2）将文化财产返还给出借人之前，但在给予返还承诺的最长期限内，根据本法律或其他法律规定不允许对文化财产提起返还、扣留、抵押和查封的法律诉讼以及行政处分或扣留。

（3）租用合同到期后的出口不受第 24 条所述许可义务的限制。

第八章　数据保护，通用程序，海关

第 77 条　含个人数据的信息的收集与处理

（1）在下列必需的情况下，负责实施本法的联邦和州行政机关可以收集、处理并使用含个人数据的所有信息

1. 依照本法、保护可移动文化财产的地方法规、欧盟和欧共体现行法规，履行含有禁止和限制内容的职责时，以及

2. 依照基于本法制定的法规履行职责时。

（2）保护个人数据的相关规定不受影响。

第 78 条　向主管机关传送含个人数据的信息资料

（1）根据 2003 年 1 月 14 日公布的《德国联邦数据保护法》官方文本第 2 条（《联邦法律公报》，第一卷，第 66 页），2015 年 2 月 25 日最近一次修改的第一章（《联邦法律公报》，第一卷，第 162 页）的规定，公共机构可以将含有个人数据的信息资料传送给需要这些信息资料的联邦及州的行政机关，以保障其履行本法第 77 条所述的职责。

（2）当联邦及州相关行政机关履行其职责，需要获取违反进出口规定已经或将要进口或出口的文化财产的相关信息，公共机构应立即提供。

（3）负责启动和实施处罚或罚款程序的有关部门应根据法律规定，将检察机关、法院或负责对违法行为进行追踪和惩处的有关管理机关审理与办结涉及文化财产的处罚和罚款程序的相关情况，立即告知负责的联邦及州行政机关。对于最高只可判处 1000 欧元罚款的违法行为，其程序不适用第 1 句的规定。

（4）收到来自另一成员国或缔约国的法律协助请求时，适用第 3 款规定的指示，告知联邦文化和媒体最高管理局。在收到缔约国法律协助请求时，应告知外交部。

第 79 条　联邦及州的通用程序

（1）为全面保护国家文化财产，根据《德国电子政务法》第 11 条的规定，联邦与州共同实施通用程序，且有权在通用程序中处理含个人数据的信息。

（2）参与通用程序的联邦及州的相关机关分别对各自收集、处理和使用数据的合法性负责。

（3）参与通用程序的联邦及州的相关机关将受到《德国联邦数据保护法》的约束。根据《德国电子政务法》第 11 条第 5 款第 2 句的规定，经联邦授权负责数据保护和信息自由的机关有权对通用程序涉及数据保护规定的遵守情况进行监管。此外，经联邦授权的负责数据保护和信息自由的机关，其所拥有的管辖权不受经联邦州授权的负责数据安全的机关的管辖权影响。

（4）在通用程序的框架内，除用于文化财产鉴定的数据外，也可处理所有人的个人数据及必要时国家文化财产占有人的个人数据。特别是其姓名和住址。

（5）通用程序的细节，特别是依照《德国电子政务法》第 11 条第 4 款第 1 句第 1 项的规定，各负责部门对专业技术规定的制定、修改、后续开发和遵守，依照第 4 条第 4 款的规定，由对所有联邦州具有约束力的管理委员会的决定进行规范。

第 80 条　向成员国和缔约国提交含个人数据的信息资料

（1）联邦文化与媒体最高管理局，根据合理请求，向成员国相关中央机构提供信息，

1. 当该信息为相关检查所必需，可作为情报，是否

   a）已满足文化财产返还请求或诉讼的前提条件或者

   b）已满足依照 2009 年 116 号法令给予出口许可的前提条件，以及

2. 可为寻获并返还被盗或非法进口到联邦境内的文化财产提供有效信息的情报。

若相关信息为其他成员国有关机构检查工作所必需，依照第 1 句第 1 项和第 2 项的规定，该情报信息除了非个人数据外，还应包含现任或前任所有人或占有人的姓名和真实有效的通信地址。

（2）外交部依据合理请求向缔约国提供情报，

1. 为其审查工作所必需的情报是否满足返还请求或返还诉讼的前提条件，以及

2. 可为寻获并返还被盗或非法进口到联邦境内的文化财产提供有效信息的情报。

（3）只有在依法请求返还文化财产的实施过程中必须用到个人数据信息时，才可向成员国和缔约国有关机构转交该数据。在转交数据时还应满足《德国联邦数据保护法》第 4b 条和第 4c 条规定的要求。

第 81 条　海关部门的参与以及对文化财产的扣留

（1）海关部门在其权限范围对文化财产的进出口进行监管，并受本法或基于本法制定的法令条例的禁止或限制。一旦因实施本法或基于本法制定的法律条令的需要，海关部门应将其在监管职责范围内所收集的包括可能是税务秘密在内的信息提交给主管部门。

（2）联邦文化和媒体最高管理局可向海关最高主管部门提交详细的关于国家的、商品的或个人的风险提示。

（3）在海关监管过程中，如发现有违反本法或基于本法所制定的法令条例的线索，海关应立即通知已扣留文化财产的国家主管部门。

（4）在第 3 款所述情况下，海关扣留该货物、运输工具与包装材料以及货物所附的有关支配权的费用和风险文件。海关也可将所扣留的货物以及其运输工具、包装材料交由第三方保管。适用本法第 39 条的规定。

（5）海关应退还已扣留的文化财产、运输工具和包装材料以及所附文件，当其满足各项手续和要求，并且

1. 主管部门通知，依照本法第 33 条的规定确认扣押该文化财产，
2. 主管部门通知，确认不扣押该文化财产，或者
3. 依照第 3 款的规定，自下达通知起 3 个工作日后，主管机关未作出进一步通知，或者
4. 依照第 3 款的规定，自下达通知起 10 个工作日后，主管机关未依照本法第 33 条的规定，作出有关该文化财产扣押情况的进一步通知。

（6）禁止破坏、毁坏依照第 4 款规定扣留的文化财产，或暂时和轻微改变其外观。

第 82 条　与第三国进行文化财产交易的进出口申报义务

（1）在相关海关部门进行文化财产的申报登记，其属于

1. 直接从第三国进口并需经该国许可从原产国出口的或者

2. 需从第三国出口并依照本法或者欧盟官方公告、欧共体现行法律规定的需要从已授权的国内市场出口的。

（2）由文化财产的进口或出口人进行申报登记。登记时应提交进出口所必须的许可文件或其他档案资料。

（3）按海关部门的要求出示所申报的文化财产。

第九章　处罚和罚款规定

第 83 条　处罚规定

（1）有下列行为之一的，将处以最长五年监禁或处罚款，

1. 违反本法第 21 条第 1、2、4 或 5 项的规定出口文化财产的，

2. 违反本法第 21 条第 3 项的规定出口文化财产，且知晓依照本法第 32 条第 1 款第 1 或 2 项的规定为非法进口的，

3. 违反本法第 28 条的规定进口文化财产，且知晓其行为违反当地相关法律规定的，

4. 违反本法第 40 条第 1 款的规定运输文化财产，且该文化财产属于遗失或当事人知晓该文化财产为非法盗掘或依照本法第 32 条第 1 款第 1 或 2 项的规定为非法进口的，或者

5. 违反本法第 40 条第 3 款的规定，达成文化财产义务交易或使用权交易，而该文化财产是以第 1 或第 2 项所述行为出口的。

（2）违反联邦参议院 2008 年 12 月 18 日制定的，2009 年生效的第 116 条关于文化财产出口条例第 2 条第 1 款的规定（2009 年 2 月 10 日修订，第 1 页第 1 节第 39 条）出口文化财产的，同样应受到处罚。

（3）违反本法第 18 条第 1 款的规定，并结合第 2 款的规定，损坏、毁坏或改变文化财产的，处以最长三年监禁或处罚款。

（4）犯罪未遂的，亦应处罚。

（5）根据本条第1款第4项的规定，以下情形可判处一至十年监禁

1. 专业从事非法活动或者

2. 作为犯罪团伙成员长期从事此类非法活动的。

（6）因渎职导致本条第1款第1项或第2款所述职业犯罪行为发生的，最高可处三年监禁或处罚款。

（7）若作案人立即将文化财产带回联邦领土，法院可依照《刑法典》第49条第1款的规定，减轻依照本条第1款第1项对所述犯罪情形的处罚，或免于处罚。

第84条　罚款规定

（1）对于违反法律的行为，任何人

1. 违反本法第15条第2款的规定，知情不报、误报、瞒报或不及时报告的，

2. 违反本法第42条第1款第1句第1项的规定，不提供或不及时确认相关人员姓名或通信地址的，

3. 违反本法第42条第1款第1句第2项的规定，不提供或不及时给出描述或图像的，或者

4. 违反本法第42条第1款第1句第7项的规定，不提供或不及时做出所需的相关解释的。

（2）对于违反法律的行为，任何人因故意或过失

1. 违反第30条第1句的规定，在进口文化财产时知晓或按理应当知晓，该文化财产被某成员国或缔约国分级或定义为国宝级文化财产，而未提交检查部门所要求的文件或者，

2. 违反本法第82条第3款的规定，不提交或不及时提交所要求文件的。

（3）对于上述违法行为，依据本条第1款第2至4项的规定，最高可处30,000欧元罚款，在其他情形下，最高可处100,000欧元罚款。

第 85 条　没收和扩大追缴

（1）若发生依照本法第 83 条所述的犯罪行为或发生依照本法第 84 条第 1 或 2 款所述的违法行为，依法可没收下列物品：

1. 犯罪行为或违法行为所涉及的物品，或者
2. 由犯罪行为或违法行为所产生的或者实施或准备过程中所需的或者为此而确定的物品。

适用《刑法典》第 74a 条及《秩序违反法》第 23 条的规定。

（2）本法第 83 条第 5 款第 2 项所述情形适用《刑法典》第 73d 条的规定。

第 86 条　使用文化财产的特殊前提

（1）依照本法第 85 条的规定没收或查抄的文化财产，仅允许在经相关部门同意的情况下使用。

（2）上述同意可撤销。通常对有下列情形的文化财产，可撤销同意，

1. 依照本法第 24 条的规定已获准出口，且因尚未通过最终审查而未被列入国家珍贵文化财产名录的，
2. 依照本法第五章的规定可要求返还，且该返还要求未满 4 年有效期或该要求尚未撤销的，或者
3. 依照本法第 40 条的规定禁止该文化财产的流通，或者依照本法第 44 条的规定增加了其流通中的注意义务的。

（3）在使用外国文化财产之前，应听取外交部和主管文化与媒体的联邦最高当局的意见。

（4）依照其他法规，在没收和查抄文化财产时适用本条第 1 至 3 款的规定。

（5）仅当依照本条第 2 款的规定通过最终审查后，方可使用相关部门依照本法所没收的文化财产。

第 87 条　海关部门的职责和权限

（1）对于犯罪行为和违法行为，依照本法第 83 条、第 84 条的规定，检察机关也可委托海关总署或海关调查办公室依照《刑事诉讼法》第 161

条第 1 款第 1 句的规定，对本法第 83 条第 1 款第 1 项、第 2 项或第 3 项结合第 4 款和第 6 款，以及本法第 83 条第 2 款结合第 4 款所述情形进行调查。依照本法第 36 条第 1 款第 2 项或第 2 款的规定，处置违法行为的相关管理机关也可委托海关总署或海关调查办公室，对第 1 句所述情形进行调查。

（2）相应适用 2013 年 6 月 6 日通过的德国《对外贸易法》第 21 条第 2 款（见《联邦法律公报》，第一部分，第 1482 页），于 2015 年 8 月 31 日为该法规第 297 条所修改的规定（见《联邦法律公报》，第一部分，第 1474 页）。

第 88 条　处罚和罚款程序

依照本法第 83 条的规定，若州法院在其辖区内已设立地方法院，若该地方法院客观上有权处罚犯罪行为，则其拥有属地管辖权。州政府可以通过法律条例规范拥有属地管辖权的地方法院，使其在考虑当地经济及交通条件，管理建设或其他地方需求的情况下合理适当地行使权力。州政府也可将该授权移交给州司法管理部门。

第十章　评估，过渡和排除规定

第 89 条　评估

联邦文化与媒体最高管理局告知德国联邦议院和联邦参议院，该法生效后 5 年的法律适用情况并预先告知生效后 2 年的管理开支范围。

第 90 条　至今已流失文化财产保护的效力与时限

（1）根据 1999 年 7 月 8 日公布的官方文本（见《联邦法律公报》，第一部分，第 1754 页），最近一次于 2007 年 5 月 18 日修改该法律第 2 条（见《联邦法律公报》，第一部分，第 757 页），为保护德国文化财产免遭流失，将其列入国家珍贵文化财产名录，登录于

1. 国家珍贵文化财产名录或者

2. 州国家珍贵档案名录。

（2）至迟在 2025 年 12 月 31 日前，下列文化财产的出口仍须获得出口许可

1. 艺术作品，根据德国政府于 1919 年 12 月 11 日通过（见《德国法律公报》，第 1961 页），最后一次更新为 1932 年 12 月 20 日的法令条例（见《德国法律公报》，第一部分，第 572 页）有关延续效力的规定，已登录和尚未决定是否登录进国家珍贵文化财产名录的艺术作品，以及

2. 依照 1980 年 7 月 3 日通过的《文化财产保护法》（见《法律公报》，第一部分，第二十条，第 191 页）的规定，已登录和尚未决定是否登录进国家宝贵文化财产名录的文化财产。

（3）对于截至 2016 年 8 月 6 日已采用且已公布的审理程序，适用根据 1999 年 7 月 8 日公布的官方文本（见《联邦法律公报》，第一部分，第 1754 页），最后一次修改为 2007 年 5 月 18 日的法律第 2 条（见《联邦法律公报》，第一部分，第 757 页）有关保护德国文化财产免遭流失的法律规定，直至审理程序结束。

第 91 条　对不一致的州法律的排除

州法律不得违背本法第 7 条至第 17 条，第 22 条至第 27 条及第 73 条至第 76 条所涉及的管理程序规则。

第二项
对《建立“德国联邦环境基金会”法》进行修订

对 1990 年 7 月 18 日《建立“德国联邦环境基金会”法》（见《联邦法律公报》，第一部分，第 1448 页）第 2 条第 2 款中的字句进行修改，将“- 鉴于环境的有害影响保存和保护国家宝贵文化财产（试行）”修改为“- 鉴于环境的有害影响保存和保护国家珍贵文化财产（试行）”。

第三项
对《1954 年 5 月 14 日〈武装冲突情况下保护文化财产的公约〉》的修订

对 1967 年 4 月 11 日通过的《1954 年 5 月 14 日〈武装冲突情况下保护文化财产的公约〉》第 2 条第 5 款（见《联邦法律公报》，1967 年，第二部分，第 1233 页），最近一次于 2004 年 4 月 27 日修改了该法第 4 条（见《联邦法律公报》，第一部分，第 630 页），作如下表述：

“（5）联邦民众保护与灾害救助局负责

1. 依照该公约第 25 条所述，传播公约条文及其实施细则，当其无法依据第 4 款 b 目的规定实施时，
2. 在中央救助地点将备份介质进行包装、制成档案、存储及保留。”

第四项
对《法院组织法实施细则》的修订

对《联邦法律公报》第三部分、分类编号为 300-1 的《法院组织法实施细则》官方文本第 14 条第 1 款第 9 项，最近一次于 2015 年 8 月 31 日修改了第 130 条（见《联邦法律公报》，第一部分，第 1474 页），其中“气候与地形”的表述修改为“气候与地形及文化财产”。

第五项
对《国际法律援助法》的修订

对 1994 年 6 月 27 日公布官方文本的《国际法律援助法》（见《联邦法律公报》，第一部分，第 1537 页）第 56b 条第 2 款，最近一次于 2015 年 8 月 31 日修改了第 163 条（见《联邦法律公报》，第一部分，第 1474 页），作如下表述：

“（2）依照《文化财产保护法》第 6 条第 1 款第 1 项的规定，2016 年 7 月 31 日达成的关于国家文化财产的协定，必须经过联邦文化和媒体最高管理局的批准。”

第六项
对《FIDE 目录条例》的修订

对 2011 年 10 月 5 日通过的《FIDE 目录条例》第 1 条第 1 款第 8 项（见《联邦法律公报》，第一部分，第 2057 页），最近一次于 2015 年 1 月 21 日修改了第 2 条第 6 款（见《联邦法律公报》，第一部分，第 10 页），作如下表述：

“8. 依照于 2016 年 7 月 31 日（见《联邦法律公报》，第一部分，第 1914 页）通过的《文化财产保护法》第 83 条第 1 款第 1 项，触犯商品流通中文化财产保护规定的犯罪行为。”

第七项
对《所得税法》的修订

对 2009 年 10 月 8 日公布官方文本的《所得税法》中第 10g 条第 1 款第 2 句第 4 项（见《联邦法律公报》，第一部分，第 3366 页和第 3862 页），最近一次于 2015 年 8 月 31 日修改了第 234 条（见《联邦法律公报》，第一部分，第 1474 页），其中的字句“或者列入国家珍贵文化财产名录或名录档案”修改为“或者依照于 2016 年 7 月 31 日（见《联邦法律公报》，第一部分，第 1914 页）通过的《文化财产保护法》第 7 条第 1 款作为国家珍贵文化财产列入国家珍贵文化财产名录”。

第八项
对《继承和赠与税法》的修订

对 1997 年 2 月 27 日公布官方文本的《继承和赠与税法》（见《联邦法律公报》，

第一部分，第 378 页），最近一次于 2015 年 11 月 2 日修改了第 10 条（见《联邦法律公报》，第一部分，第 1834 页），其修订内容如下：

1. 第 13 条第 1 款第 2 项 b 目 bb 表述如下：

"bb）为家庭所有至少已达 20 年时间或依照于 2016 年 7 月 31 日（见《联邦法律公报》，第一部分，第 1914 页）通过的《文化财产保护法》第 7 条第 1 款规定列入国家珍贵文化财产名录至少已达 20 年时间的物品。"

2. 第 37 条增加第 11 款：

"（11）依照于 2016 年 8 月 6 日生效的官方文本中第 13 条第 1 款第 2 项 b 目 bb 所述规定，自 2016 年 8 月 5 日后继承所产生的继承税适用本规定。"

第九项
对《工商业管理条例》的修订

对 1999 年 2 月 22 日公布官方文本的《工商业管理条例》第 29 条第 1 款第 5 项（见《联邦法律公报》，第一部分，第 202 页），最近一次于 2015 年 8 月 31 日修改了第 626 条第 3 款（见《联邦法律公报》，第一部分，第 1474 页），作如下表述：

"（5）只要该工商业行为依照《文化财产保护法》第 42 条第 1 款进行。"

第十项
法律的生效、失效

本法律自公布之日起生效。同时废止

1. 1999 年 7 月 8 日公布官方文本《保护德国文化财产免遭流失的法律》（见《联邦法律公报》，第一部分，第 1754 页），最近一次于 2007 年 5 月 18 日修改了第 2 条（见《联邦法律公报》，第一部分，第 757 页），

2. 2007 年 5 月 18 日通过的《文化财产返还法》（见《联邦法律公报》，第一部分，第 757 页，第 2547 页），2013 年 6 月 6 日修改了第 2 条第 8 款（见

《联邦法律公报》，第一部分，第 1482 页），

3. 2008 年 10 月 15 日通过的《文化财产名录条例》（见《联邦法律公报》，第一部分，第 2002 页），以及

4. 2007 年 5 月 18 日对《1954 年 5 月 14 日〈武装冲突情况下保护文化财产的公约〉法》的修订案（见《联邦法律公报》，第一部分，第 757 页，第 762 页，第 2574 页）。

四、瑞 士

述 评

长期以来，瑞士秉承较为宽松的文物市场管理政策，也没有专门规范文物进出境的法律法规。此举为瑞士的文物市场带来一定繁荣的同时，也滋生了大量非法文物交易，他国文物被非法转运到瑞士，得不到瑞士政府的有效保护，引起他国不满。同时瑞士对参与国际公约的消极态度，也导致其本身的文物权益得不到保障。随着国际文物保护与打击非法文物交易的势头逐渐明朗，为了维护本国文化权益和外交权益，树立正面的国际形象，瑞士联邦议会专门成立"关于实施《1970年公约》工作组"，根据工作组建议，2003年瑞士加入《1970年公约》。2003年6月20日，瑞士通过了《文化财产国际转让法》(Federal Act on the International Transfer of Cultural Property，即Cultural Property Transfer Act，CPTA)，又于2005年4月13日通过了CPTA的实施条例——《文化财产国际转让条例》(Ordinance on the International Transfer of Cultural Property，即Cultural Property Transfer Ordinance，CPTO)。2005年6月1日，《文化财产国际转让法》及其实施条例正式生效。《文化财产国际转让法》以《1970年公约》为蓝本制定，共11节34条，内容涉及文化财产的范围、登记、进出口管理及转让、非法流转文化财产的返还，有关机构的执法、监督等职责，以及相应的刑事处罚等。瑞士联邦希望通过该法在联邦层面上有效实施《1970年公约》，使国内法律规范与国际公约规定的最低国际标准保持一致，保护人类文化财产，遏制文化财产非法转让，加强文化财产转让领域的国际合作，促进公开和公平的国际文化财产交流。但是，根据该法只有与瑞士签订双边协议的国家才能提起文物返还之诉，这在一定程度上限制了该法的适用范围。

《文化财产国际转让法》

联邦法之文化财产国际转让法[①]

（文化财产转让法，CPTA）

（徐书林　初校）

日期：2003 年 6 月 20 日

瑞士联邦议会，

根据《瑞士联邦宪法》【1】第 69 条第 2 款和第 95 条第 1 款的规定，在执行 1970 年 11 月 14 日【2】签订的联合国教科文组织《关于禁止和防止非法进出口文化财产和非法转让其所有权的方法的公约》（简称 1970 年《联合国教科文组织公约》）的过程中，对 2001 年 11 月 21 日【3】的瑞士联邦委员会信息进行检查后，

决定：

第 1 节　总则

第 1 条　范围和目的

1. 本法的适用范围包括将文化财产进口到瑞士，从瑞士转移和出口文化财产，以及将文化财产从瑞士返还至其本国。

2. 瑞士联邦希望通过本法，对保护人类文化遗产及阻止盗窃、掠夺、非法进出口文化财产做出贡献。

---

① 中译本源于《文化财产国际转让法》的英文译本，原始法律文本采用德语、法语、意大利语等瑞士官方语言书写，若有出入，以官方语言书写的文本为准。

第 2 条　术语

1. 文化财产，是指根据宗教的或世俗的理由，明确指定为具有重要考古、史前史、历史、文学、艺术或科学价值的财产并属于 1970 年《联合国教科文组织公约》第 1 条所述类别。

2. 文化遗产，是指 1970 年《联合国教科文组织公约》第 4 条所述类别的文化财产整体。

3. 缔约国，是指已批准 1970 年《联合国教科文组织公约》的国家。

4. 专门机构，是指负责执行第 18 条中所列任务的行政管理机构。

5. 非法进口，是指违反第 7 条的协议规定，或第 8 条第 1 款 a 项措施的进口行为。

第 2 节　文化财产的登记

第 3 条　联邦登记簿

1. 对文化遗产具有重要意义[①]的瑞士联邦文化财产应登记在联邦登记簿中。

2. 文化财产登记具有以下效果：

a. 登记文化财产不因时效取得或善意取得方式获得所有权；

b. 登记文化财产的返还之诉不受诉讼时效的限制[②]；

c. 永久禁止登记文化财产从瑞士出口。

3. 联邦登记簿中登记的文化财产符合以下条件时，可撤销登记：

a. 该文化财产对文化遗产不再具有重要作用；

b. 合并处理整体效果更佳；

① 按照瑞士联邦文化部公布的标准，如果某物品适于或值得在博物馆展出、其流失将导致国家文化财的损失、对于公众有特殊利益、具有稀缺性时，该文化财产就具有“重要意义”。

② 在《文化财产转让法》生效之前，文化财产视为其他普通动产，动产原所有人自动产被盗或遗失之日起 5 年内可要求返还该动产（瑞士民法典 934 条 1 款）。如果该动产是通过公开拍卖或是在公共市场或从出售同类商品的商人处购得，申请人就只有在偿还购买人支付的价金后才能申请返还动产（瑞士民法典 934 条 2 款）。

c. 瑞士联邦已丧失或放弃该文化财产的所有权。

4. 专门机构以电子数据库的形式对联邦登记簿进行维护并发布。

第 4 条　州登记簿

1. 为了简化边境检查，在州境内监管文化财产出口的各州可连接联邦数据库，查看：

a. 各州文化财产登记簿；

b. 私人文化财产登记簿，但必须获得私人当事方的授权。

2. 各州可宣布任何人不得通过时效占有或善意取得方式获得其登记簿中登记文化财产的所有权，登记文化财产的返还之诉不受诉讼时效的限制。

第 3 节　进口与出口

第 5 条　联邦登记簿中登记文化财产的出口许可

1. 凡欲从瑞士出口联邦登记簿中登记文化财产，必须获得专门机构的授权。

2. 如果满足以下条件，方可取得出口授权：

a. 系临时出口文化财产；并且

b. 文化财产出口旨在研究、保护、展览或类似目的。

第 6 条　瑞士的文化财产返还请求权

1. 如果联邦登记簿中登记文化财产从瑞士非法出口，瑞士联邦委员会可向所有其他缔约国追索该文化财产。由此产生的一切赔偿和费用将由瑞士联邦承担。

2. 如果州登记簿中登记文化财产从瑞士非法出口，瑞士联邦委员会可应该州的请求，向所有其他缔约国追索该文化财产。由此产生的一切赔偿和费用将由提出追索请求的州承担。

第 7 条　协议

1．为保护文化和外交权益，确保文化遗产的安全，瑞士联邦委员会可与缔约国签订关于文化财产进口与返还的国际条约（或协议）。

2．必须满足以下条件：

a. 协议所保护的必须是对于相关缔约国文化遗产十分重要的文化财产；

b. 文化财产必须符合相关缔约国为了保护文化遗产而制定的出口规定；以及

c. 缔约国必须给予对等权利。

第 8 条　限制措施

1．为了防止国家文化遗产免受突发状况破坏，瑞士联邦委员会可以：

a. 授权进口、转移和出口文化财产，并且规定相关的条件、限制或禁例；

b. 根据 1970 年《联合国教科文组织公约》第 9 条规定参与共同国际行动。

2．上述措施必须有时间限制。

第 9 条　基于协议的文物返还请求权

1．如果某人占有非法进口至瑞士的文化财产，则该文化财产的出口国可对此人提起返还之诉。提起诉讼的国家必须特别说明：该文化财产对其本国的文化遗产具有十分重要的意义，且该文化财产系非法进口。

2．文化财产在返还过程中不再处于危险状态，法院可暂停返还。

3．提起诉讼的国家需承担为保护、维护和返还文化财产所采取的必要措施产生的费用。

4．一国的返还之诉申请自该国主管部门发现该文化财产所在地和占有人身份之日起 1 年内提出。但是，诉讼最长有效期为文化财产非法出口之日起 30 年。

5. 即使是善意取得的文化财产也必须返还，但在返还同时，善意取得人可以要求补偿，补偿额根据购买价格以及必要的保管和维护费用确定。

6. 提起诉讼的国家必须支付补偿金。在此之前，文化财产的占有人有权保留该文化财产。

第 4 节　归还保证书

第 10 条　申请

如果缔约国的文化财产临时出借给瑞士某博物馆或其他文化机构展出，借用该文化财产的机构可申请专门机构按照租借协议规定向出借机构签发展期内归还保证书。

第 11 条　公示和异议程序

1. 上述申请需在《瑞士联邦公报》公示。公示内容包括对文化财产的精确描述及其来源。

2. 如果申请明显不符合签发归还保证书的条件，则该申请将被拒绝且不会公示。

3. 申请人可根据 1968 年 12 月 20 日《联邦行政程序法》【4】的规定自公示之日起 30 日内向专门机构书面提出异议。

4. 未提出异议的，且异议未被接受的，禁止申请人采取进一步行动。

第 12 条　签发

1. 专门机构决定是否依申请签发归还保证书。

2. 下列情况中，可签发归还保证书：

   a. 没有人提出异议主张该文化财产的所有权；

   b. 文化财产系合法进口；

   c. 租借协议规定，展览结束后，文化财产将归还给文化财产原主缔约国。

3. 瑞士联邦委员会可提出补充要求。

第 13 条　效力

归还保证书意味着，只要该文化财产在瑞士，行政相对人和官方机构都不得主张该文化财产的所有权。

第 5 节　有利于维护文化遗产的财政援助

第 14 条

1. 瑞士联邦可在以下情况提供财政援助：

   a. 提供给临时受托保管属于他国文化遗产的文化财产的瑞士博物馆或类似机构，且该文化财产在该国正因突发状况处境危险；

   b. 提供给用于维护其他缔约国文化遗产的项目；

   c. 在突发情况下提供财政援助，以帮助减轻缔约国修复文化遗产的压力。

2. 只有当受托保管符合以下条件时，才能提供第 1 款 a 项规定的财政援助：

   a. 其他国家的官方机构同意；或

   b. 获得联合国教科文组织或其他旨在文化财产保护的国际组织的赞助。

第 6 节　文化财产的转让

第 15 条　转让给联邦机构

1. 禁止联邦机构取得或展出以下文化财产：

   a. 失窃、不慎遗失，或者非法挖掘的文化财产；

   b. 属于某国文化遗产组成部分，并且从该国非法出口的文化财产。

2. 获得此类文化财产的联邦机构必须立即向专门机构汇报。

第 16 条　勤勉义务

1. 在艺术品交易和拍卖活动中转让该文化财产的前提是，转让人确信该文化财产：

a. 不属于失窃、不慎遗失，或者非法挖掘的；

b. 不属于非法进口的。

2. 从事艺术品交易和拍卖活动的人有义务：

a. 确认供应方或卖方的身份，并且要求供应方或卖方书面声明享有该文化财产处分权；

b. 将缔约国现有进出口规则告知客户；

c. 将文化财产的购买情况做书面记录，记录文化财产的来源、供应方或卖方的名称和地址，以及文化财产的相关描述和售价；

d. 向专门机构提供与此类勤勉义务履行情况有关的所有必要信息。

3. 相关记录和收据必须保存30年。《瑞士义务法》【5】第962条第2款规定也同样适用。

第17条　审查

1. 为了审查勤勉义务履行情况，专门机构有权进入从事艺术品交易和拍卖活动的人的商务房间和仓库。

2. 当专门机构合理怀疑存在本法规定的犯罪活动时，可向刑事检察机关提起控告。

第7节　官方机构

第18条　专门机构

瑞士联邦任命专门机构执行本法，具体承担以下任务：

a. 就文化财产转让事宜为联邦机构提供建议和支持，并且协调相应工作；

b. 就文化财产转让事宜向州机构提出建议，并且与该机构协同合作；

c. 就文化财产转让事宜代表瑞士与国外机构进行面对面磋商；

d. 与其他国家的官方机构协作，以保护这些国家的文化遗产；

e. 向从事艺术品交易和拍卖活动以及其他相关人员提供文化财产转

让的相关信息；

f. 保存信息中心关于已报道的被盗文化财产的清单；

g. 以电子数据库的形式管理联邦登记簿，并且公布（参见本法第3条）；

h. 签发归还保证书（参见本法第10至13条）；

i. 审查从事艺术品交易和拍卖活动的人是否遵守勤勉义务（参见本法第16条和17条）。

第19条　海关

1. 海关在边境检查文化财产转让情况。

2. 在文化财产进口、转移和出口期间，海关有权扣留有疑点的文化财产，并且报告给刑事检察机关。

3. 根据本法，一旦文化财产进入海关仓库，该文化财产即被视为已进口。

第20条　刑事检察机关

1. 如果刑事检察机关怀疑某件文化财产是在违背所有者意愿情况下被盗窃、遗失的，或者是通过非法途径进口至瑞士的，则命令没收该文化财产。

2. 需将没收情况立即向专门机构报告。

第8节　官方和法律援助

第21条　瑞士官方援助

来自瑞士联邦、各州和各市镇的主管机构向对方以及相关监管机构提供执行本法需要的所有资料。

第22条　国际官方和法律援助

1. 负责执行本法的联邦机构可配合国外主管机构、国际组织和国际机构协助调查，条件是：

a. 这是执行本法所需要的；和

b. 这些国外机构、国际组织或国际机构受官方机密约束，或者需要遵守相应的保密义务。

2. 联邦机构可能要求国外机构提供所需要的资料。作为交换，联邦机构也可为国外机构提供尤其涉及以下方面的资料：

a. 文化财产的质量、数量、使用目的地和地点、使用目的以及接收人；

b. 参与文化财产交付或购买活动的人；

c. 交易上的财务安排。

3. 联邦机构可根据第 2 款规定主动提供，或应其他国家要求提供相关资料，条件是该国家：

a. 保留互惠权利；

b. 保证只会在本法框架内处理这些资料；以及

c. 保证只会在刑事诉讼程序中使用这些资料，前提是刑事诉讼程序中的法律援助不会因犯罪类型而遭遇阻碍。这种情况下，联邦行政主管机构应就刑事诉讼程序中法律援助的可能性提前与联邦司法局进行协商。

第 23 条　与《法律援助法》的关系

国外主管机构可获得法律援助，以处理违反本法的违规行为。根据 1981 年 3 月 20 日《法律援助法》第 3 条第 3 款的规定【6】，这些违规行为不视为货币犯罪、贸易犯罪或经济犯罪。本法程序上的规定也适用。

第 9 节　刑事处罚

第 24 条　轻罪

1. 若该罪行在其他法律条款中没有更高的处罚，则有以下行为者将处以 1 年有期徒刑，并处罚金 10 万瑞士法郎：

a. 进口、出售、分销、采购、取得或出口被盗或遗失的文化财产的；

b. 根据《瑞士民法典》第 724 条规定占用挖掘发现物的【7】；

c. 非法进口文化财产，或者在进口及转移期间对文化财产进行错误申报的；

d. 非法出口联邦登记簿中列出的文化财产，或者在出口期间对文化财产错误申报的。

2. 过失犯罪的，处罚金 2 万瑞士法郎。

3. 故意犯罪的，处 2 年有期徒刑，并处罚金 20 万瑞士法郎。

第 25 条　违规行为

1. 若该罪行在其他法律条款中没有更高的制裁，则艺术品交易或拍卖活动中有以下行为的，处罚金 2 万瑞士法郎：

a. 忽视勤勉义务（参见第 16 条）；

b. 妨碍审查（参见第 17 条）。

2. 犯罪未遂、帮助行为和教唆行为均应受到处罚。

3. 程度较轻的违规行为可免除处罚。

第 26 条　商业违规行为

商业违规行为适用 1974 年 3 月 22 日《联邦法行政处罚法典》第 6 条和第 7 条【8】。

第 27 条　刑事诉讼

各州负责根据本法对犯罪活动提起诉讼并进行评估。

第 28 条　文化财产和资产的没收

根据《瑞士刑法典》第 58 条和第 59 条【9】被没收的文化财产和资产上交瑞士联邦。瑞士联邦委员会谨遵本法负责管理没收文化财产和资产。

第 29 条　披露要求

海关和刑事检察机构需要向专门机构披露违反本法的情况。

第 10 节 上诉和资料保护

第 30 条

1.《联邦司法系统组织法》的一般规定适用于因根据本法作出的法院裁定而提起的申诉程序。

2. 有关资料保护的法律适用于个人资料的处理。

第 11 节 最后条款

第 31 条 实施

瑞士联邦委员会应制定实施细则。

第 32 条 法律的修订

以下法律修订如下：

1.《瑞士民法典》【10】

第 724 条第 1 和 1bis 款

1 具有科学价值的自然遗体或文物古迹，属于其被发现时所在州的财产。

1bis 未经相关州主管机构允许，不得进行出售。这些物品不可通过时效占有或善意取得方式获得。要求归还上述物品的请求权不受诉讼时效的限制。

第 728 条第 1ter 款

1bis 在保留法定例外情况下，根据 2003 年 6 月 20 日《文化财产转让法》第 2 条第 1 款规定【11】，文化财产的逆占有期限为 30 年。

第 934 条第 1bis 款

1bis 根据 2003 年 6 月 20 日《文化财产转让法》第 2 条第 1 款的规定【12】，要求归还违背所有者意愿遗失的文化财产的请求权，具有 1 年诉讼时效，从所有者知晓该文化财产所在地和所有权情况之日起计算。但是，该诉讼时效最长为该文化财产遗失之日起 30 年。

2.《瑞士义务法》【13】

第 196a 条

c. 关于文化财产

符合 2003 年 6 月 20 日《文化财产转让法》第 2 条第 1 款规定【14】的文化财产，确保出售权利的请求权自买方发现过错时起算有效期为 1 年。但是，在任何情况下，该项权利最长有效期为合同签署后 30 年。

第 210 条第 1bis 款

1bis 符合 2003 年 6 月 20 日《文化财产转让法》第 2 条第 1 款规定【15】的文化财产，相关请求权自买方发现过错时起算有效期为 1 年。但是，在任何情况下，该项权利最长有效期为合同签署后 30 年。

3.1987 年 12 月 18 日《联邦国际私法》【16】

第 98a 条

3. 文化财产

被告居住地、注册地、文化财产所在地法院，对根据 2003 年 6 月 20 日《文化财产转让法》第 9 条规定【17】提起的请求归还文化财产的诉讼具有管辖权。

4.1966 年 7 月 1 日《联邦自然区和来源地保护法》【18】

第 24 条第 1 款 c 项

1 若无正当理由且有以下行为者，则处以 1 年有期徒刑并处罚金 10 万瑞士法郎：

c. 破坏或严重损坏地下具有科学价值的古生物化石或文物古迹（参见第 724 条第 1CC 款【19】）；

第 33 条　不溯及既往

本法不具有溯及力。具体而言，本法不适用于生效前发生的购买活动。

第 34 条　公投和生效日期

1. 本法案须经公民投票决定。
2. 瑞士联邦委员会规定生效日期。

公示日期：2003 年 7 月 1 日【20】

注释：

【1】联邦立法系统汇编 101

【2】联邦立法系统汇编 0.444.1

【3】官方公报 2002 535

【4】联邦立法系统汇编 172.021

【5】联邦立法系统汇编 220

【6】联邦立法系统汇编 351.1

【7】联邦立法系统汇编 210

【8】联邦立法系统汇编 313.0

【9】联邦立法系统汇编 311.0

【10】联邦立法系统汇编 210

【11】联邦立法系统汇编 444.1

【12】联邦立法系统汇编 444.1

【13】联邦立法系统汇编 220

【14】联邦立法系统汇编 444.1

【15】联邦立法系统汇编 444.1

【16】联邦立法系统汇编 291

【17】联邦立法系统汇编 444.1

【18】联邦立法系统汇编 451

【19】联邦立法系统汇编 210

【20】联邦法律官方汇编 2005 1881（官方公报 2003 4475）

五、加拿大

述 评

1975 年 6 月 19 日，加拿大制定并通过了《文化财产进出口法》。加拿大既是文物市场国，同时也是文物原主国，因此在制定文物进出境法律的时候要充分注意既有效保护本国文物，又保证文物合法流通的前提下防止他国文物非法进口至加拿大。该法最近一次修正是在 2019 年 10 月。这部法律分为 17 个部分，构建出一个相对完善的许可证出口管理机制，还对已非法进口到加拿大的外国文化财产退还原主国的程序问题作出规定。加拿大遗产部为主管机关，负责本法实施，加拿大海关、执法机构和文化遗产社团在各自职责范围内通力合作。加拿大后又为《文化财产进出口法》制定了《加拿大文物财产出口控制清单》和《文化财产出口条例》等配套法规。

1978 年 5 月 28 日，加拿大正式批准《1970 年公约》，同年 6 月 28 日，公约对加拿大生效，加拿大成为《1970 年公约》的成员国。

《文化财产进出口法》

文化财产进出口法

（荣煜　初校）

第 51 章[①]

本法规定文化财产从加拿大出口以及文化财产非法进口到加拿大的相关内容。

简略标题

简略标题

1. 本法可引称为《文化财产进出口法》。

1974-75-76 年第 50 章第 1 条。

解释

定义

2. 在本法中，

“控制清单”是指依据本法第 4 条制定的《加拿大文化财产出口控制清单》；

“专家审查员”是指依据本法第 6 条指定的个人或机构；

“出口许可证”是指由许可官员依据本法规定签发的出口许可证件；

“普通许可证”是指由部长依据本法第 17 条签发的出口许可证件；

---

① 本法收录进 1985 年《加拿大法规修订汇编》第 51 章。《加拿大法规修订汇编》即 Revised Statute of Canda, 简称 R.S.C.。每 15 年或 20 年整理出版一次。1985 年之前出版的，每章序号前加上本章法律首字母，因此，确切地说，本法为汇编第 C-51 章。1985 年之后编制的汇编章序号前不再加首字母。

“机构”是指以文化教育为宗旨、由公共所有的，为了便于收藏、展示或公众接触藏品（objects）[①]而设立的公益性机构；

“部长”是指总督为实现本法宗旨而在加拿大枢密院成员中任命的人；

“许可官员”是指依据本法第5条任命的人；

“公共主管部门”是指加拿大或加拿大某省的代理人，如加拿大的市政当局、在加拿大境内履行政府职能的公立机构或公共团体，或者为了加拿大或加拿大某省权益履行职责的公司；

“加拿大居民”是指经常居住地在加拿大的自然人，或者总部在加拿大的公司，或者在加拿大设有一个或一个以上机构，且该机构职工的工作与公司日常业务相关；

“复审委员会”是指依据本法第18条设立的加拿大文化财产出口复审委员会。

1974-75-76年第50章第2条；SI/80-153；1984年第40章第21条。

适用范围（HER MAJESTY）

约束力

3. 本法在加拿大或加拿大各省均有拘束力。

1974-75-76年第50章第2条。

《加拿大文化财产出口控制清单》

《控制清单》的制定

4.（1）经与外交部部长咨询，部长可以建议总督命令制定《加拿大文化财产出口控制清单》。

内容

（2）依本条第（3）款的规定，总督为保护加拿大国家遗产，可将本款所列的总督认为有必要实施出口控制的任何物品或物品种类列入《控制清单》，无论

① 编者认为，此处的objects意指cultural property，即文化财产。但为了忠于原条文，翻译为“某物”。

其源于何地：

（a）在加拿大境内领土、领海、内陆或内水出土（出水）的具有考古、史前、历史、艺术或科学价值的物品；

（b）由加拿大原住民制造，或（d）项规定的与加拿大原住民相关的物品，并且在加拿大正常市场价超过 500 加元的物品；

（c）在加拿大现有领土内制作的、具有 100 年以上历史的装饰艺术品：

（i）在加拿大正常市场价超过 500 加元的玻璃器皿、陶具、纺织品、木制及金属制品；以及

（ii）在加拿大正常市场价超过 2000 加元的家具、木雕作品、贵金属制品以及其他装饰艺术品；

（d）在加拿大正常市场价超过 500 加元的图书、档案、文献、照片（正片及底片）、音频及其他此类物品；

（e）在加拿大正常市场价超过 1000 加元的图画、雕塑、原始印刷品和水彩画；以及

（f）在加拿大正常市场价超过 3000 加元的任何物品。

例外

（3）如果某件物品的历史不足 50 年或者制造该物品的自然人仍然健在的，则该物品不应纳入《控制清单》。

推定条款

（4）为了本法目的，凡属《控制清单》所规定种类的物品都应被看作是在《控制清单》中。

修订法规，1985 年第 C-51 章第 4 条；1995 年第 5 章第 25 条；2001 年第 34 章第 37（F）条。

许可官员

指定许可官员

5. 经公共安全与应急准备部部长同意，部长可以在加拿大边境服务局雇佣的

任何人员或某类人员中，指定某人或某类人为许可官员，依照本法受理出口许可证申请事宜并颁发出口许可证。

修订法规，1985 年第 C-51 章第 5 条；1994 年第 13 章第 7 条；1999 年第 17 章第 121 条；2005 年第 38 章第 59 条第 145 款。

专家审查员

指定专家审查员

6.（1）为了本法的目的，部长可以任命任何加拿大居民或加拿大境内的任何机构为专家审查员。

报酬

（2）专家审查员不是加拿大或加拿大某省的代理人或雇员，也不是其代理人的雇员，故加拿大或加拿大某省应支付本法项下经财政委员会同意的服务报酬。

费用

（3）专家审查员或其代理人（当专家审查员为某机构时）为提供本法服务的需要而离开其日常居所的，有权在财政委员会同意的限度内获得离开期间所支付的差旅、生活费用。

1974-75-76 年第 50 章第 5 条。

出口许可证

立即签发出口许可证

7. 许可官员收到加拿大居民的出口许可证申请后，如果申请人能使许可官员确信某物属于以下情形的，许可官员应立即签发出口许可证：

（a）在申请日之前 35 年内进口到加拿大，且在这次进口之前，不曾利用依据本法签发的许可证从加拿大出口；

（b）系某人出借给加拿大境内的机构或公共主管部门，且在出借时，该人并非加拿大居民；或

（c）为某一法定目的在一段时期内移出加拿大，且这段时期并未超过为本款目的而可能规定的时间段。

1974-75-76 年第 50 章第 6 条。

许可官员的决定

8.（1）许可官员收到加拿大居民出口某件物品的申请后，若没有依据本法第 7 条的规定签发许可证，且在申请日之前的 2 年内，不曾收到本法第 13 条第（1）款规定的拒绝该物品的出口通知，则许可官员应该确定该物品是否在《控制清单》中。

未在《控制清单》物品的出口许可

（2）若许可官员认为申请出口的物品不在《控制清单》中，则应立即签发出口许可证。

提交给专家审查员

（3）若许可官员认为申请出口的物品包括或可能包括在《控制清单》中，则应立即将该申请提交给专家审查员。

1974-75-76 年第 50 章第 7 条。

专家审查员的决定

9. 若出口许可申请依据本法第 8 条第（3）款的规定被提交给专家审查员，专家审查员应立即确认申请出口的物品是否在《控制清单》中。

1974-75-76 年第 50 章第 8 条。

申请出口的物品不在《控制清单》中

10. 若专家审查员认为提交其审查的申请出口的物品不在《控制清单》中，应立即以书面形式建议提交该申请的许可官员签发出口许可证，并将建议副本

送交复审委员会和部长。

1974-75-76 年第 50 章第 8 条。

申请出口的物品在《控制清单》中

11.（1）若专家审查员认为提交其审查的申请出口的物品在《控制清单》中，则应进一步查证：

（a）该物品是否与加拿大历史及民族生活具有密切联系、是否具有美学特性或具有艺术、科学研究价值，并因此具有重大意义；以及

（b）该物品所具有的国家意义的重要性是否达到一旦出口将会严重减损加拿大国家遗产价值的程度。

拟签发出口许可证

（2）若专家审查员认为提交其审查的申请出口的物品不具有本条第（1）款第（a）项所规定的重要意义，或对国家的重要性未达到本条第（1）款第（b）项所规定的程度，则应立即以书面形式建议提交该申请的许可官员签发出口许可证，并将建议副本送交复审委员会和部长。

拟拒签出口许可证

（3）若专家审查员认为申请出口的物品具有本条第（1）款第（a）项所规定的重要意义，或对国家的重要性达到了本条第（1）款第（b）项所规定的程度，则应立即以书面形式建议提交该申请的许可官员不得签发出口许可证，并向许可官员说明理由。

1974-75-76 年第 50 章第 8 条；1980-81-82-83 年第 47 章第 53 条。

签发出口许可证

12. 依本法第 14 条和第 16 条的规定，许可官员接到专家审查员建议后或在复审委员会作出指示后，应立即签发出口许可证。

1974-75-76 年第 50 章第 9 条。

拒签通知

13.（1）若许可官员依据第 11 条第（3）款规定的专家审查员的意见拒绝签发出口许可证，则该许可官员应将书面拒绝通知送交给申请人，通知应包括专家审查员提供的拒绝理由。

送交复审委员会的副本

（2）许可官员应将本条第（1）款规定的拒绝通知副本立即送交复审委员会。

1974-75-76 年第 50 章第 10 条。

复件留存

14. 除了根据本法第 7 条签发出口许可证之外，任何一件在《控制清单》中的、本法第 39 条（d）项所规定的几类物品，只有在申请人将该物品的复制品交存于部长指定的机构，方可签发出口许可证。

1974-75-76 年第 50 章第 11 条。

部长对许可证的变更及通知

15. 除依照复审委员会指示而签发的出口许可证外，部长可以修正、暂停、撤销或恢复出口许可证，并应第一时间书面通知受此影响的许可证申请人。

1974-75-76 年第 50 章第 12 条。

两年内禁止签发许可证

16. 在拒绝通知依第 13 条第（1）款规定送达之日起 2 年内，不得给在《控制清单》中的物品签发出口许可证。除非根据第 7 条签发出口许可证，或根据第 29 条或第 30 条规定的复审委员会的指示签发出口许可证。

1974-75-76 年第 50 章第 13 条。

普通许可证

普通出口许可证

17.（1）部长可以向任何申请许可证的加拿大居民签发普通出口许可证，出口《控制清单》中的物品。部长也可以视情况在任何时间内修正、暂停、撤销或恢复该许可证。

开放普通出口许可证

（2）在征得外交部部长同意后，部长可以普遍性地向所有人签发普通出口许可证出口属于《控制清单》中规定的和许可证中特指的种类的物品。部长在征得外交部部长同意后，可以视情况在任何时间内修正、暂停、撤销或恢复该许可证。

修订法规，1985 年第 C-51 章第 17 条；1995 年，第 5 章，第 25 条。

复审委员会

复审委员会的设立

复审委员会的设立

18.（1）加拿大文化财产出口复审委员会由主席和不超过 9 名委员组成，委员由总督根据部长的推荐而任命。

委员

（2）主席和 1 名委员应从加拿大居民中随机挑选，同时：

（a）在现任或曾任艺术馆、博物馆、档案馆或其他收藏机构的官员、成员或雇员的加拿大居民中最多挑选出 4 名委员；以及

（b）在现任或曾任艺术品、古董或其他构成国家遗产一部分的物品的经销商或收集者的加拿大居民中最多挑选出 4 名委员。

代理主席

（3）在主席缺席、无能力履行职务或空缺时，复审委员会可以授权 1 名委员代行主席职责。

法定人数

（4）复审委员会法定人数为 3 人，其中至少有 1 人是本条第（2）款（a）项所指人员，至少有 1 人是本条第（2）款（b）项所指人员。

修订法规，1985 年第 C-51 章第 18 条；1995 年第 29 章第 21 条第 22© 款；2001 年第 34 章第 38 条。

报酬

19.（1）复审委员会委员不是加拿大或加拿大某省的雇员，也不是其代理人的雇员，故加拿大或加拿大某省应为其支付经由总督确定的薪水或其他报酬。

费用

（2）复审委员会每一位成员均有权在财政委员会规定的限度内，获得其为履行复审委员会职责而在离开日常居所期间所支付的差旅、生活费用。

1974-75-76 年第 50 章第 16 条。

职责

职责

20. 复审委员会应申请人的要求，

（a）应当依本法第 29 条的规定，审查出口许可证的申请；

（b）应当依本法第 30 条的规定，确定购买该物品的公平现金价格；以及

（c）应当依本法第 32 条的规定，为《所得税法》第 39 条第（1）款（a）项（i.1）目和第 110.1 条第（1）款（c）项的目的，确定该法第 118.1 条第（1）款和第 118.1 条第（10）款中“纯粹文化赠与”定义。

修订法规，1985 年第 C-51 章第 20 条；1991 年第 49 章第 216 条。

总部和会议

总部

21.（1）复审委员会总部应依总督命令设在加拿大境内某地。

开会

（2）复审委员会可在其认为对合理尽职必要或需要的时间、地点开会。

1974-75-76 年第 50 章第 18 条。

顾问

专家建议

22.（1）复审委员会可以召集具有专业、技术或其他专长的人就某些问题提供咨询协助。

评估师

（2）部长应复审委员会要求，可确定评估专家的酬金。评估专家协助复审委员会确定本法第 30 条规定的公平现金出价，或第 32 条规定的处置或拟处置给机构或公共主管部门物品的公平市价。

修订法规，1985 年第 C-51 章第 22 条；1991 年第 49 章第 217 条。

行政

行政服务

23. 部长应当为复审委员会提供行政服务。

1974-75-76 年第 50 章第 20 条。

规则和程序

规则

24. 复审委员会为执行本法中规定的程序、履行规定的义务和职能，可以在不与本法相抵触的情况下，制定规则。

1974-75-76 年第 50 章第 21 条。

复审委员会可以接受的信息

25. 复审委员会可以接受与其处理的问题相关的以口头和书面形式提交的任何信息，且不受证据法律规则或技术规定的约束。

1974-75-76 年第 50 章第 22 条。

向申请者提供信息

26. 复审委员会应将其收到的、与待处理的问题相关信息的实质内容要旨，告知该问题涉及的标的物出口许可证申请人，或者根据具体情况，告知依本法第 32 条第（1）款规定申请裁决的个人、机构或公共主管部门（视情况而定）。在复审委员会对该问题作出处理之前，应给予该人、机构或公共主管部门陈述对该信息意见的机会。

1974-75-76 年第 50 章第 22 条。

听证除外

27. 复审委员会可以拒绝与正在处理的问题无直接利害关系的任何人参加听证，除非出口许可证申请人要求公开听证，且实际上也进行了公开听证。

1974-75-76 年第 50 章第 22 条。

复审委员会应不拘形式地、迅速地处理问题

28. 复审委员会，在情况允许和保证公平的前提下，应遵从自己的内心迅速地、不拘形式地对需要解决的问题作出处理。

1974-75-76 年第 50 章第 22 条。

出口许可证申请的审查

要求复审委员会进行审查

29.（1）收到本法第 13 条规定的拒绝通知或第 15 条规定的通知后，出口许可证申请人可在通知送达之日起 30 日内，以书面形式提请复审委员会对申请进行审查。

复审应在四个月内进行

（2）复审委员会应当对出口许可证申请进行审查，且应在收到第（1）款所规定的申请之日起 4 个月内作出决定，除非个案有其他要求。

复审委员会的决定

（3）对出口许可证申请进行审查时，复审委员会应当确认申请出口的物品：

（a）是否在《控制清单》中；

（b）是否因第 11 条第（1）款第（a）项规定的一个或一个以上的理由而具有显著的重要性；以及

（c）是否达到第 11 条第（1）款第（b）项规定的重要程度。

不符合标准的物品

（4）若复审委员会认为某物品未达到本法第（3）款规定的一项或多项标准，则应立即指示许可官员签发该物品的出口许可证。

符合标准的物品

（5）若复审委员会认为该物符合本法第（3）款规定的全部标准，

（a）如果认为自作出决定之日起 6 个月内，加拿大有关机构或公共主管部门可能以公平价格购买这个物品，应确定一个 2 个月至 6 个月的延缓期，在此期间，复审委员会将不会作出签发许可证的指示；或

（b）在其他任何情况下，应指示许可官员立即签发该物品的出口许可证。

延缓期间的通知

（6）如果复审委员会依据本条第（5）款第（a）项确定了一个延缓期，则应书面通知出口许可证申请人和部长延缓期的期限。该通知应当包括复审委员会认为该物符合第（3）款全部标准的理由。

延缓期间的通知

（7）部长一收到第（6）款规定的通知，就应将延缓期和或延缓期所涉及的物品通知给其认为适合的加拿大境内机构和公共主管部门。

1974-75-76 年第 50 章第 23 条。

申请确定公平交易价格

30.（1）如果复审委员会根据第 29 条第（5）款（a）项确定了延缓期，且在该期间内相关机构或公共主管部门确定了该物品的交易价格，但是出口许可证申请人无法接受该价格，那么申请人、机构和公共主管部门均可通过书面形式要求复审委员会确定该物品的公平交易现金价格。

提出申请的时间

（2）本条第（1）款规定的提出申请，不得晚于第 29 条第（5）款（a）项所规定的延缓期届满前 30 日。

复审委员会的决定

（3）复审委员会收到第（1）款所规定的申请后，应确定申请出口物品的公平交易现金价格，且将该价格通知给出口许可证申请人，或提出报价购买该物品的机构或公共主管部门。

出口许可的指示

（4）若复审委员会根据第 29 条第（5）款（a）项确定了延缓期，且在该期间内没有收到第（1）款规定的申请，则延缓期结束后，应依照第 29 条第（1）款的申请，指示许可官员立即签发该物品的出口许可证。

出口许可的指示

（5）若复审委员会根据第 29 条第（5）款（a）项确定了延缓期，且收到了第（1）款规定的申请，则在延缓期届满后，或在确立了第（3）款所规定的某物品的公平交易现金价格之后（以较晚时间为准），根据第 29 款第（1）项规定请求，指示许可官员立即签发出口许可证。除非复审委员会确信在申请提出之前，相关机构或公共主管部门已经提出以等于或高于复审委员会确定的价格来购买该物品。

1974-75-76 年第 50 章第 24 条。

出口许可证的限制

31. 复审委员会不得指示许可官员签发出口许可证，根据第 29 或第 30 条签发的除外。

1974-75-76 年第 50 章第 25 条。

与《所得税法》有关的决定

要求复审委员会作出决定

32.（1）为《所得税法》第 39 条第（1）款（a）项（i.1）目和本法第 110.1 条第（1）款（c）项的目的，以及为确定该法第 118.1 条第（1）款和第 118.1 条第（10）款中“纯粹文化赠与”的定义。若某人将申请出口的物品处置或拟处置给本条第（2）款指定的机构或公共主管部门，那么该人、该机构或公共主管部门均可通过书面形式要求复审委员会确定该物品是否符合第 29 条第（3）款（b）（c）两项规定的标准，同时确定该物品的公平市场价。

指定主管部门和机构

（2）为《所得税法》第 39 条第（1）款（a）项（i.1）目和本法第 110.1 条第（1）款（c）项的目的、确定该法第 118.1 条第（1）款和第 118.1 条第（10）款以及第 207 条第 3 款中“纯粹文化赠与”的定义，部长可以任意地或在一定时间内或为特定的目的，指定任何机构或公共主管部门。

撤回指定

（3）部长可以在任何时间内撤回根据本条第（2）款所作指定。

在四个月内作出决定

（4）复审委员会应当审查本条第（1）款规定的要求，除非特殊情况，应当在收到申请书之日起 4 个月内作出决定，将该决定以书面或电子方式送交给处置或拟处置该物品的人。若上述审查要求是由指定的机构或公共主管部门提出的，则还应当送达给该机构或公共主管部门。

重新作出决定

（5）若复审委员会已依据第（4）款的规定，确定了处置或拟处置物品的公平市场价，则其：

（a）应该在已将该物品处置或拟处置给指定机构或公共主管部门的人提出书面申请时，或其为本目的而指定的代理人提出书面申请时，在前款规定的通知送达之日起 12 个月内重新确定该物品的公平市场价；以及

（b）可以在任何时间内主动确定某物品的公平市场价。

在四个月内重新作出决定以及决定结果的通知

（6）若依据第（5）条第（a）款规定需要重新决定某物品的公平市场价，除非有特殊情况，复审委员会应当在申请之日起 4 个月内做出，且应将最新决定以书面形式或电子方式通知申请人。

主动作出的重新决定的通知

（7）若复审委员会依据本条第（5）款（b）项的规定重新作出决定，则该决定应以书面或电子方式送达给处置或拟处置的申请人；若（1）款规定的申请由指定机构或公共主管部门提出，则重新决定还应送给该机构或公共主管部门。

限制

（8）除非有特殊情况，复审委员会不应多次重新确定某物品的公平市场价。

终局的、确定性的决定

（9）本条第（5）款规定的、有关拟处置的决定，不得上诉，也不受任何法庭的审查。

修订法规，1985 年第 C-51 章第 32 条；1991 年第 49 章第 218 条；1995 年第 38 章第 1 条。

所得税确认书

所得税确认书

33.（1）若复审委员会确定了或依第 32 条规定的申请确定了某物品的公平市场价，且认为该物符合第 29 条第（3）款第（b）项和第（c）项所规定的标准，如该物品已被不可撤销地处置给指定的机构或公共主管部门，则复审委员会应以国家税务部长指定的方式，向处置该物之人发放确认书，证实该品的公平市场价以及该物品符合规定的标准。

国家税务部长送达副本

（1.1）复审委员会应将第（1）款规定的确认书副本送交国家税务部长。

当存在一个以上的确认书

（1.2）若复审委员会针对某物品签发的第（1）款所确认书不止一个，则最后一次签发的应视为与该物品唯一确认书。

交换信息

（2）为有效实施《所得税法》，加拿大遗产局的官员或复审委员会的委员，可以同加拿大税务局交换信息。这些信息是为实施本条和第 32 条、第 33.1 条和第 33.2 条的规定，而依据本法收集来的。

修订法规，1985 年第 C-51 章第 33 条；1991 年第 49 章第 219 条；1995 年第 11 章第 45 条，第 38 章第 2 条；1999 年第 17 章第 122 条；2005 年第 38 章第 138 条。

上诉至加拿大税收法院

请求重新确定公平市场价的上诉

33.1（1）若某物品的公平市场价已经按照第 32 条第（5）款的规定重新确定，并且该物品不可撤销地处置给指定机构或公共主管部门，处置人可在第 33 条第（1）款规定的确认书签发之日起 90 日内向加拿大税收法院提出上诉，请求重新确定该物品的公平市场价。

法院的决定

（2）接受本条第（1）款规定的上诉请求后，加拿大税收法院依《所得税法》的宗旨可以确认或改变该物品的公平市场价，法院所确定的价格应视为复审委员会确定的处置该物品的公平市场价。

1995 年第 38 章第 2 条。

上诉期的延长

33.2（1）若处置人没有在第 33.1 条规定的期限内提出上诉，则可以申请加拿大税收法院延长上诉期。法院可以通知延长，也可以附加适当条件。

申请书的内容

（2）本条第（1）款所提申请中应列明未能在第 33.1 条所规定的期限内提出上诉的原因。

如何提出申请

（3）第（1）款所提申请应根据《加拿大税收法院法》，在加拿大税收法院登记处登记提出，同时应附上申请书的三份副本以及上诉通知的三份副本。

向助理司法部长提交副本

（4）加拿大税收法院应将本条规定的申请书副本提交给加拿大助理司法部长办公室。

下发命令的情形

（5）下述情形中，方可下发命令：

（a）在第 33.1 条规定的上诉期届满后 1 年内提出申请；以及

（b）申请人能够证明：

（i）在第 33.1 条规定的上诉期内，申请人

（A）确实不能上诉，或者委托他人以申请人的名义代为上诉，或

（B）出于善意提起上诉，

（ii）申请书中所列明的理由和案件具体情况能够证明申请是正确且适当的，

（iii）条件一旦成熟即提出申请，以及

（iv）有适当理由提出申请。

1995 年第 38 章第 2 条；2000 年第 30 章第 159 条。

向部长报告

向部长报告

34. 复审委员会主席，每年 3 月 31 日之后，应尽快向部长提交关于上一年度复审委员会运转情况的报告，如果有建议，还应在报告中附上建议。

修订法规，1985 年第 C-51 章第 34 条；1995 年第 29 章第 22© 条。

财政

财政拨款资助与贷款

35. 部长可以将国会拨款资助或借贷给加拿大某机构或公共主管部门，以购买依照本法被拒发出口许可证的物品，或加拿大境外的与国家遗产相关的文化财产。

1974-75-76 年第 50 章第 29 条。

设立加拿大遗产保护捐赠帐户

36.（1）应在加拿大国家帐户中专门设立一个“加拿大遗产保护捐赠帐户”。

记入加拿大遗产保护捐赠帐户的款项

（2）记入加拿大遗产保护捐赠帐户的款项有：

（a）女王收到的赠与、遗赠，以及为购买被拒发出口许可证的物品或为购买境外的与加拿大遗产相关的物品而拨付或贷给该机构或公共主管部门使用的款项；

（b）为（a）项的目的，女王持有的证券出售收入及其他收益，以及

（c）存款利息，该利息是按照总督参照财政大臣建议所定的利率计算出来的。

可记入加拿大遗产保护捐赠帐户的款项

（3）除依据本法第 35 条规定，资助某机构或公共主管部门以购买拒发出口许可证的物品，或加拿大境外的与加拿大国家遗产相关的物品支出外，部长的其他支出也可计入加拿大遗产保护捐赠帐户。

1974-75-76 年第 50 章第 30 条。

《武装冲突情况下保护文化财产的公约》及其《附加议定书》

定义

36.1（1）以下定义适用于本条。

“公约”是指 1954 年 5 月 14 日在海牙订立的《武装冲突情况下保护文化财产的公约》。《公约》第 1 条见本法附件。

“第一议定书”是指 1954 年 5 月 14 日在海牙订立的附属于《公约》的第一项议定书。

“第二议定书”是指 1999 年 3 月 26 日在海牙订立的附属于《公约》的第二项议定书。

“缔约国”是指《公约》以及《第一议定书》或《第二议定书》的签约国。

出口或转移文化财产

（2）任何人均不得故意出口《公约》第1条第（a）项指定的文化财产或以其它方式将其从《第二议定书》缔约国境内转移出去，除非此种出口或转移符合该国法律或对该财产的保护或保存而言是必要的。

加拿大境外的违法行为视为在加拿大发生的违法行为

（3）尽管本法和其他法案有任何规定，某人在加拿大境外的某一行为或不作为（疏忽）如果在加拿大境内发生则违反第（2）款规定，或预谋或企图从事该违法行为，或者事后协助、庇护这种违法行为的，以下情形中上述行为或不作为应视同发生在加拿大：

（a）行为人是加拿大公民；

（b）行为人不属于任何国家的公民但长期居住加拿大；或

（c）行为人属于《移民及难民保护法》第2（1）款定义的常住居民，并且在犯罪后，仍在加拿大。

文化财产返还之诉

（4）如果缔约国政府向部长提出书面申请要求收回和归还从该缔约国境内出口到加拿大且被加拿大任何个人、机构或公共主管部门控制的任何文化财产，加拿大司法部长可以在联邦法院或省高级法院提起诉讼，以返还缔约国要求的财产。

诉讼通知

（5）根据本条提起的诉讼，司法部长应当将通知依照受理法院规定的方式送达当事人，如果没有既定送达规则，则按照法院法官裁定方式送达。

文化财产返还令

（6）根据本条受理案件的法院，在听取了与本案有利害关系的所有当事人的意见后，如果认为该财产出口到加拿大系违反缔约国相关法律或者该财产是为了获得保护或保存而进口到加拿大，且已支付本条第（7）款确定的金额（如有），法院可以判决返还诉讼所涉及的财产，或者作出其它足以保证财产返还给缔约国的判决。

补偿

（7）根据本条受理该案的法院如合理认为购买财产的个人、机构或公共主管部门是善意购买人或享有诉讼所涉及财产的有效所有权，并且在购买财产或获得财产所有权之时对以下情况并不知情，那么法院可判定缔约国应支付给该个人、机构或公共主管部门公正补偿：

（a）该财产的出口违反了缔约国相关法律；或

（b）该财产是为获得保护或保存而进口到加拿大的。

保全

（8）在本条规定的诉讼中，法院可以在最后判决之前的任何时间，命令将诉讼涉及的财产移交给部长保管或保存。

出口许可证

（9）收到法院依据本条第（6）款所做命令的副本之后，部长应向诉讼相关缔约国的委托人签发出口许可证，授权他将法院命令所涉财产运回缔约国。

不适用的限制条款

（10）《联邦法院法》第 39 条不适用于依照本条提起的任何诉讼。

2005 年第 40 章第 4 条。

外国文化财产

定义

37.（1）在本条中，

“文化财产协定”与其他国家相关，是指加拿大与其他国家签订的双边协定，或加拿大与其他国家均参加的国际协议，该协议旨在防止国际间非法转让文化财产；

“外国文化财产”与加拿大互惠国相关，是指被该国指定具有考古、史前、历史、文学、艺术、科学价值的物品；

“互惠国”是指作为文化财产协定成员国的其他国家。

非法进口

（2）文化财产协定在加拿大和互惠国生效后，任何外国文化财产从互惠国非法出口并进口到加拿大的均属非法进口。

外国文化财产的返还之诉

（3）若任何外国文化财产像本条第（2）款规定那样非法进口到加拿大，并被加拿大境内的任何个人、机构或公共主管部门所有或受其控制，互惠国政府以书面形式向部长提出寻找并返还请求，加拿大司法部长可以在联邦法院或省高级法院提起诉讼，以返还互惠国请求的财产。

诉讼通知

（4）根据本条提起的诉讼，司法部长应当将通知依照管辖法院则规定的方式送达当事人，如果没有既定送达规则，则按照该法院法官裁定方式送达。

指定财产返还令

（5）根据本条代表互惠国利益受理该案的法院，在听取了当事人和利害关系人意见后，如果认定该财产系依本条第（2）款非法进口到加拿大，且已经支付本条第（6）款确定的金额（如有），则法院可以为互惠国的利益判决返还涉案财产，或者作出其它足以保证财产返还给互惠国的判决。

补偿

（6）若任何个人、机构或公共主管部门能够使审理法院相信：

（a）他（它）是涉案财产的善意购买人，而且在购买该财产时，不知道

该财产是从互惠国非法出口的，正是为了该互惠国的利益启动了本次诉讼，或

（b）他（它）持有涉案财产的有效所有权，且在得到该所有权时，不知道该财产是从互惠国非法出口的，正是为了该互惠国的利益启动了本次诉讼，

那么，法院在认为公证合理的范围内，可以判定由该互惠国向上述个人、机构或公共主管部门支付一笔金额作为补偿。

保全

（7）在本条规定的诉讼中，法院可以在最后判决之前的任何时间，命令将涉案财产移交给部长保管或保存。

出口许可证

（8）收到本条第（5）款规定的法院命令副本后，部长应向诉讼相关互惠国委托人签发出口许可证，以授权他将涉案财产运回互惠国。

不适用的限制条款

（9）《联邦法院法》第 39 条不适用于依照本条提起的任何诉讼。

修订法规，1985 年第 C-51 章第 37 条；2002 年第 8 章第 182 条。

文化财产的确定

文化财产的确定

38. 为了《禁止和防止非法进口文化财产和非法转让其所有权的方法的公约》第 1 条的目的，《控制清单》中的任何物品均被加拿大指定为具有考古、史前、历史、文学、艺术或科学意义。

1974-75-76 年第 50 章第 32 条。

规则

规则

39. 总督根据部长和外交大臣的建议，可以制定规则，要求提供以下信息：

（a）申请者依本法申请许可证或确认书时应当提交的信息、文件或保证书，申请、签发许可证或确认书的程序，适用条件和术语，以及许可证的有效期；

（b）根据本法取得许可证的人需提供必要的信息情况和信息类型；

（c）为本法第 7 条第（c）款的目的，在一定期间内将某物移出加拿大的目的及其期间；

（d）为本法第 14 条规定的目的，各种手稿、原始文件、档案、照片及其底片、胶片和录音。

修订法规，1985 年第 C-51 章第 39 条；1995 年第 5 章第 25 条；1998 年第 19 章第 261 条。

犯罪与惩罚

出口或企图出口

40. 除非根据本法签发的许可证或授权，任何人不得从加拿大出口或企图出口《管制清单》中的任何物品。

1974-75-76 年第 50 章第 34 条。

不得转让许可证

41. 依据本法所签发的许可证授权从加拿大出口物品的人，不得转让该许可证或允许非授权人使用。

1974-75-76 年第 50 章第 35 条。

虚假信息

42. 以下情形中，任何人不得故意提供伪造的、误导性的信息资料，或者故意作错误表述：

（a）在请求依照本法规定签发许可证的申请书中；

（b）根据本法取得许可证过程中；或

（c）在依照使用本法签发的许可证或处置与此类许可证有关物品时。

1974-75-76 年第 50 章第 36 条。

进口或企图进口外国文化财产

43. 任何人不得进口或企图进口本法第 37 条第（2）款规定的、非法进口到加拿大的任何财产。

1974-75-76 年第 50 章第 37 条。

出口或企图出口

44.（1）已经根据本法第 37 条第（3）款提起诉讼，且诉讼正在进行中的，任何人不得从加拿大出口或企图出口涉案财产。

出口或企图出口

（2）除非有部长依据本法第 37 条第（8）款签发的许可证或许可证授权，任何人不得从加拿大出口或企图出口本法第 37 条第（5）款判决所涉及的财产。

1974-75-76 年第 50 章第 38 条。

犯罪与惩罚

45.（1）凡违反本法第 36 条第 1 款第 2 项以及第 40 条至第 44 条规定的均构成犯罪，则

（a）依照简易程序定罪的，判处 5000 加元以下的罚金，或 / 并处 12 月以下监禁；

（b）依照公诉程序定罪的，判处 25 000 加元以下的罚金，或 / 并处 5 年以下监禁。

诉讼有效期

（2）第（1）款（a）规定的诉讼可在起诉事由发生之日起3年内提出。

修订法规，1985年第C-51章第45条；2005年第40章第5条。

法人犯罪

46. 当法人触犯本法规定的罪名，无论该法人是否被起诉或被判有罪，法人中指挥、授权、批准、默许或直接参与犯罪的官员、董事或代理人均属有罪，并将依照简易程序或者公诉程序受到相应处罚。

1974-75-76年第50章第40条。

审判地点

47. 因触犯本法规定的罪名而进行的任何诉讼，可在加拿大境内的案发地，或者诉讼时犯罪嫌疑人在加拿大境内的住所地、经常居住地、办公地或者营业地提起、审理或判决。

1974-75-76年第50章第41条。

证据

48.（1）在本法有关货运单据物品运送的诉讼中，提货单、海关文件、商业发票或其他文件的正本和副本（本条中称为“货运单据”），为可采信证据，可证明：

（a）物品是从加拿大送出、运出或运入加拿大的；

（b）承运人、托运人或收货人将该物品从加拿大送出、运出或带入加拿大；或

（c）物品被送到或运到指定目的地或个人。

事实证据

（2）若无相反的证据，依本条第（1）款而采信的证据，将被看作货运单据所涉及的、本条第（1）款（a）、（b）、（c）项所述事实的证据。

1974-75-76年第50章第42条。

附则

其他法律义务

49. 依本法签发的出口许可证或其它可出口物品的许可证，不得影响出口人根据其它法律为出口某物品而取得的任何执照、许可证或合格证中规定的义务，也不影响其因出口某物品而应按照任何法律要求缴纳赋税、关税、通行费或其他费用的义务。

1974-75-76 年第 50 章第 43 条。

海关官员的责任

50.《海关法》所指官员，在许可某物品出口之前，若有理由怀疑该物品的进出口违反本法及相关规则，那么，有权要求出口人或进口人证明该物品的进出口并不违反本法及相关规则的任何规定，且完全符合该物品的所有要求。

修订法规，1985 年第 C-51 章第 50 条；修订法规，1985 年第 1 章（第 2 次增补）第 213 条。

《海关法》相关权力的适用

51.《海关法》所指的每一位官员对适用本法的任何物品都享有《海关法》赋予的有关货物进出口的任何权力；对以下物品，有权根据实际需要行使《海关法》及相关规则规定的搜查、扣押、没收或征用的权力：

（a）拟出口或拟进口的物品、已出口或已进口的物品，或其它没有依照本及其规则的规定进行处置的物品；以及

（b）（a）项所述物品的相关文件。

修订法规，1985 年第 C-51 章第 51 条；修订法规，1985 年第 1 章（第 2 次增补）第 213 条。

向国会提交报告

52. 部长收到复审委员会主席依本法第 34 条而提交的报告后，应即尽快拟定并向国会提交一份可行报告，该报告包括本法在复审委员会主席报告所在财

年内的执行情况，还包括复审委员会主席的报告。

修订法规，1985 年第 C-51 章第 52 条；1995 年第 29 章第 22 条（c）款。

附件

（第 36.1 条第（1）款）

《武装冲突情况下保护文化财产的公约》第 1 条，1954 年 5 月 14 日，海牙

第 1 条文化财产的定义

为本《公约》目的，“文化财产”，不论其来源或所有权，应包括：

（a）对各国人民的文化遗产具有重大意义的动产或不动产，例如建筑、艺术或历史上的纪念物，不论是宗教性的或者是世俗的；考古遗址；具有历史或艺术上价值的整套建筑物；艺术品；手稿、书籍和其他具有艺术、历史或考古价值的其他物品；以及科学珍藏和书籍或档案的重要珍藏或者上述各物的复制品；

（b）其主要目的为保存或展览（a）款所述的可移动文化财产的建筑物，例如博物馆、大型图书馆和档案库，以及发生武装冲突时准备用以掩护（a）款所述的可移动文化财产的保藏所；

（c）用以存放大量的（a）（b）两款所述文化财产的中心站，称为“纪念物中心站”。

2005 年第 40 章第 6 条。

相关条款

—1991 年第 49 章第 216 条第（2）款：（2）所述法案第 20 条（c）项的规定应被认为与第 118.1 条第（10）款的规定无关，除此之外，对本条第（1）款所规定的、在 1990 年 2 月 21 日之前完成的赠与，本条第（1）款只在 1988 年 12 月 11 日之后适用。

—1991 年第 49 章第 217 条第（2）款：（2）本条第（1）款于 1990 年 2 月 20 日以后生效。

—1991 年第 49 章第 218 条第（3）款和第（4）款:（3）法案第 32 条第（1）款应被认为与“复审委员会对某物品的公平市场价的确定无关”，除此之外，对本条第（1)款所规定的、在 1990 年 2 月 21 日之前完成的赠与，本条第（1）款只在 1988 年 12 月 11 日以后适用。

—1991 年第 49 章第 218 条第（3）款和第（4）款:（4）本条第（2）款的规定适用于 1990 年 2 月 20 日之后完成的赠与。

—1991 年第 49 章第 219 条第（2）款:（2）本条第（1）款所涉及的、法案第 33 款第（1）项的规定在 1990 年 2 月 20 日以后适用。

—1995 年第 38 章第 8 条第（1）款至第（3）款:

过渡

8.（1）若某物品在 1992 年 1 月 1 日至本条生效期间，已由加拿大文化财产复审委员会依照《加拿大文化财产进出口法》第 32 条，确定或重新确定了公平市场价，且在本条规定生效之前，该物品已被不可撤销地处置给指定的机构或公共主管部门，则处置该物品的人可以在本条规定生效之日起 6 个月内，上诉至加拿大税收法院，以确定或重新确定该物品的公平市场价。

过渡

（2）若某物品在 1992 年 1 月 1 日至本条生效期间，已由加拿大文化财产复审委员会依照《加拿大文化财产进出口法》第 32 条，确定或重新确定了公平市场价，且在本条规定生效之日起 6 个月内，该物品已被不可撤销地处置给指定的机构或公共主管部门，则处置该物的人可以在处置该物品之日起 6 个月内，上诉至加拿大税收法院，以确定或重新确定该物的公平市场价。

部分条款的适用

（3）在本法第 2 条中所涉及的、《文化财产进出口法》第 33 条第（2）款和第 33.1 条第（2）款以及第 33.2 条，在根据实际情况作出这样修改的情况下，适用本条第（1）款和第（2）款规定的上诉。

六、澳大利亚

述 评

澳大利亚重视保护本国文物，制定了详尽严格的文物出境管控措施，对于非法进境文物，一经发现并核实，澳大利亚政府即没收并主动归还给原属国。1986年，澳大利亚专门制定了《可移动文物保护法》，历经多次修正[①]，最近一次修正启动于2014年，新修正的法律于同年7月1日生效，该法共6部分，规定了相关定义、法律适用、文物进出口控制、国家文物委员会职能、国家文物专项资金、法律的实施等。其中涉及文物进出境管理的条款主要集中于本法第二部分以及第16、41条。

从立法、监管、鉴定、执法到支持机构，澳大利亚拥有一套完整的文物保护体系。澳大利亚通讯与艺术部（Communications and Arts）主管澳大利亚的博物馆和艺术馆，是可移动文物的监管部门，艺术部部长还可根据需要任命特别巡视员，对条例的执行情况进行检查——澳大利亚联邦警察局及各州、领地警察局的警官都被视为巡视员。澳大利亚海关与边境保护署承担着侦查、发现文物非法进出境的重任，联邦警察局在必要的情况下，配合其他政府部门，对非法进出境文物展开调查和收缴。澳大利亚政府还设立了国家文物专项资金，为收藏机构提供资助，以购入那些未能获得出境许可的文物，确保那些有价值的文物能够留在澳大利亚境内，供专家研究和全体国民欣赏。该资金总额为每年50万澳元，各类收藏机构均可申请，如博物馆、美术馆、图书馆、档案馆等。大量国家级、州级文化机构，非营利性文化机构均得到过该专项的资助，私立机构所获得的资金总额占到30%以上。[②]此外，根据《可移动文物保护法》设立的国家文物委员会，负责《国家文物控制清单》的制定和调整，与国家文物专项资金的运行，对文物进出境管理起到必不可少地辅助作用。

---

① 详见澳大利亚《可移动文物保护法》尾注3和尾注4。

② 林瑞华：《澳大利亚：严苛出入境为文物上双保险》，载于《中国文化报》，2016年1月11日。

《可移动文物保护法》

1986年可移动文物保护法

1986年第11号修正案

（陈锐达　初校）

编纂开始日期：2014年7月1日

修订截止：2014年第62号法案

（堪培拉议会法律顾问办公室编写）

关于本次编纂

本次编纂

本法为《1986年可移动文物保护法》的编纂，于2014年7月1日生效。本次编纂包括该日期前对本法编纂所有已启动的有效修订。

本次编纂于2014年8月13日开始筹备。

本次编纂最后的注释（尾注）包括有关修正案和各修正条款的修正历史信息。

未启动的修订

未启动的修正案的效力没有体现在已编法律文本中，但尾注包含了该修订的文本。

条款及修正案的适用、保留和过渡性条款。

如果条款和修正案的执行受已编法律中未包含的适用、保留和过渡性条款的影响，详见尾注。

更改

已编法律被现行法律更改的，详见尾注。

失效条款

根据本法有关条款，已编法律某条款已过期或失效的，详见尾注。

本法对澳大利亚可移动文物保护、支持外国可移动文物保护及相关用途作出规定。

第一部分　前言

1. 简称

本法可引称为《1986 年可移动文物保护法》。

2. 生效

本法于公告确定的生效日期生效。

3. 释义

（1）本法中，除非出现相反用意：

飞行器是指依靠空气反应或浮力在大气中获得支撑的机器或装置。

任命包括再次任命。

澳大利亚包括除诺福克岛以外的外部领地。

澳大利亚保护文物是指 A 类文物或 B 类文物。

证明文件是指根据第 12 条生效的证明文件。

主席是指委员会主席。

A **类文物**是指包括在控制清单“A 类文物”序列中的文物。

B **类文物**是指包括在控制清单“B 类文物”序列中的文物。

沿海海域在澳大利亚是指：

（a）澳大利亚领海；及

（b）澳大利亚领海向陆地一侧的海域。

委员会是指根据第 15 条规定成立的国家文物委员会。

条件，在许可证中是指许可条件。

控制清单是指第 8 条规定的现行有效的《国家文物控制清单》。

专家鉴定人是指在第 22 条规定的名册上登记了姓名的人。

出口是指从澳大利亚出口。

进口是指向澳大利亚进口。

澳大利亚内水包括澳大利亚沿海海域向陆一侧的所有水域。

检查员是指第 28 条规定的检查员。

成员是指委员会成员。

国家文物账户是指根据第 25 条建立的账户。

许可证是指根据第 11 条有效的许可证。

主要收藏机构是指根据联邦法律、州法律或领地法律成立的

（a）公共艺术馆；或

（b）公共博物馆；或

（c）公共图书馆；或

（d）公共档案馆；

受保护文物是指受澳大利亚保护的文物或受外国保护的文物。

受外国保护文物是指构成外国可移动文化遗产一部分的文物。

结构包括固定在海床上的平台或其他海上操作平台。

船只是指任何能够在水上装载或运输人员或货物的（交通工具），包括气垫船或类似船只。

（2）本法所赋予的权利，可由权利人自行决定行使该权利。

（3）违反本法或违反本法有关罪行，包括违反：

（a）《1914 年犯罪法》第 6 条；或

（b）附属犯罪（参见《刑法典》规定的含义）

视为违反本法该规定或违反本法的罪行（视情况而定）。

（3A）违反本法的罪行，包括违反与本法有关的《刑法典》第 148.1 条、第 148.2 条、第 147.1 条或第 149.1 条的犯罪。

（4）为了本法目的，法人团体实施本法时，在不影响其他任何非法人团体的个人责任的情况下：

（a）代表该法人团体利益的个人作出的声明或提交的文件，视为该法人团体作出的声明或提交的文件；且

（b）任何受该法人团体雇用或与其管理有关的人知悉的情形，视为该法人团体知悉的情形。

（5）本法中提及的外国可移动文物，指对该国或该国特定领域具有重要性的物品，基于：

（a）民族的、考古的、历史的、文学的、艺术的、科学的或技术的；或

（b）其他任何法定理由。

（6）本法中文物进出口条款，虽然某物品从一国运至澳大利亚是为了转运到其他国家，或者该文物是作为船只或飞行器的仓储或设备的一部分而运至澳大利亚，也适用本法文物进出口条款。

4. 本法约束王权

英联邦、各州、北方领地和诺福克岛之王权受本法约束。

5. 适用

本法适用于澳大利亚国内和国外。

6. 扩大适用于各领地

本法适用扩展到除诺福克岛之外的各外部领地。

6A.《刑法典》的适用

《刑法典》第 2 章适用于违反本法的所有罪行。

注：《刑法典》第 2 章规定了刑事责任的一般原则。

第二部分　进出口控制

第一节　出口

7. 澳大利亚可移动文物

（1）本法第 8 条所称澳大利亚可移动文物，是指对澳大利亚或澳大利亚某一领域具有重要民族、考古、历史、文学、艺术、科学或技术价值的物品，属于以下一个或多个类别：

（a）从下列地点发现的物品：

（i）澳大利亚的土地或内水；

（ii）澳大利亚沿海海域或大陆架覆盖水域；或

（iii）第（ii）段中的海域或水域的海床或底土；

（b）与澳大利亚原住民和托勒斯海峡群岛上原住民后裔有关的物品；

（c）民族艺术品或民族物品；

（d）军事物品；

（e）装饰艺术品；

（f）美术作品；

（g）有科学技术价值的物品；

（h）图书、档案、文献或照片、图像、影视资料或录音；

（j）其他规定的类别。

（2）第（1）款（j）项的范围不受第（1）款中其他各项的限制。

8. 国家文物控制清单

（1）根据本法第（2）款，依法编制一份属于澳大利亚可移动文物并应受出口限制的物品清单，称为《国家文物控制清单》。

（2）控制清单将此类文物分为两个级别，即：

（a）A 类文物，只能依据证明文件出口的文物；及

（b）B 类文物，只能依据许可证或证明文件出口的文物。

（3）第（2）款的规定并不妨碍将 A 类文物和 B 类文物进一步分级，或者按其他类别划分。

（4）本条任何规定，不构成对《1901 年法律解释法》第 33 条第（3A）款的适用限制。

9. **非法出口**

（1）没有按照许可证或证明文件出口澳大利亚保护文物，该文物将被没收。

（2）企图不按照许可证或证明书出口澳大利亚保护文物，该文物将可能被没收。

（3）有以下行为的人即为犯罪：

（a）出口或企图出口文物；且

（b）该文物为澳大利亚保护文物；且

（c）不按照许可证或证明文件实施（a）项行为。

（3A）有以下行为的人即为犯罪：

（a）持有关于澳大利亚保护文物的许可证或证明文件；且

（b）行为人实施某一行为；且

（c）该行为违反了许可证或证明文件的条件。

（3B）行为人被裁定违反第（3）款或第（3A）款规定的：

（a）个人违法的，判处 1,000 个罚款单位以下的罚金，或 / 并处 5 年以下监禁；

（b）法人团体违法的，判处 2,000 个罚款单位以下的罚金。

注：简易审判庭的量刑标准参见第 46 条第（4）款。

（4）为本条的目的，文物在以下时间视为出口：

（a）该文物已被放置在位于澳大利亚某处的船只或飞行器上，将由该船只或飞行器将该文物带离澳大利亚，且该船只或飞行器已开始离港；或

（b）该文物已作为邮递物品被送至位于澳大利亚某处的澳大利亚邮政公司控制范围内，欲以邮寄方式带离澳大利亚，且已开始从该地

点邮寄该文物。

（5）在对本条所指的企图出口文物的含义不作限制的情况下，企图出口该文物或明知该文物企图被出口而运送或持有该文物的，视为企图出口该文物。

（6）为了本条的目的，出口或企图出口澳大利亚保护文物的，视为不按照许可证或证明文件出口或企图出口，除非在出口或企图出口之前出示批准出口的许可证或证明文件：

（a）非从境外领地出口的，向海关官员出示；或

（b）从境外领地出口的，向负责澳大利亚保护文物出口的检查人员出示。

（7）本条中：

“实施某一行为”指：

（a）采取某一行动；或

（b）疏于采取某一行动。

10. 向特定文物颁发许可证

（1）出口B类文物的，可向部长申请B类文物出口许可证。

（2）应按规定的书面格式申请，没有规定格式的，按部长批准的格式申请。

（3）部长收到申请后，应转交给委员会，由委员会转交一名或多名专家鉴定人。

（4）专家鉴定人或者鉴定人向委员会提交关于申请的书面报告，由委员会将该报告及委员会书面建议（如有）一并转交给部长。

（5）部长审议该报告和建议（如有），并：

（a）颁发许可证，准许按照部长规定的条件（如有）出口该文物；或

（b）拒绝颁发许可证。

（6）专家鉴定人、委员会和部长评议申请时：

（a）除须考虑的其他事项外，应参阅第7条第（1）款中与申请文物

相关的规定；及

（b）若确信该文物对澳大利亚或澳大利亚的某一领域具有重要价值，一旦失去该文物将导致澳大利亚文物的重大损失，则不建议颁发许可证，或颁发许可证，使该文物永久出口（视情况而定）。

（7）如果部长拒绝颁发许可证，应在作出决定后的规定期限内向申请人送达书面通知，并列明拒绝的理由。

10A 向机构颁发一般许可证

（1）主要收藏机构可向部长申请许可证，以便出口该机构收藏的B类文物。

（2）对于不是法人团体的主要收藏机构，该机构的经营负责人可依第（1）款提出申请。

（3）应按规定的书面格式申请，没有规定格式的，按部长批准的格式申请。

（4）部长收到申请后，必须转交给委员会。

（5）委员会必须向部长提交关于申请的书面报告。

（6）部长必须对报告进行审议，并：

（a）向申请人颁发许可证，准许出口该机构负责收藏的B类文物；或

（b）拒绝颁发许可证。

（7）颁发许可证须符合以下条件：

（a）出借B类文物用于研究、公开展览或出于类似目的；及

（b）部长在许可证中规定的其他条件（如有）。

（8）如果部长拒绝颁发许可证，必须在作出决定后的规定期限内向申请人送达书面通知，并列明拒绝的理由。

11. 许可证

（1）根据第10条或第10A条颁发的许可证，应为规定格式的书面许可证，没有规定格式的，按部长批准的格式颁发。

（2）根据第 10 条或第 10A 条颁发的许可证，自颁发之日起生效，并在许可证规定的期限内有效，没有有效期的，则持续有效。

12. 豁免证明

（1）计划进口澳大利亚受保护文物的行为人：

（a）用于暂时性目的；或

（b）计划随后即出口该文物；

可向部长申请授权出口该文物的证明文件，以批准出口该文物。

（2）应按规定的书面格式申请，没有规定格式的，按部长批准的格式申请。

（3）部长收到申请后，应：

（a）根据部长规定的条件（如有）颁发证明书；或

（b）拒绝颁发证明书。

（4）证明文件应为规定的书面格式，没有规定格式的，按部长批准的格式颁发。

（5）证明文件自颁发之日起生效，在其规定的期限内有效。

（6）如果部长拒绝颁发证明书，应在作出决定后的规定期限内向申请人送达书面通知并列明拒绝的理由。

13. 许可证或证明文件的条件和期限的变更等

（1）部长在许可证或证明书的有效期内，以书面形式通知许可证或证明文件持有人后，可：

（a）增加许可证或证明文件应遵守的条件；

（b）变更或撤销许可证或证明文件的某项条件；

（c）变更许可证或证明文件的有效期；或

（d）撤销许可证或证明文件。

（2）第（1）款的通知于送达许可证或证明文件持有人之日起或通知中指定的较晚的日期（如有）生效。

（3）除非许可证或证明文件的持有人按照规定的书面格式申请，没有规定格式的，按部长批准的格式申请，否则部长不得行使第（1）款的权力。

13A. 通知送达地址

（1）为本部分之目的，申请人根据第 10 条或第 10A 条申请许可证或根据第 12 条申请证明文件的，必须指定其位于澳大利亚的地址。

（2）为本部分之目的，申请人已按照第（1）款的规定指定地址或已在先前的申请中指定地址的，可随时向部长提交书面通知，指定与最后一次指定地址不同的位于澳大利亚的地址。

（3）根据本节规定最后一次指定的地址，视为申请人的住所地或营业地，将根据本部分的规定向申请人送达通知。

第二节　进口

14. 非法进口

（1）凡：

（a）从外国出口受该国保护的文物；

（b）此类出口被该国文化财产法律禁止；且

（c）该文物已进口到澳大利亚；

则该文物可能被没收。

（2）凡进口文物时明知：

（a）从外国出口的文物受该国保护；且

（b）此类出口被该国文化财产法律禁止；

文物进口人即为犯罪，应受以下惩处：

（a）自然人违法的，判处 100,000 澳元以下罚金，或 / 并处 5 年以下监禁；

（b）法人团体违法的，判处 200,000 澳元以下的罚金。

（3）本条不适用于以下文物进口：

（a）根据以下当事方签订协议的文物进口：

（i）联邦、州、领地、主要收藏机构或展览协办方；与

（ii）其他任何人或机构（包括政府）；且

（b）该协议规定向联邦、州、领地、主要收藏机构或展览协办方（视情况而定）出借该物品，用于在澳大利亚的公开展览，出借期限不超过 2 年。

（4）第（3）款中：

展览协办方是指常通过以下方式，在澳大利亚安排将澳大利亚之外收藏的文物举办公开展览的机构：

（a）与个人或机构（包括政府）签订借用该类文物的进口协议；且

（b）与联邦、州或领地签订协议，根据协议，联邦、州或领地同意就因履行（a）项中的协议或在澳大利亚进行公开展览而造成该文物丢失或损坏，应向（a）项中的人员或机构进行赔偿。

第三部分　管理

15. 国家文物委员会

应设立一个委员会，称为国家文物委员会。

16. 委员会的职能

委员会的职能包括：

（a）主动或应部长要求，向部长提出以下方面的建议：

（i）本法的实施问题；

（ii）在控制清单中列入或删除文物；

（iii）列入控制清单的文物分类和重新分类；及

（iv）国家文物账户的运行问题；

（b）根据第 10 条第（4）款和第 10A 条第（5）款向部长提出建议；

（c）建立并维护第 22 条规定的名册；及

（d）就其职能相关事项，与联邦、州和领地的相关部门以及其他组织、机构和个人磋商与合作。

17. 委员会章程

（1）委员会应包括：

（a）4 名分别代表不同收藏机构的成员；

（b）1 名澳大利亚大学校长委员会成员；

（c）1 名负责执行《1986 年原住民土地授予法（杰维斯湾领地）》（Aboriginal Land Grant <Jervis Bay Territory>）的部长代理人；及

（d）4 名具有澳大利亚文物保护经验的专家。

（1A）第（1）款（c）项中的人必须是：

（a）澳大利亚原住民；或

（b）托勒斯海峡群岛原住民的后裔。

（2）委员会的成员：

（a）由部长任命；

（b）兼职工作；

（c）任期不超过 4 年，具体由任命文件规定；且

（d）可以连任。

（3）部长应书面指定 1 名成员担任主席。

（5）以下原因不会单独导致委员会行使权力或履行职能的无效：

（a）属于第（1）款（b）项或（c）项的成员职位空缺未超 3 个月；或

（b）属于第（1）款（a）项或（d）项的成员人数少于 4 人的情况未超 3 个月。

（6）为本条之目的，在收藏机构担任收藏部门高级职位的人，视为代表该收藏机构。

（7）本条中，收藏机构指：

（a）公共艺术馆；

（b）公共博物馆；

（c）公共图书馆；或

（d）公共档案馆。

18. 罢免与辞职

（1）部长可因品行不端或身体或精神原因罢免某一名成员。

（2）应负责执行《1986 年原住民土地授予法（杰维斯湾领地）》的部长要求，部长可罢免第 17 条第（1）款（c）项中的成员。

（3）如一成员无正当理由违反第 20 条的规定，部长应罢免该成员。

（4）委员会成员可向部长递交本人签字的书面申请后辞去其职务。

19. 薪酬与津贴

（1）委员会成员按薪酬审理委员会确定的标准领取薪酬。

（2）委员会成员按规定领取津贴。

（3）第（1）款和第（2）款依《1973 年薪酬审理委员会法》执行。

20. 利益披露

（1）与委员会审议或即将审议的事项有直接或间接经济利益关系的成员，在知晓该情况后，应尽快在委员会会议上披露该利益的性质。

（2）根据第（1）款作出的披露，应记录在委员会会议纪要上，除非部长或委员会另有决定，该成员不得：

（a）在委员会审议该事项时出席；或

（b）参与委员会关于该事项的任何决议。

（3）委员会根据第（2）款作出与根据第（1）款履行披露义务的成员相关的决定时，与该披露事项有直接或间接经济利益关系的成员不得：

（a）在委员会为作出决定而进行审议时出席；或

（b）参与委员会决定。

21. 会议

（1）委员会会议通常根据委员会决定的时间和地点召开。

（2）主席可随时召集会议。

（3）会议法定出席人数为5人。

（4）除第（5）款规定的情形外，所有会议应由主席主持。

（5）如主席缺席会议，应从出席会议的成员中选举1人主持会议。

（6）会议中提出的问题，应由出席会议的成员投票表决，多数通过方可决定。

（7）主持会议的成员所投票为普通票；票数相同时，主持会议的成员所投票为决定票。

21A. 会议形式

（1）委员会可规定其认为适合的会议议程。

（2）在对第（1）款不造成限制的前提下，委员会可准许成员以下列任何通讯方式参加委员会的特别会议或所有会议，并计入法定人数：

（a）电话；

（b）闭路电视；

（c）委员会决定的任何其他通讯方式。

（3）准许以第（2）款的方式参加会议的成员，视为出席该会议。

21B. 无需开会即可作出的决议

（1）如果除第（3）款外的所有委员会成员签署一份声明文件，表示支持文件中与根据第10条或10A条提出的申请有关的建议或报告，则视为签署当天召开的委员会会议批准了该建议或报告，如各成员签署日期不同，批准时间以最后一个成员签署时为准。

（2）为第（1）款之目的，如果存在两份或多份独立文件包含上述声明，每份文件由1名或多名成员签署，则这些文件视为构成一份声明文件，每一份构成文件分别由不同成员在不同时间签署。

（3）根据第20条，如果某一成员被认为与某一事项有直接或间接经济利益关系，该成员不得签署批准该事项的建议或报告的声明文件。

（4）有资格签署文件的委员会成员少于5名时，不适用本条规定。

22. 专家鉴定人名册

（1）为了本法之目的，委员会应依法维护由委员会确定为专家鉴定人的人员名册。

（2）第（1）款中的“人员”包括：

（a）机构或团体的成员，无论该机构或团体是否组建成立；及

（b）居住或定居在澳大利亚之外的人。

23. 专家鉴定人

专家鉴定人的职责是，就委员会咨询的事项向委员会提出建议。

24. 授权

（1）部长可以书面文件通过一般形式或授权文件规定的其他形式向下列人员授权：

（a）担任或行使部门秘书办公室职能的人；或

（b）在部门中担任或代理高级行政人员的人；

行使本法规定的部长的全部或任何职权，但不包括进行授权职权或第 17 条、第 18 条、第 28 条第（3）款、第（4）款或第（5）款、第 38 条或第 47 条规定的职权。

（2）在本法中，被授权人行使授予的职权，视为部长行使。

（3）本条规定的授权不得妨碍部长行使职权。

第四部分　国家文物账户

25. 建立国家文物账户

（1）根据本法建立国家文物账户。

（2）该账户是为《2013 年公共管理、绩效和责任法》之目的设立的特别账户。

25A. 计入账户

凡以下内容必须计入国家文物账户：

（a）从州或领地，或者从州或领地的主管部门收取的、用于该账户的所有钱款；及

（b）以赠与、遗赠或其他形式收取的、用于该账户的所有钱款；及

（c）如从该账户中计出款项用于投资，投资产生的利润。

注：如果特别账户的任何用途属于拨款法规定的用途，则应计入特别账户的金额由拨款法规定。

25B. 账户的用途

国家文物账户内的款项也可用于收购澳大利亚保护文物以展示或保存。

26. 税务

国家文物账户的收入和交易可免除联邦、州或领地任何法律规定的税务。

27. 通过电话颁发搜查证

（1）根据本条规定，在紧急情况下，如果检查员认为有必要，可以通过电话向地方法官申请搜查证。

（2）在电话申请搜查证前，检查员应先根据第 30 条第（1）款的要求宣誓告发，阐述颁发搜查证的依据，在必要时，可在宣誓告发前提出申请。

（3）根据第（1）款提出申请后，如果地方法官：

（a）在分析根据第（1）款提供的信息后；及

（b）在收到地方法官颁发搜查证所需依据的进一步信息（如有）后；

认为有颁发搜查证的合理理由且该申请符合第 30 条的规定，地方法官应根据第 30 条制作并签发搜查证。

（4）如地方法官根据第（3）款的规定签发搜查证：

（a）地方法官应将搜查证的条款与签署的日期和时间告知检查员，

并记录颁发搜查证的原因；且

（b）检查员应根据地方法官提供的条款填写搜查证表格，并填写地方法官的姓名和签署搜查证的日期和时间。

（5）检查员根据第（4）款的规定填写搜查证表格的，应在不迟于搜查证到期日的次日向签发搜查证的地方法官提交其填写的搜查证表格及正式宣誓的与搜查证有关的信息。

（6）收到根据第（5）款提供的文件后，地方法官应附上由其签署的搜查证，并按照第30条规定的申请搜查证的程序处理上述文件。

（7）检查员根据第（4）款的规定正确填写的搜查证表格，如果符合地方法官签署的搜查证的条件要求，可作为经签署的搜查证授权进行搜查、入户或扣押的依据。

（8）在任何诉讼程序中，如果法庭亟待证明搜查、入户或扣押根据本条规定获得了授权，但由地方法官根据本条签署的授权搜查、入户或扣押的搜查证并未作为证据，则法庭有权认为搜查、入户或扣押行为未获得所述搜查令的授权，除非能够作出相反证明。

第五部分　本法的实施

28. 释义

（1）本部分中（除第35条、第36条、第37条和第38条），“没收”包括应予没收。

（2）根据《1901年海关法》第203T条规定，在特定时间，海关官员向检查员移交文物，或文物的所有人、持有人、保管人或控制人主动向检查员上交文物的，为本部分之目的，视为该检查员依本法即时扣押该文物。

29. 检查员

（1）部长可通过书面文件任命检查员。

（2）根据本款规定以下人员为检查员：

（a）澳大利亚联邦警察机构的成员或特别成员；及

（b）州或领地警察队伍的成员；

（3）部长可与国家部长根据本法协议安排州官员行使检查员的职权并履行其职责。

（4）协议的内容可包括部长和国家部长认为必要的附带规定或补充规定。

（5）部长可与国家部长协议变更或撤销正在生效的协议。

（6）上述协议及其变更或撤销应以书面形式作出，并在公报上公布相应文件的副本。

30. 身份证明

（1）部长应向非警察身份的检查员颁发身份证明，其证明格式由部长以书面文件批准。

（2）不再担任检查员的人员，应立即将身份证明归还部长。

（3）违反第（2）款规定的，属于犯罪行为，可判处 100 澳元以下罚金。

（4）第（3）款中的违法行为适用严格责任。

注：关于“严格责任”，参见《刑法典》第 6.1 条[①]。

31. 搜查证

（1）如果地方法官收到宣誓告发，称有合理理由怀疑当时或在未来 24 小时内，在任何土地上或在任何房屋、其他建筑物、船只、飞行器或车辆上部或其内部，有某件物品，或是某类特殊物品应该予以没收或涉嫌违反本法的规定，且提供了证据，地方法官可颁发搜查证，授权搜查证上署名的检查员在其认为必要的情形下，提供援助甚至使用强制力：

（a）进入该块土地或该房屋、其他建筑物、船只、飞行器或车辆；

（b）在该块土地或该房屋、其他建筑物、船只、飞行器或车辆内搜查上述物品；

（c）扣押有合理理由认为应予没收或涉嫌犯罪的物品。

---

① 严格责任又称结果责任，是英美法系刑法中的一种无罪过责任。强调行为和结果之间的关系，而与主观过错无关，即只要行为人实施了造成危害结果的行为，不论其是否有罪过，均应当追究刑事责任。

（2）地方法官只有在以下条件下，才得根据第（1）款的规定颁发搜查证，除非：

（a）举报人或其他人通过口头或书面证词向地方法官提供更多情报（如有），这些情报可作为地方法官颁发搜查证所需的依据；且

（b）地方法官认为有颁发搜查证的合理依据。

（3）根据本条规定颁发的搜查证上应注明：

（a）颁发搜查证的目的，包括关于授权进入并搜查应予没收物品的性质和犯罪的性质；

（b）授权进入时间是在白天或夜晚的任意时间还是特定时间；

（c）对授权扣押物品的描述；及

（d）搜查证失效的日期，不超过颁发后1个月。

（4）在使用根据本节规定颁发的搜查证对搜查证上注明的应予没收或涉嫌犯罪的特定种类物品进行搜查的过程中，如果存在有合理理由认为应予没收或涉嫌违法的任何其他物品；即使该物品不属于搜查证上注明的种类，或涉嫌其他违反本法的行为，且检查员有合理理由认为急需立即扣押以防止该物品出口、进口、藏匿、遗失或损坏，或防止该物品被用于实施、继续实施或重复实施上述犯罪行为或用于其他犯罪行为，检查员可扣押该物品。

（5）就本条而言，以下物品涉嫌犯罪：

（a）与已发生的犯罪行为相关的物品；

（b）构成犯罪行为的证据的物品；或

（c）用于或意图用于犯罪行为目的的物品。

（6）本条中，“犯罪”包括有合理理由认为已经或将要发生的犯罪行为。

32. 紧急搜查

（1）检查员可：

（a）对怀疑携带任何应被没收或涉嫌违反本法物品的人，进行搜身或搜查其衣物和随身携带的财产；或

（b）进入有合理理由认为应被没收或涉嫌违反本法的任何物品所在

的任何土地或房屋、其他建筑物、船只、飞行器或车辆；

并且在下列情况下，扣押在搜查中或在土地上或房屋中、其他建筑中、船只、飞行器或车辆上发现的任何此类物品，视情况而定；

（c）检查员有合理依据认为有必要如此行事，以防止应没收或涉嫌违反本法的任何物品出口、进口、藏匿、丢失或破坏；

（d）在重要紧急情况下进行的搜查或入户，如在未经法庭或根据本法颁发的搜查证授权或命令的情况下须立即进行搜查或入户的情况。

（2）执行第（1）款时，检查员可拦截任何人、船只、飞行器或车辆。

（3）第 30 条第（5）款和第（6）款的情形同样适用于本条。

33. 逮捕权

（1）存在以下合理理由，检查员可在没有逮捕证的情况下逮捕任何人：

（a）行为人正在实施或已经实施违反本法的行为；及

（b）无法在诉讼中有效传唤；

（2）在根据第（1）款逮捕行为人后，检查员应立即将其送交地方法官或其他合法机构，依法进行处理。

（3）在不对第（1）款表述限制性解释的情况下，一旦：

（a）检查员发现行为人正在实施违反本法的行为或有合理理由认为其已实施违反本法的行为，若不知道该行为人的姓名或经常居住地，检查员可要求其交代姓名或经常居住地（视情况而定）；且

（b）行为人：

（i）拒绝或未能按要求交代姓名或经常居住地；或

（ii）无论是否按要求或声称按要求交代了一个名字或地点作为其姓名或经常居住地（视情况而定），但检查员有合理理由认为在重要情节存在不实或误导；

为第（1）款（b）项之目的，如果认为行为人无法在诉讼中有效传唤，可视为检查员有合理理由。

（4）本条规定不影响依据任何其他法律逮捕嫌犯。

34. 扣押受保护文物

检查员如果有合理理由认为受保护文物应予没收，即可先行扣押。

35. 保留权

（1）下列情况中，根据本法扣押的物品可先予以保留[①]：

（a）根据第 9 条第（1）款为没收而扣押的受保护文物，将保留至法庭命令归还该文物或根据第 38 条进行处置为止；

（b）任何其他受保护文物，保留至法庭命令归还该文物或该文物被没收为止；或

（c）任何其他物品，可保留至扣押后 60 天，如果在该期限内就该物品提起诉讼，则保留至诉讼程序（包括就该诉讼向法院提起上诉）终结为止。

（2）部长可通过书面文件批准将根据本法扣押的任何物品（不包括被没收的受保护文物）归还给被扣押前的所有人以及持有人、保管人或控制人，因而，第 36 条和第 37 条的规定不适用该物品或根据案件要求不适用于该物品。

36. 扣押通知

（1）本条中，“相关人员”指部长或由部长书面指定的人员。

（2）根据本条规定，检查员根据本法扣押受保护文物后，应立即向其被扣押前的所有人以及持有人、保管人或控制人发送书面通知：

（a）确定扣押的文物及日期；

① 此处“保留”的英文是 retain（名词形式是 retention），与第 34 条的“扣押”（动词形式 seize，名词形式 seizure）和“没收”（动词形式 forfeit，名词形式 forfeiture）三个词之间既有联系又有区别。三者在时间环节上是层层递进的，例如，首先对涉嫌违法财产进行扣押（seize），接着经过一定的程序（比如美国的民事没收程序 civil forfeiture）后，被扣押的财产可能被判定没收（forfeit），或者判定“不予没收”。没收后，其中一种处理结果是 retention（保留），以联邦保留（federal retention）为例，就是财产被没收后，由美国联邦政府保留。可见，没收是扣押的结果之一，保留是没收后的一种处置方法。

（b）说明扣押的理由；

（c）阐明第 37 条第（1）款的规定；及

（d）在适用第（5）款时，阐明第（5）款的规定，明确相关人员及其地址，陈述按本款规定将发送至该人员的通知。

（3）经检查员认为必要的盘问后，如果其无法获得充分信息，则无需根据第（2）款发出通知。

（4）凡：

（a）检查员没有根据第（2）款送达通知；且

（b）在该文物被扣押后 30 天内，声称有权接收该通知的人以书面形式向相关人员提供了充分信息，使通知满足送达条件；

相关人员应立即向检查员转达该信息。

（5）在扣押了根据第 9 条第（2）款或第 14 条第（1）款应予没收的受保护文物，并就该文物发出第（2）款规定的通知后，该文物将被没收，除非该文物被扣押前的所有人以及持有人、保管人或控制人在通知送达后 30 天内：

（a）以书面通知的形式向第（2）款规定的通知中明确的相关人员主张该文物；或

（b）提起文物返还之诉。

（6）根据本法在扣押受保护文物后 30 天期限届满时，如：

（a）未就该文物发出第（2）款规定的通知；且

（b）声称有权接收该通知的人未能向相关人员提供充分信息，未能使通知送达；

该文物即被没收。

（7）如某人根据第（5）款向相关人员提出主张，相关人员应向其发出书面通知，阐明第（8）款的规定。

（8）凡：

（a）根据第（7）款就该文物向某人发出通知；且

（b）其在通知送达后 4 个月内未提起文物返还之诉；

该文物即被没收。

37. 审判程序

（1）凡：

（a）受保护文物根据本法被扣押；且

（b）该文物尚未被根据第 36 条或本条规定没收；

则该文物被扣押前的所有人以及持有人、保管人或控制人可向具有管辖权的法院以该文物不能被没收或不应被没收为由向联邦提起文物返还之诉。

（2）凡：

（a）根据第 9 条第（2）款或第 14 条第（1）款，应予没收的受保护文物被扣押；

（b）某人提起文物返还之诉；且

（c）继而又终止诉讼；

该文物即被没收。

（3）针对提起的文物返还之诉，法庭应权衡各种可能性，以确定：

（a）该文物是否根据第 9 条第（1）款被没收；或

（b）该文物是否根据第 9 条第（2）款或第 14 条第（1）款应予没收；

法庭认为：

（c）符合本款（a）项没收条件的，驳回文物返还的请求；

（d）符合本款（b）项应予没收条件的，指令没收该文物；或

（e）若存在其他情况，可指令归还该文物。

（4）如某人被判违反第 9 条第（3）款的规定企图出口受保护文物或被判违反第 14 条第（2）款有关受保护文物的规定，法庭应指令没收该文物。

38. 没收后的处置

受保护文物依据本法被没收后：

（a）该文物所有权益皆归联邦所有，无需进一步诉讼程序；

（b）根据部长的指示处置该文物；且

（c）联邦在运输或处置该文物时产生的一切费用，为该文物被没收前的所有人对联邦的债务，联邦可通过具有管辖权的法院请求履行债务。

39. 出示许可证

（1）检查员有合理理由怀疑某人试图出口、正在出口或已经出口澳大利亚受保护文物，可要求其出示批准出口的许可证或证明文件，或出示证据证明其持有该许可证或证明文件及其内容。

（2）未按照第（1）款提供的，属犯罪行为，可判处1000澳元以下罚金。

（3）如行为人存在合理理由，则第（2）款不适用。

注：被告对第（3）款的情形负有举证责任（参见《刑法典》第13.3条第（3）款）。

（4）第（2）款中的违法行为适用严格责任。

注：关于“严格责任”，参见《刑法典》第6.1条。

40. 职权证明

检查员（不包括着制服的警察队伍成员）无权对任何人行使第32条、第33条、第34条、第39条或第43条中的任何权力，除非：

（a）如果该检查员为警察队伍成员，须出示书面证据，证明其为警察队伍成员，以供当事人检查；或

（b）在其他情况下，须出示身份证明，以供当事人检查。

41. 外国要求返还文物

（1）检查员对受外国保护文物不得行使本部分授予的权力，除非有合理理由认为联邦已经收到该国政府文物返还请求。

（2）不得以违反第14条规定为由对受外国保护文物启动诉讼程序，除非联邦已经收到该国政府文物返还请求。

（3）在任何诉讼程序中，为证明由部门秘书签署且声明联邦已经收到某国政府文物返还请求而出示的文件，仅作为主张事实的初步证据。

43. 协助检查员

检查员根据本部分规定对房屋、其他建筑物、船只、飞行器或车辆等财产行使或准备行使职权时，可要求该财产的所有人或负责人提供合理协助，该当事人应按要求予以配合。

处罚：判处 2,000 澳元罚金，或 / 并处 12 个月监禁。

46. 可起诉罪行

（1）违反第 9 条第（3）款、第 9 条第（3A）款或第 14 条第（2）款的行为，为可起诉的罪行。

（2）违反第 43 条的行为，适用简易程序处罚。

（3）即使是属于第（1）款的可起诉罪行，如果简易审判庭认为由其审理适当且经被告和公诉人同意，可由简易审判庭审理和裁判。

（4）根据第（3）款的规定，如果简易审判庭判定当事人犯有第（1）款规定的犯罪行为，则：

（a）个人违法的，判处 50 个罚款单位以下罚金，或 / 并处 2 年以下监禁；或

（b）法人团体违法的，判处 200 个罚款单位以下罚金。

第六部分　其他事项

47. 年度报告

（1）每年 6 月 30 日后，部长应尽快组织编写本法上一年度工作报告，报告时间截止到当年 6 月 30 日。

（2）部长必须在收到报告后的 15 个议会日内安排呈交议会议员阅。

48. 行政上诉审裁处

（1）可向行政上诉审裁处申请审查：

（a）部长拒绝颁发许可证或证明文件的决定；

（b）部长根据第 10 条第（5）款（a）项、第 10A 条第（7）款（b）项或第 12 条第（3）款（a）项增加规定条件的决定；或

（c）部长根据第 11 条第（2）款、第 12 条第（5）款或第 13 条第（1）款作出的决定。

（2）在通知当事人第（1）款所列举的决定时，部长应向其阐明可根据《1975 年行政上诉审裁处法》，向行政上诉审裁处申请审查该决定。

（3）未根据第（2）款要求阐明的，不影响决定效力。

49. 法规

总督可制定与本法不相冲突的法规，对以下事项做出规定：

（a）本法要求或允许作出规定的事项；或

（b）本法实施或生效必要的或有利于其实施或生效的事项。

尾　注

尾注 1——关于尾注

尾注提供了本法立法及其条款的历史沿革详情。

以下为历次编纂中都包括的尾注：

尾注 1——关于尾注

尾注 2——缩写表

尾注 3——立法历史

尾注 4——修法历史

尾注 5——未启动的修改

尾注 6——修正

尾注 7——误述的修改

尾注 8——其他

如某个尾注下没有信息，会在尾注标题后的方括号内注明“无”。

缩写表——尾注2（略）

尾注中的缩写表列出了尾注中可能使用的缩写。

立法历史和修订历史——尾注3和尾注4

立法历史和修订历史中对修订法律进行注释。

尾注3中的立法历史提供了关于已修订法律的每一条法律信息。该信息包括修订法律的启动细节以及未包含在已编法律中的任何适用、保留或过渡性条文的细节。

尾注4中的修订历史提供了条文层面上的修订信息，还包括根据条文已经过期或失效的信息。

未启动的修订——尾注5

未启动的修正案的效力不能体现在已编法律文本中，但尾注5包含了该修订的文本。

修正——尾注6

如果已编纂法律为现行有效的法律所更改，该更改的细节包括在尾注6中。

误述的修订——尾注7

如果已编纂的法律文本不能纳入修正案的效力，则该修正案为误述的修订。尾注7中包括所有误述的修订。

其他——尾注8

尾注8中包括对读者有帮助的所有关于编纂的其他信息。

尾注 3——立法历史

法案	编号和年份	批准日期	实施日期	适用、保留和过渡性条款
1986 年可移动文物保护法	1986 年第 11 号	1986 年 5 月 13 日	1987 年 7 月 1 日（参见 1987 年公报第 S138 号）	
1988 年邮政服务法修正案	1988 年第 126 号	1988 年 12 月 14 日	第 4 条，第 5 条，第 9–11 条，第 21 条第（2）款和第 22 条第（1）款：1989 年 1 月 1 日（参见 1988 年公报第 S402 号） 第 12 条，第 21 条第（3）款和第 22 条第（2）款：1989 年 6 月 30 日（参见 1988 年公报第 S216 号）其余：御准	
1990 年艺术、环境、旅游和国土立法修正案	1990 年第 88 号	1990 年 11 月 20 日	第 7 部分（第 14–23 条）：御准（a）	
1991 年艺术、体育、环境、旅游和国土立法修正案（第 2 号）	1991 年第 179 号	1991 年 11 月 25 日	1991 年 11 月 25 日	
1992 年艺术、体育、环境、旅游和国土立法修正案	1992 年第 21 号	1992 年 4 月 10 日	1992 年 5 月 8 日	
1996 年成文法修正案	1996 年第 43 号	1996 年 10 月 25 日	附表 4（第 123 项）：御准（b）	
1999 年可移动文物保护法修正案	1999 年第 101 号	1999 年 7 月 16 日	1999 年 7 月 16 日	附表 1（第 9 项）
1999 年公共就业法（重大及过渡性）修正案	1999 年第 146 号	1999 年 11 月 11 日	附表 1（第 752 项）：1999 年 12 月 5 日（见 1999 年公报第 S584 号）（c）	
2000 年刑法典（盗窃、诈骗、贿赂和相关犯罪）修正案	2000 年第 137 号	2000 年 11 月 24 日	第 1–3 条，附表 1（第 1,4,6,7,9–11,32 项）：御准 其他：2001 年 5 月 24 日	附表 2（第 418, 419 项）
2001 年通讯和艺术（实施刑法典）立法修正案	2001 年第 5 号	2001 年 3 月 20 日	第 4 条和附表 1（第 40–49 项）：（d）	第 4 条
2005 年财政体系立法修正案	2005 年第 8 号	2005 年 2 月 22 日	第 4 条和附表 1（第 313, 314, 496 项）：御准	第 4 条和附表 1（第 496 项）
2011 年成文法修正案	2011 年第 5 号	2011 年 3 月 22 日	附表 7（第 113,114 项）：2011 年 4 月 19 日	
2011 年法案解释修正案	2011 年第 46 号	2011 年 6 月 27 日	附表 2（第 937,938 项）和附表 3（第 10,11 项）：2011 年 12 月 27 日	附表 3（第 10,11 项）

续表

法案	编号和年份	批准日期	实施日期	适用、保留和过渡性条款
2012 年成文法修正案	2012 年第 136 号		附表 1（第 108 项）：御准	
2014 年成文法修正案（第 1 号）	2014 年第 31 号	2014 年 5 月 27 日	附表 3（第 2,3 项）和附表 7（第 8 项）：2014 年 6 月 24 日	
2014 年公共管理、绩效和责任法（重大及过渡性条款）	2014 年第 62 号	2014 年 6 月 30 日	附表 11（第 79−81 项）和附表 14（第 1−4 项）：2014 年 7 月 1 日（第 2（1）条第 6,14 项）	附表 14（第 1−4 项）

（a）《1986 年可移动文物保护法》由《1990 年艺术、环境、旅游和国土立法修正案》第 7 部分（第 14-23 条）修订，其中第 2 条第（1）款规定如下：

（1）第 1,4,5,6,7 和 8 部分于本法获御准之日开始实施。

（b）《1986 年可移动文物保护法》由《1996 年成文法修正案》附表 4（第 123 项）修订，其中第 2 条第（1）款规定如下：

（1）根据第（2）条和第（3）条的规定，本法于获御准之日开始实施。

（c）《1986 年可移动文物保护法》由《1999 年公共就业法（重大及过渡性）修正案》附表 1（第 752 项）修订，其中第 2 条第（1）款和第（2）款规定如下：

（1）本法中，“开始实施的时间”指《1999 年公共服务法》开始实施的时间。

（2）根据本条规定，本法于该时间开始实施。

（d）《1986 年可移动文物保护法》由《2001 年通讯和艺术（实施刑法典）立法修正案》附表 1（第 40-49 项）修订，其中第 2 条第（1）款第（a）项规定如下：

（1）根据本条规定，本法案于以下时间中的最晚时间开始实施：

(a)《2000 年刑法典（盗窃、诈骗、贿赂和相关违法）修正案》附表 1 第 15 项开始实施后；

第 15 项于 2001 年 5 月 24 日开始实施。

尾注 4——修法历史

受影响的条款	影响程度
第一部分	
第 3 条	由 1990 年第 88 号；1999 年第 101 号；2000 年第 137 号；2001 年第 5 号；2011 年第 46 号修正
第 6A 条	由 2001 年第 5 号增加
第二部分 第一章	
第 9 条	由 1988 年第 126 号；2001 年第 5 号修正
第 10 条	由 1990 年第 88 号修正
第 10A 条	由 1990 年第 88 号增加
第 11 条	由 1990 年第 88 号修正
第 13A 条	由 1990 年第 88 号修正
第二章	
第 14 条	由 1990 年第 88 号修正
第三部分	
第 16 条	由 1990 年第 88 号；1999 年第 101 号修正
第 17 条	由 1990 年第 88 号；2014 年第 31 号修正
第 18 条	由 2014 年第 31 号修正
第 19 条	由 1996 年第 43 号修正
第 21A 条	由 1991 年第 179 号增加
第 21B 条	由 1999 年第 146 号；2011 年第 5 号增加
第 24 条	由 1999 年第 146 号；2011 年第 5 号增加
第四部分	
第四部分的标题	由 1999 年第 101 号废除并取代
第 25 条	由 1999 年第 101 号废除并取代 由 2014 年第 62 号修正
第 25A 条	由 1999 年第 101 号增加 由 2005 年第 8 号；2014 年第 62 号修正
第 25A 条注	由 2005 年第 8 号增加 由 2014 年第 62 号修正
第 25B 条	由 1999 年第 101 号增加
第 26 条	由 1999 年第 101 号修正
第五部分	
第 27 条	由 2012 年第 136 号修正
第 29 条	由 2001 年第 5 号修正

续表

受影响的条款	影响程度
第 39 条	由 2001 年第 5 号修正
第 41 条	由 2011 年第 5 号修正
第 42 条	由 2001 年第 5 号废除
第 44，45 条	由 2000 年第 137 号废除
第 46 条	由 2000 年第 137 号；2001 年第 5 号修正
第六部分	
第 47 条	由 1999 年第 101 号修正
第 48 条	由 1990 年第 88 号修正

尾注 5——未启动的修改【无】

尾注 6——修正

《自治（重大过渡性）法规（1989 年第 3 号）》

尾注 7——误述的修订【无】

尾注 8——其他【无】

七、埃　及

述 评

埃及是世界上著名的文明古国，拥有法老、希腊、罗马基督教与伊斯兰教的文明历史，悠久的历史和灿烂的文化留下了丰富文化遗产。但是从18世纪开始，西方国家大量掠取埃及的珍贵文物。如今，尚存海外的大部分埃及文物主要是在埃及人尚未意识到文物价值的过去三个世纪里流失的。其中，一些文物是在没有监督的情况下非法挖掘并通过各种渠道走私出去的。还有一些文物则是昔日商人"合法交易"和旧政权统治者无知的"慷慨馈赠"外流的。历史上，欧洲列强以"合法"与"非法"手段从埃及掠夺的文物数量十分惊人。[①]1835年8月15日，当时的统治者穆罕默德·阿里曾下令禁止非法将本国文物偷运出境，同时命令在开罗建立一个宝库用以储藏文物，这可能是埃及政府最早采取的文物保护措施。颁布于1912年6月12日的《第14号文物管理法》中第14条规定：未经文物部门特别授权，禁止文物出口，任何企图带出埃及国境的文物一律收归国有。1951年埃及又颁布了关于文物保护的第215号法令。1983年8月12日生效的埃及《文物保护法》是一部旨在保护埃及文物的综合性法律，对文物范畴作出明确界定，并明确规定禁止文物买卖和收藏（除祖传外）。而1983年以前，埃及法律是一直允许文物交易的。

但是因为种种原因，上述法律政策的实施效果都不是十分理想，埃及的文化遗产未能得到有效保护，埃及一直受到文物掠夺和文物被盗的困扰。2010年1月26日，埃及文物最高委员会制定1983年《文物保护法》修正案，经埃及人民议会法律委员会审议后通过，于2010年2月14日公布，即2010年《文物保护法》。该法进一步加大了考古和文物的管理力度，以及对文物盗窃和走私活动的打击力度。2010年《文物保护法》共4章52条，对文物的范

① 马海兵：《尽全力追回被盗掠文物——埃及文物保护一瞥》，南京博物院官网，网址：http://www.njmuseum.com/html/News_content%40NewsID%4086108050-5d7f-4662-a52d-2b8077521d6c.html，2018年12月20日最后访问。

围，文物的占有、收藏和处置，文物的登记、修缮和调查，考古发掘，法律责任等方面作出了具体规定。

2010年《文物保护法》明显加大了对文物盗窃、走私犯罪分子的惩罚力度，服刑期限从原来的7年以下有期徒刑延长到7年以上有期徒刑，罚金的最高额由原先的5万埃镑增加升到100万埃镑，同时，监禁和罚金的判罚也由可单处，改为并处。

为防止外国考古人员与国际、国内文物贩子勾结盗掘本国文物，埃及最高文物委员会于2009年推出了新的外国考古队在埃及考古条例。该条例强化了对境内外国考古人员的管理，规定外国考古队必须在埃及文物最高委员会的直接监督下开展工作，外国考古人员只能在该委员会下属的研究中心或埃及大学的研究机构进行相关研究，发现的任何文物必须马上向该委员会报告并专门登记造册。

埃及有关文物保护和追索流失海外文物的机构也在实践中逐渐得到完善。19世纪50年代末，埃及政府成立了一个专门负责文物保护的机构，即"文物服务局"，70年代初期被更名为"埃及文物局"，根据1983年《文物保护法》，文物局"系负责管理各博物馆、文物仓库、古遗址和历史文物地区（包括偶然发现的文物考古区）的一切与文物考古有关的事务的专门机构"，"负责调查地面上的文物古迹以及勘探埋藏在地下、内水和埃及领海内的文物，经由常设委员会同意，文物局理事会主席可向本国或外国的专门机构颁发许可证，允许在指定地区按规定期限进行文物考古研究和调查。"1994年，根据埃及总统第28号令，文物局更名为现在的"埃及最高文物委员会"，由文化部长兼任该委员会主席。该委员会的重要职能之一是负责对非法出口文物或被盗文物的返还进行监督。为了提高海外流失文物追索效率，埃及最高文物委员会成立了文物归还管理局，主要负责查询境外所有经营文物的拍卖公司的记录；对埃及驻世界各国使领馆提供的有关埃及流失海外文物的信息进行统计；并追踪世界上经营文物的主要网络交易站点，以便在最短的时间内发现是否有埃及流失文物。2010年新文物保护法实施后，埃及成立专职常设委员会，隶属于埃及最高文物委员会，并专门立法规定其设立和职能等事宜。

《文物保护法》

引言

成功留住自己的文化和遗产，是衡量一个国家发展水平的标准，我认为埃及是世界上极少数能保护其文化遗产的国家之一。在文化部部长法罗克·霍斯尼（FaroukHosni）的领导下，经过不懈努力，我们已经有能力保护文化遗产并向世界展示这个伟大国家的辉煌历史，以及在这片土地上曾经孕育的最重要的文明。这种文明对于地球上每一个人都是极其重要的。法国报纸《费加罗报》（Le Figaro）不久前刊登了一篇文章，称赞了埃及对遗迹修复和维护的质量以及来自埃及团队的考古新发现。

在建立博物馆、管理考古遗址、实施考古认知计划以及返还走私文物方面，我们为全世界树立了榜样。

我认为当前最重要的是保护埃及文化遗产，这些文化遗产先前并未得到有效保护，并且遭受着掠夺和偷窃。这促使我们建立了超过 36 个具有世界级维护、修复和电子保护功能的仓库，这些仓库还配备了保护实验室和摄影实验室，以供学术之用。此外，我们在文物登记中心通过一个由一批训练有素，尽职尽责的年轻人带领下的国家项目进行文物登记。我们发现从埃及出境的大部分文物都是通过开罗和亚历山大附近的港口走私出境，于是我们在机场、港口和边境通道处设置了 29 个以上的（文物进出境管理）机构，以防止从国内走私文物。我们还新雇用了大约 8000 名安保人员，给了他们空前优厚的报酬以确保他们能为埃及文化遗产的安全尽心竭力。

2003 年，为了修改文物保护法，文化部部长法罗克·霍斯尼先生成立了文物委员会，成员包括著名考古学家、法律专家和社会知名人士。在过去的 8 年内，我们多次召开会议并讨论，最终完成修法准备工作。修法草案被提交至最高行政法院[①]（State Council）和部长会议（Council of Minister），再提交到人民议会（People's Assembly）。我们主要是对法律具体条款进行修改，而非整体修订。

对于审议最重要的条款之一是废止外交使团可保留 10% 发现物的协议，尽力阻止文物交易并宣布文物交易属于犯罪行为，另一个重要条款是公民个人所有文物需要在法律颁布的 6 个月内进行登录。我们专门成立了一个负责处理此类事务的新部门，并负责接收公民的登录请求，同时进行大规模媒体宣传，以使公民意识到自己有责任记录和检查其所有的文物。目前正在编制该法律的实施细则，以便更为高效地执行新条款。部分文物已被复制并用作商业用途，并且只有埃及最高文物委员会（the Supreme Council of Autiquities）被允许 1:1 复制文物。

与众多考古学家一样，我也希望对盗窃和走私文物处以更严重的惩罚，因为那是对埃及历史荣耀的侵害。令人遗憾的是，当前的惩罚机制并不能遏制文物从我国流出。但总体而言，我们为了保护埃及的遗产已迈出了重要的一步。我在这里感谢人民议会在野党成员、独立人士及缔约国在讨论文物保护法时给予的支持与关注。我希望所有公民共同协助维护文化遗产并帮助我们找到仍流失在外的文物。保护本国遗产的人将得到报酬奖励。祖国的记忆是后代子孙的权利，我们的责任是保持这段历史的生机和活力。

札希·哈瓦斯（Zahi Hawass）

通知

根据埃及最高文物委员会的法律顾问（意见）

按照埃及法律规定，随附翻译版本[②]仅供参考。

因此，若阿拉伯语版本与翻译版本存在任何不一致之处，则应以阿拉伯语版

① 埃及有三个最高法院：最高宪法法院（the Supreme Constitutional Court），上诉法院（Court of Cassation），最高行政法院（Supreme Administrative Court）。其中最高宪法法院专门负责判决法律的合宪性，上诉法院是普通法院系统的最高法院，最高行政法院是行政法院系统的最高法院，又被称为 the State Council.

② 本书中关于《埃及文物保护法》的中文翻译即从英文版而来。其中 1983 年《埃及文物保护法》中未被修改的条款，本书参考了《外国保护文化遗产法律文件选编》（国家文物局法制处编，紫禁城出版社 1995 年出版）的译文。

本为准。

2010 年 6 月 **ACHRAF EI-ACHMAWI**

2010 年关于颁布文物保护法的第 3 号法令

1983 年第 117 号法律被本法修改

（陈月迷　初校）

以人民的名义

共和国总统

在查阅《宪法》，

《民法典》，

《刑法典》，

1953 年第 529 号法律“关于文物服务的组织”，由 1955 年第 192 号法律和 1970 年第 27 号法律修订，

1956 年第 86 号法律“关于矿山和采石场”，

1963 年第 66 号法律颁布的《海关法》，

1973 年第 93 号法律“关于国家总预算”，

1983 年第 117 号法律《文物保护法》，

1990 年第 10 号法律“符合公众利益的财产没收”，

1990 年第 11 号法律颁布的《一般销售税法》，

1994 年第 4 号法律《环境法》，

2002 年第 82 号法律颁布的《知识产权保护法》，

2006 年第 144 号《拆除年久失修建筑设施和保护建筑遗产法》，

2008 年第 119 号《统一建筑法》，

和 1994 年设立埃及最高文物委员会的第 82 号总统令之后，

经部长议会的批准，

并根据最高行政法院意见，

法令

本法已由人民议会通过，现予公布。

第一条 1983年第117号《文物保护法》第一条、第二条和第三条的规定以及第1、4、5、6、7、8、10、16、17、25、32条、第34条第c款，以及第35、36、39、41、42、43、44和45条中规定均按以下规定被替代。

在本法范围内，“委员会”和“至委员会”代替词组“文物局”和“至文物局”，“委员会负责人”和“最高文物委员会”分别代替“文物局局长”和“文物局”。

第二条 在本法实施过程中，大写名词和术语含义如下：

– **“部长”**系指主管文化事务的部长。

– **“委员会”**系指最高文物委员会。

– **“委员会负责人”**系指文化部部长、最高文物委员会董事会主席。

– **“董事会”**系指最高文物委员会董事会。

– **“秘书长”**系指最高文物委员会秘书长。

– **“专职常设委员会”**根据法律规定，系指古埃及、希腊和罗马文物常设委员会，或者伊斯兰和科普特文物常设委员会。

– **“文物保护区”**系指专职常设委员会为确保文物安全在其附近划定的区域。

– **“文物公共设施用地”**系指依据同期存在的考古证据被证实是考古用地的国有土地。

– **“周边空间或土地”**系指位于考古遗址范围之外的区域，可延伸距离由委员会决定，并由规划和城市发展最高委员以法令形式公布，旨在确保文物安全（无论是对于居民区还是其他任何区域）。

– **“经批准的文物美化区”**系指文物古迹周围的一定区域（区域大小由委员会确定），以确保文物古迹的艺术风貌。上述土地应视为文物古迹区。

第三条 为实施本法，主管文化事务的部长有权发布行政法规以及作出必要的决定。

第四条 在1983年第117号《文物保护法》中增加以下内容：

–第5条之二，

–“在不损害不可移动文物所有人获得合理补偿权利的原则下”一句放在第13条开始，

–“依据规划和城市发展最高委员会规定的条件和情况以及部长的建议”一句放在第20条开始，

–“依据规划和城市发展最高委员会规定的条件和情况”一句放在第22条开始，

–第36条之二、第44条之二、第45条之二和第52条。

第五条 删除1983年第117号《文物保护法》第（9）条。

第六条 本法在官方公报上予以公布，并于公布第二日起生效。

本法加盖国印，作为一项国法实施。

2010年2月14日发布。

共和国总统

胡斯尼·穆巴拉克（HosniMubarak）

第一章 总则

第1条 在实施本法时，凡满足以下条件的不动产或动产均视为文物：

1. 在埃及领土上出现的，史前、历史上各时代直至一百年前的埃及文明或历代文明的产物，或者与艺术、科学、文学和宗教有关。

2. 具有考古或艺术价值或是具有历史意义，可反映埃及文明，或是在埃及领土上诞生的其他文明的某一方面。

3. 在埃及领土上产生并成长的人类遗骸和同时期的生物遗骸也视为依本法登记的文物。

第 2 条 在保护和保存任何具有历史、科学、宗教、艺术和文学价值的动产或不动产的工作中，一旦发现对国家有利，可根据主管文化事务的部长的建议，经总理批准，将其视为文物，不受前款时代规定的限制，并根据本法规定予以登记。此决定要以挂号信函通知文物所有者本人并签收回执。自所有者收到通知之日起，文物所有者要负责文物的保护，不得对文物进行任何改变。

第 3 条 凡属国家所有及本法实施前作出的决定、命令，或根据主管文化事务的部长的建议，经总理批准视为文物古迹区的土地，根据本法均属文物古迹区。该地区内的任何一块土地，如经委员会核实，其内没有文物古迹或被划在经批准的文物美化区外，根据主管文化事务的部长的建议，经总理批准，可划为非文物古迹区或非文物公益区。

第 4 条 古建筑指的是在本法实施前依照法令和决定登记的建筑物或根据本法项下的法令进行登记的建筑物。一旦国家发现具有历史意义的建筑物或遗址关涉国家利益，委员会可改变其被占有状态，也不再征用，在找到合适的替代地点或提供合理补偿之日起的 1 年内应终止有关租赁关系。

第 5 条 考虑到本法第 32 条的规定，委员会系负责管理各博物馆、文物库房，地上或地下、内水和埃及领海内的考古遗址区域，以及偶然发现文物等一切与文物事务相关的专门机构。委员会负责陆地考古调查和发掘（即使土地为他人所有），也负责在考古遗址或文物保护区进行的任何文化、旅游、商业或推广活动。本法实施条例规定考古遗址的修复和安保工作。

第 5 条之二 最高文物委员会有权终止考古遗址区域的任何性质的占有合同关系，包括民用、商业、工业和任何其他形式占有，并给予合理补偿，不论当事人是谁。

考古遗址禁止摊贩或动物进入，但在本法实施条例规定的条件和情况下，并在其允许的地点除外。

第6条 所有可移动和不可移动的文物，和被视为文物古迹区域的土地均为公共财产，但瓦克夫和私人财产不在此列。只有在本法规定的条件和情况下，以及本法实施条例允许的范围内才能收藏、占有、处置文物。

第7条 最高文物委员会成立两个常设委员会，其中一个负责古埃及、希腊和罗马文物，另一个负责伊斯兰、科普特人和犹太人遗迹。实施条例应规定各委员会的设立与职能。

第8条 根据本法，禁止任何文物的交易、销售和（国际间）贸易，其中包括作为私有财产持有的文物，以及在本法或源自本法的其他法律生效时已经合法收藏的文物。任何文物的所有人或收藏人都不得处置、毁损或丢弃文物，否则上述行为将被视为非法。根据部长所提解决方案的程序、条件和情况、并在得到委员会的书面同意后60天内实施的除外。

可假设任何情况下上述交易、销售、贸易或处理文物会千方百计将文物运出国外。

在任何情况下，委员会可从文物占有人或收藏人处优先获取文物，并做合理补偿。

任何根据本法规定占有文物的人，必须自2010年3月初开始的6个月内向委员会进行文物申报，并负责保护直到委员会根据本法规定登记为止。

此外，一旦董事会发现对国家有利，委员会可根据专职常设委员会建议，从文物占有人或收藏人处收回从建筑物上拆下来的文物（部件），并做合理补偿。

第10条 经总统批准，在采取必要措施确保文物安全后，规定期限内可将部分文物运往国外展览，文物孤品和专职常设委员会确定的（不可出境）文物除外。可与其他国家、阿拉伯国家和外国博物馆、教育机构交换部分可移动文物的复制品。

第 11 条　团体或个人以捐赠或象征性出售方式将具有历史意义的不动产所有权转让给最高文物委员会，或将所有权交由委员会支配，支配期限在 50 年以上的，若对国家有利，最高文物委员会可予接受。

第 12 条　根据董事会的建议，经主管文化事务的部长的批准，方可进行文物登记。通过行政手段将不可移动文物登记的决定通知到文物所有人或其代理人，并在埃及官方公报上公布文物登记决定，同时在不动产局的不动产登记册上注明。

第 13 条　在不损害不可移动文物所有人获得合理补偿权利的原则下，根据本法第 11 条规定，登记不可移动文物和通知所有人，还必须遵守下列规定：

1. 不得拆毁不动产的全部或部分，不得将其部分运出阿拉伯埃及共和国。

2. 不得以除国家利益之外的其他利益为由征用土地或房产。征用与之相邻的土地，需根据最高文物委员会董事会建议并由主管文化事务的部长批准，方可进行。

3. 不得在不动产上设立第三人的地役权。

4. 经专职常设委员会同意、委员会负责人批准，方可对不动产进行翻新或对其部分原貌加以改变。经批准的施工要在委员会代表直接监督下进行。有关方面如未经批准进行上述施工，委员会负责恢复该区域原貌，所需费用由违反者负担，但不得与赔偿权抵触或违反本法有关刑罚的规定。

5. 不动产所有权人需得到委员会的书面批准，并上报受让方的姓名、住址，方可处置不动产。所有人要通知受让方该不动产业经登记注册。自申请使用不动产报告提交之日起 30 日内，委员会应对申请表态，预期不答复的，视为拒绝此申请。

6. 委员会在任何时侯均有权对文物古迹进行必要维护，费用自理。

即使古迹内文物已移出，上述各款仍适用。

第 14 条 注销已登记的不可移动文物或其部分，要征求专职常设委员会的意见，并根据董事会建议由主管文化事务的部长批准。注销决定应在官方公报上公布，并将此决定通知登记人和有关方面；在委员会文物登记册和不动产局不动产登记册上注明。

第 15 条 个人或团体已使用考古遗址的，并不能因为使用而享有所有权，如有必要，委员会可让其迁出，并做合理补偿。

第 16 条 根据主管文化事务部长的建议，规划和城市发展最高委员会有权对考古遗址附近的不动产和文物保护区内的历史建筑物的使用权作出安排决定，并做合理补偿，以确保维护不动产的艺术特征和风貌。上述决定要划定被使用的不动产或其部分，规定使用权范围以及不动产所有人或占用人应遵守的条件。

第 17 条 在不违反本法或其他法律有关刑罚规定的情况下，委员会负责人或秘书长在得到专职常设委员会同意后，有权通过行政手段取缔对考古遗址或文物古迹的任何侵占，并将取缔决定通知地方行政长官。地方主管部门负责执行取缔决定，侵占行为人应处 10 日以下拘留，若地方主管部门未能执行，委员会将通过其所属机构或其它机构执行，请求警方拘留，费用由违法者承担。

第 18 条 个人所有的土地如具有文物考古价值，可征用该土地。也可由共和国总统批准临时占有直至完成征用手续。自临时占有之日起，该块土地属文物区域，应支付合理补偿。被征用土地中如有文物将不再作价。

第 19 条 根据董事会的决定，主管文化事务的部长可作出决定划定公共文物和考古遗址的美化范围，在此范围内的土地属文物古迹区，本法有关规定对这类土地适用。

第 20 条　按照规划和城市发展最高委员会规定的特殊条件以及部长的建议，不得发放考古遗址和文物古迹区内进行建筑的许可证。

禁止他人在考古遗址、文物古迹区、文物公益区和经批准的文物美化区范围的土地上建设施工、修坟墓、铺道路或种植。未经委员会许可和没有文物局的监督，不得在上述地区植树、砍伐、清理瓦砾、取土沙及肥料或进行其他改变考古遗址、文物古迹区原貌的工程。对与上述地区毗邻的非居住区 3 公里或由委员会划定的距离范围内的地域可适用前款规定，以保护这些文物地区的环境。

如果委员会研究认为某地区地下可能埋藏文物，主管文化事务的部长可决定该地区按本条规定处理。对沙漠地区和经许可进行采石的地区，本条规定也适用。

第21条　改变城市、居住区和村镇规划时，要照顾其范围内的考古遗址、文物保护区和有历史价值的地域及建筑物。未经委员会书面同意，不得在文物古迹区、具有历史意义的地区及其边沿地区进行新规划、扩建或改建工程。如进行此类工程，要照顾到委员会的使用权。

委员会应在收到进行上述工程申请之日起 3 个月内答复，在此期限内如未答复，申请人可向主管文化事务的部长请示，由部长作出决定。

第 22 条　禁止在居住区内的与考古遗址毗邻区进行建筑施工，专业机构获得规划和城市发展最高委员特许并经委员会同意的除外。有关方面获取的许可须符合委员会的条件，即保证建筑物的高度适当，不得影响文物古迹或有损其外貌。保证留出适当的参观游览场地，同时要考虑到历史文物区划和文物保护。委员会应自许可申请书提交之日起 60 天内予以答复，否则视为不予许可。

第 23 条　任何人发现未经登记的文物古迹，应当向委员会报告。这类文物属国家所有，委员会应当采取措施加以保护。委员会有权在 3 个月内将属于个人所有的文物搬出，或采取措施征用有文物的土地，或就地保存并按本法规定予以登记注册。被征用的土地要作价，但该土地上发现的文物不予作价。委员会可向文物古迹发现者颁发奖赏，奖赏由专职常设委员会确定。

第 24 条 任何人如偶然发现可移动文物，或不可移动文物的一部分和若干部分，应当在 48 小时内就近向行政机关报告并负责保管文物，直至有关机构前来接收。如不报告，则以未经许可收藏文物论处。上述行政机关接到报告后应立即通知委员会。

文物属于国家财产，委员会有权向其发现者颁发奖赏，奖赏由专职常设委员会确定。

第 25 条 由主管文化事务的部长批准成立的一个委员会（委员会成员包括董事会）负责现行法律第 4 条、第 5 条之二、第 8 条、第 13 条、第 15 条、第 16 条和第 18 条规定的补偿事宜。

补偿金由国库承担。补偿金额应以挂号信函的形式通知当事人，如当事者对金额有异议，自通知之日起 60 天内可向有关部长申诉，逾期不申诉的，该补偿金额即生效。

总之，在最终确定赔偿金额之日起 3 年内未提起申诉，丧失申诉权利。

第二章 文物登记、修缮和调查

第 26 条 不可移动文物和可移动文物的统计、照相、描绘、登记以及归档等工作由委员会负责。登记工作按董事会批准的规定和条件进行。本法生效前已有专门登记的文物，属于登记文物。

委员会要对考古遗址和文物古迹进行普遍测量，划定其位置，确定文物古迹面貌，并在应当归纳概括考古遗址的相关调查，确定并将上述文物古迹的地点和特征记录于地图中，同时将地图复制分送地方主管部门和城市规划总局，以备制定总体规划时参考。

委员会要按重要性，为每处考古遗址设资料档案，包括周围的环境、建筑和其他有影响的因素。

第 27 条 委员会负责安排开放登记的文物古迹区、考古遗址和具有历史价值的建筑用于参观、研究，但不得影响其安全和保养。委员会要尽力展现出文物古迹的艺术和历史特征。

委员会要充分利用文物古迹和博物馆进行文物考古知识教育。

第 28 条 可移动文物和由于客观原因需迁移的古建筑和文物应保存在委员会的博物馆和文物库房内。委员会负责用科学方法进行管理和安排展出，并负责保养、维修和必要的安全保卫；负责举办临时内部展览。委员会可委托埃及各大学负责其大学内的博物馆的组织管理以及展品登记、安全保卫工作。这些博物馆和文物库房均属国家财产。

第 29 条 委员会负责保护文物、博物馆、文物库房、考古遗址和具有历史价值的建筑，通过专职文物警察以及根据有关规定批准的私人值班、看守人员负责警卫工作。委员会要划定每处文物的最大看管范围，以保证在看管区的行动方便和便于对文物的检查。根据董事会的决定，划出每一处考古遗址的范围，并由委员会安排警卫。经与旅游局协商后，上述考古遗址可收取门票费，对埃及人的收费不得超过 5 埃镑，对外国人的收费不得超过 100 埃镑或等值外币。收取办法不得与本法第 39 条关于门票收取的规定相抵触。

第 30 条 只有委员会负责所有登记文物、考古遗址和具有历史价值的建筑进行必要的保养和修缮。

宗教捐赠基金部（即“瓦克夫部”）、埃及宗教基金委员会、何普特教基金局承担所属登记文物古迹和历史建筑物的修缮、保养费用。

委员会应承担已登记的由个人或其他机构占用的历史建筑物的修缮费用。如因占用者使用不当，需进行维修，费用由占用者负担，具体费用由专职常设委员会确定。

经专职常设委员会的同意，委员会董事会主席可批准专门的科学团队在委员会的监督下进行修缮和保养，也可向有专长的个人颁发修缮保养许可证。

第 31 条 有关团队或机构在最易受环境危害和最易受国家建设项目扩展影响的地区进行考古勘探的优先权，由委员会根据董事会的决定按时间顺序和客观情况进行安排。

第 32 条 委员会负责调查地上文物以及发掘地下和水下（包括内水和领海）文物。根据本法实施条例规定的条件和情况，在获得专职常设委员会的批准后，董事会可允许任何国内外专业的科研机构和大学根据持有的特殊许可证在特定期限、特定范围内发掘、调查文物古迹，许可证不得转让。只有在确定申请许可证的机构或大学具备丰富的科学、技术、财务和考古实践经验后，才能将向其颁发许可证。

即使调查、发掘不在文物古迹区，上述规定同样适用。

许可证持有人可在许可期限内，对其发现的文物进行研究、描绘和拍照。从在考古工地第一件文物发现之日起 5 年内，许可证持有人有权就其考古发掘在科学刊物上发表文章。

第 33 条 规定委员会的董事会制定颁发考古发掘许可证必须遵循的条件和应履行的义务；规定文物调查区域的范围、期限、在该区域内工作的最低要求；规定应向委员会交纳的保险金；制定在限定区域进行发掘和完成发掘工程的条件，保证登记的连续性，承担警卫、维修工作；向委员会提供完整的登记以及经许可的各项工作的全面的科学报告。

第 34 条 向外国文物调查、勘探团队颁发许可证需遵循下列原则：

a）各团体应当在委员会相关机构的监督和合作下，修复和保护其在工作期间内发现的文物古迹。各团队对发现的古建筑、可移动文物，在完成考察工作之前，应与委员会专业机构合作、并在其监督下及时进行维修、保养；

b）任何外国团队制定在埃及进行考古勘探工作计划时，要制定相应计划，以便在委员会批准或由委员会参加的情况下，对已发现的文物进行一定的维修，或对施工区及其附近地区进行考古测量、文物统计和文物登记；

c）专职常设机构有权评估每个许可机构的工作。

第35条　外国或埃及科学考古团队发现的一切文物属国家所有。

第36条　委员会制作的考古复制品以及委员会所有的考古文物和古文化遗址照片均享有知识产权、商标权和按照符合委员会利益的方式进行使用的权利（根据2002年第82号法律规定）。本法实施条例作出具体规定。

第36条之二　为了实现目的，委员会有权成立特殊性质的生产厂家。本法实施条例规定了上述生产厂家的组建和工作系统规则。

第37条　根据委员会董事会的法令，考古发掘机构、团队在工作期间如有违法行为，在不违反对非法侵占文物或走私文物的惩罚规定的情况下，委员会可吊销其工作许可证。考古团队或外国文物古迹博物馆如被查实参与或协助其成员进行法律规定的违法行为，委员会可禁止该机构或博物馆最低5年以内不得在阿拉伯埃及共和国进行考古发掘工作。考古发掘机构、团队在工作期间如有违章行为，委员会的董事会可决定吊销其工作的许可证。在不违反关于对无理侵占文物或走私文物的惩罚规定的情况下，考古团队或外国博物馆的成员犯有本法列举的任何一种罪行，一经核实，委员会可禁止该机构或博物馆在阿拉伯埃及共和国进行考古发掘工作，禁期不得少于5年。

第38条　最高文物委员会、各埃及大学团队因考古发掘、维修古建筑和历史遗址工作的需要，以及为装备博物馆及其所属文物中心、举办文物艺术展览，从国外进口工具、设备、仪器可免交海关税。外国团队因考古发掘、维修的需要以及为进行与文物考古有关的正常研究，将工具、设备带进埃及，海关署予以临时免税放行。外国团队如将这些工具、设备处理转让给委员会或埃及大学的考古队，可最终免交海关税。如外国团队在工作期满后将工具、设备处置给非文物考古单位，须按规定交纳海关税。

第 39 条 经委员会董事会批准，根据部长决议，可确定埃及人和外国人参观博物馆和考古遗址的门票费。埃及人门票费不超过 1000 埃镑，外国人门票费则不超过 5000 埃镑或等值外币。

第三章 刑罚

第 40 条 在不违反刑法和其他法律规定的任何最严厉惩罚的情况下，凡违反本法各条款者按下列条款判处刑罚。

第 41 条 凡向埃及共和国境外走私文物，并明知此行为的，判处情节加重的有期徒刑，并处 100,000 埃镑以上、不超过 1,000,000 埃镑的罚金。走私文物、作案使用的设备、工具、仪器、车辆应被没收归委员会所有。

第42条 以走私为目的盗窃国家所有的登记文物或是委员会、许可团队、机构或大学登记文物或是其考古挖掘所发现文物的全部或其组成部分的，判处有期徒刑，并处 50,000 埃镑以上、不超过 500,000 埃镑罚金。凡为走私而窝藏文物或其组成部分的，判处 7 年以上有期徒刑。上述情况中，应没收涉案文物以及涉案机器、工具、设备、车辆归委员会所有。

下述行为判处 1 年以上、7 年以下有期徒刑，并处 50,000 埃镑以上、不超过 100,000 埃镑罚金：

1. 故意破坏或损毁文物，毁坏文物或者改变文物原貌的，拆散文物部件的。

2. 未经许可，为寻找文物而进行考古挖掘的。

对于上述情况，如作案人系最高文物委员会的工作人员、考古团队的职员及工人或委员会的承包人员及他们的工人，则判处有期徒刑，并处 100,000 埃镑以上、不超过 250,000 埃镑罚金。

第 42 条之二 盗窃国家所有的文物或其组成部分的，判处 7 年以下有期徒刑，并处 50,000 埃镑以上、不超过 250,000 埃镑罚金。

除罚款外，凡藏匿犯罪所得的文物或其组成部分的，判处 5 年以下有期徒刑。上述情况中，应没收涉案文物以及涉案机器、工具、设备、车辆归委员会所有。

第 43 条 凡有下列行为的，判处 1 年以上、5 年以下有期徒刑，并处 10,000 埃镑以上、不超过 100,000 埃镑罚金。

1. 未经委员会书面批准将国家所有的文物或登记文物迁移、挪动。

2. 未经许可，将古建筑、文物古迹所在地或其部分改变为住宅、圈厩、仓库、工厂或将其用于种植、备作种植，或在上面植树、修水池、挖排灌渠，或进行其他工程以及其他任何形式的侵占。

3. 为行骗伪造古文物。

第 44 条 凡违反本法第 6 条、第 8 条、第 13 条、第 17 条和第 20 条规定的，判处本法第 43 条规定的刑罚。上述情况中，应没收涉案文物，以及涉案机器、工具、设备、车辆归委员会所有。

第 44 条之二 任何人违反本法第 5 条第二款、第 24 条和第 36 条规定，判处 1 年以下有期徒刑，并处 5,000 埃镑以上、不超过 20,000 埃镑罚金，或单处。上述情况中，应没收涉案文物以及涉案机器、工具、设备、车辆归委员会所有。

第 45 条 下述凡有下列行为的，判处 1 年以下有期徒刑，并处 1,000 埃镑以上、不超过 50,000 埃镑罚金，或单处：

1. 在文物上张贴广告、宣传画。

2. 在文物上书写、刻画或涂抹。

3. 损毁或破坏可移动或不可移动文物，或造成文物部件的拆散。

4. 未经委员会许可或超出采石场许可限度从考古遗址或文物古迹区盗取残砖碎瓦、肥料、泥土、沙子或其他材料，或者在该区域堆放肥料、泥土、垃圾或其他材料；

以上情形中，行为人应为其违法行为造成的损害承担赔偿责任。

第 45 条之二　凡在调查开始前向主管机构或调查机构坦白其罪行的，豁免本法第 41 条和第 42 条规定的处罚。如果上述行为人承认其导致委员会没收涉案文物的罪行或协助找回涉案文物（无论处于国内还是国外），那么法院可豁免其处罚。

第 46 条　国家工作人员违反本法第 18 条、第 19 条和第 20 条的规定，判处 2 年以上有期徒刑，并处 100 埃镑以上、不超过 500 埃镑罚金，并责其赔偿损失。

第 47 条　违反第 7 条、第 21 条和第 22 条规定的，判处没收文物，文物归最高文物委员会所有。

第四章　附则

第 48 条　委员会董事会主席、各文物局局长、博物馆馆长、副馆长、书记、各文物区主任、文物巡视员和助理巡视员均有权根据本法和为施行本法制定的细则中所列举的违法犯罪行为进行司法逮捕。

第 49 条　根据本法判处的罚金和本法第 29 条和第 39 条规定的门票收入均上交委员会所属的文物考古和博物馆工程资助基金会。委员会可利用此款奖赏在侦讯、破获违法行为工作中作出贡献的人员。奖赏的条件由委员会的董事会制定，奖金额由董事会主席决定。

第 50 条 委员会为实施本法所需一切费用可在行政费中取得。

第 51 条 委员会负责与规划、住房、旅游、公共、福利、治安的有关部门的协调工作，以确保文物、博物馆和历史建筑物免受震动、潮湿、污染、工业危害的影响，保护其历史和考古环境，妥善处理城市发展需要和保护文物需要之间的平衡。

第 52 条 委员会有权建立负责检测考古物品、犯罪主体的技术考古委员会。上述委员会应在检测后编制有关结果的技术考古报告，并将报告提交至法院和调查机构。上述委员会的组建程序由本法实施条例具体规定。

八、日 本

述 评

日本自明治维新以来，传统的历史文化受到西方文明的巨大冲击，历经文物保护与经济发展的冲突矛盾，日本逐渐意识到文物保护的重要性，1871（明治四年），日本政府制定《古器旧物保存方》，对以古代美术工艺品和古代建筑为核心的31个门类有形文化财进行登记保护。这是日本最初的一部由政府颁布的与文化财保护相关的法律，它对文化财历史价值的再认识和保护思想的启蒙起到了重要作用。1897年（明治三十年），日本又颁布了《古社寺保存法》，修复和保存古社寺内所有的建筑及宝物，确立了文化财保护和向公众公开的两项基本原则。由内务大臣指定其中的最具历史见证和美术典范价值的为“特别保护建造物”或“国宝”，初步建立了文化财指定制度。该法中关于指定物的管理、规制、公开展示和资金援助等条款成为战后日本文化财保护制度的原型。1919年（大正八年）颁布《史迹名胜天然纪念物保存法》，规定内务大臣指定史迹名胜天然纪念物，并且指定地方的公共团体负责史迹名胜天然纪念物的管理。这一指定程序与《古社寺保存法》中国宝的认定程序相同，说明政府对历史遗迹、人文或自然景观保护的重视程度与国宝相当。

1929年（昭和四年）颁布的《国宝保存法》取代了《古社寺保存法》，将指定国宝范围扩大到现存国家、团体及个人所有的全部物品，规定未经文部大臣许可，禁止出口与转让国宝。1933（昭和八年），为遏制大量极具价值的美术品因未被指定而流失海外的现状，颁布《重要美术品保存法》。该法规定历史上或在美术上有特别价值的美术作品，未经文部大臣许可不得出口，同时还创建了文部省、大藏省和海关等政府部门联合防止美术品流失海外的协同配合体制。[①]

1950年5月30日，为了“保护文化财并促使其得到充分利用，提高国民

① 于小川：“从法令规制的角度看日本文化财的保护及利用——二战前日本文化财保护制度的成立”，《北京理工大学学报（社会科学版）》，2005年6月第7卷第3期。

的文化素质，对世界文化的进步有所贡献”，日本颁布《文化财保护法》(法律第214号)，这是日本文化财法律中最重要的法律之一。在第二次世界大战刚刚结束之际，日本即制定文化财保护的法律，力图加强文化财保护利用，并将视野扩大到对世界文化的贡献上，其立法思路是比较先进的。其后，《文化财保护法》几乎每隔一两年就就会修改一次，至2018年(平成30年)6月8日(号外法律第42号)的修改，已历经40次重大修订，立法目的始终未变。现行《文化财保护法》共计13章，203条，另有附则。本法将文化财分为有形文化财、无形文化财、民俗文化财、纪念物、文化景观和传统建造物群等六大类并分别作出定义，并对指定、认定、登录、选定、报告以及进出境管理等重要制度作出明确规定。其中涉及文化财进出境管理的法条主要有第44、82、168、179、193、194条。

1954年6月29日，日本根据《文化财保护法》制定了《关于国宝或重要文化财的变更现状、出口及重要有形民俗文化财的出口的许可申请等规则》(文化财保护委员会规则第3号)。2005年3月28日，该规则以文部科学省令第11号被修正。

2002年(平成14年)7月3日，以法律第81号公布《非法进出口文化财产规制法》，共7条，加附则，旨在采取有效措施防止从《1970年公约》缔约国博物馆、公共纪念馆或类似机构盗窃文化财产非法进口，以及返还这些文化财产，落实公约精神。该法于2004年(平成16年)5月28日以号外法律第61号修正，最终于2005年(平成17年)4月1日起施行。该法明确了在本法调整范围内的“文化财产”的内涵，主要规定了如何指定“特定的外国文化财”，以及在这类文化财产的进口和善意取得规则。但是该法的不足之处为适用范围有限，只涉及《1970年公约》缔约国被盗文化财产的返还问题，并不包括从以上国家非法出口文化财产的进出境限制与归还。

日本文物进出境管理的相关机构在国家层面主要是文化厅。文化厅具体负责日本文化财保护工作，文化厅直属文部科学省，其职责、组织机构在《文部科学省设置法》《文部科学省组织指令》《文部科学省设置法实施规则》中有明确规定。文化厅设置文化部和文化财部两个部门。文化财部中设部长、文化财监查官各一人，下设传统文化科、美术学艺科和纪念物科和建筑物参事官。这三个科室和一个参事官共同承担文化财的保护职责。比如日本的老旧书画等出口，向美术学艺科提出申请，该部门负责审核。在各科和参事官室又分别配备了负责专业领域的文化财调查官，从事由国家指定、选定文化财等工作，也负责向地方政府进行指导、建议等。[①]在地方，到1977年（昭和五十二年），所有的都道府县都设置了文化艺术、文化财专管科，大部分市镇村设置了文化财专管负责人，部分设置专管科。[②]

① 国家文物局第一次全国可移动文物普查工作办公室编译：《日本文化财保护制度简编》，北京，文物出版社，2016年7月第1版，第92页。

② 同上，第97页。

（一）《文化财[①]保护法》*

文化财保护法

（周超　翻译校对）

1950 年（昭和 25 年）5 月 30 日法律第 214 号［制定］

1951 年（昭和 26 年）12 月 24 日法律第 318 号［第一次修改］

1952 年（昭和 27 年）7 月 31 日号外法律第 272 号［第二次修改］

1953 年（昭和 28 年）8 月 10 日法律第 194 号

［根据国有财产法的修改法附则第 2 条的修改］

1953 年（昭和 28 年）8 月 15 日法律第 213 号

［根据实施地方自治法修改法的相关法律整理法第 6 条的修改］

1954 年（昭和 29 年）5 月 29 日法律第 131 号［第三次修改］

1956 年（昭和 31 年）6 月 12 日法律第 148 号

［根据实施地方自治法修改法的相关法律整理法第 47 条的修改］

1956 年（昭和 31 年）6 月 30 日法律第 163 号

［根据实施地方教育组织法的相关法律整理法第 9 条的修改］

1958 年（昭和 33 年）4 月 25 日号外法律第 86 号

［根据特别职位职员工资法修改法第 5 条的修改］

---

① 目前，国内在“文化财”这一名词的翻译上存在不同意见，有的翻译成“文化财产”，有的翻译成“文化遗产”，还有的直接用“文化财”。鉴于日本的文化财含义丰富，既包括有形遗产，也有无形遗产，既包括可移动遗产，也有不可移动遗产，既包括自然遗产，也有保存技术，其保护对象与“文物”、“文化财产”和“文化遗产”都有不同，因此本法翻译直接采用“文化财”一词。

* 本书有关日本文化财的法律法规，均由重庆大学法学院周超副教授翻译，为 2018 年度国家社科基金艺术学项目（批准号：18BH154）的阶段性成果。本书翻译的日本《文化财保护法》体现了 2018 年的最新修改成果。

1959年（昭和34年）4月20日号外法律第148号

[根据实施国税征收法的相关法律整理法第58条的修改]

1961年（昭和36年）6月2日法律第111号

[根据国家行政组织法修改法第19条的修改]

1962年（昭和37年）5月16日法律第140号

[根据实施行政事件诉讼法修改法的相关法律整理法第29条的修改]

1962年（昭和37年）9月15日号外法律第161号

[根据实施行政不服审查法的相关法律整理法第67条的修改]

1965年（昭和40年）3月31日号外法律第36号

[根据实施所得税及法人税法的相关法律整理法第38条的修改]

1968年（昭和43年）6月15日号外法律第99号

[根据行政机关简政之总理府设置法的修改法第17条的修改]

1971年（昭和46年）5月31日法律第88号

[根据环境厅设置法附则第15条的修改]

1971年（昭和46年）6月1日号外法律第96号

[根据许可、认可等整理法第14条的修改]

1971年（昭和47年）6月3日法律第52号

[根据公害等调整委员会法附则第9条的修改]

1975年（昭和50年）7月1日法律第49号[第四次修改]

1983年（昭和58年）12月2日号外法律第78号

[根据实施国家行政组织法修改法的相关法律整理法第68条的修改]

1993年（平成5年）11月12日号外法律第89号

[根据实施行政手续法的相关法律整理法第78条的修改]

1994年（平成6年）6月29日号外法律第49号

[根据实施地方自治法修改法的相关法律整理法第13条的修改]

1994年（平成6年）11月11日号外法律第97号

[根据许可、认可等整理法第4条的修改]

1996年（平成8年）6月12日号外法律第66号[第五次修改]

1999年（平成11年）7月16日号外法律第87号

[根据推进地方分权的相关法律整理法第 135 条的修改]

1999 年（平成 11 年）7 月 16 日号外法律第 102 号

[根据中央省厅改革的行政组织关系法律整备法第 69 条的修改]

1999 年（平成 11 年）12 月 22 日号外法律第 160 号

[根据中央省厅改革关系法实施法第 522 条的修改]

1999 年（平成 11 年）12 月 22 日号外法律第 178 号

[根据独立行政法人国立博物馆法附则第 9 条的修改]

1999 年（平成 11 年）12 月 22 日号外法律第 179 号

[根据独立行政法人文化财研究所法附则第 8 条的修改]

2000 年（平成 12 年）5 月 19 日号外法律第 73 号

[根据城市规划以及建筑基准法修改法附则第 11 条的修改]

2002 年（平成 14 年）2 月 8 日号外法律第 1 号

[根据促进利用日本电信电话株式会社股票销售收入的社会资本整备特别措施法修改法第 20 条的修改]

2002 年（平成 14 年）7 月 3 日号外法律第 82 号 [**第六次修改**]

2004 年（平成 16 年）5 月 28 日号外法律第 61 号 [**第七次修改**]

2004 年（平成 16 年）6 月 9 日号外法律第 84 号

[根据行政事件诉讼法修改法附则第 17 条的修改]

2006 年（平成 18 年）5 月 31 日号外法律第 46 号

[根据为改善城市秩序的城市规划法修改法附则第 13 条的修改]

2006 年（平成 18 年）6 月 15 日号外法律第 73 号

[根据遗失物法附则第 5 条的修改]

2007 年（平成 19 年）3 月 30 日号外法律第 7 号

[根据独立行政法人国立博物馆法修改法附则第 10 条的修改]

2011 年（平成 23 年）5 月 2 日号外法律第 37 号

[根据为改革、推进以及提高地方自主性的相关法律整备法第 10 条的修改]

2014 年（平成 26）6 月 4 日号外法律第 51 号

[根据为改革、推进以及提高地方自主性的相关法律整备法第 5 条的修改]

2014 年（平成 26 年）6 月 13 日号外法律第 69 号

[根据实施行政不服审查法修改法的相关法律整备法第 108 条的修改]

2018年（平成30年）6月8日号外法律第42号*

［根据文化财保护法以及地方教育行政组织运营法的修改法第1条的修改］

第一章　总则（第一条～第四条）

【立法目的】

第一条　为了保护文化财并促使其得到充分利用，为了提高国民的文化素质，同时也为了对世界文化的进步有所贡献，特制定本法。

【文化财定义】

第二条　本法中的“文化财”包括以下各项内容：

（一）在我国历史上或艺术方面具有较高价值的建筑物、绘画、雕刻、工艺品、书法、典籍、古文书以及其他有形文化成果（包括与其形成一个整体而具有价值的土地和其他物件）、考古资料和其他具有较高学术价值的历史资料（以下称为“有形文化财”）。

（二）在我国历史上或艺术方面具有较高价值的戏剧、音乐、工艺技术及其它无形的文化成果（以下称为“无形文化财”）。

（三）为理解我国国民生活的变迁与发展，与民众衣食住行、生产、信仰、节假日等风俗习惯、民俗技艺以及再现其所不可或缺的服饰、器具、房屋和其他物品（以下称为“民俗文化财”）。

（四）在我国历史上或学术方面具有较高价值的贝塚、古墓、都城遗址、城址、旧民居及其他遗迹；在我国艺术或观赏方面具有较高价值的庭园、桥梁、峡谷、海滨、山岳及其他名胜地以及具有较高学术研究价值的动物（包括其栖息地、繁殖地及迁徙地）、植物（包括其生长地）及地质矿物（包括产生特殊自然现象的土地）等（以下称为“纪念物”）。

（五）为理解我国国民生活、生产所不可或缺的地域民众的生活、生产以

---

* 此次改正新增一节一款条文59条，修改36条，核心内容是增设了各类文化财的“保护利用计划”的“认定制度”。修改后的新法施行日期为2019年4月1日。

及由该地域风土所形成的景观地等（以下称为“文化景观”）。

（六）与周围环境风貌共同形成具有历史风格和很高价值的传统建造物群（以下称为“传统建造物群”）。

2. 本法规定（除第二十七至二十九条、第三十七条、第五十五条第一款第四项、第一百五十三条第一款第一项、第一百六十五条、第一百七十一条以及附则第三条外）的“重要文化财”包括“国宝”。

3. 本法规定（除第一百〇九条、第一百条、第一百一十二条、第一百二十二条、第一百三十一条第一款第四项、第一百五十三条第一款第七项、第八项、第一百六十五条以及第一百七十一条外）的“史迹名胜天然纪念物”包括“特别史迹名胜天然纪念物”。

【政府及地方公共团体之任务】

第三条 政府及地方公共团体不仅要充分认识到文化财是我国历史、文化的重要组成部分，同时也要认识到文化财是文化发展之基础，为了使文化财得到真正保护，必须为切实执行本法的具体规定而付出努力。

【国民、所有人等的责任】

第四条 为实现本法之立法目的，政府及地方公共团体所实施的各项行政措施，一般国民必须诚实地予以协助。

2. 文化财所有人及其他关系人应该自觉地认识到文化财是全体国民的贵重财产，为了全体国民的共同利益其不仅应妥善保护文化财，同时也应该尽可能地公开展示文化财以实现其文化价值的充分利用。

3. 在本法的实施过程中，政府及地方公共团体必须尊重文化财关系人的所有权及其他财产权。

第二章 删除①

① 本章原为“文化财保护委员会”组织法。“文化财保护委员会”是在文部省之外设置的专门负责文化财保护的国家组织，1968 年因行政机构简化与文部省文化局统合为现在的“文化厅”。

第三章　有形文化财（第二十七条～第七十条）

第一节　重要文化财（第二十七条～第五十六条）

第一款　指定（第二十七条～第二十九条）

【指定】

第二十七条　文部科学大臣可将有形文化财中的重要者指定为“重要文化财”。

2．从世界文化的角度考虑，文部科学大臣可将重要文化财中那些具有很高价值且无以伦比的国民之宝指定为国宝。

【公告、通知及指定证书之交付】

第二十八条　根据前条规定作出的指定，文部科学大臣不仅要在《官报》上公告，还要将指定结果通知国宝或重要文化财的所有人。

2．根据前条规定作出的指定，自上款规定的公告之日起生效；但对国宝或重要文化财所有人而言，指定自收到上款规定的通知之日起生效。

3．根据前条规定作出的指定，文部科学大臣应当向被指定国宝或重要文化财的所有人交付指定证书。

4．指定证书上所应记载事项以及其他涉及指定证书的必要事项，均由文部科学省政令规定。

5．根据第三款规定收到国宝指定证书的国宝所有人，必须在收到证书之日起30日内将被指定为国宝的原重要文化财指定证书返还给文部科学大臣。

【撤销】

第二十九条　当国宝或重要文化财失去其作为国宝或重要文化财的价值或者发生其他特殊事由时，文部科学大臣可以撤销国宝或重要文化财指定。

2．根据前款规定的指定撤销，除在《官报》上发布公告外，还需将撤销指定通知国宝或重要文化财的所有人。

3. 根据第一款规定的指定撤销，准用前条第二款规定。
4. 所有人在收到第二款规定的通知后，必须在 30 日内将被撤销的指定证书返还给文部科学大臣。
5. 根据第一款规定撤销的国宝指定、但未撤销重要文化财指定的，文部科学大臣应当立刻向文化财所有人交付重要文化财指定证书。

第二款　管理（第三十条 ~ 第三十四条）

【管理方法之指示】

第三十条　在重要文化财的管理上，文化厅长官可以指示重要文化财所有人实施必要的管理方法。

【所有人的管理义务及管理责任人】

第三十一条　重要文化财的所有人必须根据本法、文部科学省政令以及文化厅长官的指示等，对重要文化财进行妥善管理。
2. 为妥善管理该重要文化财，重要文化财所有人认为必要时，可选任第一百九十二条之二第一款所规定的文化财保存利用支援团体或其他适当人选、代替自己承担管理重要文化财的责任（在本节及第一百八十七条第一款第一项中称为“管理责任人”）。
3. 根据前款规定选任管理责任人后，重要文化财所有人与被选任的管理责任人必须在 20 日内上报文化厅长官提交连署的文部科学省政令所规定的、记载必要事项的书面文件。解任管理责任人时也同样适用。
4. 前条及本条第一款的规定，准用于管理责任人。

【所有人或管理责任人之变更】

第三十二条　当重要文化财所有人发生变更时，新所有人必须在 20 日内向文化厅长官提交文部科学省政令所规定的变更所有人申报表，并添附原所有人的指定证书。
2. 重要文化财所有人在变更管理责任人时，必须在 20 日内向文化厅长官提交与新管理责任人连署的由文部科学省政令所规定的变更管理责任人申报表。该情况不适用前条第三款规定。

3. 重要文化财的所有人或管理责任人的姓名、名称或住所发生变更时，必须在 20 日内向文化厅长官提交文部科学省政令所规定的变更所有人或管理任人的名称或住所申请表。如果姓名、名称或住所的变更涉及重要文化财所有人的，变更申请材料中必须添附指定证书。

【管理团体的管理】

第三十二条之二 在难以判明重要文化财所有人或者认为所有人、管理责任人对重要文化财的管理陷入困难或明显管理不当时，为保存该重要文化财，文化厅长官可以指定适当的地方公共团体或其他法人对该重要文化财实施必要管理（包括对那些由该重要文化财所有人所有或者管理人管理的、为保存该重要文化财所必需的设施、设备及其他物品等的管理）。

2. 在实施前款规定的指定时，文化厅长官必须事先征得该重要文化财所有人（无法判明所有人的除外）、合法占有人以及被指定管理团体的同意。

3. 根据第一款规定的指定，文化厅长官不仅应在《官报》上公告，还要将指定结果通知该重要文化财所有人、占有人以及被指定团体。

4. 根据第一款规定的指定，准用第二十八条第二款。

5. 重要文化财的所有人或者占用人，若无正当理由不得拒绝、妨碍或规避接受第一款指定的地方公共团体及其他法人（本节以下及第一百八十七条第一款第一项中称为“管理团体”）对重要文化财的管理以及为管理而实施的必要措施。

6. 对于管理团体，准用第三十条及第三十一条第一款规定。

第三十二条之三 当前条第一款规定的事由已经消灭或又出现其他特殊事由时，文化厅长官可撤销对管理团体的指定。

2. 前款规定的指定撤销，准用前条第三款以及第二十八条第二款规定。

第三十二条之四 除本法有特别规定外，管理团体实施管理工作所需费用由管理团体承担。

2. 前款规定并不妨碍管理团体与所有人通过协议的方式约定在所有人受益的

范围内由所有人承担部分管理费用。

【灭失、损毁等】

第三十三条　当重要文化财全部或部分灭失、损毁、丢失、被盗时，重要文化财所有人（包括管理责任人、管理团体等）必须自发现之日起 10 日内，用文部科学省政令所规定的书面材料上报至文化厅长官。

【所在地之变更】

第三十四条　重要文化财的所有人（包括管理责任人、管理团体等）试图变更重要文化财所在地时，必须在准备变更之日的前 20 日内，准备文部科学省政令所规定的文件材料并添附指定证书上报至文化厅长官；但如果文部科学省政令的规定中不需要上报、上报时未要求添附指定证书或者根据文部科学省政令规定可在变更所在场所后再上报即可。

第三款　保护（第三十四条之二 ~ 第四十七条）

【修缮】

第三十四条之二　重要文化财的修缮由所有人实施，但有管理团体的则由该管理团体实施。

【管理团体的修缮】

第三十四条之三　管理团体在修缮重要文化财时，必须将修缮日期及修缮方法事先告知重要文化财的所有人（除难于判明所有人外）或合法占用人，并听取其意见。

2. 管理团体进行修缮时，准用第三十二条之二第五款、第三十二条之四的规定。

【管理或修缮之补贴】

第三十五条　当重要文化财所有人或管理团体无法承担重要文化财的巨额管

理费、修缮费以及出现其他特殊情况时，政府应当对重要文化财所有人或管理团体给予适当的财政补贴以保证其有充足的管理费或修缮费。

2. 在交付前款财政补贴时，文化厅长官可对管理或修缮工作适时地作出必要指示，并可将该指示作为财政补贴条件。

3. 文化厅长官认为必要时，可以指挥和监督依据第一款规定获得财政补贴的重要文化财的管理或修缮。

【管理的命令或建议】

第三十六条 因不能胜任管理工作或因管理失误可能造成重要文化财灭失、损毁或存在失盗之虞的，文化厅长官可以命令或建议该重要文化财所有人、管理责任人或管理团体等选任或变更重要文化财管理人、改善管理方法、设置必要的防火设施或其他保护性设施。

2. 前款命令或建议中的措施实施费用，文部科学省可通过政令形式决定由国家承担其全部或部分。

3. 前款规定的由国家承担的全部或部分的费用，准用前条第三款规定。

【修缮的命令或建议】

第三十七条 国宝有损毁迹象，文化厅长官认为有保存必要的，可命令或建议所有人或管理团体对该国宝进行修缮。

2. 对于除国宝外的重要文化财有损毁迹象，文化厅长官认为有保存必要的，可建议所有人或管理团体对该重要文化财进行修缮。

3. 前二款中的修缮费用，可由文部科学省以政令形式决定由国家承担全部或部分。

4. 对于前款所规定的由国家承担全部或部分的费用，准用第三十五条第三款规定。

【由文化厅长官实施的国宝修缮等措施】

第三十八条 有下列情况之一者，文化厅长官可决定亲自对国宝进行修缮，或者采取措施防止国宝灭失、损毁或被盗等。

（一）所有人、管理责任人或管理团体不服从前两条命令的。

（二）当国宝正在损毁或者存在灭失、损毁或被盗之虞，所有人、管理责任人或管理团体被认为拒不采取措施防止国宝灭失、损毁或被盗的。

2. 根据前款规定，文化厅长官在准备修缮国宝或采取其他保护措施时，必须事先将载有该国宝名称、修缮或采取保护措施内容、修缮日期及其他认为必要事项的政令告知国宝所有人、管理责任人或管理团体，并通知该国宝的合法占有人。

第三十九条　实施前条第一款规定的修缮或保护措施时，文化厅长官必须在文化厅职员中任命有能力实施修缮或保护措施者为该国宝修缮的管理责任人。

2. 根据前款规定所选择的责任人，在修缮国宝或采取其他保护措施时，必须携带身份证明，应国宝相关人员要求出示其身份证明，并必须尊重相关人员的正当意见。

3. 前条第一款规定的修缮或实施其他保护措施，准用第三十二条之二第五款规定。

第四十条　第三十八第一款规定的修缮或实施其他保护措施所需费用由国家承担。

2. 根据文部科学省政令规定，文化厅长官可向国宝所有人（若为管理团体时，则向管理团体）征收部分费用以承担第三十八条第一款规定的修缮或实施其他保护措施所需费用；但征收仅限于该条第一款第二项所规定的国宝所有人、管理责任人、管理团体等对国宝的修缮或实施其他保护措施等负有责任，而且国宝所有人和管理团体有承担该部分费用的能力的情形。

3. 前款规定的费用征收，准用《行政代执行法》① 第五条、第六条规定。

第四十一条　因第三十八条第一款规定的国宝修缮或实施其他保护措施给相关人造成损害的，由国家对所产生的损害进行补偿。

2. 前款规定的补偿额度，由文化厅长官决定。

3. 不服前款决定的补偿额度的，可通过诉讼方式要求增加补偿，但仅限于自收到前款补偿决定通知之日起 6 个月内行使。

---

① 1948（昭和 23）年 5 月 15 日法律第 43 号。

4. 前款之诉的被告为国家。

【重要文化财转让时补助金等的返还】

第四十二条 已接受国家根据第三十五条第一款、第三十六条第二款、第三十七条第三款及第四十条第一款规定的实施修缮或实施防止灭失、损毁及被盗等措施（以下本条中为“修缮等”）交付补助金、保护措施实施费、修缮费的重要文化财所有人、继承人、受遗赠人、受赠人（包括再继承的继承人、再遗赠的受遗赠人、再赠与的受赠人。以下本条同，称为“所有人等”），有偿转让重要文化财时，可通过文部科学省政令要求所有人等向国家返还国家承担的补助金及修缮费（第四十条第一款规定的相关费用中应扣除该条第二款向所有人征收的部分，以下本条同），但应扣除国家在实施修缮等措施后所有人等个人再次进行修缮而支出的费用（以下本条中称为“返还金”）。

2. 前款中的“补助金及修缮费”，是指该维修补助金及修缮费的总金额除以文化厅长官决定实施修缮等后该文化财的耐用年数、再乘以耐用年数减去自实施修缮等后至转让时的所剩年数（不足一年的舍去）的金额。

3. 在利用“补助金及修缮费”实施修缮等行为后，因非所有人等的责任造成重要文化财价值明显降低或所有人等将重要文化财让渡给国家的，文化厅长官可决定免除所有人等应返还的全部或部分返还金。

4. 未在文化厅长官指定的期限内返还上述金额的，可按国税滞纳标准征收滞纳金。征收滞纳金的先取特权顺位为先国税、后地税。

5. 当返还金交纳人为继承人、受遗赠人或受赠人时，其返还金的金额总数应扣除下列第一项所规定的继承税额或赠与税额与第二项所规定金额差、除以第三项所规定的年限、再乘以第四项所规定年限。

（一）取得该重要文化财时已交纳或应交纳的继承税额或赠与税额。

（二）当前项税额课税基础的课税价格中包括该重要文化财继承、赠与行为发生前、已获得第一款规定的国家补助金的应扣除该补助金之后的、该重要文化财全部或部分所应缴纳的继承税税额或赠与税税额。

（三）第二款所规定的由文化厅长官确定的该重要文化财全部或部分的

耐用年限中减去修缮等后至继承、赠与时的年限后所获年数（不足一年的舍去）。

（四）第二款所规定的有关该重要文化财全部或部分的剩余耐用年数。

6. 前款第二项中所列举的第一款中的修缮费、补助金等，准用本条第二款规定，此时该款中的“转让时”替换为“继承、遗赠或赠与时”。

7. 在计算本条第一款规定的返还金缴纳人因转让该重要文化财所得税时，按照《所得税法》[①]第三十三条第一款规定的转让所得金额计算，依据本条第一款规定的返还金作为该条第三款规定的资产转让所需费用。

【现状变更等的限制】

第四十三条　变更重要文化财现状或实施某种对该重要文化财的保存环境有影响的行为，必须事先取得文化厅长官的许可；但变更现状是重要文化财的维持措施、避免自然灾害给其造成破坏而采取的应急措施、且对保存环境的影响轻微的，则不在此限。

2. 前款但书中的“维持措施”范围，由文部科学省政令规定。

3. 文化厅长官在下达第一款的许可时，可对该款所规定的现状变更及对保存环境有影响的行为作出必要指示，并以此作为许可的条件。

4. 若接受第一款许可的被许可人不服从前款规定的必要指示，文化厅长官可以命令停止变更现状以及停止实施对保存环境有影响的行为，或者撤销该许可。

5. 因未能获得第一款规定许可或者因被要求服从第三款所规定的许可条件而遭受一般性损失的，由国家给予补偿。

6. 前款中的国家补偿，准用本法第四十一条第二款至第四款规定。

【修缮之申请】

第四十三条之二　当重要文化财需要修缮时，其所有人或管理团体必须在预定修缮开工之前30日内向文化厅长官提出修缮申请，但前条第一款规定必须

① 1965（昭和40）年3月31日法律第33号。

获得许可、并由文部科学省政令规定的，则不在此限。

2. 对于前款修缮申请，文化厅长官认为必要时，可就重要文化财修缮提出技术性指导或建议。

【出境禁止】

第四十四条 禁止重要文化财出境；但因国际文化交流或其他事由等获得文化厅长官特别许可的，则不在此限。

【环境保护】

第四十五条 就重要文化财的保护问题，文化厅长官认为必要时，可以命令在一定地域内限制或禁止某种行为，或者命令建设必要的保护设施。

2. 因前款命令而使相关人受到财产损失的，由国家对所产生的一般性损失给予补偿。

3. 前款的损失补偿，准用本法第四十一条第二款至第四款规定。

【向国家出让之申请】

第四十六条 有偿转让重要文化财时，出让人必须事先将受让人、预定价格（若预定价格为金钱以外的其他物品的，则按时价标准确定金额，以下同）及其他文部科学省政令所规定的事项，以书面形式告知文化厅长官并提出向国家出让的申请。

2. 在前款规定的书面申请中，可阐明希望让渡给对方的理由。

3. 文化厅长官认为前款书面申请中的让渡理由充分时，应在收到该申请后30日内通知出让人国家不予购买的决定。

4. 在出让人提出向国家出让申请的30日内，若文化厅长官将该重要文化财由国家购买的决定通知出让人的，则视为国家以相当于申请书所载价格购买该重要文化财的买卖合同成立。

5. 在前款所规定的期限（该期限的截止日期为文化厅长官作出不购买决定的通知之日）内，第一款中的出让人不得转让该重要文化财。

【管理团体购买的财政补贴】

第四十六条之二 为保护重要文化财、特别是作为重要文化财管理团体的地方公共团体或其他法人有必要购买其所管理的重要文化财（仅限于建筑物、土地附着物以及被指定为重要文化财的土地）时，国家认为必要可以对其购买所需经费给予适当补贴。

2. 前款国家补贴，准用本法第三十五条第二款、第三款及第四十二条规定。

【管理、修缮的委托或技术指导】

第四十七条 在文化厅长官规定的条件下，重要文化财所有人（若为管理团体的则为该管理团体）可向文化厅长官提出重要文化财的管理（除管理团体外）或修缮委托。

2. 文化厅长官认为有必要时，可以在明示一定条件的情况下，向重要文化财所有人建议其（若为管理团体的则为该团体）向文化厅长官提出该重要文化财的委托管理（除管理团体外）或委托修缮。

3. 前两款规定的文化厅长官接受的委托管理或委托修缮，准用本法第三十九条第一款、第二款规定。

4. 重要文化财所有人、管理责任人及管理团体可根据文部科学省政令规定，请求文化厅长官对重要文化财的管理、修缮等进行技术性指导。

第四款 公开展示（第四十七条之二～第五十三条）

【公开展示】

第四十七条之二 重要文化财的公开展示由所有人实施；但若为管理团体的则由管理团体实施。

2. 前款规定并不妨碍重要文化财所有人及管理团体之外的其他人依据本法规定对该重要文化财进行公开展示。

3. 管理团体在公开展示其管理的重要文化财时，可对参观者收取一定费用。

【由文化厅长官实施的公开展示】

第四十八条　文化厅长官可以建议所有人（若为管理团体的则为该团体）提供其重要文化财，由文化厅长官主持在国立博物馆（独立行政法人国立文化财机构设立的博物馆，本条以下同）或其他机构内，实施为期1年以内的公开展示。

2. 文化厅长官可以命令由国家承担全部或部分费用，或接受补助金进行管理、修缮的重要文化财所有人，提供其重要文化财，由文化厅长官主持在国立博物馆或其他机构内实施为期1年以内的公开展示。

3. 文化厅长官认为必要时，可以决定延长前款规定的1年以内公开展示期，但连续不得超过5年。

4. 在作出第二款命令、前款的公开展示期间更新决定后，重要文化财所有人（若为管理团体的则为该团体）必须提供该项重要文化财以便公开展示。

5. 在前四款规定的情形之外，文化厅长官认为重要文化财所有人（若为管理团体的则为该团体）申请希望在国立博物馆或其他机构、由文化厅长官主持实施重要文化财公开展示的理由合理时，可允许其公开展示。

第四十九条　文化厅长官根据前条规定公开展示重要文化财时，除本法第一百八十五条规定的情形外，必须任命文化厅的工作人员承担公开展示该重要文化财期间的管理责任。

第五十条　根据第四十八条规定的公开展示所需费用由国家承担，其费用标准由文部科学省以政令形式规定。

2. 政府根据文部科学省政令规定的费用标准，向根据第四十八条规定出展重要文化财的所有人或管理团体支付相关出展费。

【所有人等的公开展示】

第五十一条　文化厅长官可以建议重要文化财所有人或管理团体实施为期3个月以内的重要文化财公开展示。

2. 文化厅长官可以命令由国家承担全部或部分费用，或接受补助金进行重要文化财管理、修缮的重要文化财所有人实施为期3个月以内的公开展示。

3. 前款公开展示，准用第四十八条第四款规定。

4. 文化厅长官可以对重要文化财所有人或管理团体根据前三款规定的公开展示以及与公开展示相关的管理事宜等给予必要指示。

5. 重要文化财所有人或管理责任人不服从前款指示的，文化厅长官可以命令停止或中止该公开展示。

6. 根据文部科学省政令的相关规定，本条第二款及第三款的公开展示所需费用的全部或部分可由国家承担。

7. 除前款规定的情形外，根据文部科学省的政令规定，重要文化财所有人或管理团体公开展示其所有或管理的重要文化财所需费用的全部或部分也可由国家承担。

第五十一条之二 除前条规定的公开展示外，为便于重要文化财向公众公开展示而根据第三十四条规定提出变更重要文化财所在地申请的，可准用前条第四款、第五款规定。

【损失的补偿】

第五十二条 对于因第四十八条、第五十一条第一款、第二款以及第三款规定的出展、公开展示等引起的重要文化财灭失、损毁的，国家应对该重要文化财所有人的合理损失给予补偿；但如果是因重要文化财所有人、管理责任人或管理团体的原因引起的，则不在此限。

2. 前款所规定的情形，准用本法第四十一条第二款至第四款规定。

【所有人等以外的其他人之公开展示】

第五十三条 重要文化财所有人、管理团体等以外的其他人在其主办的展览会或其他展览中公开展示重要文化财时，必须获得文化厅长官的许可；但如果文化厅长官以外的其他国家机关、地方公共团体等在已经获得文化厅长官承认的博物馆或其他机构（以下称为“承认的公开展示之机构”）主办的展览上进行公开展示的，则不在此限。

2. 在前款但书中，公开展示的主办人（除文化厅长官外）应在公开展示结束之日的次日起20日内，填写文部科学省政令所规定的书面材料，向文化厅长官作出汇报。

3. 文化厅长官在进行第一款规定的许可时，作为许可条件，可对该重要文化财公开展示或与之有关的管理工作给予必要指示。

4. 获得第一款许可而不服从前款指示的，文化厅长官可以命令停止公开展示或撤销许可。

第五款　重要文化财保护利用计划（第五十三条之二—第五十三条之八）

【重要文化财保护利用计划的认定】

第五十三条之二　重要文化财的所有者（若为管理团体则为该管理团体）可根据文部科学省政令的规定，制定重要文化财保护利用计划（以下称为“重要文化财保护利用计划”），并向文化厅长官申请予以认定。

2. 前款重要文化财保护利用计划应记载以下事项：

（一）该项重要文化财的名称、所在地；

（二）为保护和利用该项重要文化财而实施的具体措施；

（三）计划实施周期；

（四）文部科学省政令规定的其他事项。

3. 前款第二项中的具体措施内容，应记载以下事项：

（一）对该重要文化财的现状变更或保存产生影响的相关行为事项；

（二）对该重要文化财的维修事项；

（三）以公开该重要文化财（除建造物之外。下一款第六项同）为目的的委托管理合同事项。

4. 本条第一款的重要文化财保护利用计划的认定申请，符合以下条件的，文化厅长官可以予以认定。

（一）该重要文化财的保护利用计划的实施，有利于该重要文化财的保护与利用；

（二）该重要文化财的保护利用计划被认为能够得到确实、可行、顺利地实施；

（三）若存在本法第一百八十三条之二第一款规定的文化财保护利用大纲

或者第一百八十三条之五第一款规定的文化财保护利用区域规划，该保护利用计划应符合大纲或规划要求；

（四）该重要文化财保护利用计划中可能影响该重要文化财的现状变更或保存的、前款第一项所规定的相关行为，应符合文部科学省政令规定基准；

（五）该重要文化财保护利用计划所列举的、前款第二项所载重要文化财维修事项，应符合文部科学省政令规定的基准；

（六）该重要文化财保护利用计划所列举的、以公开重要文化财为目的的委托管理合同内容，应当符合文部科学省政令规定的标准；

5. 文化厅长官作出前款认定后，应立刻将认定结果通知申请人、不得延迟。

【获得认定的重要文化财保护利用计划之变更】

第五十三条之三　获得前条第四款认定的重要文化财所有者或者管理团体，若要变更（除文部科学省政令规定轻微变更外）其重要文化财保护利用计划，必须获得文化厅长官认定。

2. 前款认定，准用前条第四款、第五款规定。

【现状变更等的许可之特例】

第五十三条之四　本法第五十三条之二第三款第一项所规定的、影响该重要文化财的现状变更或保存的行为事项，在获得第四款认定（包含前条第一款的变更认定。本款以及第一百五十三条第二款第六项同）的情况下，实施影响重要文化财的现状变更或保存行为时，可无视第四十三条第一款必须获得许可的规定，只需在影响重要文化财的现状变更或保存行为终了后，立刻根据文部科学省政令的规定、向文化厅长官书面报告。

【维修申报之特例】

第五十三条之五　在实施第五十三条之二第三款第二项所记载的、获得第四款认定的重要文化财维修事项时，可无视第四十三条之二第一款必须获得许可的规定，只需在该维修行为结束后，根据文部科学省政令规定立刻向文化厅长官书面报告。

【被认定的重要文化财保护利用计划之实施状况的报告】

第五十三条之六 文化厅长官可以要求获得本法第五十三条之二第四款认定的重要文化财的所有者或管理团体，报告其已获认定的重要文化财保护利用计划（如有变更则为变更后的计划。在下一条以及第五十三条之八中称为“认定的重要文化财保护利用计划”）的实施情况。

【认定的撤销】

第五十三条之七 文化厅长官认为被认定的重要文化财保护利用计划不再符合第五十三条之二第四款所规定的各项条件时，可以撤销该认定。

2．文化厅长官根据前款规定撤销认定的，应立刻将认定撤销决定通知被认定人，不得延迟。

【对所有者等的指导或建议】

第五十三条之八 根据重要文化财所有者或者管理团体的请求，都、道、府、县以及市（含特别行政区，以下同）、町、村教育委员会（根据《地方教育行政组织法》[①]第二十三条第一款规定，为负责管理和执行文化财保护事务的地方公共团体［以下称为“特定地方公共团体”］及其负责人。除本法第一百四十三条第三款、第一百八十三条之八第四款、第一百九十条第一款以及第一百九十一条第一款外，以下同）可以就重要文化财保护利用计划的制定、所制定的保护利用计划能够得到确实、顺利实施等，提供必要的指导和建议。

2．根据重要文化财所有者或管理团体的请求，文化厅长官必须努力就重要文化财保护利用计划的指定、所认定的重要文化财保护利用计划能够得到确实、顺利实施等，提供必要的指导和建议。

---

① 1956年（昭和31年）6月20日法律第162号。

第六款 调查（第五十四条~第五十五条）

【为保护而实施的调查】

第五十四条 文化厅长官认为必要时，可要求重要文化财所有人、管理责任人或管理团体报告重要文化财的现状、管理、修缮及保存环境等。

第五十五条 发生下列情形之一的，根据前条报告无法确定重要文化财现状、也无其他方法进行确认时，文化厅长官可以指派调查人员进入重要文化财所在地对该重要文化财的现状、管理、修缮及保存环境等进行实地调查。

（一）已申请改变重要文化财现状或实施了影响重要文化财保存环境行为的；

（二）重要文化财正在被损毁或其现状、所在场所等已发生变更的；

（三）重要文化财存在灭失、损毁以及被盗之虞的；

（四）因特别事由有必要对国宝或重要文化财的价值重新鉴定的。

2. 根据前款规定，调查人员在进行实地调查时，应携带其身份证明，向相关人员出示，并当充分尊重相关人员的正当意见。

3. 对于因第一款的调查所造成的正常损失，由国家给予适当补偿。

4. 前款的补偿，准用本法第四十一条第二款至第四款规定。

第七款 其他事项（第五十六条）

【所有人等变更后权利义务的继承】

第五十六条 重要文化财所有人变更后，文化厅长官依据本法所作出的命令、建议、指示及其他处分等方式赋予原所有人在该重要文化财上的所有权利与义务由新所有人继承。

2. 原所有人移交重要文化财给新所有人时，必须同时移交该重要文化财的指定证书。

3. 针对管理团体的指定或指定解除等准用第一款规定，但当管理团体被指定时，属于原所有人的权利义务则不在此限。

第二节　登录有形文化财（第五十七条~第六十九条）

【有形文化财的登录】

第五十七条　鉴于重要文化财以外的其他有形文化财（除本法第一百八十二条第二款规定的由地方公共团体指定的有形文化财外）的文化价值以及对其保护和利用的必要等，文部科学大臣可将其登录在“文化财名录”上。

2．文部科学大臣在实施前款登录时，应事先听取相关地方公共团体的意见，但当该登录的有形文化财与第一百八十三条五第一款规定的登录提案相关时，则不在此限。

3．“文化财名录”的应登载事项由文部科学省政令规定。

【公告、通知以及登录证的交付】

第五十八条　在进行前条第一款登录后，应迅速在《官报》上公告并就所登录的有形文化财（以下称为“登录有形文化财”）结果通知该有形文化财所有人。

2．前条第一款规定的登录自前款《官报》公告之日起生效，但对该登录有形文化财所有人而言则自其收到前款通知之日起生效。

3．进行前条第一款登录时，文部科学大臣应向该有形文化财所有人交付登录证书。

4．登录证书上所记载内容以及其他与登录证书相关事项等，由文部科学省政令规定。

【有形文化财的登录撤销】

第五十九条　根据本法第二十七条第一款规定，当登录有形文化财被文部科学大臣指定为重要有形文化财时，原有形文化财的登录应予撤销。

2．根据本法第一百八十二条第二款规定，当登录有形文化财被地方公共团体指定时，文部科学大臣应撤销该登录；但当文部科学大臣认为有必要对登录有形文化财采取保护和利用措施、且所有人同意的，则可以不予撤销。

3．当有形文化财所采取措施的必要性丧失或者发生其他特殊事由时，文部科学大臣可以撤销该登录。

4. 根据前三款规定撤销登录的，应迅速在《官报》上公告并将撤销登录的结果通知该登录有形文化财所有人。

5. 根据第一款至第三款的登录撤销准用前条第二款规定。

6. 登录有形文化财的所有人在收到第四款通知后，必须在30日内将登录证书上缴文部科学大臣。

【登录有形文化财的管理】

第六十条 登录有形文化财所有人必须根据本法以及基于本法的文部科学省政令管理登录有形文化财。

2. 为适当管理登录有形文化财，登录有形文化财的所有人可以选择本法第一百九十二条之二第一款规定的文化财保护利用支援团体或者其他适当管理团体（本节中称为“管理责任人”）代自己管理登录有形文化财，并承担管理责任。

3. 当登录有形文化财所有人无法判明或者所有人、管理责任人的管理陷入困境或管理明显不当时，为保护和利用该登录有形文化财，登录有形文化财所在地的地方公共团体提出申请的，文化厅长官可以在征求相关地方公共团体意见的基础上，指定适当的地方公共团体或其他法人实施必要管理（包括由登录有形文化财所有人所有或管理的、为保护和利用该登录有形文化财的必要设施、设备以及其他物件等。本节以下称为“管理团体”）。

4. 对登录有形文化财的管理，准用本法第三十一条第三款、第三十二条、第三十二条之二第二款至第五款、第三十二条之三、第三十二条之四的规定。

5. 有关登录有形文化财的管理责任人以及管理团体，准用第一款规定。

【登录有形文化财的灭失、损毁等】

第六十一条 登录有形文化财全部或部分灭失、损毁或丢失以及被盗的，所有人（若是管理责任人或管理团体的则为该管理责任人或管理团体）应当根据文部科学省政令规定，自知道上述事实发生的次日起，10日内向文化厅长官书面报告。

【登录有形文化财所在地之变更】

第六十二条 登录有形文化财所有人（若为管理责任人或管理团体的则为该管理责任人或管理团体）若要变更登录有形文化财所在地，应当在决定变更之日前 20 日内，依据文部科学省政令规定，向文化厅长官提交书面报告并添附登录证书。若文部科学省政令有特别规定无需报告、添附登录证书或者可以在变更所在地之后报告的，则不在此限。

【登录有形文化财的修缮】

第六十三条 登录有形文化财的修缮由所有人实施，但若为管理团体的则由该团体实施。

2. 管理团体对登录有形文化财的修缮，准用本法第三十二条之二第五款、第三十二条之四以及第三十四条之三第一款规定。

【登录有形文化财的现状变更申请】

第六十四条 试图改变登录有形文化财现状者，必须根据文部科学省政令规定在改变现状之日前 30 日内，向文化厅长官提出申报；但若改变现状仅是为实施修缮、防止灾害等的必要应急措施或者为实施依据其他政令的改变现状命令而采取措施的，则不在此限。

2. 前款但书中的"修缮"措施范围，由文部科学省政令规定。

3. 为保护登录有形文化财，文化厅长官认为有必要时，可对第一款所规定的、登录有形文化财的现状变更予以指导、提出意见或给予建议。

【登录有形文化财的出境申请】

第六十五条 根据文部科学省政令规定，试图将登录有形文化财运出境外者，必须在运出境外之日起、提前 30 日向文化厅长官提起出境申请。

2. 文化厅长官如果认为必要，为保护登录有形文化财可对前款登录有形文化财的出境予以指导、提出意见或给予建议。

【登录有形文化财的管理或修缮的技术性指导】

第六十六条 根据文部科学省政令规定，登录有形文化财的所有人、管理责任人或管理团体可以请求文化厅长官就登录有形文化财的管理或修缮给予技术性指导。

【登录有形文化财的公开展示】

第六十七条 登录有形文化财的公开展示由所有人实施；但若为管理团体的则由管理团体实施。

2. 前款规定并不妨碍登录有形文化财所有人、管理团体之外的其他人在取得所有人（若为管理团体的则为该管理团体）同意的情况下，公开展示该登录有形文化财。

3. 管理团体公开展示其管理的登录有形文化财，准用本法第四十七条之二第三款规定。

4. 为合理利用登录有形文化财，文化厅长官认为有必要可对所有人或者管理团体进行登录有形文化财的公开展示以及与公开展示相关的管理等，予以必要指导或提供建议。

【登录有形文化财保护利用计划的认定】

第六十七条之二 登录文化财的所有者（如为管理团体则为该管理团体）可根据文部科学省政令规定，制定登录有形文化财保护利用计划（以下称为“登录有形文化财保护利用计划”），并申请文化厅长官认定。

2. 登录有形文化财保护利用计划应记载以下事项：

（一）该登录有形文化财的名称、所在地；

（二）为保护和利用该登录有形文化财而实施的具体措施；

（三）计划的实施周期；

（四）文部科学省政令规定的其他事项。

3. 前款第二项中的具体措施，应该记载以下事项：

（一）登录有形文化财的现状变更事项；

（二）具有历史、艺术以及学术价值的登录有形文化财（除建造物之外。

下一款第五项同）的公开展出委托合同所载事项；

（三）以公开该登录有形文化财（除建造物之外。下一款第六项同）为目的的委托保管合同事项。

4. 符合以下条件的第一款登录有形文化财保护利用计划的认定申请，文化厅长官应予以认定。

（一）登录有形文化财保护利用计划的实施，有利于该登录有形文化财的保护与利用；

（二）登录有形文化财保护利用计划的实施被认为可以顺利且能够得到确实实施的；

（三）若存在第一百八十三条之二第一款规定的文化财保护利用大纲或者第一百八十三条之五第一款规定的文化财保护利用区域规划时，该保护利用计划应符合大纲或规划要求。

（四）登录有形文化财保护利用计划中列举的前款第一项所载的变更现状事项，应当适合登录有形文化财的现状变更，并符合文部科学省政令所规定的标准；

（五）登录有形文化财保护利用计划中列举的前款第二项所载的委托保管合同事项，其内容应能够保障登录有形文化财的公开展示，并符合文部科学省政令所规定的标准；

5. 文化厅长官作出前款认定后，应立刻将认定结果通知申请人，不得延迟。

【被认定的登录有形文化财保护利用计划之变更】

第六十七条之三　获得前条第四款认定的登录有形文化财所有者或管理团体，若要变更已获认定的登录有形文化财保护利用计划，必须获得文化厅长官的认定。

2. 前款的认定准用前条第四款、第五款规定。

【现状变更的报告特例】

第六十七条之四　本法第六十七条之二第三款第一项所记载的登录有形文化财保护利用计划，在获得同条第四款认定（包含前条第一款的变更认定。

本节以及本法第一百五十三条第二款第七项中，相同）的情况下，实施被认定的影响登录有形文化财现状变更或保存的行为时，可忽略依据本法第六十四条第一款规定的必须提交报告的规定，只需在登录有形文化财的现状变更结束后，根据文部科学省政令规定立刻向文化厅长官报告。

【被认定的登录有形文化财保护利用计划之实施状况的报告】

第六十七条之五　文化厅长官可要求获得本法第六十七条之二第四款认定的登录有形文化财的所有者或管理团体，报告其已获认定的登录有形文化财保护利用计划（如有变更则为变更后的计划。在下一条第一款以及第六十七条之七中称为“被认定的登录有形文化财保护利用计划”）的实施情况。

【认定的撤销】

第六十七条之六　文化厅长官认为被认定的登录有形文化财保护利用计划不再符合本法第六十七条之二第四款规定的各项条件时，可撤销该认定。

2. 根据前款规定撤销认定的，文化厅长官应立刻将认定撤销决定通知被认定人，不得延迟。

【对所有者等的指导或建议】

第六十七条之七　根据登录有形文化财所有者或者管理团体的请求，都、道、府、县以及市、町、村教育委员会可就登录有形文化财保护利用计划的制定，以及所认定的保护利用计划能够得到确实、顺利实施等，向登录有形文化财所有者或者管理团体提供必要的指导或建议。

2. 根据登录有形文化财所有者或管理团体请求，文化厅长官必须努力就登录有形文化财保护利用计划的制定，所认定的登录有形文化财保护利用计划能够得到确实、顺利实施等，向登录有形文化财所有者或者管理团体提供必要的指导或建议。

【登录有形文化财之现状等的报告】

第六十八条　文化厅长官认为必要时，可要求登录有形文化财所有人或管理团体报告其所有或管理的登录有形文化财的管理或修缮等现状。

【伴随所有人变更的登录证书之移交】

第六十九条 登录有形文化财的所有人发生变更后，旧所有人必须在向新所有人移交该登录有形文化财的同时移交该登录有形文化财的登录证书。

第三节 重要文化财及登录有形文化财之外的其他有形文化财（第七十条）

【技术性指导】

第七十条 重要文化财及登录有形文化财之外的其他有形文化财所有人，可请求文化厅长官在该有形文化财的管理或修缮上给予技术性指导。

第四章 无形文化财（第七十一条~第七十七条）

【重要无形文化财的指定等】

第七十一条 文部科学大臣可以指定无形文化财中的重要者为重要无形文化财。

2. 根据前款规定，文部科学大臣指定重要无形文化财时，必须同时认定该重要无形文化财的保持者或保持团体（若由无形文化财保持者构成的团体，则认定其代表者，以下同）。

3. 第一款的指定应在《官报》上公告，并通知被认定的重要无形文化财的保持者或保持团体（若为保持团体的则为其代表者）。

4. 根据第一款规定，文部科学大臣在指定了重要无形文化财后，若认为某人或某团体仍可作为该项重要无形文化财的保持者或保持团体的，可追加认定其为保持者或保持团体。

5. 前款所规定的追加认定准用第三款规定。

【重要无形文化财之指定等的撤销】

第七十二条 当重要无形文化财丧失其作为重要无形文化财价值或存在其他特别事由时，文部科学大臣可以撤销该重要无形文化财指定。

2. 文部科学大臣认为保持者因身心障碍不再适合作为保持者、保持团体因成员变动而不宜再作为适合保持团体或存在其他特别事由时，可以撤销对保持者或保持团体的认定。

3. 第一款规定的指定撤销或第二款规定的认定撤销，应在《官报》上公告，并应将撤销结果通知该重要无形文化财的保持者或保持团体的代表者。

4. 保持者死亡或保持团体解散（包括不复存在的情形，本条以下同）的，视为保持者或保持团体的认定被撤销；所有保持者死亡或所有保持团体解散的，则视为该重要无形文化财的指定被撤销。对于上述撤销，文部科学大臣应在《官报》上公告。

【保持者姓名等的变更】

第七十三条 保持者的姓名、住所发生变更或者死亡，或者发生文部科学省政令规定事由的，保持者或其继承人应当依据文部科学省政令所规定的书面格式，在该事由发生之日起20日内向文化厅长官提交书面报告。保持团体的名称、所在地或其代表者发生变更，或其构成人员发生变动，或者团体解散等，保持团体代表者（保持团体解散时，则为其代表者）也应按前述规定上报。

【重要无形文化财的保存】

第七十四条 文化厅长官认为重要无形文化财有保存必要时，可亲自记录该重要无形文化财、培育或采取其他适当保护措施；国家对重要无形文化财保持者、保持团体或地方公共团体以及其他与该重要无形文化财保存有关的单位和适当个人（本章以下称为“保持者等”）实施保存措施时所需费用给予部分财政补贴。

2. 前款财政补贴的交付，准用本法第三十五条第二款、第三款规定。

【重要无形文化财的公开展示】

第七十五条 文化厅长官可建议重要无形文化财保持者或保持团体公开展示其重要无形文化财，也可建议重要无形文化财记录的所有人公开其记录。

2. 重要无形文化财保持者或保持团体公开展示其重要无形文化财时，可准用本法第五十一条第七款规定。

3. 重要无形文化财记录的所有人公开其记录的，国家对其公开记录所需经费给予部分财政补贴。

【重要无形文化财保存的意见和建议】

第七十六条 文化厅长官可就重要无形文化财的保存，向重要无形文化财保持者等给予必要意见与建议。

【重要无形文化财保护利用计划的认定】

第七十六条之二 重要无形文化财的保持者可根据文部科学省政令规定，制定重要无形文化财保护利用计划（本章以及第一百五十三条第二款第八项以下称为“重要文化财保护利用计划”），并申请文化厅长官予以认定。

2. 前款重要无形文化财保护利用计划应记载以下事项：

（一）该重要无形文化财的名称、保持者或保持团体；

（二）为保护和利用该重要无形文化财而实施的具体措施；

（三）计划的实施周期；

（四）文部科学省政令规定的其他事项。

3. 根据第一款之规定的重要无形文化财保护利用计划的认定申请，符合以下条件的，文化厅长官应予以认定。

（一）重要无形文化财保护利用计划的实施，有利于该重要无形文化财的保护与利用；

（二）该重要无形文化财保护利用计划被认为能够得以确实、顺利地实施；

（三）若存在第一百八十三条之二第一款规定的文化财保护利用大纲或者第一百八十三条之五第一款规定的文化财保护利用区域规划时，该保护利用计划应符合大纲或规划要求。

4. 文化厅长官作出前款之认定后，应立刻将认定结果通知申请人，不得延迟。

【被认定的重要无形文化财保护利用计划之变更】

第七十六条之三 获得前条第三款认定的重要无形文化财保持者，若要变更（除文部科学省政令规定轻微变更外）重要无形文化财保护利用计划，必须获得文化厅长官的认定。

2．前款认定，准用前条第三款、第四款规定。

【被认定的重要无形文化财保护利用计划的实施状况之报告】

第七十六条之四 文化厅长官可要求获得本法第七十六条之二第三款认定的重要无形文化财保持者，报告其已获认定（包括前条第一款的变更认定。在下一条以及第一百五十三条第二款第八项中，相同）的重要无形文化财保护利用计划（如有变更的则为变更后的计划。在下一条以及第七十六条之六中称为"被认定的重要无形文化财保护利用计划"）的实施情况。

【认定的撤销】

第七十六条之五 文化厅长官认为被认定的重要无形文化财保护利用计划不再符合本法第七十六条之二第三款所规定的各项条件时，可以撤销该认定。

2. 根据前款规定的撤销认定，文化厅长官应立刻将认定撤销决定通知被认定人，不得延迟。

【对保持者等的指导或建议】

第七十六条之六 根据重要无形文化财保持者等的请求，都、道、府、县以及市、町、村教育委员会可就重要无形文化财保护利用计划的制定，以及所认定的保护利用计划能够得到确实、顺利实施等，提供必要的指导和建议。

2．根据重要文无形化遗产保持者的请求，文化厅长官必须努力就重要无形文化财保护利用计划的制定、所认定的保护利用计划能够得到确实、顺利实施等，提供必要的指导和建议。

【重要无形文化财以外的无形文化财之记录等】

第七十七条　文化厅长官可选择重要无形文化财以外的无形文化财中特别有必要的，亲自对其进行记录、保存或者公开展示；国家对适合保存的保存者记录、保存及公开展示无形文化财的，给予部分财政补贴。

2. 前款规定的部分经费财政补助，准用本法第三十五条第二款、第三款规定。

第五章　民俗文化财（第七十八条~第九十一条）

【重要有形民俗文化财及重要无形民俗文化财的指定】

第七十八条　文部科学大臣可以指定有形民俗文化财中特别重要者为重要有形民俗文化财；可以指定无形民俗文化财中特别重要者为重要无形民俗文化财。

2. 前款重要有形民俗文化财的指定，准用本法第二十八条第一款至第四款规定。

3. 根据第一款规定的重要无形民俗文化财的指定，应在《官报》上公告。

【重要有形民俗文化财及重要无形民俗文化财的指定之撤销】

第七十九条　重要有形民俗文化财或重要无形民俗文化财在失去其作为重要有形民俗文化财或重要无形民俗文化财的价值或者存在其他特别事由时，文部科学大臣可以撤销对该重要有形民俗文化财或重要无形民俗文化财的指定。

2. 前款规定的重要有形民俗文化财的指定撤销，准用本法第二十九条第二款至第四款的规定。

3. 根据第一款规定的重要无形民俗文化财的指定撤销，应在《官报》上公告。

【重要有形民俗文化财的管理】

第八十条　重要有形民俗文化财的管理，准用本法第三十条至第三十四条规定。

【重要有形民俗文化财的保护】

第八十一条 试图变更重要有形民俗文化财现状、实施对其保存环境造成影响行为的，必须在上述行为实施之日的前20日以内，根据文部科学省政令所规定的格式要求向文化厅长官提出书面申请。但文部科学省政令另有规定的除外。

2. 文化厅长官认为必要时，可对前款中的重要有形民俗文化财现状改变、实施对重要有形民俗文化财保存环境造成影响的行为申请，给予必要指示。

第八十二条 试图将重要有形民俗文化财运出国境的，必须获得文化厅长官的许可。

第八十三条 有关重要有形民俗文化财的保护，准用本法第三十四条之二至第三十六条、第三十七条第二款至第四款、第四十二条、第四十六条以及第四十七条规定。

【重要有形民俗文化财的公开展示】

第八十四条 重要有形民俗文化财的所有人或管理团体（本法第八十条中准用第三十二条之二条第一款接受指定的地方公共团体及其他法人，本章[除第九十条之二第一款外]以下及第一百八十七条第一款第二项）以外的其他人在其主办的展览会或以其他方式向公众公开展示该重要有形民俗文化财时，必须在其公开展示之日前30日内，根据文部科学省政令规定的格式向文化厅长官提出书面申请。但文化厅长官之外的其他国家机关或地方公共团体以及事先取得文化厅长官许可无需事前申请的博物馆及其他机构（以下称为“事先免除公开展示申请的机构”）主办的展览会或以其他方式公开展示的，在其公开展示结束之日起20日内向文化厅长官报告即可。

2. 前款申请，准用本法第五十一条第四款以及第五款规定。

第八十五条 重要有形民俗文化财的公开展示，准用本法第四十七条之二至第五十二条规定。

【重要有形民俗文化财保护利用计划的认定】

第八十五条之二 重要有形民俗文化财的所有者（若为管理团体的则为管理团体）可根据文部科学省政令规定，制定重要有形民俗文化财的保护利用计划（以下称为“重要有形民俗文化财保护利用计划”），并申请文化厅长官予以认定。

2. 前款重要有形民俗文化财保护利用计划应记载以下事项：

（一）该项重要有形民俗文化财的名称及其所在场所；

（二）为保护和利用该项重要有形民俗文化财而实施的具体措施；

（三）计划的实施周期；

（四）文部科学省政令规定的其他事项。

3. 前款第二项中的具体措施，可记载影响该重要有形民俗文化财现状的变更或保存的相关行为事项；

4. 根据本条第一款规定的重要有形民俗文化财保护利用计划的认定申请，符合以下条件的，文化厅长官应当予以认定。

（一）该重要有形民俗文化财保护利用计划的实施，有利于该重要有形民俗文化财的保护与利用；

（二）该重要有形民俗文化财保护利用计划被认为能够得以确实、顺利实施；

（三）若存在第一百八十三条之二第一款规定的文化财保护利用大纲或者第一百八十三条之五第一款规定的文化财保护利用区域规划时，该保护利用计划应符合该大纲或规划要求。

（四）当该重要有形民俗文化财保护利用计划中列举前款所载事项时，其行为内容应适当并符合文部科学省政令规定的标准；

5. 文化厅长官作出前款认定后，必须立刻将认定结果通知申请人，不得延迟。

【现状变更等的报告之特例】

第八十五条之三 前条第三款所规定的、记载影响该重要有形民俗文化财现状的变更或保存的行为，在获得前条第四款认定（包括下一条中准用本法第五十三条之三的变更认定。在本法第一百五十三条第二款第十二项中相同）的情况下，根据认定实施影响重要有形民俗文化财的现状变更或保存行为必须获得本法第八十一条第一款报告时，可忽略本款规定，只需在影响重要有形民俗文化财的现状变更或保存行为结束后，根据文部科学省政令规定立刻向文化厅长官书面报告即可。

【准用】

第八十五条之四 重要有形民俗文化财保护利用计划，准用本法第五十三条之三以及第五十三条之六至第五十三条之八的规定。准用时，第五十三条之三第一款中的“前条第四款”应替换为“第八十五条之二第四款”、同条第二款中的“前条第四款、第五款”应替换为“第八十五条之二第四款、第五款”、第五十三条之六中的“第五十三条之二第四款”应替换为“第八十五条之二第四款”、第五十三条之七中的“第五十三条之二第四款”替换为“第八十五条之二第四款。

【重要有形民俗文化财调查、所有人变更后的权利义务继承】

第八十六条 为保存重要有形民俗文化财而实施的调查，准用本法第五十四条规定；重要有形民俗文化财的所有人变更、管理团体的指定以及指定撤销，准用本法第五十六条规定。

【重要无形民俗文化财的保存】

第八十七条 文化厅长官认为重要无形民俗文化财有保存必要的，可亲自记录该重要无形民俗文化财或实施其他适当的保存措施，国家对地方公共团体或其他被认为适当的保存者（第八十九条以及第八十九条之二第一款中称为“保存地方公共团体等”）保存重要无形民俗文化财所需费用给予部分财政补贴。

2. 前款财政补贴的交付，准用本法第三十五条第二款以及第三款规定。

【重要无形民俗文化财之记录的公开】

第八十八条 文化厅长官可劝告重要无形民俗文化财记录的所有人公开其记录。

2. 重要无形民俗文化财记录的所有人公开其记录的，准用本法第七十五条第三款规定。

【有关重要无形民俗文化财保存的意见、建议】

第八十九条　为保存重要无形民俗文化财，文化厅长官可对保存地方公共团体等提供必要意见或建议。

【重要无形民俗文化财保护利用计划之认定】

第八十九条之二　根据文部科学省政令规定，保存地方公共团体等可制定重要无形民俗文化财的保护利用计划（在本章以及第一百五十三条第二款第十三项中称为“重要无形民俗文化财保护利用计划”），并申请文化厅长官予以认定。

2. 前款重要无形民俗文化财保护利用计划应记载以下事项：

（一）该项重要无形民俗文化财的名称；

（二）为保护和利用该项重要无形民俗文化财而实施的具体措施；

（三）计划的实施周期；

（四）文部科学省政令规定的其他事项。

3. 符合以下条件的重要无形民俗文化财保护利用计划的认定申请，文化厅长官应予以认定。

（一）该重要无形民俗文化财保护利用计划的实施，有利于该重要无形民俗文化财的保护与利用；

（二）该重要无形民俗文化财保护利用计划被认为能够得以确实、顺利实施；

（三）若存在第一百八十三条之二第一款规定的文化财保护利用大纲或者第一百八十三条之五第一款规定的文化财保护利用区域规划时，该保护利用计划应符合大纲或规划要求。

4. 文化厅长官作出前款认定后，应立刻将认定结果通知申请人，不得延迟。

【准用】

第八十九条之三　重要无形民俗文化财保护利用计划，准用本法第七十六条之三至第七十六条之六的规定。准用时，第七十六条之三第一款中的“前条第三款”应替换为“第八十六条之二第三款”，同条第二款中的“前条第三款、第四款”应替换为“第八十九条之二第三款、第四款”，第七十六条之四款中的“第七十六条之二第三款”应替换为“第八十九条之二第三款”、“下一条以及第一百五十三条第二款第八项”应替换为“下一条”，第七十六条之五第一款中的“第七十六条之二第三款各项”应替换为“第八十九条之二第三款各项”。

【登录有形民俗文化财】

第九十条　文部科学大臣对重要有形民俗文化财以外的有形民俗文化财（本法第一百八十二规定由地方公共团体指定的除外）中、具有文化价值并有保存与利用必要的，可以在文化财名录上予以登录。

2. 前款登录，准用本法第五十七条第二款、第三款规定。

3. 根据前两款规定的登录有形民俗文化财（以下称为“登录有形民俗文化财”），准用本法第三章第二节（除第五十七条以及第六十七之二至第六十七之七外）规定。在准用中，第六十四条第一款与第六十五条第一款中的“30日内”应替换为“20日内”；第六十四条第一款但书中的“实施修缮措施、非常灾害的必要应急措施或者为实施依据其他政令的现状改变命令而采取措施的”应替换为“文部科学省政令规定的情况”。

【登录有形民俗文化财保护利用计划的认定】

第九十条之二　根据文部科学省政令规定，登录有形民俗文化财的所有者（或管理团体）可制定登录有形民俗文化财的保护利用计划（以下称为“登录有形民俗文化财保护利用计划”），并申请文化厅长官予以认定。

2. 前款登录有形民俗文化财保护利用计划应记载以下事项：

（一）该项登录有形民俗文化财的名称及其所在场所；

（二）为保护和利用该项登录有形民俗文化财而实施的具体措施；

（三）计划的实施周期；

（四）文部科学省政令规定的其他事项。

3. 前款第二项中的具体措施，可记载影响该登录有形民俗文化财的现状变更的相关事项；

4. 登录有形民俗文化财保护利用计划的认定申请，符合以下条件的，文化厅长官应当予以认定。

（一）该登录有形民俗文化财保护利用计划的实施，有利于该登录有形民俗文化财的保护与利用；

（二）该登录有形民俗文化财保护利用计划被认为能够得以确实、顺利实施；

（三）若存在第一百八十三条之二第一款规定的文化财保护利用大纲或者第一百八十三条之五第一款规定的文化财保护利用区域规划时，该保护利用计划应符合大纲或规划要求。

（四）当该登录有形民俗文化财保护利用计划中列举有前款所载事项时，其行为内容应适当并符合文部科学省政令所规定的标准；

5. 文化厅长官作出前款认定后，应立刻将认定结果通知申请人，不得延迟。

【现状变更的报告之特例】

第九十条之三　前条第三款所规定的、记载影响该登录有形民俗文化财现状的变更或保存的行为，在获得前条第四款认定（包含下一条中准用本法第六十七条之三第一款的变更认定。在本法第一百五十三条第二款第十四项中相同）的情况下，根据认定实施影响登录有形民俗文化财的现状变更或保存的行为必须获得本法第九十条第三款中准用第六十四条第一款规定的报告时，可忽略本款规定，只需在影响登录有形民俗文化财的现状变更或保存行为结束后，立刻根据文部科学省政令向文化厅长官书面报告。

【准用】

第九十条之四　登录有形民俗文化财保护利用计划，准用本法第六十七条之三、第六十七条之五至第六十七条之七的规定。准用时，第六十七条之三第一款中的“前条第四款”应替换为“第九十条之二第四款”、同条第二款中的“前条第四款、第五款”应替换为“第九十条之二第四款、第五款”、第六十七条之五中的“第六十七条之二第四款”应替换为“第九十条之二第四款”、第六十七条之六第一款中的“第六十七条之二第四款各项”应替换为“第九十条之二第四款各项”。

【重要无形民俗文化财以外的无形民俗文化财之记录的作成等】

第九十一条 重要无形民俗文化财以外的无形民俗文化财的记录等，准用本法第七十七条规定。

第六章 埋藏文化财（第九十二条～第一百〇八条）

【为调查的发掘申请、指示及命令】

第九十二条 调查或发掘埋藏地下的文化财（以下称为“埋藏文化财”）的调查者或发掘者，必须根据文部科学省政令规定，在决定发掘的前30日内向文化厅长官提出书面申请；但文部科学省政令另有规定的，则不在此限。

2. 文化厅长官认为在埋藏文化财的保护上有特别必要时，可就与前款申请相关的必要发掘事项及申请报告等作出指示，或者命令禁止、停止或中止发掘。

【因土木工程等埋藏文化财的发掘之申请及指示】

第九十三条 因土木工程以及其他调查埋藏文化财以外目的，发掘贝塚、古墓等周知的文化财埋藏地（以下称为“周知的文化财埋藏地”）的，准用前条第一款规定；准用时，该款中的“30日内”应替换为“60日内”。

2. 文化厅长官认为对埋藏文化财有特别保护的必要时，可就前款的准用前条第一款的相关发掘申请、在该发掘实施前为记录埋藏文化财而进行的发掘调查以及其他相关事项等，给予必要指示。

【国家机关等发掘之特例】

第九十四条 国家机关、地方公共团体或者国家或地方公共团体根据政令规定设立的法人等（本条以下及第九十七条中称为“国家机关等”），根据前条第一款规定，在周知的文化财埋藏地发掘埋藏文化财时，不适用该条规定；国家机关等决定前述发掘时，必须事先向文化厅长官报告其发掘实施计划。

2. 文化厅长官在收到前款报告后，如果认为有特别保护必要，可通知国家机关等就其制定发掘实施计划等进行磋商。

3. 国家机关等在接到前款磋商要求后，必须就其发掘实施计划等与文化厅长官进行磋商。

4. 除第二款规定的情形外，文化厅长官在收到第一款报告后，可对其发掘实施计划中的埋藏文化财保护，给予必要建议。

5. 当前各款中的国家机关等为各省、厅长官（《国有财产法》[①] 第四条第二款规定的各省、厅长官，以下同）时，各款中的报告、磋商或建议等应通过文部科学大臣实施。

【文化财埋藏地的周知】

第九十五条 为了全社会能够了解文化财埋藏地，国家及地方公共团体必须努力收集整理相关资料并采取必要宣传措施。

2. 地方公共团体实施前款各项措施，国家可给予指导、建议及其他必要援助。

【有关遗址发现的报告、停止命令等】

第九十六条 除本法第九十二条第一款调查中发现的情形外，土地所有人或占用人因遗物出土等发现贝塚、古墓、旧居或其他遗址时，不得改变遗址现状，必须根据文部科学省政令所规定的格式向文化厅长官书面报告，不得延迟。但如果是为防止灾害发生而采取应急措施的，可以在一定限度内对遗址现状进行必要变更。

2. 文化厅长官接到前款报告后，如认为所报告的遗址重要、有实施调查必要的，可禁止该土地的所有人或占用人在一定期限内及划定的区域内，实施任何改变现状的行为，但所限定的期限不得超过 3 个月。

---

① 1948 年（昭和 23 年）年 6 月 30 日法律第 73 号。

3. 文化厅长官在作出前款禁止命令前，必须事先听取相关地方公共团体的意见。

4. 第二款的禁止命令必须在第一款的报告之日起 1 个月内作出。

5. 若第二款中的调查未能在规定期限内完成，且有继续调查必要的，文化厅长官可命令延长调查期限，但只能延长一次、且整个调查期限累计不得超过 6 个月。

6. 第二款及前款的期间计算，包含从第一款报告日到第二款命令发布日的期间。

7. 文化厅长官未收到第一款报告的，也可采取第二款及第五款所规定的措施。

8. 除第二款措施外，文化厅长官收到第一款报告时，可就遗址保护作出必要指示。除前款规定的采取第二款措施外，即便是未收到第一款规定的报告，文化厅长官也可就遗址保护作出必要指示。

9. 对于因第二款命令所遭受的一般性损失，国家应该给予补偿。

10. 前款的国家补偿，准用本法第四十一条第二款至第四款的规定。

【国家机关等发现遗址的特别规定】

第九十七条 国家机关等发现前条第一款遗址的，可不适用该条规定；除第九十二条第一款或第九十九第一款规定的因调查发现的遗址外，不得改变其现状、立刻报告文化厅长官，不得迟延。但为防止灾害发生而采取应急措施的，则可以在一定限度内对遗址现状进行必要变更。

2. 文化厅长官在收到前款报告后，认为所发现的遗址特别重要且为了保护有调查必要的，可要求国家机关等就该遗址的调查、保存等事项与文化厅进行磋商。

3. 收到前款磋商要求的国家机关等必须与文化厅长官进行磋商。

4. 文化厅长官在接到第一款报告后，除前两款规定的情形外，可就该遗址的保护提供必要建议。

5. 前述各款规定的情形，准用本法第九十四条第五款规定。

【文化厅长官实施的发掘】

第九十八条 文化厅长官认为埋藏文化财具有特别高的历史和学术价值、对其调查在技术上存在难度、且有必要由国家实施调查的，可对其实施土地发掘调查。

2. 实施前款土地发掘时，文化厅长官必须事先就实施发掘目的、发掘方法以及发掘开始日期等书面通知文化财埋藏地的所有人或者合法占有人。

3. 第一款调查实施，准用第三十九条（包括该条第三款中准用第三十二条之二第五款规定）及第四十一条规定。

【由地方公共团体实施的发掘】

第九十九条 除文化厅长官根据前条第一款规定实施的发掘外，地方公共团体认为有必要调查埋藏文化财的，可对可能埋藏文化财的土地进行发掘调查。

2. 当前款发掘调查的埋藏文化财所在地属国家所有并被国家机关所占有时，地方公共团体教育委员会必须事先与相关各省、各厅长官及其他国家机关就发掘目的、发掘方法、发掘日期及其他必要事项进行协议。

3. 地方公共团体可以要求相关事业单位就本条第一款规定的发掘等，提供协助。

4. 由地方公共团体实施的发掘，文化厅长官可提供必要的指导与建议。

5. 由地方公共团体实施的发掘，国家可以给予部分财政补贴。

【返还或通知等】

第一百条 对于根据第九十八条第一款规定发掘的埋藏文化财，在判明所有人时，文化厅长官应将其返还给该所有人；在无法判明所有人的情况下，可不受《遗失物法》① 第四条第一款规定的约束，直接通知警察署长。

2. 如果根据前条第一款规定，都、道、府、县或《地方自治法》② 第

---

① 2006年（平成18年）6月15日法律第73号。

② 1947年（昭和22年）4月17日法律第67号。

二百五十二条之十九第一款规定的指定都市（以下称为“指定都市”）或第二百五十二条之二十二第一款规定的中心城市（以下称为“指定城市等”）的教育委员会通过发掘发现埋藏文化财时，准用前款规定。

3. 警察署长在收到第一款（包括前款准用）通知时，必须根据《遗失物法》第七条第一款，立刻公告。

【提交】

第一百〇一条 根据《遗失物法》第四条第一款，如果所提交的埋藏物属于文化财，警察署长必须立刻将埋藏物提交给被发现所在地都、道、府、县的教育委员会（若为指定都市等则是该指定都市等的教育委员会，以下同），但若能判明所有人的，则不受此限。

【鉴定】

第一百〇二条 都、道、府、县教育委员会必须对前条中所提交的埋藏物是否属于文化财进行鉴定。

2. 经过鉴定，都、道、府、县教育委员会认为该埋藏物为文化财的，必须将这一结果通知警察署长。如果都、道、府、县教育委员会认为该埋藏物不属于文化财，则必须将其返还给警察署长。

【移交】

第一百〇三条 当第一百条第一款、第二款以及前条第二款所规定的文化财所有人请求警察署长返还其文化财时，文化厅长官、都、道、府、县教育委员会或指定都市教育委员会等必须将该文化财移交给警察署长。

【所有权的国家归属与褒赏金】

第一百〇四条 在无法判明第一百条第一款、第一百〇二条第二款所规定的文化财（仅限于国家机关或独立行政法人国立文化财机构因调查而发现的埋藏文化财）所有人的情况下，其所有权归国家所有；但文化厅长官应将埋藏文化财的发现情况通告土地所有人，并向其支付埋藏文化财价格二分之一的金钱作为褒赏金。

2. 前款褒赏金的金额以及救济等，准用本法第四十一条第二款至第四款规定。

【所有权的都、道、府、县归属与褒赏金】

第一百〇五条 在无法判明第一百条第二款、第一百〇二条第二款规定的文化财（除前条第一款规定的文化财外）所有人的情况下，其所有权归发现地都、道、府、县所有；但都、道、府、县教育委员会应将该文化财的发现通告发现人或发现地的土地所有人，并向其支付价格相当的金钱作为褒赏金。

2. 前款规定的发现人与土地所有人不是同一人时，所支付的褒赏金一人一半。

3. 第一款中的褒赏金金额，由都、道、府、县教育委员会决定。

4. 关于前款褒赏金的金额，准用第四十一条第三款规定。

5. 因准用第四十一条第三款规定而提起的诉讼，都、道、府、县为被告。

【让与等】

第一百〇六条 除有必要由国家有效保护的、第一百〇四条第一款所规定的、归属于国家所有的文化财外，政府可以在相当于发现该文化财所支付褒赏金的价格范围内，将该文化财让与文化财发现地的土地所有人。

2. 前款中的让与价格为扣除第一百〇四条规定的褒赏金金额后的余额。

3. 除有必要由国家有效保护的、第一百〇四条第一款所规定的、归属于国家所有的文化财外，独立行政法人国立文化财机构或发现地的地方公共团体，可以申请以低于市场价格获得该文化财的政府让与。

第一百〇七条 除有必要由都、道、府、县有效保护的，第一百〇五条第一款所规定的，归属于都、道、府、县所有的文化财外，都、道、府、县教育委员会可以在相当于发现该文化财所支付褒赏金的价格内，将该文化财让与文化财发现地的土地所有人。

2. 前款中的让与价格为扣除第一百〇五条规定的褒赏金金额后的余额。

【遗失物法的适用】

第一百〇八条 除本法有特别规定外，埋藏文化财适用《遗失物法》。

第七章 史迹名胜天然纪念物（第一百〇九条~第一百三十三条）

【指定】

第一百〇九条 文部科学大臣可以指定纪念物中的重要者为史迹、名胜地及天然纪念物（以下称为“史迹名胜天然纪念物”）。

2. 文部科学大臣可以在被指定的史迹名胜天然纪念物中指定特别重要者为特别史迹、特别名胜及特别天然纪念物（以下称为“特别史迹名胜天然纪念物”）。

3. 前两款的指定应在《官报》上公告，并将指定结果通知史迹名胜天然纪念物和特别史迹名胜天然纪念物的所有人或合法占有人。

4. 因前款通知人数众多而不宜个别通知的，文部科学大臣可将该通知内容在该特别史迹名胜天然纪念物或史迹名胜天然纪念物所在地的市、町、村办公场所的公告栏中公告，公告两周后则视为通知送达。

5. 第一款、第二款指定自第三款所规定的公告之日起生效。但对该特别史迹名胜天然纪念物及史迹名胜天然纪念物所有人或合法占有人，则自第三款所规定的通知送达之日起生效。

6. 在名胜或天然纪念物指定前，如果所指定的名胜或天然纪念物具有很高环境保护价值的，文部科学大臣必须与环境大臣进行磋商。

【临时指定】

第一百一十条 在前条第一款的指定之前，都、道、府、县教育委员会（如果所指定的纪念物在指定都市区域内的，则为该指定都市教育委员会。除第一百三十三条外，以下本章同）认为存在紧急事由的，可以对史迹名胜天然纪念物进行临时指定。

2. 都、道、府、县教育委员会在进行前款临时指定后，必须直接向文部科学大臣报告。

3. 根据第一款的临时指定，准用前条第三款至第五款规定。

【所有权等的尊重与其他公共利益的协调】

第一百一十一条 文部科学大臣或都、道、府、县教育委员会在根据第一百〇九条第一款、第二款或前条第一款的规定进行指定或临时指定时，不仅要特别注意尊重关系人的所有权、矿业权及其他财产权，同时也必须特别注意其与国土开发及其他公共事业相关部门之间关系的协调。

2. 当文部科学大臣或文化厅长官认为有必要保护和整备与名胜或天然纪念物相关的自然环境的，可以向环境大臣陈述自己的意见。文化厅长官在陈述上述意见时，应通过文部科学大臣。

3. 从自然环境保护出发，对有较高价值的名胜或天然纪念物，环境大臣认为有保护和利用必要时，可向文部科学大臣或通过文部科学大臣向文化厅长官陈述意见。

【指定或临时指定的撤销】

第一百一十二条 当特别史迹名胜天然纪念物或史迹名胜天然纪念物失去其价值或出现其他特别事由时，文部科学大臣或都、道、府、县教育委员会可以撤销指定或临时指定。

2. 当第一百一十条第一款规定的临时指定被第一百〇九条第一款规定的指定取代，或者临时指定自被指定后 2 年内未被正式指定的，该临时指定的效力丧失。

3. 当文部科学大臣认为第一百一十条第一款的临时指定不当时，可以撤销该临时指定。

4. 第一款或前款的指定及临时指定的撤销，准用第一百〇九条第三款至第五款规定。

【由管理团体实施的管理或修复】

第一百一十三条 在史迹名胜天然纪念物的所有人或根据第一百一十九条第二款规定选任的管理人的管理陷入困难或者管理明显不当，甚至无法判明所有人等情况下，为保存该史迹名胜天然纪念物，文化厅长官可以指定适当的地方公共团体或其他法人对其进行必要的管理或修复（包括为保存该史迹名胜天然纪念物的必要设施、设备以及其他物件中属于该史迹名胜天然纪念物所有人所有或管理的设施、设备以及其他物件的管理与修复）。

2. 对于前款指定，文化厅长官必须事先征得被指定地方公共团体或其他法人的同意。

3. 第一款的指定，除应在《官报》上公告外，还应通知该史迹名胜天然纪念物所有人、合法占有人以及被指定的地方公共团体或其他法人。

4. 第一款的指定，准用第一百〇九条第四款、第五款规定。

第一百一十四条　当前条第一款规定的事由已经消灭或出现其他新事由时，文化厅长官可以撤销对管理团体的指定。

2. 前款规定的指定撤销，准用前条第三款、第一百〇九条第四款、第五款规定。

第一百一十五条　根据第一百一十三条第一款规定，接受管理团体指定的地方公共团体或其他法人（除第一百三十三条之二第一款外，本章以及第一百八十七条第一款第三项中称为“管理团体”）必须依据文部科学省政令所规定的标准，设置管理所需的必要标识、说明板、界标、围栏以及其他设施。

2. 被指定为史迹名胜天然纪念物的地域内土地所在、地名及面积等发生变化时，管理团体必须根据文部科学省政令，向文化厅长官报告。

3. 管理团体在修复史迹名胜天然纪念物时，必须事前就修复方法、修复日期等事项听取该史迹名胜天然纪念物所有人（所有人不明的除外）或合法占有人的意见。

4. 史迹名胜天然纪念物的所有人或占有人无正当理由，不得拒绝、妨碍或回避管理团体实施的管理或修复以及与之相关的其他必要措施。

第一百一十六条　除本法有特别规定外，管理团体实施管理或修复所需费用由管理团体承担。

2. 前款规定并不妨碍所有人与管理团体通过协商，由所有人在管理团体实施管理或修复措施而受益的范围内承担部分管理或修复费用。

3. 管理团体可以对参观其所管理的史迹名胜天然纪念物民众，征收参观费。

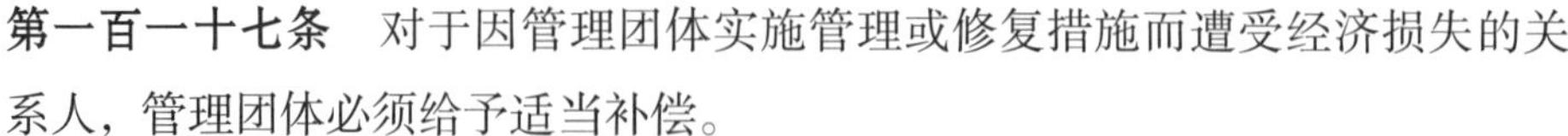

第一百一十七条 对于因管理团体实施管理或修复措施而遭受经济损失的关系人，管理团体必须给予适当补偿。

2．前款的补偿额度由管理团体（管理团体为地方公共团体时则为该地方公共团体的教育委员会）决定。

3．根据前款规定的补偿额度，准用第四十一条第三款规定。

4．因前款准用第四十一条第三款规定而提起的诉讼，管理团体为被告。

第一百一十八条 管理团体实施的管理，准用第三十条、条三十一条第一款及第三十三条规定；管理团体实施的管理与修复，准用第三十五条、第四十七条规定；管理团体的指定或者指定的撤销，准用第五十六条第三款规定。

【由所有人实施的管理或修复】

第一百一十九条 除管理团体外，史迹名胜天然纪念物的所有人也可以对史迹名胜天然纪念物进行管理或修复。

2．为了该史迹名胜天然纪念物必要且适当的管理，前款规定的管理史迹名胜天然纪念物的所有人可以选任本法第一百九十二条第一款规定的文化财保护支援团体以及其他合适人选代替自己承担对该史迹名胜天然纪念物的管理责任（在本章及第一百八十七条第一款第三项中称为“管理责任人”）。管理责任人的选任，准用第三十一条第三款规定。

第一百二十条 所有人实施的管理，准用第三十条、第三十一条第一款、第三十二条、第三十三条、第一百一十五条第一款及第二款（除该条第二款有管理责任人外）规定；所有人实施的管理与修复，准用第三十五条及第四十七条规定；伴随所有人变更而产生的权利义务继承，准用第五十六条第一款规定；由所有人选任的管理责任人实施的管理，准用第三十条、第三十一条第一款、第三十二条第三款、第三十三条、第四十七条第四款及第一百一十五条第二款规定。

【有关管理的命令或建议】

第一百二十一条 因管理不当使史迹名胜天然纪念物有灭失、损毁、消亡或被盗之虞的，文化厅长官可命令或建议管理团体、所有人或管理责任人改善其管理方法、设置保护设施或采取其他适当管理措施等。

2. 前款命令或建议，准用第三十六条第二款及第三款规定。

【有关修复的命令或建议】

第一百二十二条 当特别史迹名胜天然纪念物存在损毁或消亡现象时，文化厅长官认为有保护必要的，可命令或建议该特别史迹名胜天然纪念物的管理团体或所有人对其进行修复。

2. 当特别史迹名胜天然纪念物以外的史迹名胜天然纪念物存在损毁或消亡现象时，文化厅长官认为有保护必要的，可建议该管理团体或所有人实施必要修复措施。

3. 前二款的管理或修复，准用第三十七条第三款及第四款规定。

【由文化厅长官实施的修复等】

第一百二十三条 发生下列情形之一的，文化厅长官可亲自对特别史迹名胜天然纪念物进行修复，实施防止其灭失、损毁、消亡及被盗的措施。

（一）管理团体、所有人或管理责任者不服从前两条命令的。

（二）特别史迹名胜天然纪念物正在发生损毁、消亡或者有灭失、损毁、消亡或被盗之虞，管理团体、所有人或管理责任人采取的修复或防止灭失、损毁、消亡及被盗等措施不当的。

2. 前款中的相关措施，准用第三十八条第二款、第三十九条至第四十一条规定。

【史迹名胜天然纪念物让渡时补助金的返还】

第一百二十四条 根据第一百一十八条及第一百二十条中准用第三十五条第一款规定，国家对采取修复或防止史迹名胜天然纪念物灭失、损毁、消亡或失盗措施的管理团体给予资金补助；根据第一百二十一条第二款中准用第三十六条第二款、根据第一百二十二条第三款中准用第三十七条第三款或根据前条第二款中准用第四十条第一款规定，国家承担了与史迹名胜天然纪念物相关费用的，准用第四十二条规定。

【限制改变现状以及恢复原状等命令】

第一百二十五条　改变史迹名胜天然纪念物的现状或为保护史迹名胜天然纪念物实施对其有影响的行为时，必须获得文化厅长官的许可。但是，如果改变现状是为维护史迹名胜天然纪念物或为预防非常灾害而实施的对其保存影响轻微的措施的，则不在此限。

2. 前款但书中的维护措施范围，由文部科学省政令规定。

3. 第一款中的许可，准用第四十三条第三款规定；接受第一款许可者，准用第四十三条第四款规定。

4. 根据第一款规定，在处理相关利益关系时，准用第一百一十一条第一款规定。

5. 对于未获第一款许可，或因第三款中准用第四十三条第三款规定实施许可条件而遭受经济损失的，国家应予适当经济补偿。

6. 有关前款的经济补偿，准用第四十一条第二款至第四款规定。

7. 对于未获第一款许可，或者不服从第三款中准用第四十三条第三款所规定的许可条件的，文化厅长官可命令其恢复原状，并可就该恢复给予必要指示。

【相关行政机构的通知】

第一百二十六条　根据前条第一款规定，对于必须获得许可方可实施的行为，在其他政令规定的许可中，或必须接受其他政令规范的情况下，拥有相关职权的行政机关或其受托人，应该依据政令规定，将其相关决定通告文化厅长官（由第一百八十四条第一款规定，当前条第一款中的许可由都、道、府、县教育委员会或市教育委员会做出时，则为该都、道、府、县教育委员会或市教育委员会）。

【修复之申请等】

第一百二十七条　根据文部科学省政令规定，管理团体或所有人修复史迹名胜天然纪念物时，必须在修复开始前30日向文化厅长官提出修复申请。但根据第一百二十五条第一款规定必须获得许可或文部科学省政令规定的其他情形的，则不在此限。

2. 文化厅长官认为史迹名胜天然纪念物有保护必要时，可以对前款申请的史迹名胜天然纪念物修复，给予技术性指导或修复意见。

【环境保全】

第一百二十八条 为保护史迹名胜天然纪念物，文化厅长官可以命令划定一定范围，并在该范围内限制或禁止一定行为，或者设置其他必要保护性设施。

2. 因前款行政命令遭受经济损失的，国家给予适当经济补偿。

3. 违反第一款限制或禁止规定的，准用第一百二十五条第七款规定；前款经济补偿，准用第四十一条第二款至第四款规定。

【由管理团体收购的财政补贴】

第一百二十九条 作为管理团体的地方公共团体或其他法人认为为保护所管理的史迹名胜天然纪念物而有必要收购与该史迹名胜天然纪念物相关的土地、建造物或其他地上定着物的，国家可以对其收购所需费用给予部分财政补贴。

2. 关于前款财政补贴，准用第三十五条第二款、第三款以及第四十二条规定。

【史迹名胜天然纪念物保护利用计划的认定】

第一百二十九条之二 史迹名胜天然纪念物的管理团体或所有者，可以根据文部科学省政令规定，制定史迹名胜天然纪念物保护利用计划（以下称为“史迹名胜天然纪念物保护利用计划”），并申请文化厅长官予以认定。

2. 史迹名胜天然纪念物保护利用计划应记载以下事项：

（一）该史迹名胜天然纪念物的名称以及所在地；

（二）为保护和利用该史迹名胜天然纪念物而实施的具体措施；

（三）计划的实施周期；

（四）文部科学省政令规定的其他事项。

3. 前款第二项中的具体措施，可记载影响该史迹名胜天然纪念物现状的变更或保存的相关行为事项；

4. 根据本条第一款规定的史迹名胜天然纪念物保护利用计划的认定申请，符合以下条件的，文化厅长官应予认定。

（一）史迹名胜天然纪念物保护利用计划的实施，有利于该史迹名胜天然纪念物的保护与利用；

（二）史迹名胜天然纪念物保护利用计划被认为是能够得到确实、顺利实施的；

（三）若存在第一百八十三条之二第一款规定的文化财保护利用大纲或者第一百八十三条之五第一款规定的文化财保护利用区域规划时，该保护利用计划符合大纲或规划要求；

（四）史迹名胜天然纪念物保护利用计划中列举的前款所载的现状变更事项，应当适合史迹名胜天然纪念物的现状变更，并符合文部科学省政令所规定之标准；

5. 文化厅长官作出前款认定后，应立刻将认定结果通知申请人，不得延迟。

【被认定的史迹名胜天然纪念物保护利用计划之变更】

第一百二十九条之三　获得前条第四款认定的史迹名胜天然纪念物的管理团体或所有者，若要变更已获认定的史迹名胜天然纪念物保护利用计划（除文部省政令规定的轻微变更外），必须获得文化厅长官的认定。

2. 前款认定，准用前条第四款、第五款规定。

【现状变更报告之特例】

第一百二十九条之四　本法第一百二十九条之二第三款所载事项，在获得该条第四款认定（含前条第一款的变更认定。本章以及本法第一百五十三条第二款第二十三项中相同）后，实施所许可的影响史迹名胜天然纪念物现状变更或保存的行为时，可忽略依据本法第一百二十五条第一款所规定的必须提交报告的规定，只需在史迹名胜天然纪念物的现状变更结束后，根据文部科学省政令规定立刻向文化厅长官书面报告。

【被认定的史迹名胜天然纪念物保护利用计划之实施状况的报告】

第一百二十九条之五 文化厅长官可以要求获得本法第一百二十九条之二第四款认定的史迹名胜天然纪念物的管理团体或所有者，报告其已获认定的史迹名胜天然纪念物保护利用计划（如有变更则为变更后的计划。在下一条第一款以及第一百二十九条之七中称为“被认定的史迹名胜天然纪念物保护利用计划”）的实施情况。

【认定的撤销】

第一百二十九条之六 文化厅长官认为被认定的史迹名胜天然纪念物保护利用计划不再符合本法第一百二十九条之二第四款所规定的各项条件时，可以撤销该认定。

2. 根据前款规定撤销认定的，文化厅长官应立刻将认定撤销决定通知被认定人，不得延迟。

【对管理团体等的指导或建议】

第一百二十九条之七 根据史迹名胜天然纪念物的管理团体或所有人的请求，都、道、府、县以及市、町、村教育委员会可以就史迹名胜天然纪念物保护利用计划的制定，以及所认定的保护利用计划能够得到确实、顺利实施等，提供必要的指导与建议。

2. 根据史迹名胜天然纪念物管理团体或所有者的请求，文化厅长官必须努力就史迹名胜天然纪念物保护利用计划的制定，以及所认定的史迹名胜天然纪念物保护利用计划能够得到确实、顺利实施等，提供必要的指导和建议。

【为保护而实施的调查】

第一百三十条 文化厅长官认为必要时，可以要求管理团体、所有人或管理责任人，报告史迹名胜天然纪念物的现状、史迹名胜天然纪念物的管理、修复或者环境保全的状况等。

第一百三十一条 存在下列情形之一，且文化厅长官根据前条报告不能确认史迹名胜天然纪念物的现状，也无其他确认方法的，可指派调查员进入该史迹名胜天然纪念物所在地或其邻接地，对其现状、管理、修复或者环境保全等进行实地调查，并可以就相关土地的开发、障碍物的清除或为实现调查而采取必要的措施，但所采取的措施不得明显危害相关土地所有人、占有人及其他关系人的利益。

（一）申请改变史迹名胜天然纪念物现状或实施影响其保护环境行为的。

（二）史迹名胜天然纪念物有损毁或消亡迹象的。

（三）史迹名胜天然纪念物有灭失、损毁、消亡或被盗之虞的。

（四）因特别事由，有必要重新调查特别史迹名胜天然纪念物或史迹名胜天然纪念物价值的。

2. 因前款调查或实施的措施遭受经济损失的，国家给予适当经济补偿。

3. 第一款调查，准用第五十五条第二款规定；前款补偿，准用第四十一条第二款至第四款规定。

【登录纪念物】

第一百三十二条　文部科学大臣对史迹名胜天然纪念物（包含都、道、府、县教育委员会根据第一百一十条规定临时指定的）以外的纪念物（除地方公共团体根据第一百八十二条第二款规定指定的纪念物外）中具有文化财价值并有必要加以保存与利用的，可以登录在文化财名录上。

2. 前款登录，准用第五十七条第二款及第三款、第一百〇九条第三至第五款、第一百一十一条第一款规定。

第一百三十三条　根据前条规定登录的纪念物（以下称为“登录纪念物”），准用第五十九条第一款至第五款、第六十四条、第六十八条、第一百一十一条第二款第三款以及第一百一十三条至第一百二十条规定。准用时，第五十九条第一款中的“根据第二十七条第一款被指定为重要文化财”应替换为“根据第一百〇九条第一款指定的史迹名胜天然纪念物（包括根据第一百一十条第一款规定由都、道、府、县教育委员会临时指定的史迹名胜天然纪念物）”、该条第四款中的“通知所有人”应替换为“通知所有人及合法占有人，但若被通知方人数明显过多不宜逐一通知的，文部科学大臣可以在该登录纪念物所在地的市、町、村办公地公告栏公告，公告两周后视为通知送达”；该条第五款中的“关于撤销，准用前条第二款规定”应替换为“根据前款规定，撤销自在《官报》上公告之日起生效。但根据前款规定，自通知送达或视为送达该登录纪念物所有人或合法占有人起生效”；第一百一十三条第一款中的“被认为明显不当时”应替换为“因明显不当相关地方团体提出申请时，应该听取相关地方公共团体的意见”；第一百一十八条及第一百二十条中的“第三十条、第三十一条第一款”应替换为“第三十一条第一款”、“准用”应替换为“准用，在这种情况下，第三十一条第一款中‘服从文部科学省政令及文化厅长官指示’应替换为‘服从文部科学省政令’”；第一百一十八条中的“准用第三十五条、第四十七条规定；关于管理团体的指定或者指定的撤销，准用第五十六条第三款之规定”应替换为“第四十七条第四款”；第一百二十条中的“准用第三十五条、第四十七条规定；所有人变更后权利义务继承，准用第五十六条第一款规定”应替换为“第四十七条第四款”。

【登录纪念物保护利用计划的认定】

第一百三十三条之二　登录纪念物的管理团体（前条准用第一百一十三条第一款的被指定的地方公共团体以及其他法人）或所有人可根据文部科学省政令规定，制定登录纪念物的保护利用计划（以下称为“登录纪念物保护利用计划”），并申请文化厅长官予以认定。

2. 前款登录纪念物保护利用计划应记载以下事项：

（一）该登录纪念物的名称及其所在场所；

（二）为保护和利用该登录纪念物而实施的具体措施；

（三）计划的实施周期；

（四）文部科学省政令规定的其他事项。

3. 前款第二项中的具体措施，可记载影响该登录纪念物的现状变更的相关事项；

4. 根据前款规定的登录纪念物保护利用计划的认定申请，符合以下条件的，文化厅长官应当予以认定。

（一）该登录纪念物保护利用计划的实施，有利于该登录纪念物的保护与利用；

（二）该登录纪念物保护利用计划被认为能够得以确实、顺利实施；

（三）若存在第一百八十三条之二第一款规定的文化财保护利用大纲或者第一百八十三条之五第一款规定的文化财保护利用区域规划时，该保护利用计划应符合大纲或规划要求。

（四）当该登录纪念物保护利用计划中列举有前款所载事项时，其内容应适当并符合文部科学省政令所规定的标准；

5. 文化厅长官作出前款认定后，必须立刻将认定结果通知申请人，不得延迟。

【现状变更的报告之特例】

第一百三十三条之三 前条第三款所规定的、记载影响该登录纪念物现状的变更或保存行为，在获得前条第四款认定（包含下一条中准用本法第六十七条之三第一款的变更认定。在本法第一百五十三条第二款第二十四项中相同）的情况下，根据认定实施影响登录纪念物的现状变更或保存行为必须获得本法第一百三十三条中准用第六十四条第一款规定的报告时，可忽略本款规定，只需在影响登录纪念物的现状变更或保存行为结束后，立刻根据文部科学省政令规定向文化厅长官书面报告。

【准用】

第一百三十三条之四 登录纪念物保护利用计划，准用本法第六十七条之三、第六十七条之五至第六十七条之七的规定。准用时，第六十七条之三第一款中的“前条第四款”应替换为“第一百三十三条之二第四款”、同条第二款中的“前条第四款、第五款”应替换为“第一百三十三条之二第四款、第五款”、第六十七条之五中的“第六十七条之二第四款”应替换为“第一百三十三条之二第四款”、第六十七条之六第一款中的“第六十七条之二第四款各项”应替换为“第一百三十三条之二第四款各项”。

第八章　重要文化景观（第一百三十四条～第一百四十一条）

【重要文化景观的选定】

第一百三十四条　根据都、道、府、县或市、町、村的申请，文部科学大臣在参照文部科学省政令规定标准的基础上，可以选定都、道、府、县或市、町、村根据《景观法》[①]第八条第一款第一项、第六十一条第一款规定的景观规划区或景观区中，那些采取必要保护措施、且特别重要的文化景观为重要文化景观。

2．前款规定的选定，准用第一百〇九条第三款至第五款规定。在准用时，第三款中的“合法占有人”替换为“合法占有人及根据第一百三十四条第一款规定提出申请的都、道、府、县及市、町、村”。

【重要文化景观选定的撤销】

第一百三十五条　当重要文化景观失去其价值或出现其他特殊事由时，文部科学大臣可以撤销其选定。

2．前款撤销，准用前条第二款规定。

【灭失或损毁】

第一百三十六条　重要文化景观全部或部分灭失或损毁的，所有人或合法占有人（以下称为“所有人等”）必须在知道上述事实之日起10日内，就文部科学省政令所规定的记载事项，书面向文化厅长官报告。但文部科学省政令规定的、明显不会对重要文化景观保存产生重大影响的，则不在此限。

【有关管理之建议或命令】

第一百三十七条　因管理不当，文化厅长官认为重要文化景观有灭失、损毁

① 2004年（平成16年）6月18日法律第100号。

之虞的，可以对该重要文化景观所有人等，就管理方法的改善或采取其他管理措施等提出建议。

2. 收到前款建议的所有人等，无正当理由不实施相关建议或与建议相关的、被认为必要的措施的，文化厅长官可以命令其实施。

3. 文化厅长官在作出第一款建议或第二款命令时，必须事前听取根据第一百三十四条第一款规定提出重要文化景观选定申请的都、道、府、县或市、町、村的意见。

4. 第一款建议及第二款命令的相关费用的承担，准用第三十六条第二款、第三款规定。

【让渡重要文化景观时补助金的退还】

第一百三十八条　根据前条第四款中准用第三十六条第二款规定，国家承担了为防止重要文化景观灭失、损毁而实施必要措施所需的费用，准用第四十二条规定。

【现状变更之申请】

第一百三十九条　试图改变重要文化景观现状或实施影响重要文化景观保存行为的行为人，根据文部科学省政令规定，必须在实施前述行为的前 30 日向文化厅长官申请。但如果重要文化景观的现状改变、维持措施等是为防止自然灾害发生而采取的必要应急措施，或是根据政令被命令变更、且对重要文化景观的保存影响轻微的，则不在此限。

2. 前款但书所规定的维持措施的范围，由文部科学省政令规定。

3. 在重要文化景观的保护上，文化厅长官认为必要时可以就与第一款申请相关的现状改变或影响其保存的行为，给予指导、建议或意见。

【现状之报告等】

第一百四十条　文化厅长官认为必要时，可以要求重要文化景观所有人等，报告其重要文化景观的现状、管理或修复等状况。

【与其他公益的协调】

第一百四十一条 文部科学大臣根据第一百三十四条第一款规定，选定重要文化景观时，必须尊重相关主体的所有权、采矿权以及其他财产权，还应注意与国土开发及其他公益间的关系协调、以及与农林水产业及其他领域产业间的利益关系协调。

2. 有鉴于重要文化景观的特性，文化厅长官在根据第一百三十七条第一款、第二款以及第一百三十九条第三款规定提出建议或发布命令时，必须考虑与国土开发及其他公益间的协调，同时也必须从协调农林水产业及其他领域产业的协调发展出发，根据相关政令规定，事先与各相关省厅长官进行协商。

3. 都、道、府、县或市、町、村为保存重要文化景观、特别是那些为保存重要文化景观所必须物件的管理、维修，景观的维护与修复等所需经费，国家应给予部分财政补贴。

第九章　传统建造物群保存地区（第一百四十二条~第一百四十六条）

【传统建造物群保存地区】

第一百四十二条 本章“传统建造物群保存地区”是指，市、町、村根据第一百四十三条规定，决定有保存必要的传统建造物群以及与之形成一体的、具有保存价值的区域。

【传统建造物群保存地区的决定及其保护】

第一百四十三条 根据《城市规划法》[①] 第五条或第五条之二的规定，市、町、村可以在被指定的城市规划区域或准城市规划区域内，确定传统建造物群保存地区。在这种情况下，为保存该区域，市、町、村根据政令所规定的标准，可以通过制定条例规制变更地区现状的行为或实施其他必要的保存措施。

2. 市、町、村可根据自己制定的条例，在前款规定的城市规划区域及准城市

---

① 1968年（昭和43年）6月15日法律第100号。

规划区域外，确定传统建造物群保存地区。该确定，准用前款后段规定。

3. 都、道、府、县知事根据《城市规划法》第十九条第三款规定，同意第一款的传统建造物群保存地区规划的，必须事先听取都、道、府、县教育委员会的意见，但该都、道、府、县为特定地方公共团体时则不在此限。

4. 市、町、村在确定或撤销传统建造物群保存地区、制定或废除与传统建造物群保存地区条例时，必须向文化厅长官报告。

5. 文化厅长官及都、道、府、县教育委员会可以对市、町、村保存传统建造物群保存地区等，给予必要指导或建议。

【重要传统建造物群保存地区的选定】

第一百四十四条 根据市、町、村的申请，文部科学大臣可以在传统建造物保存地区的区域内，选定具有特别价值的为"重要传统建造物群保存地区"。

2. 前款的选定结果，要在《官报》公告并通知提出申请的市、町、村。

【选定的撤销】

第一百四十五条 在重要传统建造物群保存地区失去其特别价值或存在其他特别事由时，文部科学大臣可撤销该选定。

2. 前款选定的撤销，准用前条第二款规定。

【有关管理等的财政补助】

第一百四十六条 为保护重要传统建造物群保存地区，国家对于都、道、府、县或市、町、村管理、维护、修复该地区内的建造物以及与传统建造物群等形成一体环境的其他必要物件等所需经费，可以给予部分财政补贴。

第十章 文化财的保存技术之保护（第一百四十七条～第一百五十二条）

【保存技术的选定等】

第一百四十七条 文部科学大臣可以选定保存文化财所不可或缺、且有必要采取保护措施的传统保存技术或技能为“选定保存技术”。

2. 根据前款规定，文部科学大臣在选定所要保护的文化财保存技术的同时，必须认定选定保存技术的保持者或保存团体（包括以保存选定保护技术为目的的组织、含财团的代表者或管理人所确定的主体，以下同）。

3. 第一款选定保存技术的前款认定，可以并列认定保持者与保存团体。

4. 根据第一款的选定以及根据第二款的认定，准用第七十一条第三款至第五款规定。

【选定等的撤销】

第一百四十八条 当文部科学大臣认为所选定的保存技术没有必要再予以保存或存在其他特别事由时，可撤销该选定。

2. 当选定的保存技术的保持者因身心障碍不再适合作为保持者或保持团体不再适合作为保持团体以及存在其他特别事由时，文部科学大臣可以撤销保持者或保持团体的认定。

3. 前二款撤销，准用第七十二条第三款规定。

4. 根据前条第二款规定，只认定了保持者而所认定的保持者全部死亡、只认定了保持团体而所认定的保持团体解散（包括终止、以下同），或者既认定了保持者又认定了保持团体但所有被认定的保持者死亡且保持团体也解散的，文部科学大臣可以撤销对该选定保存技术的选定。对于该选定的撤销，文部科学大臣必须在《官报》上公告。

【保持者姓名的变更等】

第一百四十九条 当保持者的姓名、保持团体的名称等发生变更的，准用第七十三条规定。准用时，该条后段中的“代表人”应替换为“代表人或管理人”。

【选定保存技术的保存】

第一百五十条 文化厅长官认为选定保存技术有保存必要时，可以亲自记录选定的保存技术、培育传承人或采取适当的被认为必要的其他保护措施。

【选定保存技术之记录的公开】

第一百五十一条 选定保存技术记录的所有人公开其记录的，准用第八十八条规定。

【选定保存技术之保存的援助】

第一百五十二条 对于选定保存技术的保持者、保持团体、地方公共团体或其他被认为适当的保存者，国家可以给予必要指导、意见或其他被认为必要的援助。

第十一章 向文化审议会咨询（第一百五十三条）

第一百五十三条 文部科学大臣必须事先就下列事项咨询文化审议会。

（一）国宝或重要文化财的指定以及指定撤销；

（二）登录有形文化财的登录及登录撤销（除第五十九条第一款、第二款所规定的登录撤销外）；

（三）重要无形文化财的指定及指定撤销；

（四）重要无形文化财保持者及保持团体的认定及认定撤销；

（五）重要有形民俗文化财或重要无形民俗文化财的指定及其指定撤销；

（六）登录有形民俗文化财的登录及登录撤销（除第九十条第三款准用第五十九条第一款、第二款所规定的登录撤销外）；

（七）特别史迹名胜天然纪念物、史迹名胜天然纪念物的指定及指定的解除；

（八）史迹名胜天然纪念物暂时指定的解除；

（九）登录纪念物的登录及登录的撤销（除第一百三十三条准用第五十九条第一款、第二款所规定的登录撤销外）；

（十）重要文化景观的选定及选定撤销；

（十一）重要传统建造物群保存地区的选定及选定撤销；

（十二）选定保存技术的选定及选定撤销；

（十三）选定保存技术的保持者或保持团体的认定及认定撤销。

2. 文化厅长官必须事先就以下所列事项咨询文化审议会。

（一）重要文化财的管理或国宝修缮命令；

（二）文化厅长官实施的国宝修缮或为防止国宝灭失、损毁或被盗而实施的相关措施；

（三）重要文化财的现状改变许可或实施影响重要文化财保存行为的许可；

（四）为保全重要文化财环境，而限制、禁止或建设必要设施的命令；

（五）国家收购重要文化财；

（六）重要文化财保护利用计划的第五十三条之二第四款的认定；

（七）登录有形文化财保护利用计划的第六十七条之二第四款的认定；

（八）重要无形文化财保护利用计划的第七十六条之二第三款的认定；

（九）在重要无形文化财之外的无形文化财中，由文化厅长官选择记录或给予记录财政补助的；

（十）重要有形民俗文化财的管理命令；

（十一）收购重要有形民俗文化财；

（十二）重要有形民俗文化财保护利用计划的第八十五条之二第四款的认定；

（十三）重要无形民俗文化财保护利用计划的第八十九条之二第三款的认定（含第八十九条之三中准用第七十六条之三第一款的变更的认定）；

（十四）登录有形民俗文化财保护利用计划的第九十条之二第四款的认定；

（十五）在重要无形民俗文化财之外的无形民俗文化财中，由文化厅记录或给予记录财政补助的；

（十六）命令停止改变史迹现状行为或延长禁止命令期间的；

（十七）为调查埋藏文化财，由文化厅长官施行发掘的；

（十八）有关史迹名胜天然纪念物的管理或特别史迹名胜天然纪念物的修复命令；

（十九）由文化厅长官修复特别史迹名胜天然纪念物或实施为防止其灭失、损毁、消亡及被盗措施的；

（二十）许可改变史迹名胜天然纪念物现状或实施影响其保存行为的；

（二十一）为保全史迹名胜天然纪念物环境，限制、禁止或建设必要设施命令；

（二十二）未获得改变史迹名胜天然纪念物的现状或实施影响其保存环境的行为的许可，或者因不符上述许可条件或为保存史迹名胜天然纪念物的环境，违反限制或禁止性规定时恢复现状的命令；

（二十三）史迹名胜天然纪念物保护利用计划的第一百二十九条之二第四款的认定；

（二十四）登录纪念物保护利用计划的第一百三十三条之二第四款的认定；

（二十五）有关重要文化景观管理的命令；

（二十六）第一百八十三条之三第一款规定的文化财保护利用地域计划的该条第五款之认定（包含第一百八十三条之四第一款的变更认定）。

（二十七）第一百八十四条第一款政令（仅限于该款第二号、第一百八十四条第一款第二项所列举的与事务相关的事项）的制定、修改与废止的草案。

第十二章　补则（第一百五十四条~第一百九十二条）

第一节　听证、意见听取及异议申请（第一百五十四条~第一百六十一条）

【听证之特例】

第一百五十四条　文化厅长官（根据第一百八十四条第一款规定，当都、道、府、县或市教育委员会行使属于文化厅长官权限时则为该都、道、府、县或市教育委员会）在实施以下各项行政行为时，无论是否适用《行政程序法》[①]第十三条第一款所规定的意见听取程序，都必须举行听证。

（一）根据第四十五条第一款或第一百二十八条第一款规定的，针对特定对象的限制、禁止或命令；

① 1993年（平成5年）11月12日法律第88号。

（二）根据第五十一条第五款（包括第五十一条之二、第八十四条第二款以及第八十五条中的准用）规定的公开展出的中止命令；

（三）根据第九十二条第二款规定的禁止或中止发掘命令；

（四）根据第九十六条第二款规定的停止或禁止调查命令、或者根据该条第五款的延长期间命令；

（五）根据第一百二十五条第七款（包括第一百二十八第三款中的准用）规定的恢复原状命令。

2. 文化厅长官（根据第一百八十四条第一款、第一百八十四条之二第一款规定、文化厅长官的权限由都、道、府、县或市、町、村教育委员会行使时，则为该都、道、府、县或市、町、村教育委员会。下一条同）在举行前款规定的听证以及第四十三条第四款（包括第一百二十五第三款中的准用）或第五十三条第四款规定的许可撤销听证时，必须提前10日根据《行政程序法》第十五条第一款规定通知听证参与人，并公告听证内容、听证日期以及听证地点。

3. 前款听证的审理，必须公开进行。

【意见听取】

第一百五十五条　文化厅长官在采取以下措施时，必须公开听取相关关系人及其代理人的意见。

（一）根据第三十八条第一款或第一百二十三条第一款规定，采取修缮或修复措施时；

（二）根据第五十五条第一款或第一百三十一条第一款规定，进行实地调查或为实地调查实施其他必要措施时；

（三）根据第九十八条第一款规定，进行发掘时；

2. 文化厅长官在听取前款意见时，必须提前10日就实施各项措施的理由、所采取措施的内容以及听取意见的日期以及场所等，通知各相关关系人，且公告所实施措施的内容以及听取意见的日期及场所。

3. 在听取第一款中相关关系人及其代理人的意见时，相关关系人及其代理人可以陈述并说明自己的意见，而且也可以提供相关证据材料。

4. 相关关系人及其代理人无正当理由，不回应第一款所规定的意见听取的，文化厅长官可以在未听取相关各方意见的情况下，实施第一款所规定的各项措施。

【异议审查申请中的意见听取】

第一百五十六条 根据《行政不服审查法》[①]第二十四条规定，第一款中的处分或者不作为、第二款中的处分异议审查请求等的裁决等（除裁决或决定驳回审查请求外），审查员（该法第十一条规定的审查员）或审查厅（该法第九条第一款规定的都、道、府、县或市、町、村教育委员会的则为审查厅）必须在受理审查请求或异议申请之日（根据该法第二十三条规定，若有被要求补充材料的则为补充材料补充之日）起30日以内，公开听取审查请求人以及参加人（根据该法第十三条第四款规定的参加人，以下同）、异议申请人以及代理人的意见后才能作出裁决或决定。

（一）根据第四十三条第一款或第一百二十五条第一款规定的现状改变或实施影响保存环境行为的许可或不许可；

（二）根据第一百一十三条第一款（包括第三十三条中的准用）规定的管理团体的指定。

2. 前款意见听取的实施者，必须提前10日，就该意见听取的日期以及听取场所，通知审查请求人、参加人、异议申请人以及相关参与人，且公告被审查或异议的事项内容以及听取意见的日期及场所等。

3. 第一款中的审查请求，不适用《行政不服审查法》第三十一条；该款中的意见听取，准用《行政不服审查法》第三十一条第二款至第五款（包含根据《行政不服审查法》第九条第三款规定的替换适用的情况）规定。

【参加】

第一百五十七条 除审查请求人、异议申请人、参加人及代理人外的其他利害关系人，要在前条第一款的意见听取中陈述自己意见者，必须按照文

① 2014年（平成26年）6月13日法律第68号。

部科学省政令所规定的格式，向文化厅长官提出书面申请并获得许可后方可参加。

【证据的提示等】

第一百五十八条 在第一百五十六条第一款规定的听取意见的过程中，文化厅长官必须向审查请求人、异议申请人、参加人、前条的意见听取的参加人以及各自的代理人提示相关证据，并给予其充分陈述意见的机会。

【裁决或决定前的协商等】

第一百五十九条 在协调与矿业及采石业者之间关系的审查请求、异议申请的裁决或决定（除裁决或决定驳回外），必须在事先同公害等调整委员会磋商后才能做出。

2. 相关行政机关长官可以对相关审查请求或异议申请的事项，陈述自己的意见。

【程序】

第一百六十条 除第一百五十六条至前条以及《行政不服审查法》的规定外，有关审查请求以及异议申请程序，由文部科学省政令规定。

第一百六十一条 删除

第二节 有关国家的特例（第一百六十二条~第一百八十一条）

【有关国家的特例】

第一百六十二条 对国家或国家机关适用本法时，若本节有特别规定的则依该规定。

【有关重要文化财的国家之特例】

第一百六十三条 当重要文化财、重要有形民俗文化财、史迹名胜天然纪念物或重要文化景观等为《国有财产法》所规定的国有财产时，由文部科学大臣管理。但根据《国有财产法》第三条第二款规定，以上物品为文部科学大臣之外的其他人管理的行政财产、也有特别必要应由文部科学大臣之外的其他人管理时，文部科学大臣、相关省厅长官及财务大臣应该通过协商决定这些物品由相关省厅长官管理还是由文部科学大臣管理。

第一百六十四条 根据前条规定，由于重要文化财、重要有形民俗文化、史迹名胜天然纪念物以及重要文化景观由文部科学大臣管理，其所属或所管发生变动时，会计上的变更可以无偿进行，不受《国有财产法》第十五条的规定影响。

第一百六十五条 当指定国家所有的有形文化财、有形民俗文化财为国宝或为重要文化财或重要有形民俗文化时，根据第二十八条第一款、第三款（包括第七十八条第二款中的准用）规定，所应该通知及交付指定证书的对象为管理该有形文化财、有形民俗文化财的各省各厅长官。其中收到国宝指定证书的各省各厅长官，必须立刻将被指定为国宝的重要文化财的指定证书上交文部科学大臣。

2. 在国家所有的国宝、重要文化财或重要有形民俗文化财指定被撤销后，根据第二十九条第二款（包括第七十九条第二款中的准用）、第五款规定，所应该通知及交付指定证书的对象为管理该国宝、重要文化财或重要有形民俗文化财的各省各厅长官。此时各省各厅长官必须立刻将指定证书上交文部科学大臣。

3. 根据第一百〇九条第三款（包括第一百一十第三款、第一百一十二条第四款中的准用）规定，将国家所有或占有的指定、临时指定为特别史迹名胜天然纪念物或史迹名胜天然纪念物时，其所有人或占有人应该为通知对象；当撤销指定或临时指定时，则以管理该特别史迹名胜天然纪念物或史迹名胜天然纪念物的各省各厅长官为通知对象。

4. 在国家所有或占有的重要文化景观被选定或选定被撤销后，根据第一百三十四条第二款（包括第一百三十五条第二款中的准用）中准用第一百〇九条第三款规定，对其所有人或占有人的通知对象为管理该重要文化景观的各省各厅长官。

第一百六十六条 管理重要文化财、重要有形民俗文化财、史迹名胜天然纪念物以及重要文化景观的各省各厅长官，必须根据本法以及根据本法制定的文部科学省政令以及文化厅长官的建议，对重要文化财、重要有形民俗文化财、史迹名胜天然纪念物以及重要文化景观进行管理。

第一百六十七　下列各项通知，相关各省各厅长官必须通过文部科学大臣通知文化厅长官。

（一）取得重要文化财、重要有形民俗文化财或史迹名胜天然纪念物时；

（二）接受重要文化财、重要有形民俗文化财或史迹名胜天然纪念的管理或转移所属时；

（三）所管理的重要文化财、重要有形民俗文化财、史迹名胜天然纪念物以及重要文化景观全部或部分灭失、损毁或者消亡、遗失及被盗时；

（四）变更所管理的重要文化财或重要有形民俗文化财的管理场所时；

（五）修缮或修复所管理的重要文化财、史迹名胜天然纪念物时（除根据下一条第一款第一项规定，必须获得文化厅长官同意或者文部科学省政令规定的其他情形外）；

（六）变更所管理的重要有形民俗文化财、重要文化景观之现状或者实施对其保存有影响的行为时；

（七）所管理的史迹名胜天然纪念物的指定地域土地的登记（所在地、登记号吗、土地用途以及土地面积）发生变更时。

2. 前款第一项、第二项中的通知，准用第三十二条第一款（包括第八十条以及第一百二十条中的准用）规定；前款第三项中的通知，准用第三十三条（包括第八十条以及第一百二十条中的准用）以及第一百三十六条规定；前款第四项中的通知，准用第三十四条（包括第八十条中的准用）规定；前款第五项中的通知，准用第四十三条之二第一款、第一百二十七条第一款规定；前款第六项中的通知，准用第八十一条第一款、第一百三十九条第一款规定；前款第七项中的通知，准用第一百一十五条第二款规定。

3. 有关第一款第五项、第六项的通知相关的事项，文化厅长官可以给予必要之建议。

第一百六十八　相关各省各厅长官必须事前就以下事项，通过文部科学大臣获得文化厅长官同意。

（一）变更重要文化财、史迹名胜天然纪念物现状或者实施对其保存有影响的行为时；

（二）出口所管理的重要文化财、重要有形民俗文化财时；

（三）出租、交换、出售、让与或以其他方式处分所管理的重要文化财、重要有形民俗文化财、史迹名胜天然纪念物时；

2．各省各厅长官之外的国家机关变更重要文化财、史迹名胜天然纪念物现状或实施对其有影响的行为时，必须事先征得文化厅长官同意。

3．第一款第一项以及前款规定的同意，准用第四十三条第一款但书以及第二款、第一百二十五条第一款但书以及第二款规定。

4．文化厅长官在同意第一款第一项、第二项所规定的相关措施，作为同意实施相关措施的条件可以给予必要建议。

5．相关各省各厅长官以及其他国家机关，必须充分尊重前款文化厅长官的建议。

第一百六十九 文化厅长官认为必要时，可以就以下所列事项通过文部科学大臣对各省各厅长官给予必要建议。

（一）所管理的重要文化财、重要有形民俗文化财、史迹名胜天然纪念物的管理方法；

（二）所管理的重要文化财、重要有形民俗文化财、史迹名胜天然纪念物以及重要文化景观的修缮、修复或者采取防止其灭失、损毁、消亡以及被盗的措施；

（三）重要文化财以及史迹名胜天然纪念物的环境必要保全的设施；

（四）展出或公开所管理的重要文化财、重要有形民俗文化财。

2．前款规定的建议，准用前条第五款规定。

3．根据第一款规定，基于文化厅长官建议而实施的第二、第三项行为所需费用的承担，由文部科学大臣与各省各厅长官协商。

第一百七十条 有下列情形之一的，文化厅长官可以亲自修缮或修复国宝、特别史迹名胜天然纪念物，或者采取防止其灭失、损毁、消亡以及被盗措施。当该文化财由文部科学大臣以外的其他各省各厅长官管理时，文化厅长官必须事先就修缮、修复的内容、时间以及其他必要的事项等，通过文部科学大臣与管理该文化财的相关各省各厅长官协商；当该文化财由文部科学大臣管理时，除文部科学大臣规定的情形外，必须获得文化厅长官的承认。

（一）相关各省各厅长官不听从文化厅长官根据前条第一款第二项规定的修缮、修复建议的；

（二）对于国宝、特别史迹名胜天然纪念物的损毁、消亡或者存在灭失、损毁、消亡或被盗之虞，而相关各省各厅长官实施的修缮、修复等措施被认为不当的。

第一百七十条之二 根据文部科学省政令规定，管理国家所有的重要文化财、重要有形民俗文化财以及史迹名胜天然纪念物的各省各厅长官可制定重要文化财保护利用计划、重要有形民俗文化财保护利用计划以及史迹名胜天然纪念物保护利用计划，并通过文部科学大臣、请求文化厅长官同意。

2. 对于根据前款规定的请求，当重要文化财保护利用计划、重要有形民俗文化财保护利用计划以及史迹名胜天然纪念物保护利用计划，分别符合第五十三条之二第四款各项、第八十五条之二第四款各项或第一百二十九条之二第四款各项规定的，文化厅长官应当同意其计划。

第一百七十条之三 获得前条第二款同意的各省各厅长官，若要变更其获得同意的重要文化财保护利用计划、重要有形民俗文化财保护利用计划以及史迹名胜天然纪念物保护利用计划（除文部科学省政令规定轻微变更外）时，必须通过文部科学大臣获得文化厅长官的同意。

2．前款规定的同意，准用前条第二款规定。

第一百七十条之四 本法第五十三条之二第三款第一项规定的影响重要文化财保护利用计划、第八十五条之二第三款规定的影响重要有形民俗文化财保护利用计划，以及第一百二十九条之二第三款规定的影响史迹名胜天然纪念物保护利用计划的行为，在获得第一百七十条之二第二款同意（包含前条第一款的同意变更。在下一条以及第一百七十条之六中相同）的情况下，实施影响重要文化财、重要有形民俗文化财以及史迹名胜天然纪念物等现状的行为时，可忽略第一百六十七条第一款（仅限于第六项相关部分）所要求的必须通知以及第一百六十八条第一款（仅限于第一项相关部分）所要求的必须同意的规定，只需在影响其现状变更或保存行为结束后，根据文部科学省政令的规定，通过文部科学大臣向文化厅长官书面通告。

第一百七十条之五　第五十三条之二第三款第二项所记载的重要文化财保护利用计划在获得第一百七十条之二第二款同意的情况下，实施该重要文化财的维修以及所记载事项行为的，可忽略本法第一百六十七条第一款（仅限于第五项相关部分）必须通知规定，只需在该影响重要文化财的现状变更或保存行为结束后，根据文部科学省政令规定，通过文部科学大臣向文化厅长官书面通告。

第一百七十条之六　文化厅长官可以要求获得本法第一百七十条之二第二款同意的各省各厅长官报告其已获同意的重要文化财保护利用计划、重要有形民俗文化财保护利用计划以及史迹名胜天然纪念物保护利用计划（如有变更则为变更后的计划）的实施情况。

第一百七十一条　在指定或选定国家所有的文化财为国宝、重要文化财、重要有形民俗文化财、特别史迹名胜天然纪念物、史迹名胜天然物或重要文化景观时，文部科学大臣认为有必要确认前述文化财现状的，可以要求相关各省各厅长官报告相关情况；除重要有形民俗文化财及重要文化景观外，文部科学大臣可以指派调查人员进行实地调查。

第一百七十二条　文化厅长官认为国家所有的重要文化财、重要有形民俗文化财有保存必要时，可以指定适当的地方公共团体或其他法人对该文化财的保存进行必要管理（包括属于国家所有或管理的保存文化财的必要设施、设备及其他物件）。

2. 根据前款指定，文化厅长官必须事先通过文部科学大臣征得管理该文化财的各省各厅长官的同意，同时也必须征得被指定地方公共团体或其他法人的同意。

3. 第一款规定的指定，准用第三十二条之二第三款、第四款规定。

4. 因第一款规定的管理而产生的收益，归该地方公共团体或其他法人所有。

5. 地方公共团体或其他法人根据第一款规定，管理重要文化财或重要有形民俗文化财时，准用第三十条、第三十一条第一款、第三十二条之四第一款、第三十三条、第三十四条、第三十五条、第三十六条、第四十七条之二第三款、第五十四条规定；管理史迹名胜天然纪念物时，准用第三十条、第三十一条第一款、第三十三条、第三十五条、第一百一十五条第一款及第二款、第一百一十六条第一款及第三款、第一百二十一条、第一百三十条规定。

第一百七十三条 前条第一款所规定的指定撤销，准用第三十二条之三的规定。

第一百七十四条 当文化厅长官认为重要文化财、重要有形民俗文化财或史迹名胜天然纪念物有特别保护的必要时，可以促使接受第一百七十二条第一款规定指定的地方公共团体或其他法人修缮或修复该文化财。

2. 根据前款规定实施的修缮或修复，准用第一百七十二条第二款规定。

3. 地方公共团体或其他法人根据第一项规定进行修缮或修复时，若为重要文化财或重要有形民俗文化财，准用第三十二条之四第一项及三十五条规定；若为史迹名胜天然纪念物，则准用第三十五条、第一百一十六条第一款以及第一百一十七条规定。

第一百七十四条之二 获得第一百七十二条第一款指定的地方公共团体或者其他法人制定的重要文化财保护利用计划、重要有形民俗文化财保护利用计划以及史迹名胜天然纪念物保护利用计划，分别准用第五十三条之二至第五十三条之八、第八十五条之二至第八十五条之四以及第一百九十二条之二至第一百九十二条之七。

2. 在根据前款准用第五十三条之二第四款、第八十五条之二第四款以及第一百九十二条之二第四款规定，进行认定（包含前款准用第五十三条之三第一款[①]以及第一百九十二条之三第一款的变更认定）时，应该事先通过文部科学大臣与管理重要文化财、重要有形民俗文化财以及史迹名胜天然纪念物的各省各厅长官进行协商。当该各省各厅长官为文部科学大臣时，即获得其承认。

第一百七十五条 根据第一百七十二条第一款规定接受指定的地方公共团体可以在管理的必要限度内，无偿地使用其所管理的、属国家所有的重要文化财、重要有形民俗文化财、史迹名胜天然纪念物以及与之相关的土地及建造物。

---

① 包含前款中准用第八十五条之四中的准用。

2. 前款中土地及建造物的使用，准用《国有财产法》第二十二条第二款、第三款规定。

第一百七十六条 根据第九十八条第一款规定进行发掘时，如果所发掘区域的土地属国家所有或由国家机关占有，文化厅长官必须事先将发掘的目的、方法、发掘时间及其他事项，通过文部科学大臣与相关各省各厅长官进行协调。但当该各省各厅的长官为文部科学大臣时，应视为接受其承认。

第一百七十七条 根据第一百〇四条第一款规定，归属于国家的文化财由文化厅长管理。但是如果为了其保存或有效地利用，有必要由其他国家机关进行管理时，则必须将该文化财移交给该机关管理。

【有关登录有形文化财等的国家之特例】

第一百七十八条 根据第五十七条第一款、第九十一条第一款规定，登录国家所有的有形文化财、有形民俗文化财后，第五十八条第一款、第三款（包括第九十条第三款中的准用）所规定的登录证书或通知的交付对象为管理该登录有形文化财、有形民俗文化财的相关各省各厅长官。

2. 根据第五十九条第一款至第三款（包括第九十条第三款中的准用）规定，撤销属国家所有的登录有形文化财、有形民俗文化财登录后，应该将第五十九条第四款（包括第九十条第三款中的准用）所规定的撤销决定通知管理该登录有形文化财、登录有形民俗文化财的相关各省各厅长官。在这种情况下，相关各省各厅长官必须立刻将登录证书上交给文部科学大臣。

3. 根据第一百三十二条第一款、第一百三十三条第一款，或者第一百三十三条中准用第五十九条第一款至第三款规定，由国家所有或占有的纪念物登录之撤销，根据第一百三十二条第二款中准用第一百〇九条第三款或者第一百三十三条中准用第五十九条第四款的规定向所有人或占有人通知的，应以管理该登录纪念物的相关各省各厅长官。

第一百七十九条 相关各省各厅长官必须就以下各项事项通过文部科学大臣通知文化厅长官。

（一）有形文化财、有形民俗文化财及纪念物取得登录时；

（二）登录有形文化财、登录有形民俗文化财及登录纪念物的所管或所属发生变更时；

（三）属自己所管理的登录有形文化财、登录有形民俗文化财及登录纪念物等全部或部分灭失、损毁或者消亡、遗失、被盗时；

（四）属自己所管理的登录有形文化财、登录有形民俗文化财的所在地发生变更时；

（五）登录有形文化财、登录有形民俗文化财及登录纪念物的现状变更时；

（六）属自己所管理的登录有形文化财、登录有形民俗文化财出境时；

（七）所管理的登录纪念物的所在土地的登记（所在地、登记号码、土地用途以及土地面积）变更时。

2. 各省各厅长官以外的国家机关试图变更登录有形文化财、登录有形民俗文化财及登录纪念物现状时，必须通知文化厅长官。

3. 第一款第一项、第二项的通知，准用本法三十二条第一款规定；第一款第三项的通知，准用本法三十三条、第六十一条（包括第九十条第三款中的准用）规定；第一款第四项的通知，准用六十二条（包括第九十条第三款中的准用）规定；第一款第五项及前款的通知，准用六十四条第一款（包括第九十条第三款及第一百三十三条中的准用）规定；第一款第六项的通知，准用六十五条第一款（包括第九十条第三款中的准用）规定；第一款第七项的通知，准用一百一十五条第二款规定。

4. 第一款第五项及第二款的现状变更，准用六十四条第一款但书及第二款规定；

5. 文化厅长官认为登录有形文化财、登录有形民俗文化财及登录纪念物有保护必要的，可以就第一款第五项、第二款所规定的现状变更，通过文部科学大臣向相关各省各厅长官以及各省各厅的长官以外的其他国家机关陈述意见。

第一百七十九条之二 根据文部科学省政令规定，管理国家所有的登录有形文化财、登录有形民俗文化财以及登录纪念物的各省各厅长官，可以制定登录有形文化财保护利用计划、登录有形民俗文化财保护利用计划以及登录纪念物保护利用计划，并通过文部科学大臣请求文化厅长官同意该计划。

2. 对于根据前款规定的请求，当登录有形文化财保护利用计划、登录有形民俗文化财保护利用计划以及登录纪念物保护利用计划分别符合本法第六十七条之二第四款各项、第九十条之二第四款各项以及第一百三十三条之二第四款各项规定的，文化厅长官应当同意其计划。

第一百七十九条之三 获得前条第二款同意的各省各厅长官，若要变更其获得同意的登录有形文化财保护利用计划、登录有形民俗文化财保护利用计划以及登录纪念物保护利用计划（除文部科学省政令规定轻微变更外）时，必须通过文部科学大臣、获得文化厅长官的同意。

2．前款规定的同意，准用前条第二款规定。

第一百七十九条之四 本法第六十七条之二第三款第一项、第九十条之二第三款以及第一百三十三条之二第三款规定的影响登录有形文化财保护利用计划、登录有形民俗文化财保护利用计划，以及登录纪念物保护利用计划，在获得第一百七十条之二第二款同意（包含前条第一款的变更同意。在下一条相同）的情况下，实施的变更登录有形文化财、登录有形民俗文化财以及登录纪念物的行为应所同意的事项，可忽略第一百七十九条第一款（仅限于第五项相关部分）所要求的必须通知的规定，只需在现状变更行为结束后，根据文部科学省政令规定，通过文部科学大臣书面通告文化厅长官。

第一百七十九条之五 文化厅长官可以要求获得本法第一百七十九条之二第二款同意的各省各厅长官报告其已获同意的登录有形文化财保护利用计划、登录有形民俗文化财保护利用计划以及登录纪念物保护利用计划（如有变更则为变更后的计划）的实施情况。

第一百八十条 文部科学大臣认为必要时，可以要求各省各厅长官报告其管理的、属国家所有的登录有形文化财、登录有形民俗文化财及登录纪念物的基本现状。

第一百八十一条 有关国家所属的登录有形文化财、登录有形民俗文化财及登录纪念物，不适用第六十条第三款至第五款、第六十三条第二款及第六十七条第三款（包括第九十条第三款中的准用）规定。

2．有关国家所有的登录纪念物，不适用第一百三十三条中准用第一百一十三条至第一百一十八条规定。

第三节 地方公共团体及教育委员会（第一百八十二条~第一百九十二条）

【地方公共团体的事务】

第一百八十二条 地方公共团体可以对文化财的管理、修缮、修复、公开及其他保存和利用所需经费给予补贴。

2. 地方公共团体可以通过制定地方条例，指定所辖地区重要文化财、重要无形文化财、重要有形民俗文化财、重要无形民俗文化财及史迹名胜天然纪念物之外的重要文化财，并采取必要的保存与利用措施。

3. 在制定、改废前款条例，指定或撤销前款文化财指定时，教育委员会必须根据文部科学省政令规定，向文化厅长官报告。

【地方债的发行】

第一百八十三条 为保证区域文化财的保存与利用事业有充足资金，在法令规定的范围内，结合保存和利用文化财的资金情况以及地方财政状况等，地方公共团体可适当发行地方债券。

【文化财保护利用大纲】

第一百八十三条之二 都、道、府、县教育委员会可以制定本辖区文化财保护利用的综合性施政大纲（在下一款及下一条中称为“文化财保护利用大纲”）。

2. 都、道、府、县教育委员会制定或变更文化财保护利用大纲后，必须及时公布并送达文化厅长官以及相关市、町、村。

【文化财保护利用区域规划之认定】

第一百八十三条之三 根据文部科学省政令规定，市、町、村教育委员会（仅限于设有地方文化财保护审议会）在考量所制定的文化财保护利用大纲的基础上，制定市、町、村文化财保护利用区域规划（本节以及第一百九十二条之六第一款中称为“文化财保护利用区域规划”），并申请文化厅长官予以认定。

2. 文化财保护利用区域规划应该包含以下各项内容：

（一）有关市、町、村区域性文化财保护利用的基本方针；

（二）为实现市、町、村区域性文化财的保护利用，市、町、村采取的具体措施；

（三）为掌握市、町、村区域性文化财情况而实施的调查事项；

（四）计划的实施周期；

（五）文部科学省政令规定的其他事项。

3. 市、町、村教育委员会在制定文化财保护利用区域规划时，必须举行听证或采取其他措施以保障听取当地居民意见，而且还必须听取地方文化财保护审议会（若组建本法第一百八十三条之九第一款规定的协议会的，则为该地方文化财保护审议会以及协议会。第一百八十三条之五第二款中相同）的意见。

4. 如果存在《保持改善地域历史风貌法》[①] 第五条第一款规定的地域历史风貌保持改善计划，文化财保护利用区域规划必须与其保持协调关系。

5. 根据第一款规定的文化财保护利用区域规划的认定申请，符合以下条件的，文化厅长官应当予以认定。

（一）该文化财保护利用区域规划的实施，有利于市、町、村区域文化财的保护与利用；

（二）该文化财保护利用区域规划被认为能够得以确实、顺利实施；

（三）若有文化财保护利用大纲，文化财保护利用区域规划必须与其相符、且内容适当。

6. 文化厅长官作出前款认定时，必须事先通过文部科学大臣与相关行政机关负责人进行协商。

7. 文化厅长官作出第五款认定后，必须立刻将认定结果通知提出申请的市、町、村教育委员会，不得延迟。

8. 市、町、村教育委员会在收到前款认定通知后，必须向当地居民公告被认定的文化财保护利用区域规划。

---

① 2008 年（平成 20 年）5 月 23 日法律第 40 号。

【获认定的文化财保护利用区域规划的变更】

第一百八十三条之四 获前条第五款认定的市、町、村（在本节以及第一百九十二条之六第二款中称为“获认定市、町、村”）教育委员会，若要变更（除文部科学省政令规定轻微变更外）其文化财保护利用区域规划，必须获得文化厅长官的认定。

2．前款认定，准用前条第三款至第八款规定。

【文化财登录之建议】

第一百八十三条之五 获认定的市、町、村教育委员会在第一百八十三条之三第五款认定（包含前条第一款的变更认定。第一百八十三条之七第一款、第二款中相同）的文化财保护利用区域规划（若有变更则为变更后的计划。在本节以及第一百九十二条之六中称为“认定的文化财保护利用区域规划”）实施期间，如果认为其辖区内有文化财符合本法第五十七条第一款、第九十条第一款以及第一百三十二条第一款规定、适合登录的，可根据文部科学省政令规定，向文部科学大臣建议将其登录在文化财登录簿上。

2. 获认定的市、町、村教育委员会根据前款规定，提起登录建议时，必须事前听取地方文化财保护审议会的意见。

3. 针对第一款建议，如果文部科学大臣认为不符合第五十七条第一款、第九十条第一款以及第一百三十二条第一款登录条件、决定不予登录的，必须立刻将不予登录决定以及理由告知提起建议的市、町、村教育委员会，不得延迟。

【认定的文化财保护利用区域规划实施状况之报告】

第一百八十三条之六 文化厅长官可要求获认定的市、町、村教育委员会，报告其已获认定的文化财保护利用区域规划的实施情况。

【认定的撤销】

第一百八十三条之七 文化厅长官认为被认定的文化财保护利用区域规划不

再符合本法第一百八十三条之三第五款所规定的各项条件时，可以撤销该认定。

2. 根据前款规定的认定撤销，文化厅长官应立刻将认定撤销决定通知市、町、村教育委员会，不得延迟。

3. 市、町、村教育委员会在收到前款认定撤销决定后必须向当地居民公告，不得延迟。

【对市、町、村的建议】

第一百八十三条之八 都、道、府、县教育委员会可对市、町、村制定文化财保护利用区域规划，确实、顺利实施认定的文化财保护利用区域规划等，提供必要建议。

2. 国家必须努力对市、町、村制定文化财保护利用区域规划，确实、顺利实施认定的文化财保护利用区域规划等，提供必要信息以及适当建议。

3. 除前两款规定外，国家，都、道、府、县以及市、町、村必须就促进文化财保护利用区域规划得到确实、顺利实施而相互协作。

4. 市、町、村责任人以及教育委员会，必须就促进文化财保护利用区域规划得到确实、顺利实施而紧密协作。

【协议会】

第一百八十三条之九 市、町、村的教育委员会可单独或共同组建有关文化财保护利用区域规划的制定、变更以及被认定的文化财保护利用区域规划的实施等进行协商的协议会（本条中称为“协议会”）。

2. 协议会由以下机构组成：

（一）该市、町、村；

（二）包含该市、町、村的都、道、府、县；

（三）第一百九十二条之二第一款规定的市、町、村教育委员会指定的文化财保护利用支援团体；

（四）文化财的所有人、学者、工商业者、旅游业者以及市、町、村教育委员会认为的其他关系者。

3. 协议会认为必要时可要求相关行政机关提供资料、表明意见、说明情况以及其他必要协助等。

4. 协议会的成员必须尊重协议会的协议结果。

5. 除上述各款规定外，有关协议会运营的其他必要事项由协议会决定。

【都、道、府、县或市的教育委员会处理的事务】

第一百八十四条 文化厅长官以下各项权限的全部或部分，可通过政令规定，由都、道、府、县或市教育委员会行使。

（一）根据第三十五条第三款（包括第三十六条第三款以及第八十三条、第一百二十一条第二款、第一百七十二条第五款中的准用，第三十七条第四款以及第一百二十二条第三种的准用，第四十六条之二第二款、第七十四条第二款、第七十七条第二款以及第九十一条中的准用，第八十三条、第八十七条第二款、第一百一十八条、第一百二十条、第一百二十九条第二款、第一百七十二条第二款、第一百七十四条第三款中的准用）的指挥与监督；

（二）根据第四十三条或第一百二十五条规定的文化财现状变更或者实施影响其保存的行为的许可、撤销许可以及命令停止相关（除现状重大变更、实施重大影响行为的许可、撤销许可外）权限；

（三）根据第五十一条第五款（包括第八十五条中准用第五十一条之二、第八十四条第二款、第八十五条中的准用）规定的公开停止命令；

（四）根据第五十三条第一款、第三款、第四款规定的公开展示许可、许可撤销、停止公开的命令；

（五）根据第五十四条（包括第八十六条、第一百七十二条第五款中的准用）、第五十五条、第一百三十条（包括第一百七十二条第五款中的准用）、第一百三十一条规定的调查或调查的必要措施；

（六）根据第九十二条第一款（包括第九十三条第一款中的准用）规定的申请受理，第九十二条第二款规定的指示或命令，第九十三条第二款规定的指示，第九十四条第一款规定的通知受理、第二款规定的通知、第三款规定的协议、第四款规定的建议，第九十六条第一款规定的申请受理、第二款或第七款规定的命令、第三款规定的意见听取、第五款或第七款规定的期限延长、第八款规定的指示，第九十七条第一款规定的通知受理、第二款规定的通知、第三款规定的协议以及第四款规定的建议。

2. 对于都道府或市的教育委员会根据前款规定实施前款第五项所列举的第五十五条、第一百三十一条所规定的实地调查或为调查而采取的必要措施等，不得根据《行政不服审查法》提起不服申请。

3. 都、道、府、县或市的教育委会根据第一款规定，处理该款第六项所列举的第九十四条第一款至第四款、第九十七条第一款至第四款所规定的事务时，不适用第九十四条第五款、第九十七条第五款规定。

4. 都、道、府、县或市的教育委员会根据第一款规定，处理以下各项事务（仅限于《地方自治法》[①]第二条第八款规定的自治性事务）给他人造成经济损失的，可无视各项后所列条款规定，都、道、府、县或市应给予适当补偿。

（一）第一款第二项列举的第四十三条、第一百二十五条规定的现状变更或实施影响其保存行为的许可（第四十三条第五款及第一百二十五条第五款）。

（二）根据第一款第五项所列举的第五十五条、第一百三十一条规定的调查或为调查而采取的必要措施（第五十五条第三款及第一百三十一条第二款）。

（三）根据第一款第六项所列举的第九十六条第二款规定的命令（该条第九款）。

5. 前款的补偿额度，由该都、道、府、县或市的教育委员会决定。

6. 根据前款规定的补偿额度，准用第四十一条第三款规定。

7. 在依据前款准用第四十一条第三款规定而提起的行政诉讼中，都、道、府、县或市为被告。

8. 都、道、府、县或市的教育委员会根据第一款规定实施的、与《地方自治法》第二条第九款第一项的法定受托事务相关的处分及行使其他公权力行为的审查请求，以文化厅长官为对象。

---

① 1947年（昭和22年）4月17日法律第67号。

第一百八十四条之二 前条第二款第二项、第四项以及第五项中所列举的、与被认定市、町、村辖区相关的属于文化厅长官各项权限的全部或者部分，在认定的文化财保护利用区域规划的实施期间内，根据政令规定，可由该市、町、村教育委员会行使。

2. 根据前款规定，市、町、村教育委员会行使相关权限时，准用前条第二款、第四款（除第三项相关部分）以及第五款至第八款规定。

3. 根据第一款规定，被认定的市、町、村教育委员会开始实施该款确定的相关事项前完成的许可等行政处分行为（本条以下称为“处分行为”）或者许可申请等行为（本条以下称为“申请等行为”），视为被认定的市、町、村教育委员会行使的处分行为或对被认定的市、町、村教育委员会的申请行为。

4. 在被认定的文化财保护利用区域规划实施期间终了后，因其他原因被认定的市、町、村教育委员会根据第一款规定的事务终了日之前的处分行为或申请行为，视为终了后的处分行为或申请行为。

【出展的重要文化财等的管理】

第一百八十五条 根据政令规定，文化厅长官可以将第四十八条（包括第八十五条中的准用）所规定的全部或部分出展的重要文化财或重要有形民俗文化财的管理事务，交由都、道、府、县或指定市等的教育委员会行使。

2. 根据前款规定，都、道、府、县或指定市等的教育委员会在实施前款管理事务时，都、道、府、县或指定市等的教育委员会必须在其职员中确定管理该重要文化财或重要有形民俗文化财的责任人。

【修缮等的委托实施】

第一百八十六条 文化厅长官认为必要时，可以将第三十八条第一款、第一百七十条的国宝修缮或者实施防止国宝灭失、损毁、被盗等措施，第九十八条第一款的实施发掘、第一百二十三条第一款或第一百七十条的特别史迹名胜天然纪念物的修复或者实施防止其灭失、损毁、消亡、被盗等措施的全部或部分，委托都、道、府、县教育委员会实施。

2. 基于前款规定的委托，都、道、府、县教育委员会在实施第三十八条第一款所规定的修缮的全部或部分、第九十八条第一款规定的发掘的全部或部分以及第一百二十三条第一款规定的修复的全部或部分，准用第三十九条规定。

【重要文化财等管理的委托或技术性指导】

第一百八十七条 根据下述人员的请求，都、道、府、县或指定市的教育委员会可接受其委托进行下列相应管理、维修等给予技术性指导。

（一）重要文化财的所有人（若为管理团体的则为该管理团体）或者管理责任人有关该重要文化财的管理（除为管理团体的情况）或维修；

（二）重要有形民俗文化财的所有人（若为管理团体的则为该管理团体）或者管理责任人（承担本法第八十条中准用第三十一条第二款所选任的承担管理责任的人员）有关该重要有形民俗文化财的管理（除为管理团体的情况）或维修；

（三）史迹名胜天然纪念物的所有人（若为管理团体的则为该管理团体）或者管理责任人有关该史迹名胜天然纪念物的管理（除为管理团体的情况）或修复；

2．根据前款规定，都、道、府、县或指定市的教育委员会接受管理、修缮、修复委托的，准用第三十九条第一款、第二款规定。

【文书等的递交】

第一百八十八条 根据本法规定，所有向文部科学大臣或文化厅长官提交的与文化财相关的书面申请以及其他书面文件及物品等，必须经由都、道、府、县教育委员会（当该文化财在指定都市的则为该指定都市教育委员会，以下同）递交。

2．都、道、府、县教育委员会收到前款规定的文书及物品后，必须附上自己的意见，一并送交文部科学大臣或文化厅长官。

3．根据本法规定，文部科学大臣或文化厅长官发出的所有与文化财相关的命令、建议、指示及其他通知等，必须经由都、道、府、县教育委员会下达。情况特别紧急的，不受此限。

【向文部科学大臣或文化厅长官呈报意见】

第一百八十九条　都、道、府、县及市、町、村的教育委员会，可以向文部科学大臣或文化厅长官呈报有关其辖区内文化财的保存和利用等意见。

【地方文化财保护审议会】

第一百九十条　都、道、府、县及市、町、村的教育委员会（除特定地方公共团体外）可通过制定相关条例，设置由文化财保护专业人士构成的地方文化财保护审议会。

2. 特定地方公共团体可根据条例规定设置地方文化财保护审议会。

3. 地方文化财保护审议会向都、道、府、县及市、町、村的教育委员会提供咨询、调查并审议与文化财保存和利用相关的重要事项，并就相关事项向都、道、府、县及市、町、村的教育委员会提供相关建议。

4. 有关地方文化财保护审议会的组织机构以及运用等必要事项，由条例规定。

【文化财保护指导委员】

第一百九十一条　都、道、府、县及市、町、村的教育委员会（当该都、道、府、县及市、町、村为特定地方公共团体时则为该特定地方公共团体）可设置文化财保护指导委员。

2. 文化财保护指导委员可随时巡视文化财，并对文化财所有人以及其他关系人就文化财保护给予指导并提供意见。同时，也可普及和提高当地居民对文化财的保护意识。

3. 文化财保护指导委员为聘任制。

【事务的区分】

第一百九十二条　根据第一百一十条第一款第二款、第一百一十二条第一款以及第一百一十条第三款、第一百一十二条第四款中准用第一百〇九条第三款第四款规定，都、道、府、县实施的临时指定、临时指定的撤销以及相关通知等事务为《地方自治法》第二条第九款第一项所规定的法定受托事务。

第四节　文化财保护利用支援团体

【文化财保护利用支援团体的指定】

第一百九十二条之二　由文部科学省政令规定的法人团体或其他相当于法人的组织，若有能力确实、顺利地实施下一条规定的各项事务，可向市、町、村教育委员会申请，指定其为文化财保护利用支援团体（本节称为“支援团体”）。

2. 市、町、村教育委员会指定了前款支援团体后，必须公示被指定支援团体的名称、住所以及主要事务所所在地等。

3. 支援团体变更其名称、住所以及主要事务所所在地时，必须事前向市、町、村教育委员会报告。

4. 市、町、村教育委员会收到前款报告后，必须公示该变更事项。

【支援团体的事务】

第一百九十二条之三　支援团体主要从事以下各项事务。

（一）在该市、町、村辖区内保护利用该市、町、村的文化财；

（二）向以保护利用该市、町、村文化财为目的的组织和个人提供资料情报、咨询等支援活动；

（三）根据文化财所有人请求，接受委托从事管理、维护、修复以及其他为保护该文化财的必要措施；

（四）有关保护利用文化财的相关调查；

（五）除以上各项事务外，保护利用该市、町、村文化财的其他必要事务。

【监督等】

第一百九十二条之四　为确保前条各项事务能够得到适当、确实实施，市、町、村教育委员会认为必要，可要求支援团体报告其业务实施情况。

2. 市、町、村教育委员会认为支援团体未适当、确实实施前条各项业务时，可命令其采取必要措施改善业务实施情况。

3. 支援团体违反前款命令，市、町、村教育委员会可撤销根据第一百九十二条之二第一款规定的支援团体认定。
4. 市、町、村教育委员会根据前款规定取消支援团体认定的，必须公告取消认定决定。

【资讯的提供等】

第一百九十二条之五 国家及地方公共团体应向支援团体就其各项业务的实施等进行指导、提供资讯以及必要建议。

【文化财保护利用区域规划的议案】

第一百九十二条之六 支援团体可就文化财保护利用区域规划的制定、认定的文化财保护利用区域规划的变更等，向市、町、村教育委员提出议案。
2. 在认定的文化财保护利用计划实施的期间内，支援团体可据文部科学省政令规定，就市、町、村辖区内根据第五十七条第一款、第九十条第一款以及第一百三十二条第一款规定而登录适当时，向市、町、村教育委员会提起第一百八十三条之五第一款规定的议案。

第十三章　罚则（第一百九十三条～第二百〇三条）

第一百九十三条 违反第四十四条规定，未经文化厅长官许可将重要文化财运出境外的，处五年以下有期徒刑或监禁、或处一百万日元以下罚金。
第一百九十四条 违反第八十二条规定，未经文化厅长官许可将重要有形民俗文化财运出境外的，处三年以下有期徒刑或监禁、或处五十万日元以下罚金。
第一百九十五条 损坏、毁弃或藏匿重要文化财的，处五年以下有期徒刑或监禁、或处一百万日元以下罚金，或者二者并罚。
2. 前款损坏、毁弃或藏匿人为该重要文化财所有人的，处二年以下有期徒刑或监禁、或处五十万日元以下罚金。
第一百九十六条 变更史迹名胜天然纪念物现状或实施的行为影响其保存环

境，造成该史迹名胜天然纪念物灭失、损毁或消亡的，处五年以下有期徒刑或监禁、或处一百万日元以下罚金。

2．造成前款史迹名胜天然纪念物灭失、损毁或消亡的为该史迹名胜天然纪念物所有人的，处二年以下有期徒刑或监禁、或处五十万日元以下罚金。

第一百九十七条 有下列行为之一的，处五十万日元以下罚金。

（一）违反第四十三条或第一百二十五条规定，未经许可或未满足许可条件改变重要文化财、史迹名胜天然纪念现状，或者实施影响其保存行为，或者不服从停止改变其现状或停止实施影响保存行为的命令的；

（二）违反第九十六条第二项规定，不服从停止或禁止改变文化财现状的命令的。

第一百九十八条 有下列行为之一的，处三十万日元以下罚金。

（一）违反第三十九条第三款（包括第一百八十六条第二款）中准用第三十二条之二第五款规定，拒绝或者妨碍国宝修缮、拒绝或者妨碍实施防止其灭失、损毁及被盗措施的。

（二）违反第九十八条第三款（包括第一百八十六条第二款）中准用第三十九条第三款中准用第三十二条二第五款规定，拒绝或妨碍实施发掘的。

（三）违反第一百二十三条第二款（包括第一百八十六条第二款）中准用第三十九条第三款中准用第三十二条之二第五款规定，拒绝或妨碍修复特别史迹天然纪念物、拒绝或妨碍实施防止其灭失、损毁、消亡及被盗措施的。

第一百九十九条 法人代表人、法人或法人代表人的代理人、使用人（职员）以及其他从业人员，就其相关业务或财产的管理，实施了违反第一百九十三条至前条所规定行为的，除处罚相关行为人外，对法人或法人代表人处以各条规定的相应罚金。

第二百条 承担第三十九条第一款（包括第四十七条第三款、第八十六条、第一百二十三条第二款、第一百八十六条第二款、第一百八十七条第二款中的准用）、第四十九条（包括第八十五条中的准用）、第一百八十五条第二款所规定的管理、修缮或修复重要文化财、重要有形民俗文化财及史迹名胜天然纪念物责任的，如果因怠慢或重大过失造成所管理、修缮、修复的重要文化财、重要有形民俗文化财及史迹名胜天然纪念物灭失、损毁、消亡或被盗的，处三十万日元以下罚金。

第二百〇一条 有下列行为之一的，处三十万日元以下罚金。

（一）无正当理由不服从文化厅长官根据第三十六条第一款（包括第八十三条、第一百七十二条第五款中的准用）或第三十七条第一款发布的重要文化财、重要有形民俗文化财的管理或者国宝的修缮等命令的。

（二）无正当理由不服从文化厅长官根据第一百二十一条第一款（包括第一百七十二条第五款中的准用）、第一百二十二条第一款发布的史迹名胜天然纪念物的管理或特别史迹名胜天然纪念的修复命令的。

（三）无正当理由不服从文化厅长官根据第一百三十七条第二款发布的重要文化景观的管理或实施相关措施的建议命令的。

第二百〇二条 有下列行为之一的，处十万日元以下罚金。

（一）无正当理由违反第四十五条第一款规定的限制、禁止或者建设必要设施命令的。

（二）违反第四十六条（包括第八十三条中的准用）规定，未向文化厅长官提出出让给国家申请；或者虽提起了申请，但在该条第五款（包括第八十三条中的准用）所规定的期限内，又将该重要文化财转让给国家以外的他人，或者提起前述出让给国家申请但有虚假内容的。

（三）违反第四十八条第四款（包括第五十一条第 3 款以及第八十五条中的准用）规定拒不出展或公开展示，或者违反第五十条第五款（包括第五十一条之二、第八十四条第二款、第八十五条中的准用）规定，不服从停止或中止公开展示命令的。

（四）违反第五十三条第一款、第三款以及第四款规定，未获得许可或者未满足获得许可条件公开展示重要文化财，或者不服从停止公开展示命令的。

（五）违反第五十三条之六（包括第八十五条之四以及第一百七十四条之二第一款中的准用）、第一百七十四条之二第一款中的准用以及第五十四条（包括第八十六条以及第一百七十二条第五款中的准用）、第五十五条、第六十七条之五（包含第九十条之四以及第一百三十三条之四中的准用）、第六十八条（包括第九十条第三款以及第一百三十三条中的准用）、第七十六条之四（包含第八十九条之三中的准用）、第一百二十九条之五（包含第一百七十四条之二第一款中的准用）、第一百三十条（包括第一百七十二条第五款中的准用）、第一百三十一条或第一百四十条规定，不报告或虚假报告，或者拒绝、妨碍、回避公务员进行实地调查或为调查实施必要措施的。

（六）违反第九十二条第二款规定，不服从禁止、停止或中止发掘命令的。

（七）无正当理由违反第一百二十八条第一款所规定的限制或禁止，或者建设相关设施命令的。

第二百〇三条 有下列行为之一的，处五万日元以下罚金。

（一）违反第二十八条第五款、第二十九条第四款（包括第七十九条第二款中的准用）、第五十六条第二款（包括第八十六条中的准用）、第五十九条第六款以及第六十九条（包括第九十条第三款中的准用）规定，未向文部科学大臣或新所有人上交或移交重要文化财、重要有形民俗文化财指定证书或者登录有形文化财、登录有形民俗文化财登录证书的。

（二）违反第三十一条第三款（包括第六十四条第四款、第九十条第三款、第八十条、第一百一十九条第二款、第一百三十三条中的准用）、第三十二条（包括第六十条第四款、第九十条第三款、第八十条以及第一百二十条、第一百三十三条中的准用）、第三十三条（包括第八十条、第一百一十八条以及第一百二十条、第一百三十三条和第一百七十二条第五款中的准用）、第三十四条（第八十条以及第一百七十二条第五款中的准用）、第四十三条之二第一款、第五十三条之四或第五十三条之五（包含该规定在第一百七十四条之二第一款中的准用）、第六十一条或第六十二条（包括第九十条第三款中的准用）、第六十四条第一款（包括第九十条第三款及第一百三十三条中的准用）、第六十五条（包括第九十条第三款中的准用）、第六十七条之四、第七十三条、第八十一条第一款、

第八十四条第一款主文、第八十五条之三（包含第一百七十四条之二第一款中的准用）、第九十条之三、第九十二条第一款、第九十六条第一款、第一百一十五条第二款（包括第一百二十条、第一百三十三条、第一百七十二条第五款中的准用）、第一百二十七条第一项、第一百二十九条之四（包含第一百七十四条之二第一款中的准用）、第一百三十三条之三、第一百三十六条、第一百三十九条第一款规定，未申请或提出虚假申请的；

（三）违反第三十二条之二第五款（包括第三十四条之三第二款、第八十三条、第六十条第四款、第六十三条第二款、第九十条第三款、第八十条、第一百一十五条第四款、第一百三十三条中的准用）之规定，拒绝、妨碍或回避管理、修缮、修复以及拒绝、妨碍或回避为管理、修缮、复原而采取必要措施的。

附则　抄

【施行日期】

第一条　本法施行日期自公布之日起 3 个月内由政令决定。

【相关法律的废止】

第二条　废止以下法律、敕令及政令。

《国宝保存法》（昭和 4 年法律第 17 号）；

《重要美术品保存法》（昭和 8 年法律第 43 号）；

《史迹名胜天然纪念物保存法》（大正 8 年法律第 44 号）；

《国宝保存法施行令》（昭和 4 年敕令第 210 号）；

《史迹名胜天然纪念物保存法施行令》（大正 8 年敕令第 499 号）；

《国宝保存会官制》（昭和 4 年敕令第 211 号）；

《重要美术品等调查审议会令》（昭和 24 年政令第 251 号）；

《史迹名胜天然纪念物调查会令》（昭和 24 年政令第 252 号）。

【伴随法令废止的其他规定】

第三条　根据本法施行前的《国宝保存法》第一条规定的“国宝之指定”（除

根据同法第十一条第一款规定指定撤销外）视为根据本法第二十七条第一款规定的“重要文化财之指定”；根据《国宝保存法》第三条、第四条的“许可”视为根据本法第四十三条、第四十四条规定的“许可”。

2. 关于本法施行前的国宝灭失、损毁以及根据《国宝保存法》第七条第一款的命令、第十五条前段的补助金交付等，同法第七条至第十条、第十五条后段规定的效力依然有效。这种情况下，第九条第二款中的“主管大臣”替换为“文化财保护委员会”。

3. 除《国宝保存法》第六条、第二十三条外，有关本法施行前的违法行为的处罚依然有效。

4. 在本法施行时，根据《国宝保存法》第一条规定的国宝所有人，必须根据委员会规则所规定的记载事项，在本法施行后 3 个月内书面向委员会报告。

5. 根据前款规定提交报告的，根据本法第二十八条规定，委员会必须向该所有人交付重要文化财指定证书。

6. 违反第四款规定，未报告或虚假报告的，处五千日元以下罚金。

7. 本法施行时，管理《国宝保存法》第一条规定的国家国宝的各省各厅长官，必须根据委员会规则所规定的记载事项，在本法施行后 3 个月内书面通知委员会，但委员会规则另有规定的，则不在此限。

8. 根据前款规定通知后，委员会必须根据第二十条规定向各省各厅长官交付重要文化财指定证书。

第四条　本法施行时，之前根据《重要美术品保存法》第二条第一款被认定的物品，其效力在一定期间内依然存在。此间有关《重要美术品保存法》适用的相关事务由文化厅长官负责，该法中的“国宝”替换为“根据《文化财保护法》所规定的重要文化财”、“主务大臣”替换为“文化厅长官”、“根据《国宝保存法》第一条规定指定的国宝及前条”替换为“前条”。

2. 在一定期间内，根据《重要美术品保存法》第二条第一款规定的与认定撤销相关的事项，由文化财审议会调查审议，并就相关必要事项向文化厅长官提供咨询意见和建议。

3. 有关《重要美术品保存法》的施行，在一定期间内，准用本法第一百八十八条规定。

第五条　本法施行前《史迹名胜天然纪念物保存法》第一条第一款的指定（除指定撤销外）可视为本法第一百〇九条第一款的指定、第一条第二款的临时指定（除临时指定撤销外）为本法第一百一十条第一款的临时指定、第三条的许可为本法第一百二十五条第一款的许可。

2. 对于本法施行前根据《史迹名胜天然纪念物保存法》第四条第一款规定发出的命令及处分，同法第四条及《史迹名胜天然纪念物保存法施行令》第四条规定继续有效。此时，该施行令第四条中的“文部大臣”替换为“文化财保护委员会”。

3. 有关本法施行前的相关行为的处罚，《史迹名胜天然纪念物保存法》中的相关规定依然有效。

【从前的国立博物馆】

第六条　除法律（包括基于法律的命令）有特别规定外，从前的国立博物馆及其职员（除美术研究所及所属职员外）视为基于本法的国立博物馆及其职员；从前国立博物馆下设的美术研究所及所属职员则成为基于本法的研究所及其职员，其前后存在持续同一性。

2. 基于本法成立的东京国立文化财研究所承担从前国立博物馆下设的美术研究所所主持的调查研究工作，其在名称上可以使用“美术研究所”。

【国家的无息借贷等】

第七条　本法第三十五条第一款所规定的给予经费补助的重要文化财，属于《利用日本电信电话株式会社股份的销售收入促进社会资本整顿的特别措施法》（昭和 62 年法律第 86 号）第二条第一款第二项所规定的补助对象的，国家在预算的范围内，对其所需的部分经费给予一定期间的无息借贷。

2. 前款无息借贷款的偿还期间在 5 年（包括 2 年以内的存放期间）以内由政令决定。

3. 除前款由政令决定的事项外，第一款中的无息借贷款的偿还方法、提前偿还以及其他与还款相关的必要事项等由政令规定。

4. 根据第一款规定，国家就重要文化财的管理借贷款给重要文化财所有人或管理团体时，其补助金额相当于该借贷款金额；该补助金交付时间为该借贷款偿还时、所交付补偿金金额为该借贷款的偿还金额。

5．根据第一款规定获得无息借贷款后，重要文化财所有人或管理团体在根据第二款、第三款所确定的偿还期间内，提前偿还上述借贷款（除政令另有规定外）涉及前款适用时，该提前偿还视为该借贷款偿还。

6．根据第一款规定，国家实施无息借贷行为时，本法第三十五条第二款中的“交付”改为“借贷”、“补助的”改为“借贷的”、“管理或维修”改为“管理”；第三十五条第三款中的“交付”改为“借贷”、“管理或维修”改为“管理”，并适用这些规定。

附则　1951 年（昭和 26 年）12 月 24 日法律第 318 号　抄

1．本法自公布之日起施行。但第二十条、第二十三条、第二十三条及第一百二十四条第二款的改正规定以及附则第三款规定，自 1952 年（昭和 27 年）4 月 1 日起施行。

2．对本法施行前行为的罚则适用，修改前的《文化财保护法》第三十四条规定仍然有效。

附则　1952 年（昭和 27 年）7 月 31 日法律第 272 号　抄

【施行日期】

1．本法自 1953 年（昭和 28 年）8 月 1 日起施行。但附则第三款规定，自公布之日起施行。

【有关东京国立博物馆分馆职员的规定】

2．本法施行时，除另有委任外，原东京国立博物馆分馆的职员，按同一工作条件成为奈良国立博物馆的职员。

附则　1953 年（昭和 28 年）8 月 10 日法律第 194 号　抄

1．本法自公布之日起施行。

附则　1953 年（昭和 28 年）8 月 15 日法律第 213 号　抄

1. 本法自 1953 年（昭和 28 年）9 月 1 日起施行。

2. 本法施行前根据从前法令所作出的许可、认可以及其他行政处置、申请、报告及其手续等，可视为根据改正后相应规定所作出的行政行为或手续。

附则　1954 年（昭和 29 年）5 月 29 日法律第 131 号　抄

1. 本法自 1954 年（昭和 29 年）7 月 1 日起施行。

2. 对于本法施行前临时指定的史迹名胜天然纪念物，除根据改正后的《文化财保护法》（以下称为《新法》）第六十九条第一款规定进行指定外，自本法施行之日起 3 年内未根据该条该款规定进行指定的，其效力自动失效。该规定不受《新法》第七十一条第二款规定的限制。

3. 对于在本法施行前 6 个月内、根据改正前的《文化财保护法》第四十三条第一款或第八十条第一款、第四十五条第一款或第八十一条第一款规定的现状变更许可或不许可、限制或禁止及命令等处分不服的，可以在本法施行之日起 30 日内向委员会提出异议申请。此时可以准用第八十五条之二第二款、第三款及第八十五条之三至第八十五条之九的规定。

4. 对在本法施行前行为的罚则适用，根据从前规定。

5. 废止 1983 年（昭和 28 年）政令第 289 号《有关史迹名胜天然纪念物的管理团体之指定等政令》。

6. 根据旧《有关史迹名胜天然纪念物的管理团体之指定等政令》第一条第一款规定，接受指定的地方公共团体、其他团体以及根据该法令附则第二款规定接受指定的地方公共团体及其他团体，则被视为根据新法第七十一条之二第一款、第九十五条第一款规定接受指定的地方公共团体及其他法人。

7. 前款所指定的团体为非法人的，在本法施行后 1 年内，可根据新法第七十一条之二第一款、第九十五条第一款及第九十五条之三第一款规定进行管理或修缮。该非法人可准用新法第七十一条之二第一款、第九十五条第一款及第九十五条之三第一款中有关接受指定的法人的规定。

附则　1956年（昭和31年）6月12日法律第148号　抄

1. 本法自《〈地方自治法〉部分改正之法律》（昭和31年法律第147号）施行之日起施行。

附则　1956年（昭和31年）6月30日法律第163号　抄

【施行日期】

1. 本法自1956年（昭和31年）10月1日起施行。

附则　1958年（昭和33年）4月25日法律第86号　抄

1. 本法自公布之日起施行，除《有关特别职位职员的工资之法律》第四条、第九条及第十四条第一款的修改规定、《文化财保护法》第十三条之后增加的修改规定、《自治厅设置法》第十六条之后增加的修改规定以及附则第二款规定外，自1958年（昭和33年）4月1日起适用。

附则　1959年（昭和34年）4月20日法律第148号　抄

【施行日期】

1. 本法自《国税征收法》（昭和34年法律第147号）施行之日起施行。

【公共课税的先取特权之顺位的修改】

7. 根据第二章规定的改正后各法令（仅限与征收金的先取特权顺位相关部分）规定，在本法施行后，适用于《国税征收法》第二条第（十二）项所规定的通过强制换价手续开始的分配手续，本法施行前已开始的该分配手续，在征收金的先取特权顺位上依照旧法规定。

附则　1961年（昭和36年）6月2日法律第111号　抄

【施行日期】

1. 本法自公布之日起施行，自1961年（昭和36年）4月1日起适用。

【《行政机关职员定编法》废止】

2.《行政机关职员定编法》（昭和24年法律第126号）废止。

【对全职职员的暂定措施】

3. 1961年（昭和36年）4月1日现在，两个月内所雇佣的全职职员，可以在一定期间内将其置于《国家行政组织法》第十九条第一款、第二款以及第二十一条第二款所确定人员编制之外。

附则　1962年（昭和37年）5月16日法律第140号　抄

1. 本法自1962年（昭和37年）10月1日起施行。

2. 除本法附则中有特别规定外，本法改正后的规定适用于本法施行前所发生的事项，但并不影响改正前已实施行为的法律效力。

3. 本法实施时仍在进行的诉讼，不受改正后新法不得提起诉讼规定的限制，仍按旧法规定执行。

4. 本法实施时正在进行的管辖权之诉，不受改正后新法的专属管辖规定的限制，仍按旧法规定执行。

5. 本法施行时有关根据旧法规定作出的、有关起诉期间的决定或裁决，按旧法规定执行，但此规定仅限于新法规定的起诉期间比旧法短的情形。

6. 本法施行前与当事人诉讼相关的决定或裁决，新法规定起诉期间的，其起诉期间从新法施行之日起计算。

7. 本法施行前提起、正在进行的撤销决定或裁决之诉，依照旧法规定进行，不受新法所确定的该法律关系当事人一方为被告的限制。但如果原告申请，允许法院可以作出变更该诉讼的诉讼当事人的决定。

8. 前款但书，准用《行政诉讼法》第十八条后段以及第二十一条第二款至第五款规定。

附则　1962年（昭和37年）9月15日法律第161号　抄

1. 本法自1962年（昭和37年）10月1日起施行。

2. 除本法附则有特别规定外，改正后的新法规定也适用于本法施行前的行政行为、与申请相关的行政机关的不作为以及本法施行前发生的其他事项等。但根据本法改正前规定已经发生效力的则不受影响。

3. 本法施行前提出的诉讼、审查请求、异议申请及其他不服申请（以下称为“诉愿等”），在本法施行后仍按旧法规定处理。对于本法施行前提起的诉愿等的裁决、决定以及其他处分（以下称为“裁决等”）或者本法施行前提起的诉愿等本法施行后作出的裁决等不服的诉愿等，也按旧法规定处理。

4．本法施行后，有关前项诉愿等可根据《行政不服审查法》提起的不服申请，在适用《行政不服审查法》以外法律的，则视为根据《行政不服审查法》提起的不服申请。

5．根据附则第三款规定，针对本法施行后提出的审查申请、异议申请及其他不服申请的裁决等，不可作为根据《行政不服审查法》规定的不服申请来对待。

6．根据本法规定，对于本法施行前的行政行为可依据改正前的规定提出诉愿、且未确定起诉期间的，其可依据《行政不服审查法》提起不服申请的期间从本法施行之日起计算。

8．对于本法施行前实施的处罚，适用旧法规定。

9．除前八款规定的事项外，有关本法施行的必要措施由政令规定。

10．若某一法律上的相关规定因本法及《有关〈行政诉讼法〉施行与相关法律的协调之法律》（昭和37年法律第140号）的施行需要改正时，首先根据本法规定进行改正，其次根据《有关〈行政诉讼法〉施行与相关法律的协调之法律》的规定进行改正。

附则　1965年（昭和40年）3月31日法律第36号　抄

【施行日期】

第一条　本法自1965年（昭和40年）4月1日起施行。

【伴随其他法令部分改正的原则】

第五条　除另有规定处，根据第二章规定，改正后的法令规定适用于1965年（昭和40年）度以后的所得税及法人税；1964年（昭和39年）度以前的所得税及法人税仍按之前规定处理。

附则　1968年（昭和43年）6月15日法律第99号　抄

【施行日期】

1．本法自公布之日起施行。

【过渡性规定】

2．本法施行后，如果没有其他委任状，那么原文部省文化局、文化财保护委员会事务局、文部省附属机关（仅限于相当本法所规定的附属于文化厅的机关）及文化财保护委员会的附属机关（除文化财审议会外）的职员在同一工作条件下成为文化厅职员。

3．在本法施行后，文化财保护委员会、文部大臣根据改正前的《文化财保护法》、《著作权法》、《有关著作权居间业务之法律》、《有关加入〈世界版权公约〉的著作权法的特例之法律》、《枪炮刀剑等持有取缔法》及《国立剧场法》的规定作出的许可、认可、指定、通知及其他行政行为，视为文部大臣、文化厅长官根据修改后的法律规定所出的许可、认可、指定、通知及其他行政行为。

4．在本法施行后，根据改正前的《文化财保护法》、《著作权法》、《有关著作权居间业务之法律》、《有关加入〈世界版权公约〉的著作权法的特例之法律》、《枪炮刀剑等持有取缔法》及《国立剧场法》的规定，向文化财保护委员会、文部大臣提出的申请、报告及其他请求，视为根据修改后的法律规定向文部大臣、文化厅长官提出的申请、报告及其他请求。

5．本法施行后，原有《文化财保护委员会规则》作为文部省的政令，依然有效。

附则　1971年（昭和46年）5月31日法律第88号　抄

【施行日期】

第一条　本法自1971年（昭和46年）7月1日起施行。

附则　1971年（昭和46年）6月1日法律第96号　抄

【施行日期】

1．本法自公布之日起施行。

附则　1971年（昭和47年）6月3日法律第52号　抄

【施行日期】

第一条　在本法公布之日起30日的范围内，由政令决定施行日期。

【有关土地调整委员会以及中央公害审查委员会的行政行为的对应措施】

第十六条 本法施行前，土地调整委员会或中央公害审查委员会根据改正前的法律规定实施的相关行政行为，除政令另有规定外，视为公害等调整委员会根据改正后的相关法律实施的行政行为。

附则 1975年（昭和50年）7月1日法律第49号 抄

【施行日期】

1. 本法自公布之日起3个月后施行。

【发现遗迹时的停止命令等特例】

2. 自本法施行之日起5年内，改正后的《文化财保护法》（以下称为"新法"）第五十七条之五第二款但书中的"3个月"改为"6个月"、第五款但书中的"6个月"改为"9个月"。在该情况下，有关自本法施行之日起5年内实施了该条第二款规定的措施的，即便是5年后，也依然以5年前的规定来处理。

【过程性措施】

3. 本法施行后，在根据改正前的《文化财保护法》（以下称为"旧法"）第五十六条之三第一款规定指定的重要无形文化财中，文部大臣认为有必要将根据旧法第五十六条之三第二款认定的"保持者"改换为根据新法第五十六条之三第二款认定的"保持团体"的，其必须在本法施行后1年内，根据旧法第五十六条之三第二款规定撤销保持者认定的同时，根据新法第五十六条之三第二项规定认定为保持团体。对于这种情况，准用新法第五十六条之三第三款及第五十六条之四第三款规定。

4. 本法施行后，根据旧法第五十六条之十第一款规定指定的"重要民俗资料"视为根据新法第五十六条之十第一款规定指定的"重要有形民俗文化财"；同时根据旧法第五十六条之十第二款中准用旧法第二十八条第三款规定所交付的"重要民俗资料指定证书"视为根据新法第五十六条之十第二款中准用新法第二十八条第三款规定所交付的"重要有形民俗文化财指定证书"。

5. 在本法施行前，与旧法第五十七条之二第一款规定的发掘相关申请，根据旧法第五十七条之二的规定来处理，不受新法第五十七条之二、第五十七条之三规定的限制。

6. 在本法施行前，有关对制定了新法第五十七条之三第一款所规定事业计划的国家机关等（除就该事业计划实施根据旧法第五十七条之二第一款规定已经提出申请外）适用新法第五十七条之三的规定，该条第一款中的“在制定该发掘计划时，事先……”改为“本法施行后不得延迟”。

7. 对于本法施行前，根据旧法第八十四条第一款规定已报告的遗迹，旧法第八十四条规定依然有效，并不受新法第五十七条之五（与旧法第八十七条所规定的各省各厅长官不对应的新法第五十七条之三第一款规定的国家机关等，新法第五十七条之六）规定的影响。

8. 有关本法施行前旧法第八十七条所规定的各省各厅长官根据旧法第九十条第一款第八项规定所认可的、与已通知相关遗迹，旧法第九十条第一款第八项通知相关的旧法第九十条第三款规定依然有效，不受新法第五十七条之六规定的影响。

9. 有关本法施行前行为的罚则适用，依据旧法规定。

10. 除前七款中的规定外，与本法施行相关的必要措施，由政令规定。

附则　1983 年（昭和 58 年）12 月 2 日法律第 78 号　抄

1. 本法（除第一条外）自 1983 年（昭和 59 年）7 月 1 日起施行。

2. 在本法施行前，根据法律规定所设置的机关与本法施行后《国家行政组织法》以及基于本法改正后相关法律所规定的政令（以下称为“相关政令”）设置的机关之间，可通过政令规范必要过渡性措施以及伴随其他法律的施行，制定、修改或废止相关政令。

附则　1993 年（平成 5 年）11 月 12 日法律第 89 号　抄

【施行日期】

1.《行政手续法》（平成 5 年法律第 88 号）自施行之日起施行。

【有关咨询等不利处分的对应措施】

2. 根据《行政手续法》第十三条规定，对于向依据本法施行前的法令而设立的审议会及其他合议制机关等提起听证、申辩及其他说明程序等而受到不利处分的，依照从前的规定处理，不受本法改正后的相关法律规定的影响。

【有关罚则的对应措施】

第十三条 有关本法施行前行为的罚则，依照之前规定。

【有关协调听证之规定的过渡性措施】

第十四条 本法施行前，根据法律规定实施的听证、意见听取、听证会（除与不利处罚相关行为外）以及与之相关的程序等，视为根据改正后相关对应法律规定实施的行为。

第十五条 除附则第二条至前条规定的事项外，有关本法施行的其他必要措施由政令规定。

附则 1994 年（平成 6 年）6 月 29 日法律第 49 号 抄

【施行日期】

1. 本法第一章及次款规定，自《地方自治法部分改正之法律》（平成 6 年法律第 48 号）中《地方自治法》第二编第十二章的改正规定施行之日起施行；本法第二章规定自《地方自治法部分改正之法律》中《地方自治法》第三编第三章的改正规定施行之日起施行。

附则 1994 年（平成 6 年）11 月 11 日法律第 97 号 抄

【施行日期】

第一条 本法自公布之日起施行。

【伴随《文化财保护法》部分改正的对应措施】

第四条 有关第四条规定施行前，根据改正前《文化财保护法》第四十六条第一款（包括第五十六条之十四中的准用）规定的“出让申请”以及改正前该条第一款但书（包括第五十六条之十四中的准用）规定的“承认申请”等，依照从前的规定处理，不受根据第四条规定改正后《文化财保护法》规定的影响。

【有关罚则的对应措施】

第二十条 对于本法（附则第一条各项列举的规定）施行前完成的行为以及依据附则第二条、第四条、第七条第二款、第八条、第十一条、第十二条第二款、第十三条及第十五条第四款规定遵照从前第一条、第四条、第八条、

第九条、第十三条、第二十七条、第二十八条及第三十条规定施行之后的行为处罚，仍然依照之前规定。

【委任立法】

第二十一条 除附则第二条至前条所规定的内容外，有关本法施行所应该采取的其他必要对应措施（包括罚则的过渡措施），由政令规定。

附则 1996 年（平成 8 年）6 月 12 日法律第 66 号 抄

【施行日期】

1. 在本法公布后 9 个月内，由政令决定开始施行日。

【有关重要文化财公开展出申请的过渡性规定】

2. 本法施行时，改正前的《文化财保护法》（以下称为“旧法”）第五十三条第一款规定的获得许可，或提出申请后，改正后的《文化财保护法》（以下称为“新法”）第五十三条第一款但书所规定的、由公开承认设施的设置者在其公开设施所举办的展览会上的公开，视为根据该条第二款规定的许可或公开。

3. 在本法实施前，根据旧法第五十三条第一款但书规定提出了公开申请的，文化厅长官以外的国家机关或地方公共团体，在主办新法第五十三条第一款但书所规定的公开承认设施举办展览会或其他展览等，视为根据该条第二款规定的公开展出申请。

4. 文化厅长官以外的国家机关或地方公共团体实施新法第五十六条之十五第一款但书规定、在免除事先公开申请的设施主办展览会或其他展览，或者免除事先公开申请的设施设置者在其免除事先公开申请的设施上实施公开的，根据本法施行前旧法第五十六条之十五第一款规定提出的公开申请，视为根据新法第五十六条之十五第一款但书规定所提出的公开申请。

【有关罚则的过渡性规定】

5. 对于本法施行前行为的处罚，适用旧法规定。

【研究】

6. 在本法施行 10 年后，政府必须总结本法的适用状况、应保护的文化财的保护状况，研究有形文化财登录的相关制度等，并在此基础上制定适合发展的措施。

附则　1999年（平成11年）7月16日法律第87号　抄

【施行日期】

第一条　本法自2000年（平成12年）4月1日起施行。但以下各项规定由该各项规定的日期开始施行。

（一）第一条中有关《地方自治法》第二百五十条以下五条、节名以及两款及款名的改正规定（仅限于与该法第二百五十条之九第一款相关、即获得参众两院同意的部分）、第四十条中《自然公园法》附则第九条、第十条的改正规定（仅限与附则第十条相关部分）、第二百四十四条规定（除《农业改良促进法》第十四条之三的改正规定相关部分外）、第四百二十七条规定（除与《市、町、村合并特例法》第六条、第八条以及第十七条的改正规定相关部分外）以及附则第七条、第十条、第十二条、第五十九条但书、第六十条第四款及第五款、第七十三条、第七十七条、第一百五十七条第四款至第六款、第一百六十条、第一百六十三条、第一百六十四条、以及第二百〇二条规定的公布日。

【《文化财保护法》部分改正的对应措施】

第五十八条　施行日之前发现的文化财、在本法施行时未判明所有人的，其所有权的归属以及相关褒赏金等，根据第一百三十五条规定，改正前的《文化财保护法》（以下称为“旧《文化财保护法》”）第五十九条第一款所规定的文化财以及根据旧《文化财保护法》第六十一条第二款所规定的文化财中，属国家机关在调查埋藏文化财发掘时发现的文化财的，根据第一百三十五条规定，适用改正后的《文化财保护法》（以下称为“新《文化财保护法》”）第六十三条规定，对于其他文化财则适用新《文化财保护法》第六十三条之二规定。

第五十九条　在由旧《文化财保护法》第六十三条第一款规定的、归属国家的文化财中，在本法施行时由地方公共团体保管（除与《物品管理法》第八条第三款或第六条所规定的物品管理官管理相关外）的文化财所有权，自本法施行之日起归属于保管该文化财的地方公共团体所有。但截至本法施行日之前，文部省政令规定该地方公共团体已经另行提出申请的，则不受此限。

【国家等的事务】

第一百五十九条　除本法改正前各项法律所规定的事项外，地方公共团体机关根据法律或法令，管理或实施国家、其他地方公共团体事务（附则第一百六十一条中称为“国家等的事务”），视为本法施行后，地方公共团体根据法律或法令，作为该地方公共团体事务来处理。

【有关处分、申请的过渡性措施】

第一百六十条　本法（附则第一条各项所列举的规定。在本条以及附则第一百六十三条中相同）施行前，根据改正前各项法律之规定的许可等具体行政行为（以下称为“具体的行政行为”）或者根据改正前的各项法律规定的许可申请等行为（以下称为“申请等行为”），在本法施行之日，与该行为相关的行政事务处理者不同的，除附则第二条至前条规定或改正后的相关法律（包括根据该法律的相关行政命令）所规定对应措施外，就本法施行后各项法律的适用问题，视为根据改正后各项法律规定所作出的具体行政行为或申请等。

2. 本法施行前，根据改正前的各相关法律规定，必须向国家机关或地方公共团体机关报告、申请或提出等其他手续的事项，在本法实施日之前未提出的，除本法及政令有特别规定外，视为根据改正后的相关法律规定的必须向国家机关或地方公共团体机关的报告、申请、或提出等其他手续，适用本法改正后的相关法律规定。

【有关不服申请的过渡性措施】

第一百六十一条　在本法施行前实施的与国家等事务相关的具体行政行为的行政机关（以下本条称为“处分厅”），在本法施行前的《行政不服审查法》中规定的上级行政机关（以下称为“上级行政厅”）实施的行政行为的不服申请，被视为本法施行后的该行政机关的上级机关实施的行政行为，适用《行政不服审查法》的规定，即将处分厅的上级行政厅被视为行政厅，作为施行日之前该处分厅的上级行政厅。

2. 当前款被视为行政厅的上级行政厅为地方公共团体机关时，该机关根据《行政不服审查法》处理的行政事务则为新《地方自治法》第二条第九款第一项规定的第一项法定受托事务。

【有关手续费的过渡性措施】

第一百六十二条 在施行前，根据改正前的各项法律（包含政令）应交纳的手续费，除本法以及基于本法的政令另有规定外，仍然依据之前规定。

【有关罚则的过渡性性规定】

第一百六十三条 对本法施行前行为的处罚，适用施行前的法律。

【其他政令委托的过渡性措施】

第一百六十四条 除附则的规定外，伴随本法施行的其他必要的过渡性措施（包括罚则的过渡性措施），由政令规定。

2. 有关适用附则第十八条、第五十一条以及第一百八十四条规定的必要事项，由政令规定。

【研究】

第二百五十条 有关新《地方自治法》第二条第九款第一项规定的“第一项法定受托事务”，在尽可能不设定新事务的同时，从推动地方分权的观点出发，适当、确实地从新思考新《地方自治法》附表（一）中所列举的事务以及基于新《地方自治法》政令所表明的事务。

第二百五十一条 为促进地方公共团体自主、自立执行地方行政事务，政府应该根据国家与地方公共团体间公共事务的分担情况，充分考虑并研究经济情势的变化、采取相应的必要措施，以确保地方拥有充足财源。

第二百五十二条 伴随医疗保险制度、年金制度等的改革，政府应立足于确保被保险人等的利益与便利、提高事务处理效率等，研讨社会保险事务的处理体制、从业人员的存在形态等，如认为必要应采取必要的改进措施。

附则 1999 年（平成 11 年）7 月 16 日法律第 102 号 抄

【施行日期】

第一条 本法自《内阁法部分修改之法律》（平成 11 年法律第 88 号）施行之日起施行。但以下各项之规定，自各项所定之日起施行。

（一）略。

（二）附则第十条第一款及第五款、第十四条第三款、第二十三条、第二十八条以及第三十条，自公布之日起施行。

【职员身份的继承】

第三条 除另有任命外，本法施行时前总理府、法务省、外务省、大藏省、文部省、厚生省、农林水产省、通商产业省、运输省、邮政省、劳动省、建设省以及自治省（以下统称为“前府省”）的职员（除《国家行政组织法》第八条所规定的审议会等的会长或委员长及委员、中央防灾会议委员、日本工业标准调查会会长及委员以及由政令规定与之类似职位外），在同等工作条件下，作为本法施行后的内阁府、总务省、法务省、外务省、财务省、文部科学省、厚生劳动省、农林水产省、经济产业省、国土交通省、环境省（以下统称为“新府省”）以及由政令设置的部局或机关的职员。

【其他过渡性措施】

第三十条 除第二条至前条的规定外，伴随本法施行的必要过渡性措施，由其他法律规定。

附则 1999年（平成11年）12月22日法律第160号 抄

【施行日期】

第一条 本法（除第二条、第三条外）自2001年（平成13年）1月6日起施行。

附则 1999年（平成11年）12月22日法律第178号 抄

【施行日期】

第一条 本法自2001年（平成13年）1月6日起施行，但附则第九条，由政令在本法施行之日起不超过6个月的范围内决定施行日。

附则 1999年（平成11年）12月22日法律第179号 抄

【施行日期】

第一条 本法自2001年（平成13年）1月6日起施行，但附则第八条规定，由政令在本法施行之日起不超过6个月的范围内决定施行日。

附则 2000年（平成12年）5月19日法律第73号 抄

【施行日期】

第一条 本法在其公布之日起不超过1年的范围内由政令决定施行日。

附则 2002年（平成14年）2月8日法律第1号 抄

【施行日期】

第一条 本法自公布之日起施行。

附则 2002年（平成14年）7月3日法律第82号 抄

本法自日本加入的《禁止和防止非法进出口文化财产和非法转让其所有权的方法的公约》生效之日起施行。

附则 2004年（平成16年）5月28日法律第61号 抄

【施行日期】

第一条 本法自2005年（平成17年）4月1日起施行。

附则 2004年（平成16年）6月9日法律第84号 抄

【施行日期】

第一条 本法在其公布之日起不超过1年的范围内，由政令决定施行日。

【研讨】

第五十条 本法施行5年后，政府应该就新法施行状况进行调研，如认为必要可根据调研结果，采取必要改进措施。

附则 2006年（平成18年）5月31日法律第46号 抄

【施行日期】

第一条 本法在其公布之日起不超过一年六个月的范围内由政令决定施行日，

但以下各项规定自该项所规定之日起施行。

（一）略。

（二）略。

（三）第一条中的《都市规划法》第五条之二第一款及第二款、第六条、第八条第二款及第三款、第十三条第三款、第十五条第一款、第十九条第三款及第五款的修改，该条第六款的删除规定以及该法第二十一条、第二十二条第一款、第八十七条之二的改正规定，第二条中的《建筑基准法》第六条第一款的改正规定、第三条、第六条、第七条中《都市再生特别措置法》第五十一条第四款的改正规定以及附则第三条、第四条第一款、第五条、第八条及第十三条规定等，自其公布之日起 6 个月内由政令规定施行日。

附则　2006 年（平成 18 年）6 月 15 日法律第 73 号　抄

【施行日期】

第一条　本法在其公布之日起一年六个月内，由政令决定施行日。

附则　2007 年（平成 19 年）3 月 30 日法律第 7 号　抄

【施行日期】

第一条　本法自 2007 年（平成 19 年）4 月 1 日起施行。

【文化财保护法部分改正的过渡性措施】

第十一条　根据前条规定，有关改正后《文化财保护法》第一百〇四条第一款规定的适用，施行日之前研究所实施发掘埋藏文化财（该法第九十二条第一款规定的埋藏文化财）调查发现的，该法第一百〇二条第二款所规定的文化财，视为机构发现的文化财。

附则　2011 年（平成 23 年）5 月 2 日法律第 37 号　抄

【施行日期】

第一条　本法自公布之日起施行。

【有关罚则的过渡性措施】

第二十三条　对于本法（附则第一条所列各项规定，在该规定）施行前行为的罚则，适用之前法律。

【法令委任】

第二十四条 除附则第二条至前条以及附则第三十六条中规定的过渡性措施外，有关本法实施的过渡性措施，由政令规定。

附则 2014年（平成26年）6月4日法律第51号 抄

【施行日期】

第一条 本法自2015年（平成27年）4月1日起施行。

【有关罚则的过渡性措施】

第八条 对于本法施行前实施行为的罚则，适用之前法律。

【法令委任】

第九条 除附则第二条至前条规定的过渡性措施外，有关本法施行的过渡性措施（包括罚则的过渡性措施），由政令规定。

附则 2014年（平成26年）6月13日法律第69号 抄

【施行日期】

第一条 本法自《行政不服审查法》（2014平成26年法律第68号）的施行日起施行。

附则 2018年（平成30年）6月8日号外法律第42号 抄

【施行日期】

第一条 本法自2019年（平成31年）4月1日起施行。

【有关罚则的过渡性措施】

第二条 对于本法施行前实施行为的罚则，适用之前法律。

【法令委任】

第三条 除前条规定外，有关本法施行的必要过渡性措施，由政令规定。

（二）《非法进出口文化财产[①]规制法》

非法进出口文化财产规制法

（周超　翻译校对）

2002 年（平成 14 年）7 月 3 日法律第 81 号 [制定]
2004 年（平成 16 年）5 月 28 日号外法律第 61 号
[根据文化财保护法修改法附则第 13 条的修改]

【目的】

第一条　为确保《禁止和防止非法进出口文化财产和非法转让其所有权的方法的公约》（以下简称“《公约》”）在国内的实施，采取必要措施限制或禁止被盗文化财产的进出口以及返还等，特制定本法。

【定义】

第二条　本法中的“文化财产”是指，国内文化财产以及《公约》缔约国（以下简称“外国”）基于《公约》第一条规定指定的物件。

2. 本法中的“国内文化财产”是指，《公约》第一条第（1）项至第（11）项所列举的各类物件中，基于《文化财保护法》[②]第二十七条第一款规定

① 鉴于日本文化財の不法な輸出入等の規制等に関する法律　（平成14年7月3日法律第81号）（即《文化财产非法进出口规制法》）提交联合国教科文法律数据库的英文版本名称为 Act Concerning Controls on the Illicit Export and Import of Cultural Property，将“文化财”翻译为“Cultural Property”（即“文化财产”），本法也是为了执行《1970 年公约》而制定，因此，本法将“文化财”翻译为“文化财产”。

② 1950 年（昭和 25 年）5 月 30 日法律 214 号。

被指定的重要文化财产、第七十八条第一款规定被指定的重要有形民俗文化财产以及第一百零九条第一款被指定的史迹名胜天然纪念物等。

【特定的外国文化财产】

第三条 外务大臣在获得《公约》第七条第（2）项、第（9）项所规定设施的文化财产被盗通知后，立刻通告文部科学大臣，不得延迟。

2. 在收到外务大臣前款通知后，文部科学大臣根据文部科学省政令规定，将该通知中的相关文化财产指定为特定外国文化财产。

3. 根据前款规定，文部科学大臣在指定时，必须与经济产业大臣进行协商。

【进口许可】

第四条 根据1949年《外汇及对外贸易法》[①]第五十二条规定，特定外国文化财产的进口者有义务在申请获得许可后才能进口。[②]

【申请的公示等】

第五条 根据《文化财保护法》第三十三条（含第八十条、第一百一十八条及第一百二十条中的准用情形）规定，文化厅长官就国内文化财产（仅限于被损毁、遗失或被盗等）的上报时，必须在《官报》上公示，同时，国内文化财产发生《公约》第七条第（2）项、第（9）项规定情形时，必须通告外务大臣。

2. 外务大臣在获得前款通报后，应该就所获通告内容通告外国。

【特定外国文化财产的善意取得规则】

第六条 特定外国文化财产的占有人就特定外国文化财产的占有具备《民法》[③]第一百九十二条规定条件，当本法第三条第一款规定的被盗被害人根据第

① 1949年（昭和24年）12月1日法律第228号。

② 当然这种情况下，证书几乎不可能颁发。

③ 1896年（明治29年）4月27日法律第89号。

一百九十三条规定请求返还的，即便被盗时起已经经过 2 年并在 10 年期限内，受害人依然可以请求占有人返还[①]。但当该特定外国文化财产进入我国境内后、依据本法第三条第二款规定已被指定的，则不在此限。

2. 在前款情形下，受害人依然可以请求占有人返还的，须先向占有人作出相应赔偿。

【为加强国民理解等的措施】

第七条 国家必须努力通过教育、宣传活动等，加强国民对防止文化财产的非法进出口和所有权非法转让的理解，并能积极协助国家防止文化财产的非法进出口和所有权非法转让等。

附则

【施行日期】

本法自《公约》在日本国生效之日起实施。

【过渡措施】

本法施行前的被盗文化财产不适用第三条规定。

本法施行前的被损毁、遗失或被盗文化财产不适用本法第五条规定。

附则 2004 年（平成 16 年）5 月 28 日法律第 61 号抄

【施行日期】

第一条 本法自 2005 年（平成 17 年）4 月 1 日起施行。

---

① 被盗的外国文化财产所有人自文化财产被盗之日起 10 年内可申请返还，突破了《日本民法典》中有关追索被盗财产 2 年的时效规定。

（三）《关于国宝或重要文化财的变更现状、出口及重要有形民俗文化财的出口的许可申请等规则》

关于国宝或重要文化财的变更现状、出口及重要有形民俗文化财的出口的许可申请等规则

（1954年6月29日文化财保护委员会规则第3号）

（周超　翻译校对）

最终修正：2005年3月28日文部科学省令第11号

根据文化财保护法（1950年法律第214号）第15条第1项及第43条第2项（含该法第91条第3项规定的比照适用情况）的规定，有关国宝或重要文化财变更现状的许可申请等事项按以下规则办理。

（国宝或重要文化财变更现状等的许可申请）

第一条　根据文化财保护法（1950年法律第214号。以下称“法”）第43条第1项规定将要申请许可的人士（以下称“变更现状等许可申请者”），应向文化厅厅长（根据法第184条第1项第2号及文化财保护法实施令（1975年政令第267号。以下称“令”）第5条第3项第1号的规定，由都道府县或指定城市等（指地方自治法（1947年法律第67号）第252条第19款第1项规定的指定城市或该法第252条第22款第1项规定的核心市。以下相同）的教育委员会进行该许可时，该都道府县或指定城市等的教育委员会）提交记载

以下事项的许可申请书。

一　国宝或重要文化财的名称及件数

二　指定日期及证书编号

三　国宝或重要文化财指定证书中记载的所在地点

四　所有者的姓名或名称及地址

五　有管理责任人时，其姓名及地址

六　有管理团体时，其名称及办公场所地址

七　变更现状等许可申请者的姓名及地址，或名称、代表者的姓名及办公场所地址

八　需要进行变更现状或对保存产生影响的行为（以下称“变更现状等”）的理由

九　变更现状等的内容及实施方法

十　现所在地点与指定证书中记载的所在地点不同时，现所在地点

十一　为变更现状等要变更所在地点时，变更后的所在地点以及变更现状等结束后应归还的所在地点及其期限

十二　开始及结束变更现状等的预定期限

十三　进行变更现状等相关工程或其他行为的实施者的姓名及地址，或名称、代表者的姓名及办公场所地址

十四　其他可参考事项

（国宝或重要文化财变更现状等的许可申请书的附件等）

第二条　上一条的许可申请书中应附上如下文件、图纸及照片。

一　变更现状等的设计说明书及设计图

二　将要变更现状等部分的照片或示意图

三　有资料可充分证明需要变更现状等的理由时，附上该资料

四　变更现状等许可申请者并非所有者时，附上所有者的承诺书

五　有管理责任人时，如变更现状等许可申请者并非管理责任人，附上管理责任人的承诺书

六　有管理团体时，如变更现状等许可申请者并非管理团体，附上管理

团体的承诺书

（国宝或重要文化财出口的许可申请）

第三条 根据法第44条补充条款规定将要申请许可的人士（以下称“重要文化财等出口许可申请者”），应向文化厅厅长提交记载以下事项的许可申请书。

一 国宝或重要文化财的名称及件数

二 指定日期及证书编号

三 有管理团体时，其名称、办公场所地址及代表者的姓名

四 重要文化财等出口许可申请者的姓名或名称及地址，其为法人时，法人代表者的姓名

五 需要出口的理由

六 出口的时期或期限

七 出口时的运送方法

八 出口后的展览会等的主办者、名称、会场及会期

九 对出口后的展览会等的管理方法

十 进行出口及展览会等时的相关保险事项

十一 对出口后的展览会等的安防措施

十二 其他可参考事项

（国宝或重要文化财出口的许可申请书的附件等）

第四条 上一条许可申请书中应附上如下文件。

一 国宝或重要文化财的照片

二 出口后的展览会等的概要及会场图纸

三 与出口后的展览会等主办者的协议

四 有资料可充分证明需要出口的理由时，附上该资料

五 重要文化财等出口许可申请者并非所有者时，附上所有者的承诺书

六 有管理团体时，如重要文化财等出口许可申请者并非管理团体，附上管理团体的承诺书

七 其他可参考资料

（重要有形民俗文化财出口的许可申请）

第五条 根据法第 82 条规定将要申请许可的人士（以下称“重要有形民俗文化财出口许可申请者），应向文化厅厅长提交记载如下事项的许可申请书。

一 重要有形民俗文化财的名称及件数

二 指定日期及证书编号

三 有管理团体时，其名称、办公场所地址及代表者的姓名

四 重要有形民俗文化财出口许可申请者的姓名或名称及地址，其为法人时，法人代表者的姓名

五 需要出口的理由

六 出口的时期或期限

七 出口地及接收者的姓名或名称及住址，其为法人时，法人代表者的姓名

八 出口后使用保管等情况的计划概要

九 其他可参考事项

（重要有形民俗文化财出口的许可申请书的附件等）

第六条 上一条的许可申请书中应附上如下文件。

一 重要有形民俗文化财的照片

二 有资料可充分证明需要出口的理由时，附上该资料

三 重要有形民俗文化财出口许可申请者并非所有者时，附上所有者的承诺书

四 有管理团体时，如重要有形民俗文化财出口许可申请者并非管理团体，附上管理团体的承诺书

五 其他可参考资料

（结束的报告）

第七条 根据法第 43 条第 1 项规定已得到许可的人士，与该许可有关的变更现状等结束时，应及时向文化厅厅长（根据法 184 条第 1 项第 2 号及令第 5

条第3项第1号的规定由都道府县或指定城市等的教育委员会进行该许可时，该都道府县或指定城市等的教育委员会）报告。

2. 前项的结束报告中应附上表示其结果的照片或示意图。

3. 根据法第44条补充条款或第82条的规定已得到许可的人士，与该许可有关的出口结束时，应及时向文化厅厅长报告。

（维护措施的范围）

第八条 法第43条第2项的维护措施的范围应符合以下情况。

一 在国宝或重要文化财损毁的情况下，将该国宝或重要文化财恢复到指定时的原状（对于指定后得到变更现状等许可的，为该变更现状等后的原状）且不影响其价值时。

二 在国宝或重要文化财损毁的情况下，为防止该损毁扩大而采取应急措施时。

（由国家机关进行的变更现状等）

第九条 各省各厅的最高长官及其他国家机关针对国宝、重要文化财或重要有形民俗文化财的变更现状等或出口，根据法第168条第1项第1号或第2号或者第2项的规定将要请求批准时，比照适用第1条至第6条的规定，根据法第168条第1项第1号或第2号或者第2项的规定已受到批准时，比照适用第7条的规定。

2. 法第168条第3项中比照适用的法第43条第2项的维护措施的范围应符合上一条所列情况。

附则

该规则自1954年7月1日起实施。

附则（1968年12月26日文部省令第31号）抄

1. 该省令自公布之日起实施。

附则（1975 年 9 月 30 日文部省令第 33 号）抄

1. 该省令自文化财保护法部分修正法案实施之日（1975 年 10 月 1 日）起实施。

附则（1978 年 9 月 12 日文部省令第 34 号）

该省令自公布之日起实施。

附则（2000 年 3 月 8 日文部省令第 8 号）

该省令自 2000 年 4 月 1 日起实施。

附则（2002 年 10 月 30 日文部科学省令第 43 号）

1. 该省令自文化财保护法部分修正法案（2002 年法律第 82 号）实施之日（2002 年 12 月 9 日）起实施。

2. 该省令实施时针对根据文化财保护法（1950 年法律第 214 号）第 44 条补充条款的规定进行的许可申请，仍遵循以往的法令。

附则（2005 年 3 月 28 日文部科学省令第 11 号）

该省令自 2005 年 4 月 1 日起实施。

九、韩　国

述 评

因为相似的文化背景，韩国历史上颁布的几部文化遗产保护法，基本上都与日本文化遗产保护法有关，有些甚至可以说就是日本人为推行自己的殖民政策而制定、移植过来的。譬如，人们从《寺刹令》中很容易看到日本《古社寺保护法》的影子；从《朝鲜宝物古迹名胜天然纪念物保存令》中，也很容易看到日本《史迹名胜天然纪念物保存法》的影子。

1962年，韩国颁布《文化财保护法》，这部韩国文物保护工作的综合法律，历经多次修订，基本上总能反映出韩国人对文化遗产的最新观点。在这部法律中，韩国人首先接受了日本人提出的“文化财”这一全新理念，同时对日本人提出的“有形文化财”、“无形文化财”、“民俗文化财”、“纪念物”等文化财分类也全盘接受，立法目的也几乎一致。《文化财保护法》从公布之后，多次被部分修正，最近的一次修正是在2018年，并于2019年4月17日公布。最新修正的《文化财保护法》共计12章，规定了本法中出现的专有名词、文化财保护的基本原则、政府职责、文化财的保护、各项文化财管理制度、相关权利与法律以及违法者需承担的法律责任等。该法涉及文化财进出境管理的法条主要集中在第6章、第8章及相关处罚规定。

1962年，韩国在制定《文化财保护法》的同时设立文化财管理局，1990年文化财管理局改制并升格为文化财厅（相当于国家文物局），隶属于中央政府文化观光部。文化财厅分为预算法律制度检查局；政策局，下设政策科、无形文化财科、发掘科、安全科；保存局，下设保存政策科、古都保存科、有形文化财科、天然纪念物科、修理技术科；活用局，下设活用政策科、宫陵文化财科、国际协力科、近代文化财科、世界遗产科、文化遗产培训科。另外还有一个人事科，一位发言人。另外还设立了国立文化财研究所等六个研究所以及针对各个大型露天有形文化财，像宫殿、楼阁、陵墓等而设立的20多个管理所，韩国传统文化学校及韩国传统文化研修院等两所培训机构以及独立运营的中央故宫博物馆。

韩国专门负责全国文物出境的鉴定审核工作的机构是文化财鉴定官室，最早于1968年2月在金浦和釜山机场设立。以后逐渐在其他对外开放口岸如机场、港口、通关邮局、南北进出境事务所等地方增设，并依据工作量配备数量不等的文化财鉴定官。2007年1月，各地文化财鉴定官室统归文化财厅，隶属文化财厅安全科直接领导，经费和物资由文化财厅统一拨付。文化财鉴定官一般属于专业任期制国家公务员，根据工作业绩及安全科名额，合同最长为5年。[①] 文化财厅对鉴定官的文化素养、专业水平要求很高。成为文化财鉴定官需要经过文化财厅严格的考核选拔。文化财鉴定官的职责是对出境物品进行文物鉴定及确认；监视并防止文物非法出境；文物非法出境宣传；相关机关业务协助（比如搜查要领培训等）。此外，文化财鉴定官还会定期对海关人员和社会公众进行培训，培训计划会在年初公布。

文化财厅下设机构国外所在文化财团（Oversea Korea Cultural Heritage Foundation）是一个致力于对韩国流失文化财进行系统调查、研究、追索以及活用的财团法人，设有主席和秘书处，秘书处下设管理部、研究部、国际合作部、日本办公室（Janpan Office）和美国办公室（United States Office）。其具体职能参见韩国《文化财保护法》第69条。

① 根据《韩国文化财鉴定官室设置运营规定》，按照国家公务员法规定被录用的、在文化财鉴定官室工作的工作人员为“全勤鉴定委员”；而不适用于国家公务员法规定、按照另行委任程序聘用的工作人员为“非全勤鉴定委员”。

《文化财保护法》

文化财保护法

（崔景日　翻译校对）

[实行 2019.4.17] [法律第 15827 号，2018.10.16，部分修正]

第 1 章　总　则

第 1 条（目的） 本法律旨在通过保存文化财、传承民族文化，提升国民文化素养，为人类文化发展做出贡献。

第 2 条（定义） ①本法律中所指的“文化财”是人工或自然形成的国家、民族或世界性遗产，应具有高的历史、艺术、学术及景观等价值，如下列各号所示。< 修正 2015.3.27.>

1. 有形文化财：指建筑物、典籍、书迹、古文书、绘画、雕刻、工艺品等有形文化性产物，应具有高的历史、艺术或学术价值，以及符合此标准的考古资料。
2. 无形文化财：指经过世代相传的无形文化遗产中，符合下列任意一目的文化财。
   1）传统表演、艺术
   2）工艺、美术等相关传统技术
   3）韩医药、农耕、捕鱼等相关传统知识
   4）口头传统及表达
   5）衣食住等传统生活习惯

6）民间信仰等社会仪式

7）传统游戏、庆典及技艺、武艺

3. 纪念物：指下列各目所定事项

1）具有高的历史、学术价值的寺址、古墓、贝冢（贝丘）、城址、宫殿遗址、陶窑遗址、遗物包含层等历史遗迹及有特殊纪念意义的设施

2）具有高的艺术价值、景致出色的地方

3）具有高的历史、景观或学术价值的动物（包括其栖息地、繁殖地、迁徙地等）、植物（包括其自生地）、地形、地质、矿物、洞窟、生物学产物或特殊的自然现象

4. 民俗文化财：了解国民生活变化的必需品，与衣食住、职业、信仰、年例行活动等有关风俗或习惯的服装、器具、房屋等

②本法律中所指的“指定文化财”是下列各号所示的内容。<修正2014.1.28.>

1. 国家指定文化财：指根据第23至第26条，由文化财厅厅长指定的文化财

2. 市、道指定文化财：根据第70条第1项，由特别市市长、广域市市长、特别自治市市长、道知事及特别自治道知事（以下称“市、道知事”）指定的文化财

3. 文化财资料：指未进入1号和2号范围的文化财中，根据第70条第2项，由市、道知事指定的文化财

③本法律中所指的“注册文化财”是，根据第53条，在非指定文化财中，由文化财厅厅长注册的文化财。

④本法律中所指的“保护区域”是，固定在地面的有形物或一定的区域被指定为文化财时，指定文化财所占面积之外的区域，旨在保护该指定文化财。

⑤本法律中所指的“保护物”是，为保护文化财而指定的建筑或设施。

⑥本法律中所指的“历史文化环境”是，需要同文化财一并被保护的文化财周边自然景观、历史及文化价值高的空间等周边环境。

⑦本法律中所指的“建设工程”是，依照总统令规定的土木工程、建筑工程、

造景工程，或者因土地、海底形态变化的工程。

⑧本法律中所指的“国外所在文化财”是，与大韩民国历史和文化有直接关联的外流至国外（第 39 条、第 60 条第 1 项的外流至国外的文化财除外）的文化财。

第 3 条（文化财保护的基本原则）文化财的保存、管理及使用，必须以保持原状为基本原则。

第 4 条（国家及地方政府等职责）①国家必须制订和实施关于文化财保存、管理及使用的综合政策。

②地方政府根据国家政策和地方特色，必须制订和实施关于文化财保存、管理及使用的政策。

③国家及地方政府计划和实施各种开发项目时，必须确保文化财及文化财的保护物、保护区域、历史文化环境不受损坏。

④为了保存和管理文化财，国民必须积极协助国家及地方政府的政策实施。

第 5 条（同其他法律的关系）①关于文化财的保存、管理及使用，除其他法律中的特殊规定外，均以本法律为准。

②关于指定文化财（包括第 32 条的临时指定文化财）的维护、实测、设计、监理及埋藏文化财的保护和调查以及无形文化财的保护及振兴，另定细则。<修正 2015.3.27.>

第 2 章　文化财保护政策的制定及推进

第 6 条（文化财基本计划的制定）①为了保存，管理和使用文化财，文化财厅厅长与市、道知事协商后，每隔 5 年制定包含下列各号所示的综合性基本计划（以下简称“文化财基本计划”）。<修订 2012. 1. 26.，2015. 3. 27.，2017. 3. 21.>

1. 关于文化财保存的基本方向和目标

2. 对以往文化财基本计划的分析及评价

3. 文化财的维修，维护及复原相关事项

4. 文化财历史文化环境保护相关事项

5. 文化财安全管理相关事项

6. 文化财记录信息化相关事项

7. 关于文化财保存的资金的筹集

7 之 2. 国外所在文化财的收回及使用相关事项

7 之 3. 南北韩文化财交流合作相关事项

8. 文化财保存、管理及使用的研发相关事项

9. 其他关于文化财保存、管理及使用所需事项

②制订文化财基本计划时，文化财厅厅长必须听取总统令规定的所有者，管理者、管理团体及专家的意见。

③制订文化财基本计划后，文化财厅厅长必须告知市、道知事，并在官报告示。

④为制订文化财基本计划，文化财厅厅长可以请求市、道知事提供管辖区域的文化财资料。

第 6 条 2（文化财的研究开发）①为有效促进文化财的保护、管理及使用等研究开发，文化财厅厅长除固有研究外，还可实施共同研究等。

②第 1 项的共同研究，选定各领域的研究课题后，与大学、产业单位、地方政府、政府研究机关等机构签署协议并实施。

③第 2 项的共同研究，文化财厅厅长在预算范围内，可以支援共同研究的全部或部分费用。

④第 2 项的共同研究的项目及必要事项，依照总统令决定。[本条新设 2017. 3. 21.]

第 7 条（文化财保存实行计划建立）①文化财厅厅长及市、道知事必须制订和实施文化财基本计划的年度计划。

②市、道知事根据第 1 项制订和实施年度计划后，必须向文化财厅厅长报告

实施结果。

③文化财厅厅长及市、道知事制订年度计划后，必须公布。

④第 2 项的年度计划实施结果的报告对象、时间及流程，以及第 3 项的公布方法等事项，依照总统令规定。

第 8 条（文化财委员会的设置）①为调查和审议下列各号所示的文化财保存、管理及使用相关内容，在文化财厅设置文化财委员会。

1. 文化财基本计划相关事项
2. 国家指定文化财的指定及解除相关事项
3. 国家指定文化财的保护物、保护区域的指定及解除相关事项
4. 删除 <2015.3.27.>
5. 国家指定文化财的状态变更相关事项
6. 国家指定文化财的出境相关事项
7. 国家指定文化财的历史文化环境保护相关事项
8. 文化财的注册及注销相关事项
9. 埋藏文化财的发掘及评价相关事项
10. 认为对国家指定文化财保存、管理的专业或技术方面有重要意义的事项
11. 文化财保存、管理及使用等，由文化财厅厅长列为审议对象的其他事项

②文化财委员会委员由文化财厅厅长在符合下列各号任意一项的人员中委任。

1. 在《高等教育法》规定的大学的文化财保存、管理及或使用相关学院里，曾任或现任的副教授以上人员
2. 从事文化财保存、管理及使用相关工作 10 年以上人员
3. 从事人类学、社会学、建筑、城市规划、观光、环境、法律、宗教、媒体领域相关工作 10 年以上，有丰富的文化财相关知识和经验的专家

③根据第 1 项中各号事项，为了对各类文化财分类调查和审议，可以在文化财委员会设立分科委员会。

④为调查和审议，第 3 项的分科委员会，可以同其他分科委员会（以下称“联

合分科委员会”）共同召开委员会。

⑤分科委员会或联合分科委员会调查、审议第 1 项第 2 号到第 11 号事项时，看作文化财委员会的行为。< 新设 2017. 11. 28.>

⑥文化财委员会、分科委员会及联合分科委员会必须完成下列各号所示的会议记录。有必要时，可以速记或录音。< 修订 2017. 11. 28.>

1. 会议时间及地点

2. 出席委员

3. 审议内容及表决事项

⑦第 6 项的会议记录必须公开。但，对特定人物的财产利益产生影响或侵犯隐私等违反总统令规定的情况时，相关委员会通过表决可以不予公开。< 修订 2017. 11.28.>

⑧文化财委员会、分科委员会及联合分科委员会的组织、分管业务和运营等事项，依照总统令决定。< 修订 2017. 11. 28.>

⑨依照文化财厅厅长或各分科委员会委员长的命令，文化财委员会可以设置从事文化财委员会所需资料的收集、调查及研究等业务的非专职委员。< 新设 2011. 7. 14.，2017. 11. 28.>

⑩文化财委员会的委员、专门委员的人数、任期及资格等有关事项，依照总统令规定。< 新设 2011. 7. 14.，2017. 11. 28.>

第 9 条（韩国文化财财团的设立）①为保护、保存、普及及使用文化财，开发传统生活文化，设立文化财厅下属机构——韩国文化财财团（以下称“财团”）。< 修正 2014.5.28.>

②规定财团为法人。< 修正 2014.5.28.>

③为达到其设立目的，财团必须开展下列各号所示业务。< 新增 2014.5.28.>

1. 对演出、展示等无形文化财活动的支援和振兴

2. 文化财相关教育、出版、学术调查研究及内容的开发、利用

3.《埋藏文物保护与调查法》第 11 条第 1 款及同条第 3 款但书的埋藏文化财的发掘

4. 传统文化商品、食物、婚姻礼仪等的开发、普及和便利设施等的运营

5. 文化财开发援助等国际交流

6. 文化财保护运动的支援

7. 传统文化活动的复原及再现

8. 国家、地方政府或公共机关等委托的业务

9. 为财团设立目的的盈利业务及其他章程规定的业务

④根据章程规定，财团设置管理人员及必要职工。< 修正 2014.5.28.>

⑤除本法律规定内容外，财团适用《民法》中关于财团法人的规定。< 修正 2014.5.28.>

⑥财团运营经费可由国库支援。< 修正 2014.5.28.>

⑦对开展财团业务有必要时，国家或地方政府可以允许其无偿使用国有财产或共有财产，并从中受益。< 修正 2014.5.28.>

[题目修正 2014.5.28.]

第 3 章　建立文化财保护基础

第 10 条（文化财基础调查）①为防止文化财消失，国家及地方政府必须调查并记录现存文化财的现况、管理状态等。

②文化财厅厅长及地方政府负责人执行第 1 项的调查时，如有必要，有权直接调查或要求文化财所有者、管理者或从事调查、发掘工作的团体等提供相关资料。

③对非指定文化财进行调查时，文化财厅厅长及地方政府负责必须需事前征得相关文化财所有者或管理者同意。

④文化财调查的具体流程及方法等相关事项，依照总统令规定。

第 11 条（文化财信息化的促进）①文化财厅厅长必须有效地利用第 10 条的调查资料和文化财保存及管理等资料，构建和管理文化财信息体系，使国民能够轻松接触和利用文化财信息。

②为构建第 1 项的文化财信息体系，文化财厅厅长有权要求有关中央行政机关负责人、地方政府负责人以及博物馆、研究所等法人及团体，提供所需资

料。被要求者无特殊情况时必须遵从。< 修订 2017. 11. 28.>
③根据第 2 项，文化财厅厅长要求提交资料时，可以对相关中央行政机关及地方政府的负责人以外的人员支付正当的报酬。< 新设 2017. 11. 28.>
④第 1 项的文化财信息体系的构建范围、运营程序以及其他必要事项，依照总统令决定。< 修订 2017. 11. 28.>

第 12 条（工程建设时的文化财保护）工程建设有导致文化财面临损坏、消失、湮没的危险，或认为有必要保护文化财的历史文化环境时，工程建设执行人必须按照文化财厅厅长的指示采取必要的措施。措施所需经费由工程建设执行人承担。

第 13 条（历史文化环境保存地区的保护）①为保护指定文化财（除属于动产的文化财及无形文化财。适用于本条内容）的历史文化环境，市、道知事同文化财厅厅长协商后，必须以条款规定历史文化环境保存区域。
②对在指定文化财外围区域（如果被指定为保护区域时，则指保护区域）的外部地区实施的建设工程，即第 1 项的市、道知事指定的历史文化环境保存区域内实施的建设工程，担任建设工程批准、许可等事务的行政机构必须在批准、许可之前，分析建设工程对指定文化财保存造成的影响，并依照总统令规定，必须听取相关专家的意见。< 修正 2014.1.28.>
③考虑指定文化财的历史、艺术、学术、景观等价值和周围环境及其他必要因素，历史文化环境保存区域的范围一般定为文化财外围 500 米以内的区域。但，考虑文化财的特点和其地理条件等因素，认为文化财外围 500 米以外的建设工程对文化财造成影响时，历史文化环境保存区域的范围可以定为文化财外围 500 米以外的区域。
④文化财厅厅长或市、道知事指定文化财后，自指定公示之日起 6 个月内，在历史文化环境保存区域内，对指定文化财的保存造成影响的行为，制订具体的行为准则并告示。
⑤ 制订第 4 项的具体行为准则时，文化财厅厅长有权要求市、道知事或市长、郡守、区长（指自治区的区长。下同），市、道知事有权要求市长、郡守、区

长提供所需资料或意见。< 新增 2014.1.28.>

⑥ 在已告示具体行为准则的地区内实施的符合第 4 项中行为准则的建设工程，可以省略第 2 项的分析。< 新增 2014.1.28.>

⑦第 5 项的材料或意见提交流程等具体事项，依照文化体育观光部令规定。< 新增 2014.1.28.>

第 14 条（火灾等预防政策的制订和教育训练、宣传的实施）①为防止指定文化财及注册文化财的火灾、灾难及盗窃（以下称“火灾等”），文化财厅厅长及市、道知事必须制定和实施必要的政策。

②文化财厅厅长及地方政府负责人必须对文化财所有人，管理者及管理团体，进行火灾等的初期应对和平时预防管理的教育训练。

③文化财厅厅长及地方政府负责人必须对国民开展防止文化财火灾等的宣传。

[专门修订 2017. 3. 21.]

第 14 条 2（火灾等应对指南的准备）①文化财厅厅长及市、道知事根据指定文化财及注册文化财的特点，制作火灾等应对指南，并采取措施，使所有者，管理者及管理团体使用。

②对第 1 项的指南的内容、需要制作指南的文化财范围、手册指南内容的定期检查和完善等必要事项，依照总统令决定。

[本条新设 2017. 3. 21.]

第 14 条 3（火灾等防止设施的安装）①为预防及扑救火灾等，指定文化财的所有人，管理人和管理团体必须依照《火灾预防，消防设施的设置、维持及安全管理的法律》的规定，安装、维持和管理防止灾难的设施。为防止指定文化财的失窃，必须依照文化体育观光部令的标准，安装、维持和管理防盗装置。

②安装第 1 项的设施后，管理者力保其设施融合到历史文化环境保存区域。

③对下列各号所示的设施以及维护、管理人员，文化财厅厅长和地方政府负责人可以在预算的范围内补助全部或部分费用。

1. 第 1 项的消防设施，灾难预防设施和防盗设施。

2. 第 14 条 4 第 2 项的禁烟区域和吸烟区域的标识。

[本条新设 2017. 3. 21.]

第 14 条 4（禁烟区域的指定）①指定文化财、注册文化财、保护物、保护区域及保管设施（本条称为“指定文化财等”）的所有者，管理者或管理团体必须把属于指定文化财等的设施或区域指定为禁烟区域。但，在确定没有火灾隐患时，仅限于居住用建筑，可以指定禁烟区域和吸烟区域。

②指定文化财等的所有者，管理者或管理团体必须设立第 1 项的禁烟区域和吸烟区域的标识。

③对违反第 2 项的人，市、道知事有权命令限期整改。

④第 2 项的禁烟区域和吸烟区域的标识设置标准及方法，依照文化体育观光部令或市、道条例制定。

⑤任何人都不许在第 1 项中的禁烟区域内吸烟。

[本条新设 2017. 3. 21.]

第 14 条 5（对相关机构的协助请求）在检查火灾等防止设施，或进行应对火灾等的训练，或发生火灾等的应急情况时，文化财厅厅长或地方政府负责人有权向以下各号所示的任意一家机关或团体请求装备、人力上的协助。被请求的机关或团体，在无特殊原因的情况下，必须提供协助。

1. 消防部门

2. 警察局

3.《灾难及安全管理基本法》第三条第 5 号规定的灾难管理负责机关

4. 总统令规定的其他文化财保护相关机构及团体

[本条新设 2017. 3. 21.]

第 14 条 6（信息构建及管理）①为有效应对火灾等文化财损失，文化财厅厅长必须定期收集文化财防灾相关信息，并构建、管理数据库，并维护数据库信息的更新。

②第 1 项规定的信息构建范围及运营步骤等具体事项，依照总统令决定。
[本条新设 2017. 3. 21.]

第 15 条（文化财保护活动的支援等）为保护、保存、普及并宣扬文化财，文化财厅厅长认为必要时，可以支援和培养相关团体。

第 16 条（文化财专门人力的培养）①文化财厅厅长可以培养保护、管理及维护文化财的专门人才。
②为培养第 1 项的专门人才，文化财厅厅长有权颁发奖学金。
③文化厅厅长认为有必要确认第 2 项规定的奖学金（以下称“奖学金”）获得者的教育和研究情况，有权要求其提交成绩证明书或研究成果报告书。
④奖学金获得者或已获得者，中断或变更依照文化体育观光部令规定的学业或研究时，必须立即向文化财厅厅长报告。
⑤中断依照文化体育观光部令规定的学业、研究、或变更内容、成绩不佳时，文化财厅厅长有权终止颁发奖学金或要求获得者返还奖学金。
⑥第 1 项至第 5 项规定的奖学金颁发对象、奖学金支付申请、奖学金支付终止、返还等事项，由文化体育观光部令规定。

第 17 条（文化财国际交流合作的推进等）①国家通过文化财相关国际机构及同其他国家合作，必须积极推进文化财相关信息及技术的交换、人才交流、共同调查研究等活动。
②为推进第 1 项规定的文化财领域合作政策，文化财厅厅长可以在预算范围内支援全部或部分所需费用。

第 17 条 2 删除 <2015.3.27.>

第 18 条（南北半岛间文化财交流合作）①国家应努力增进南北半岛间文化财领域的相互交流与合作。
②为增进南北半岛间文化财领域的相互交流与合作，文化财厅厅长必须调查

研究朝鲜的文化财相关政策、制度、现况等。
③依照总统令的规定，文化财厅厅长认为有必要开展第 1 项及第 2 项规定的交流合作及调查研究工作时，有权要求相关团体进行合作，并支付全部或部分所需经费。

第 19 条（世界遗产等的收录及保护）①文化财厅厅长根据《保护世界文化遗产及自然遗产公约》、《保护非物质文化遗产公约》或联合国教科文组织项目规定，为国内优秀文化财申请联合国教科文组织世界遗产、人类非物质文化遗产或世界记录遗产。申请对象的选定流程等相关事项，文化财厅厅长参考联合国教科文组织章程而决定。< 修正 2011.4.6.>
②文化财厅厅长必须积极推动人类文化财的保存及文化财的对外宣传，包括已列入联合国教科文组织世界遗产、人类非物质文化遗产或世界记录遗产项目的文化财（以下该条中称“世界遗产等”）。< 修正 2011.4.6.>
③世界遗产等自收录之日起，国家和地方政府必须予以维护、管理和支援。文化财厅厅长根据总统令的规定，对世界遗产和其历史文化环境的保护造成影响的人员采取必要的措施。

第 20 条（外国文化财的保护）①为保存人类文化遗产，增进国家间友谊，依照大韩民国加入的文化财保护相关国际条约（以下称“条约”）中的外国法律规定，对被指定、保护的文化财（以下称“外国文化财”）进行保护。
②将引进或已引进国内的外国文化财为非法出口，并有充分的证据时，文化财厅厅长有权扣留该文化财。
③文化财厅厅长扣留第 2 项规定的外国文化财时，必须将该文化财置于博物馆等地保存、管理。
④文化财厅厅长确认第 3 项规定的外国文化财为合法出口时，必须立即将其返还至其所有者或占有者。本项同样适用于引进的外国文化财为非法出口，但原主国没有收回意向的情况。
⑤原主国证明其出口到大韩民国的外国文化财为非法出口，并根据条约的流程，要求返还或履行返还义务时，文化财厅厅长通过相关机构的协助，根据

条约的规定，采取必要措施，确保该文化财的返还。

第 21 条（非常时期的文化财保护）①发生战争、事变或类似的非常情况时，文化财厅厅长有权命令相关文化财所有者、持有者、占有者、管理者及管理团体，将国有文化财、国有以外的指定文化财及第 32 条规定的临时指定文化财转移、埋藏于安全地区，或采取其他必要措施。

②发生战争、事变或类似的非常情况时，文化财厅厅长有权将文化财输送至国外，而无需适用第 9 条。此决定必须通过国会审议。

③第 1 项的措施或命令导致文化财受损时，受损者补偿办法参照第 46 条。但不包括战祸等不可抗力因素造成的损失。

第 22 条（支援请求）为采取第 21 条第 1 项规定的措施，文化财厅厅长或执行其命令的公务员有权要求相关机构负责人提供必要的支援。

第 4 章　国家指定文化财

第 1 节　指定

第 23 条（宝物及国宝的指定）①经文化财委员会审议，文化财厅厅长有权将有形文化财中重要的部分指定为宝物。

②从人类文化观点出发，在属于第 1 项宝物的文化财中，遴选价值高、稀少的宝物，经过文化财委员会的审议后，由文化财厅厅长将其指定为国宝。

③第 1 项和第 2 项规定的宝物、国宝的指定标准、流程等事项，依照总统令决定。

第 24 条（国家无形文化财的指定）①根据《无形文化财保护及振兴法》第 9 条，经无形文化财委员会审议，文化财厅厅长可将无形文化财中的重要部分指定为国家无形文化财。< 修正 2015.3.27.>

②删除 <2015.3.27.>

③删除 <2015.3.27.>

④删除 <2015.3.27.>

⑤删除 <2015.3.27.>

[标题修正 2015.3.27.]

第 25 条（史迹、名胜、天然纪念物的指定）①经文化财委员会审议，文化财厅厅长有权将纪念物中的重要的部分指定为史迹、名胜或天然纪念物。

②第 1 项规定的史迹、名胜、天然纪念物的指定标准及流程等事项，依照总统令决定。

第 26 条（国家民俗文化财的指定）①经文化财委员会的审议，文化财厅厅长有权将民俗文化财中重要部分指定为国家民俗文化财。< 修订 2017. 3. 21.>

②根据第 1 项的国家民俗文化财的指定标准和步骤相关事项，依照总统令决定。< 修订 2017. 3. 21.>

[题目修订 2017. 3. 21.]

第 27 条（保护物或保护区域的指定）①根据第 23 条、第 25 条和第 26 条进行指定时，为保护文化财，文化财厅厅长可以指定保护物或保护区域。

②发生人为或自然条件的变化，需要对保护物或保护区域进行调整时，文化财厅厅长根据第 1 项，调整保护物或保护区域。

③根据第 1 项及第 2 项，文化财厅厅长指定或调整保护物或保护区域后，结合下列各号所示事项，每 10 年检查指定或调整的合理性。由于特殊原因，未按时完成检查时，可以在总统令规定的期限内延期完成。

1. 相关文化财的保存价值
2. 保护物或保护区域的指定对财产权造成的影响
3. 保护物或保护区域的周边环境

④第 1 项到第 3 项规定的指定、调整及合理性检查等事项，依照总统令决定。

第 28 条（指定的公布与通知）①根据第 23 条、第 25 条至第 27 条，文化财厅厅长指定国家指定文化财（包括保护物和保护区域）时，必须在政府公报

上公示其主旨，并及时告知相关文化财所有者。< 修正 2015.3.27.>

②第 1 项规定的所有者不存在或不明确时，应告知其占有者或管理者。

[标题修正 2015.3.27.]

第 29 条（指定证书的发放）①根据第 23 条和第 26 条，文化财厅厅长指定国宝、宝物或国家民俗文化财后，必须向该文化财的所有者发放指定证书。< 修订 2017. 3. 21.>

②删除 <2015. 3. 27.>

[题目修订 2015. 3. 27.]

第 30 条（指定生效日期）对文化财所有者、占有者或管理者而言，根据第 23 条、第 25 条到第 27 条，自在政府公报上公布之日起生效。< 修正 2015.3.27.>

[标题修正 2015.3.27.]

第 31 条（指定的解除）①根据第 23 条、第 25 条或第 26 条指定的文化财，丧失作为国家指定文化财的价值，或通过价值评估有必要解除指定时，经过文化财委员会审议后，文化财厅厅长有权解除指定。

②删除 <2015.3.27.>

③删除 <2015.3.27.>

④根据第 27 条第 3 项的检查结果，认为保护物或保护区域的指定不合理，或出现其他特殊原因时，文化财厅厅长有权解除保护物或保护区域的指定或调整。解除国家指定文化财的指定时，必须及时解除对相关文化财保护物或保护区域的指定。

⑤第 1 项、第 4 项规定的指定文化财解除指定的公告及通知的生效时间等，应参照第 28 条及第 30 条。< 修改 2015.3.27.>

⑥根据第 5 项和第 28 条，国宝、宝物或国家民俗文化财的所有者收到解除通知时，自收到通知日起的 30 天内必须向文化财厅厅长返还文化财指定证书。< 修订 2017. 3.21.>

⑦删除 <2015.3.27.>

[标题修正 2015.3.27.]

第 32 条（临时指定）①根据第 23 条、第 25 条、第 26 条，具有指定意义文化财，有保持原状的必要，而且来不及通过文化财委员会审议时，文化财厅厅长有权临时指定为重要文化财。
②第 1 项规定的临时指定，从告知临时被指定为指定文化财（以下称“临时指定文化财”）的所有者、占有者或管理者之日起生效。
③第 1 项规定的临时指定，从临时指定之日起 6 个月内，没有获得根据第 23 条、第 25 条或第 26 条的指定时，则视为解除。
④第 1 项规定的临时指定的通知及临时指定书颁发相关内容，将适用第 28 条及第 29 条第 1 项在政府公报上进行公告，而无需适用第 28 条第 1 项。

第 2 节　管理及保护

第 33 条（所有者管理原则）①国家指定文化财所有者应本着善良的态度，对相关文化财进行管理、保护。
②国家指定文化财所有者根据需要，有权选任代理人，并委托文化财的管理、保护。

第 34 条（管理团体进行的管理）①国家指定文化财的所有者不明，或者其所有者、管理者难以担任或不适合管理时，文化财厅厅长有权指定地方政府、适合管理的法人或团体为管理团体。不属于国家直接管理的国家指定文化财的管理团体是，该文化财所在的特别自治市、特别自治道、市、郡、区（自治区，下同）等。但，文化财的地理位置跨 2 个以上的市、郡、区时，其所在特别市、广域市、道（特别自治市和特别自治道除外）成为管理团体。< 修正 2014.1.28.>
②被指定为管理团体的地方政府与文化财厅厅长商议后，可以将相关文化财管理工作委托适合管理的法人或团体。
③根据第 1 项，文化财厅厅长指定管理团体时，必须听取相关文化财所有者

或即将被指定为管理者的地方政府、法人或团体的意见。
④根据第 1 项，文化财厅厅长指定管理团体时，必须及时在政府公报上公示目的，并告知国家指定文化财所有者或管理者及相关管理团体。
⑤任何人不得妨碍第 1 项规定指定管理团体的管理行为。< 修正 2014.1.28.>
⑥本法律中没有另定细则时，运营费等经费由相关管理团体承担。管理团体无法承担经费时，从国家或地方政府的年度预算中拨款。< 修正 2016.2.3.>
⑦第 1 项规定的管理团体的指定生效时间将适用第 30 条。

第 34 条 2（国家进行的特别管理）①所有者、管理者及管理团体无法管理国家指定文化财，或其管理行为不恰当时，经过文化财委员会审议后，文化财厅厅长有权直接对相关文化财执行特殊管理或保护，而无需适用第 34 条第 1 项。
②第 1 项规定的国家指定文化财的管理、保护所需经费由国家承担。
[本条新增 2014.1.28.]

第 35 条（许可事项）①对国家指定文化财（除国家无形文化财，以下同本条）实施以下各号行为的人，依照总统令，必须事先获得文化财厅厅长的许可。获得许可后，变更许可内容时，也必须获得文化财厅厅长的许可。但，在国家指定文化财保护区域，实施指示牌和警告牌设置等总统令规定的轻度行为时，必须得到特别自治市市长，特别自治道知事，市长，郡守或区长的许可（包含变更许可）。< 修订 2014.1.28.，2015.3.27.，2017.11.28.>

1. 改变国家指定文化财（包括保护物、保护区域、已死的天然纪念物、以及第 41 条第 1 项规定的进口或运入的部分）的现象等依照总统令规定的行为。
2. 有可能影响国家指定文化财（不包括属于动产的文化财）的保存等依照总统令规定的行为
3. 拓本或影印国家指定文化财，或有影响保存嫌疑的拍摄行为
4. 在被指定或被临时指定为名胜或天然纪念物的区域或其保护区域内，捕获和采集动植物及矿物，并试图带出该区域的行为

②在国家指定文化财和市、道指定文化财的历史文化环境保存区域重叠的区

域内，根据第 1 项第 2 条，获得文化财厅厅长或特别自治市市长、特别自治道知事、市长、郡守、区长的许可时，将视为获得第 74 条第 2 项规定的市、道知事许可。< 修正 2014.1.28.>

③文化财厅厅长有权委托市长、道知事，在第 1 项第 2 号的有影响国家指定文化财保存嫌疑的行为中，依照总统令规定的轻度变更许可的行为。< 修正 2014.1.28.>

④文化财厅厅长和特别自治市长，特别自治道知事，市长，郡守或区长收到第 1 项规定的许可或许可变更申请时，必须在 30 天内向申请人通知许可结果。< 新设 2018. 6.12.>

⑤文化财厅厅长和特别自治市市长，特别自治道知事，市长，郡守或区长在第 4 项规定的期间内没有向申请人通知许可和变更许可的结果，或者没有通知依照信访处理相关法律申请的延期处理结果时，该期间（依照信访处理相关法律的延长或延长处理期间，指的是相关法律处理期间）结束的翌日自动获得许可或变更许可。< 新设 2018.6.12.>

第 36 条（许可标准）①文化财厅厅长、特别自治市市长、特别自治道知事、市长、郡守或区长收到第 35 条第 1 项规定的许可申请时，仅批准符合下列行为的申请。< 修正 2014.1.28.>

1. 不影响文化财的保存和管理
2. 不破坏文化财的历史文化环境
3. 符合文化财基本计划和第 7 条的年度计划

②文化财厅厅长、特别自治市市长、特别自治道知事、市长、郡守或区长在审核第 1 项规定的许可时，依照总统令规定，有权委托相关专业人士进行调查。< 新增 2014.1.28.>

第 37 条（许可事项的取消）①根据第 35 条第 1 项正文、同条第 3 项、第 39 条第 1 项但书、同条第 3 项及第 48 条第 5 项获得许可的人，违反下列各号中任意一项时，文化财厅厅长有权取消许可。< 修订 2014.1.28.，2016.2.3.，2018.6.12.>

1. 违反许可事项或许可条件时

2. 用欺骗或其它不正当手段取得许可时

3. 认为无法履行许可事项或明显损害公共利益时

②根据第 35 条第 1 项但书获得许可的人违反第 1 项任意一项时，特别自治市市长、特别自治道知事、市长、郡守或区长有权取消许可。< 新增 2014.1.28.>

③根据第 35 条第 1 项获得许可的人在许可期限内，未申报着手与否，逾期时将视为许可取消。< 修正 2014.1.28.>

第 38 条（天然纪念物动物的治疗等）①天然纪念物动物遇险时，可以在市、道知事指定的动物治疗所进行救治所需的运送、施药、手术、饲养和野外适应训练等行为（以下称“治疗”）。

②第 1 项规定的动物治疗所，应具备文化财相关专业知识，或具有天然纪念物保护活动经历和野生动物治疗经验，并符合以下各号所示任意一项。市、道知事在上述机构中指定第 1 项规定的动物治疗所，指定流程和其他事项由地方政府条例规定。

1. 取得《兽医师法》规定的兽医资格证者开设的动物医院

2. 所属员工取得《兽医师法》规定的兽医资格证的地方政府畜产相关机构

3. 所属会员取得《兽医师法》规定的兽医资格证的管理团体或动物保护团体

③天然纪念物动物遇险，采取紧急保护措施时，文化财厅厅长或特别自治市市长、特别自治道知事、市长、郡守或区长有权在未取得第 35 条第 1 项规定的变更现状许可的情况下，允许动物治疗所先进行治疗后报告。< 修正 2014.1.28.>

④国家或地方政府可以在预算范围内，为天然纪念物动物的治疗提供经费。此项中的天然纪念物动物治疗经费支出业务，有权委托文化体育观光部令规定的天然纪念物治疗保护相关团体，治疗经费的支出流程和其他事项由文化体育观光部令规定。

⑤动物治疗违反以下所示任意一项时，市、道知事有权取消指定。< 修正 2016.2.3.>

1. 用欺骗或其他不正当手段获得指定资格时

2. 未达到第 2 项规定的指定标准时

3. 故意或因重大过失，导致治疗中的天然纪念物动物死亡或致残时

4. 未报告或虚假报告第 3 项规定的治疗结果时

5. 虚报第 4 项规定的治疗经费时

6. 违反第 42 条第 1 项规定的文化财厅厅长或地方政府命令时

⑥根据第 2 项和第 5 项，市、道知事在指定动物治疗所或取消指定时，必须向文化财厅厅长报告。

第 39 条（出口等的禁止）①国宝，宝物，天然纪念物或国家民俗文化财不允许出口或携带至国外。但是，以展示等国际文化交流为目的，并从出口之日起 2 年内返还至韩国为条件时，获得文化财厅厅长许可后，允许出口。< 修订 2017.3.21.>

②根据第 1 项但书，申请文物出境许可的人，必须在出口日的 5 个月前，依照文化体育观光部令，向文化财厅厅长提交出口许可申请书。< 新设 2016.2.3.>

③根据第 1 项但书，获得出口许可的人申请延长出口期限时，出于出境目的或文化财的安全等问题考虑，文化财厅厅长仅对符合第 4 项的审核标准的情况，许可延长申请，其期限为 2 年以内。< 修订 2016.2.3.>

④第 1 项但书及第 3 项的出口及出口期限延长等许可的具体审核标准，由文化体育观光部令决定。< 新设 2016.2.3.>

⑤文化财厅厅长有权对根据第 1 项但书获得出口许可的人，要求提交相关文化财的现状及保存，管理情况等资料。收到要求的人在没有特殊理由情况下，必须遵从。< 新设 2017.11. 28.>

⑥符合下列各号所示任意一项时，获得文化财厅厅长的许可后，可以出口，而无需适用第 1 项。< 修订 2016. 2. 3.，2017. 11. 28.>

1. 获得第 35 条第 1 项第 1 号规定的许可后，将天然纪念物制作成姿态标

本或其它标本时[1]

2. 在特定设施中以研究或观赏为目的的自然繁殖的天然纪念物

⑦文化财厅厅长收到第6项许可申请时，自接收日起30天内，必须向申请人通知许可结果。<新设 2018. 6. 12.>

⑧文化财厅厅长在第7项的期间内，没有向申请人通知许可结果，或没有通知依照信访处理相关法律规定申请的延期处理结果时，该期间（依照信访处理相关法律的延长或延长处理期间，指的是相关法律处理期间）结束的翌日自动获得许可。<新设 2018. 6. 12.>

第40条（申报事项）①国家指定文化财（包括保护物及保护区域，以下同本条）的所有者，管理者或管理团体，发生下列各号任意一项时，依照总统令，必须将向文化财厅厅长申报事实和经过。但是获得第35条第1项但书规定的许可后，着手或完成该行为时，必须向特别自治市市长、特别自治道知事、市长、郡守或区长申报。<修订 2014.1.28., 2015.3.27., 2017.11.28.>

1. 委任或解聘管理者时

2. 国家指定文化财所有者变更时

3. 所有者或管理者姓名、住址变更时

4. 国家指定文化财所在地地名、土地编号、土地名称、面积等变更时

5. 保管场所变更时

6. 国家指定文化财全部或部分丢失、流失、被盗或被损坏时

7. 获得第35条第1项第1号规定的许可（包括变更许可）后，着手或完成文化财现况变更时

8. 根据第35条第1项第4号、第39条第1项，获得出口许可的文化财出口后再进口时

9. 在动植物的种被指定为天然纪念物情况下，指定日之前拥有姿态标本

---

① 根据标本不同的制作方法，可分为剥制标本、干制标本和浸制标本。剥制标本是将动物皮连同上面的毛发、羽毛、鳞片等衍生物一同剥下制成的标本，作为动物实体存在的一个证据。如果整张皮填充后还原成生活姿态的，即为真剥制，又称“姿态标本”。干制标本和浸制标本的制作方法分别为针插和液浸，此处翻译为“其它标本”。

或其它标本时

9 之 2. 对死亡的天然纪念物动物验尸时

9 之 3. 对指定为天然纪念物的动物实施总统令规定的疾病预防、保存和生存必要措施等行为时

②进行第 1 项规定的申报时，同项第 1 号规定的所有者及管理者，以及同项第 2 号规定的新、旧所有者必须共同在申请书上签字。< 新增 2014.1.28.>

③在历史文化环境保存区域内实施建设工程的人根据第 35 条第 1 项第 2 号，在保存区域获得许可（包括变更许可）后并着手实施或完成许可项目时，依照总统令规定，必须向文化财厅厅长报告其事实及经过。但，根据第 35 条第 1 项的但书，获得许可后，着手实施或完成时，必须向特别自治市市长、特别自治道知事、市长、郡守或区长申报。< 修正 2014.1.28.>

第 41 条（动物的进口、运入申报）①从国外进口或运入指定为天然纪念物的动物物种（包括亚种）时，依照总统令规定，必须向文化财厅厅长申报。

②关于第 1 项规定的申报事项，文化财厅厅长有权向相关中央行政机关，公共机关等相关机关负责人要求提供必要的资料或信息。被要求提供资料或信息的机关负责人，在没有特殊理由情况下，必须遵从。[本条新设 2017. 11. 28.]

第 42 条（行政命令）①为管理并保护国家指定文化财（包括保护物及保护区域。以下同本条一致）及其历史文化环境保存区域，文化财厅厅长或地方政府负责人有权命令执行下列各号所示的事项。< 修正 2015.3.27.>

1. 国家指定文化财管理状况不符合该文化财保存特性，或认为有其他特别必要事项时，有权禁止或限制该文化财所有者、管理者及管理团体的部分行为

2. 有权要求国家指定文化财所有者、管理者及管理团体维修、安装其他必要设施或清除障碍物

3. 有权要求国家指定文化财的所有者、管理者及管理团体采取文化财保

护必要紧急措施

4. 在未获得第 35 条第 1 项各号规定的许可的情况下，对变更国家指定文化财现象，或实行影响保存行为的人，要求终止行为，或恢复原状

②文化财厅厅长、地方政府负责人认为国家指定文化财所有者、管理者及管理团体未执行第 1 项第 1 号至第 3 号规定的命令，或其所有者、管理者及管理团体不适合实施第 1 项第 1 号至第 3 号规定的措施时，有权以国家财政实施第 1 项第 1 号至第 3 号规定的措施。< 修正 2015.3.27.>

③收到命令的人未执行第 1 项第 4 号规定的命令时，文化财厅厅长或地方政府负责人依照《行政代执行法》规定代理执行，所发生的费用由违反命令的人承担。

④地方政府负责人下达第 1 项规定的命令时，必须向文化财厅厅长报告。

第 43 条（记录的制定、保存）①文化财厅厅长、相关特别自治市市长、特别自治道知事、市长、郡守、区长及管理团体负责人必须记录并保存关于国家指定文化财保存、管理及变更事项等。< 修正 2014.1.28.>

②为保存、管理国家指定文化财，文化财厅厅长有权要求文化财专业人士或研究机构拟定国家指定文化财的记录。

第 44 条（定期调查）①文化财厅厅长必须定期进行对国家指定文化财的现状、管理、维修及其他环境保护情况等的调查。< 修正 2015.3.27.>

②第 1 项规定的定期调查结束后，文化财厅厅长认为有必要深入调查，有权要求其所属公务员重新调查相关国家指定文化财。

③根据第 1 项及第 2 项，进行调查时，必须事前向该文化财所有者、管理者及管理团体告知调查目的。如果情况紧急，可事后告知。< 修正 2015.3.27.>

④根据第 1 项、第 2 项，进行调查时，公务员有权向文化财所有者、管理者及管理团体，要求公开文化财，提供情况资料及人员出入情况等调查所需的协助。在不损坏文化财现状的情况下，可以进行测量、挖掘、清除障碍物及其他调查行为。但是在日出前或日落后进行调查时，必须获得所有者、管理者及管理团体同意。< 修正 2015.3.27.>

⑤根据第 4 项，进行调查时，公务员必须向相关人士出示具有调查权限的证件。
⑥文化财厅厅长依照总统令规定，有权将第 1 项、第 2 项的定期调查及深入调查的全部或部分，委任于地方政府、专门机构及团体。
⑦文化财厅厅长必须将第 1 项、第 2 项的定期调查及深入调查结果反映在下列各号的国家指定文化财管理业务中。

1. 文化财的指定及解除
2. 保护物或保护区域的指定及解除
3. 删除 <2015.3.27.>
4. 文化财的维修及修复
5. 对影响文化财保存行为的限制或禁止，以及相关设施的安装、解除及转移
6. 其他必要的管理事项

第 45 条（依靠职权的调查）①文化财厅厅长有权命令其所属公务员对国家指定文化财的现状、管理、维修及其他环境保护情况进行调查。<修正 2015.3.27.>
②根据第 1 项，依据职权进行调查时，调查通知、调查协助要求、调查行为范围、调查证明的携带及出示等事项，适用第 44 条第 3 项至第 5 项。

第 46 条（损失赔偿）国家对下列各号任意一项人士赔偿损失。

1. 执行第 42 条第 1 项第 1 号至第 3 号的命令受损失者
2. 因第 42 条第 2 项的措施受损失者
3. 因第 44 条第 4 项（包括适用第 45 条第 2 项的情况）的调查受损失者

第 47 条（临时指定文化财相关许可事项等准用性）临时指定文化财的管理及保护相关事项，适用第 35 条第 1 项、第 37 条、第 39 条、第 40 条第 1 项（仅限于同项第 2 号至第 4 号，第 6 号至第 8 号）、第 40 条第 2 项、第 42 条第 1 项第 1 号、第 3 号及第 46 条。<修正 2014.1.28.>

第 3 节　公开及参观费

第 48 条（国家指定文化财的公开等）①根据第 2 项，除限制公开外，在无特殊原因的情况下，必须公开国家指定文化财（不包括国家无形文化财。以下同本条一致）。< 修正 2015.3.27.>

②为保护国家指定文化财并防止其被损坏，文化财厅厅长有权限制相关文化财全部或部分的公开。该情况下，文化财厅厅长必须听取相关文化财所有者（有指定管理团体时，则指该管理团体）的意见。

③根据第 2 项，文化财厅厅长限制国家指定文化财的公开时，依照总统令规定，公示相关文化财所在地区的位置、限制期间、区域等，并告知相关文化财所有者、管理者、管理团体，以及管辖市、道知事、市长、郡守及区长。

④第 2 项规定的限制原因消除时，文化财厅厅长必须立即解除限制。依据总统令规定，文化财厅厅长必须公示解除限制的信息，并告知相关文化财所有者、管理者、管理团体，以及管辖市、道知事、市长、郡守及区长。

⑤出入第 2 项、第 3 项规定的限制区域时，必须表明出入原因，并获得文化财厅厅长的许可。

⑥文化财厅厅长对第 5 项规定的许可申请，自申请之日起 30 天内，向申请人通报许可结果。< 新设 2018.6.12.>

⑦文化财厅厅长在第 6 项规定的期间内，没有向申请人通知许可结果，或没有通知依照信访处理相关法律申请的延期处理结果时，该期间（依照信访处理相关法律的延长或延长处理期间，指的是相关法律处理期间）结束的翌日自动获得许可。< 新设 2018.6.12.>

第 49 条（参观费的征收及减免）①国家指定文化财所有者公开其文化财时，可以征收参观费。但是，有指定管理团体时，参观费征收权利属于管理团体。< 修正 2015.3.27.>

②第 1 项规定的参观费由相关国家指定文化财所有者或管理团体决定。< 修

正 2015.3.27.>

③国家有权依照文化体育观光部令，对国家所管国家指定文化财减免相关地区居民的参观费；地方政府有权依照地方条例，对地方政府所管国家指定文化财减免相关地区居民的参观费。国家和地方政府有权不适用第 1 项。< 新增 2014.1.28.>

[题目修正 2014.1.28.]

第 50 条　删除 < 2015.3.27.>

第 4 节　补助金及经费支援

第 51 条（补助金）①国家可补助下列各号所示的全部或部分经费。

1. 第 34 条第 1 项规定的管理团体，管理文化财时所需经费
2. 实施第 42 条第 1 项第 1 号至第 3 号措施时所需经费
3. 除第 1 号及第 2 号外，管理、保护、维修、使用或记录国家指定文化财时所需经费
4. 删除 < 2015.3.27.>

②补助第 1 项经费时，文化财厅厅长有权监督该文化财的维修及其他工程。

③ 第 1 项第 2 号及第 3 号规定的补助金必须通过市、道知事交付。市、道知事有权要求按照指示管理和使用。文化财厅厅长可以直接交付至所有者、管理者、管理团体，有权要求按照指示管理和使用。< 修正 2015.3.27.>

第 52 条（地方政府的经费承担）地方政府有权负担或补助其管辖区域内，非地方政府所有或管理的国家指定文化财的管理、保护、维修或使用等经费。

第 5 章　注册文化财

第 53 条（文化财的注册）①经过文化财委员会的审议后，文化财厅厅长在属于非指定文化财的有形文化财，纪念物（第 2 条第 1 项第 3 号第 2 目及第 3

目除外）及民俗文化财中，遴选特别需要保存、利用的文化财，登记为注册文化财。< 修订 2017. 3. 21.>

第 54 条（注册文化财的管理）①注册文化财的所有者或管理者等管理注册文化财的人士应努力保存注册文化财的原状。

②注册文化财没有明确的所有者或所有者、管理者无法管理注册文化财时，文化财厅厅长有权要求地方政府管理，或可以指定适合管理的法人、团体管理。

③依照文化体育观光部令，注册文化财的所有者、管理者或第 2 项规定的被指定人士（以下称“注册文化财管理团体”），有权向文化财厅厅长要求提供注册文化财管理、维修相关技术指导。

第 55 条（注册文化财的申报事项）发生下列各号所示任意一项时，注册文化财所有者、管理者或注册文化财管理团体依照总统令规定，必须向文化财厅厅长报告其事实及经过。第 1 号情况时，所有者及管理者必须在报告书上签字；第 2 号情况时，新、旧所有者必须在报告书上签字。< 修正 2014.1.28.>

1. 选任或解聘管理者时
2. 所有者变更时
3. 所有者或管理者住址变更时
4. 所在地的地名、土地编号、土地名称、面积等变更时
5. 保管场所变更时
6. 文化财的全部或部分丢失、流失、被盗或被损毁时
7. 根据第 56 条第 2 项，获得许可（包括变更许可）后，着手或已完成文化财现状变更时
8. 根据参照第 59 条第 2 项的第 39 条第 1 项但书，获得出口许可的文化财出口后再次运入时

第 56 条（注册文化财的现象变更）①下列各号所示的任意一项变更注册文化财行为，必须在 30 日前，向管辖特别自治市市长、特别自治道知事、市长、郡守或区长报告。< 修正 2014.1.28.>

1. 变更相关文化财（不包括属于动产的文化财）外观等依照总统令规定的行为

2. 拆除相关文化财（不包括属于动产的文化财），以及转移至其他地方的行为

3. 维修或保存属于动产的文化财的行为

②下列各号所示的任意一项变更注册文化财现状的行为，依照总统令规定，必须获得文化财厅厅长的许可，而无需适用第 1 项。变更许可事项也适用于本条规定。

1. 根据第 57 条，适用于在建筑物建筑覆盖率或容积率等获得特例的注册文化财

2. 根据适用第 59 条第 2 项的第 51 条，获得国家补助金支援的注册文化财

3. 国家或地方政府所有的注册文化财

③特别自治市市长、特别自治道知事、市长、郡守或区长接到第 1 项的报告后，通过市、道知事（不包括特别自治市市长及特别自治道知事）必须向文化财厅厅长报告该事实。< 修正 2014.1.28.>

④为保护注册文化财的保护，文化财厅厅长有权对第 1 项的申请变更现状的注册文化财，提供指导、建议或劝告等。

第 57 条（注册文化财的建筑覆盖率及容积率相关特例）注册文化财为建筑物时，其建筑覆盖率及容积率在可用面积允许的建筑覆盖率及容积率的 150% 的范围内，可以根据总统令的标准进行调整，而无需适用《国土计划及使用法》第 77 条至第 79 条。

第 58 条（注册注销）①注册文化财失去保存和利用价值，或有其他特殊事由时，通过文化财委员会审议后，文化财厅厅长有权注销注册。

②注册文化财被指定为指定文化财时，失去注册效力。

③注册文化财所有者收到注册注销通知时，自收到通知之日起 30 日内，必须将相关文化财的注册证返还至文化财厅厅长。

第 59 条（准用规定）①注册文化财注册、注册注销的公示及通知、注册证的交付、注册、注册注销的生效日期，适用第28条至第30条。该情况下，将“国家指定文化财”视为“注册文化财”，“指定”视为“注册”，“文化财的指定书”视为“注册证”。

②有关注册文化财所有者管理原则、注册文化财管理团体的管理、注册文化财的许可取消及出口禁止等、注册文化财的记录和保存、定期调查、依据职权的注册文化财现象等的调查、定期调查造成的损失、注册文化财参观费的征收、国家补助金的支援、地方政府的经费负担、所有者变更时权利和义务的继承等，适用第 33 条、第 34 条第 2 项至第 7 项、第 37 条、第 39 条、第 43 条至第 45 条、第 46 条第 3 号、第 49 条、第 51 条第 1 项第 1 号和第 3 号及第 2 项和第 3 项、第 52 条及第 81 条。此时“国家指定文化财”指的是“注册文化财”，“管理团体”指的是“注册文化财管理团体”。< 修订 2014.1.28., 2017.3.21.>

第 6 章　一般动产文化财

第 60 条（一般动产文化财出口等的禁止）①根据本法律规定，未指定或未注册的文化财属于动产的文化财（以下称“一般动产文化财”）时，适用第 39 条第 1 项及第 3 项。但是，以国际文化交流为目进行的活动，例如在国外展示一般动产文化财等，且符合下列各号任意一项时，获得文化财厅厅长许可的情况后，不适用以上规定。< 修正 2016.2.3.>

1. 依照《博物馆及美术馆振兴法》规定设立的博物馆等向国外博物馆等运出一般动产文化财，并自运出之日起 10 年内返还时
2. 外国政府认证的博物馆或文化财相关团体，以在本国博物馆等地展示为目的，从国内购买一般动产文化财、或被赠与一般动产文化财后运出时

②根据第 1 项但书，获得许可后，违反第 37 条第 1 项各号所示任意一项时，文化财厅厅长有权取消许可。

③第 1 项第 2 号规定的一般动产文化财的出口和运出流程等事项，由文化体

育观光部令规定。
④根据第 1 项但书，获得许可的人运出一般动产文化财后再运入时，必须向文化财厅厅长申报。
⑤可能被误认为一般动产文化财的动产出口或运出至国外时，必须事前获得文化财厅厅长确认。
⑥第 1 项及第 5 项规定的一般动产文化财的范围及确认等事项，依照总统令决定。

第 60 条 2（文化财鉴定官的配备等）①为进行防止文化财非法运出及鉴定运出动产等相关业务，文化财厅厅长有权在《航空设施法》第 2 条第 3 号规定的机场、《港湾法》第 2 条第 2 号规定的贸易港、《关税法》第 256 条第 2 项规定的通关邮局等地配备文化财鉴定官，执行鉴定工作。< 修正 2016.3.29.>
②第 1 项规定的文化财鉴定官配备及运营等必要事项，依照总统令决定。
[本条新增 2015.3.27.]

第 61 条（关于一般动产文化财的调查）①文化财厅厅长有权要求其所属公务员调查国家机构或地方政府收藏的一般动产文化财的现状、管理、维修及其他保护情况。相关国家机构或地方政府负责人则必须协助调查。
②第 1 项规定的调查结束后，文化财厅厅长认为文化财的保存及管理不妥，有权要求相关机构负责人制订文化财保存、管理相关方案。
③根据第 2 项，收到文化财厅厅长要求国家机构或地方政府负责人，必须制订相关文化财的保存、管理方案，并依照总统令规定，向文化财厅厅长报告。
④根据第 1 项，文化财厅厅长进行调查时所需的通知、调查的协助要求及其他调查事项等，适用第 44 条第 3 项至第 5 项。

第 7 章　关于国有文化财的特例

第 62 条（管理厅和总括厅）①凡属于国有的文化财（以下称“国有文化财”）由文化财厅厅长管理、总揽，而无需适用《国有财产法》第 8 条、《物品管理法》第 7 条规定。但是，国有文化财属于由文化财厅厅长以外的中央机关负责人（指《国家财政法》规定的中央行政机关负责人，下同）管理的行政财产，或属于有必要由文化财厅厅长以外的中央机构负责人特别管理时，文化财厅厅长必须同相关机构负责人及企划财政部部长协商后，确定其管理厅。

②根据第 1 项但书，确定管理厅时，文化财厅厅长必须听取文化财委员会的意见。

③文化财厅厅长有权将不属于第 1 项但书的国有文化财管理工作委托于地方政府，或委托于非盈利法人、非法人非盈利团体。该情况下，因国有文化财管理产生的收益可作为受委托方的收入。

第 63 条（会计间的无偿管理转换）为管理国有文化财，从所属不同的会计处获得管理转换时，文化财厅厅长有权进行无偿转换，而无需适用《国有财产法》第 17 条。

第 64 条（流程及方法的特例）①根据第 62 条第 1 项但书，已确定管理厅的国有文化财中，由文化财厅厅长指定或临时指定为国家指定文化财，或撤销其指定或临时指定时，根据本法律规定，对相关文化财所有者或占有者的通知传达至该文化财管理厅。

②对第 62 条第 1 项但书规定的已确定管理厅的国有文化财，适用第 40 条、第 42 条、第 45 条及第 49 条时，该文化财所有者指的是该文化财管理厅。

第 65 条（处分的限制）第 62 条第 1 项但书规定的管理厅对其管理范围内的国家指定文化财或临时指定文化财实行第 35 条第 1 项各号以外的行为时，必须事前得到文化财厅厅长的同意。

第 66 条（转让及个私权利设定的禁止）本法律中没有特别规定时，不得将国有文化财（包括其用地）转让或在其范围内行使私权。但在不影响其管理及保护前提下，仅限于公用、共用或公益事业，可以附加一定的条件实行。

第 8 章 国外所在文化财

第 67 条（国外所在文化财的保护）国家必须为保护、收回及利用国外所在文化财等而努力，并确保其所需的组织及预算。

第 68 条（国外所在文化财的调查、研究）①文化财厅厅长或地方政府负责人可对国外所在文化财的现况、保存管理实况、外流原委等进行调查研究。< 修正 2016.2.3.>

②为有效进行第 1 项的调查、研究，文化财厅厅长或地方政府负责人有权要求博物馆、韩国国际交流财团、国史编纂委员会及各大学等相关机构提供所需材料及信息，以上相关机构必须予以协助。< 修正 2016.2.3.>

第 69 条（国外所在文化财保护及收回活动的支援）①为保护和收回国外所在文化财，文化财厅厅长或地方政府负责人有权支援、培养相关机构或团体。< 修正 2016.2.3.>

②根据第 1 项，地方政府负责人选择支援、培养的机构或团体，以及实施财政支援等事项，依照相关地方政府条例决定。< 新增 2016.2.3.>

第 69 条 2（关于国外所在文化财收回及使用的意见听取）关于国外所在文化财收回及利用相关重要政策等，文化财厅厅长有权听取有关专家或机构的意见。

[专门修正 2016.2.3.]

第 69 条 3（国外所在文化财财团的设立）①为综合、系统开展与国外所在文化财相关的各项工作，包括关于国外所在文化财的现况及外流原委等事项的调查、研究，国外所在文化财的收回、使用相关的各种战略、政策研究等，设立文化财厅下属机构——国外所在文化财财团（以下称“国外文化财财团”）。

②规定国外文化财财团为法人。

③根据章程规定，国外文化财财团包括管理人员及必要职工。
④除本法律规定内容外，国外文化财财团适用《民法》中关于财团法人的规定。
⑤国外文化财财团设立及运营所需经费，可出自国家预算或由《文化财保护基金法》规定的文化财保护基金出资或提供补贴。
⑥国外文化财财团为达成其设立目的，需开展以下各号所示工作。

1. 国外所在文化财现况、外流原委等的调查研究
2. 国外所在文化财收回及保护、使用的相关研究
3. 国外所在文化财的获得及保存、管理
4. 关于收回及使用国外所在文化财团体的支援、交流及国际连带关系强化
5. 关于国外所在文化财收回及使用的宣传、教育、出版及普及
6. 外国博物馆中韩国馆的运营支援
7. 负责韩国业务的管理者派遣及教育培训
8 国外所在文化财的保存处理及宣传支援
9. 为达成国外文化财财团的设立目的，有必要开展营利性业务时，应事前获得文化财厅厅长许可。
10. 其他为达成国外文化财财团设立目的而开展的业务

⑦经过文化财厅厅长同意后，国外文化财财团有权要求相关行政机构、国外所在文化财收回及使用相关法人或团体负责人提供开展业务所需的材料。

[本条新增 2012.1.26.]

第 9 章　市、道指定文化财

第 70 条（市、道指定文化财的指定等）①对市、道知事管辖范围内的、且未被指定为国家指定文化财的文化财，市、道知事认为有保存价值时，有权将其指定为市、道指定文化财。<修正 2015.3.27.>
②根据第 1 项，对未被指定的文化财，市、道知事认为在乡土文化保存方面具有价值时，有权将其指定为文化财资料。
③经过文化财委员会审议后，对有必要的文化财，文化财厅厅长有权建议市、

道知事将其指定并保存为市、道指定文化财或文化财资料（包括保护物或保护区域，下同）。收到建议的市、道知事，在没有特殊原因的情况下，必须执行文化财的指定程序，并向文化财厅厅长报告。

④根据第 1 项至第 3 项，指定市、道指定文化财和文化财资料时，为明确文化财或文化财资料为相关特别市、广域市、特别自治市、道或特别自治道的指定，应在“指定”二字前注明相关特别市、广域市、特别自治市、道或特别自治道名称。< 修正 2014.1.28.>

⑤市、道指定文化财和文化财资料的指定及解除程序、管理、保护、培养、公开等必要事项，由相关地方政府条例规定。

⑥删除 <2015.3.27.>

第 71 条（市、道文化财委员会的设立）①为调查、审议市、道知事管辖范围内文化财的保存、管理、使用相关事项，在市、道设立文化财委员会（以下称为“市、道文化财委员会”）。

②市、道文化财委员会组织和运营等相关事项由条例进行规定，必须包括下列以下各号所示事项。

1. 文化财保存、管理及使用相关调查、审议事项
2. 委员的委任和免职相关事项
3. 分科委员会的设立和运营相关事项
4. 专家委员的委任和工作安排相关事项

③市、道知事向文化财厅厅长申请将其管辖范围内的文化财指定为国家指定文化财（包括保护物和保护区域）或解除指定时，必须经过市、道文化财委员会的事前审议。

第 72 条（经费承担）①根据第 70 条第 1 项和第 2 项，市、道指定文化财或文化财资料属于国有或公共财产时，其保存所需经费由国家或相关地方政府承担。

②在保存、管理、修缮、使用、记录市、道指定文化财或文化财资料（非国有或公共财产）时，国家或地方政府可承担全部或部分经费。< 修正

2015.3.27.>

第 73 条（报告等）①市、道知事有以下各号任意一项所示的事由时，依照总统令规定，必须向文化财厅厅长报告。

1. 指定市、道指定文化财或文化资料，或解除指定时
2. 市、道指定文化财或文化财资料所在地或保管地点变更时
3. 市、道指定文化财或文化财资料的全部或部分内容丢失、遗失、被盗、被损坏时

②文化财厅厅长认为第 1 项第 1 号和第 2 号规定的行为不恰当时，有权命令改正或采取必要措施。

第 74 条（准用规定）①关于市、道指定文化财和文化财资料的出口或运出等事项，适用第 39 条第 1 项至第 5 项。< 修订 2016.2.3.，2017.11.28.>
②关于市、道指定文化财和文化财资料的指定、解除及管理等事项，准用第 27 条、第 31 条第 1 项和第 4 项、第 32 条至第 34 条、第 35 条第 1 项、第 36、第 37 条、第 40 条、第 42 条至第 45 条、第 48 条、第 49 条及第 81 条。此时“文物厅长”指的是“市、道知事”，“总统令”指的是“市、道条例”，“国家”指的是“地方政府”。< 修订 2015.3.27.，2018.10.16.>

第 10 章　文化财交易等

第 75 条（买卖等营业许可）①专门从事属于动产的有形文化财或有形民俗文化财的买卖、交换业务（包括接受委托，专门从事买卖或交换）的人，依照总统令规定，必须获得特别自治市市长、特别自治道知事、市长、郡守或区长的文化财交易许可。< 修正 2014.1.28.>
②根据第 1 项，取得许可的人（以下称为“文化财交易者”）依照总统令规定，必须向特别自治市市长、特别自治道知事、市长、郡守或区长报告文化财的保存、买卖或交换现况。< 修正 2014.1.28.>
③根据第 2 项，特别自治市市长、特别自治道知事、市长、郡守或区长在收

到报告后，依照总统令规定，定期将收到的报告事项报告给文化财厅厅长。< 修正 2014.1.28.>

④根据第 1 项，获得许可的人，变更下列各号所示任意一项时，依照文化体育观光部令，必须向特别自治市市长、特别自治道知事、市长、郡守或区长报告变更内容。< 新设 2018.6.12.>

1. 商号变更
2. 营业地址变更

第 76 条（资格条件）①根据第 75 条第 1 项，申请文化财交易许可的人，必须满足以下各号所示任意一项条件。

1. 在国家、地方政府、博物馆或美术馆管理文化财 2 年以上者
2. 在专科以上的大学（包括研究生院）系统学习历史学、考古学、人类学、美术史学、民俗学、图书学、传统工艺学、文化财管理学知识 1 年以上者
3. 被从事文化财交易者雇用，并从事文化财管理工作 3 年以上者

②第 1 项的博物馆和美术馆范围、专业科目等相关内容，其所需事项由文化体育观光部令规定。

第 77 条（不合格理由）符合下列各号任意一项的人，不能成为文化财交易商。< 修订 2017.3.21.>

1. 被成年监护人或被限制监护人
2. 违反本法律和《刑法》第 347 条或第 362 条，被判有期徒刑，刑满释放或缓期执行未满 3 年者
3. 根据第 80 条，许可取消之日起未满 3 年者

第 78 条（遵守事项）①根据文化体育观光部令规定，文化财交易商必须准备文化财买卖、交换账簿，记录交易内容，并拍摄并附实物照片，以便确认相关文化财。< 修正 2014.1.28.>

②根据文化体育观光部令规定，文化财交易商必须每年接受关于第 1 项的买

卖、交易等账簿的检查。不从事文化财交易时，也应遵守本项规定。<新增 2014.1.28.>

第 79 条（停业申报的义务）根据第 75 条第 1 项，获得许可的人士，不再从事文化财交易时，依照文化体育观光部令规定，必须在 3 个月内向特别自治市市长、特别自治道知事、市长、郡守或区长提交停业申报书。<修正 2014.1.28.>

第 80 条（许可取消等）①符合下列各号所示的任意一项行为时，特别自治市市长、特别自治道知事、市长、郡守或区长有权取消文化财交易商的许可，或命令其停止全部或部分的营业，期限为 1 年以内。但是，属于第 1 号至第 3 号时，必须取消其许可。<修正 2014.1.28.>

1. 通过虚假或不正当方法获得许可时
2. 违反第 90 条、第 92 条及《埋藏文物保护与调查法》第 31 条，获罚款以上处罚时
3. 在停业期间营业时
4. 违反第 78 条的遵守事项时

②第 1 项的行政处分详细标准，依照文化体育观光部令决定。

第 11 章　附　则

第 81 条（权利、义务的继承）①国家指定文化财（包括保护物、保护区域及临时指定文化财）所有者变更时，新所有者将继承本法律规定的或文化财厅厅长根据本法律做出的命令、指示、处分等前所有者的权利及义务。

②根据第 34 条，指定管理团体或解除指定时，对管理团体及所有者适用第 1 项。但是，专属于所有者的权利及义务不适用第 1 项。

第 82 条（权限的委任、委托）本法律规定的文化财厅厅长权限，依照总统令规定，有权将部分权限委任于市、道知事或市长、郡守、区长，或委托于为

保护、保存、普及并使用文化财等而设立的机构、法人或团体等。

第 82 条 2（类似名称的禁止使用）非本法律规定的财团禁止使用韩国文化财财团或类似名称。
[本条新增 2014.5.28.]

第 83 条（土地的征用或使用）①文化财厅厅长或地方政府负责人为保存、管理文化财，依照《用于公益事业土地等的取得及补偿法》，有权征用或使用指定文化财或位于其保护区域的土地、建筑、树木、竹木及其他设施。
②删除 <2014.1.28.>

第 84 条（国、公有财产的借贷及使用等）①为保存、管理、使用或传承文化财，国家或地方政府有权签订借贷、使用、盈利或出售国有或公有财产的合同，而无需适用《国有财产法》或《公有财产及物品管理法》中有相关规定。
②对第 1 项规定的国有或公有财产的借贷、使用、盈利、出售等内容及条件，适用《国有财产法》或《公有财产及物品管理法》。

第 85 条（文化财防灾日）①为了安全保护文化财不被火灾等灾害破坏，同时提高国民对文化财的安全管理意识，将每年 2 月 10 日定为文化财防灾日。
②为契合文化财防灾日设立目的，国家及地方政府必须开展文化财安全检查、防灾训练等工作和活动。
③文化财防灾日活动所需事项，由文化财厅厅长或市、道知事单独决定。

第 86 条（奖金）①违反第 90 条至第 92 条、《埋藏文物保护与调查法》第 31 条的人或未遂的人被判缓期起诉处分或有罪时，文化财厅厅长在预算范围内必须向举报者及抓捕有功者颁发奖金。
②调查机关的范围、举报的处理、奖金的支付标准等奖金支付必要事项，依照总统令决定。

第 87 条（同其他法律的关系）①文化财厅厅长在《自然公园法》规定的公园区域进行下列各号所示任意一项活动，且该面积大于总统令规定时，必须与相关公园的管理厅协商。< 修正 2014.1.28.>

1. 根据第 25 条，指定一定区域为史迹、名胜、天然纪念物
2. 根据第 27 条，指定保护区域
3. 根据第 35 条第 1 项正文，获得许可或变更许可

②特别自治市市长、特别自治道知事、市长、郡守或区长对《自然公园法》规定的公园区域允许第 25 条第 1 项但书的许可或变更许可，且该面积大于总统令规定的面积区域时，必须与相关公园的管理厅协商。< 新增 2014.1.28.>
③根据第35条第1项（包括第74条第2项规定提及的准用情况），获得许可时，将视为获得下列各号规定的许可。< 修正 2014.1.28.>

1.《自然公园法》第 23 条规定的可在公园区域进行的行为许可
2.《城市公园及绿地法》第 24 条、第 27 条及第 38 条的城市公园、城市自然公园区域、绿地的占用及使用许可

④根据第 23 条，第 25 条至第 27 条或第 70 条第 1 项，被指定为国家指定文化财或市、道指定文化财，以及其保护物或保护区域属于“国土计划及使用法”第 6 条第 1 号中城市区域时，认为同法第 37 条第 1 项第 5 号的保护区。< 修订 2014.1. 28.，2017.4.18.>
⑤下列各号所示任意一项文化财买卖等交易行为，不适用《民法》第 249 条中关于善意取得的规定。但，受让人通过拍卖或出于善意从文化财交易商等处购买的，被害者或遗失者赔偿受让人损失，并要求其返还。< 修正 2014.1.28.>

1. 文化财厅厅长或市、道知事指定的文化财
2. 已公告确认被盗或遗失的文化财
3. 可以确认出处的重要部分或记录被人为损坏的文化财

⑥第 5 项第 2 号规定的公告必要事项，依照文化体育观光部令规定。< 修正 2014.1.28.>

第 88 条（听证）文化财厅厅长、市、道知事、市长、郡守或区长决定下列各

号所示任意一项处分时，必须召开听证会。

1. 根据第 35 条第 1 项、第 39 条、第 56 条第 2 项或第 60 条第 1 项但书的规定获得许可的人，违反许可事项或许可条件时，给予取消许可的处分

2. 取消第 38 条第 5 项规定的动物治疗所的指定

3. 取消第 80 条规定的文化财交易商的许可或给予停业处分

第 89 条（接受惩罚方面的公务员议题）准用《刑法》第 129 条至第 132 条，符合下列各号所示任意一项的人时，将视为公务员。< 修正 2014.1.28.>

1. 根据第 8 条第 1 项，对文化财保存及管理相关事项进行调查、审议的文化财委员会委员（包括第 71 条第 1 项的市、道文化财委员会委员）

1 之 2. 根据第 13 条第 2 项后半部分内容，针对指定文化财保存影响提出意见者

1 之 3. 根据第 36 条第 2 项，提出现状变更许可调查意见者

2. 根据第 38 条第 4 项，受委托支付天然纪念物动物治疗经费者

3. 根据第 44 条第 6 项，受委托执行文化财调查工作者

4. 根据第 82 条，接受文化财厅厅长权限委托、并从事相关委托工作者

第 12 章　处罚规定

第 90 条（非法出口等罪）①违反第 39 条第 1 项正文（包括第 59 条第 2 项及第 74 条第 1 项的准用情况）规定，向国外出口或运出指定文化财或临时指定文化财，或违反第 39 条第 1 项但书及第 2 项至第 4 项（包括第 59 条第 2 项及第 74 条第 1 项的准用情况），未在期限内将外流文化财重新运入国内时，处 5 年以上有期徒刑，并没收其文化财。< 修正 2016.2.3.>

②违反第 60 条第 1 项，向国外出口或运出文化财，或未将外流文化财重新运入国内时，处 3 年以上有期徒刑，并没收文化财。

③违反第 1 项或第 2 项，已获知向国外非法出口或运出文化财情况下，转让、接受转让相关文化财或中介的人，处 3 年以上有期徒刑，并没收文化财。

第 91 条（虚假临时指定等诱导罪）利用虚假或其他不正当手段，将文化财被指定为指定文化财或临时指定文化财时，处 5 年以上有期徒刑。

第 92 条（损坏或隐匿等罪）①损坏、窃取或隐匿国家指定文化财（不包括国家无形文化财），或利用其他方法破坏其功能，处 3 年以上有期徒刑。<修正 2015.3.27.>

②符合下列各号所示任意一项的人，处 2 年以上有期徒刑。

1. 损坏、窃取或隐匿除第 1 项规定外的指定文化财或临时指定文化财（不包括建筑物），或利用其他方法破坏其功能者
2. 在已获知文化财是一般动产文化财的情况下，损坏、窃取或隐匿一般动产文化财，或利用其他方法破坏其功能者

③符合下列各号所示任意一项的人，处 2 年以上有期徒刑或处 2 千万韩元以上、1 亿 5 千万韩元以下罚款

1. 未获得第 35 条第 1 项第 1 号规定的现状变更的许可或变更许可的情况下，剥制天然纪念物或将其制作为标本[①]者
2. 已获知违反第 1 项、第 2 项或第 1 号规定的情况下，获取、转让、接受转让或运输相关文化财者
3. 第 2 号的中间人

④在作出第 1 项及第 2 项规定的隐匿行为前，已依靠他人作出同项规定的损坏、盗取、隐匿指定文化财、临时指定文化财或一般动产文化财，或使用其他方法破坏其功能，但未受到相应处罚，相关隐匿行为者根据同项规定接受处罚。

⑤无法没收第 1 项至第 4 项规定的文化财时，则额外征收相关文化财的鉴定价格。但第 4 项规定的隐匿行为者出于善意获得相关文化财，则不适用本条规定。

第 93 条（加重罪）①显现团体或众人的威力、或携带危险物品，违反第 90 条至第 92 条时，根据各相关条例，最多可以加重二分之一的罪。

---

① 即制成“姿态标本”。

②违反第 1 项，且伤害到指定文化财或临时指定文化财的管理者、保护者时，处以无期徒刑或 5 年以上有期徒刑。致人死亡时，则处以死刑、无期徒刑或 5 年以上有期徒刑。

第 94 条（《刑法》的准用性）对下列各号所示的建筑物实施放火、溢水或破坏的人，根据《刑法》第 165 条、第 178 条或第 367 条，以及同法中的相关规定处罚。最多可以加重二分之一的罪。

1. 作为指定文化财或临时指定文化财的建筑物
2. 作为保护指定文化财或临时指定文化财的建筑物

第 95 条（史迹等的溢水罪）通过溢水，损坏文化财厅厅长指定或临时指定的史迹、名胜或天然纪念物、保护区域时，处 2 年以上、10 年以下有期徒刑。

第 96 条（其他溢水罪）通过溢水，损坏第 95 条外的指定文化财或临时指定文化财、其保护区域时，处 10 年以下有期徒刑或 1 亿韩元以下罚金。

第 97 条（犯罪未遂犯等）①第 90 条至第 92 条、第 93 条第 1 项、第 95 条及第 96 条的犯罪未遂的人必须受处罚。
②预计或图谋犯第 90 条至第 92 条、第 93 条第 1 项、第 95 条及第 96 条的人，处 2 年以下有期徒刑或 2 千万韩元以下罚金。

第 98 条（过失犯）①因过失犯第 95 条或第 96 条的人，处 1 千万韩元以下罚款。
②因工作过失或重大过失犯第 95 条或 96 条的罪行者，处 3 年以下监禁或 3 千万韩元以下罚金。

第 99 条（非法行为等罪）①符合下列各号所示任意一项的人，处 5 年以下有期徒刑或 5 千万韩元以下罚金。

1. 违反第 35 条第 1 项第 1 号或第 2 号（包括第 47 条及第 74 条第 2 项的准用情况），变更指定文化财（包括保护物、保护区域及天然纪念物中的死物）或临时指定文化财现状，而影响其保存的人。

2. 违反第 35 条第 1 项第 4 条（包括第 74 条第 2 项的准用情况），在未获得许可情况下，在被指定或临时指定为名胜、天然纪念物的区域或保护区域内，捕获动物，开采植物、矿物，或试图将其携带出区域外的人

3. 违反第 75 条第 1 项，在未获得许可情况下营业的人

②符合下列各号所示任意一项的人，处 2 年以下有期徒刑或 2 千万韩元以下罚款。

1. 第 1 项各号的情况下，文化财所有者

2. 违反第 56 条第 2 项，在未获得许可或未获得变更许可的情况下，变更注册文化财现状者

第 100 条（违反行政命令等罪）符合下列各号所示任意一项的人，处 3 年以下有期徒刑或处 3 千万韩元以下罚金。第 2 项情况，则没收其物品。

1. 在无正当理由的情况下，违反第 21 条第 1 项或第 42 条第 1 项（包括第 74 条第 2 项的准用情况）的命令的人

2. 在被指定或临时指定为天然纪念物（包括市、道指定文化财中的纪念物）的动物栖息地、繁殖地、迁徙地等引入或撒布有害物质的人

第 101 条（干扰管理行为等罪）符合下列各号所示任意一项的人，处 2 年以下有期徒刑或处 2 千万韩元以下罚金。

1. 在无正当事由的情况下，不响应第 12 条的指示的人

2. 违反第 34 条第 5 项（包括第 74 条第 2 项规定的准用情况），干扰管理团体的管理行为，或在无其他正当理由的情况下，干扰拥有指定文化财或临时指定文化财管理权力者的管理行为的人

3. 在未获得许可的情况下，作出第 35 条第 3 号规定（包括第 74 条第 2 项规定的准用情况）的行为的人

4. 拒绝第 44 条第 4 项正文规定（包括第 45 条第 2 项及第 74 条第 2 项规定的准用情况）的协助或干扰必要协助行为的人

5. 负责指定文化财或临时指定文化财管理及保存的人中，因重大过失导

致文化财丢失或受损的人

6. 虚假申报或报告的人

7. 故意损坏、移动、去除被指定为指定文化财区域或其保护区域的边界标识，或用其他手段导致该区域边界无法识别的人

8. 违反文化财厅厅长根据第 48 条第 2 项提出的公开限制公开文化财，或在未获得同条第 5 项规定的许可情况下，出入文化财的人（包括第 74 条第 2 项规定的准用情况）

第 102 条（双罚制）法人代表、法人或个人代理人、使用人、其他从业人员针对该法人或个人的工作，作出第 94 条至第 96 条或第 98 条至第 101 条规定的任意一项违反行为时，除处罚外，还针对该法人或个人根据相关条文规定处罚金刑。没有罚金刑时，则处 3 亿韩元以下罚金。但是，对防止违法行为，格外注意并监督违法工作的法人或个人，则不适用本条规定。

第 103 条（罚金）①违反下列各号所示任意一项的人，处以 500 万元以下的罚金。< 修订 2012.1.26.，2014.5.28.，2017.3.21.，2017.11.28.>

1. 不遵从第 14 条 4 第 3 项规定的施政命令的人

2. 未申报第 40 条第 1 项第 6 号、第 9 号、第 9 号的 2 或第 9 号的 3 规定（包括根据第 74 条第 2 项适用的情况）的人

2 之 2. 没有申报第 41 条第 1 项规定的运进、进口的人

3. 未申报第 55 条第 6 号规定的人

4. 未申报第 56 条第 1 项规定的人

5. 未履行第 78 条规定的遵守事项的人

6. 未申报第 79 条规定的停业的人

7. 违反第 82 条 2 的，使用韩国文化财团或者类似名称的人

②对未申报第 40 条第 1 项第 5 号规定（包括适用第 74 条第 2 项的情况）的人，处以 400 万元以下的罚金。

③对未申报第 40 条第 1 项第 7 号、第 3 项规定（包括适用第 74 条第 2 项的情况）的人，处以 300 万元以下的罚金。< 修订 2014.1.28.>

④违反下列各号任意一项的人，处以 200 万元以下的罚金。<修订 2018.6.12.>

1. 未申报第 40 条第 1 项第 1 号至第 4 号及第 8 号规定（包括适用第 74 条第 2 项的情况）的人

2. 未申报第 55 条第 1 号至第 5 号、第 7 号或第 8 号规定的人

3. 未申报第 60 条第 4 项规定的人

4. 未申报第 75 条第 4 项规定的变更内容的人

⑤根据第 14 条 4 第 5 项，对在禁烟区吸烟的人处以 10 万韩元以下的罚款。<新设 2012.1.26.，2017.3.21.>

第 104 条（罚金的收缴、征收）第 103 条的罚金，根据总统令规定，由文化财厅厅长、市、道知事或市长、郡守、区长收缴、征收。

附则 <第 15827 号，2018.10.16.>

第 1 条（实行日）本法自公布 6 个月后实行。

第 2 条（关于继承权力、义务的准用例）自本法实行后，如果市、道指定文化财和文化财资料的所人发生变更，或者指定、解除管理单位时，将准用第 74 条第 2 项的修正规定。

十、欧 盟

述　评

1957 年 3 月 25 日，法国、联邦德国、意大利、荷兰、比利时和卢森堡六国政府首脑和外长在罗马签署《欧洲经济共同体条约》和《欧洲原子能共同体条约》，被后人统称为《罗马条约》。条约于 1958 年 1 月 1 日生效，被认为欧洲共同体（简称欧共体，即欧盟前身）由此诞生。欧共体成立后，各成员国间的商品贸易、文化交流等各种生产要素的流动更加活跃，但文物走私、非法贩运和不正当交易等状况也随之而来，同时各成员国对文物进出口管制宽严不一，尽管《罗马条约》第 36 条关于商品自由流动的相关规定并不排除为保护具有艺术、历史或考古价值的国宝（National Treasure）而制定的货物进出口或过境的禁令或限制。为此，欧共体理事会于 1992 年 12 月 9 日颁布了《文物出口条例》（即 3911/92 条例），1993 年又颁布《关于返还从成员国境内非法转移文物的指令》（即 93/7/EEC 指令）。2008 年 12 月 18 日，欧盟理事会修改 3911/92 条例，并以 116/2009 号公布。2014 年 5 月 15 日，欧盟理事会颁布《关于返还从成员国境内非法转移文物的指令》（2014/60/EU 指令），对 93/7/EEC 指令作出了重大修改，以便文义清晰，方便执行。具体修改之处在其前言中有明确说明。近几年来，德国、法国等欧盟国家纷纷修订本国文物保护法律，对文物进出境采取较为严格的限制管理措施，并对他国文物的保护力度加大，返还非法进口的他国文物也比较积极，这些动态无疑释放出一个强烈的信号：欧盟国家的文物进出口政策由宽严不一逐渐转向从严管控。

（一）《关于文物出口的第 116/2009 号理事会条例》

关于文物出口的第 116/2009 号理事会条例

2008 年 12 月 18 日

（修订）

（王成岳　初校）

欧盟理事会

根据欧共体成立条约，特别是第 133 条，

根据欧盟委员会的提案，

鉴于：

（1）1992 年 12 月 9 日欧盟关于文物出口的第 3911/92 号理事会条例【1】已经得到多次实质性修改【2】。为确保条例明确、合理，应对该条例进行修订。

（2）为维护内部市场，须建立与第三方国家的贸易规则，以保护文物。

（3）有必要采取措施确保向欧盟以外区域的文物出口得到统一管控。

（4）本体系要求在出口本条例规定的文物之前出示相关成员国颁发的许可证。为此，有必要明确该措施的范围和实施程序。实施本体系时应尽可能简便有效。

（5）应根据 1999 年 6 月 28 日理事会决议 1999/468/EC 采取实施本条例的必要措施，上述决议规定了欧盟委员会行使本条例权利的程序【3】。

（6）考虑到成员国的主管部门在执行 1997 年 3 月 13 日第 515/97 号理事

会条例（关于成员国各行政管理部门的互惠协助以及成员国行政管理部门与欧盟委员会之间关于确保正确适用海关和农业事务法律的合作）【4】中具有丰富的经验，本条例应适用此事项。

（7）本条例附录 I 旨在明确在与第三国贸易中应受特别保护的文物类别，但成员国不得因此歪曲《条约》第 30 条中对国宝（national treasure）的定义[①]。

特通过本条例：

第 1 条　定义

在不与《条约》第 30 条规定的成员国权利相抵触的情况下，就本条例而言，"文物"指附录 I 中所列物品。

第 2 条　出口许可证

1. 向欧盟共同关税区以外出口文物的，须出示出口许可证。

2. 经当事方请求，出口许可证应由以下部门颁发：

（a）某成员国相关主管部门，且 1993 年 1 月 1 日申请出口文物已经合法且明确地位于该成员国境内；

（b）或者，在此之后，某成员国相关主管部门，且该文物经从其他成员国合法转移、从第三国进口，或由其他成员国通过合法途径转移至第三国后复又从第三国进口至该成员国境内。

然而，在不与第 4 款冲突的情况下，对于附录 I 中类别 A.1 下第一和第二行规定的文物，如果申请出口文物的考古价值或科学价值有限，也并非直接来自该成员国境内的发掘、发现或考古遗址，并且该文物可以在市场上进行合法交易，则第一项（a）或（b）中的相关成员国有权对出口许可证不做要求。

为实现本条例的目的，如申请出口文物是在该成员国受法律保护的具有

① 这里的《条约》即《罗马条约》（Treaty of Rome），条约第 36 条规定，不排除对进出口和运送中的货物施加禁止或限制，只要符合保护具有历史或考古意义的国宝。然而条约并未就"国宝"作出明确定义，留待各国根据本国情况确定。《罗马条约》几经修改，最初的第 36 条改为第 30 条。

艺术、历史或考古价值的国宝，可以拒发出口许可证。

必要时，第一项（b）中的相关主管部门应与申请出口文物所在成员国的相关主管部门联系，尤其是1993年3月15日的关于返还从成员国境内非法转移的文物的理事会93/7/EEC指令中规定的相关主管机关。【5】

3. 出口许可证制度在欧盟全境内有效。

4. 在不与第1、2、3款冲突的情况下，从欧盟共同关税区内直接出口并非本条例规定的文物的具有艺术、历史或考古价值的国宝，须遵从出口成员国的国内法律。

第3条　主管部门

1. 成员国应向欧盟委员会提交有权颁发文物出口许可证的机关名单。

2. 欧盟委员会应在《欧盟公报》'C'辑中发布名单及其修订情况。

第4条　出示许可证

办理海关出口手续时，应向接收出口申报单的海关出示申报单和出口许可证。

第5条　对相关海关的限制

1. 成员国可限制有权办理文物出口手续的海关数量。

2. 成员国选择第1款做法的，应将其授权的海关告知欧盟委员会。

委员会应在《欧盟公报》'C'辑中发布该信息。

第6条　行政合作

为本条例实施的目的，原则上适用第515/97号条例的规定，尤其是关于信息保密性的规定。

除上款规定的合作外，成员国还应采取多种措施，在已建立的相互关系的基础上，促进93/7/EEC指令第4条规定的海关部门和相关主管部门建立合作。

第 7 条　实施措施

应根据第 8 条第 2 款规定的程序采取实施本条例的必要措施，尤其是实施形式（如模式和技术性能）。

第 8 条　专门委员会

1. 应成立一个专门委员会协助欧盟委员会工作。
2. 引用本款时，适用 1999/468/EC 决议第 3 条和第 7 条。

第 9 条　处罚

成员国应制定违反本条例的处罚原则，并采取必要措施确保其实施。规定的处罚措施必须有效、适当并有劝诫作用。

第 10 条　报告

1. 各成员国应将其根据本条例采取的措施告知欧盟委员会。
欧盟委员会应将此信息分享给其他成员国。
2. 欧盟委员会每 3 年向欧盟议会、理事会与欧盟经济和社会委员会报告本条例的实施情况。
应欧盟委员会的提议，欧盟理事会根据欧盟的经济和货币指标每 3 年对附录 I 进行一次审查，适当时可对数量进行更新。

第 11 条　废止

第 3911/92 号条例因被附录 II 中条例修改，现予废止。
引用已废止条例的，视为引用本条例，并按附录 III 中相关表项解读。

第 12 条　生效

本条例将于在《欧盟公报》公布后的第 20 天生效。
本条例全文具有法律约束力，并直接适用于所有成员国。

2008 年 12 月 18 日，布鲁塞尔

欧盟理事会

主席

M. Barnier

注释：

【1】第 L395 号《欧盟公报》，1992 年 12 月 31 日，第 1 页。

【2】见附录 II。

【3】第 L184 号《欧盟公报》，1999 年 7 月 17 日，第 23 页。

【4】第 L82 号《欧盟公报》，1997 年 3 月 22 日，第 1 页。

【5】第 L74 号《欧盟公报》1993 年 3 月 27 日，第 74 页。

附录 I

第 1 条规定的文物种类

A.	1.	100 年以上的考古文物，来源于：		
		— 陆地或水下发掘和发现		9705 00 00①
		— 考古遗址		9706 00 00
		— 藏品		
	2.	100 年以上的、具有艺术、历史或宗教价值的湮没古迹的组成部分		9705 00 00 9706 00 00
	3.	以任何手法运用任何材料纯手工制作的图画和绘画，且不属于第 4 或 5 类 (1)		9701
	4.	运用任何材料纯手工制作的水彩画、水粉画和蜡笔画(1)		9701
	5.	运用任何材料纯手工制作的镶嵌画，且不属于第 1 或 2 类，以及以任何手法运用任何材料纯手工制作的图画 (1)		6914 9701
	6.	雕版、印刷品、绢网印花和石版画原作，及带有其相应图版或原版招贴画 (1)		第 49 章②
				9702 00 00
				8442 50 99
	7.	雕塑或雕像原作以及用原作同样手法制作的复制品(1)，且不属于第 1 类		9703 00 00
	8.	照片、胶卷及其底片 (1)		3704
				3705
				3706

① 出口文物类别序号。

② 《欧盟公报》中的章节。

续表

				4911 91 80
	9.	古籍和手稿，包括地图和乐谱的单行本或丛书[1]		9702 00 00
				9706 00 00
				4901 10 00
				4901 99 00
				4904 00 00
				4905 91 00
				4905 99 00
				4906 00 00
	10.	100 年以上的书籍，包括单行本或丛书		9705 00 00
				9706 00 00
	11.	200 年以上的印刷地图		9706 00 00
	12.	50 年以上的、任何种类或载体的档案及档案的任何组成部分		3704
				3705
				3706
				4901
				4906
				9705 00 00
				9706 00 00
	13.	（a）具有动物学、植物学、矿物学或解剖学价值的藏品[2]和标本		9705 00 00
		（b）具有历史、古生物学、人种学或古钱币学价值的藏品[2]		9705 00 00
14. 75 年以上的运输工具				9705 00 00
				第 86–89 章

续表

15.A.1 到 A.14 类之外的任何其他文物			
	（a）50 至 100 年		
		玩具、游戏用品	第 95 章
		玻璃器皿	7013
		金银器	7114
		家具	第 94 章
		光学、照相或电影设备	第 90 章
		乐器	第 92 章
		钟表及部件	第 91 章
		木器	第 44 章
		陶器	第 69 章
		挂毯	5805 00 00
		地毯	第 57 章
		墙纸	4814
		武器	第 93 章
	（b）100 年以上		9706 00 00

A.1 至 A.15 类中的文物，只有在其价值等于或高于 B 中规定的最低经济价值时，才适用本条例。

B. 适用于 A 中具体类别文物的最低经济价值（以欧元计）：

价值：

— 1（考古实物）

— 2（湮没的古迹）

— 9（古籍和手稿）

— 12（档案）

15 000

— 5（镶嵌画和绘画）

— 6（雕版）

— 8（照片）

— 11（印刷地图）

30 000

— 4（水彩画、水粉画和蜡笔画）

50 000

— 7（雕像）

— 10（书籍）

— 13（藏品）

— 14（运输工具）

— 15（任何其他文物）

150 000

— 3（图画）

申请出口许可证时，必须对是否达到一定经济价值进行评估。经济价值指第 2 条第（2）款规定的位于成员国境内的文物的经济价值。

成员国不以欧元作为本国货币的，附录 I 中以欧元计算的价值应按 2001 年 12 月 31 日《欧洲共同体公报》公布的汇率兑换为其本国货币计算。自 2001 年 12 月 31 日起，每 2 年审查一次以该国货币兑换的情况。计算兑换价时，应在 12 月 31 日修改汇率前，按 8 月最后一天之前 24 个月的该国货币的日平均值计算，以欧元表示。这种计算方法应由文物咨询委员会根据欧盟委员会的提案进行审议，原则上于首次启用该汇率 2 年后审议。每次修改汇率后，应在该修改生效前，于 11 月的第一天定期在欧盟公报上公布欧元价和各成员国货币兑换价。

注释：

【1】50 年以上且不属于其创作者。

【2】第 252/84 号判决将“藏品”定义如下：“收藏人收藏的符合《共同海关税则》的物品，此种物品具有藏品的必要特点，即相对稀缺、多不适用原有用途、属于类似实用品普通交易之外的特殊交易、具有较高价值。”

附录 II

废止条例的修改情况

第3911/92号欧盟理事会条例（第L395号《欧盟公报》，1992年12月31日，第1页）

第2469/96号欧盟理事会条例（第L335号《欧盟公报》，1996年12月24日，第9页）

第974/2001号欧盟理事会条例（第L137号《欧盟公报》，2001年5月19日，第10页）

第806/2003号欧盟理事会条例（第L122号《欧盟公报》，2003年5月16日，第1页）附录I，仅第2点

附录 III

相关表

第 3911/92 号理事会条例	本条例
第 1 条	第 1 条
第 2（1）条	第 2（1）条
第 2（2）条，第 1 小款，序言	第 2（2）条，第 1 小款，序言
第 2（2）条，第 1 小款，第 1 项	第 2（2）条，第 1 小款，第（a）项
第 2（2）条，第 1 小款，第 2 项	第 2（2）条，第 1 小款，第（b）项
第 2（2）条，第 2 小款	第 2（2）条，第 2 小款
第 2（2）条，第 3 小款	第 2（2）条，第 3 小款
第 2（2）条，第 4 小款	第 2（2）条，第 4 小款
第 2（3）条	第 2（3）条
第 2（4）条	第 2（4）条
第 3 至 9 条	第 3 至 9 条
第 10 条，第 1 款	第 10（1）条，第 1 小款
第 10 条，第 2 款	第 10（1）条，第 2 小款
第 10 条，第 3 款	第 10（2）条，第 1 小款
第 10 条，第 4 款	—
第 10 条，第 5 款	第 10（2）条，第 2 小款
—	第 11 条
第 11 条	第 12 条
附录，A.1、A.2 、A.3	附录 I，A.1、A.2、A.3

续表

第 3911/92 号理事会条例	本条例
附录，A.3A	附录 I，A.4
附录，A.4	附录 I，A.5
附录，A.5	附录 I，A.6
附录，A.6	附录 I，A.7
附录，A.7	附录 I，A.8
附录，A.8	附录 I，A.9
附录，A.9	附录 I，A.10
附录，A.10	附录 I，A.11
附录，A.11	附录 I，A.12
附录，A.12	附录 I，A.13
附录，A.13	附录 I，A.14
附录，A.14	附录 I，A.15
附录，B	附录 I，B
—	附录 II
—	附录 III

（二）《返还从成员国境内非法转移文物指令》

欧洲议会和欧盟理事会于2014年5月15日颁布的关于返还从成员国境内非法转移的文物的2014/60/EU指令以及经修订的欧盟第1024/2012号条例

（重编）

（王成岳　初校）

欧洲议会和欧盟理事会，

参考《欧洲联盟运作条约》，特别是其第114条；

参考欧盟委员会的建议，

将立法草案提交给各成员国议会后，

遵循普通立法程序【1】

鉴于：

（1）93/7/EEC指令【2】已被欧洲议会和欧盟理事会的96/100/EC指令【3】和2001/38/EC指令【4】[①]进行了重大修改，且还会作出进一步修改。因此，为了文义清晰，重编本指令。

（2）欧盟内部市场指的是没有内部边界区，根据《欧洲联盟运作条约》（TFEU），该区域内商品、人员、服务及资本可自由流动。依据TFEU第36条，商品自由流动的相关规定并不排除为保护具有艺术、历史或考古

① 修订关于返还从成员国境内非法转移的文物的93/7/EEC指令的欧洲议会和理事会2001年6月5日2001/38/EC指令（第L 187号《欧盟公报》，2001年7月10日，第43页）。

价值的国宝而制定货物进出口或过境禁令或限制。

（3）根据 TFEU 第 36 条，成员国保留如何定义国宝以及采取何种必要保护措施的权利。尽管如此，欧盟在促进各成员国就保护欧洲文物（上述国宝属于文物）方面的合作中起着十分重要的作用。

（4）93/7/EEC 指令规定一系列措施，确保成员国能将文物返还至本国境内。前述“文物”必须属于 TFEU 第 36 条定义下的国宝，且应属于该指令附件所列述的文物常见类别，而且这些文物已经被非法出口，违反了所在国家的保护措施或违反了第 116/2009 号理事会条例【5】。该指令同样适用于虽然不属于该指令附件所列述的文物常见类别，但同样被认定为国宝并且是公共藏品或基督教教会机构财产的组成部分。

（5）93/7/EEC 指令促使各成员国之间建立关于国宝事务的行政合作，并与国际刑警组织以及被盗艺术品领域内的其它相关组织（特别是在文物遗失、被盗或非法转移方面，而前述文物属于国宝和公共藏品）。

（6）93/7/EEC 指令规定的程序只是在各成员国之间建立内部市场方面合作的第一步，旨在促进各成员国进一步相互认可相关国内立法。

（7）第 116/2009 号理事会条例以及 93/7/EEC 指令建立了一个保护成员国文物的欧盟运作体系。

（8）93/7/EEC 指令的目的是确保将非法从成员国境内转移的文物返还其原主国，不受上述文物财产权的影响。但是，该指令仅适用于文物返还。该指令的实施报告指出，其附件规定的条件、提出返还诉讼的短暂期限以及返还诉讼费用导致本指令适用范围受到限制，也因此适用率不高。

（9）应当将本指令的适用对象扩大到按照成员国国内法律或行政法规分类或界定为国宝的一切文物，且该文物应该符合 TFEU 第 36 条规定，并具有艺术、历史或考古价值。因此，本指令应当适用于具有历史、古生物学、人种学、古钱币或科学价值的物品，只要其被划分或界定为国宝，无论是公共藏品或其它藏品的组成部分还是单一物品，无论是来自合法发掘或是盗掘，都应适用本指令。此外，为了实现本指令文物返还的目的，被划分或界定为国宝的文物不再需要必须符合关于年限和 / 或经济价值的条件。

（10）对于保护国宝的国家间协定，其多样性被 TFEU 第 36 条认可。为了增进成员国之间的互信、合作意愿和互相理解，应在 TFEU 第 36 条的框架下确定术语“国宝”的范围。成员国还应当协助返还从其他成员国境内非法转移的文物（无论该成员国何时加入欧盟），并应当确保文物返还不会产生不合理的费用。根据 TFEU 的相关规定，成员国也可能返还被划分或界定为国宝以外的文物以及在 1993 年 1 月 1 日前非法转移的文物。

（11）加强成员国之间的行政合作，以便本指令高效、统一实施。因此，各成员国中央机关之间应当加强合作，并利用欧洲议会和欧盟理事会第 1024/2012 号条例提供的内部市场信息系统（“IMI”）交流非法转移文物的相关信息【6】。为了完善本指令的实施，应当为文物建立专门的 IMI 系统模型。在适当情况下，成员国的其它主管机关也可使用该系统。

（12）为确保个人数据安全，主管机关之间的行政合作和信息交流应当符合欧洲议会和欧盟理事会 95/46/EC 指令规定的各项规则【7】，使用 IMI 时应当符合第 1024/2012 号条例规定。欧洲议会和欧盟理事会 95/46/EC 指令和第 45/2001 号条例使用的定义【3】同样适用于本指令。

（13）实践中，用于认定在另一成员国境内发现的文物是否属于 93/7/EEC 指令界定的文物的期限过短。因此，认定期限应当延长至六个月。更长的期限使成员国有时间采取必要的文物保护措施，同时，也可在适当时候避免逃避返还程序的行为。

（14）境内发生文物非法转移的成员国，在知道文物的位置以及其收藏人或拥有人的身份的情况下，提起返还诉讼的期限应延长至 3 年。期限延长的目的是促进文物返还并打击非法转移国宝的行为。明确起见，应当规定提起返还诉讼的期限自该成员国中央机关了解到上述信息之日起算。

（15）93/7/EEC 指令规定，如果从成员国境内非法转移文物的时间超过 30 年，则不可提出返还诉讼。但是，如果文物属于公共藏品的组成部分或成员国基督教教会机构财产的组成部分，且在成员国境内，受到本国立法的特殊保护，那么在特定情况下，返还诉讼的最长期限可能延长。由于成员国也可依其本国立法为除基督教教会机构以外的其他宗教机构安排特殊保护安排，故本指令也适用于其他宗教机构。

（16）根据 2011 年 12 月 13 日和 14 日作出的预防和打击文物犯罪决议，理事会认为有必要采取措施以便更加有效地预防和打击文物犯罪。建议欧盟委员会支持各成员国预防和打击非法交易以及促进落实配套措施（在必要情况下），以有效保护文物。此外，理事会建议各成员国考虑批准 1970 年 11 月 17 日在巴黎签订的联合国教科文组织（Unesco）《关于禁止和防止非法进出口文物和非法转让其所有权的方法的公约》和国际统一私法协会（UNIDROIT）于 1995 年 6 月 24 日在罗马签订的《关于被盗或非法出口文物的公约》。

（17）在文物的市场交易中，交易主体应持谨慎和注意的态度。如果收藏人能证明其在交易中已尽到谨慎注意的义务，并已接受补偿，那么将仅仅对从非法来源处购买文物的当事人进行劝诫。因此，为实现欧盟预防和打击文物非法交易的目标，本指令应当规定文物收藏人必须举证证明其在购买文物时已尽到谨慎注意义务，唯此才能获得补偿。

（18）能够便利地查阅被成员国划分或界定为国宝的文物的相关公开信息，对于任何人，特别是市场活动主体都是有益的。成员国应当努力为查阅信息提供便利。

（19）为了便于统一解释“谨慎注意”这一概念，本指令应当规定用于判断收藏人在购买文物时是否做到谨慎注意的非穷尽标准。

（20）由于成员国无法完全实现本指令的目标，即：归还从成员国境内非法转移的、被划分或界定为国宝的文物。且由于规模和影响力的原因，欧盟可以更好地实现这一目标。故欧盟可按照《欧洲联盟条约》第 5 条规定的辅助性原则采取措施。但按照该条规定的比例原则，本指令的规定不得超出实现本指令目标的必要限度。

（21）由于删除 93/7/EEC 指令的附件导致第 116/2009 号理事会条例规定的委员会任务作废，委员会解散。但为了维持各成员国执行本指令实践经验的交流平台，委员会应当成立一个专家小组，专家来自于各成员国负责执行本指令的中央机关。专家小组应参与包括定制文物 IMI 系统模型在内的各种活动。

（22）由于第 1024/2012 号条例附件包含一个运用 IMI 执行欧盟法案中行政合作的法律规范清单，故应对该附件作出修改以便清单中包括本指令。

（23）各成员国必须将本指令经过实质性修改的规定转换为其国内立法，未变更的规定转换义务仍依据原指令。

（24）本指令不得影响之前指令中附件一 B 规定的成员国进行国内立法转换的时限义务。

适用以下指令。

第 1 条

本指令适用于被成员国划分或定义为国宝、从其境内非法转移的文物的归还，具体如第 2 条第（1）点所述。

第 2 条

根据本指令，适用下述定义：

（1）“文物”系指不论在从成员国境内非法掠夺之前或之后，已被该成员国国内立法或行政法规根据 TFEU 第 36 条划分或界定为具有艺术、历史或考古价值的国宝的物品；

（2）“从成员国境内非法转移”系指：

（a）违反成员国国内国宝保护规范或欧盟第 116/2009 号条例从成员国境内转移；或

（b）在临时合法转移结束后未予以归还或违反关于临时转移的其他条件；

（3）“请求成员国”系指从其境内非法转移文物的成员国；

（4）“被请求成员国”系指从另一成员国非法转移的文物目前所在的国家；

（5）“归还”系指将文物实际归还至请求成员国境内；

（6）“收藏人”系指以自己的名义实际持有文物的人；

（7）“持有人”系指为第三方实际持有文物的人；

（8）“公共藏品”系指根据成员国法律被定义为公有物，且属成员国国家、地方或区域权威机关所有，或位于成员国境内的机构所有的藏品，机构是归成员国、地方或区域机关所有或得到其资金支持。

第 3 条

应按照本指令规定的程序和条件归还从成员国境内非法转移的文物。

第 4 条

每个成员国均应指定一个或多个中央权力机构负责履行指令赋予的职责。
成员国应将根据本条指定的所有中央权力机构通知给欧盟委员会。
欧盟委员会应在《欧盟公报》“C”辑上发布上述中央权力机构名单及其任何相关更改。

第 5 条

成员国的中央权力机构应互惠合作并推动成员国主管机关之间的磋商。各成员国主管机关尤其在以下方面应做到：

（1）根据请求成员国申请，寻找从其境内非法转移的指定文物，并确定所有人和 / 或持有人的身份。申请必须包括为利于寻找非法转移文物所需的全部信息，特别是文物的实际位置或推测位置；

（2）在某成员国境内发现有合理理由认为是从另一成员国境内非法转移的文物时，通知在其境内发现非法转移文物的成员国；

（3）请求成员国的主管机关有权在第（2）点规定之通知后的 6 个月内审查和认定争议物品是否为文物，如果未在规定期限内完成检查，那么第（4）点和第（5）点不再适用；

（4）采取一切必要措施并与相关成员国合作，维护文物安全；

（5）采取必要的临时措施以防发生妨碍文物返还程序进行的一切行为；

（6）就文物归还事宜，在收藏人和 / 或持有人与请求成员国之间充当协调人。为此，被请求成员国的主管机关可在不违反第 6 条规定的原则下，首先按照被请求成员国的国内法律推动启动仲裁程序，但前提是请求成员国和收藏人和 / 或持有人正式同意。

为了相互合作和磋商，成员国的中央权力机构应当利用专门为文物设计的内部市场信息系统（“IMI”）（依据欧盟第 1024/2012 号条例建模）进行合作和交流。还可在 IMI 公布其境内文物盗窃或文物非法转移案件相关信息。根据本指令，成员国有权决定其他成员国主管机关是否可以使用 IMI。

第 6 条

为确保归还从其境内非法转移的文物，请求成员国可向被请求成员国境内管辖法院起诉收藏人或持有人。

但只有在起诉文件随附下述资料的情况下方可提起诉讼：

（a）描述请求返还物品以及证明其为文物的文件；

（b）请求成员国主管机关发表的该文物系从其境内非法转移的声明。

第 7 条

请求成员国的中央权力机构应立即通知被请求成员国的中央权力机构确保争议物品返还诉讼已提起。

被请求成员国的中央权力机构应立即通知其他成员国的中央机关。

使用 IMI 进行信息交流时，应遵守保护个人数据与隐私的法律规定。中央权力机构亦可使用 IMI 以外的其它通信手段。

第 8 条

1. 成员国应在立法中规定，自请求成员国的中央权力机构知道文物位置及其收藏人或持有人身份之日起 3 年内，可依本指令提起文物返还诉讼。若文物从请求成员国境内被非法转移超过 30 年的，任何情况均不可提起上述诉讼。

但是，如果文物属于第 2 条第（8）点规定的公共藏品的组成部分或成员国国内法提供特殊保护安排的基督教教会机构或其它教会机构财产，则返还诉讼的最长期限为 75 年。此处 75 年期限不适用于未设起诉期限的成员国或签订了包括超过 75 年起诉期限的双边协议的成员国。

2. 如果起诉时，从请求成员国境内转移该文物已不再属于违法行为，则不再提起返还诉讼。

第 9 条

争议文物符合第 2 条第（1）点，且非法转移出境的，有管辖权的法院应判决返还。第 8 条和第 14 条中情形除外。

第 10 条

若判决返还文物，被请求成员国境内具有管辖权的法院则应根据案件的具体情况判决给予收藏人合理补偿，但收藏人应证明在取得该文物时已尽到谨慎注意的义务。

在确定收藏人是否尽到谨慎注意义务时，应考虑取得文物的各种情况，特别是关于文物来源的文件、请求成员国关于文物出口许可的法定文件、交易各方性质、交易价格、收藏人是否查阅任何可接触到的被盗文物登记册以及其他可以合理获得的相关信息，或是否采取了在同样情况下理性第三人应当采取的其他措施。

收藏人若是通过捐赠或继承获得文物，则不应享有优于捐赠人或继承人的地位。

文物返还后，请求成员国应承担相应补偿。

第 11 条

请求成员国应承担因执行文物返还决议产生的费用，还应承担因采取第 5 条第（4）点规定措施产生的费用。

第 12 条

在支付合理补偿以及第 10 条和第 11 条规定的费用后，请求成员国可以向非法转移文物的行为人追偿。

第 13 条

请求成员国依法确定返还文物的所有权。

第 14 条

本指令仅应适用于 1993 年 1 月 1 日及其后从成员国境内非法转移的文物。

第 15 条

1. 每个成员国均可将本指令规定的安排应用于归还除第 2 条第（1）点所述文物以外的文物。
2. 每个成员国均可将本指令的规定应用于请求归还 1993 年 1 月 1 日之前从其他成员国境内非法转移的文物。

第 16 条

本指令不应影响请求成员国和 \ 或被盗文物所有人根据成员国法律提起的任何民事或刑事诉讼。

第 17 条

1. 截至 2015 年 12 月 18 日及其后每隔 5 年，成员国应将关于执行本指令的报告提交至欧盟委员会。
2. 欧盟委员会应每 5 年向欧盟议会、理事会和欧盟经济和社会委员会提交一份报告，用以审查本指令的执行情况和效果。必要时，报告应附合理建议书。

第 18 条

应将下一点增添到第 1024/2012 号条例附件：

‘8. 欧盟议会和理事会 2014 年 5 月 15 日颁布的关于返还从成员国境内非法转移的文物的 2014/60/EU 指令以及经修订的第 1024/2012 号条例（*）：第 5 条和第 7 条。

（*）第 L159 号《欧盟公报》，2014 年 5 月 28 日，第 1 页。’

第 19 条

1. 截至 2015 年 12 月 18 日，成员国应制定实施相应的法律、法规和行政规定，以落实本指令第 2 条第（1）点、第 5 条第 1 款第（3）点、第 5 条第 2 款、第 7 条第 3 款、第 8（条第 1 款、第 10 条第 1 款和第 1 款以及第 17 条第 1 款的要求。

上述法律、法规和行政规定一旦生效，成员国应立即通知委员会。

成员国制定上述规范时，应参照本指令，或在正式公布时引用本指令。在上述规范中还应包括一份声明，声明在引用已由本指令废止的现行法律、法规和行政规定时，视为引用本指令。成员国应确定如果参照本指令以及如何拟定声明。

2. 成员国应将其在本指令涉及领域中制定的国内法律的主要内容通知委员会。

第 20 条

在不影响成员国义务（关于将 B 部分附件一所述指令转换为国家法律的期限）的原则下，自 2015 年 12 月 19 日起，废除 93/7/EEC 指令（已由 A 部分附件一所列指令修正）。

引用已废除指令的，视为引用本指令，并应结合附件二的表项解读。

第 21 条

本指令在刊登于《欧盟公报》后的第 20 天生效。

第 2 条、第 3 条和第 4 条的第（2）点至第（8）点、第 5 条第 1 款第（1）点、第（2）点、第（4）点至第（6）点、第 6 条、第 7 条第 1 款和第 2 款、第 8 条第 2 款、第 9 条、第 10 条第 3 款和第 4 款以及第 11 条至第 16 条应自 2015 年 12 月 19 日起生效。

第 22 条

本指令发送至各成员国。

于2014年5月15日在布鲁塞尔完成。

欧盟议会	理事会
主席	会长
M. SCHULZ	D. KOURKOULAS

注释：

【1】2014年4月16日欧洲议会的态度（未在《欧盟公报》中发布）及理事会2014年5月8日的决定。

【2】1993年3月15日关于返还从成员国境内非法转移的文物的93/7/EEC指令（第L 74号《欧盟公报》，1993年3月27日，第74页）。

【3】修订关于返还从成员国境内非法转移的文物的93/7/EEC指令的欧洲议会和理事会1997年2月17日96/100/EC指令（第L 60号《欧盟公报》，1997年3月1日，第59页）。

【4】修订关于返还从成员国境内非法转移的文物的93/7/EEC指令的欧洲议会和理事会2001年6月5日2001/38/EC指令（第L 187号《欧盟公报》，2001年7月10日，第43页）。

【5】2008年12月18日修订的关于文物出口的第116/2009号理事会条例（第L 39号《欧盟公报》，2009年2月10日，第1页）。

【6】欧洲欧盟议会和欧盟理事会关于在内部市场信息系统方面的行政合作的第1024/2012号条例，废止2008/49/EC委员会决议（即IMI条例）（第L136号《欧盟公报》，2012年11月14日，第1页）。

【7】欧洲议会和欧盟理事会于1995年10月24日颁布的关于个人数据加工及传输的95/46/EC指令（第L281号《欧盟公报》，1995年11月23日，第74页）。

【8】欧洲议会和欧盟理事会于2000年12月18日颁布的关于社会组织和机构进行个人数据加工及传输的第45/2001号条例。

附件一

A
已废止指令及其修正案清单
（详见第20条）

理事会93/7/EEC指令	（第L74号《欧盟公报》，1993年3月27日，第74页）
欧盟议会和欧盟理事会96/100/EC指令	（第L60号《欧盟公报》，1997年3月1日，第59页）
欧盟议会和欧盟理事会2001/38/EC指令	（第L187号《欧盟公报》，2001年7月10日，第43页）

B
转换为各国国内法律的期限一览
（详见第20条）

指令	转换期限
93/7/EEC	1993年12月15日（1994年3月15日，比利时、德国和荷兰）
96/100/EC	1997年9月1日
2001/38/EC	2001年12月31日

附件二

对比表

93/7/EEC 指令	本指令
	第 1 条
第 1 条，第（1）点，第一项	第 2 条，第（1）点
第 1 条，第（1）点，第二项，引言部分	—
第 1 条，第（1）点，第二项，第一项，第一个词组	—
第 1 条，第（1）点，第二项，第一分项，第二个词组	第 2 条，第（8）点
第 1 条，第（1）点，第二项，第二分项	—
第 1 条，第（2）点，第一项	第 2 条，第（2）（a）点
第 1 条，第（2）点，第二项	第 2 条，第（2）（b）点
第 1 条，第（3）点至第（7）点	第 2 条，第（3）点至第（7）点
第 2 条	第 3 条
第 3 条	第 4 条
第 4 条，开头部分	第 5 条，第一款，开头部分
第 4 条，第（1）点和第（2）点	第 5 条，第一款，第（1）点和第（2）点
第 4 条，第（3）点	第 5 条，第一款，第（3）点
第 4 条，第（4）点至第（6）点	第 5 条，第一款，第（4）点至第（6）点
—	第 5 条，第二款
第 5 条，第一款	第 6 条，第一款
第 5 条，第二款，第一项	第 6 条，第二款，第（a）点
第 5 条，第二款，第二项	第 6 条，第二款，第（b）点
第 6 条，第一款	第 7 条，第一款
第 6 条，第二款	第 7 条，第二款
—	第 7 条，第三款

续表

93/7/EEC 指令	**本指令**
第 7（1）和（2）条	第 8（1）和（2）条
第 8 条	第 9 条
第 9 条，第一款	第 10 条，第一款
第 9 条，第二款	—
—	第 10 条，第二款
第 9 条，第三款和第四款	第 10 条，第三款和第四款
第 10 条至第 15 条	第 11 条至第 16 条
第 16（1）和（2）条	第 17（1）和（2）条
第 16（3）条	—
第 16（4）条	—
第 17 条	—
—	第 18 条
第 18 条	第 19 条
—	第 20 条
—	第 21 条
第 19 条	第 22 条
附件	—
—	附件一
—	附件二